JUVENILE JUSTICE IN AMERICA

FIFTH EDITION

Clemens Bartollas
University of Northern Iowa

Stuart J. Miller
Washington & Jefferson College

PEARSON

Prentice
Hall

Upper Saddle River, New Jersey 07458

Library of Congress Cataloging-in-Publication Data

Bartollas, Clemens.
   Juvenile justice in America / Clemens Bartollas, Stuart J. Miller.—5th ed.
      p. cm.
   Includes bibliographical references and index.
   ISBN 0-13-225694-0
  1. Juvenile justice, Administration of—United States.   2. Juvenile delinquency—United States.
  3. Juvenile delinquents—United States.   I. Miller, Stuart J.   II. Title.
   HV9104.B347 2007
   364.360973—dc22   2006039741

Editor-in-Chief: Vernon R. Anthony
Senior Acquisitions Editor: Tim Peyton
Assistant Editor: Mayda Bosco
Editorial Assistant: Jillian Allison
Marketing Manager: Adam Kloza
Production Editor: Donna Leik, Techbooks
Production Liaison: Barbara Marttine Cappuccio
Managing Editor: Mary Carnis
Manufacturing Manager: Ilene Sanford
Manufacturing Buyer: Cathleen Petersen
Senior Design Coordinator: Christopher Weigand
Cover Design: Rob Aleman
Cover Image: Lonnie Duka, Jupiter Images-ImageState
Composition: Techbooks
Printer/Binder: Courier/Westford

Pearson Education Ltd.
Pearson Education Singapore Pte. Ltd.
Pearson Education Canada, Ltd.
Pearson Education—Japan

Pearson Education Australia Pty. Limited
Pearson Education North Asia Ltd.
Pearson Educación de Mexico, S. A. de C.V.
Pearson Education Malaysia Pte. Ltd.

10 9 8 7 6 5 4
ISBN 0-13-225694-0

Dedicated to Kristin, Kathryn Leigh,
Andrea Lyn, and Laura Ann,
our children

CONTENTS

CHAPTER 7: JUVENILES IN ADULT COURT   165

PART III: COMMUNITY-BASED CORRECTIONS

CHAPTER 8: JUVENILE PROBATION   187

**PART V: TOWARD AN UNDERSTANDING OF THE
YOUTHFUL OFFENDER**

PREFACE

Juvenile justice is part of a broader human rights movement that is concerned with far more than society's response to juvenile lawbreaking. Indeed, as globalization, urbanization, industrialization, and worldwide communications increase, the world's attention increasingly is directed to the plight of all children, regardless of circumstances. This concern is extremely late in coming. Approximately one-half of the world's population today is age fifteen or younger, and the magnitude of the problems these youths face is staggering. Poverty, racism, sexism, ethnocentrism, and religious differences all influence how children are treated. The reality is that in many societies, children are considered to be economic hindrances and expendable. Local, municipal, state, provincial, territorial, and national governments often lump together the needy, the dependent and neglected, the status offender, the mentally ill, the violent, and the victim of abuse. These children are discriminated against, victimized, persecuted, and sometimes executed by citizens, police, and paramilitary forces. The problems youths face go to the core of cultural thinking, far beyond the needs of societies simply to fine-tune agencies and rules for the handling of youths in need.

English-speaking countries such as the United States provide many of the ideals that are behind current world efforts to reform the world's approach to juvenile justice. Unfortunately, even world leaders often fall far short of their own ideals. In this regard, the United States is an excellent case study of what is and what could be in juvenile justice in the world today.

GOALS AND OBJECTIVES

Our primary purposes in writing this edition are the following:

1. To present the structures, procedures, and philosophies of juvenile justice agencies in the United States
2. To explore and define the important components of and debates over juvenile justice in the United States

3. To examine the issues and challenges facing juvenile justice agencies today
4. To maintain a balance between theory, research, law, and practice in our examination of juvenile justice
5. To provide the most up-to-date materials possible and, at the same time, to make this text interesting for the student

ORGANIZATION OF THE TEXT

The fifth edition of *Juvenile Justice in America* has sixteen chapters.

- Chapter 1 presents the history of juvenile justice and several historical themes of juvenile justice, examines juvenile justice agencies and functions, and reviews the most widely held philosophies and strategies on correcting juveniles.
- Chapter 2 examines the measurement of juvenile crime, considers the dimensions of law-violating behaviors, and takes a look at the victimization of children at home and in the school.
- Chapter 3 provides a broad review of the causes of juvenile crime, including an application of the theory to the practice of working with juveniles.
- Chapter 4 discusses the role of the police in dealing with juveniles. It covers police attitudes, the legal rights of juveniles in dealing with the police, how police process juveniles, and the role of community-oriented policing.
- Chapter 5 examines the main U.S. Supreme Court cases related to the handling of juveniles who come before the juvenile court, considers how status offenders have been handled, presents information on the judge and other key personnel in the juvenile court, and discusses the pretrial procedures of the juvenile court.
- Chapter 6 focuses on the adjudicatory hearing, disposition hearing, and judicial alternatives of the juvenile court. This chapter also looks at the rights of appeal a juvenile has and the current juvenile sentencing structure. Then it provides a defense of the juvenile court and suggestions concerning what is needed for the juvenile court to achieve excellence.
- Chapter 7 extends the discussion to juveniles who are waived to adult court. The issue of transfer receives major attention, but a youthful offender system, life for a juvenile in prison, changes in the death penalty for juveniles, and a proposed adult court for juveniles are also examined.
- Chapter 8 considers the administration, functions, and risk control focus of probation today. The job of the probation officer is described, and the rights of probationers, the role of volunteers, and the effectiveness of probation are considered.
- Chapter 9 examines the various aspects of community-based programs, including prevention, diversion, day treatment, and residential programs.
- Chapter 10 evaluates the various aspects of juvenile institutionalization, both short-term and long-term, for juveniles. The chapter concludes with a discussion of juvenile aftercare or parole.

- Chapter 11 considers and evaluates the various types of treatment modalities.
- Chapter 12 extends the discussion to juvenile gangs, revealing their history, the types and background of urban and emerging gangs, and the toxicity of gang involvement. The chapter concludes by considering what communities can do to prevent and control youth gangs.
- Chapter 13 examines drugs and youthful offending. The main types of drugs, the extent of drug use among juveniles, the relationship between drug use and delinquency, and an explanation of why youngsters use drugs are some of the subjects of this chapter.
- Chapter 14 combines an examination of gender, race/ethnicity, and class. It includes explanations of adolescent female offending, a feminist theory of delinquency; the most important dimensions of female delinquent behavior, how gender bias affects the processing of the female offender, and the influence of class and race on how juveniles are handled by the justice system.
- Chapter 15 discusses juvenile justice in Canada, England and Wales, Australia, South Africa, China, India, and Brazil.
- Chapter 16 provides a review of the text, considers the problems facing juvenile justice now, and considers what juvenile justice will look like in the future.

WHAT'S NEW IN THIS EDITION

- Chapter 1 now includes a review of the history of juvenile justice, followed by several historical themes.
- Chapter 2 has a new box on juvenile violence and updates recent statistics, with new data on the victimization of children in the home and at school.
- Chapter 3 has a new section on delinquency across the life course and includes a section applying the theories of causation to the lives of youngsters, as well as the programs in juvenile justice agencies.
- Chapter 4 places greater emphasis on how the police process juveniles, focusing on the rights of juveniles, and places more importance on community-oriented policing and juvenile lawbreaking.
- Chapter 5 now includes the courtroom team (described in Chapter 6 in previous editions) and discusses the pretrial procedures in greater detail.
- Chapter 6 extends the discussion of the adjudicatory hearing and includes a new box on achieving excellence in the juvenile court.
- Chapter 7 places greater emphasis on transfer procedures and frames the discussion of the juvenile death penalty in the context of *Roper v. Simmons.*
- Chapter 8 provides new material on restitution and electronic monitoring.
- Chapter 9 includes a new section on prevention programs, presenting the exciting new findings of the *Blueprint for Violence Prevention* programs.
- Chapter 10 in the fourth edition is now incorporated in the new Chapter 10 on Juvenile Institutionalization and Aftercare.

- Chapter 11 includes a section on intervention with juvenile sex offenders as part of the discussion of treatment modalities.
- Chapter 12 no longer has a section on female gangs, which now appears in the new Chapter 14.
- Chapter 13 is a new chapter on drugs and youthful offending. It examines the most important factors in adolescents' use of alcohol and drugs.
- The former Chapter 14 on the juvenile offender has been dropped, with materials on violent juveniles, status offenders, and sex offenders being placed in other chapters. The new Chapter 14 focuses on gender, race/ethnicity, and class. Beginning with a discussion of gender and juvenile justice, the chapter also considers the influence of class and race on the handling of juvenile offenders.
- Chapter 16 has a new section on what juvenile justice looks for in the twenty-first century.

LEARNING TOOLS

This text contains a number of features that are designed to help students in the learning process.

FOR STUDENTS

Chapter Objectives and Key Terms

Chapter-Opening Quotation. Each chapter opens with a quotation, frequently from a youthful offender or someone who works with juveniles, to set the tone for the chapter.

Chapter Summary. The concepts and insights of the chapter are summarized to help students learn the text.

Focus on Law. There are a number of boxes on the law related to juvenile justice.

Focus on Policy. These boxes are a reminder of the importance of what needs to be done to improve the handling of juveniles by society.

Focus on the Offender. When relevant, youthful offenders are given a voice.

Focus on Intervention. These boxes examine what can be done to intervene more effectively with youthful offenders.

Web Links. At the end of the chapter are usually several Web sites that can be used to help students understand the material.

Critical Thinking Questions. These are found at the end of boxes, following some sections, and at at the end of the chapters.

SUPPLEMENTS

FOR STUDENTS

Voices in the Juvenile Justice System. Youthful offenders and professionals contribute twenty-six "stories" to this supplement; sixteen from individuals who talked about their childhoods, the crimes they committed, and the contacts they had with the police and juvenile justice system. The other ten statements are from those who either have or who presently work with youthful offenders, ranging from police officers to a juvenile court judge, a chief of juvenile probation, a superintendent of a training school, a founder and director of a residential facility, two staff members in residential facilities, a therapist who has worked with sex offenders, a former juvenile court prosecutor from New York City, and a Deputy Commissioner of Probation in New York City.

Study Guide. This edition, like the previous one, includes a student study guide.

Online Progress Checks. These checks are provided for each chapter to help students understand the progress they are making in assimilating the materials.

Webcasts. The authors identify the online home sites and webcast locations that add insights to students' understanding of course materials. These webcasts include both brief PowerPoint presentations and videos supplementing course materials.

FOR INSTRUCTORS

Instructor's Manual. This manual includes summaries of chapter contents, test questions, and an updated film.

Interactive PowerPoint Slides. Five hundred interactive PowerPoint slides outline the text and are available to the instructor.

Webcasts. The authors identify the online home sites and webcast locations that add insights to students' understanding of course materials. These webcasts include both brief PowerPoint presentations and videos supplementing course materials.

Voices in the Juvenile Justice System. This intriguing supplement of voices from juveniles and professionals may well be the instructor's best friend in getting the student actively engaged in course materials.

Although no author is totally value-free, every attempt has been made to be fair and provide a balanced presentation of the juvenile justice system. Before juvenile justice can develop more just systems and a more humane present and future for juveniles, its characteristics, procedures, policies, and problems must be carefully examined. This is the task of this text.

ACKNOWLEDGMENTS

Many individuals have contributed to the writing of this book. We are profoundly grateful to our wives, Linda Dippold Bartollas and JoAnn Miller. Both were constant sources of support and encouragement throughout the many phases involved in the publication of this fifth edition. Linda Bartollas also conducted interviews with juvenile offenders in three states.

We are grateful to those participants of the juvenile justice system who were willing to be interviewed, who contributed materials for this edition, or who assisted us in replicating scenes from the halls of justice for photographs for this volume. Special thanks are due to North Franklin, Pennsylvania, former Police Chief Roger Cuccaro; current Police Chief Mark Kavakich; Sgt. Richard Horner; Lt. Kirk Hessler and Officer Jerry Cavanaugh; Claysville, Pennsylvania, Police Chief David Danley and Patrolman Donald Cooper;

Pennsylvania Magistrate Jay Dutton; Probation Officer Steven Tkatch; Washington County Correctional Facility Treatment Supervisor Dave Talpus; Mall Managers Richard Conrady and David Graham; Mall Security Officer Rich Keys; Willard (Buzz) Holbert and Shane Bane; and Mel Blount Youth Home Directors Mel Blount and Carol Lockett. Special thanks are also due to Trevor Onest and David Kraueter, current and past reference librarians at Washington & Jefferson College, as well as to those students who were willing to be models for various photographs throughout this book: Mary Murphy, Jessica, Melody, and Thomas Butterfield, Tommy Suitek, Anne Moore, Danielle King, Tanya Terchanik, Jeffrey Pollack, Azzorrahhnove Livingstone, Andrea Miller, Nelson Downey, Richard Kelley, and Alanna Santee. Katie Miller and Heather Dengle provided photographs for this and past editions.

At the University of Northern Iowa, we thank Betty Heine for all the tasks that she and her staff performed to keep the manuscript moving without interruption. Michael Pottman was especially helpful. At Washington & Jefferson College, Emily Bloom, Rachel Guyton, Alanna Santee, Allyson Kolljeski, and Desiree Dornetta, diligently performed research and sent out permission requests to sources. Alanna Santee also typed, developed questions for the test manuals, and assisted in writing several boxes. Debbie Trent, Margie Mahramus, Sunny Sefzik, and Barbara Rea provided invaluable assistance in preparation of the text, instructor's manual, and index; as did Katie Miller, Andrea Miller, and Laura Miller. Willie T. Barney, Robert Quirk, Hanna Bengston, Jamie Miller, Matthew Beals, and Domenick Lombardo also played key roles in the development of the manuscript. We would also like to thank the following reviewers: Mahfuzul I. Khondaker, Ph.D., Assistant Professor, Department of Criminal Justice and Social Work, Kutztown University, Pennsylvania; Professor Lori Guevara, Fayetteville State University, Fayetteville, NC; Professor Lynn S. Urban, Central Missouri State University, Warrensburg, MO. Finally, we are grateful to Neil Marquardt and Kim Davies, our former editors at Prentice Hall; and Tim Peyton, our present editor, and his associate, Mayda Bosco.

1

JUVENILE JUSTICE
An Overview

The Division of Juvenile Justice [of the California Department of Corrections and Rehabilitation] has many good people working for it—hard working, dedicated, and well meaning. The current leadership is professional, knowledgeable, and committed to reform. But if reform is to happen, they will need help. For this is not a system that needs tinkering around the edges, this is a system that is broken almost everywhere you look. It is a system with:

- *High levels of violence and fear in its institutions*
- *Unsafe conditions for both residents and staff*
- *Antiquated facilities unsuited for any mission*
- *An adult corrections mentality with an adult/juvenile mix*
- *Management by crisis with little time to make changes*
- *Frequent lockdowns to manage violence with subsequent program reductions*
- *Time adds for infractions adding over eight months to average lengths of stay*
- *Lengths of stay almost triple the average for the nation*
- *Hours on end when many youths have nothing to do*
- *Vocational classrooms that are idle or running half speed*
- *Capitulation to gang culture with youths housed by gang affiliation*
- *Low levels of staffing and huge living units*
- *Abysmal achievement despite enormous outlays for education*
- *Information systems incapable of supporting management*
- *Little partnership with counties and a fragmented system*
- *Poor re-entry planning and too few services on parole*
- *Enormous costs with little to show for it*

It is not just reform that is needed. Everything needs to be fixed.[1]

OUTLINE

OBJECTIVES

1. To retrace the journey of juvenile justice in the United States
2. To reveal the historical themes that have guided the development of juvenile justice in the United States
3. To present the structure and procedures of juvenile justice agencies in this nation
4. To examine the various philosophies and strategies for correcting juvenile offenders

KEY TERMS

adjudicatory hearing
aftercare officers
arrest
balanced and restorative
  justice model
commitment
cottage system
crime control model
dangerous poor

detention
dispositional hearing
house of refuge
just desserts
justice model
juvenile court officer
least-restrictive approach
medical model
minor

parens patriae
parole
petition
petitioner
positivist
respondent
status offenders
taking into custody
treatment model

The chapter-opening statement of a 2006 evaluation of the juvenile justice system in California, especially its correctional institutions for juveniles, is a devastating critique of the experiences that youths and young adults are having in this state's facilities. Long a model for other juvenile justice systems across the United States, California has made the decision to implement major reform in the structure and philosophy of confining youths and young adults.[2] Yet California is just one of many states in which juvenile justice systems are currently confronting massive criticism.

This widespread criticism is actually focused more on the juvenile court, as well as on its rehabilitative *parens patriae* ("the state as parent") philosophy. Indeed, one characteristic of juvenile justice today is the proposal, from both liberals and conservatives, to reduce the scope of the juvenile court's responsibilities. Conservatives wanted to refer more law-violating youths to adult court, while many liberals recommend divesting the juvenile court of its jurisdiction over **status offenders** (juveniles who have engaged in behaviors for which adults would not be arrested).

Some also believe that the adult court could do a much better job than the juvenile court with youthful offenders. Juvenile offenders, according to this position, would at least receive their constitutionally guaranteed due process rights.

It is not surprising that few are happy with the performance of juvenile justice today. To express this another way, precious little support is given to keeping the juvenile court and the juvenile system the way they are now.[3] The fact is that the juvenile justice system will experience major changes in the next few years. How it will change and whether the changes will be helpful to the youth of this nation are critical questions to be answered.[4]

The juvenile justice system is responsible for controlling and correcting the behavior of troublesome juveniles. What makes this mission so difficult to accomplish in the twenty-first century are the complex forces that intrude on any attempt either to formulate goals or to develop effective programs. Juvenile violence remains a serious problem, although homicides committed by juveniles began to decline in the mid-1990s. Even though juvenile gangs declined in numbers and membership across the nation in the final four years of the twentieth century, these gangs continue to be a problem in many communities. Juveniles' increased use of weapons has also become a serious concern, and there are those who believe that "getting the guns out of the hands of juveniles" is the most important mandate that the juvenile justice system currently has. The use of drugs and alcohol among the juvenile population declined in the final decades of the twentieth century, but beginning in the mid-1990s and continuing to the present, there is evidence that the use of alcohol and drugs, especially marijuana and methamphetamine, is rising in the adolescent population. Furthermore, the fact that there are conflicting philosophies and strategies for correcting juvenile offenders combines with the social, political, and economic problems that American society faces today to present other formidable challenges to the juvenile justice system.

Yet, while presenting the challenges of juvenile justice and the often disturbing results of working with youth in trouble, let it be clear that the authors are not promoting a "nothing works" or "everything is terrible" thesis. There are stirring accounts of youths who started out in trouble and were able to turn things around. In some cases, it was a program that worked with them; in others, it was an adult who made a difference in their lives; and in still others, it was the youths themselves who made the decision to live a crime-free life.

A heartwarming success story is found in Focus on Offenders 1–1. The youth in this case had more than his share of troubles with the law as an adolescent. He ended up being sent to one of the toughest juvenile correctional institutions in the United States. Upon his release at the age of eighteen, this youth could have continued his law-violating activities into his adult years and spent the remainder of his life in and out of prison. Instead, he was motivated to make something of himself. His goals were not always achieved in the ways he intended, but he persisted. He earned a B.S. degree and eventually was awarded an M.B.A. With his educational achievements came job success, a happy marriage, and the joys of fatherhood.

This chapter examines four topics: a historical sketch of juvenile justice, several historical themes, the organizational structure of juvenile justice agencies, and the philosophical approaches to treating youthful offenders. What these topics have in common is that they present the contexts (past and present) that have shaped juvenile justice in the United States.

FOCUS ON OFFENDERS   1–1
I AM DETERMINED TO MAKE SOMETHING OF MYSELF

I returned to Cincinnati when I left TICO [Training Institution, Central Ohio, a maximum security training school of the Ohio Youth Commission] in August 1977. Since I was 18, I opted for independent status and stayed at the Fryar's Club for six months and then moved into my own apartment that I shared with a friend. I had a regular job, both while I was staying at the Fryar's Club and after I moved out. I started college at Thomas More College in Erlanger, Kentucky, in the fall of 1978, and commuted from Cincinnati.

I applied for and received a grant but finally started to run out of money. I majored in chemistry and was hoping to get a job working in a lab. I was not able to find anything local, so after a year and a half at Thomas More, I moved to New Jersey, where my mother lived with my two younger sisters. I got a job as a chemist. My mother was able to get me a job at the company she worked for. I had only intended to stay for a year and then return to school. Somehow, that never happened.

I got laid off from the one company and landed a job with another chemical company. After a little over a year and a half, I was in a motorcycle accident and was out of work for three months. When I was ready to return, they had filled my position. I decided that I would go back to school, but I would do it in New Jersey. I went to the local two-year school, which was where I met my wife. I then landed a job in chemistry with Colgate-Palmolive, [which] had come recruiting on campus. [It was] located very close to Rutgers, and my intention was to work and go to school at night. School and work proved to be a bit more than I could deal with, so I stopped going to school after about a year.

I stayed at Colgate for about six years, during which time my wife and I were married in May of 1987. I left Colgate and went to work for another chemical company. After being there only a short time. I decided that I was tired of working in a lab, so I went back to school at night for a degree in Information Systems.

My wife and I bought our house in the late full of 1990. Our daughter was born in April of 1992. I finished my B.S. [Bachelor of Science degree] in the spring of 1993. I was able to make the transition from the lab to IT [information technology] while I was at FMC. That fall I decided to go to graduate school and get an M.B.A. Our son was born in January of 1994. There was a change in management at the company I was with, so I left and joined a consulting firm doing IT consulting. I finished my graduate degree in 1996.

I was promoted and moved to a more senior level position within the consulting firm I was working for. I had started to specialize in pharmaceutical clinical data management systems and was leading a team of six other consultants. I left that firm and joined another consulting firm that I am currently with now. I am currently consulting for a major pharmaceutical company as an IT project manager.

Source: Letter received from a former institutionalized delinquent. Used with permission; the writer chooses to remain anonymous.

Critical Thinking Questions:
Why do you believe that this person turned his life around? What attributes does he appear to have that many delinquents who go on to criminal careers do not have? Does this focus have any lessons for those in the juvenile justice system?

HOW DID JUVENILE JUSTICE DEVELOP IN THE UNITED STATES?

Throughout history, there has rarely been an emphasis on the special needs of juveniles. Adults and juveniles who violated the law were typically processed in the same manner and were subject to the same types of punishments, including whippings, mutilation, banishment, torture, and death.[5]

In the fifth century A.D., the age was fixed at seven for determining whether youths would be exempted from criminal responsibility under certain conditions. With the onset of puberty at the age of twelve for girls and fourteen for boys, youths were held totally responsible for their socially unacceptable behaviors.

This understanding of children and criminal responsibility continued in medieval Europe. For example, during the entire period between 700 and 1500 A.D., children were not viewed as a distinct group with special needs and behaviors. Although little is known about the peasant families of the Middle Ages, it is clear that children were expected to assume adult roles in the family early in life and apprentice themselves in crafts or trades to wealthier families. The landowners of the country, then, assumed control over children and their welfare and, at the same time, lifted the burden of child care from their parents.

These early medieval traditions eventually influenced the shaping of juvenile justice in England. Both the Chancery court, which eventually became responsible for overseeing the general welfare of the citizenry, and the concept of *parens patriae* which focused on the sovereign as the one who protected his or her subjects, played a prominent role in the shaping of English juvenile justice.

Because children and other incompetents were under the protective control of the sovereign, it was not difficult for English kings to justify interventions in their lives. With the passage of time, the concept of *parens patriae* was increasingly used to justify interventions in peasants' families.

The common law tradition in England eventually concurred with earlier law that children under seven should not face legal penalties. Children between seven and fourteen were deemed another matter, and their responsibility was determined by other considerations: severity of the crime, maturity, capacity to distinguish between right and wrong, and evidence of blatant malice.

A sad page in the history of English juvenile justice is that some 160 to 200 capital offenses were listed in the statutes for which children could be executed. Although many juveniles sentenced to die were later pardoned or transported to another country, some children were executed. For example, eighteen of the twenty people executed in London in 1785 were under the age of eighteen.[6] The executions of children continued, but only occasionally, into the 1800s.

Juvenile justice in the United States began in the colonial period and continued English practices. The family, the cornerstone of the community in colonial times, was the source and primary means of social control of children. The law was uncomplicated; the only law enforcement officials were town fathers, magistrates, sheriffs, and watchmen; and the only penal institutions were jails for prisoners awaiting trial or punishment. Juvenile lawbreakers did not face a battery of police, probation, or **aftercare officers** (the juvenile equivalent of adult parole officers), nor did they have to worry that practitioners of the juvenile justice system would try to rehabilitate or correct them. They only had to concern themselves with being sent back to their families for punishment.[7]

As children got older, however, the likelihood increased that they would be dealt with more harshly by colonial law. The state, even in those early days, clearly was committed to raising its children correctly and making

Punishment in the good ol' days was swift and certain. (Photo by Stuart Miller.)

them follow society's rules. Indeed, this early practice appears to have been incorporated into the early Massachusetts Puritan code, which was a model for the U.S. Constitution of 1787.[8]

The state became even more concerned about the welfare of its children in the 1800s. Increased urbanization, industrialization, and bureaucratization were changing the face of America. In the cities particularly, increasing numbers of youths were seemingly out of control. Reformers searched for ways to teach them traditional values, and the asylum and the training school were developed to help the state maintain its control.

The courts were by now heavily involved with the juvenile problem. The concept of *parens patriae* was formalized by *ex parte Crouse* in 1838 and gave the courts a legal basis for intervening in the lives of children. The Bill of Rights, the court ruled, did not apply to minors, and the state could legitimately confine minors who, according to the ruling, did not have the right to counsel or trial by jury, and who could be confined even in the absence of criminal behavior.

By the end of the 1800s, much of the U.S. population lived in urban areas and worked in factories. Cities were large and growing, and waves of immigration were inundating the nation's shores with millions of people destined to remain poor. Conditions in the cities were shocking; there was much poverty, crime, disease, mental illness, and dilapidation. The cities' children were viewed as unfortunate victims of the urban scene.

How Did the Juvenile Court Develop?

Anthony Platt, in *The Child Savers*, adds greatly to our understanding of the origins of the first juvenile court in Chicago. The Chicago court was created, he argues, partly because the middle and upper classes wanted to control the increasing numbers of immigrants and the poor. In addition, the conditions of the Cook County Jail and the Chicago House of Correction, in which children were placed with adults, were deplorable. Increased numbers of youths were being confined with hardened adult felons who corrupted and exposed them to debauchery, crime, and sin.[9]

These reformers were primarily middle- and upper-class women who had achieved a certain amount of power and freedom. Women such as Jane Addams, Louise Bowen, and Julia Lathrop were committed to rescuing the urban American family and its youth by restoring rural values to them. They wanted to reaffirm parental authority, restore the role of the woman in the home, ensure the proper training of youths, and, most important, save youths from the sins they were exposed to on the streets.[10] Focus on the Law 1–2 reveals the moral behaviors that the early juvenile courts attempted to instill in the youth brought before them.

FOCUS ON THE LAW   1–2
PROHIBITIVE BEHAVIORS IN EARLY JUVENILE CODES

- Violating any law or ordinance
- Being habitually truant from school
- Associating with vicious or immoral persons
- Being incorrigible
- Demonstrating behavior that is beyond parental control
- Leaving home without consent of parents
- Growing up in idleness or crime
- Participating in behavior that injures or endangers the health, morals, or safety of self or others
- Using vile, obscene, or vulgar language in public
- Entering or visiting a house of ill repute
- Patronizing a place where liquor is sold
- Patronizing a gaming place
- Wandering in the streets at night not on lawful business (curfew violations)
- Engaging in immoral conduct at school or in other public places
- Smoking cigarettes or using tobacco in any form
- Loitering
- Sleeping in alleys
- Using intoxicating liquor
- Begging
- Running away from a state or charitable institution
- Attempting to marry without consent, in violation of law
- Indulging in sexual irregularities
- Patronizing public pool rooms
- Wandering about railroad yards or tracks
- Jumping a train or entering a train without authority
- Refusing to obey a parent or guardian

Critical Thinking Questions:
Which of these offenses do you believe should be defined as delinquent behavior? How many of these behaviors did you engage in when you were a teenager?

Cook county court 1899

The reformers were aided in their quest by a new emerging philosophy. In the past, the classical school of criminology had argued that laws were violated because people willfully chose to violate them. People were presumed to operate on the basis of free will, having total control over their actions; punishment was required to get them to follow the law. The emerging **positivist** school, in contrast, contended that people were pushed into crime by forces beyond their control. It argued that the causes of crime could be discovered through the use of the scientific method and that the biological, psychological, social, economic, political, and other environmental causes of crime could be discovered through rigorous and precise measurement. Once the causes of crime were discovered, this school argued, experts could then step in and cure the offender of his or her problem. Proponents of this philosophy believed that the juvenile court should use these assumptions in attacking the problems of youth.

Everything was in place. The *parens patriae* doctrine had been accepted by the courts for more than a half century. Social conditions had generated an underclass of people who appeared unable to help themselves. Conservative, humanitarian, and religious philosophies had justified the need and had provided the power necessary for change. Jails and prisons clearly were no places for children. And finally, the positivist philosophy held out the promise that if the right mechanism could be developed, wayward children could be saved.

The Cook County Juvenile Court was founded in 1899. Its premises were that the *parens patriae* doctrine permitted it to take charge of children in need, that the causes of the children's problems could be discovered and treated, and that the court had to develop a different set of procedures and terminology from those of the adult courts to achieve these goals.

Accordingly, the Illinois court was set up to operate on an informal basis. First, this meant that traditional courtrooms were not used; all that was actually required were a table and chairs where the judge, the child, and his or her parents and probation officers could sit together and discuss the case. Second, children could be brought before the court on the basis of complaints of citizens, parents, police, school officials, or others. Third, the children's hearings were not public, and their records were kept confidential because children coming before the court were not considered criminal. Fourth, proof of the child's criminality was not required for the child to be considered in need of the court's services. Fifth, the court had great discretion in determining what kinds of services the child required and had wide latitude in determining a disposition. Sixth, lawyers were not required because the hearings were not adversarial. Finally, the standards and procedures long in use in adult courts were missing in the juvenile courts; the standard of proof beyond a reasonable doubt was not required, and hearsay evidence was permitted.

The attractiveness of the juvenile court philosophy resulted in almost all states setting up juvenile courts. In fact, by 1928, only two of thirty-one states had not passed a juvenile court statute.[11] Those that did closely followed the wording and intent of the Chicago statute and its amendments. These were civil courts, usually a family court, and their purpose was rehabilitation, not punishment. The neglected, the dependent, the misbehaving youngster, the status offender, and the delinquent were all subject to the courts' dictates. But the public was assured that programs would be developed to solve the problems of wayward youth so that they would be released to the community as respectable citizens.

Juvenile courts attempted to live up to their mandate for the next sixty years. For about the first twenty years, the court was aided by religiously motivated volunteers who brought strong moral commitments to their work with juveniles. Confidence in the juvenile court began to erode in 1911 and 1912, with exposés detailing the court's deplorable conditions and practices.[12] Another negative influence on the juvenile court following World War I was the general disenchantment with the idea that society was improving.

Immediately following World War I, volunteers were replaced with paid social work professionals called "social adjusters." The social work orientation of these professionals enabled them to help redefine the juvenile court as a social agency and to lobby successfully for more paid social workers. In the 1920s, the field of social work adopted Freudian psychoanalysis, which focused on the client's emotional feelings. Thus, instead of attempting to deal with social environmental problems as the cause of delinquency, as did earlier reformers, social workers began to focus on the inner mental workings of the child.

WHAT IS THE HISTORY OF JUVENILE CONFINEMENT?

At the time of the American Revolution, the penal system in the colonies was modeled after that in England. The larger urban jails, county jails, and prisons contained men, women, and juveniles, whether they were felons or misdemeanants, insane or sane—sometimes all mixed together. Smaller rural counties, however, had less need for larger jails and prisons and temporarily housed their wayward citizens in small rural jails.

In neither city nor county, however, were youths expected to get into trouble. If they did, they were subject to the same punishments as adults. Beyond that, normal community processes were thought to be sufficient to keep them in line. Community norms were enforced through gossip, ridicule, and other informal social pressures, and little formal social control was needed. Local enforcers consisted of watchmen, magistrates, and sheriffs. All those who were caught, including youths, received fines, beatings, and floggings; were put in stocks; were driven through town in carts to be ridiculed by the citizenry; and in extreme cases were hanged, burned, mutilated, or banished from the community. After punishment, some youths were apprenticed to local craftsmen; until the mid-1800s others were sent on extended whaling voyages; and still others were placed with relatives or farm families.[13]

In the late 1700s and early 1800s, the United States was in a period of transition. The rural way of life was threatened, and the changes were having an irreversible effect on the structure of society. Concern about what to do with the growing number of juveniles who were abandoned, were runaways, or had run afoul of community norms increased and placed the young nation in a dilemma. On the one hand, thinkers reasoned that the natural depravity of humans made attempts at rehabilitation useless and that banishing the guilty was simpler than either punishment or rehabilitation. On the other hand, some hoped to find specific causes for deviancy, and the family was believed to be the primary source of the problem. Common sense and the examination of case histories indicated that older offenders usually had been problem children. The idea emerged that if institutions could be used for the poor, perhaps similar institutions could be set up for children using the well-adjusted family as the model.[14]

Regardless of the source of the problem, the situation demanded a solution. The growing number of delinquents and other children running in the streets of larger cities, the increasing population, and the changing character of U.S. society were all putting greater pressure on existing facilities. Conditions in the jails and prisons were deplorable. Youths were sentenced for fixed periods of time and were confined with the worst criminals society had to offer. Some youths died of disease, and morals were corrupted as children ten to eighteen years old were confined with adult felons.

The House of Refuge

When citizens and reformers became concerned about these inhumane conditions, their solution was the **house of refuge.** This facility was for all children, not just delinquents. Benevolence and compassion, along with concern over the degrading conditions in the jails and prisons, motivated the reformers to establish the houses of refuge.

New York City started the first school for males in 1825, followed by Boston in 1826 and Philadelphia in 1828. Other cities, including Bangor, Richmond, Mobile, Cincinnati, and Chicago, followed suit over the years. Twenty-three houses of refuge were built in the 1830s and thirty more in the 1840s. Of these, the vast majority were for males, with an occasional institution reserved for females. Their capacity ranged from ninety at Lancaster, Massachusetts, to 1,000 at the New York House of Refuge, with a median number of 210. The promise of these institutions seemed so great that youths with every type of problem were placed in them. The New York House of Refuge accepted children adjudicated guilty of committing crimes as well as those who simply were in danger of getting into trouble. The poor, destitute, incorrigible, and orphaned were all confined. Admissions policies were obviously quite flexible, and little concern was shown for due process; some youths simply were kidnapped off the streets. Not until later did these institutions begin to limit their rosters to those who had committed crimes.

The children generally were confined for periods ranging from less than six weeks to about twenty-four months, although some stayed longer. In some institutions the youths were taught trades, such as manufacturing shoes, brushes, and chairs, or were readied for apprenticeships to local craftsmen. Sentences were indeterminate, and superintendents of the institutions decided whether the apprenticed youths would be released or returned to the institution.

The first of the houses of refuge set aside for females was chartered in New York in 1824. Some schools were biracial, but many, especially those in the southern states, were segregated. Even in the North, African Americans often were sent to the state prisons and county jails rather than to the new houses of refuge.

These juvenile institutions accepted the family model wholeheartedly, for reformers desired to implant the order, discipline, and care of the family in institutional life. The institution, in effect, would become the home, peers would become the family, and staff would become the parents. Orphanages and houses of refuge substituted a rigorous system of control and discipline for the disordered life of the community.

Discipline was severe when the rules were disobeyed, but the reformers believed that once the authority of the superintendents was established, they would be looked on admiringly and as friends. Belief in these principles was so great that parents for the first time had to surrender their authority to superintendents and could not participate in the upbringing of their unruly children.

The first houses of refuge did not differ greatly from the existing state prisons and county jails. Built to hold inmates securely, some were surrounded by walls, and their interiors were designed to implant the notions of order and rationality in their charges:

> The buildings were usually four stories high, with two long hallways running along either side of a row of cells. The rooms, following one after another, were all five by eight feet wide, seven feet high, windowless, with an iron-lattice slab for a door and flues for ventilation near the ceiling. Each group of eleven cells could be locked or unlocked simultaneously with one master key; every aperture within an inmate's reach was guarded by iron. On the first

floor of each wing was a huge tub for bathing, sizeable enough to hold fifteen to twenty boys; on the fourth floor were ten special punishment cells.[15]

These institutions were based on the congregate system, with large numbers of clients sharing a single room or cell. Some later facilities, especially those built after 1850, were based on the cottage system, which is discussed later in this chapter.

Treatment of the youths paralleled the routine nature of the facility's physical plant. When the youths entered, they were dressed in institutional clothing and given identical haircuts. Troublemakers were punished; placing offenders on a diet of bread and water or depriving them of meals altogether were milder forms of discipline, but they were coupled with solitary confinement if a severe punishment was deemed necessary. Corporal punishments, used alone or in combination with other corrections, consisted of whipping with a cat-o'-nine-tails or manacling with a ball and chain. The worst offenders were shipped off to sea.

The school, the workshop, and the church were all brought into the house of refuge to teach order, obedience, and discipline. Routines were established, schedules were organized, and the institutions began to resemble military organizations rather than families. Youths were awakened by bells, and their days were partitioned by the ringing of bells. They awoke at sunrise, marched to washrooms, paraded in ranks for inspections, marched to chapel, attended school for an hour, and went to breakfast when the bells rang again at seven o'clock. From seven-thirty until noon the boys worked in the shops, making nails and other needed items of the day, and the girls sewed, did laundry, cooked, and cleaned. The lunch hour was from noon until one o'clock, and then work was continued until five o'clock. A half hour was allotted for washing and eating, following which there were two and a half hours of evening classes. After the evening prayer, youths were marched back to their cells, were locked in, and were expected to be quiet for the night until the routine began again.[16]

The specific order of daily events varied from institution to institution, but all followed the same basic schedule and routine. In some, youths were counted frequently to make sure that none had escaped, and in many facilities silence was maintained at all times, even during the recreation and exercise periods. Eating at times other than regularly scheduled mealtimes was forbidden, and youths who wanted extra food had to raise their hands. In school everyone recited in unison.

Reformers were enthusiastic about the house of refuge, but the residents apparently did not share their positive feelings. Hutchins Hapgood, sent to the New York House of Refuge in the nineteenth century, viewed this setting as a "school for crime," in which "unspeakably bad habits were contracted there. The older boys wrecked the younger ones," and children who were orphans had an especially hard time. The residents, he added, were overworked while making overalls and were beaten frequently. He bluntly concluded, "I say without hesitation that lads sent to an institution like the House of Refuge, the Catholic Protectory, or the Juvenile Asylum might better be taken out and shot."[17]

The Reformatory or Training School

Reformatories, also called *training schools* or *industrial schools*, developed in the mid-nineteenth century. The new reformatories were essentially a continuation of the houses of refuge, although they did stress a longer period of schooling, usually half a day. Another change is that the contracting of inmates' labor became more exploitative, as manufacturers often inflicted cruelty and violence on juveniles during working hours. The cat-o'nine-tails, for example, was used on youths who slacked off on their work in the reformatory shops.

In spite of the questionable nature of these institutions, states continued to build reformatories or training schools. In 1847 Massachusetts opened the first state-operated training school, the Lyman School for Boys, and in 1856 established the State Industrial School for Girls at Lancaster. New York built an industrial school in 1849, and by 1870 Connecticut, Indiana, Maryland, Nevada, New Hampshire, New Jersey, Ohio, and Vermont had opened training schools for delinquents. By 1890 nearly every state outside of the South had established a training school.[18]

The Cottage System

Introduced in 1854, the **cottage system** spread throughout the country. Reformers had succeeded in placing the industrial schools outside cities, their rationale being that youths on farms would be reformed when exposed to the rural virtues, the simple way of life, and the bounty of Mother Nature. With the new cottage system, the process of individual reform could be furthered, as residents were housed in separate buildings, usually no more than twenty to forty per cottage. The training schools were no longer supposed to be fortresslike either in physical design or in the relationships among residents and staff. The first cottages were log cabins; later ones were made of brick or stone. This form of organization was widely accepted and is the basic design for many juvenile facilities even today.

Three major changes began to affect juvenile institutions in the closing decades of the nineteenth century—the increasing size of institutional populations, a decrease in funding from state legislatures, and the admission of more dangerous offenders. As a result, the industrial school became custodial, and superintendents had to accept custodianship as an adequate goal.[19] Yet faith in the industrial school continued into the twentieth century.

HOW DID PROBATION DEVELOP?

John Augustus, a Boston cobbler, is considered to be the father of probation in this country. He spent considerable time in the courtroom and in 1841 accepted his first probation client, whose offense was "yielding to his appetite for strong drink."[20] Beginning with this "common drunkard," he was able to devote himself to the cause of probation as he became convinced that many lawbreakers needed only the interest and concern of another to be able to stop drinking, straighten out their lives and become model citizens. Augustus worked with women and children as well as with male offenders; in fact, he was willing to work with all types of offenders—drunkards, petty thieves, prostitutes, and felons—as long as he met a contrite heart. Augustus instigated such services as investigation and screening, supervision of probationers, interviewing, and arranging for relief, employment, and education—all of which are still provided today.

The state of Massachusetts, very much impressed with Augustus's work, established a visiting-probation-agent system in 1869. The philosophy of this system, which was set up to assist both youths and adults, was that first offenders who showed definite promise should be released on probation. Youths would be allowed to return to their parents and to live at home as long as they obeyed the injunction "Go and sin no more."[21]

Probation was regulated by statute for the first time in 1878, when the mayor of Boston was authorized to appoint a paid probation officer to the police force, to serve under the police chief. In 1880, the authority to appoint probation officers was extended to all cities and towns in Massachusetts. By 1890, probation had become statewide, with the authority to appoint resting with the courts rather than with municipal authorities. Soon thereafter, Vermont, Missouri, Illinois, Minnesota, Rhode Island, and New Jersey enacted probation statutes.

Although probation was radically extended in the wake of the juvenile court movement, probation systems varied from one jurisdiction to another. Probation officers generally considered themselves servants of the juvenile court judge rather than defenders of the rights of children. Thus, they would gather relevant facts and opinions on each case to help the judge make his decision, sometimes blatantly disregarding the due process safeguards of the law. Judges, in turn, saw nothing objectionable about returning children to the care of the probation officer who had placed them at the court's mercy in the first place. Most juvenile courts relied at first on volunteer juvenile probation officers. One observer said that their work "is the chord upon which all the pearls of the Juvenile Court are strung. It is the keynote of a beautiful harmony; without it the Juvenile Court could not exist."[22] Probation volunteers, however, largely disappeared by the second decade of the twentieth century, not to return until the late 1950s.

The spread of probation was marked by the founding in 1907 of the National Association of Probation Officers (renamed the National Probation Association in 1911). Homer Folks, one of the early advocates of probation, summarized the perception of probation in the early twentieth century: "Probation provides a new kind of reformatory, without walls and without much coercion."[23] Nevertheless, the idea of coercion lurked close to the surface, and force was used without hesitation if the delinquent continued to disobey the law. "When sterner treatment was demanded," said one officer, "the friendly advisor became the official representative of the court with the demand that certain conditions be observed or that the probationer be returned to the court."[24]

After World War I, there was an ever-increasing demand for trained social workers to serve as probation officers. These social workers, trained under the medical model, began to treat juvenile probationers as disturbed children who needed psychiatric therapy. The philosophy and administration of probation thus retained the older concern with helping children adjust to their environment as it added a new concern with helping them resolve their emotional problems.

In addition to a greater concern for treating children's problems, twentieth-century probation theory also includes the idea of more responsibility for the delivery of services to probationers, a greater consciousness of standards, and a desire to upgrade the probation officer and restore the volunteer to probation services.

WHAT IS THE HISTORY OF AFTERCARE?

Juvenile aftercare is as old as the juvenile institution. Superintendents of the early houses of refuge had the authority to release youths when they saw fit. Some youths were returned directly to their families; others were placed in the community as indentured servants and apprentices. After such service, they were released from their obligations and reentered the community as free citizens. For some, placement amounted to little more than slavery. They were sent to stores, factories, or farms that needed cheap labor. For others, the situation was more favorable, and some youths in trouble benefited from placement with caring and responsible families. Nevertheless, the system was not at all formalized; only in the 1840s did states begin to set up inspection procedures to keep watch on those with whom youths were placed.[25]

Parole, the period of time after institutional release when offenders are still under the control of the courts or state, continued to be used throughout the 1800s and into the 1900s. With the formation of the juvenile court, parole generally was called aftercare. Professionally trained individuals were added to the juvenile court to deal with released juveniles in the early 1900s. In addition, aftercare officers generally mirrored probation officers in trying to utilize current popular treatment modalities. Aftercare officers' caseloads were generally extremely high, and few resources were available to them. Even today, aftercare officers in many jurisdictions have the task of monitoring extremely large caseloads.

The development of aftercare programs was far from rapid, and the system remains underdeveloped even today. Citizens and professionals perhaps thought that institutionalization was sufficient for youth, or they may have been more concerned about adults, whom they feared and mistrusted more. Whatever the reason, not until fairly recently have innovative efforts been undertaken to improve juvenile aftercare systems.

WHAT ARE THE HISTORICAL THEMES OF JUVENILE JUSTICE?

A number of themes can be discovered by examining the emergence of juvenile justice in the United States. The most important of these themes are the increased authority of the state, the cycles of reform and retrenchment, the tendency to get tough with serious juvenile offenders and to go soft for minor offenders and status offenders, the fear of the dangerous poor, and the unsolvable nature of youth crime.

INCREASED AUTHORITY OF THE STATE

Ever since the colonial period, society has gradually *taken authority away from the family* and given it to the state for correcting the behaviour of children. There is little reason to believe that the three-hundred-year-old legacy of taking authority away from the family is likely to change in the near future. Even if the state were receptive to relinquishing some of its power (all indicators point to the fact that the state wants to increase rather than decrease its power over citizens), the American family is under greater pressure than ever before. Its mounting problems include high rates of divorce and single-parent families, alarming rates of abuse and neglect of children, problems with drug and alcohol abuse among both parents and children, and large numbers of adolescent out-of-wedlock births.

REFORM AND RETRENCHMENT

It is sometimes claimed that the history of juvenile justice has been a steady march toward more humane and enlightened conceptions of childhood and democracy, but a more reliable reading of history shows that a period of reform has inevitably led to a period of retrenchment.[26] To express this another way, the history of juvenile justice appears to go through cycles of reform and retrenchment.

Thomas J. Bernard's *The Cycle of Juvenile Justice* is a perceptive analysis of what drives these cycles of reform and retrenchment. According to Bernard, a cycle begins when both juvenile officials and the general public believe that youth crime is at an exceptionally high level and that many harsh punishments are used but few lenient treatments exist for youthful offenders. In this context, many minor offenders avoid punishment because justice officials believe that harsh punishment will make them worse. A period of reform

Table 1–1   *The Cycle of Juvenile Justice*

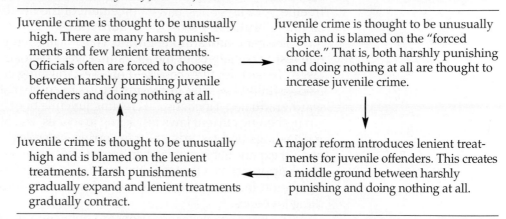

Juvenile crime is thought to be unusually high. There are many harsh punishments and few lenient treatments. Officials often are forced to choose between harshly punishing juvenile offenders and doing nothing at all.	Juvenile crime is thought to be unusually high and is blamed on the "forced choice." That is, both harshly punishing and doing nothing at all are thought to increase juvenile crime.
Juvenile crime is thought to be unusually high and is blamed on the lenient treatments. Harsh punishments gradually expand and lenient treatments gradually contract.	A major reform introduces lenient treatments for juvenile offenders. This creates a middle ground between harshly punishing and doing nothing at all.

Source: Thomas J. Bernard, *The Cycle of Juvenile Justice.* Copyright © 1992 by Oxford University Press, Inc. Used by permission of Oxford University Press, Inc.

arrives when the solution is seen as introducing lenient treatments for youthful offenders.[27]

Justice officials and the public, according to Bernard, always believe that (1) youth crime is "at an exceptionally high level, (2) present juvenile justice policies make the problem worse, and (3) changing these policies will reduce juvenile crime."[28] It does not take them long, however, to conclude that lenient treatments are the reason for the remaining high levels of juvenile crime. With that awareness, a period of repression begins to replace reform. Responses to serious youthful offenders are gradually "toughened up" so that these youths receive harsh rather than lenient punishments. The response to less serious forms of youth crime is also toughened up so that they too receive harsh punishments. When juvenile officials are forced to choose between harshly punishing juvenile offenders and doing nothing at all, the cycle has returned to where it started (see Table 1–1 for further explanation of these cycles).

S. I. Singer examined juvenile justice policy during the 1980s and 1990s by analyzing effects of the 1978 New York State Juvenile Offender Act (1978 N.Y. Laws). In the late 1970s, legislators responded to several highly publicized murders committed by youths in New York City by increasing sanctions for violent juvenile crimes. According to Singer, these changes reflected the desire of society and its policymakers to "recriminalize" delinquency. Recriminalization is characterized by increasing punishments to juveniles, including waiving more juveniles to adult court. Singer argues that the acceptance of treatment and punishment-oriented policies is contingent on political attitudes and beliefs about adolescent law-violating behaviors.[29]

The period from the 1960s to the mid-1970s was characterized by a liberal agenda. This reform agenda emphasized the reduced use of training schools, the diversion of status offenders and minor offenders from the juvenile justice system, and the reform of the juvenile justice system.

The liberal agenda ended in the 1980s and was followed by a get tough approach. One of the contributing causes of this shift from reform to repression was the failure of the reform agenda of the 1970s to address violent youth crime and repeat offenders.[30] Thus, the inability of the reformers to provide meaningful programs and policies aimed at persistent and serious youth crime proved to be the Achilles heel of the reform process.[31] The get tough approach continued into the 1980s. The main thrusts of the Reagan administration's crime control policy for juveniles were preventive detention, transfer of violent and repeat juvenile offenders to the adult court, mandatory and determinate sentences for serious and repeat juvenile offenders, increased long-term confinement for juveniles, and enforcement of the death penalty for juveniles who commit "brutal and senseless" murders.

The get tough attitude toward youth crime led to a number of federal juvenile justice initiatives in the 1990s that went beyond those implemented in the 1980s. These initiatives consisted of (1) establishing curfews, (2) passing parental responsibility laws, (3) increasing efforts to combat street gangs, (4) moving toward graduated sanctions, (5) creating juvenile boot camps, (6) maintaining and strengthening current laws restricting juveniles' use of guns, (7) opening juvenile proceedings and records, (8) transferring juveniles to criminal or adult courts, and (9) expanding sentencing authority over juveniles. The popularity of the get tough approach is reflected in the fact that in the 1990s nearly every state enacted legislation incorporating these federal initiatives into the social policy for handling juveniles.[32]

In sum, the cyclical relationship between reform and retrenchment in juvenile justice seems to hinge upon society's dissatisfaction with the ill-fated promises of reform, followed a generation or two later by rejection of retrenchment's lack of benevolence. Perhaps the key to this shift is that society and its policymakers want social order, but, at the same time, they want special treatment for children.

GET TOUGH AND GO SOFT APPROACHES

Although reform and retrenchment alternate as official policies for juvenile justice in this nation, the get tough approach for serious juvenile offenders and the go soft strategy for minor offenders and status offenders have characterized the sentencing practices of juvenile courts in recent decades. The **least-restrictive** (or go soft) **approach** first became popular in the 1960s. When professionals and students became aware of the extent of youth crime, the negative impact of delinquency labels, and the criminogenic and violent nature of juvenile institutions, many of them began to reappraise what should be done with juvenile lawbreakers. Studies on hidden delinquency and middle-class lawbreaking also taught a valuable lesson—nearly all juveniles break the law, but only a few are caught.

David Matza, Edwin Schur, and others developed a theoretical framework for the least-restrictive approach.[33] The philosophy behind this approach is that fate and chance are the only reasons that many juveniles are caught. The lucky break the law and get away with it, but those who are caught are labeled and processed through the juvenile justice system. A great many of these offenders, according to this theory, begin to live up to their labels, which then become self-fulfilling prophecies. Offenders become committed to delinquent behavior, particularly when they are placed in juvenile institutions or detention facilities with youths who have committed much more serious crimes.

For these reasons, supporters of this approach urge a least-restrictive philosophy—do not do any more than necessary with youthful offenders. If possible, leave them alone.[34] If their offense is too serious to permit this course of action, use every available resource before placing them in detention or in institutions. Keeping status offenders (juveniles who run away, violate a curfew, are ungovernable at home, or are truant from school) out of the juvenile justice system is one of the predominant concerns of proponents of this philosophy. Providing juveniles with all the procedural safeguards given to adults is also a vital concern. Adherents, of course, urge the use of community resources in working with juvenile offenders, an approach believed by many to be the best for juvenile justice.

On the other end of the spectrum, however, juveniles who commit serious crimes or continue to break the law are presumed to deserve punishment rather than treatment because they possess free will and know what they are doing. Their delinquencies are viewed as purposeful activity resulting from rational decisions in which the pros and cons are weighed and the acts that promise the greatest potential gains are performed.

THREAT OF THE DANGEROUS POOR

Early in the history of this nation, crime was blamed on the poor, especially on those who were newcomers to America. The fact that these individuals came from different cultural, ethnic, and religious backgrounds also made them appear dangerous. It was reasoned that institutions were needed to protect society against the behavior of these so-called **dangerous poor**.[35]

Significantly, until the late nineteenth century, each succeeding wave of immigration that brought impoverished newcomers was perceived as threatening a new crime wave. Anthony Platt's classic work, *The Child Savers*, makes the point that the behaviors the child savers selected to be penalized—sexual license, roaming the streets, drinking, begging, fighting, frequenting dance halls and movies, and staying out late at night—were found primarily among lower-class children. From the very beginning, according to this interpretation, juvenile justice engaged in class favoritism that resulted in poor children being processed through the system while middle-class children were more likely to be excused.[36]

The association of poverty with dangerousness has continued to the present day. It is expressed, especially, with the fear of violence and gang behaviors from African-American and Hispanic underclass children. Elijah Anderson describes the fear that young African-American males create in others:

> An overwhelming number of young black males in the Village [in Philadelphia] are committed to civility and law-abiding behavior. They often have a hard time convincing others of this, however, because of the stigma attached to their skin color, age, gender, appearance, and general style of self-presentation. Moreover, most residents ascribe criminality, incivility, toughness, and street smartness to the anonymous black male, who must work hard to make others trust his common decency. . . .
>
> When young black men appear, women (especially white women) sometimes clutch their pocketbooks. They may edge up against their companions or begin to walk stiffly and deliberately. On spotting black males from a distance, other pedestrians often cross the street or give them a wide berth as they pass. When black males deign to pay attention to passersby, they tend to do so directly, giving them a deliberate once-over; their eyes may linger longer than the others consider appropriate to the etiquette of "strangers in the streets." Thus, the black males take in all the others and dismiss them as a lion might dismiss a mouse. Fellow pedestrians in turn avert their eyes from the black males, deferring to figures who are seen as unpredictable, menacing, and not to be provoked—predators.[37]

THE UNSOLVABLE NATURE OF YOUTH CRIME

The get tough and go soft policies illustrate that the United States has a history of seeking cure-alls to solve the crime problem. Unfortunately, no simple solutions to this age-old problem exist. The search for a panacea began in the early nineteenth century—the Jacksonian period—when the young American nation was thought to have an unlimited capacity to solve its social problems.[38] The institutions that emerged to create better environments for deviants represented an attempt to promote the stability of society at a time when traditional ideas and practices seemed to be outmoded, constricted, and ineffective.

Legislators, philanthropists, and local officials all were convinced that the nation faced both unprecedented dangers and unprecedented opportunities. It was hoped that the penitentiary for adults and the house of refuge for juveniles, as well as the almshouse for the poor, the orphan asylum, and the insane asylum, would restore a necessary balance to the new republic and, at the same time, eliminate long-standing problems. The fact that these institutions eventually came to be viewed as failures did not prevent another generation of reformers from seeking new ways to cure the crime problem.[39] Ysabel Rennie aptly summarizes this history of seeking a cure-all for crime:

> There is nothing more disconcerting than the realization that what is being proposed now for the better management of crime and criminals—to get tough, to increase sentences and make them mandatory, and to kill more killers—has been tried over and over again and abandoned as unworkable. It is sad but true that the reformation of criminals through education, psychology, and prayer has not worked either. As for that great rallying-cry of the positivists, the individualization of punishment, its chief, if not its only, effect, has been an unconscionable disparity in judicial sentences. Thus, we are left to contemplate the evidence that we have for centuries been going in circles.[40]

✓**Progress Check 1.1**
Review this section at
www.prenhall.com/bartollas

WHAT ARE THE JUVENILE JUSTICE AGENCIES AND FUNCTIONS?

The Constitution of the United States gives both the federal government and the states the authority to draw up laws and the mechanisms for enforcing those laws. The primary laws with which this book is concerned are laws governing delinquent and criminal behaviors and the three subsystems—the police, the courts, and correction departments—that carry out the mandates of the laws.

These three subsystems have between ten thousand and twenty thousand public and private agencies, with annual budgets totaling hundreds of millions of dollars. Many of the forty thousand police departments have juvenile divisions, and more than three thousand juvenile courts and about one thousand juvenile correctional facilities exist across the nation. More than thirty thousand of the fifty thousand employees in the juvenile justice system are employed in juvenile correctional facilities; sixty-five hundred are juvenile probation officers, and the remainder are aftercare officers and residential staff in community-based programs. Several thousand more employees work in diversion programs and privately administered juvenile justice programs.[41]

THE POLICE

The functions of the three subsystems are somewhat different. The basic responsibilities of the police consist of enforcing the law and maintaining order. The law enforcement function requires that the police deter crime, make arrests, obtain confessions, collect evidence for strong cases that can result in convictions, and increase crime clearance rates. The maintenance of order function involves such tasks as settling family disputes, directing traffic, furnishing information to citizens, providing emergency ambulance service, preventing suicides, giving shelter to homeless persons and alcoholics, and checking the homes of families on vacation. Police–juvenile relations require the police to deal with juvenile lawbreaking and to provide services needed by juveniles.

THE JUVENILE COURTS

The juvenile courts must dispose of cases referred to them by intake divisions of probation departments, make detention decisions, deal with child neglect and dependency cases, and monitor the performance of juveniles who have been adjudicated delinquent or status offenders. The *parens patriae* philosophy, which has undergirded the juvenile court since its founding at the end of the nineteenth century, charges that juvenile judges treat rather than punish juveniles appearing before them. This treatment arm of the juvenile court generally does not extend to those committing serious crimes or persisting in juvenile offenses, however; such hard-core juveniles may be sent to training schools or transferred to the adult court.

CORRECTION DEPARTMENTS

Correction departments are responsible for the care of juvenile offenders sentenced by the courts. Juvenile probation supervises offenders released to probation by the courts, ensuring that they comply with the courts' imposed conditions of probation and refrain from unlawful behavior in the community. Day treatment and residential programs have the responsibility of preparing juveniles for their return to the community.

Training schools have similar responsibilities, but the administrators of these programs are generally also charged with deciding when each juvenile is ready for institutional release and with ensuring that residents receive their constitutionally guaranteed due process rights. Aftercare officers are delegated the responsibility of supervising juveniles who have been released from training schools so that they comply with the terms of their aftercare agreements and avoid unlawful behavior.

Juvenile justice agencies, because they have been developed by more than fifty state and federal government legislative bodies, do differ rather significantly across the nation. The structure of the juvenile court, as well as its administrative responsibilities, vary widely from one state to the next. Most juvenile probation departments emphasize restitution and community service programs as conditions of probation, but some juvenile probation departments provide intensive supervision programs and may even have house arrest and electronic monitoring programs. Some states hire private agencies to implement community-based programs, and most states are increasingly using private institutional placements for status offenders. Finally, a number of organizational structures are used to administer juvenile correctional institutions and aftercare services.

Much similarity exists between the juvenile and adult justice systems. Both consist of three basic subsystems and interrelated agencies. The flow of justice in both is supposed to be from law violation to police apprehension, judicial process, judicial disposition, and rehabilitation in correctional agencies. The basic vocabulary is the same in the juvenile and adult systems, and even when the vocabulary differs, the intent remains the same.

Note the following terms that refer to the juvenile and adult systems:

Adjudicatory hearing is a trial.

Aftercare is parole.

Commitment is a sentence to confinement.

Detention is holding in jail.

Dispositional hearing is a sentencing hearing.

Juvenile court officer is a probation officer.

A **minor** is a defendant.

Petition is an indictment.
A **petitioner** is a prosecutor.
A **respondent** is a defense attorney.
Taking into custody is **arresting** a suspect.

Both the juvenile and adult systems are under fire to get tough on crime, especially on offenders who commit violent crimes. Both must deal with excessive caseloads and institutional overcrowding, must operate on fiscal shoestrings, and face the ongoing problems of staff recruitment, training, and burnout. Focus on Practice 1–3 further describes the common ground and differences between the juvenile and adult justice systems.

FOCUS ON PRACTICE   1-3
SIMILARITIES AND DIFFERENCES BETWEEN THE JUVENILE AND ADULT JUSTICE SYSTEMS

Similarities

- Police officers use discretion with both juvenile and adult offenders.
- Juvenile and adult offenders receive *Miranda* and other constitutional rights at time of arrest.
- Juveniles and adults can be placed in pretrial facilities.
- The juvenile court and the adult court use proof beyond a reasonable doubt as the standard for evidence.
- Plea bargaining may be used with both juvenile and adult offenders.
- Convicted juvenile and adult offenders may be sentenced to probation services, residential programs, or institutional facilities.
- Boot camps are used with juvenile and adult offenders.
- Released institutional juvenile and adult offenders may be assigned to supervision in the community.

Differences

- Juveniles can be arrested for acts that would not be criminal if they were adults (status offenders).
- Age determines the jurisdiction of the juvenile court; age does not affect the jurisdiction of the adult court.
- Parents are deeply involved in the juvenile process but not in the adult process.
- Juvenile court proceedings are more informal, while adult court proceedings are formal and open to the public.
- Juvenile court proceedings, unlike adult proceedings, are not considered criminal; juvenile records are generally sealed when the age of majority is reached. Adult records are permanent.
- Juvenile courts cannot sentence juveniles to jail or prison; only adult courts may issue such sentences.

Critical Thinking Questions:
How much harm would it do juveniles if juvenile proceedings were abolished and juveniles were handled in adult court? What would the advantages be to juvenile offenders to be handled with adult proceedings and procedures?

HOW ARE JUVENILE OFFENDERS PROCESSED?

The means by which juvenile offenders are processed by juvenile justice agencies are examined throughout this text. The variations in the juvenile justice systems across the nation make describing this process difficult. Focus on Practice 1–3 shows the similarities and differences of these two systems. The process begins when the youth is referred to the juvenile court; some jurisdictions permit a variety of agents to refer the juvenile, whereas others charge the police with this responsibility. The more common procedure is that the youth whose alleged offense has already been investigated is taken into custody by the police officer who has made the decision to refer the juvenile to the juvenile court. After adjudication, a youth is placed in juvenile detention or moved out of detention and into probation, residential placement, or the adult system, and then released (see Figure 1–1).

The intake officer, usually a probation officer, must decide whether the juvenile should remain in the community or be placed in a shelter or detention facility. A variety of options exist for determining what to do with the youth, but in more serious cases, the juvenile generally receives a petition to appear before the juvenile court.

The juvenile court judge, or the referee in many jurisdictions, hears the cases of those juveniles referred to the court. The transfer of a juvenile to the adult court must be done before any juvenile proceedings take place. Otherwise, an adjudicatory hearing, the primary purpose of which is to determine whether the juvenile is guilty of the delinquent acts alleged in the petition, takes place. The court hears evidence on these allegations. The *In re Gault* case (see Chapter 5) usually guarantees to juveniles the right to representation by counsel, freedom

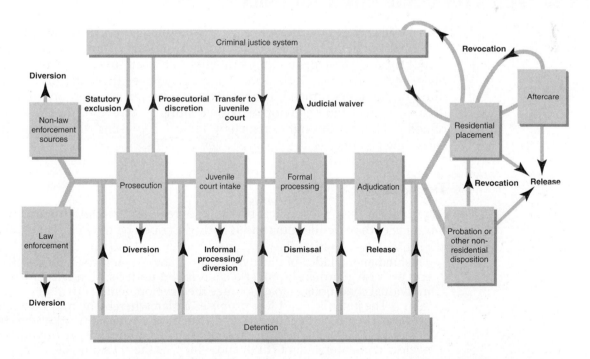

Figure 1–1   *What Are the Stages of Delinquency Case Processing in the Juvenile Justice System?*

Note: This chart gives a simplified view of caseflow through the juvenile justice system. Procedures vary among jurisdictions.

Source: Howard N. Snyder and Melissa Sickmund, *Juvenile Offenders and Victims: 2006 National Report* (Washington, DC: Office of Juvenile Justice and Delinquency Prevention, 2006), p. 105.

from self-incrimination, the right to confront witnesses, and the right to cross-examine witnesses. Some states also give juveniles the right to a jury trial.

A disposition hearing takes place when a juvenile has been found delinquent in the adjudicatory stage. Most juvenile court codes now require that the adjudicatory and disposition hearings be held at different times. The number of dispositions juvenile judges have available to them varies from one jurisdiction to the next. In addition to the standard dispositions of warning and release, placement on juvenile probation, or adjudication to the department of youth services or corrections, some judges can place juveniles in a publicly or privately administered day treatment or residential program. Some jurisdictions even grant juvenile judges the authority to send a juvenile to a particular correctional facility.

A juvenile adjudicated to a training school is generally treated somewhat differently in small and large states. In small states with one training school for males and usually one for females, a youth adjudicated to a training school is usually sent directly to the appropriate school. But large states that have several facilities for males and perhaps more than one for females may send the youth to a classification, or diagnostic, center to determine the proper institutional placement. Training school residents currently are not confined as long as they were in the past and are frequently released within a year. Institutional release takes place in a variety of ways, but a juvenile released from a training school is generally placed on aftercare status. To be released from this supervision, the juvenile must obey the rules of aftercare and must avoid unlawful behavior.

WHAT ARE THE MOST WIDELY HELD PHILOSOPHIES AND STRATEGIES ON CORRECTING JUVENILES?

Four basic correctional models exist in juvenile justice: the treatment model, the justice model, the crime control model, and the balanced and restorative justice model. These conflicting strategies handicap juvenile justice and are a major reason that no single policy or set of policies presently guide the handling of offenders. Indeed, nearly everyone has an opinion on what can be done to correct the behavior of law-violating youths; pet theories and folk remedies abound throughout society. Table 1–2 presents the philosophies of correcting juveniles in the various juvenile codes.

THE TREATMENT MODEL

Parens patriae, the philosophical basis of the **treatment model**, emerged with the founding of the juvenile court and is aptly described by the following statement:

> The fundamental idea of the juvenile court law is that the state must step in and exercise guardianship over a child found under such adverse social or individual conditions as to encourage the development of crime.
> . . . The juvenile court law proposes a plan whereby he may be treated, not as a criminal, or legally charged with crime, but as a ward of the state, to receive practically the care, custody, and discipline that are accorded the neglected and dependent child, and which, as the act states, "shall approximate as nearly as may be that which should be given by his parents."[42]

The state, represented by the juvenile court, was to deal with children differently than it did with adults by substituting a more informal and flexible procedure. In the juvenile court, a fatherly and benevolent juvenile judge

Table 1–2 *Juvenile Code Philosophies*

States' juvenile code purpose clauses vary in their emphasis

BARJ features	Juvenile Court Act language	Legislative Guide language	Accountability/ protection emphasis	Child welfare emphasis
Alabama	Arkansas	Arkansas	Connecticut	Dist. Of Columbia
Alaska	California	Maine	Hawaii	Kentucky
California	Florida	Montana	North Caronlina	Massachusetts
Florida	Georgia	New Hampshire	Texas	West Virginia
Idaho	Illinois	New Jersey	Utah	
Illinois	Iowa	New Mexico	Wyoming	
Indiana	Louisiana	North Dakota		
Kansas	Maine	Ohio		
Maryland	Massachusetts	Tennessee		
Minnesota	Michigan	Texas		
Montana	Minnesota	Vermont		
New Jersey	Mississippi	Wyoming		
Oregon	Missouri			
Pennsylvania	Nevada			
Washington	New Jersey			
Wisconsin	Rhode Island			
	South Carolina			

- The Balanced and Restorative Justice (BARJ) advocates public safety, individual accountability to victims and the community, and development of skills to help offenders live law-abiding and productive lives.
- Juvenile Court Act language suggests that each child should receive care, guidance, and control conducive to his or her welfare and, if removed from the home, receive care equivalent to that which normally would be given by parents.
- The *Legislative Guide* recommends providing for the care, protection, and wholesome mental and physical development of children involved with the juvenile court; substituting supervision, care, and rehabilitation for punishment; leaving children in their homes unless clearly unfeasible; and guaranteeing all children their constitutional and legal rights.
- Accountability/protection focuses on community safety, offender accountability, crime reduction, deterrence, and punishment.
- Child welfare emphasizes the promotion of the child's welfare, not his or her criminality, as the sole purpose of the juvenile court system.

Source: Authors' adaptation from Howard N. Snyder and Melissa Sickmund, *Juvenile Offenders and Victims: 2006 National Report* (Washington, DC: U.S. Department of Justice, Office of Justice Programs, Office of Juvenile Justice and Delinquency Prevention, 2006), pp. 98–99. Originally from Griffin and Bozynski, *National Overview: State Juvenile Justice Profiles.* Nation Center for Juvenile Justice (Sep. 23, 2003) at http://ncjj.org/stateprofiles/overviews/faq9.asp

would gently, and in a friendly manner, probe the roots of the child's difficulties. According to Warren H. Dunham, the court's purposes were "to understand the child, to diagnose his difficulty, to treat his condition, and [to] fit him back into the community."[43] The court, acting in lieu of a child's parents, was to engage in individualized justice; delinquency was viewed as a symptom of some underlying personality problem.

The juvenile court, then, was to serve as a social clinic. Its task was to call up the scientific expert to provide the necessary treatment for the child. *Child saving reformers,* a term used by Anthony Platt, were confident that the combination of *parens patriae* philosophy and the treatment provided by the scientific expert would lead to the salvation of wayward children.[44]

The **medical model,** the first treatment model to develop from the *parens patriae* philosophy, argues that youth crime is caused by factors that can be identified, isolated, and treated as though they were a disease. Punishment is to be avoided because it gives youths a negative image and does nothing to solve their problem. By diagnosing the causes of youths' behavior, advocates believe that they can cure youths and prevent them from committing additional crimes. Most supporters of this model also assume that juvenile lawbreakers do not have the ability to exercise freedom of choice or to use reason.

The treatment model, including the medical model as well as the methods of treatment described in Chapter 11, is based on the belief that the basic mission of juvenile justice is to rehabilitate youthful offenders. The treatment model also proposes that the legal definition of delinquency should be broad and that victimless crimes and status offenses, as well as crimes against victims, should remain on the books. Proponents of this model do not believe in the frequent use of detention facilities; these facilities should be reserved for children who need special care and custody.

How Does the Treatment Model Work?

The mental, physical, and social needs of the child are the focus of the treatment model, and many are implemented before the juvenile is processed into the system. Police officers may recommend community programs to youths and their parents that help youths in need with their special problems. Intake officers, probation officers, prosecutors, judges, and aftercare officers also may either informally or formally request that juveniles, status as well as delinquent offenders, attend drug and alcohol, tutoring, anger management, and other after-school programs; youths who are institutionalized also often receive drug and alcohol, sexual offending, and other treatment modalities such as those discussed in Chapter 11.

THE JUSTICE MODEL

The *parens patriae* philosophy was challenged by due process philosophy from the very founding of the juvenile court. Those promoting the due process approach wanted to give juveniles better protection through due process provisions and procedural safeguards. In the 1970s, proponents of due process were troubled by the contradictions of juvenile justice philosophy and by the inequities and inadequacies of juvenile justice law, policy, and practice.[45] These reformers turned to David Fogel's **justice model** and its concept of **just desserts.** Fogel believes that both juvenile and adult offenders are volitional and responsible human beings and, consequently, deserve to be punished if they violate the law. The punishment they receive, however, must be proportionate to the seriousness of the offense. Fogel also proposed the end of the indeterminate sentence and parole, the initiation of uniform sentencing, and the establishment of correctional programming based solely on the compliance of inmates.[46] Fogel reasons, "If we cannot coercively treat with reliability, we can at least be fair, reasonable, humane, and constitutional in practice."[47]

Judge Charles E. Springer has urged the adoption of the justice model in juvenile justice:

> A number of reasons are advanced in favor of adopting the justice model in dealing with the young people who violate the law. The main idea is that committing a crime, whether as an adult or a child, is wrong and deserves punishment. Most of us understand this; and certainly young delinquents do—except insofar as they have been told otherwise by the juvenile court. . . .
>
> Officially recognizing justice as the legitimate end of the juvenile court process certainly does not mean that every lollipop thief will be brought before the bar of justice; it does not mean a palpable move from "tears to teargas" in juvenile court jurisprudence. The call for justice is not a call for thumbscrews; rather, it is a call for a more certain, prompt, proportionate response to criminal misconduct.[48]

How Does the Justice Model Work?

Proponents of the justice model are now advocating a number of changes to bring more fairness to juvenile justice:

- Limit the enormous discretion granted to juvenile justice practitioners.
- Divert increasing numbers of youthful offenders from the justice system to voluntary services.
- Remedy common deficiencies in due process to ensure greater fairness in the transactions among the justice system, the family, and the juvenile offender.
- Curb indeterminate sentencing practices of juvenile courts and give juveniles a fixed sentence by the court at the time of disposition.
- Decriminalize status offenses.
- Change the governing principle of sentencing to one of *proportionality,* which means that there must be a relationship between the seriousness of the offense committed and the severity of the sanction imposed.
- Make training schools safer and more humane.
- Allow programs offered in training schools to be voluntary in nature and to have nothing to do with the release of a youth.
- Require restitution and community service sanctions of more juvenile lawbreakers; these sanctions have the potential for fairness because they give youthful offenders opportunities to atone or make amends for the damage or harm they have inflicted upon others.[49]

Many of these proposed changes are found in the standards developed by the Institute of Judicial Administration and the American Bar Association Joint Commission on Juvenile Justice Standards. These standards are also outlined in the report of the Task Force on Sentencing Policy Toward Young Offenders formed by the Twentieth Century Fund.[50] The mandatory sentencing law for violent juvenile offenders in the state of New York, the determinate sentencing law for juveniles in the state of Washington, and the institutional release policy adopted in the state of Minnesota are other indicators of the increasing national acceptance of the justice model.

THE CRIME CONTROL MODEL

The **crime control model** emphasizes punishment as the remedy for juvenile misbehavior. Punishment philosophy actually originated well before the eighteenth century, but it gained popularity in the 1970s because of the assumed rise of youth crime. Although this approach has had different connotations at various times, supporters today maintain that punishment is beneficial because it is educative and moral. Offenders are taught not to commit further crimes, whereas noncriminal citizenry receive a demonstration of what happens to a person who breaks the law; punishment, proponents believe, deters crime.

The supporters of punishment philosophy claim that the juvenile court has abandoned punishment in favor of individual rehabilitation. They argue for severity and certainty of punishment and advocate a greater use of incarceration. Other fundamental assumptions of punishment philosophy propose that those who become involved in unlawful behavior are abnormal and few in number; that this unlawful behavior reflects a character defect that punishment can correct; that punishment can be helpful in teaching a youth to be responsible, diligent, and honest; and that the deterrence of youth crime depends on the juvenile justice system apprehending and punishing youthful offenders with greater speed, efficiency, and certainty.

How Does the Crime Control Model Work?

The crime control model holds that the first priority of justice should be to protect the life and property of the innocent. Accordingly, proponents of this model support the police and are quick to isolate juvenile offenders, especially those who have committed serious crimes, in detention homes, jails, and training schools. The increased use of transfers to adult court and the adoption of mandatory sentencing laws specifying extended confinements for serious crimes are recent crime control policies.

Many states are now using a combination of the crime control and justice models to deal with violent and hard-core juvenile offenders. In a personal correspondence with one of the authors, Donna Hamparian, coauthor of *The Violent Few,* put it this way:

> The important point, I think, is that there is a shift from rehabilitation, or *parens patriae,* to punishment. It is much more difficult to talk about rehabilitating the juvenile armed robber than it is to talk about rehabilitating the status offender. I think much of the shift from the resultant legislative changes can be attributed to the news media, particularly, large newspapers, such as the *New York Times.* At least half of the states have changed the provisions with serious offenders in the last ten years. These changes have not all been more punitive, but certainly the states making major changes have moved to more specific ways to deal with "violent" kids. At the same time, several states have increased the age of juvenile court jurisdiction from 15, to 17, to 18.[51]

THE BALANCED AND RESTORATIVE JUSTICE MODEL

A traditional New Zealand approach to juvenile offending, the **balanced and restorative justice model,** is rapidly expanding throughout the United States and, indeed, throughout the world. "Balanced" refers to system-level decision making by administrators to "ensure that resources are allocated equally among efforts to ensure accountability to crime victims, to increase competency in offenders, and to enhance community safety." These three goals are summarized in the terms *accountability*, *competency*, and *community protection.*[52]

Accountability refers to a sanctioning process in which offenders must accept responsibility for their offenses and the harm caused to victims, and make restitution to the victims, assuming that community members are satisfied with the outcome. *Competency* refers to the rehabilitation of offenders, that is, when offenders improve their educational, vocational, emotional, social, and other capabilities and can perform as responsible adults in the community. *Community protection* refers to the ability of citizens to prevent crime, resolve conflict, and feel safe because offenders have matured into responsible citizens. Subsequently, the overall mission of the balanced and restorative justice model is to develop a community-oriented approach to the control of offenders rather than rely solely on punishment either by confinement or by individual rehabilitation through counseling. The juvenile justice system, in implementing this model, meets the needs of the community, the victim, and the offender in the most cost-effective manner possible.

How Does the Balanced and Restorative Justice Model Work?

This approach is an alternative to processing youths through the juvenile justice systems of their communities. Once a juvenile is identified as being a perpetrator of a delinquent act, a police officer, probation officer, community volunteer, or other

Table 1–3 *New Roles in the Balanced and Restorative Justice Model*

The Co-Participants	
Victim	Active participation in defining the harm of the crime and shaping the obligations placed on the offender.
Community	Responsible for supporting and assisting victims, holding offenders accountable, and ensuring opportunities for offenders to make amends.
Offender	Active participation in reparation and competency development.

Juvenile Justice Professionals	
Sanctioning	Facilitate mediation; ensure that restoration occurs (by providing ways for offenders to earn funds for restitution); develop creative and/or restorative community service options; engage community members in the process; educate community on its role.
Rehabilitation	Develop new roles for young offenders which allow them to practice and demonstrate competency; assess and build on youth and community strengths; develop partnerships.
Public Safety	Develop [a] range of incentives and consequences to ensure offender compliance with supervision objectives; assist school and family in their efforts to control and maintain offenders in the community; develop prevention capacity of local organizations.

Source: G. Bazemore, 1997. "What's 'New' About the Balanced Approach?" *Juvenile & Family Court Judge,* Vol. 48, No 1. p. 13.

designated person initiates the restorative process (see Table 1–3). The victim, the offender, the offender's family, a law enforcement representative, or a volunteer brings all the parties together to begin discussing the problem at hand.

This model, in other words, calls for a new framework of community organization and a restructuring of practitioner roles throughout the juvenile justice system. It calls for a new set of values that emphasize a commitment to all—the offender, the victim, and the community. Importantly, offenders are viewed as clients whose crime is a symptom of family breakdown, community disorganization, and community conflict, and these problems must be addressed if juvenile crime is to be reduced. Figure 1–3 shows the types of roles the balanced and restorative justice model calls for from all the components of the system.

Gordon Bazemore provides us with a practical example of the model in action:

> In cities and towns in Pennsylvania, Montana, and Minnesota—as well as in Australia and New Zealand—family members and other citizens acquainted with an offender or victim of a juvenile crime gather to determine what should be done in response to the offense. Often held in schools, churches, or other community-based facilities, these *Family Group Conferences* are facilitated by a community justice coordinator or police officer and are aimed at both ensuring that offenders are made to hear community disapproval of their behavior and developing not only an agreement for repairing the damage to victim and community but also a plan for reintegrating the offender.[53]

Bazemore goes on to identify some different techniques generated by the model's values. In some jurisdictions, victim/offender mediation is set up so that victims can express their feelings and the harm done to them. Once this is accomplished, an agreement is signed with the offender on how the victim can be "made whole" again. A second approach involves *family group conferencing.* This process is initiated and carved out by a facilitator who guides the victim, his or her family, and the community in developing the restorative sanction with the offender. A third process is *circle conferencing*. This approach, used in Canada, is a sentencing and problem-solving procedure enacted by a judge or community member. This facilitator calls together for problem solving the victim, the offender, their families, and local citizens who want to resolve the problem in the community. A fourth mechanism, *community reparation boards*, used in Vermont, consists of citizen sentencing, panels that encourage nonfelony offenders to recognize the harm the victims suffered and that help devise a way the offender can help restore the community. Another system is *reparative court hearings.* These are often special hearings implemented by judges in an informal community setting during the dispositional phase of the adjudication process. The hearing's purpose is to determine the type of reparation due the victim by the offender. Many other possibilities exist, but the major difference between the balanced and restorative justice model and other approaches is the model's equal weighing of the roles of the victims, the offender, and the community in preventing and responding to criminal acts.[54]

COMPARISON OF THE FOUR MODELS

The treatment model is most concerned that juvenile offenders receive therapy rather than institutionalization. The crime control model emphasizes punishment because it argues that juveniles must pay for their crimes. Proponents of this model support long-term confinements rather than short-term confinements for juvenile offenders. The justice model strongly supports the granting of procedural safeguards and fairness to juveniles who have broken the law. Yet proponents of this model also believe that the punishment of juveniles should be proportionate to the gravity of their crimes. The balanced and restorative justice model also contends that juveniles have free will and know what they are doing and, therefore, should receive punishment for their antisocial behavior. The advantages of this model, according to its proponents, are that it includes the punishment approach of the crime control and justice models, supports the due process emphasis of the justice model, and places consequences on behavior to encourage juveniles to become more receptive to treatment.

Each of the models has supporters. The crime control model, or the hard line, is used with violent and repetitive juvenile offenders. The treatment model, or the soft line, is primarily used with status offenders and minor offenders. Some jurisdictions show support for the justice model in juvenile justice, but the balanced and restorative justice model is making the most extensive advances. Nevertheless, on a day-to-day basis, juvenile justice practitioners continue to pick and choose from each of the four models in designing how they work with juvenile offenders. These conflicting approaches, as well as the intolerance of those who follow a different course of action, create inefficiency and confusion in juvenile justice.

✓**Progress Check 1.2**
Review this section at
www.prenhall.com/bartollas

SUMMARY

- The influences affecting the juvenile justice system can be traced back to the Middle Ages.
- The common law tradition in England eventually concluded that children under seven should not face legal penalties.
- However, the responsibility of children between seven and fourteen was determined by such considerations as the severity of the crime, maturity, capacity to distinguish between right and wrong, and evidence of blatant malice.

- The family was the source and primary means of social control of children in the colonial period.
- The concept of *parens patriae* gave the courts a legal basis for intervening in the lives of children.
- The premises of the *parens patriae* doctrine permitted the juvenile court to take charge of children in need so that the causes of their problems could be discovered and treated.
- The juvenile courts had to develop different procedures and terminology from those of the adult courts to achieve their goals.
- The attractiveness of the juvenile court philosophy resulted in almost all states setting up juvenile courts.
- Juvenile confinement goes back to the nineteenth century, when houses of refuge were established to separate juveniles from adult offenders in jails and prisons.
- The cottage system, in which residents were housed in separate buildings, usually included no more than twenty to forty per cottage.
- Later nineteenth-century juvenile institutions were called reformatories or industrial schools.
- Probation and aftercare were also early developments of juvenile justice; their focus was on treating youthful offenders in the community.
- The most important early themes of juvenile justice were the increased authority of the state, the cycles of reform and retrenchment, the tendency to get tough with serious juvenile offenders and go soft on minor offenders and status offenders, the fear of the dangerous poor, and the unsolvable nature of youth crime.
- The juvenile justice system has been given the mandate to correct and control youthful offenders.
- The conflicting philosophies and methods of correcting juvenile offenders make it difficult to succeed in correcting juveniles in trouble.
- Crime control policies of the past twenty years have proposed a get tough strategy, especially with violent juveniles.

WEB SITES OF INTEREST

To find information and resources on general areas of interest about juvenile justice and delinquency, go to the OJJDP home page at

http://ojjdp.ncjrs.org

Information on the Office of Juvenile Justice Programs and its mission can be found at

http://www.ojp.usdoj.gov/index.htm

CRITICAL THINKING QUESTIONS

1. The juvenile justice system has devised four ways to deal with youth crime: the treatment model, the justice model, the crime control model, and the balanced and restorative justice model. Which do you think works the best? Why?
2. Why is justice so important to the juvenile justice system? How can the juvenile justice system become more just, fair, and effective?
3. What do you believe can be done about reconciling the different approaches to juvenile justice?

NOTES

1. Christopher Murray, Chris Baird, Ned Loughran, Fred Mills, and John Platt, *Safety and Welfare Plan: Implementing Reform in California* (Sacramento: California Department of Corrections and Rehabilitation, 2006), 1.
2. Ibid., 8–39.
3. For an evaluation of the juvenile court, see Chapters 5 to 7.
4. In a number of chapters, positive changes are recommended to improve the functioning of the juvenile court.
5. The section on the early history of juvenile justice is based on William Wakefield and J. David Hirschel, "England," in *International Handbook on Juvenile Justice*, edited by Donald J. Shoemaker (Westport, CT: Greenwood Press, 1996), 91.
6. Leon Radzinowicz, *A History of English Criminal Law and Its Administration from 1750–1833* (London: Stevens and Sons, 1948), 14.
7. David Rothman, *The Discovery of the Asylum* (Boston: Little, Brown, 1971), 46–53.
8. Edwin Powers, *Crime and Punishment in Early Massachusetts, 1620–1692*, (Boston: Beacon Press, 1966), 94, 529.
9. Frederick L. Faust and Paul J. Brantingham, eds., *Juvenile Justice Philosophy* (St. Paul, MN: West, 1974), 569–75.
10. Anthony M. Platt, *The Child Savers* (Chicago: University of Chicago Press, 1969), 121–36.
11. Ibid., 98.
12. Sanford J. Fox, "Juvenile Justice Reform: An Historical Perspective," *Stanford Law Review* 22, no. 6 (June 1970), 1187–1239.
13. Rothman, *The Discovery of the Asylum*. See also Barbara M. Brenzel, *Daughters of the State* (Cambridge, MA: MIT Press, 1983), and Alexander W. Pisciotta, "Treatment on Trial: The Rhetoric and Reality of the New York House of Refuge, 1857–1935," *American Journal of Legal History* 29 (1985), 151–81.
14. Rothman, *The Discovery of the Asylum*, 53–54. For the origins of juvenile justice in California, see Daniel Macallair, "The San Francisco Industrial School and the Origins of Juvenile Justice in California: A Glance at the Great Reformation," *UC Davis Journal of Juvenile Law & Policy* 7 (Winter 2003), 1–60.
15. Ibid., 226.
16. Ibid., 225–27.
17. Hutchins Hapgood, *Autobiography of a Thief* (New York: Fox, Duffield, 1903), 71–72.
18. National Conference of Superintendents of Training Schools and Reformatories, *Institutional Rehabilitation of Delinquent Youth: Manual for Training School Personnel* (Albany, NY: Delman, 1962).
19. For this same tendency in the State Industrial School for Girls in Lancaster, Massachusetts, see Brenzel, *Daughters of the State*.
20. *John Augustus, First Probation Officer* (Montclair, NJ: Patterson-Smith Company, 1972), 4–5.
21. Board of State Charities of Massachusetts, *Sixth Annual Report, 1869, 269*.
22. Robert M. Mennel, *Thorns and Thistles* (Hanover: University of New Hampshire Press, 1973), 140.
23. Homer Folks, "Juvenile Probation," *NCCD Proceedings, 1906*, 117–22.
24. Mennel, *Thorns and Thistles*, 142.
25. Frederick Howard Wines, *Punishment and Reformation: Rise of the Penitentiary System* (Boston: Thomas Y. Crowell, 1985), 222.

26. Barry Krisberg and James Austin, *The Children of Ishmael: Critical Perspectives on Juvenile Justice* (Palo Alto, CA: Mayfield, 1978), 569.

27. Thomas J. Bernard, *The Cycle of Juvenile Justice* (New York: Oxford University Press, 1992), 3.

28. Ibid., 4.

29. S. I. Singer, *Recriminalizing Delinquency: Violent Juvenile Crimes and Juvenile Justice Reform* (New York: Cambridge University Press, 1996).

30. R. B. Coates, A. D. Miller, and L. E. Ohlin, *Diversity in a Youth Correctional System: Handling Delinquents in Massachusetts* (Cambridge, MA: Ballinger, 1978), 190.

31. Barry Krisberg et al., "The Watershed of Juvenile Justice Reform," *Crime and Delinquency* 32 (January 1986), 40.

32. National Crime Justice Association, *Juvenile Justice Reform Initiatives in the States 1994–1996* (Washington, DC: Office of Juvenile Justice and Delinquency Prevention, 1997), 9.

33. David Matza, *Delinquency and Drift* (New York: Wiley, 1964); Edwin M. Schur, *Radical Non-Intervention: Rethinking the Delinquency Problem* (Upper Saddle River, NJ: Prentice Hall, 1973).

34. Schur, *Radical Non-Intervention.*

35. Rothman, *The Discovery of the Asylum,* 78.

36. Platt, *The Child Savers.*

37. Elijah Anderson, *Street Wise: Race, Class, and Change in an Urban Community* (Chicago: University of Chicago Press, 1990), 163–64.

38. Rothman, *The Discovery of the Asylum,* 78.

39. Ibid.

40. Ysabel Rennie, *The Search for Criminal Man* (Lexington, MA: Lexington Books, 1978), 273.

41. See Kathleen Maguire and Ann L. Pastore, *Sourcebook of Criminal Justice Statistics—1994* (Washington, DC: Government Printing Office, 1995).

42. Roscoe Pound, "The Juvenile Court and the Law," *National Probation and Parole Association Yearbook* 1 (1944), 145.

43. Warren H. Dunham, "The Juvenile Court: Contradictory Orientation in Processing Offenders," *Law and Contemporary Problems* 23 (Summer 1958), 508–27.

44. Anthony M. Platt, *The Child Savers,* 2d ed. (Chicago: University of Chicago Press, 1977).

45. Charles Shireman, "The Juvenile Justice System: Structure, Problems and Prospects," in *Justice as Fairness,* edited by David Fogel and Joe Hudson (Cincinnati: W. H. Anderson, 1981), 136–41.

46. David Fogel, ". . . *We Are the Living Proof . . .": The Justice Model for Corrections* (Cincinnati: W. H. Anderson, 1975).

47. Fogel, "Preface," in *Justice as Fairness,* viii.

48. Charles E. Springer, *Justice for Juveniles* (Rockville, MD: National Institute for Juvenile Justice and Delinquency Prevention, 1987), 82–83.

49. Adapted from Shireman, "The Juvenile Justice System."

50. A shortened version of the standards developed by the Institute of Judicial Administration and the American Bar Association Joint Commission on Juvenile Justice Standards is listed in the juvenile court chapters and was published in 1977 by Ballinger Press; Twentieth-Century Task Force on Sentencing Policy on Young Offenders, *Confronting Youth Crime: Report of the Twentieth-Century Force on Sentencing Policy on Young Offenders* (New York: Holmes and Meier, 1978).

51. Personal correspondence was received from Ms. Hamparian and is used with permission.

52. Adapted from D. Maloney, D. Romig, and T. Armstrong, "Juvenile Probation: The Balanced Approach," *Juvenile and Family Court Journal* 39 (1988), 5; G. Bazemore, "On Mission Statements and Reform in Juvenile Justice: The Case for the Balanced Approach," *Federal Probation* 56 (1992), 64–70. G. Bazemore, "What's 'New' about the Balanced Approach?" *Juvenile and Family Count Judge* (1997), 2, 3.

53. Bazemore, "What's 'New' about the Balanced Approach?," 2, 3.

54. Ibid.

2

THE MEASUREMENT OF JUVENILE CRIME AND VICTIMIZATION

What countless human tragedies, what immeasurable sorrow are concealed upon a page of statistics? Often the very size of the numbers acts to immunize us from the pain; for how can we identify with the broken lives, the periods of repeated confinement, the furtive and violent struggles against authority, the hardened acts of victimization against fellow men, of men whose namelessness is turned into figures and percentages on one page and table after another? A single person, called John or James or David or whatever, a name created to conceal the identity, emerges when his story is revealed. We feel his pain no matter how strongly we feel the pain of those who have been his victims, we cry out against some cosmic injustice that has brought him to his wretched status, and whether some of us feel responsible for him because we are our brother's keeper, or issue words of condemnation motivated by the need for personal and social defense, he emerges in all his pathetic dimensions: the violent criminal among us. But multiply him by hundreds, or by some 1,500 in this instance, remove the fictional name and the details of his own case history, make no mention of an intoxicated father who beat a child or an unemployed youth filled with rage. Instead, dehumanize the individual, place him with hundreds under some social microscope, tell us whether the time between the first and second arrest was greater if the first arrest was for this crime or that one, and what have you? With scores of meticulously constructed tables, with tests of significance that tape the most sophisticated techniques, we have the stuff out of which social science is built, but it shall be a human and humane science only if we bring the fore that each number on the page, each column in the table, is a coalescence behind which are found these human beings, the forces that shaped them, and the people into whose lives they introduced great harm.

—Edward Sagarin[1]

OUTLINE

33

OBJECTIVES

1. To examine the extent of official juvenile lawbreaking
2. To reveal the findings of unofficial studies of juvenile lawbreaking
3. To compare official and unofficial findings of juvenile lawbreaking
4. To explore the extent to which juveniles are the victims of crime

KEY TERMS

age of onset
bullying
chronic offenders
cohort studies
delinquent offense
desistance from crime

escalation of offenses
Juvenile Court Statistics
*National Crime Victimization
    Survey*
official statistics
school safety

self-report studies
specialization of offenses
status offense
transition to adult crime
Uniform Crime Reports

The chapter-opening quote from one of the Dangerous Offender Project's publications illustrates well how statistics can dehumanize the offenders and victims of crime. It is a reminder that all statistical measurements of crime must retain the individuals behind the statistics if criminologists are to be part of a humane science. Another equally vexing problem is the difficulty of obtaining accurate information about crime. A simple enumeration of the data is interesting and sometimes illuminating, but it is often notable for the information *not* conveyed. A responsible researcher must make use of many different sources of data to understand fully the crime problem. Nowhere is this more true than with respect to juvenile crime. Debates persist over what juvenile crime is and should be, where the causes of crime can be found, and what special issues concern juveniles, such as gangs, drugs, guns, and schools. The result is that many different sources of information are available today to provide us with insights into juvenile misbehaviors. All sources must be studied, their strengths and weaknesses analyzed, and their contributions to understanding stated clearly.

Our understanding starts with distinguishing between juveniles who are *status offenders* and juveniles who are *delinquents*. Early juvenile courts did not make this distinction, as all youths coming before them were considered in need of care. Today, however, abused and neglected youths, and those who are incorrigible, run away, talk back to their parents, smoke cigarettes, and engage in other behaviors for which adults would not be arrested are called *status offenders*; society is not quite certain what to do with these youths, but more and more frequently, they are kept out of the juvenile justice system. On the other hand, youths who commit crimes such as murder, robbery, burglary, auto theft, and other serious crimes for which they can be arrested the same as adults are considered *delinquents*. This chapter and book focus primarily upon delinquents, but we also consider the plight of status offenders, for many still end up behind bars with delinquents and, sometimes, adult felons. The purpose of this chapter is to unmask the amount, the nature, and the extent of juvenile lawbreaking in the United States. Official juvenile lawbreaking is youthful misbehavior violating the legal norms of society that comes to the attention of justice authorities and is recorded. Unofficial juvenile lawbreaking is youthful behavior that does not result in youths' names or behaviors being recorded in official records; these youths are handled informally by those in the justice system.

The various studies on officially undetected delinquency find that adolescents should not be divided into offenders and nonoffenders, because the majority of youths occasionally commit minor offenses.[2] The evidence, in fact, suggests that the youth who never violates the law is a rarity. Some are minor offenders, some break the law regularly, a few commit violent or predatory crimes, and a few support themselves through crime and are committed to crime as a way of life.[3] Studies also demonstrate that the victims of crime frequently are juveniles. Whether minority or white, male or female, infant or adolescent, the very young are harmed more by crime than are their older counterparts.

In this chapter, we identify the main tools used to measure juvenile crime, and we discuss the problems of these statistical approaches. Finally, we examine juvenile victims and address the most important questions related to the future of juvenile crime.

HOW AND WHAT DO WE KNOW ABOUT JUVENILES? THE MEASUREMENT OF JUVENILE CRIME

WHAT DO WE KNOW ABOUT THE EXTENT OF JUVENILE CRIME?

Juveniles are studied by a wide variety of agencies. Traditionally, the *Uniform Crime Reports*, collated by the Federal Bureau of Investigation (FBI), were known as **official statistics** and were the primary source of our knowledge. Over the past seventy-five years, however, many more data collection sources came online to contribute to our knowledge of juveniles and their problems. *Juvenile Court Statistics* were developed to show what happens to juveniles who come to the attention of authorities. Victimization surveys focused on "hidden" or nonreported crime. Yet other governmental agencies such as the National Center for Education Statistics, the National Clearinghouse on Child Abuse and Neglect, and the Office of Juvenile Delinquency and Prevention also do research on juveniles. In addition, research funded by federal and state governments and private foundations takes place in private research institutes and in universities across the nation. This chapter looks at these research efforts and their findings on children in trouble.

UNIFORM CRIME REPORTS

The *Uniform Crime Reports,* or UCRs, have been our major source of information on the amount of crime in society since 1930. Then, in an effort to better understand the nature and extent of the crime problem, the International Association of the Chiefs of Police recommended that national crime statistics be collected and reported. The FBI was chosen as the clearinghouse for these data, and police departments across the United States were requested to report all arrests to the FBI. This information is published by the FBI on both a quarterly and a yearly basis and is probably the most popular of all the crime statistics. Reports of offenses are not always sent from the local police directly to the FBI. Some states have state reporting agencies; the locals report to the state agency, and it, in turn, reports to the FBI.

The UCRs classify crimes into Part I and Part II offenses. This classification is used to differentiate very serious from less serious crimes for the purpose of national statistics. Part I offenses include murder, rape, aggravated assault, robbery, burglary, larceny, auto theft, and arson. Part II offenses include all crimes not listed as Part I, such as simple assaults; buying, receiving, and possessing stolen property; carrying and possessing weapons; fraud; forgery; and counterfeiting. All states classify these behaviors as crimes and call for their prosecution.

In addition to reporting arrest data, the UCRs provide data on the age, sex, and race of offenders, as well as on the amount of crime they commit. Information also is available on whether the total amount of crime is increasing or decreasing, as well as on the amount of crime by size of city and by the sex and race of the offenders. In addition to the FBI, the Office of Juvenile Justice and Delinquency Prevention, and the Bureau of Justice Statistics also use these data in their analysis of juvenile crime.

Crime Rates by Age Group

The UCRs reveal that in 2004 juveniles (individuals under age eighteen) were arrested for 1.6 million crimes. This demographic age group constituted about 26 percent of the population and accounted for 17.3 percent of all persons arrested nationally in 2004.[4] These youths accounted for 14.6 percent of all index crimes; more specifically, youths were responsible for 15.5 percent of the violent crimes and 27.5 percent of the index property crimes. Juvenile arrests were highest for larceny-theft, other assaults, drug abuse, curfew violations, disorderly conduct, liquor law violations, and vandalism. Juveniles constituted 28 percent of burglary arrests, 23 percent of robbery arrests, 23 percent of weapons arrests, 10.5 percent of murder arrests, and 14 percent of aggravated assault arrests in 2004. Juvenile arrests for murder declined 8.3 percent between 2000 and 2004, when they reached one of their lowest levels since 1987.[5] These numbers continued to decrease through 2003 but appeared to spike slightly in 2004, increasing 21.6 percent over 2003.[6] Focus on Research 2–1 analyses the characteristics and circumstances of juvenile murders and suicides.

Crime Rates by Sex

The UCR data for juveniles and adults *combined* for 2004 show that males account for 82.2 percent of violent crimes and 68 percent of property crimes. Males under age eighteen had a total of about 1,121,000 arrests; females under age eighteen accounted for 477,000 arrests.[7] These data indicate further that males under the age of fifteen were arrested for approximately 346,000 offenses, whereas females under the age of fifteen were arrested for 163,000 offenses.

Focusing on juvenile violence, the UCR's report showed that violent crime index arrests for females under eighteen decreased 4 percent between 2000 and 2004, whereas those for males decreased 6 percent. Overall, however, female arrest rates tended either to increase slightly compared to males or not to decline as much as those of males over this time period. Females increased their share of robbery and aggravated assault arrests proportionate to that of males; the one offense for which youthful females are arrested more often than males is running away.[8] Although juvenile arrests decreased 9.1 percent between 2000 and 2004, the rate decreased 1.9 percent between 2003 and 2004; male and female crime rates for adults and juveniles began to drop in most categories in 1994 and continue, with some notable exceptions, to decrease today.[9]

FOCUS ON RESEARCH

JUVENILE HOMICIDES ARE DECLINING

2–1

The National Center for Injury Prevention and Control (within the Centers for Disease Control and Prevention) reported that homicide was the fourth leading cause of death of children ages one to eleven in 2002. Only deaths caused by cancer, congenital anomalies, and unintentional injury were more common for young children. In that same year, homicide was the third leading cause of death of juveniles ages twelve to seventeen. Only unintentional injury and suicide were more common causes of death in this age group.

- In 2002, four juveniles, on average, were murdered daily in the United States.
- More than half (51 percent) of juvenile murder victims in 2002 were white, 45 percent were African American, and 4 percent were either American Indian or Asian American.
- Given that white youth constituted 78 percent of the U.S. resident juvenile population in 2002 and African-American youth 16 percent, the murder rate for African-American youth in 2002 was more than four times the white rate.
- This disparity in race/ethnicity was seen across victim age groups and increased with victim age.
- Almost half (48 percent) of all juveniles murdered in 2002 were killed with a firearm, and 22 percent were killed by the offender's hands or feet (beaten/kicked to death or strangled).
- Persons ages seven to seventeen are about as likely to be victims of suicide as they are to be victims of homicide. In most states, juvenile suicides are more common than juvenile homicides.
- Between 1980 and 2002, the deadliest year for juveniles was 1993, when an estimated 2,800 were murdered.
- Between 1980 and 2001, for every ten white juveniles murdered, twenty-six were suicide victims. In contrast, for every ten African-American juveniles murdered, one was a suicide victim. For every ten Hispanic juveniles murdered, there were three juvenile suicide victims.
- In 2001, students were safer in school than they were in 1992.
- Between 1980 and 2002, about 2,000 juveniles were murdered annually in the United States.
- The number of juvenile homicides in 2002 was 44 percent below the peak year of 1993 and at its lowest level since the mid-1980s.

Source: Howard N. Snyder and Melissa Sickmund, *Juvenile Offenders and Victims: 2006 National Report* (Washington, DC: National Center for Juvenile Justice and Delinquency Prevention, 2006), pp. 20–25.

Critical Thinking Questions:

An important question is: Why did juvenile homicides decline from 1994 to the present? There are those who claim that the limited availability of guns was the most significant factor. Do you agree? Do you anticipate that the growth of the young population in the next several decades will result in an increase in juvenile homicides?

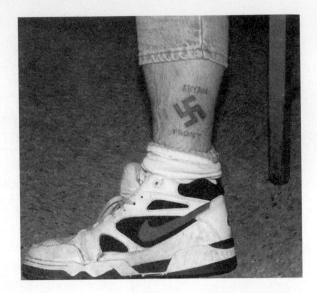

The skinhead with this swastika on his leg was arrested for holding up a restaurant with other skinheads to raise money for their cause. (Photo courtesy of the North Franklin Police, Washington, Pennsylvania.)

Crime Rates by Race

The UCRs examined juveniles under eighteen years of age and found that whites experienced 1,104,000 arrests for 69 percent of all juvenile arrests in 2004. This is compared to 447,290 or 28 percent for African Americans; 19,700 or 1.2 percent for Native Americans; and 23,000 or 1.2 percent for Asian Americans. Whites accounted for 52 percent of violent offenses; African Americans, 46 percent; Native Americans, 0.9 percent; and Asian Americans, 1.3 percent. The data for property crimes were whites, 69 percent; African Americans, 28 percent; Native Americans, 1.4 percent; and Asian Americans, 1.8 percent.[10] This arrest pattern of juveniles parallels that of adults; minority members of the U.S. population clearly are arrested in disproportionately high numbers relative to their percentage of the population.[11]

Trends in Juvenile Arrest Rates

Some major trends noted by the UCRs are as follows:

1. Juvenile arrest rates climbed up in the mid-1990s but dropped 22 percent overall since 1995. The drop was 9.1 percent from 2000 to 2004.
2. The juvenile violent crime arrest rate decreased 31 percent between 1995 and 2004.
3. Female arrest rates increased relative to those of males between 1995 and 2004 in most categories; just as with males, female violent crime arrest rates now appear to have stabilized or are even increasing.[12]
4. Juvenile arrests for drug use increased over the past ten years, roughly 22 percent of all arrests for drugs. The majority of all arrests are for drug possession rather than for manufacturing or selling. Juvenile arrests for cocaine and opium use have declined, while those for marijuana use have increased; drug use among juveniles has increased over the past decade.[13]
5. The number of arrests for homicide decreased dramatically between 1995 and 2004, but more recent data indicate that homicide rates today may be increasing.[14]

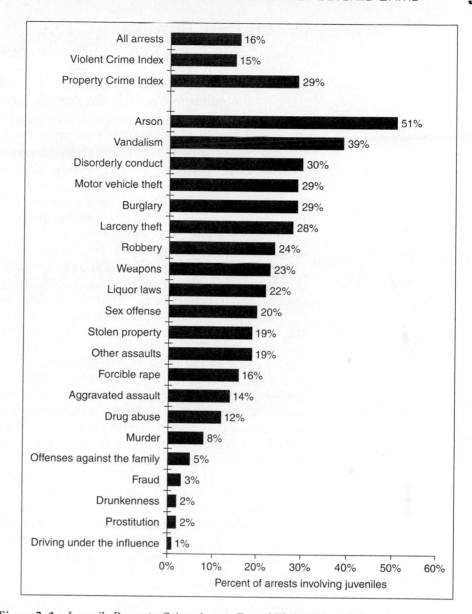

Figure 2–1 *Juvenile Property Crime Arrests Exceed Their Violent Crime Arrests*

In 2003 juveniles were involved in one in six arrests for a violent crime, one in three arrests for a property offense, and one in four arrests for a weapons law violation.

Note: Running away from home and curfew violations are not presented in this figure because, by definition, only juveniles can be arrested for these offenses.

Source: http://www.ncjrs.gov/html/ojjdp/209735/contents.html

Several reasons exist for challenging the validity of the UCRs' findings. For example, the police can make arrests only when crimes come to their attention (which results in an underestimation of the actual amount of youth crime in this nation). The police also arrest only those offenders who commit serious crimes and ignore many lesser offenses committed by juveniles. Furthermore, youth crime rates are inflated because youthful offenders are easier to detect in the act of committing a crime. Finally, juveniles frequently commit offenses in groups, and the reporting of all the groups' members may actually overestimate the amount of youth crime. Even so, new reporting procedures and computerization make the reporting and recording of offenses easier than ever before, resulting in the improved accuracy of UCR data.

JUVENILE COURT STATISTICS

Juvenile Court Statistics was first published in 1929. Its purpose was threefold:

- To furnish an index of the nature and extent of the problems brought before courts with juvenile jurisdiction
- To show the nature and extent of the services provided by these courts in such a way that significant trends could be identified
- To show the extent to which the services provided by these courts have been effective in correcting social problems[15]

These data were collected by the Children's Bureau in the Department of the Census, and from the very beginning, the report included such information as the age, sex, and race of the offender, as well as the reasons for referral, the child's living arrangements, the source of the referral, where the child was detained while awaiting adjudication, how the case was handled, and the case's disposition. In addition, information was recorded on each delinquency, status offense, and dependency case that came before the courts.

In 1974, the stage was set for the current system of data collection. After the Juvenile Justice and Delinquency Prevention Act of 1974 was passed, the Department of Justice took over the *Juvenile Court Statistics* series, which was now located in the Department of Health, Education and Welfare. The National Center for Juvenile Justice requested that state agencies complete the juvenile justice statistics form and send the information to the Center. Most state agencies not only did this but also indicated that they would send case-level information they had collected for their own purposes. These new data permitted the National Center for Juvenile Justice to reach the original goals set forth in 1923. Today, the National Center for Juvenile Justice constructs national estimates of the number of delinquency offenders brought to the nation's juvenile courts and the outcomes of the judicial processing of these offenders; the status offense data estimates are based on data from 1985 to 2000. Following are examples of their findings for both status and delinquency offenses. The estimates of delinquency offenses and their outcomes are based on yearly nonprobability sampling of more than 2,000 courts across the country.[16]

Status Offenses

Status offenses are behaviors for which juveniles, but not adults, may be arrested. However, the way juveniles actually get to juvenile court varies by jurisdiction. Although police take many juveniles into custody and may refer them to juvenile court, school officials, parents, and other members of the community also may decide that a particular youth needs help; depending upon the jurisdiction, juveniles may get to juvenile court by one of two paths. In many communities, after police or other referrals, juveniles are screened by the intake unit of the local juvenile court; the intake unit decides whether to handle the case informally or to petition the case to court. In other jurisdictions, the decision on what to do with the juvenile is made outside the juvenile court in police departments, special offices, child welfare agencies, and so on. In these jurisdictions, the intake decision often is to send the juvenile to outside agencies for counseling and treatment. This very frequently happens with status offenders.

An examination of status offenses reveals that the largest number are liquor law violations, followed by truancy, running away, and ungovernable behavior. Other status offenses include such behaviors as curfew violations and sexual misbehavior. Running away, truancy, and ungovernability peak at age fifteen and then drop off dramatically, while liquor law violations rise rapidly up to the age of seventeen.[17]

Delinquency Cases

In 2002, juvenile courts in the United States disposed of over almost 1.6 million delinquency cases.[18] Calculations on the data in Figure 2–2 indicate that 41 percent of **delinquent offenses** were property offenses, 23 percent were person offenses; 24 percent were public order offenses; and 12 percent were drug offenses. Of the person offenses, the largest percentage consisted of simple assaults, followed by aggravated assaults and then robberies; larceny-theft made up the largest number of property offenses, followed by burglary and vandalism. Obstruction of justice and disorderly conduct comprised the largest percentages

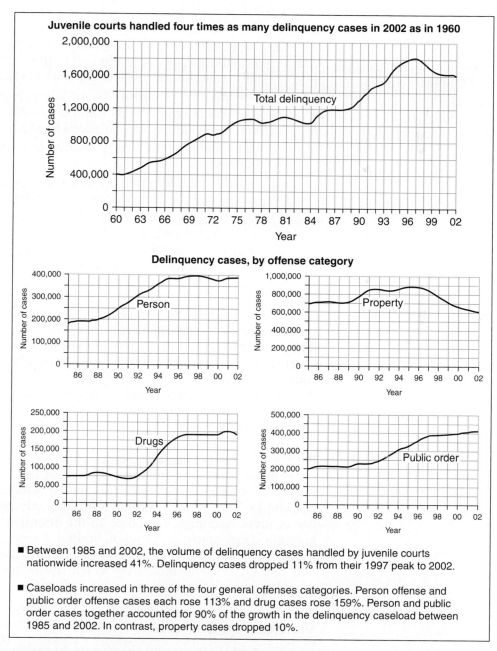

- Between 1985 and 2002, the volume of delinquency cases handled by juvenile courts nationwide increased 41%. Delinquency cases dropped 11% from their 1997 peak to 2002.

- Caseloads increased in three of the four general offenses categories. Person offense and public order offense cases each rose 113% and drug cases rose 159%. Person and public order cases together accounted for 90% of the growth in the delinquency caseload between 1985 and 2002. In contrast, property cases dropped 10%.

Figure 2–2   *Juvenile Courts and Delinquency Cases Over Time*

Source: Howard N. Synder and Melissa Sickmund, *Juvenile Offenders and Victims: 2000 National Report* (Washington, DC: National Center for Juvenile Justice and Office of Justice Programs, 2006) p. 150; adapted from Stahl et al.'s *Juvenile Court Statistics 2001–2002*.

of the public order offenses. Figure 2–2 reveals that the long-term growth for juvenile court caseloads has been tempered by recent declines.

Juvenile Court Statistics 2002 depicts what happens to the cases brought into the system. For example, 58 percent of the delinquency cases are petitioned; that is, the youths come into the juvenile court as a result of the filing of a petition, complaint, or other legal instrument requesting the court to declare the child a delinquent or a dependent or to transfer the child to an adult court.[19] In the nonpetitioned delinquency cases, 42 percent of the total are informally handled cases in which authorized court personnel screen a case prior to the filing of a formal petition and decide not to prosecute the offender. Juvenile court statistics are as follows:

1. Delinquency increases with age.
2. The number of cases appearing before the juvenile court increased until the mid-1970s, leveled off until the late 1980s, rose dramatically from the late 1980s to the mid-1990s, and then decreased through 2002.[20]
3. Of status offenses, truancy and ungovernability rates peak at age fifteen, while liquor law violations increase continuously with age.
4. Males are more frequently referred to the juvenile court than are females.
5. Females are referred to juvenile court for truancy and ungovernability at about the same rate as males; across the board, female rates are increasing relative to male rates.
6. White males are referred to the juvenile court roughly in proportion to their numbers in the population; black males are referred to juvenile court at rates highly disproportionate to their numbers in the population.

The findings of juvenile court statistics parallel those of the UCRs. The advantage of the court statistics, however, is that they reveal not only who the offenders are but also what types of dispositions are handed down. The juvenile court statistics are able further to track the number of offenders coming to the courts over specific periods of time, as well as to follow trends in the changing characteristics of offenders and the dispositions handed down. The latter data are helpful in determining the success of suggested and mandated social policy changes in who should come to court and what should happen to them.

Juvenile court statistics do have serious limitations. The usual time lag in the publication of the statistics lessens their usefulness; in addition, these cases make up only a small percentage of the total number of juvenile offenses. Moreover, the data collected by the National Institute of Juvenile Justice and Delinquency Prevention represent only an estimate of the total number of juvenile crimes that come to the attention of juvenile courts. Finally, juvenile court statistics provide limited information about juvenile court transactions and the characteristics of referred juveniles. Yet these statistics still provide a useful means by which researchers can examine youths and what happens to them relative to juvenile court.

VICTIMIZATION SURVEYS

In 1972, the U.S. Bureau of the Census began victimization studies to determine as accurately as possible the extent of crime in the United States. This new data set was needed because the UCRs measured police activity, that is, the number of arrests that police made, not the actual amount of crime committed. The volume of "hidden crime" has long been known to be great, as people often do not report crimes to the police. The **National Crime Victimization Survey** was set up to overcome this problem and give policymakers a better idea of just how much crime actually is committed.

The *National Crime Victimization Survey* of 2004 selected a random sample of 149,000 residents in 84,360 households across the United States.[21] Data from these individuals are used to measure all crimes—whether or not reported to the police—in the previous six-month period. To collect the data, representatives of the Bureau of the Census interview all household residents twelve years of age or older in the selected sample.

The *National Crime Victimization Survey* reports that in 2004, persons twelve years of age or older experienced nearly 24.0 million crimes, of which 18.6 million were property crimes, 5.2 million were violent crimes, and approximately 224,000, were personal thefts.[22] Overall, the number of offenses reported to the police was much lower than the total number of offenses uncovered by the victimization surveys.

Juveniles, as might be expected, were highly overrepresented compared to other age groups in the population. Table 2–1 shows that juveniles between the

Table 2–1 *Victimization Rates for Persons Age Twelve and Over, by Type of Crime and Age of Victims*

Type of Crime	Rate Per 1,000 Persons in Each Age Group						
	12–15	16–19	20–24	25–34	35–49	50–64	65 and over
All personal crimes	**53.1**	**54.4**	**45.0**	**27.4**	**19.0**	**10.5**	**2.5**
Crimes of violence	51.6	53.0	43.3	26.4	18.5	10.3	2.0
Completed violence	16.2	16.4	15.2	8.1	5.2	2.7	0.8*
Attempted/threatened violence	35.5	36.6	28.2	18.3	13.3	7.6	1.1
Rape/sexual assault	1.2*	1.3*	1.7	1.6	0.6	0.4*	0.1*
Rape/attempted rape	0.8*	0.7*	1.2*	1.0	0.2*	0.2*	0.1*
Rape	0.6*	0.6*	0.7*	0.7*	0.1*	0.1*	0.1*
Attempted rape[a]	0.2*	0.2*	0.4*	0.3*	0.2*	0.1*	0.0*
Sexual assault[b]	0.3*	0.6*	0.5*	0.6*	0.4*	0.2*	0.0*
Robbery	5.2	5.1	6.4	2.5	1.7	1.4	0.7*
Completed/property taken	3.2	3.7	4.3	1.5	0.9	0.8	0.8*
With injury	1.5*	1.3*	1.9	0.8	0.3*	0.3*	0.4*
Without injury	1.7*	2.4	2.4	0.7*	0.7	0.5*	0.2*
Attempted to take property	2.0	1.4*	2.1	1.0	0.8	0.6*	0.1*
With injury	0.6*	0.4*	0.5*	0.4*	0.1*	0.1*	0.0*
Without injury	1.5*	1.0*	1.5*	0.6*	0.7	0.5*	0.1*
Assault	45.3	46.6	35.3	22.3	16.1	8.5	1.2
Aggravated	8.9	11.9	9.8	8.0	3.8	1.6	0.1*
With injury	2.7	3.4	3.4	2.2	1.4	0.3*	0.0*
Threatened with weapon	6.1	8.5	6.4	3.8	2.4	1.2	0.1*
Simple	36.4	34.7	25.5	16.3	12.3	7.0	1.1
With minor injury	9.5	8.3	6.2	3.1	2.5	1.3	0.2*
Without injury	26.9	26.4	19.3	13.2	9.9	5.7	0.9*
Purse snatching/Pocket picking	1.5*	1.4*	1.6	1.0	0.5	0.3*	0.5*
Population in each age group	17,084,330	16,210,780	19,786,270	39,449,790	65,780,190	46,736,200	34,258,430

Note: Detail may not add to total shown because of rounding.
*Estimate is based on about 10 or fewer sample cases.
[a]Includes verbal threats of rape.
[b]Includes threats.

ages of sixteen and nineteen experienced the highest victimization rate per one thousand population of any age group for all violent crimes. Youths between twelve and fifteen had the next highest rate, with rates then dropping with the increasing age of the victim. (See Table 2–1 for the rates of victimization by age and type of violent offense.) Within the adolescent population itself, older adolescents (ages sixteen to nineteen) had higher overall violent-crime victimization rates than did younger ones (ages twelve to fifteen).[23] Data also show that adolescents were more likely than adults to commit violent crimes against peers and to report knowing their assailants. Crimes against adolescents also were less likely to be reported to the police than crimes against adults.[24]

Victimization surveys have not been as widely used in analyzing youth crime as have the other means of the measurement of youth crime, but they do add to what is known about crime in the United States. Some of the principal findings of victimization surveys are as follows:

1. Much more crime is committed than is recorded.
2. The discrepancy between the number of people who say they have been victimized and the number of crimes known to the police varies with the type of offense.
3. The probability of being victimized varies with the type of crime and one's place of residence. The centers of U.S. cities are the more probable sites of violent crimes.
4. Juveniles are more likely to be victimized than any other age group.

✓ **Progress Check 2.1**
Review this section at
www.prenhall.com/bartollas

Victimization studies do have limitations. Information on status offenses is not included; victims may forget the victimization they have experienced; or victims may state that a specific crime took place within the research year when it took place before or after that period.

WHAT ARE SELF-REPORT AND COHORT MEASURES OF JUVENILE CRIME?

Self-report and cohort studies are other main sources of information on delinquent behavior. Self-report studies ask juveniles to tell about offenses they committed in a previous period of time. Cohort studies mostly utilize raw police files along with a variety of other data.

SELF-REPORT STUDIES

Self-report studies have been used since the 1940s to measure hidden youth crime. The reason for their use is to obtain a fuller and more accurate picture of the amount of crime than can be obtained through the UCRs. The UCRs, for example, generally show that lower-class youths commit more crime than do middle- or upper-class youths. Researchers can test this finding by going to different classes of youths and asking them about the number and type of offenses they have committed. Researchers also can obtain considerable information on offender characteristics such as age, sex, and race, as well as on the amount of gang delinquency and the extent of drug and alcohol abuse. In this section, we look at self-reporting and offenders' demographic characteristics.

One of the most significant findings of all the self-report studies is that the amount of youth crime is much greater than that indicated by the UCRs. Indeed, practically every youth commits some type of crime. Very few, however, ever come to the attention of the authorities.[25] This means that little

Veteran female shoplifter distracts sales clerk while her accomplice pockets an item. (Photo by Kathryn Miller.)

reason exists for dividing youths into offenders and nonoffenders, as many students of the juvenile justice system are prone to do. The self-report studies contradict or expand on the UCRs in other ways as well.

Self-Report Studies and Race

Official statistics tend to show that the differences between African Americans and whites are greater than self-report studies indicate. In looking at race, for example, David Huizinga and Delbert S. Elliott's examination of the National Youth Survey concluded that "there are few if any substantial and consistent differences between the delinquency involvement of different racial groups."[26] The *Monitoring the Future Project* for 1994 also found that differences in the amount of crime between African Americans and whites were not as great as suggested by the UCRs. In examining African-American and white responses to sixteen questions, for example, the two groups of subjects were within 8 percentage points of each other in fourteen of the sixteen questions.[27] Two other national studies reported involvement in seventeen delinquent behaviors with similar frequencies, but further analysis of the data revealed that the seriousness of self-reported delinquency was slightly greater for African-American males than for white males.[28] Delbert Elliott and Suzanne Ageton's study revealed that the offense rate was greater for African Americans because they were more likely to be involved in serious property crime and because they were more likely to be chronic or repeat offenders.[29]

Sex and Self-Report

Similar discrepancies appear between official data and self-report studies when examining the sex of youthful offenders. Self-report studies show that female delinquency is higher than reported in official data.[30] Steven Cernkovich and Peggy Giordano's self-report study of midwestern youths found that the ratio of male to female arrests was about one-half as large as the 4:1 ratio found in the UCRs.[31] Self-report studies do show that females are less likely to be involved in serious crime. For example, the findings of *Monitoring the Future Project* for 1994 revealed that female high school students reported being involved in fewer fights in school, being involved in fewer fights between groups, hurting someone badly less frequently, and using a weapon less frequently.[32]

Social Class and Delinquency

The finding that unlawful behavior is unrelated or only slightly related to a juvenile's social class is one of the most significant findings of self-report studies.[33] Travis Hirschi's survey of four thousand junior and senior high-school students in Richmond, California, found little association between self-reported delinquencies and income, education, and occupation.[34] Richard E. Johnson, in redefining social class as underclass and earning class, added: "The data provide no firm evidence that social class, no matter how it is measured, is a salient factor in generating delinquent involvement."[35]

Elliott and Ageton's national study, however, found a different pattern when youths were asked how many times they had violated that law during the previous year. The average number of delinquent acts reported by lower-class juveniles, according to these researchers, exceeded that reported by working-class or middle-class youths. Indeed, the average number of crimes against persons reported by lower-class youths was one and one-half times greater than that reported by working- or middle-class youths.[36]

Evaluation of Self-Report Studies

The realization that official statistics on juvenile delinquency have serious limitations led to a growing reliance on the use of self-report studies. These studies have revealed the following conclusions:

1. A significant amount of undetected delinquency exists in the United States.
2. Middle-class juveniles are involved in a considerable number of juvenile offenses.
3. Hidden delinquency also includes a large number of serious crimes each year that elude detection by the police.
4. The differences between the offenses of African Americans and those of whites are less in self-report than in official statistics.
5. Girls commit more delinquent acts than official statistics indicate, but boys commit more delinquent acts and commit more serious youth crimes than girls do.

COHORT STUDIES

Cohort studies are another valuable tool of researchers. These studies do not start by counting offenses or by asking who has been victimized. Rather, they identify every juvenile born in a certain time frame in a particular city and then follow those juveniles for many years. Depending on the goals of the study, police files, school records, and/or socioeconomic data are collected and then scrutinized for all the juveniles. These data and any evidence that the youths have gotten into trouble are collected by the researchers for their study. The result is a wealth of information not attainable through the use of official statistics.[37] Three of the most important older cohort studies involve data collected on cohorts of youths in Philadelphia; Columbus, Ohio; and Racine, Wisconsin.[38] For more recent cohort studies, see Focus on Research 2–2.

FOCUS ON RESEARCH   2–2
HIGHLIGHTS FROM DENVER, PITTSBURGH, AND ROCHESTER YOUTH SURVEYS

Denver

The Denver study follows 1,527 boys and girls from high-risk neighborhoods in Denver who were seven, nine, eleven, thirteen, and fifteen years old in 1987. In exploring the changes in the nature of delinquency and drug use from the 1970s to the 1990s, the Denver study's findings are as follows:

- Overall, there was little change in the prevalence rates of delinquency, including serious delinquency and serious violence. However, the prevalence rate of gang fights among males doubled (from 8 percent to 16 percent).
- The level of injury from violence offenses increased substantially.
- The prevalence of drug use decreased substantially: alcohol, from 80 percent to 50 percent; marijuana, from 41 percent to 18 percent; and other drug use, from 19 percent to 4 percent.
- The relationships between drug use and delinquency have changed in that a smaller percentage (from 48 percent to 17 percent) of serious delinquents are using hard drugs other than marijuana, and a greater percentage (from 27 percent to 48 percent) of hard drug users are serious offenders.
- More than half (53 percent) of the youth in the study ages eleven through fifteen in 1987 were arrested over the next five years.

Pittsburgh

The Pittsburgh study, a longitudinal study of 1,517 inner-city boys, followed three samples of boys for more than a decade to advance knowledge about how and why boys become involved in delinquency and other problem behaviors. Its chief findings are as follows:

- There were no differences between African-American and white boys at age six, but differences gradually developed, the prevalence of serious delinquency at age sixteen reaching 27 percent for African-American boys and 19 percent for white boys.
- As prevalence increased, so did the average frequency of serious offending, which rose more rapidly for African-American boys than for white boys.
- The onset of offending among the boys involved in serious delinquency occurred by age fifteen, when 51 percent of African-American boys and 28 percent of white boys committed serious delinquent acts.
- The boys generally developed disruptive and delinquent behavior in an orderly, progressive fashion, with less serious problem behaviors preceding more serious problem behaviors.
- Three groups of developmental pathways were identified that displayed progressively more serious problem behaviors:
  Authority Conflict: Youths on this pathway exhibit stubbornness prior to age twelve, then move on to defiance and avoidance of authority.
  Covert: This pathway includes minor acts, such as lying, followed by property damage and moderately serious delinquency.
  Overt: This pathway includes minor aggression followed by fighting and violence.

Rochester

The Rochester study, a longitudinal study of one thousand urban adolescents, investigates the causes and consequences of adolescent delinquency and drug use by following a sample of high-risk urban adolescents from their early teenage years through their early adult years. Its chief findings are as follows:

- Attachment and involvement were both significantly related to delinquency. Children who were more attached to and involved with their parents were less involved in delinquency.
- The relationship between family process factors and delinquency was bidirectional—poor parenting increased the probability of delinquent behavior and delinquent behavior further weakened the relationship between parent and child.
- The impact of family variables appeared to fade as adolescents became older and more independent of their parents. Weak school commitment and poor school performance were associated with increased involvement in delinquency and drug use.
- Associating with delinquent peers was strongly and consistently related to delinquency, in part because peers provide positive reinforcements for delinquency. There is a strong relationship between gang membership and delinquent behavior, particularly serious and violent delinquency.

Sources: Katharine Browning, Terence P. Thornberry, and Pamela K. Porter, "Highlights of Findings from the Rochester Youth Development Study," *OJJDP Fact Sheet* (Washington, DC: Office of Juvenile Justice and Delinquency Prevention, 1999); Katharine Browning and Rolf Loeber, "Highlights from the Pittsburgh Youth Study," *OJJDP Fact Sheet* (Washington, DC: Office of Juvenile Justice and Delinquency Prevention, 1999); and Katharine Browning and David Huizinga, "Highlights from the Denver Youth Study," *OJJDP Fact Sheet* (Washington, DC: Office of Juvenile Justice and Delinquency Prevention, 1999).

Critical Thinking Questions:
What do the findings of these three studies have in common? How do they differ? What would you say are the most important findings overall?

DELINQUENCY IN THE PHILADELPHIA COHORT. Marvin Wolfgang and colleagues conducted two important cohort studies. The first study consisted of all males born in 1945 who resided in the city of Philadelphia from their tenth through their eighteenth birthdays. The second study consisted of all males and females born in 1958 in Philadelphia who resided in the city from their tenth through their eighteenth birthdays.[39]

Cohort I. Of the nearly ten thousand cohort subjects, Wolfgang and colleagues found that 35 percent had at least one contact with the police at some time during the span of their juvenile court age. Significantly, 6.3 percent of the total cohort were responsible for 51 percent of the total number of delinquent acts. **Chronic offenders,** as these recidivists were called, were responsible for 71 percent of the homicides, 73 percent of the rapes, 82 percent of the robberies, and 69 percent of the aggravated assaults.

Cohort II. Of the 13,160 male subjects, 33 percent had at least one police contact before reaching their eighteenth birthday. Of the 14,000 females in the cohort, about 14 percent had at least one police contact before age eighteen. The 1958 cohort contained 982 male chronic offenders, or 7.5 percent of the males, and 147 female chronic delinquents, or 7.5 percent of the females.

In sum, Wolfgang and colleagues found that a few youths committed at least half of all juvenile offenses and an even higher percentage of the violent juvenile offenses in Philadelphia. Overall, youthful offenders in Cohort II committed much more serious and more frequent offenses than those in Cohort I, and in both cohorts, males committed more frequent and more serious offenses than females did. Finally, both studies found that if an individual had been arrested before the age of nineteen, he was three times more likely to be arrested as an adult.

Evaluation of Cohort Studies

The cohort studies conducted in Columbus, Ohio, and Racine, Wisconsin, generally agree with the following conclusions of the two Philadelphia cohort studies:

1. A few youths commit at least half of all juvenile offenses and an even higher percentage of the violent juvenile offenses.
2. African-American urban youths as a group commit more frequent and more serious delinquent offenses than do whites.
3. Females typically have fewer contacts and less serious involvement with the police than do males.
4. The more frequent and more serious the police contacts are that a juvenile has, the more likely it is that that youth will continue on to adult crime.
5. Interventions by the justice system appear to raise the likelihood of the frequency and seriousness of unlawful behavior in the future.

Cohort studies, like other forms of crime statistics, have two major problems. First, their findings cannot be generalized confidently beyond the persons in the cohort. Second, cohort studies are extremely expensive and time-consuming. Indeed, keeping track of a sample of individuals even up to age thirty-five is almost impossible because names and addresses change, some people die, and others simply drop out of sight. Still, even with these drawbacks, cohort studies remain a useful addition to other official and unofficial measurements of crime.

WHAT ARE THE DIMENSIONS OF LAW-VIOLATING BEHAVIORS?

A century of study enables researchers to identify variables and patterns important in the understanding of juvenile crime. The age of onset, escalation of offenses, specialization of offenses, desistance from crime, and transition to adult crime all help focus attention on some key patterns in juvenile crime and provide some guides to our understanding of the causes of crime and the recidivism of offenders.

AGE OF ONSET

Several studies have found that the earlier juveniles began law-violating behaviors (their **age of onset**), the more likely they were to continue such behaviors. Marvin E. Wolfgang, Terence P. Thornberry, and Robert M. Figlio followed a 10 percent sample of Cohort I (of the Philadelphia cohort study) to the age of thirty and found that the average number of offenses tended to decline almost uniformly as the age of onset increased.[40] Alfred Blumstein, David P. Farrington, and Soumyo Moitra also showed that one of the factors predicting who became chronic offenders was offending at an early age.[41] Farrington further found that those who were first convicted at the earliest age (ten to twelve) consistently offended at a higher rate and for a longer time period than did those who were first convicted at later ages.[42]

ESCALATION OF OFFENSES

The findings on **escalation of offenses** (an increase in the number of crimes committed by an individual) are less consistent than those on age of onset. Official studies have typically found that the incidence of arrest accelerates at age thirteen and peaks at about age seventeen, but this pattern is less evident in self-report studies. For example, Ageton and Elliott found that the incidence of some offenses, such as assault and robbery, increased with age, whereas that of others peaked between ages thirteen and fifteen.[43]

SPECIALIZATION OF OFFENSES

The findings on **specialization of offenses** (the tendency to repeat one type of crime) are more consistent than those on escalation. The cohort studies, especially, revealed little or no specialization of offenses among delinquents.[44] Some evidence exists, however, that specialization was much more typical of status offenders. Susan K. Datesman and Michael Aickin's examination of a sample of status offenders found that the majority, regardless of sex and race, were referred to court within the same offense category 50 to 70 percent of the time. Females, especially white females, specialized in official offense behavior to a greater extent than did males; 35 percent of the white females were referred to court for the same offenses, a sizable proportion of them for running away.[45]

DESISTANCE FROM CRIME

Desistance from crime, or the age of termination of delinquency, has become a recent concern of researchers. A major problem in establishing desistance is the difficulty of distinguishing between a gap in a delinquent career and true termination. Crime-free intervals are bound to be present in the course of delinquent careers. Theorists have proposed several explanations for change in offending over time, or desistance, which we will consider by category.

- *Maturation and Aging Accounts of Desistance.* These accounts have long been popular in explaining the desirability of pursuing a conventional lifestyle or the undesirability of continuing with unlawful activities.
- *Developmental Accounts of Desistance.* One of the popular accounts of developmental explanations of desistance is that identity changes account for reduction in or cessation of crime. Peggy C. Giordano and her colleagues, in a longitudinal study of serious female offenders, found that desistance took place when cognitive shifts occurred in these offenders.[46]
- *Rational Choice Account of Desistance.* The rational choice theory is that the decision to give up or continue with crime is based on a person's conscious reappraisal of the costs and benefits of criminal activity. Proponents of this theory see persisters and desisters as "reasoned decision makers."
- *Social Learning Accounts of Desistance.* Social learning accounts incorporate all of the major elements of the rational choice and deterrence framework, including moral reasoning. According to this

framework, the basic variables explaining initiation into crime are essentially the same ones that account for desistance from crime.[47]

- *Life-Course Account of Desistance.* The life-course perspective, whose framework will be discussed in Chapter 3, as expressed by Robert Sampson and John Laub, is that "offenders desist as a result of individual actions (choice) in conjunction with situational contexts and structural influences linked to key institutions that help sustain desistance."[48]

TRANSITION TO ADULT CRIME

Studies have identified three groups of criminal offenders. One group offends only during their juvenile years; a second group offends only during their adult years; and a third group persistently offends during both periods.[49] Some scholars argue that juvenile offenders' **transition to adult crime** is due to their prior participation in unlawful activities. This prior participation, according to this position, reduces inhibitions against engaging in future unlawful behavior. Other scholars contend that some individuals have a higher propensity to delinquency than do others and that this higher propensity persists over time. This higher propensity is related to such factors as poor parental supervision, parental rejection, parental criminality, delinquent siblings, and low IQ.[50] For an examination of chronic offenders, the group of youthful offenders who violate the law more frequently and seriously and are more likely to go on to adult crime, see Focus on Chronic Offenders 2–3.

WHAT ARE THE ORIGINS OF JUVENILE VICTIMS?

Victimization surveys indicate that children too frequently are the targets of crime. In many countries throughout the world, in fact, attention to the plight of children is increasing the focus on the victimization of youths in dysfunctional families, in schools, in their neighborhoods, and by authorities. Emotionally damaged as a result of neglect and abuse, children often are unable to relate to adults and peers, to perform in school, and to make realistic plans for the future. Many of these juveniles become involved in law-violating behaviors.

THE FAMILY AND THE VICTIMIZATION OF CHILDREN

Reports by child protective agencies indicate that the maltreatment of children increased 155 percent between 1980 and 1993.[51] According to the National Center on Child Abuse and Family Violence, the amount of childhood victimization stabilized through 1994 and began dropping through 1999, only to rise slightly in 2000.[52] More recent data suggest that a slight decrease in child maltreatment is occurring; experts disagree as to whether the decrease is real or an artifact of reporting procedures.[53] Whatever the direction, the magnitude of child abuse and neglect remains unacceptably high, with almost 3 million referrals of alleged victims in 2000. Citizens, doctors, and hospitals continue to report offenses, as states now mandate the reporting of abuse when discovered. The problem of parental maltreatment of children can be divided into several different categories. The Childrens' Bureau reports that in 2004, roughly 60 percent of reported maltreatment stemmed from neglect, 18 percent from physical abuse, 10 percent from sexual abuse, and 5 percent from emotional maltreatment; 15 percent fell into an "other" category that included such factors as medical neglect, abandonment, and "congenital drug addiction."[54]

FOCUS ON CHRONIC OFFENDERS   2–3

CHRONIC OFFENDERS: NOTES ON THEIR BACKGROUNDS

The chronic offender is known by many labels: *serious delinquent, repeat offender, violent offender, dangerous offender, hard-core delinquent*, and *career delinquent*. Whatever the label, the predominant characteristics of these youths are their commitment to crime and their involvement in one crime after another, often very serious crimes against persons and property. Their initial participation in crime constitutes the budding of a lifestyle centered on violence and "making it big" in the criminal world. Chronic offenders expect to engage in criminal careers for at least several years, if not for the rest of their lives.

Chronic offenders become committed to criminal careers through one of two routes. In the first, noncriminal and situational offenders move from casual involvement with other offenders on the streets, to being processed with them through the system, to perceiving crime as a way of life, and finally to being willing to stand up for this involvement. Usually these youths have been picked up by the police many times, have been in courts and detention halls several times, and have had one or more institutional stays. The decisions they make at each stage move them closer to a delinquent career.

The second route is quite different. Some youths become absorbed in crime before they have contact with the justice system. These offenders often grow up a ghetto area and, surrounded by vice and crime, become involved with peers in unlawful acts at an early age. Frequently, they come from impoverished families. They tend to feel that life is a struggle and that only the strong survive; therefore, they are always on guard against being hurt or exploited by others, and they develop a hostile and suspicious view of the world around them. They seem to accept a commitment to crime without any apparent episodes of decision making.

Chronic offenders typically come from lower-class backgrounds and in many cases have grown up in urban pockets of poverty. They most often are minority males who have lived on the streets with insufficient parental support and with a history of failure in social institutions. An inability to function in school either in acceptable academic performance or in satisfactory relationships with teachers and peers characterizes their school experiences. A history of school dropout is followed by a pattern of unemployment. Part of this inability to find jobs is the lack of marketable skills. These juveniles contribute to the disturbing high rates of unemployment among urban African Americans.

The attitudes of chronic offenders, of course, do vary. Some are more bitter or angry than others, and this variation seems to be affected greatly by the amount of love and acceptance they received at home and the injustices they have experienced. In addition, some chronic offenders have more hope than others. Youths with histories of drug addiction generally do not demonstrate the positive attitudes of those without such histories. Chronic offenders who are closest to institutional release, not surprisingly, are more hopeful than those who face long periods of continement. Chronic offenders who have developed positive goals for the future are also more hopeful than those who lack such goals. Finally, the more that chronic offenders see life as a "give me" experience, the less they seem able to develop positive relationships with others or to pursue noncrime options.

Source: One of the authors of this textbook has formed these impressions of chronic offenders, based on his work with them in both institutional and community-based contexts over the past thirty-five years.

Critical Thinking Questions:
Why is the chronic offender so difficult to treat in the juvenile justice system? Why does this category of offenders so frequently go on to adult crime? Is long-term incarceration the only possible means to deter their criminal behaviors as juveniles and adults?

Lured to a mall after several months of contact on the Internet, this young girl could well be in extreme danger. (Photo by Kathryn Miller.)

Finkelhor, Omrod, and Turner, in a representative national sample of 2,030 youths ages two to seventeen, give us a different view of child victimization. Their study found that over half of the sample were the victims of physical assault; one-fourth were victims of a property offense, 12 percent of child maltreatment, and 8 percent of sexual victimization; over one-third either witnessed violence or were affected by victimization indirectly.[55] In yet another twist, Finkelhor and others have examined sibling violence. While the usual sibling fights over the last cookie or who is going to wear what clothes seem innocuous enough, some siblings experience repeated and prolonged violence, the effects of which may accompany them for the rest of their lives.[56] In addition to these studies, the 2004 Crime Reports present some preliminary studies on infanticide in the United States.

Homicide is the most serious victimization of children. The UCRs indicate that 1,365 people under the age of eighteen were murdered in 2004, accounting for almost 10 percent of all murders in the United States in that year. This averages almost four juveniles murdered each day.[57] Other estimates suggest that significantly more than two thousand children are killed each year.[58] The discrepancies among these estimates stem from the fact that the deaths of many young children and infants may be attributed to sudden infant death syndrome or other accidental causes instead of being labeled as deliberate maltreatment by parents or others (importantly, recent studies indicate that over 50 percent of abuse and neglect deaths are not reported); an additional analysis by the UCRs for 2004 indicates that 48 percent of the murdered children were under the age of twelve and 30 percent were between the ages of thirteen and sixteen.[59] For ages seventeen and older, the number of youths murdered each year increased dramatically.

In 2004, 79 percent of all child murder victims were killed by their parents, 7 percent by relatives, 4 percent by unmarried partners of parents, and the remaining percent by acquaintances or unknown assailants.[60] Females were twice as likely as males to be killed by family members; in addition, children under age eight were more likely to die as a result of neglect or repeated abuse, whereas children over age eight more frequently died as a result of physical or sexual abuse. Younger children generally died at the hands of family members, whereas older children were more likely to be murdered by non-family members.

The consequences for the *survivors* of child abuse and neglect can be severe. Although some victims of abuse appear to survive their victimization with only minor damage, evidence is mounting that the majority suffer serious problems of negative self-concept, an inability to form normal relationships with other people, depression, anxiety, and self-destructive behavior. Furthermore, evidence is emerging that the victims of violence and neglect are arrested more frequently than are individuals who escaped maltreatment in their early childhoods.[61]

Cathy Spatz Widom's study of 908 victims of childhood abuse demonstrates clearly that any type of maltreatment of children puts them at greater risk for arrest—both as juveniles and as adults. Widom found that 16.8 percent of a control group of 667 children who had experienced no abuse of any kind were arrested as juveniles. In contrast, 28.4 percent of neglected youths experienced arrest, as did 19.9 percent of physically abused children and 22.2 percent of sexually abused children. Similarly, as adults, 21 percent of the control group was arrested, along with 30.7 percent who had experienced neglect, 27.4 percent of the physically abused, and 20.3 percent of the sexually abused.[62] Studies continue to show this relationship between victimization and crime.[63]

THE SCHOOL AND VICTIMIZATION

In the past, the major problems teachers and administrators in the nation's school systems faced were those of juveniles running the halls, leaving class without permission, writing graffiti on the walls, and occasionally fighting. Today's students, however, are likely to experience the same problems in the schools as on the streets. Drugs, alcohol, suicide, rape, robbery, assault, arson, and bomb threats combine with knives and guns to change the atmosphere of schools and to generate fear on the part of parents, who worry about their children's safety.

In addition, as suggested by George Knox and others, schools in the 1990s became fertile soil for the violence of youth gangs.[64] Gangs perpetrate school violence in a number of ways. First, gang members frequently bring concealed weapons to school.[65] Second, gangs are always recruiting new members, and nongang students may be assaulted if they refuse to join. Third, conflict takes place on a regular basis if more than one group is present in a school. Warring gang members may start a mass riot, in which stabbings and shootings take place. Finally, conflicts among rival gangs in different schools commonly lead to drive-by shootings.[66] It is little wonder that schools no longer are perceived as havens of safety and learning for juveniles.

All of these events do happen, yet we must ask just how dangerous our schools really are. Are children likely to be murdered or assaulted when out of parents' sight and behind school walls? Part of the problem society faces today is separating fact from fiction. The reality is that the media contribute to a frenzy of fear by publicizing the slightest incident as well as the most tragic event. The national scope of reporting means that a parent in northern Maine hears about events in southern California. Students too hear about these events and fear for their safety.

Nonfatal Crime in the Schools

A 2006 report on school crime and **school safety** by the Bureau of Justice Statistics and the National Center for Education Statistics helps us put the amount of crime in schools in perspective. The United States has roughly fifty-four million children potentially subject to criminal victimization in about 125,000 elementary and secondary schools. Data on this victimization follow those of the UCRs and victimization surveys, reporting that the amount of crime reported in schools dropped from the mid-1990s steadily through 2002; some offenses appeared to stabilize through 2003.[67]

Overall, roughly 5 percent of all students report victimization in school, far more of which is crimes of theft rather than of violence. Other data reveal that students experience more theft in school than out of school, but the amount of violent victimization is greater out of school than in school; serious violent victimizations such as rape, sexual assault, robbery, and simple assault are experienced by less than 1 percent of all students. In terms of numbers, thefts are committed against forty-five out of every one thousand students and acts of violence (serious violent victimizations as well as less serious violent acts such as simple assaults) against twenty-eight of every one thousand students; and three very serious violent crimes (rape, robbery, and aggravated assault) affect far less than 1 percent of all students.[68]

Males are more likely to be victims of violence than females, but males and females are the victims of theft about equally. Students in the higher grades are less likely to be victims of violence than younger youths, and white students are more likely than Hispanics to be victims of theft. Somewhat predictably, students from urban schools are exposed to greater amounts of victimization than those in rural schools.[69]

Death in the Schools

As might be guessed from the above discussion, death in the schools is a rarity; less than one death occurs per million students. Except for a small increase in the number of deaths in the schools in the late 1990s, between twenty-eight and thirty-four homicides yearly, the number of deaths has dropped since then and currently hovers between fourteen and seventeen per year. In 2001–2002, seventeen homicides and five suicides occurred, and in 2002–2003, schools experienced fifteen homicides and eight suicides. The small number of child deaths that takes place in the schools as opposed to those occurring in the community is dramatic.[70] The vast majority of serious violence involving juveniles, including suicide, takes place in the community rather than in the schools.[71] Unfortunately, as seen in Focus on Public Policy 2–4, the few acts of violence that do happen dramatically color our perception of the safety of schools.

Bullying

Bullying as a major problem burst onto the scene in the 1990s because of its apparent connection with school shootings by bullying victims. Basically, **bullying** occurs when a stronger, more aggressive child induces fear, distress, or harm in a weaker child through physical, verbal, or psychological intimidation.[72] The motivating factor for most bullies appears to be the desire to gain power over others. Subsequently, they tease, call their targets names, and kick, punch, slap, and push them. Bullies often make fun of their victims' clothes, faces, friends, parents, homes, foods, or anything else that allows them to feel superior to those they consider weak. Recently, cyberbullies have gone online to harass and intimidate their targets, directing instant messages, personal Web pages, blogs, and e-mail messages with sexual and racial epithets at students, teachers, and school administrators.[73]

Not only is physical harm done by bullies, but their threats and violence induce distress and fear in their victims to the point where the targets are afraid to attend classes, walk the hallways, play during recess, or walk home after school. Students soon learn to avoid certain areas of the schools such as the parking lot, entrances, gyms, restrooms, and specific locker areas. At home, students may avoid their computers.

Roughly 7 percent of all students experience bullying during any given year. Although data are not available for grades one through five, recent research suggests that bullying may well begin in the first grade and continue to

---

FOCUS ON PUBLIC POLICY

SHOOTINGS IN SCHOOL

2–4

Luke Woodham's October 1, 1997, shooting in Pearl, Mississippi, in which he killed two classmates and wounded seven, has received wide media coverage. During his trial, a letter from Woodham to a friend was read in which he said, "All through my life I've been ridiculed. I was always beat on and hated. I am malicious because I am miserable." He also proclaimed, "Murder is gutsy."

This was another in a long line of shootings that have taken place in schoolyards in the United States. Previous shootings in the mid-1990s were in Grayson, Kentucky (two dead); Amityville, New York (one dead, one wounded); Redland, California (one dead, one wounded); Blackville, South Carolina (two dead, one wounded); Lynnville, Tennessee (two dead, one wounded); Mises Lake, Washington (three dead, one wounded); and Bethel, Alaska (two dead, two wounded). Subsequent to the Pearl, Mississippi, shooting, three students were killed and five wounded on December 1, 1997, in West Paducah, Kentucky; five students were killed and ten wounded in the March 1998 ambush in Jonesboro, Arkansas; two students were killed and twenty-four wounded on May 21, 1998, in Springfield, Oregon; and twelve students, a teacher, and two gunmen were killed and twenty-three wounded in the massacre that took place in Columbine High School in Littleton, Colorado. The savage way in which Eric Harris and Dylan Klebold laid brutal siege to Columbine High, armed with guns and bombs, shocked the nation.

No further large-scale shootings by students have taken place like those at Columbine to this date, but shootings in the nation's public schools continued throughout the 2002–2003 academic year at about the same frequency as in the years before 1999 and Columbine. The 2003–2004 school year began with a string of shootings, stabbings, and other attacks. Starting in mid-August, when the public schools opened for the school year, eighteen violent deaths took place, more than the total deaths in either of the previous two years. About fifty nonfatal incidents also took place. In addition, police held wounded, armed students in standoffs at Spokane, Washington, and Sacramento, California. Throughout 2005 and 2006, police and local school authorities continued to thwart planned attacks on schools by juveniles.

Source: Authors' composite of media articles; see also Carol Morello, "Sobbing Miss. School Killer Proclaims Love for Victims," *USA Today*, 4A, June 12, 1998; and Greg Toppo, "Spate of Violence Raises Alarm," *USA Today*, 1D, October 21, 2003.

Critical Thinking Questions:
Is there something going on among youngsters in today's schools so that even in a relatively safe environment, more homicides seem to be taking place than in the past? Do you agree with the experts who claim that school shootings are related to the lack of impulse control in today's children? Or do you hold to such explanations as the breakdown of the family, the many guns in the hands of young people, or the overexposure to violence on television?

rise until the sixth grade; the extent of bullying in the sixth grade clearly is higher than that in succeeding years. From the sixth grade on, evidence of bullying drops off fairly steadily through the twelfth grade.

School environment is related to reports of bullying. The presence of street gangs in schools results in higher rates of bullying, as does the presence of students who are afraid of becoming the victims of attacks either at or on the way to school. Another important factor is students who carry guns to school. Students may avoid classes and other school activities because of bullying. However, whether these factors are the causes or effects of bullying behavior is unclear. Somewhat surprising is the finding that increased security, such as the

✓**Progress Check 2.2**
Review this section at
www.prenhall.com/bartollas

presence of security guards, hallway monitors, and metal detectors, apparently is unrelated to the evidence of bullying.[74] The most dramatic outcome of this mix of factors, of course, is shootings in the schools. The more pervasive outcome of bullying, however, may well be millions of children who are damaged educationally and emotionally by the consequence of bullying.

SUMMARY

- The vast majority of all youths misbehave while they are growing up. Most end up being ignored or reprimanded lightly by their families and communities. Some find themselves in the custody of the police, some are held for juvenile court, and a few are remanded to adult courts.

- Official statistics have contributed important findings about youth crime in American society:

  1. Juveniles commit a disproportionate number of property and violent offenses.
  2. Lower-class youths are involved in slightly more frequent and more serious offenses than are middle-class youths.
  3. African-American youths commit more frequent and more serious offenses than do white youths.
  4. Urban youths commit more frequent and more serious offenses than do suburban or rural youths.
  5. A small group of youthful offenders, primarily lower-class minority youths, commit at least half of the serious offenses in urban areas.
  6. The interventions by the juvenile justice system frequently make youths worse rather than better.

- Self-report studies have revealed that most youths are involved in delinquent behavior and that almost 90 percent of delinquent acts are undetected or ignored.

  Self-report studies also indicate that girls commit more delinquent acts than are recorded in official accounts of delinquency, but boys still appear to commit more serious crimes than girls do.

- Victimization surveys reveal nearly four times as many victims each year as the UCR statistics show.

- These surveys also reveal that juveniles are more likely than adults to become victims.

- Together, these unofficial measurements of delinquency add to what is known officially about juvenile crime in the United States. As we continue to seek out the parameters of youth crime, important data are well developed in the area of drug use, and comprehensive data are beginning to emerge on school violence and bullying.

WEB SITE OF INTEREST

The student interested in examining statistics and research findings on juvenile crime, new data from the Bureau of Justice Statistics, or information on drugs and crime facts should go to the Bureau of Justice Statistics at

http://www.ojp.usdoj.gov/bjs/

and click on the subject link of interest, for example, for new data, click on the link titled "What's new." See also *The Statistical Briefing Book*, an updated source of statistics from OJJDP, published online.

CRITICAL THINKING QUESTIONS

1. What do the UCRs generally show about youth crime in the United States?
2. What do juvenile court statistics show about youth crime in the United States?
3. What can self-report studies tell us that official accounts of youth crime cannot?
4. What do you believe the connection is between the maltreatment of children in their homes and on the streets and their involvement in crime and delinquency?

NOTES

1. Edward Sagarin, "Foreword," in *Careers of the Violent: The Dangerous Offender and Criminal Justice*, edited by Stuart J. Miller, Simon Dinitz, and John P. Conrad (Lexington, MA: Lexington Books, 1982), ix.
2. LaMar T. Empey, *Studies in Delinquency: Alternatives to Incarceration* (Washington, DC: U.S. Department of Health, Education and Welfare, Office of Juvenile Delinquency and Youth Development, 1967), 27–32; Maynard L. Erickson and LaMar T. Empey, "Court Records, Undetected Delinquency and Decision-Making," *Journal of Criminal Law, Criminology and Police Science* 54 (December 1963), 456–469.
3. William T. Pink and Mervin F. White, "Delinquency Prevention: The State of the Art," in *The Juvenile Justice System*, edited by Malcolm W. Klein (Beverly Hills, CA: Sage Publications, 1976), 9.
4. *Crime in the United States 2004* (Washington, DC: Government Printing Office, 2005), Table 38, 290. Percentages calculated from Table 38, 290 (online at www.fbi.gov/ucr/cius_04/documents/CIUS2004.pdf).
5. Ibid., Table 34, 286.
6. Ibid., Table 36, 288.
7. Ibid., Tables 39, 40, 292–95.
8. Ibid., Table 35, 286–87.
9. Ibid., Tables 32, 34, 36, and 37, 284–89.
10. Ibid., Table 43, 299.
11. Ibid., Table 43, 298–99.
12. Ibid., Tables 32–40, 284–95.
13. Ibid., Table 32, 349–57.
14. Ibid., Table 32, 284.
15. Howard N. Snyder et al., *Juvenile Court Statistics, 1984* (Washington, DC: Office of Juvenile Justice and Delinquency Prevention, 1987).
16. The data noted below are for 2000, the last year for which they are published. See Charles Puzzanchera, Anne L. Stahl, Terrence A. Finnegan, Nancy Tierney, and Howard N. Snyder, *Juvenile Court Statistics 2000* (Washington, DC: Office of Juvenile Justice and Delinquency Prevention, 2004), 3.
17. Ibid. The data noted are for 1997, the last year for which these data are published. See Charles Puzzanchera, Anne L. Stahl, Terrence A. Finnegan, Howard N. Snyder, Rowen S. Poole, and Nancy Tierney, *Juvenile Court Statistics 1997* (Washington, DC: Office of Juvenile Justice and Delinquency Prevention, 2000), 7. Also see Charles Puzzanchera, Anne L. Stahl, Terrence

A. Finnegan, Nancy Tierney, and Howard N. Snyder, *Juvenile Court Statistics 2000* (Pittsburgh: National Center for Juvenile Justice, 2004), 57–71.

18. Ibid., 7

19. Ibid.

20. A. Stahl, T. Finnegan, and W. Kang, "Easy Access to Juvenile Court Statistics: 1985–2002, 2005" (online at www.ojjdp.ncjrs.gov/ojstatbb/ezajcs/asp).

21. Shannan M. Catalano, "Criminal Victimization, 2004" (Washington, DC: Bureau of Justice Statistics, National Crime Victimization Survey, September, 2005).

22. Ibid.

23. Ibid.

24. Ibid.

25. Austin L. Porterfield, "Delinquency and Its Outcome in Court and College," *American Journal of Sociology* 49 (November 1947), 199–208; James F. Short, Jr., "A Report on the Incidence of Criminal Behavior, Arrests, and Convictions in Selected Groups," *Research Studies of the State College of Washington* 22 (June 1954), 110–18; James F. Short, Jr., and F. Ivan Nye, "Extent of Unrecorded Juvenile Delinquency: Tentative Conclusions," *Journal of Criminal Law, Criminology, and Police Science* 49 (November–December 1958), 296–302; James F. Short, Jr., and F. Ivan Nye, "Reported Behavior as a Criterion of Deviant Behavior," *Social Problems* 5 (Winter 1957–1958), 207–13; LaMar T. Empey, *Studies in Delinquency: Alternatives to Incarceration* (Washington, DC: Government Printing Office, 1967), 27–32; Maynard L. Erickson and LaMar T. Empey, "Court Records, Undetected Delinquency, and Decision Making," *Journal of Criminal Law, Criminology, and Police Science* 54 (December 1963), 456–69.

26. David Huizinga and Delbert S. Elliott, "Juvenile Offenders: Prevalence, Offender Incidence, and Arrest Rates by Race," *Crime and Delinquency* 33 (April 1987), 208, 210; Franklin W. Dunford and Delbert S. Elliott, "Identifying Career Offenders Using Self-Report Data," *Journal of Research in Crime and Delinquency* 21 (February 1984), 57–82, 215.

27. Jerald G. Bachman, Lloyd D. Johnston, and Patrick M. O'Malley, *Monitoring the Future 1994* (Ann Arbor: Institute for Social Research, University of Michigan, 1994). Prepublication data received from the project staff of *Monitoring the Future 1995* just prior to the publication of the second edition of this book indicated that the trends for 1995 were, for the most part, within two percentage points of those noted in 1994.

28. J. R. Williams and Martin Gold, "From Delinquent Behavior to Official Delinquency," *Social Problems* 20 (1972), 202–29; Martin Gold and David J. Reimer, *Changing Patterns of Delinquent Behavior Among Americans 13 to 16 Years Old* (Ann Arbor: Institute for Social Research, University of Michigan, 1974).

29. Delbert S. Elliott and Suzanne S. Ageton, "Reconciling Race and Class Differences in Self-Reported and Official Estimates of Delinquency," *American Sociological Review* 45 (February 1980), 103.

30. Gary Jensen and Raymond Eve, "Sex Differences in Delinquency: An Examination of Popular Sociological Explanations," *Criminology* 13 (1976), 427–88; Michael Hindelang, "Age, Sex, and the Versatility of Delinquent Involvements," *Social Problems* 18 (1979), 522–35; J Short and Nye, "Reported Behavior as a Criterion of Deviant Behavior."

31. Steven Cernkovich and Peggy Giordano, "A Comparative Analysis of Male and Female Delinquency," *Sociological Quarterly* 20 (1979), 136–07.

32. Bachman et al., *Monitoring the Future 1994.*

33. Short and Nye, "Reported Behavior as a Criterion of Deviant Behavior"; F. Ivan Nye, James Short, Jr., and Virgil Olsen, "Socio-Economic Status and Delinquent Behavior," *American Journal of Sociology* 63 (1958), 381–89; Robert Dentler and Lawrence Monroe, "Social Correlates of Early Adolescent Theft," *American Sociological Review* 26 (1961), 381–89.

34. Travis Hirschi, *Causes of Delinquency* (Berkeley: University of California Press, 1969).

35. Richard E. Johnson, "Social Class and Delinquent Behavior: A New Test," *Criminology* 18 (May 1980), 91.

36. Elliott and Ageton, "Reconciling Race and Class Differences in Self-Reported and Official Estimates of Delinquency."

37. For a more complete examination of cohort studies, see Clemens Bartollas, *Juvenile Delinquency,* 7th ed. (Boston: Allyn & Bacon, 2006), 41–42.

38. Marvin E. Wolfgang, Robert M. Figlio, and Thorsten Sellin, *Delinquency in a Birth Cohort* (Chicago: University of Chicago Press, 1972); Donna Martin Hamparian et al., *The Violent Few: A Study of Dangerous Juvenile Offenders* (Lexington, MA: Lexington Books, 1980); Lyle W. Shannon, *Assessing the Relationships of Adult Criminal Careers to Juvenile Careers: A Summary* (Washington, DC: Government Printing Office, 1982).

39. See Paul E. Tracy, Marvin E. Wolfgang, and Robert M. Figlio, *Delinquency in Two Birth Cohorts: Executive Summary* (Washington, DC: Government Printing Office, 1985).

40. Marvin E. Wolfgang, Terence P. Thornberry, and Robert M. Figlio, eds., *From Boy to Man, from Delinquency to Crime* (Chicago: University of Chicago Press, 1987), 37, 39.

41. Alfred Blumstein, David P. Farrington, and Soumyo Moitra, "Delinquency Careers: Innocents, Amateurs, and Persisters," in *Crime and Justice: An Annual Review,* 6th ed., edited by Michael Tonry and Norval Morris (Chicago: University of Chicago Press, 1985), 187–220.

42. D. P. Farrington, "Offending from 10 to 25 Years of Age," in *Prospective Studies of Crime and Delinquency,* edited by K. T. Van Dusen and S. A. Mednick (Boston: Kluwer-Nijhoff, 1983).

43. Suzanne S. Ageton and Delbert S. Elliott, *The Incidence of Delinquent Behavior in a National Probability Sample of Adolescents* (Boulder, CO: Behavioral Research Institute, 1978).

44. See Wolfgang et al., *Delinquency in a Birth Cohort,* and Hamparian et al., *The Violent Few.*

45. Susan K. Datesman and Michael Aickin, "Offense Specialization and Escalation Among Status Offenders," *Journal of Criminal Law and Criminology* 75 (1984), 1260–73.

46. Peggy C. Giordano, Stephen A. Cernkovich, and Jennifer L. Rudolph, "Gender, Crime, and Desistance: Toward a Theory of Cognitive Transformation," *American Journal of Sociology* 107 (January 2002), 1055.

47. Ronald L. Akers, *Social Learning and Social Structure: A General Theory of Crime and Deviance* (Boston: Northeastern University Press, 1998).

48. John H. Laub and Robert J. Sampson, "Turning Points in the Life Course: Why Change Matters to the Study of Crime," *Criminology* 31 (August 1993), 301–20.

49. See Wolfgang et al., *From Boy to Man,* 21.

50. Daniel S. Nagin and Raymond Paternoster, "On the Relationship of Past to Future Participation in Delinquency," *Criminology* 29 (May 1991), 163, 165.

51. U.S. Department of Health and Human Services, Administration on Children, Youth and Families, *Child Maltreatment 2003* (Washington, DC: Government Printing Office, 2005).

52. Clearing House on Child Abuse and Neglect Information, *Child Maltreatment, 2003*, 2 (online at http://nccanch.acf.hhs.gov/pubs/factsheets/fatality.cfm).

53. Child Welfare Information Gateway, *Child Maltreatment, 2004: Summary of Key Findings* (published 2006) online at http://www.childwelfare.gov/pubs/factsheets/canstats.cfm.

54. Child Welfare Information Gateway, *Child Maltreatment, 2004: Summary of Key Findings* (online at http://www.childwelfare.gov/pubs/factsheets/canstats.cfm).

55. David Finkelhor, R. Ormrod, and H. Turner, "Victimization of Children and Youth: A Comprehensive National Survey," *Child Maltreatment* 10 (February 2005), 5–25.

56. Katy Butler, "Beyond Rivalry, a Hidden World of Sibling Violence," *New York Times,* February 28, 2006 (online at http://www.nytimes.com).

57. Federal Bureau of Investigation, *Crime in the United States 2004: Uniform Crime Reports* (Washington, DC: U.S. Department of Justice, 2005), 17, 19.

58. John Langstaff and Tish Sleeper, "The National Center on Child Fatality Review," 2001, http://www.ncjrs.gov/html/ojjdp/209735/contents.html. See T. Crume, C. diGuiseppi, T. Byers, A. Sirotnak, and C. Garrett, "Underascertainment of Child Maltreatment Fatalities by Death Certificates, 1990–1998," *Pediatrics,* 110(2), 2002 (online at pediatrics.aappublications.org/cgi/reprint/110/2/e18.pdf).

59. Federal Bureau of Investigation, *Crime in the United States 2004,* 19.

60. Child Welfare Information Gateway, "Child Maltreatment 2004: Summary of Key Findings" (published 2006) online at http://www.childwelfare.gov/pubs/factsheets/canstats.cfm.

61. Calculated from Federal Bureau of Investigation, *Crime in the United States 2004,* Table 2–10, 19.

62. Cathy Spatz Widom and Michael Mansfield, *The Cycle of Violence Revisited* (Washington, DC: National Institute of Justice, 1996).

63. Cathy Spatz Widom, "Victims of Childhood Sexual Abuse—Later Criminal Consequences," *Research Brief* (Washington, DC: National Institute of Justice, Office of Justice Programs, 1995), 4–5. For continuing updates on the consequences of child maltreatment, go online to the Child Maltreatment Center of the University of New Hampshire.

64. George G. Knox, *An Introduction to Gangs* (Berrien Springs, MI: Vande Verde, 1993).

65. G. Knox, D. Laske, and E. Tromanhauser, "Chicago Schools Revisited," *Bulletin of the Illinois Public Education Association* 16 (Spring 1992).

66. For more information on drive-by shootings, see William B. Sanders, *Gangbangs and Drive-By: Grounded Culture and Juvenile Gang Violence* (New York: Aldine De Gruyter, 1994).

67. J. F. DeVoe, K. M. Noonan, P. Kaufman, T. D. Snyder, and K. Baum, *Indicators of School Crime and Safety: 2005,* NCES 2006–1007/NCJ 210697 (Washington, DC: Government Printing Office, 2006; online at http://nces.ed.gov or http://www.ojp.usdoj.gov/bjs).

68. Ibid.

69. Ibid.

70. Ibid.

71. Ibid.

72. D. P. Farrington, "Understanding and Preventing Bullying," in *Crime and Justice: A Review of Research* (vol. 17), edited by M. Tonray (Chicago: University of Chicago Press, 1993), 381–458, cited in U.S. Department of Education, National Center for Education Statistics, *Are America's Schools Safe? Students Speak Out: 1999 School Crime Supplement* (NCES 2002–331), by Lynn A. Addington, Sally A. Ruddy, Amanda K. Miller, and Jill F. DeVoe, Project Officer: Kathryn A. Chandler (Washington, DC: U.S. Department of Education, 2002), 55.

73. John Swartz, "Schoolyard Bullies Get Nastier Online," *USA Today,* posted online March 6, 2005 (http://www.usatoday.com/tech/news/2005-03-06-cover-cyberbullies..._x.htm). DeVoe et al., *Indicators of School Crime and Safety: 2005;* Andrea Cohn and Andrea Canter, "Bullying: Facts for Schools and Parents" Bethesda, MD: National Association of School Psychologists, 2003; (online at http://www.naspcenter.org/factsheets/bullying_fs.html); Noelle M. Bidwell, "The Nature and Prevalence of Bullying in Elementary Schools," Summary of a Master's thesis, SSTA Research Centre Report #97-06, (online at http://www.ssta.sk.ca/research/school_improvement/97-06/htm).

74. See Farrington, "Understanding and Preventing Bullying."

3

CAUSES OF JUVENILE CRIME

I made up my mind the last time I was released from Fairfield that I was going to stay out of trouble. I went home and told my friends that I was going to stay clean. Then, my mother got sick, needed an operation, and couldn't work. I am older than my brothers and sisters and someone had to put food on the table. Instead of telling my friends to stay out of my face, I agreed to pull an armed robbery with them. We got caught and here I am.

—Nineteen-year-old institutionalized male

I got to the point that I was drug dependent. I went from pot to pills. Crystal (meth) is what really hooked me. To get money for drugs, I sold drugs, robbed houses, and did everything but sell my body. When you are drug dependent, you are willing to do anything to get your drugs. Even when I was arrested and sat in jail at 18 for a drug bust, I didn't know if I could walk away from drugs. But I knew if I didn't, the next step was the penitentiary.

—Twenty-two-year-old female college senior

We robbed the liquor store because we knew we wouldn't get caught. The owner of this store was half blind and old. He didn't move too good. He had a gun, but we knew there was no way he could hit us. If he went for his gun, we would have blown him away. Man, robbing that place was like taking candy from a baby.

—Seventeen-year-old male on aftercare[1]

OUTLINE

63

OBJECTIVES

1. To understand the role free will has in the classical school's understanding of delinquent behavior
2. To be able to discuss the main forms of positivism
3. To examine how each form of positivism explains juvenile lawbreaking
4. To be able to determine what types of juvenile offenders are more responsible for their actions
5. To understand how rational choice theory differs from positivism

KEY TERMS

autonomy
biological positivism
containment theory
criminal opportunity theory
cultural deviance theory
delinquency across the life
   course
deterministic view
differential association theory
excitement

fate
felicific calculus
free will
labeling perspective
Marxist perspective
positivism
psychoanalysis
rational choice theory
reinforcement theory
routine activity approach

smartness
social control theory
social disorganization theory
sociobiologists
sociopath
strain theory
trouble
toughness
turning point

The three juvenile offenders in the chapter-opening quotes had some understanding of why they were violating the law. The first suggested that he committed the armed robbery because his mother became sick, and, as the oldest sibling, he felt responsible for putting food on the table. The second offender was aware that she committed crimes to support her drug habit. With the assistance of another youth, the third offender committed the armed robbery because it made sense to rob a store in which the owner had poor sight and was old.

More typically, juvenile offenders do not know why they broke the law. An institutional social worker confronted Leo, a repetitive juvenile offender: "How could you rape that woman who had been so good to you? You told me she had given you cookies and milk on your way home from school for years. She was a good friend of your family and she was in her mid-seventies. Why in the world did you rape her?" The youth responded, "I don't know." "And in my mind," the social worker added, "it is even more disturbing to me that you brag about it." "I don't brag about it," the youth interrupted. The social worker, shaking his head and dropping his voice, retorted, "I heard you talking with your peers yesterday about it. You were joking and laughing about what you had done." The youth said nothing.[2]

Even adult offenders are frequently unable to explain why they broke the law. Richard Speck, the murderer of seven student nurses in Chicago during the mid-1960s, reported to one of the authors: "I don't remember the crime. I don't remember killing those girls. I was stoned and drunk at the time. People think I'm some kind of monster. I don't know why I did it."[3]

Four explanations have been widely used to explain why juveniles commit crimes. First, some hold that juveniles commit crimes because they have free will and rationally choose to do so. Second, biological and psychological causes have long had support for those seeking explanations for youth crime.

This position supports the view that juvenile offenders either are biologically different from other youths or have experienced emotional damage in their early years. Third, social structural explanations argue that these youths are out of step with the norms of society because they are inadequately socialized, have been influenced by antisocial peers, or are poor and have no stake in the system. Finally, multidimensional explanations are needed to understand why juveniles violate the law. Integrated explanations of delinquent behavior imply the combination of two or more existing theories on the basis of their perceived commonalities.

However, whether talking about youth crime arising from free will, biological or psychological inferiority, social causes, or integrated explanations (two or more existing theories), it is clear that any particular theory only accounts for some of the reasons for juvenile offenses. Some explanations are more powerful than others in explaining youth crime, but even the most powerful amounts to only a small piece in the larger puzzle of why juveniles commit youth crime.

WHAT IS THE RELATIONSHIP BETWEEN THEORY AND RESEARCH?

Throughout history, civilizations have developed many techniques for seeking truth. Magic and superstition; the divine right of kings; the guidance of prophets, priests, and philosophers; intuition; and common sense have all been called on to provide the answers to the great questions. The failure of these methods to provide reliable and valid knowledge has led thinkers to search for other, better sources of truth. The contemporary solution is called *science*, the proponents of which contend that it provides more accurate answers than any other method yet discovered.

The two basic tools of science are theory and research, which are inextricably bound. Each helps to guide and direct the other. Research finds methods to collect data, helps to identify variables to be studied, tests variables for their worth, analyzes related variables, and suggests new directions for theory. Theory points the way to new research, helps derive new variables, builds interconnections among variables, interprets new and old ideas, builds systems of thought, and leads the way to new social and theoretical conclusions. Research collects and theory analyzes; research discovers and theory explains; research disproves and theory reorders. The process is never-ending. Without it, we would be likely to wallow in ignorance, personal prejudice, and inaccurate information. We would also be doomed to repeat harmful and even dangerous practices.

Thus, the main task of a theory is to explain the events in the world. A theory attempts to explain the cause of past events and predicts when, where, and how future events will occur.[4] A theory is a basic building block indispensable for the advancement of human knowledge, but because social science theories can rarely be proven or rejected with the same finality as theory in the natural sciences, there exist several competing theories.

One of the most critical theoretical debates in the study of crime is over that of determinism versus free will. The basic issue is whether humans freely choose or whether other factors determine their choices. The concept of free will is based on the notion that we choose how to act. Crime or delinquency is viewed as purposeful activity resulting from rational decisions in which the pros and cons are weighed and the acts that promise the greatest potential gains are performed. Because juveniles and adults possess free will, make choices, and know what they are doing, those who commit crime are presumed to deserve punishment rather than treatment.

In contrast, the **deterministic view** holds that individuals cannot help committing criminal or delinquent acts because they are controlled either by internal factors (biological or psychological imbalances) or by external factors (poverty, learning crime from others, strain, or societal labeling). To put it another way, offenders are objects that react like billiard balls in response to different forces.[5] They, then, are presumed to need treatment rather than punishment because they are driven into crime. Our interpretation of this free will debate determines how we explain why individuals commit crime and what can be done about crime. Focus on Causation 3–1 examines the life of Lee Malvo, one of the snipers who terrorized the southeastern part of the nation during the fall of 2002.

IS JUVENILE CRIME RATIONAL BEHAVIOR?

The association between criminal behavior and the rationality of crime has roots in the eighteenth-century classical school of criminology. More recently, there have been a number of approaches to the rationality of crime, especially rational choice theory.

CLASSICAL SCHOOL OF CRIMINOLOGY

Cesare Beccaria and Jeremy Bentham were the founders of the classical school of criminology. These scholars viewed humans as rational creatures who were willing to surrender enough liberty to the state so that society could establish rules and sanctions for the preservation of the social order.

In 1763, Cesare Bonesana Beccaria, Marquis of Beccaria, then only twenty-six and just out of law school, published *On Crimes and Punishment*. This essay was read avidly and translated into the languages of Europe.[6] Beccaria based the legitimacy of criminal sanctions on the social contract. The authority of making laws rested with the legislator, who should have only one view in sight: "the greatest happiness of the greatest number." Beccaria also saw punishment as a necessary evil and suggested that "it should be public, immediate, and necessary: the least possible in the case given; proportioned to the crime; and determined by the laws."[7] He then defined the purpose and consequences of punishment as being "to deter persons from the commission of crime and not to provide social revenge. Not severity, but certainty and swiftness in punishment best secure this result."[8]

In 1780, the Englishman Jeremy Bentham published *An Introduction to the Principles of Morals and Legislation*, which further developed the philosophy of the classical school.

Believing that a rational person would do what was necessary to achieve the most pleasure and the least pain, Bentham contended that punishment would deter criminal behavior, provided it was made appropriate to the crime. He stated that punishment has four objectives: (1) to prevent all offenses if possible, (2) to persuade a person who has decided to commit an offense to commit a less rather than a more serious one, (3) "to dispose [a person who has resolved upon a particular offense] to do no more mischief than is necessary to his purpose," and (4) to prevent the crime at as small a cost to society as possible.[9]

The basic theoretical constructs of the classical school of criminology were developed from the writings of Beccaria and Bentham: First, human beings were all looked on as rational creatures who, being free to choose their actions, could be held responsible for their behavior. This doctrine of **free will**

FOCUS ON CAUSATION

3—

THE MAKING OF A SNIPER: IS ANYONE TO BLAME?

Lee Boyd Malvo was born February 18, 1985, on the island of Jamaica. Malvo was raised in a single-parent home by his mother, Una James, because his father, Leslie Samuel Malvo, had abandoned him at an age when a son really needed his father. While trying to make money, Una James left her son alone on many occasions, sometimes for months at a time. One can only imagine the desperation, heartache, and feeling of not being wanted that a young boy would experience. Watching gangster rap on TV was one of the only hobbies Lee had in those early days, and he began to act out his aggressions at the age of fourteen; he reportedly smashed large holes in the walls of the apartment where he was living after the landlord shut off the electricity because of unpaid rent.

John Muhammad had his own problems. He had survived the Gulf War but apparently experienced many problems, including being a loner, unemployed, homeless, friendless, and, very likely, feelings of powerlessness and alienation; he also was divorced and, according to news reports, likely to lose contact with his children. Muhammad apparently felt a need for someone to control or, as some have argued, manipulated Malvo so that Muhammad's ex-wife could be a sniper victim.

Local media reports said that Malvo and John Muhammad might have met one another in Antigua, where his mother left Malvo when he was younger. Malvo and Muhammad became very close in a short period of time, and it wasn't long before Malvo was referring to Muhammad as "Dad." Getting rid of his Jamaican accent to sound more like Muhammad, Lee did whatever he could to make this new friend, who was now a dominant father figure in his life, happy. Becoming intrigued by Muhammad's books, Malvo started to read the Qu'ran instead of the Bible. We can only speculate at this time what Muhammad told, taught, or convinced Malvo to think and do.

Malvo and Muhammad moved to Washington State and lived in a homeless shelter. Learning how to shoot a gun and working out every day, Lee became very strong and very good with a rifle. Muhammad nicknamed Malvo "Sniper" and introduced him as such to friends; their shooting spree across the United States began shortly thereafter.

Arrested on October 24, 2002, Lee Malvo and John Muhammad were accused of at least twenty shootings, including thirteen deaths. At the time of the incidents, Malvo was seventeen years of age. After turning eighteen in 2003, he was transferred to adult court in Virginia, where he was found guilty of the charges and sentenced to life in prison without parole. Malvo may now be tried in Maryland and Louisiana. Muhammad was sentenced to death in Virginia.

Source: Alanna Santee and Stuart Miller prepared the above materials especially for this volume from the following sources, as well as materials in the public domain.

Newsweek, "Father, Where Are Thou?", Fox News Channel, Associated Press, Bio: Lee Malvo, ABC News, "Brainwashed? Accused Sniper's Former Guardian Believes Malvo Was Influenced," www.abcnews.com, and from NewsMax.com, "Sniper Malvo's Double Life Revealed," PRNewswire.

Critical Thinking Questions:

Think through the theories of this chapter. Why did Malvo join with Muhammad to commit their murders? Did he have free will? Or was he programmed to commit his crimes because of the lack of a father, poor nurturing from his mother, or brainwashing by a substitute father? What do you think?

was substituted for the widely accepted concept of theological determinism, which saw humans as predestined to certain actions. Second, punishment was justified because of its practical usefulness, or utilitarianism. No longer was punishment acceptable on the grounds of vengeful retaliation or as expiation on the basis of superstitious theories of guilt and repayment. The aim of punishment was the protection of society, and its dominant theme was deterrence. Third, the human being was presumed to be a creature governed by a **felicific calculus** oriented toward obtaining a favorable balance of pleasure and pain. Fourth, a rational scale of punishment was proposed that should be painful enough to deter the criminal from further offenses and to prevent others from following his or her example of crime. Fifth, sanctions should be proclaimed in advance of their use; these sanctions should be proportionate to the offense and should outweigh the rewards of crime. Sixth, equal justice should be offered to everyone. Finally, proponents of the classical school urged that individuals should be judged by the law solely for their acts, not for their beliefs.

According to the principles of the classical school, then, juveniles who commit serious crimes or continue to break the law are presumed to deserve punishment rather than treatment, because they possess free will and know what they are doing. Their delinquencies are viewed as purposeful activity resulting from rational decisions in which the pros and cons are weighed and the acts that promise the greatest potential gains are performed.[10]

RATIONAL CHOICE THEORY

Rational choice theory, largely borrowed primarily from the utility model in economics, is one of the hottest present-day topics in criminology. In its pure form, rational choice theory can be seen, at least in part, as an extension of the deterrence doctrine found in the classical school to include incentives as well as deterrence and to focus on the rational calculation of payoffs and costs before delinquent and criminal acts are committed.[11]

Philip J. Cook has developed what he calls **criminal opportunity theory.** He claims that "criminals tend to be somewhat selective in choosing a crime target and are most attracted to targets that appear to offer a high payoff with little effort or risk of legal consequence."[12] He sees the interaction between potential offenders who respond to the net payoff to crime and potential victims who take actions to modify the payoff to crime as akin to the interaction between buyers and sellers in a marketplace. Thus, in using the market perspective to examine the interaction between potential victims and offenders, criminal opportunity theory emphasizes individual choice guided by the perceived costs and benefits of criminal activity.[13]

Lawrence E. Cohen and Marcus Felson are guided by ecological concepts and the presumed rationality of offenders in developing a **routine activity approach** for analyzing crime rate trends and cycles. This approach links the dramatic increase in crime rates since 1960 to changes in the routine activity structure of U.S. society and to a corresponding increase in target suitability and a decrease in the presence of "guardians," such as neighbors, friends, and family. The decline of the daytime presence of adult caretakers in homes and neighborhoods is partly the result of a trend toward increased female participation in the labor force.

Cohen and Felson believe that the volume and distribution of predatory crime are related to the interaction of three variables relating to the routine activities of U.S. life: the availability of suitable targets, the absence of capable guardians, and the presence of motivated offenders.[14]

Steven F. Messner and Kenneth Tardiff used the routine activities approach to help interpret patterns of homicides in Manhattan (New York City) and found that the routine activities approach does indeed provide a useful framework for interpreting the social ecology involved in urban homicides. They found that people's lifestyles affected their chances of being victimized. People who frequently tended to go out more often were victimized by strangers, whereas those who preferred to stay at home were more likely to be killed by someone they knew.[15]

Ronald L. Akers's examination of rational choice theory led him to conclude that a key issue is whether or not the rational choice perspective proposes a purely "rational man" theory of criminal behavior. He asks: Does it argue for a direct resurrection of classical criminology in which each person approaches the commission or noncommission of a crime with a highly rational calculus? Is rational choice theory essentially free of all constraining elements? Does it propose that each individual chooses, with full free will and knowledge, to commit or not to commit a crime, taking into account a carefully reasoned set of costs and benefits?[16]

Akers answers these questions by saying that current rational choice models emphasize "limitations and constraints on rationality through lack of information, structural constraints, values, and other 'non-rational' influences?" "Indeed," Akers adds, "the rational choice models in the literature . . . paint a picture of partial rationality with all kinds of situational and cognitive constraints and all kinds of positivistic and deterministic notions of causes."[17]

Derek B. Cornish and Ronald V. Clarke's *The Reasoning Criminal* is probably the most frequently cited source on rational choice and crime. Yet in both the preface and the introductory essay, Cornish and Clarke say that the starting assumption of their model is that

> offenders seek to benefit themselves by their criminal behavior; that this involves the making of decisions and choices, however rudimentary, on occasion, these processes might be; and that these processes exhibit a measure of rationality, albeit constrained by limits of time and ability and the availability of relevant information.[18]

They perceive offenders as "reasoning decision makers" based on the assumption that criminals or delinquents "exercise some degree of planning and foresight."[19]

In sum, rational choice theory in criminology has recently moved away from the strictly rational, reasoning model of behavior to a more limited and constrained role for rational thought. Rational choice theory does not even assume that all or even most delinquent or criminal acts result from clear, planned, well-informed, and calculated choices.[20] It can still be argued, of course, that the rational choice model places more emphasis on rationality and free will than do other theories of delinquent behavior and that this degree of rationality is not present in most juvenile crimes.[21]

HOW HAS DETERMINISM INFLUENCED THE DEVELOPMENT OF THE POSITIVE SCHOOL?

Beginning with a brief introduction to the theoretical constructs of the positive school, the biological, psychological, and sociological explanations of delinquency and crime are examined in this section.

DEVELOPMENT OF POSITIVISM

According to **positivism,** human behavior is but one more facet of a universe that is part of a natural order, but human beings can study behavior and discover how natural laws operate. Two positions diverge at this point of natural law. One view states that, because a natural order with its own laws exists, to change human behavior is impossible. The other view is that, just as laws operate in the medical, biological, and physical sciences, laws govern human behavior, and these laws can be understood and used. The causes of human behavior, once discovered, can be modified to eliminate or ameliorate many of society's problems. This second position is the one most scientists accept. The concept, as it applies to juvenile justice, is called positivism.

Positivism became the dominant philosophical perspective of juvenile justice at the time the juvenile court was established at the beginning of the twentieth century. During the Progressive Era (the period from about 1890 to 1920), the wave of optimism that swept through U.S. society led to the acceptance of positivism. The doctrines of the emerging social sciences assured reformers that through positivism their problems could be solved. The initial step was to gather all the facts of the case. Equipped with these data, reformers were then expected to analyze the issues in scientific fashion and discover the right solution.[22]

Armed with these principles, reformers set out to deal with the problem of delinquency, confident that they knew how to find its cause. Progressives looked first to environmental factors, pinpointing poverty as the major cause of delinquency. Some Progressives were attracted also to the doctrine of eugenics and believed that the biological limitations of youthful offenders drove them to delinquency. But eventually the psychological origins of delinquency came to be more widely accepted than either the environmental or the biological origins.[23]

Positivism has three basic assumptions.[24] First, the character and personal backgrounds of individuals explain delinquent behavior. Positivism, relegating the law and its administration to a secondary role, looks for the cause of deviancy in the actor.

Second, the existence of scientific determinism is a critical assumption of positivism. Delinquency, like any other phenomenon, is seen as determined by prior causes; it does not just happen. Because of this deterministic position, positivism rejects the view that the individual exercises freedom, possesses reason, and is capable of choice.

Third, the delinquent is seen as fundamentally different from the nondelinquent. The task then is to identify the factors that have made the delinquent a different kind of person. In attempting to explain this difference, positivism has concluded that wayward youths are driven into crime by something in their physical makeup, by aberrant psychological impulses, or by the meanness and harshness of their social environment.[25]

BIOLOGICAL POSITIVISM

Positivism was first applied to the study of crime with the writings of Cesare Lombroso, who is frequently acknowledged as the father of criminology. Lombroso insisted that all criminals were "born" criminal or atavistic, a reversion to an earlier evolutionary level; that is, the characteristics of primitive human beings periodically reappeared in certain individuals. He identified these characteristics as enormous jaws, high cheekbones, prominent superciliary arches, solitary lines in the palms, extreme size of the orbits, handle-shaped or sensile ears, insensibility to pain, extreme acute sight, tattooing, excessive idleness, love of orgies, and the irresistible craving for evil for its own sake.[26] Early **biological positivism,** like Lombroso's theory of the born criminal, was quickly dismissed. The physical signs that Lombroso claimed identified the born criminal have been pointed out to be a result of social environment and poor nutrition rather than part of an individual's constitutional makeup.

Charles Goring studied three thousand English convicts, with students and sailors serving as controls, and his results did not confirm Lombroso's assertion concerning the atavistic (or born) criminal.[27]

In the second half of the twentieth century, **sociobiologists** began to link genetic and environmental factors; they claimed that criminal behavior, like other behaviors, has both biological and social aspects. These sociobiologists have investigated the relationship between antisocial behavior and biological factors and environment through studies of twins and adoption, chromosomal abnormalities, electrodermal activity and pyschopathy, minimal functioning, intelligence, physique, and chemical imbalances in the body.

In the twenty-first century, the two areas of sociobiology that are receiving the most attention are neuropsychological factors and delinquency and the relationship between temperament and negative behavior.

Terrie E. Moffitt's work on neuropsychological factors and delinquency is highly regarded. Moffitt and colleagues' examination of the neuropsychological status of several hundred New Zealand males between the ages of thirteen and eighteen found that poor neuropsychological scores "were associated with early onset of delinquency" but were "unrelated to delinquency that began in adolescence."[28] Moffitt's developmental theory views delinquent behavior as proceeding along two developmental paths. On one path, children develop a lifelong pattern of delinquency at an age as early as three. They may begin to hit and bite at age four, shoplift and be truant at age ten, sell cars and steal cars at age sixteen, rob and rape at age twenty-two, and commit fraud and child abuse at age thirty.[29] According to Moffitt, these "life-course-persistent" (LCP) delinquents continue their illegal acts throughout the conditions and situations they face. During childhood, they may also exhibit such neuropsychological problems as deficit disorders or hyperactivity and learning problems in schools. On the other path, the majority of delinquents begin offending during the adolescent years and desist from delinquent behaviors around the eighteenth birthday. Moffitt refers to these youthful offenders as "adolescent-limited" (AL) delinquents.[30]

Activity and emotionality are two behaviors that identify a child's temperament. *Activity* refers to motor movements, such as the movement of arms and legs, crawling, or walking. Children who exhibit an inordinate amount of movement compared with peers are often labeled *hyperactive* or as having an attention deficit disorder (generally referred to as *attention deficit hyperactivity disorder* or ADHD). *Emotionality* ranges from very little reaction to intense emotional reactions that are out of control.

The hyperactive child remains a temperamental mystery. This child's three behaviors are impulsivity (shifts quickly from one activity to another), inattention (is easily distracted and does not want to listen), and excessive motor activity (cannot sit still, runs about, is talkative and noisy). Educators note that ADHD children have difficulty staying on task, sustaining academic achievement in school, maintaining control over their behavior, and remaining cognitively organized.[31]

In sum, early biological positivism was replaced by sociobiology and has more support in the criminological community. However, criminologists generally are reluctant to place much credence in biological explanations of delinquent behaviors because they generally omit social explanations.

PSYCHOLOGICAL POSITIVISM

Psychological factors have always been more popular in the United States in explaining juvenile offending than have biological or sociobiological factors. An early psychological explanation of juvenile offending was the psychoanalytic explanation. More recently, psychopathic factors, sensation seeking and delinquency, and reinforcement theory have received considerable attention.

Psychoanalytic Explanations

Sigmund Freud, in developing **psychoanalysis,** contributed three insights that have shaped the handling of juvenile delinquents: (1) the personality is made up of three components; (2) all normal children pass through three psychosexual stages of development; and (3) a person's personality traits are developed in early childhood.

Freud's theory of the personality involves the id, the ego, and the superego. The id has to do with the person's raw instincts and primitive drives; it wants immediate gratification of its needs and therefore tends to be primitive and savage. The ego and superego, the other two components, have the express purpose of controlling the primitive drives of the id. The ego mediates between the id and the superego and is important in the socialization of the child. The superego, or the conscience, internalizes the rules of society. Thus, as a child develops, he or she learns to distinguish socially acceptable behavior from socially unacceptable behavior.[32]

Freud identified the oral, anal, and phallic stages as the life stages that shape personality development. The first stage, the oral one, is experienced by the newborn infant. In this stage, pleasure is achieved through eating, sucking, and chewing. In the anal stage, normally occurring between one and three years of age, urinary and bowel movements replace sucking as the basic source of pleasure for the child. During the phallic stage, which normally takes place between the ages of three and six, the child receives pleasure from the genitals. Each stage brings increased social demands on the child and affects the way in which he or she deals with basic, innate drives. The sexual and aggressive drives, in particular, create tensions that a child must learn to resolve in socially acceptable ways.[33]

Freud also contended that by age five, all of the essential ingredients of a child's adult personality are determined. Consequently, what a child has experienced emotionally by the age of five will affect that child the rest of his or her life. If emotional traumas are experienced in childhood, they are likely to cause lifelong psychological problems.[34] Offending across the life course, according to this position, is continually affected by what a person has experienced as a young child.

Freud's followers have identified four ways in which emotional problems developed in childhood might lead to delinquent behavior.[35] First, delinquent behavior is related to neurotic development in the personality. Freud established a relationship between desire and behavior; that is, youths may feel guilty about a socially unacceptable desire and, as a result, seek out situations in which to be punished and then follow their punishments up with inappropriate and self-defeating behaviors.

Second, Freudians attribute delinquent behavior to a defective superego. The failure to develop a normally functioning superego can result in the inability to feel guilt, to learn from experience, or to feel affection toward others.[36] Such individuals, sometimes called *sociopathic* or *psychopathic*, may express aggressive and antisocial behavior toward others.

Third, violent delinquent behavior is sometimes explained by the tendency of children with an overly developed superego to repress all negative emotional feelings throughout childhood to the degree that these repressed feelings explode in a violent act in adolescence. So-called model adolescents occasionally become involved in violent crimes toward parents and neighbors, sometimes horribly mutilating their victims.[37] (See Focus on Causation 3–2.)

FOCUS ON CAUSATION 3–2

KEEPING THE LID ON THE ID

The authors have worked with and are familiar with a number of youths whose behavior appears to be explained by Freudian theory. The theory, it may be remembered, argues that the internal forces of the id constantly are seeking expression in society. Some of these forces are instinctual in nature, with some being destructive and some pleasure seeking. All of us, in other words, come into society ready and desiring to be destructive on the one hand and to seek pleasure on the other. Society, however, cannot permit these types of behavior and still survive, so society and its agents—the family, religion, education, and other institutions—attempt to shape our desires in socially acceptable directions. The results can sometimes be disastrous.

A fairly common scenario therapists experience is that of youths who, for seemingly unexplained reasons, suddenly break out into violent and uncontrollable behaviors. One youth the authors worked with was an Eagle Scout, straight "A" student, Sunday school teacher, and all-around good kid.

One day, however, he took a rifle and shot his mother through the kitchen window and went back to the family's garage and killed his father. Upon examination, therapists found that his parents, who were rigidly fundamentalist, always demanded perfection from him and never permitted him to express his own feelings and desires. Freud would argue that his feelings were totally suppressed by his ego and superego. As time went on, his rage built until his ego and superego could no longer contain it. The rage finally broke through his defenses, and the result was the killing of his parents.

Fourth, unlawful activities can be related to a search for compensatory gratification. According to Freud, individuals who were deprived at an early age of development will later seek the gratification they missed. The Freudian interpretation is that an adolescent may become an alcoholic to satisfy an oral craving or may become sadistic because of poor toilet training received during the anal period.

Sensation Seeking and Delinquency

Sensation seeking can be defined "as an individual's need for varied, novel and complex sensations and experiences and the willingness to take physical and social risks for the sake of such experience."[38] Derived from optimal arousal theory, this construct assumes that organisms are driven or motivated to obtain an optimal level of arousal.[39]

Recently, the relationship between sensation seeking and crime has received frequent attention. M. J. Hindelang found that delinquents are more pleasure seeking than are nondelinquents.[40] Helene Raskin White, Erich W. Labouvie, and Marsha E. Bates found that both male and female delinquents have higher rates of sensation seeking and lower rates of inhibited behavior than nondelinquents.[41]

Jack Katz's controversial book, *Seduction of Crime*, conjectures that when individuals commit a crime, they become involved in "an emotional process—seductions and compulsions that have special dynamics." It is this "magical" and "transformative" experience that makes crime "sensible," even sensually "compelling." For example, he states that for many adolescents, shoplifting and vandalism offer an exciting experience, not because of the act, but because if adults see them do it and the youths still can get away with it, the youths will feel they have proved their competence in society.[42]

Katz is arguing that instead of approaching criminal or delinquent behavior from the traditional focus on background factors, what needs more consideration are the foreground or situational factors that directly precipitate antisocial acts and reflect crimes' sensuality. According to Katz, offenders' immediate social environment and experiences encourage them to conceive of crimes as sensually compelling.[43]

The Psychopath

The psychopath (also known as the **sociopath**, *antisocial personality*, *person with a conduct disorder*, and a host of other names) is acknowledged as the personality of the hard-core juvenile offender. The claim is made that these are chiefly the unwanted, rejected children, who grow up but remain undomesticated "children" and never develop trust in or loyalty to other adults.[44] Hervey Cleckley gave the most complete clinical description of this type of personality. He indicated that the psychopath is charming and of good intelligence; is not delusional or irrational; is unreliable; is insecure and cannot be trusted; lacks shame and remorse; will commit all kinds of misdeeds for astonishingly small stakes and sometimes for no reason at all; has poor judgment, never learns from experience, and will repeat over and over again patterns of self-defeating behavior; has no real capacity for love; lacks insight; does not respond to consideration, kindness, or trust; and shows a consistent inability to make or follow any sort of life plan.[45]

The continuity between childhood symptoms of emotional problems and adult behavior emerged in L. N. Robins' thirty-year follow-up of 526 white childhood patients in a St. Louis, Missouri, guidance clinic in the 1920s. Robins was looking for clues to the adult "antisocial personality," or "sociopathy."[46] Excluding cases involving organic brain damage, schizophrenia, mental retardation, or symptoms that appeared only after heavy drug or alcohol use, she found that the adult sociopath is almost invariably an antisocial child grown up. Indeed, she found no case of adult sociopathy without antisocial behavior before the age of eighteen. Over 50 percent of the sociopathic males showed an onset of symptoms before the age of eight.[47]

Linda Mealey argues that there are two kinds of sociopaths: primary and secondary. Primary sociopaths have inherited traits that predispose them to illegal behavior; that is, they have a genotype that predisposes them to antisocial behavior. Secondary sociopaths, in contrast, are constitutionally normal but are influenced by such environmental factors as poor parenting. Thus, she argues that one type of sociopathic behavior has a genetic basis and the other is environmentally induced.[48]

Reinforcement Theory

James Q. Wilson and Richard Herrnstein's *Crime and Human Nature* combines biosocial factors and psychological research with rational choice theory to redevelop reinforcement theory.[49] Wilson and Herrnstein consider potential causes of crime and of noncrime within the context of **reinforcement theory**, that is, the theory that behavior is governed by its consequent rewards and punishments, as reflected in the history of the individual.

The rewards of crime, according to Wilson and Herrnstein, are found in the form of material gain, revenge against an enemy, peer approval, and sexual gratification. The consequences of crime include pangs of conscience, disapproval of peers, revenge of the victim, and, most important, the possibility of punishment. The rewards of crime tend to be more immediate, whereas the rewards of noncrime generally are realized in the future. The authors are quick to dismiss evidence that is inconsistent with their theoretical framework, but, as few have done in the field of criminology, they are able to show how gender, age, intelligence, families, schools, communities, labor markets, mass media, and drugs, as well as variations across time, culture, and race, greatly influence the propensity to commit crimes, especially violent offenses.[50]

Wilson and Herrnstein's theory does have serious flaws. Most important, it consistently shows a disdain for the social context in which crime occurs. What Wilson and Herrnstein do, in effect, is to factor society out of their considerations of crime. Instead of examining criminal behavior as part of complex social mechanisms and attempting to understand the connection, they typically conclude that no conclusion is possible from the available data, and therefore no programs for reducing criminality among groups perceived as major sources of crime are worth their costs.[51] In Focus on the Offender 3–3, some of the emotional problems that contribute to unlawful behaviors are documented.

✓**Progress Check 3.1**
Review this section at
www.prenhall.com/bartollas

FOCUS ON THE OFFENDER   3–3
EMOTIONAL PROBLEMS OF DELINQUENTS

We've the kids that mental health has called untreatable. We've the severe type of kids who have been involved in some heavy acts. They've pulled knives on people and are physically aggressive.

—Alternative school teacher

A lot of our kids realize that they really can't cope like the other kids their age and that they've inadequacies. They don't feel very good about themselves and have poor self-concepts. Their façade is a means of overcompensation for some of their inadequacies.

—Alternative school teacher

They've real problems dealing with authority. You've got to relate with them differently. You don't want to diminish your authority in any way, but yet you can't come across as being rigid and unyielding. You have to maintain the view that you'll call the shots. It's also important for you to communicate that you want to work with them and that their opinion is important.

—Alternative school teacher

I had a 15-year-old boy on my caseload who committed a lot of burglaries and then eventually killed his father. He had been terribly abused all his life.

—Probation officer

Gang kids were like other kids the first time you met them, but then as you got to know them you realized that they really had a lot of emotional problems. The way they looked at life was a negative sort of way. Their basic theme was to rip off everyone you can because they would rip you off if you gave them a chance.

—Probation officer

Source: Interviewed between 1985 and 1988 in a Midwestern state.

Critical Thinking Questions:

Do the individuals who work with these youths make the point that their emotional problems caused their behaviors? What would it take (degree of emotional problems) for adolescents to no longer be considered responsible for their negative behaviors?

SOCIOLOGICAL POSITIVISM

Social structure, social process, and conflict theories are the three main divisions of the sociological explanations of crime and delinquency. The basic flaw of explanations based on the individual, according to these sociological theories, is that such interpretations fail to come to grips with the underlying social and cultural conditions giving rise to youthful offending. These sociological theories add that the overall crime picture reflects conditions requiring collective social solutions and that therefore social reform, rather than individual counseling, must be given the highest priory in efforts to reduce crime problems.

Social Structural Theories

Using official statistics as their guide, social structure theorists claim that such forces as social disorganization, cultural deviance, and status frustration are so powerful that they induce lower-class individuals to become involved in criminal and delinquent behaviors.

1. *Social disorganization theory.* Clifford R. Shaw and Henry D. McKay's **social disorganization theory** views crime as resulting from the breakdown of social control by the traditional primary groups, such as the family and the neighborhood, because of the social disorganization of the community. Shaw and McKay's studies revealed that high-delinquency areas are found in disorganized communities characterized by physically deteriorated and condemned buildings, economic dependence, population mobility, heterogeneous populations, high rates of school truancy, infant mortality, and tuberculosis.[52]

2. *Cultural deviance theory.* Walter B. Miller contends that the lower class has its own cultural history and that the motivation to become involved in criminal activities is intrinsic to lower-class culture. Miller's **cultural deviance theory** argues that the lower-class culture is characterized by a set of focal concerns, or values, that command widespread attention and a high degree of emotional involvement. The focal concerns consist of trouble, toughness, smartness, excitement, fate, and autonomy.[53]

Trouble: Getting into and out of trouble represents a major preoccupation of the lower class, and fighting, drinking, and sexual adventures are basic causes of trouble for this class.

Toughness: The "tough guy" who is hard, fearless, undemonstrative, and a good fighter is the ideal personality in the eyes of lower-class males.

Smartness   This value among the lower class involves the desire to outsmart, outfox, con, and dupe others.

Excitement: The quest for excitement leads to the widespread use of alcohol and drugs by both sexes and to extensive gambling.

Fate: Lower-class individuals feel that their lives are subject to a set of forces over which they have little control.

Autonomy: Desire for personal independence is an important concern for lower-class persons because they feel controlled so much of the time.[54]

Marvin Wolfgang and Franco Ferracuti also agree that a subculture of violence exists among males in the lower class that legitimizes the use of violence in various social situations. The subculture's norms, according to Wolfgang and Ferracuti, are separated from the larger societal value system. An always-present theme of violence influences lifestyles, the socialization

Table 3–1   *Merton's Theory of Anomie*

1. Conformity	+	+
2. Innovation	+	−
3. Ritualism	−	+
4. Retreatism	−	−
5. Rebellion	±	±

Source: This material appears in Robert K. Merton, "Social Structure and Anomie," *American Sociological Review* 3 (1938), p. 676.

process, and interpersonal relationships. It is anticipated that violence will be used to solve social conflicts and dilemmas. Indeed, those who fail to turn to violence, especially when they are threatened or insulted, will encounter rejection by their peer group.[55]

3. *Status frustration theory.* In an early version of **strain theory**, Robert K. Merton theorized that cultural goals and the means to achieve these goals must be reasonably well integrated if a culture is to be stable and smooth-running. If individuals feel that a particular goal is important, they should have legitimate means of attaining it. The cultural goal of American society, according to Merton, is success, but the inequality of life in this nation produces structural pressures toward deviation in criminal behavior. In Table 3–1, types of individual adaptation are listed: a plus (+) signifies acceptance, a minus (−) signifies rejection, and a plus-and-minus (±) signifies a rejection of the prevailing values and a substitution of new ones.

Richard A. Cloward and Lloyd E. Ohlin added that lower-class cultures are asked to orient their behavior toward the prospect of accumulating wealth, while they are largely denied the means of doing so legitimately. Thus, delinquent subcultures develop as collective social adjustments to the strains of blocked opportunity.[56] Albert K. Cohen's status frustration (or strain) theory suggests that the destructive and malicious behavior of lower-class delinquent subcultures is a reaction to their failure to achieve middle-class norms and values.[57]

Social Process Theories

Social process theories examine the interactions between people and their environment that influence individuals to become involved in criminal or delinquent behaviors. These sociopsychological theories became popular in the 1960s because they provided a mechanism for understanding how environmental factors influence individual decision making. Differential association, containment, social control, and labeling theories are the social process theories that have been the most widely received.

1. *Differential association theory.* According to Edwin H. Sutherland's **differential association theory,** criminals and youthful offenders learn crime from others. Thus, crime, like any other form of behavior, is a product of social interaction. Sutherland began with the notion that criminal behavior is to be expected of those individuals who have internalized a preponderance of definitions favorable to law violations. That is, individuals are taught their basic values, norms, skills, and perceptions of self from others; therefore, it makes sense that they also learn crime from "significant others."[58]

The life of Jack Henry Abbott aptly shows how individuals learn crime from others. While in prison, Abbott wrote *In the Belly of the Beast*, a convincing narration and a penetrating insight into the brutality of prison life. His book gained him a reputation as a skilled author and a rehabilitated inmate. Praised

Dilapidated and unsafe areas of the city are associated with drugs and violence. (Photo by Heather Dengel.)

in the high circles of New York's literary elite, he was soon granted an early parole by state officials. Shortly after his release, Abbott became engaged in a verbal dispute with a New York City waiter. Abbott wanted to use the restaurant's restroom, but the waiter informed him that there was none available. Although accounts differ about what happened next, the result was that Abbott fatally knifed the waiter in the alley. When he was apprehended and charged with the murder, Abbott claimed that he acted as he did because he had learned to act that way. He had spent most of his life in juvenile and adult correctional institutions, and it was this experience that taught him to act the way he did.[59]

    2. *Containment theory.* Walter C. Reckless developed **containment theory** in order to explain why individuals do not commit crime and delinquent acts. He argued that individuals are affected by a variety of forces, some driving them toward—and others restraining them from—crime. As a control theory, which can explain both conforming behavior and deviance, containment theory has two elements: an inner control system and an outer control system. Internal containment is made up of self-control, a positive self-concept, ego strength, a well-developed superego, high frustration tolerance, and a high sense of responsibility. External containment represents the buffers in the person's immediate environment that are able to hold him or her within socially acceptable bounds. The assumption is that strong internal containment and reinforcing external containment provide insulation against delinquent or criminal behavior.[60]

    Containment theory involves both outer and inner containment, but inner containment, or self-concept, has received far more attention than has outer containment. Walter C. Reckless, Simon Dinitz, and their students spent over a decade investigating the effects of self-concept on delinquent behavior.

The subjects for this study were sixth-grade boys living in the area of Columbus, Ohio, that had the highest white delinquency rate. Teachers were asked to nominate those boys who, from their point of view, were insulated against delinquency. In the second phase of the study, teachers in the same-area schools were asked to nominate sixth-grade boys who appeared to be heading toward delinquency. Both the "good boy" group and the "bad boy" group were given the same battery of psychological tests; the mothers of members of both groups too were interviewed.[61]

Reckless and Dinitz concluded from these studies that one of the preconditions of law-abiding conduct is a good self-concept. This "insulation" against delinquency may be viewed as an ongoing process reflecting an internalization of nondelinquent values and conformity to the expectations of significant others—parents, teachers, and peers. Thus, a good self-concept, the product of favorable socialization, steers youths away from delinquency by acting as an inner buffer or containment against delinquency.

3. *Social control theory.* Travis Hirschi developed another version of control theory that examines the individual's ties to conventional society. In *Causes of Delinquency,* Hirschi outlined **social control theory,** in which he linked delinquent behavior to the bond an individual has with conventional social groups, such as the family and the school. The social bond, according to Hirschi, is made up of four main elements: attachment, commitment, involvement, and belief.[62]

An individual's attachment to conventional others is the first element of the social bond. Sensitivity toward others, argues Hirschi, relates to the ability to internalize norms and to develop a conscience.[63] Attachment to others also includes the ties of affect and respect children have to parents, teachers, and friends. The stronger the attachment to others, the more likely that an individual will take this into consideration when and if he or she is tempted to commit a delinquent act.[64]

Commitment to conventional activities and values is the second element of the bond. An individual is committed to the degree that he or she is willing to invest time, energy, and the self in conventional activities, such as educational goals, property ownership, or reputation building. When a committed individual considers the cost of delinquent behavior, he or she uses common sense and thinks of the risk of losing the investment already made in conventional behavior.[65]

Involvement also protects an individual from delinquent behavior. Because time and energy are limited, involvement in conventional activities leaves no time for delinquent behavior. "The person involved in conventional activities is tied to appointments, deadlines, working hours, plans, and the like," reasoned Hirschi, "so the opportunity to commit deviant acts rarely arises. To the extent that he is engrossed in conventional activities, he cannot even think about deviant acts, let alone act out his inclinations."[66]

The fourth element is belief. Delinquency arises from the absence of effective beliefs that forbid socially unacceptable behavior. Respect for the law and for the social norms of society are important components of belief. This respect for the values of the law and legal system is derived from intimate relations with other people, especially parents.[67]

4. *Labeling perspective.* Labeling theory contends that society creates deviants by labeling those who are apprehended as "different" from others, when in reality they are different only because they have been "tagged" with a criminal label. Edwin Lemert and Howard Becker are the chief proponents of the view that formal and informal societal reactions to criminal behavior can influence the subsequent attitudes and behaviors of criminals and delinquents.[68]

Lemert focused attention on the interaction between social control agents and rule violators and the way certain behavior came to be labeled "criminal" or "deviant." His concept of primary and secondary deviation is regarded as one of the most important insights of this **labeling perspective.** According to Lemert, *primary deviation* refers to the behavior of the individual, and *secondary deviation* is society's response to that behavior. Lemert contended that society's reaction to the deviant forces a change in the status or role of the individual and, in effect, causes the person to pursue deviant or criminal behavior.[69] Thus, the social reaction to the criminal is crucial in understanding the progressive commitment of a person to a criminal way of life.

Becker adds that once a person is caught and labeled, that person becomes an outsider and gains a new social status, with consequences for both one's self-image and one's public identity. The person is regarded as a different kind of person, and he or she finds it difficult to regain social acceptance. Hence, society's labeling ultimately forces a juvenile or an adult into a deviant career.[70]

Conflict Theory

A great deal of variation exists among conflict theories. Some theories emphasize the importance of socioeconomic class, some focus primarily on power and authority, and others emphasize group and cultural conflict.

1. *Socioeconomic class and Marxist criminology.* Karl Marx, who wrote very little on the subject of crime as the term is defined today, inspired a new school of criminology that is variously defined as "Marxist," "radical," "critical," "left-wing," "socialist," or "new." The **Marxist perspective** views the state and the law itself as ultimately tools of the economic interests of the ownership class. It is capitalism, rather than human nature, that produces egocentric, greedy, and predatory human beings. The ownership class is guilty of the crime of the brutal exploitation of the working class. Conventional crime, according to this perspective, is caused by extreme poverty and economic alienation, products of the dehumanizing and demoralizing capitalist system.

2. *Power and authority relationships.* Ralf Dahrendorf and Austin T. Turk have emphasized the relationships between authorities and their subjects. Dahrendorf contends that power is the critical variable explaining crime. He argues that although Marx built his theory on only one form of power (property ownership), a more useful perspective could be constructed by incorporating broader concepts of power.[71]

3. *Group and cultural conflict.* Another dimension of the conflict perspective focuses on group and cultural conflict. Thorsten Sellin and George Vold advocated this approach to the study of crime. Sellin argued that to understand the cause of crime, it is necessary to understand the concept of *conduct norms*. This concept refers to the rules of a group concerning how its members should act under particular conditions. The violation of these rules guiding behavior arouses a group reaction.[72]

George Vold views society "as a congeries [an aggregation] of groups held together in a shifting, but dynamic equilibrium of opposing group interests and efforts."[73] He formulated a theory of group conflict that contends that "the whole political process of law making, law breaking, and law enforcement directly reflects deep-seated and fundamental conflicts between interest groups and the more general struggles for the control of the police power of the state."[74] See Table 3–2 for a comparison of the biological, psychological, and sociological theories.

Table 3–2   *Comparison of Biological, Psychological, and Sociological Theories*

Theory	Proponents	Causes of Crime Identified
Atavistic, or born criminal	Lombroso	The atavistic criminal is a reversion to an earlier evolutionary form.
Developmental	Moffitt	Delinquent behavior proceeds along two developmental paths: On one path, early-age delinquents develop a lifelong pattern of delinquency; on the other, the adolescent develops a limited path and desists from delinquency around eighteen years of age.
Psychoanalytic	Freud	Unconscious motivations resulting from early childhood experiences
Emotional process and situational factors	Katz	Delinquency becomes an emotional process that is seductive and sensually compelling.
Psychopathic personality	Cleckley	Inner emptiness as well as biological limitations
Reinforcement	Wilson and Herrnstein	Several key constitutional and psychological factors
Social disorganization	Shaw and McKay	Delinquent behavior becomes an alternative mode of socialization through which youths who are part of disorganized communities are attracted to delinquent values and traditions.
Cultural deviance	Miller	The lower class has a distinctive culture of its own, and its local concerns, or values, make lower-class boys more likely to become involved in delinquent behavior.
Strain	Merton	Social structure exerts pressure on those individuals who cannot attain the cultural goal of success to engage in nonconforming behavior.
Delinquency opportunity	Cloward and Ohlin	Lower-class boys seek out illegitimate means to attain middle-class success goals if they are unable to attain them through legitimate means.
Status frustration	Cohen	Lower-class boys are unable to attain the goals of middle-class culture, and therefore they become involved in nonutilitarian, malicious, and negative behavior.
Differential association	Sutherland	Criminal behavior is expected of those individuals who have internalized a preponderance of definitions favorable to law violations.
Containment	Reckless	Strong inner and reinforcing external containment provides an insulation against delinquent behavior.
Social control	Hirschi	Delinquent acts result when individuals' bond to society is weak or broken.
Labeling	Lemert and Becker	Society creates deviants by labeling those who are apprehended as different from other juveniles, when in reality, they are different only because they have been given a deviant label.
Marxist perspective	Marx	Conventional delinquency and crime are caused by extreme poverty and economic alienation.
General theory of crime	Gottfredson and Hirschi	Lack of self-control is the common factor underlying problem behaviors.
Integrated social process theory	Elliott and colleagues	Integrates the strongest elements of strain, social control, and social learning perspectives into a single paradigm that accounts for delinquent behavior and drug use
Interactional theory	Thornberry	Associations with delinquent peers and delinquent values make up social delinquency; especially prolonged serious delinquency is learned and reinforced.

In sum, when social structural, social process, and social conflict theories are considered separately, a piece of the puzzle of how the environment influences a youth to become involved in crime is missing. Together, they provide a more satisfactory explanation than do biological or psychological explanations, for why juveniles become involved in delinquency.

HOW DOES INTEGRATED THEORY EXPLAIN JUVENILE CRIME?

The theoretical development of integrated explanations of juvenile crime has been one of the most highly praised concepts in criminology. Theory integration generally implies the combination of two or more already existing theories on the basis of their perceived commonalities. The overarching purpose of theoretical integration is the development of a new theory that improves on the constituent theories from which the reformulated theory is derived. The ultimate goal of theory integration, then, is the advancement of our understanding of crime and delinquency.[75]

Travis Hirschi has identified three types or forms that theoretical integration may take: side-by-side or parallel integration, end-to-end or sequential integration, and up-and-down or deductive integration. *Side-by-side integration* refers to the dividing of the subject matter into constituent types or forms; offender topologies are the most common expression of side-by-side integration. *End-to-end integration,* perhaps the most widely used type today, refers to placing causal variables in a temporal order so that the independent variables of some theories are used to become the dependent variables of the integrated theory. The process of integrating macrolevel causes with microlevel causes is another common use of the end-to-end approach. *Up-and-down integration* refers to the process of consolidating into one formulation the ideas of two or more theories by identifying a more abstract or general perspective from which at least parts of the theories can be deducted. This strategy is not frequently used because of the difficulty in compromising different assumptions.[76]

Several integrated theories for delinquent behavior have been developed. Three of the most important are Michael Gottfredson and Travis Hirschi's general theory of crime, Delbert Elliott's integrated social process theory, and Terence P. Thornberry's interactional theory.[77]

GOTTFREDSON AND HIRSCHI'S GENERAL THEORY OF CRIME

In their 1990 publication, *A General Theory of Crime,* Gottfredson and Hirschi define lack of self-control as the common factor underlying problem behaviors.[78]

> People who lack self-control will tend to be impulsive, insensitive, physical (as opposed to mental), risk-taking, short-sighted, and nonverbal, and they will tend, therefore, to engage in criminal and analogous acts [which include smoking, drinking, using drugs, gambling, having children out of wedlock, and engaging in illicit sex]. Since these traits can be identified prior to the age of responsibility for crime, since there is [a] considerable tendency for these traits to come together in the same people, and since the traits tend to persist through life, it seems reasonable to consider them as comprising a stable construct useful in the explanation of crime.[79]

Thus, self-control is the degree to which an individual is "vulnerable to the temptations of the moment."[80] The other pivotal construct in this theory of crime is crime opportunity, which is a function of the structural or situational circumstances encountered by the individual. In combination, these two

The "projects" in lower class areas often are associated with higher crime rates. Youths from these areas often require multiple services. (Photo by Stuart Miller.)

constructs are intended to capture the simultaneous influence of external and internal restraints on behavior.[81]

More than two dozen studies have been conducted on general theory, and the vast majority have been largely favorable.[82] It has been found that self-control is related to self-reported crime among college students, juveniles, and adults; tends to predict future criminal convictions and self-reported delinquency; and is related to social consequences other than crime.

Gottfredson and Hirschi's theory of self-control is part of a trend that pushes the causes of crime and delinquency further back in the life course into the family. In some respects, it is a return to the emphasis found in the works of the Gluecks and also resembles the important themes in Wilson and Herrnstein's reinforcement theory. This emphasis on early childhood socialization as the cause of crime, of course, departs from the emphasis on more proximate causes of crime found in rational choice theory and in most sociological theories.[83] Gottfredson and Hirschi's focus on a unidimensional trait also departs from the movement toward multidimensional and integrated theories of crime.[84]

Criticisms of general theory have focused largely on its lack of conceptual clarity.[85] It is argued that key elements of the theory remain to be tested,[86] that the theory does not have the power to explain all forms of delinquency and crime,[87] and that "questions remain regarding the ubiquity of self-concept."[88] Nevertheless, in spite of these criticisms, general theory will likely continue to spark continued interest and research.

ELLIOTT AND COLLEAGUES' INTEGRATED SOCIAL PROCESS THEORY

Delbert Elliott and colleagues offer "an explanatory model that expands and synthesizes traditional strain, social control, and social learning perspectives into a single paradigm that accounts for delinquent behavior and drug use."[89] They argued that all three theories are flawed in explaining delinquent behavior. Strain theory is able to account for some initial delinquent acts but does not adequately explain why some juveniles enter into delinquent careers, whereas others avoid them. Control theory is unable to explain prolonged involvement in delinquent behavior in light of there being no reward for this behavior, and learning theories portray delinquents as passive and susceptible to influence when they are confronted with delinquency-producing reinforcements.

Integrating the strongest features of these theories into a single theoretical model, Elliott and colleagues contended that the experience of living in socially disorganized areas lead youths to develop weak bonds with conventional groups, activities, and norms. High levels of strain, as well as weak bonds with conventional groups, lead some youth to seek out delinquent peer groups. These antisocial peer groups provide both positive reinforcement for delinquent behavior and role models for this behavior. Consequently, Elliott and colleagues theorize, there is a high probability of involvement in delinquent behavior when bonding to delinquent groups is combined with weak bonding to conventional groups.[90]

This theory represents a pure type of integrated theory. It can be argued that both general theory and interactional theory are not fully integrated theories but are rather elaborations of established theories. In contrast, there is no question that integrated social process theory is an integrated theory.

Examinations of this theory have generally been positive. Yet some question has been raised about its application to various types of delinquent behaviors. Questions have even been raised about its power and utility with different types of drug activity. For example, integrated social process theory explained 59 percent of the variation in marijuana use but only 29 to 34 percent of the distribution of hard drug use.[91]

THORNBERRY'S INTERACTIONAL THEORY

In Thornberry's interactional theory of delinquency the initial impetus toward delinquency comes from a weakening of the person's bond to conventional society, represented by attachment to parents, commitment to school, and belief in conventional values. Associations with delinquent peers and delinquent values make up the social setting in which delinquency, especially prolonged serious delinquency, is learned and reinforced. These two variables, along with delinquent behavior itself, form a mutually reinforcing causal loop that leads toward increasing delinquency involvement over time.[92]

Moreover, this interactive process develops over the person's life cycle. During early adolescence the family is the most influential factor in bonding the youngster to conventional society and reducing delinquency. But as the youth matures and moves through middle adolescence, the world of friends, school, and youth culture becomes the dominant influence over behavior. Finally, as the person enters adulthood, commitment to conventional activities and to family, especially, offer new avenues to reshape the person's bond to society and involvement with delinquent behavior.[93]

Finally, interactional theory holds that these process variables are systematically related to the youngster's position in the social structure. Class, minority group status, and the social disorganization of the community all affect the initial values of the interactive variables as well as the behavioral trajectories. It is argued that youths from the most socially disadvantaged backgrounds begin the process least bonded to conventional society and most exposed to the world of delinquency. The nature of the process increases the chances that they will continue on to a career of serious criminal involvement;

on the other hand, youths from middle-class families enter a trajectory that is oriented toward conformity and away from delinquency.

Thornberry's theory essentially views delinquency as the result of events occurring in a developmental fashion. Delinquency is not viewed as the end product; instead, it leads to the formation of delinquent values, which then contribute to disconnections in social bonds, more attachments to antisocial peers, and additional involvement in delinquent behavior. As found in other developmental theories, some variables affect unlawful behavior at certain ages and other factors at other ages.[94]

Interactional theory has several positive features that should assure its continued examination. It seems to make sense of much of the literature on explanations of delinquent behavior. In addition, studies that use an interactional framework are not only more commonly used among delinquency researchers, but also are being increasingly used in interdisciplinary research. Furthermore, interactional approaches are consistent with the social settings in which individuals live and interact with others.[95]

Interactional theory has several shortcomings. Most significantly, interactional theory fails to address the presence of middle-class delinquency and basically ignores racial and gender issues. Its viewpoint that delinquency will persist throughout adolescence and into adulthood, with which Hirschi and Gottfredson would find agreement, leaves little room for short-term discontinued or permanent termination of illegal behavior patterns.[96]

WHY HAS DELINQUENCY ACROSS THE LIFE COURSE BECOME SO IMPORTANT IN STUDYING THE THEORIES OF JUVENILE CRIME?

The life course perspective represents a major change in how we think about and study lives.[97] Until recently, sociological research largely neglected the life histories and future trajectories of individuals. However, the many sociological publications of Glen H. Elder, Jr., and his colleagues have done much to stimulate the use of life course theory as an appropriate research base in the study of individuals and groups.[98] Drawing on the increased numbers of longitudinal studies that examine the lives of young children, including their conduct disorders, and following these cohorts sometimes for decades, many researchers are using the life course perspective in the study of delinquent behavior and of how this behavior affects subsequent life experiences.[99]

Delinquency across the life course, or life-course criminology (DLC), is particularly concerned with documenting and explaining within-individual changes in offending throughout life. The analysis of Robert J. Sampson and John H. Laub of the Gluecks' classic longitudinal study of one thousand men has been a major impetus to the life course perspective.[100]

Sampson and Laub sought to explain both the continuity of delinquency into adult criminality and noncriminality, or change, in adulthood for those who were delinquent as children. Their basic thesis is threefold:

1. Structural context mediated by informal family and school social control explains delinquency in childhood and adolescence.
2. In turn, there is continuity in antisocial behavior from childhood through adulthood in a variety of life domains.
3. Informal social bonds in adulthood to family and employment explain changes in criminality over the life span despite early childhood propensities.[101]

Using life history data drawn from the Gluecks' longitudinal study, Laub and Sampson found that although adult crime is connected to childhood behavior, both incremental and abrupt changes still take place through changes in adult social bonds. The emergence of strong social bonds to work and family among adults deflects early behavior trajectories. Laub and Sampson also argue that the events that trigger the formation of strong adult bonds to work and family commonly occur by chance or luck.[102]

The concept of a **turning point** in the life course is one of the fascinating contributions of Laub and Sampson's research. A turning point involves a gradual or dramatic change and may lead to "a modification, reshaping, or transition from one state, condition, or phase to another."[103] In seeking to unravel the mechanisms that operate at key turning points to shift a risk trajectory to a more adaptive path, Laub and Sampson found that stable employment and a good marriage, or changing roles and environment, can lead to investment of social capital or relations among persons.[104]

APPLICATION OF THEORY TO PRACTICE

One advantage of the *Voices in the Juvenile Justice System* as a supplement to this text is that some of the stories record the accounts of individuals across their life course. A few stories describe how individuals made decisions that resulted in their being arrested, adjudicated delinquent, sent to jail or detention, and placed in residential programs. A couple of stories include accounts of how decision making resulted in a prison sentence.

With nearly every story, questions can be raised: How did this person's family background influence the course of his or her behaviors? How did success or failure in school influence subsequent behaviors? How was he or she affected by the environment? Why did he or she become involved in a youth gang? Why did this person become a drug user? What influenced this person to stop taking drugs or becoming involved in other illegal behaviors?

More specifically, what theory found in this chapter seems to apply closely to the choices that this person made? If more than one theory is required to explain behavior, what theories would you use? If none of the theories found in this chapter seem to apply to a particular story, what theoretical constructs are needed to understand this behavior?

An examination of this text further reveals a number of prevention and treatment programs that are based on a theoretical construct. The Chicago Area Projects were based on Shaw and McKay's studies of the effects of social disorganization on community life.[105] The National Juvenile Justice Assessment Centers has developed a typology for conceptualizing and organizing approaches to delinquency prevention according to the causes of delinquency they address.[106] Rational emotive therapy is a cognitive restructuring strategy that is based on rational choice theory.[107] The labeling perspective has influenced the policy of radical non-intervention, which simply means, "Leave the kids alone whenever possible."[108] Finally, conflict theory argues that the high rates of crime of lower-class youngsters are directly related to the oppressions they experience, and this has given birth to a variety of programs for these youngsters.[109]

✓**Progress Check 3.2.**
Review this section at
www.prenhall.com/bartollas

SUMMARY

This chapter has described three different explanations for why juveniles become involved in unlawful acts. These explanations include the following:

- Delinquency is a rational act stemming from free will.

- The juvenile's illegal behavior arises from biological, psychological, and sociological causes.
- The behavior, then, was determined, which would remove or reduce the juvenile's responsibility for what he or she has done.
- More multidimensional explanations, which are found in integrated theories, are required for understanding why juveniles violate the law.
- In addition to addressing these basic explanations for crime causation, other social factors exist that cannot be dismissed.
- The nurturing that does or does not take place in a family setting is an important factor.
- So is the degree of success that a juvenile attains in the school setting. Those who do poorly in school are more likely to become involved in delinquency than those who do well.
- Those juveniles who become involved in drug use or a gang are also more likely to become involved in delinquent behavior.
- Delinquency across the life course has become an important empirical consideration in understanding why juveniles pursue delinquent and later criminal behaviors.

WEB SITES OF INTEREST

Check this Crime Theory Web site to learn more about the classical school of criminology.

http://www.homestead.com/rouncefield/files/a_soc_dev_10.htm

Read about opportunity and strain theory in greater detail from the Hewett School of Norwich, Norfolk, UK.

http://www.hewett.norfolk.sch.uk

Learn more about social control theory from the University of Washington site. **Go to the Web site and click search and type in social control theory.** Learn more about labeling theory on the University of Missouri, St. Louis site.

www.washington.edu

CRITICAL THINKING QUESTIONS

1. What is the labeling perspective's definition of why adolescents become delinquent? Do you agree with this interpretation?
2. Which of the three integrated theories make the most sense to you? What are the advantages of integrated theory? What are its disadvantages?
3. Should poverty exclude an adolescent from responsibility for delinquent behavior? Why or why not?
4. Why have the juvenile courts been so quick to apply the concept of free will and rationality to violent juvenile criminals?
5. To what extent do you believe juveniles are rational in their behavior? What are the implications of your answer for the justice system?

NOTES

1. Interviewed in three midwestern states in the late 1990s.
2. Incident that took place when one of the authors was an institutional social worker.

3. Interviewed in 1981 at Stateville Correctional Center, Joliet, Illinois.

4. Jonathan H. Turner, *The Structure of Sociological Theory* (Homewood, IL: Dorsey, 1974), 2.

5. Michael Phillipson, *Understanding Crime and Delinquency* (Chicago: Aldine, 1974), 18.

6. Cesare Bonesana Beccaria, *On Crimes and Punishment*, translated by H. Paolucci (1764); reprinted ed., Indianapolis, IN: Bobbs-Merrill, 1963.

7. Ysabel Rennie, *The Search for Criminal Man: A Conceptual History of the Dangerous Offender* (Lexington, MA: Lexington Books, 1978), 15.

8. Beccaria, *On Crimes and Punishment*, 179.

9. Rennie, *The Search for Criminal Man*, 22.

10. Edward Cimler and Lee Roy Bearch, "Factors Involved in Juvenile Decisions about Crime," *Criminal Justice and Behavior* 8 (September 1981), 275–86.

11. Ronald L. Akers, "Deterrence, Rational Choice, and Social Learning Theory: The Path Not Taken," paper presented at the annual meeting of the American Society of Criminology, Reno, NV (November 1989), 2–3.

12. Phillip J. Cook, "The Demand and Supply of Criminal Opportunities," in *Crime and Justice* 7, edited by Michael Tonry and Norval Morris (Chicago: University of Chicago Press, 1986), 2.

13. Ibid., 2–3.

14. Lawrence E. Cohen and Marcus Felson, "Social Change and Crime Rate Trends: A Routine Activity Approach," *American Sociological Review* 44 (August 1979), 588–609.

15. Steven E. Messner and Kenneth Tardiff, "The Social Ecology of Urban Homicides: An Application of the 'Routine Activities' Approach," *Criminology* 23 (1985), 241–67.

16. Akers, "Deterrence, Rational Choice, and Social Learning Theory," 8.

17. Ibid., 8–9.

18. Derek B. Cornish and Ronald V. Clarke, eds., *The Reasoning Criminal: Rational Choice Perspectives on Offending* (New York: Springer, 1986), 1–2.

19. Ibid., 13.

20. Akers, "Deterrence, Rational Choice, and Social Learning Theory," 12.

21. Akers, however, questions this in his paper, "Deterrence, Rational Choice, and Social Learning Theory," 11.

22. See David J. Rothman, *Conscience and Convenience: The Asylum and Its Alternatives in Progressive America* (Boston: Little, Brown, 1980), 32.

23. Ibid., 43–60.

24. David Matza, *Delinquency and Drift* (New York: Wiley, 1964), 5.

25. Donald C. Gibbons, "Differential Treatment of Delinquents and Interpersonal Maturity Level: A Critique," *Social Services Review* 44 (1970), 68.

26. Cesare Lombroso, Introduction to C. Lombroso-Ferrero, *Criminal Man According to the Classification of Cesare Lombroso* (New York: Putnam, 1911), xiv.

27. Charles Goring, *The Criminal Convict: A Statistical Study* (Montclair, NJ: Patterson Smith, 1972).

28. Terrie E. Moffitt, Donald R. Lynam, and Phil A. Silva, "Neuropsychological Tests Predicted Persistent Male Delinquency," *Criminology* 32 (May 1994), 277.

29. Terrie E. Moffitt, "Adolescent-Limited and Life-Course-Persistent Antisocial Behavior: A Developmental Taxonomy," *Psychological Review* 100 (1993), 277.

30. Terrie E. Moffitt, "The Neuropsychology of Conduct Disorder," *Development and Psychopathology* 5 (1993), 135–51.

31. Curt R. Bartol and Anne M. Bartol, *Delinquency and Justice: A Psychosocial Approach,* 2d ed. (Upper Saddle River, NJ: Prentice Hall, 1998), 89.

32. Sigmund Freud, *An Outline of Psychoanalysis*, translated by James Strachey (1940 reprint, New York: W. W. Norton, 1963).

33. Ibid.

34. Ibid.

35. LaMar T. Empey, *American Delinquency: Its Meaning and Construction* (Homewood, IL: Dorsey Press, 1982), 172–73.

36. Herbert Cleckley, *The Mask of Sanity*, 3d ed. (St. Louis, MO: Mosby, 1935), 382–417.

37. See Kathleen M. Heide, "Parents Who Get Killed and the Children Who Kill Them," *Journal of Interpersonal Violence* 8 (December 1993), 531–44.

38. Marvin Zuckerman, *Sensation Seeking Beyond the Optimal Level of Arousal* (Hillsdale, NJ: Lawrence Erlbaum, 1979), 10.

39. Ibid.

40. M. J. Hindelang, "The Relationship of Self-Reported Delinquency to Scales of the CPI and MMPI," *Journal of Criminal Law, Criminology and Police Science* 63, (1972), 75–81.

41. Helene Raskin White, Erich W. Labouvie, and Marsha E. Bales, "The Relationship between Sensation Seeking and Delinquency: A Longitudinal Analysis," *Journal of Research in Crime and Delinquency* 22 (August 1985), 195–211.

42. Jack Katz, *Seductions of Crime: Moral and Sensual Attractions in Doing Evil* (New York: Basic Books, 1988).

43. Ibid.

44. Richard L. Jenkins, "Delinquency and a Treatment Philosophy," in *Crime, Law and Corrections*, edited by Ralph Slovenko (Springfield, IL: Charles C Thomas, 1966), 135–36.

45. Cleckley, *The Mask of Sanity,* 132–37.

46. L. N. Robins, *Deviant Children Grown Up: A Sociological and Psychiatric Study of Sociopathic Personality* (Baltimore: Williams & Wilkins, 1966), 256.

47. L. N. Robins et al., "The Adult Psychiatric Status of Black Schoolboys," *Archives of General Psychiatry* 24 (1971), 338–45.

48. Linda Mealey, "The Sociobiology of Sociopathy: An Integrated Evolutionary Model," *Behavioral and Brain Sciences* 18 (1995), 523–40.

49. James Q. Wilson and Richard J. Herrnstein, *Crime and Human Nature* (New York: Simon & Schuster, 1985).

50. Ibid.

51. Edgar Z. Friedenberg, "Solving Crime," *Readings: A Journal of Reviews* (March 1986), 21.

52. Clifford R. Shaw and Henry D. McKay, *Juvenile Delinquency and Urban Areas* (Chicago: University of Chicago Press, 1942).

53. Walter B. Miller, "Lower-Class Culture as a Generating Milieu of Gang Delinquency," *Journal of Social Issues* 14 (1958), 9–10.

54. Ibid.

55. Marvin Wolfgang and Franco Ferracuti, *Subculture of Violence* (London: Tavistock, 1957).

56. Richard A. Cloward and Lloyd E. Ohlin, *Delinquency and Opportunity: A Theory of Delinquency* (New York: Free Press, 1960).

57. Albert K. Cohen, *Delinquent Boys: The Culture of the Gang* (New York: Free Press, 1955).

58. Edwin H. Sutherland, *Principles of Criminology* (Philadelphia: J. B. Lippincott Company, 1947).

59. Jack Henry Abbott, *In the Belly of the Beast: Letters from Prison* (New York: Vintage, 1981).

60. The principles of containment theory are described in Walter C. Reckless, "A New Theory of Delinquency and Crime," *Federal Probation* 24 (December 1952), 133–38.

61. Simon Dinitz and Betty A. Pfau-Vicent, "Self-Concept and Juvenile Delinquency: An Update," *Youth and Society* 14 (December 1982), 133–38.

62. Travis Hirschi, *Causes of Delinquency* (Berkeley: University of California Press, 1969).

63. Ibid., 18.

64. Ibid., 83.

65. Ibid., 20.

66. Ibid., 22.

67. Ibid., 198.

68. Edwin L. Lemert, *Social Pathology* (New York: McGraw-Hill, 1951); and Howard S. Becker, *Outsiders* (New York: Free Press, 1958).

69. Lemert, *Social Pathology.*

70. Becker, *Outsiders.*

71. Ralf Dahrendorf and A. T. Turk, *Class and Class Conflict in Industrial Society* (Palo Alto, CA: Stanford University Press, 1959).

72. Thorsten Sellin, *Culture, Conflict, and Crime* (New York: Social Science Research Council, 1938), 28.

73. George B. Vold, *Theoretical Criminology*, 2d ed., prepared by Thomas J. Bernard (New York: Oxford University Press, 1979), 283.

74. Ibid., 288.

75. Margaret Farnworth, "Theory Integration versus Model Building," in *Theoretical Integration in the Study of Deviance and Crime: Problems and Prospects* (Albany: State University of New York at Albany Press, 1989), 93.

76. Cited in Thomas J. Bernard and Jeffrey B. Snipes, "Theoretical Integration in Criminology," in *Crime and Justice: A Review of Research*, Volume 20, edited by Michael Tonry (Chicago and London: University of Chicago Press, 1994), 307.

77. Michael G. Gottfredson and Travis Hirschi, *A General Theory of Crime* (Stanford, CA: Stanford University Press, 1990); Delbert S. Elliott, David Huizinga, and Suzanne S. Ageton, *Explaining Delinquency and Drug Use* (Beverley Hills, CA: Sage, 1985); Delbert S. Elliott, Suzanne S. Ageton, and Rachelle J. Canter, "An Integrated Theoretical Perspective on Delinquent Behavior," *Journal of Research in Crime and Delinquency* 16 (1979), 3–27; Terence P. Thornberry, "Toward an Interactional Theory of Delinquency," *Criminology* 25 (1987), 862–91; and Terence P. Thornberry, Alan J. Lizotte, Marvin D. Krohn, Margaret Farnworth, and Sung Joon Jang, "Testing Interactional Theory: An Examination of Reciprocal Causal Relationships among Family, School and Delinquency," *Journal of Criminal Law and Criminology* 82 (1991), 3–35.

78. Gottfredson and Hirschi, *A General Theory of Crime.*

79. Ibid., 90–91.

80. Ibid., 87.

81. Ibid., 87.

82. For a review of these studies, see T. David Evans, Francis T. Cullen, Velmer S. Burton, Jr., R. Gregory Dunaway, and Michael L. Benson, "The Social

Consequences of Self-Control: Testing the General Theory of Crime," *Criminology* 35 (1997), 476–77.

83. Harold G. Grasmick, Charles R. Tittle, Robert J. Bursik, Jr., and Bruce J. Arneklev, "Testing the Core Empirical Implications of Gottfredson and Hirschi's General Theory of Crime," *Journal of Research in Crime and Delinquency* 30 (February 1993), 5.

84. See Ronald L. Akers, "Self-Control as a General Theory of Crime," *Journal of Quantitative Criminology* 7 (1991), 191–211.

85. Donald J. Shoemaker, *Theories of Delinquency: An Examination of Explanations of Delinquent Behavior,* 5th ed. (New York: Oxford University Press, 2005), 53.

86. Dennis M. Giever, Dana C. Lynskey, and Danette S. Monnet, "Gottfredson and Hirschi's General Theory of Crime and Youth Gangs: An Empirical Test on a Sample of Middle-School Students," unpublished paper sent to the authors, 1998.

87. Michael Polakowski, "Linking Self- and Social Control with Deviance: Illuminating the Structure Underlying a General Theory of Crime and Its Relation to Deviant Activity," *Journal of Quantitative Criminology* 10 (1994), 41–77.

88. Ibid., 41.

89. Delbert S. Elliott, Suzanne S. Ageton, and Rachelle J. Canter, "An Integrated Theoretical Perspective on Delinquent Behavior," *Journal of Research in Crime & Delinquency* 16 (1979), 862–91.

90. Ibid.

91. Cynthia Chien, "Testing the Effect of the Key Theoretical Variable of Theories of Strain, Social Control and Social Learning on Types of Delinquency," paper presented at the annual meeting of the American Society of Criminology, Baltimore (November 1990).

92. Thornberry, "Toward an Interactional Theory of Delinquency," 886.

93. Ibid.

94. Shoemaker, *Theories of Delinquency,* 161–63.

95. Ibid., 262–63.

96. Ibid., 262.

97. Glen H. Elder, Jr., Monica Kirkpatrick Johnson, and Robert Crosnoe, "The Emergence and Development of Life Course Theory," in *Handbook of the Life Course,* edited by Jeylan T. Mortiner and Michael J. Shanahan (New York: Kluwer Academic/Plenum, 2003), 3.

98. See G. H. Elder, Jr., *Children of the Great Depression: Social Change in Life Experience,* 25th anniversary ed. (Boulder, CO: Westview Press, 1999); and G. H. Elder, Jr., and E. D. Conger, *Children of the Land: Adversity and Success in Rural America* (Chicago: University of Chicago Press, 2000).

99. The two most influential studies of the life course are Robert J. Sampson and John H. Laub, *Crime in the Making: Pathways and Turning Points through Life* (Cambridge, MA: Harvard University Press, 1993); and John H. Laub and Robert J. Sampson, *Shared Beginnings, Divergent Lives, Delinquent Boys to Age 70* (Cambridge, MA: Harvard University Press, 2003).

100. Sampson and Laub, *Crime in the Making;* and Laub and Sampson, *Shared Beginnings, Divergent Lives, Delinquent Boys to Age 70.*

101. Sampson and Laub, *Crime in the Making,* 7.

102. John H. Laub and Robert J. Sampson, "Turning Points in the Life Course: Why Change Matters to the Study of Crime," *Criminology* 31 (August 1993), 309.

103. Ibid., 309.

104. Ibid., 310.

105. See Harold Finestone, *Victims of Change: Juvenile Delinquents in American Society* (Westport, CT: Greenwood Press, 1976).

106. See J. David Hawkins et al., *Report of the National Juvenile Justice Assessment Centers: A Typology of Cause-Focused Strategies of Delinquency Prevention* (Washington, DC: Government Printing Office, 1980).

107. See Derek B. Cornish and Ronald V. Clarke, eds., *The Reasoning Criminal: Rational Choice Perspectives on Offending* (New York: Springer, 1986).

108. See Edwin Schur, *Radical Nonintervention* (Upper Saddle River, NJ: Prentice Hall, 1973).

109. See Barry Krisberg and James Austin, eds., *Children of Ishmael: Critical Perspectives on Juvenile Justice* (Palo Alto, CA: Mayfield, 1978).

4

THE POLICE

How does one explain the raw excitement of being a cop? This is an excitement so powerful that it consumes and changes the officer's personality. For the officer all five senses are involved, especially in dangerous situations. They are stirred in a soup of emotions and adrenaline and provide an adrenaline rush that surpasses anything felt before. You are stronger and more agile; your mind functions on a higher level of quickness and alertness. Afterwards, the grass seems greener; the air fresher; food tastes better; and the spouse and children are even more precious. It is an addictive feeling that makes the runner's high in comparison feel like a hangover. Police work gets into the blood and possesses the spirit. You become the job and the job becomes you, until the day you die.

—Veteran police officer[1]

OUTLINE

OBJECTIVES

1. To examine juveniles' attitudes toward the police
2. To discuss police intervention with the various types of juvenile offenders
3. To examine the legal rights of arrested juveniles
4. To portray the various ways that police departments handle juvenile crime

KEY TERMS

community-oriented policing (COP)
cycle of alienation
discretion
fingerprinting
gang detail

gang unit
interrogation
lineup
photographs
police process

problem-oriented policing
restorative justice
school searches
search and seizure
Youth Service Program

The veteran police officer in the chapter-opening quote makes a passionate statement about the joys of becoming a police officer. He clearly sees policing more as a calling than as a job or a set of bureaucratically defined duties. He believes that policing demands the very best that a person has to offer. Once it gets into your blood, he warns, it will change your identity and self-image and will stay with you for the rest of your life.

This officer, despite his positive attitude about a police career, has little interest in working with juveniles. With him, as well as with many officers, many problems exist in policing juveniles. Juvenile crimes are viewed as minor, and the arrest of a juvenile is not considered a real arrest. The due process rights accorded juveniles in recent decades also make the police feel that their crime-fighting hands are tied. Furthermore, police officers are distrusted by many juveniles, some of whom view the police as the enemy. The police then must deal with juveniles' hostile attitudes, which can become explosive and violent at a moment's notice. Finally, the nature of juvenile crime is changing; the spread of malls, the explosion of drugs, and the proliferation of gangs have complicated the lives of police officers across the country.

Police officers are faced with juveniles whose behaviors range from drinking in parks to murder. At one end of the spectrum are status offenders who have conflicts with their parents, schools, and community but who are not true criminals in either behavior or intent. At the other end are the violent, repetitive offenders. These youths commit murder, aggravated assault, rape, and grand theft; some are in organized crime, and some deal in drugs. Between these extremes are varieties of runaways and mentally ill, dependent, neglected, abused, victimized, and delinquent youths.

The history of the police in the United States is reviewed in this chapter, followed by juveniles' attitudes toward the police, the cycle of alienation, factors that influence discretion, the informal and formal dispositions of juvenile offenders, and the changing legal rights of juveniles. The final sections of this chapter consider police organizations and functions as they relate to juveniles, as well as the special challenges that juveniles' drug use, gang involvement, and gun possession bring to community-based policing.

WHAT IS THE HISTORY OF POLICE–JUVENILE RELATIONS?

The earliest Puritan communities in the United States used informal methods of controlling juveniles. Probably the most effective of these informal methods was *socialization*, by which youths were taught the rules of society from the time they were born until the rules became internalized. If a youth violated a law, the family, church, and community stepped in to bring the youth back into line. The family was expected to punish the youth, and if the family failed, church and community elders turned to other punishments.

The industrialization and urbanization that began in the late 1700s reduced the effectiveness of informal social controls. As the population increased and cities grew, the traditional tight-knit family and community structures became disorganized and street crime increased. Religious, ethnic, and political violence also increased, leading the society to look for other methods of social control.[2] Police forces were created to help solve the problem.

In the 1830s and 1840s, full-time police forces were established in larger cities, such as Boston, New York, and Philadelphia; by the 1870s, all the major cities had full-time forces, and many of the smaller cities had part-time forces. Social control had moved from the family to police officers walking the beat. The police emerged as a coercive force employed to keep youthful criminals, gangs, ethnic minorities, and immigrants in line.

Police officers had the power to arrest juveniles, but they still used many informal techniques of social control. Some officers undoubtedly were effective in striking up friendships with juveniles and convincing them to mend their ways. In other cases, police reprimanded juveniles verbally or turned them over to their parents or parish priests. Unfortunately, the power of police officers at this time was virtually unlimited; some officers talked abusively to children, roughed them up, or beat them in alleys. Added to the corruption found in many police departments, the result was that considerable tension existed between police officers and the communities they patrolled. Few, if any, efforts to remedy this problem occurred before the 1900s.

In the first three decades of the twentieth century, the Portland, Oregon; New York City; and Washington, DC, police departments started to address the problem of juvenile crime. Police chiefs began to think in terms of prevention instead of merely control. Policewomen were hired to work with delinquents and runaway and truant children by patrolling amusement parks, dance halls, and other places where juveniles might be corrupted. The job of these officers was to dissuade the youths from engaging in a life of crime.[3]

The idea of prevention was so popular that 90 percent of the nation's largest cities had instituted some type of juvenile program by 1924.[4] The Police Athletic League was launched in the 1920s, and by the 1930s, most large police departments had either assigned welfare officers to difficult districts, initiated employment bureaus for youthful males, assigned officers to juvenile courts, or set up special squads to deal with juvenile crime.[5] Other innovations included instituting relief programs, giving poor children gifts at Christmas, and developing programs whereby police spoke to various groups of youths, such as Boy Scouts and Campfire Girls.[6]

A major development occurred in the mid-1920s. Until this time, departments had not effectively organized their juvenile crime prevention efforts. Chief August Vollmer of the Berkeley, California, Police Department is credited with being the first chief to bring together the various segments of a police force to form a youth bureau.[7] The concept spread to other urban areas, and soon youth bureaus, often called *youth aid bureaus, juvenile bureaus, juvenile control bureaus, juvenile divisions,* or *crime prevention bureaus,* were found throughout major cities in the United States. The police in these bureaus were the forerunners of the modern juvenile officers.

Two developments formalized the increasingly important role of juvenile officers in the United States. In 1955, the Central States Juvenile Officer's Association was formed, followed soon after by the International Juvenile Officer's Association in 1957. Meetings were held by these and similar groups at regional, national, and international levels. For the first time, the responsibilities, standards, and procedures necessary in juvenile work were being developed. In addition, the increase in social science research on youths highlighted the necessity of training juvenile officers better, as these officers were expected to help, rather than punish, youthful offenders.

Preventive police work with juveniles continued through the 1960s. Programs were developed to reduce delinquency and to improve the way youths viewed the police. Police officers volunteered to speak to elementary, junior high, and high school students, and some departments developed special programs for these purposes. The Police Athletic League expanded its athletic programs and set up courses in leadership and moral training for youths. Furthermore, some police agencies helped youths find jobs and worked with schools to reduce truancy. Programs to fight drugs and alcohol and to show the consequences of drinking and driving were also developed.

In the 1970s, 1980s, and 1990s, severe budgetary restrictions forced many police departments to reduce their emphasis on juvenile programs. Some dropped their juvenile divisions altogether, whereas others limited their activity to dependent, neglected, and abused children, which had commenced in response to the increasingly recognized problems of domestic violence. By the late 1990s and the first decade of the twenty-first century, some police departments were experimenting with community-based or **problem-oriented policing** as well as restorative justice practices.

WHAT ARE JUVENILES' ATTITUDES TOWARD THE POLICE?

Researchers began studying the public's attitudes toward the police more than forty years ago.[8] Numerous charges of police corruption, police brutality, violation of citizens' rights, and rising crime rates generated much discussion over the role of the police in modern society. In addition, public administrators were well aware of a "we versus they" mentality that shaped relations between the police and the public and inhibited their cooperation. Administrators wanted to reduce this split and to increase the public's willingness to report victimization and cooperate with the police in preventing as well as more effectively combating crime and delinquency. Since then, numerous surveys of the public and of juveniles have been conducted. Juveniles are of particular concern because they are disproportionately involved in crime and because they will eventually be adults whose cooperation would be greatly appreciated by the police.

One of the most important early studies was conducted by Robert Portune on one thousand junior high school students in Cincinnati. Portune concluded that hostility toward the law and police increased from grades seven through nine; that whites had much more favorable attitudes than did African Americans; that girls had more favorable attitudes than did boys; that better students had more favorable attitudes than did poorer students; and that the higher the occupational status of the father, the more favorable was the child's attitude toward the police.[9]

In a more detailed study, Donald Bouma and his associates administered ten thousand questionnaires to Michigan schoolchildren in ten cities. These students, most of whom were in grades seven through nine, were asked about their attitudes, their parents' attitudes, and their friends' attitudes toward the police. The findings of this study, which agreed with all the major findings of Portune's research, additionally established the following:

1. Even though hositility toward the police significantly increased as students moved through the junior high years, the majority of students would still cooperate with the police if they saw someone other than a friend commit a crime.

2. Most youths perceived friends to be more antagonistic toward the police than they were, and they perceived the attitudes of their parents toward the police to be quite similar to their own.

3. A majority of students believed that the police were "pretty nice guys." In fact, more than half of all students believed that the police were criticized too often.

4. One-third of the white youths and two-thirds of the African-American youths believed that the police accused students of things they did not do.

5. Although two out of every three students believed that the city would be better off with more police officers, only 8 percent reported that they would like to be police officers.[10]

L. Thomas Winfree, Jr., and Curt T. Griffiths's 1977 study of students in seventeen high schools found that, to a considerable degree, juveniles' attitudes toward the police were shaped by contacts with police officers. Juveniles' attitudes were influenced more by negative contacts than by sex, race, socioeconomic status, or residence, and the negative contacts were twice as important as positive contacts in determining juveniles' attitudes toward police officers.[11]

William T. Rusinko and colleagues' 1978 examination of twelve hundred ninth-grade students in three junior high schools in Lansing, Michigan, explored the importance of police contact in formulating juveniles' attitudes toward the police. They found that positive police contact with the white youths in their study neutralized negative encounters. But positive police contact did not reduce the tendency for African-American youths to be less positive in their opinions of police. These findings agree with those of several other studies that show the development of a culturally accepted view of police among African Americans independent of their arrest experience.[12]

Scott H. Decker, in a 1981 review of literature on attitudes toward the police, concluded that youths had more negative attitudes toward the police than did older citizens and that race, the quality of police services, and previous experiences with the police also affected citizens' attitudes.[13] In 1990, however, James R. Davis found in a very small sample of New Yorkers younger than twenty years of age that attitudes toward the police were not statistically related to age.[14]

Komanduri S. Murty, Julian B. Roebuck, and Joann D. Smith found in an Atlanta study that "older, married, white-collar, highly educated, and employed respondents reported a more positive image of the police than did their counterparts—younger, single, blue-collar, low-educated, unemployed/underemployed respondents."[15] Murty and colleagues offered support for previous findings that younger African-American males are particularly hostile toward the police. These researchers demonstrated that the chances that respondents will have negative attitudes toward the police also vary, in descending order, with residence in high-crime census tracts, single marital status, negative contacts with the police, and blue-collar occupations.[16]

Michael J. Leiber, Mahesh K. Nalla, and Margaret Farnworth challenged the traditional argument that juveniles' interactions with the police are the primary determinant of their attitudes toward law enforcement officers. Instead, they saw juveniles' attitudes toward authority and social control developing in a larger sociocultural context. In their sample of Iowa youths who were accused of delinquency and adjudicated as delinquents, they found that social background variables (particularly minority status) and subcultural preferences (particularly commitment to delinquent norms) affected juveniles' attitudes toward the police both directly and indirectly (through police–juvenile interactions).[17]

Data from the *Monitoring the Future Project* survey of high school seniors from the late 1980s through the mid-1990s indicate that high school seniors' attitudes toward the police became more negative during that period across all subsets of the sample. For example, to the question about their attitudes toward the police and law enforcement agencies, the percentage of youths responding "good" and "very good" tended to decline throughout the 1980s and into the early 1990s across the categories of gender, race, and geographic region.[18] However, these general downward trends showed some improvement in later years. The *Monitoring the Future Project* data for 2001 revealed that 33.2 percent of high school seniors (up from 26.6 percent in 1996) responded either "good" or "very good." If the 33.7 percent of "fair" responses were added to the "good" and "very good" categories, roughly 67 percent of high school seniors could be considered to have a positive attitude toward the police.[19]

Susan Gaurino-Ghezzi and Bryan Carr argue, on the basis of a study conducted in Boston called "Make Peace with Police," that the way police interact with juveniles alienates youths who are already alienated from the wider society, and the results are incorporated into the youths' subculture. Three factors set the stage for what Guarino-Ghezzi and Carr call a **cycle of alienation.** First, when police arrest lower-level juvenile drug dealers, leaving upper-level suppliers untouched, youths believe the police to be ineffectual and corrupt because they do not go after the upper-level dealers and incompetent because the police are able only to arrest young kids. Second, youths are affected by police "attitudes, behaviors, and policies" in action. Arrogant, disrespectful, or rude officers quickly alienate and repulse juveniles. Third, most inner-city areas are disorganized and lack positive, structured activities. Youths cannot trust that their families, counselors, teachers, or others in the community will assist them if they are in trouble; they certainly do not feel they can trust the police. With no one to turn to in times of trouble, youths accept that they must protect themselves and handle their own problems, even if death is the result. This cycle of alienation is particularly dominant in many delinquent subcultures, especially those of gangs. It is through these feelings of alienation that juveniles react to and create new myths in relation to the police. Table 4–1 summarizes some of Guarino-Ghezzi and Carr's findings.[20]

To sum up: As Leiber and colleagues point out, juveniles' attitudes toward the police are formed in a larger sociocultural context. Gaurino-Ghezzi and Carr's study finds that police interactions with youths alienated from the wider society often results in a cycle of alienation resulting in their greater alienation from society. Yet most youths appear to have positive attitudes toward the police. Younger juveniles are more positive than older ones, white juveniles are more positive than African Americans, and female juveniles are more positive than males. A positive attitude also seems to be influenced by social class, for middle-class youths tend to be more positive than lower-class youths. Generally, juveniles who have not had contact

Table 4–1   *The Cycle of Alienation*

Delinquent Subcultural Framework	Arrests of Neighborhood Drug Dealers	High Rate of Unsolved Crime	Police Inconsistency	Neighborhood Vulnerability
Juvenile Experience	The community's crime rate is high; few arrests; abuse, harassment, and lack of respect from police	No protection if someone is after you; cops are ignorant and cannot help; only snitches talk to police	Inconsistent policing; cops act randomly and arbitrarily; judge all youths as bad	Police are crooked; police sell drugs and guns they get from kids; police want personal power
Myth	Police "benefit" from arresting small-time drug dealers; let upper-level dealers alone on purpose	Police can't protect you (denial of own lifestyle as risky)	Kids end up in the juvenile justice system as a result of police randomness; not punishment for anything done wrong	It's a game of cops and robbers; a contest between police and kids; only one will win
Lesson	Stay away from police; they abuse their power	Solve your own problems; retaliate and be retaliated against; keep police out	Kids will be arrested whether they commit crimes or not	If police don't live by the law, why should the youths?
Rituals	Confront and intimidate police; interpret police officers' fear as weakness	Trust only your friends; tell stories of police ineffectiveness	Test consistency of police by defiance, baiting, and manipulation	Act tough toward cops; look for fear and weakness; disrespect and don't listen to police

Source: Adapted from Susan Guarino-Ghezzi and Bryan Carr, "Juvenile Offenders vs. the Police: A Community Dilemma," *Caribbean Journal of Criminology and Social Psychology* 1 (July 1996), pp. 24–43.

with the police are more positive than those who have had police contact. The most hostile attitudes are typically those of youths with extensive histories of law-violating activities who have had contact with the police, or who are involved in youth gangs.

HOW DOES POLICE DISCRETION AFFECT THE POLICE RESPONSE TO JUVENILES?

Police **discretion** can be defined as the choice between two or more possible means of handling a situation confronting the police officer. By exercising discretion, the police officer can use various methods to keep juveniles out of the juvenile justice system or to involve them in it. Although it is sometimes argued that the police abuse their broad powers of discretion with juveniles, studies generally estimate that only 10 to 20 percent of police–juvenile encounters become official contacts.[21] Two major aspects of policing are the factors that influence police discretion and the ways in which police process juveniles who come to their attention.

FACTORS THAT INFLUENCE POLICE DISCRETION

The police officer's disposition of the juvenile is largely determined by nine factors: the nature of the offense; citizen complainants; the juvenile's sex, race, socioeconomic status, and other individual characteristics; the nature of the interaction between the police officer and the juvenile; departmental policy; and external pressures in the community.

The Nature of the Offense

The most important factor that influences the disposition of the youthful offender is the seriousness of the offense. Research has consistently documented that the probability of arrest increases with the legal severity of the alleged offense.[22]

Citizen Complainants

Another important factor influencing the disposition of the youth is a citizen's presence or filing of a complaint against a youth.[23] If a citizen initiates a complaint, remains present, and wishes the arrest of a juvenile, the likelihood increases that the juvenile will be arrested and processed.[24]

Sex

Police officers generally are less likely to arrest a young female than a young male if she has committed an offense, but they are more likely to arrest a female if she violates traditional role expectations for females, such as failing to obey parents, being sexually promiscuous, or running away from home.[25]

Race

Studies differ in their findings on the importance of race in determining juvenile dispositions.[26] One of the problems in appraising the importance of race is that African Americans and members of other minority groups appear to be involved in more serious crimes more often than whites are. Nevertheless, it does seem that racial bias makes minority juveniles the special targets of the police.[27] See Focus on Practice 4–1 for a discussion of the influence of racial profiling.

Socioeconomic Status

What makes it difficult to establish the effect of class on the disposition of cases involving juveniles is that most studies examine race and socioeconomic status together. Nevertheless, some evidence supports the long-standing conclusion that lower-class juveniles receive different justice than do middle- or upper-class juveniles. Lower-class youths are dragged into the net of the system for the same offenses for which middle- and upper-class juveniles are often sent home.

Individual Characteristics

A prior arrest record, previous offenses, prior police contacts, age, peer relationships, family situation, and the conduct of parents also may influence how the police officer handles a juvenile offender.[28] The juvenile most likely to be arrested is older, has a serious record, and fits the image of a delinquent and dangerous person.[29]

Nature of Police–Juvenile Interaction

Juveniles who defer to a police officer reduce the likelihood of a formal disposition.[30] Juveniles who are hostile increase the likelihood that they will be referred to the juvenile court.[31] One study found that in encounters in which no evidence linked a juvenile to an offense, the demeanor of the juvenile was the most important determinant of whether formal action was taken.[32]

Departmental Policy

Departmental policy also may influence police handling of juveniles.[33] Some evidence suggests that the more professional departments had higher numbers of juveniles referred to the juvenile court because they used discretion less often than did the departments that were not as professional.[34]

FOCUS ON PRACTICE
RACIAL PROFILING AND THE POLICE

4-1

Minority motorists, especially African Americans, have complained for decades that the police have stopped them for no legitimate reason. This practice, known as *racial profiling*, seems to exist particularly in suburban areas. Furthermore, during such stops, African Americans may be subjected to detailed questioning and searches and given little or no explanation for why they were stopped. This phenomenon has gained such notoriety among African Americans that it is called *driving while black*.

A Bureau of Justice Statistics survey of police–public contact found that in 1999 African Americans were somewhat more likely than Hispanics and whites to report being stopped by the police. African Americans who had been stopped were more likely than whites to report that they had been ticketed, handcuffed, arrested, or searched by police officers. They also were more likely to say that officers had threatened or used force against them. In addition, African Americans were also much less likely than whites or Hispanics to feel that the search of the vehicle was legitimate. Ronald Weitzer and Steven T. Tuch's recently analyzed national survey data on citizens' view of racial profiling found that both race and personal experience were strong predictors of attitudes toward profiling. Even middle-class African Americans feel they have experienced racial profiling when driving through predominantly white areas.

Source: Tom R. Tyler and Cheryl J. Wakslak, "Profiling and Police Legitimacy: Procedural Justice, Attributions of Motive, and Acceptance of Police Authority," *Criminology* 42 (May 2004), 253–81; Ronald Weitzer and Steven A. Tuch, "Perceptions of Racial Profiling: Race, Class, and Personal Experience," *Criminology* 40 (May 2002), 435–56.

Critical Thinking Questions:
Is it racial profiling when a police officer tells a group of African-American juveniles hanging around a street corner to scatter and go home? Does your answer change if the police officer believes that these particular juveniles are members of a gang?

External Pressures in the Community

The status of the complainant or victim, the attitudes of the press and the public, and the philosophy and available resources of referral agencies also may influence the disposition of the law-violating youth.

In sum, this portrait of police–juvenile contacts reveals that the seriousness of the offense and complaints by citizens appear to be the most important factors influencing police action toward juveniles. Other, less influential factors are the individual characteristics of the juvenile, departmental policy, and external pressures in the community. The sex, race, and socioeconomic status of the offender do not appear to be as influential today as they were in the past (see Table 4–2).

✓**Progress Check 4.1**
Review this section at
www.prenhall.com/bartollas

HOW DO POLICE PROCESS JUVENILES?

The studies on police discretion reveal many inconsistencies, some legitimate and some not. For example, few would argue that true justice should not take into consideration factors such as the friendliness of juveniles, their race, sex, social class, or community reputations; nevertheless, these biases do creep into police work and are under much criticism today. On the other side of the coin is the complexity of police work. Police working their beat come into contact daily with many different types of juveniles in various situations. Some youths obviously are mentally ill or mentally handicapped; some come from families

Table 4–2   *Factors That Influence the Disposition of Juvenile Offenders*

Individual Factors
Personality characteristics of the juvenile
Personality characteristics of the police officer
Interaction between the police officer and the juvenile

Sociocultural Factors
Citizen complaints
Gender of the juvenile
Race/ethnicity of the juvenile
Socioeconomic status of the juvenile
The influence of cultural norms in the community and values of the wider society on both juveniles and police officers
External pressures in the community to arrest certain types of juvenile offenders

Organizational Factors
Nature of the offense
Departmental policy

torn apart by alcohol, drugs, and other addictive disorders; some youths are neglected; and some are abused physically, emotionally, or sexually. Some youths have no family members to turn to in times of need, and some find school a frightening, frustrating, and valueless experience; conversely, many find gang experiences rewarding, emotionally satisfying, and a way to gain the respect of peers. Police officers must deal effectively with all of these youths.

INFORMAL OPTIONS: ON THE STREETS

Police view youths in the context of their community. This means that officers see how youths interact in their neighborhoods with friends and family and witness the many different ways the youths get along with others. The good beat officer knows who belongs to various peer groups and gangs, who is stable and who is unstable, who is belligerent and who is not; these officers also often know the circumstances of youths' lives. These factors affect how the **police process** a particular event or incident. For example, some of the following police actions are informal responses to youthful misbehavior and no permanent record of the incident will be kept, nor will juveniles be held for further actions by the juvenile court.

- Kids clowning around on the sidewalk are simply ignored by a passing officer.
- Police officers suggest that youths take their sidewalk soccer game into a nearby playground or vacant lot if they are bothering people, if someone could get hurt, or if a citizen has complained.
- An officer might talk to a youth bullying others and suggest that the bully change his or her ways.
- Some officers strike up friendships with local youths, sit and talk with them, and sometimes go to their school or sporting events.
- Officers who see youths fighting or stealing something might talk to them about the harm they are causing and how they might get into trouble as a result.
- An officer might write down the juvenile's name and address in a notepad for future reference.

INFORMAL OPTIONS: AT THE STATION (STATIONHOUSE ADJUSTMENT)

- Youths are taken to the police station, where their situation is discussed with them and their parents; the youths are then sent home with their parents.
- In larger departments, youths are sent to a police youth bureau that consists of specially trained officers or other personnel who counsel the youths and their parents but who permit the youths to remain in the community.
- Police officers or youth bureau personnel unofficially refer or direct youths and/or their parents or guardians to anger management classes, vocational training programs, shelters, or counseling programs for alcohol, drug, mental illness, or other problems.
- Police or youth service personnel contact and work with school personnel in getting truant youths back in schools or into special programs. (School personnel may initiate these contacts, and special programs may be set up in cooperation with police departments.)
- Police contact the probation department informally to access probation department programs for a youth in question. (The probation department also handles many cases informally.)
- Police unofficially contact children and youth services to get dependent and neglected or other children in need of supervision proper care.

COMBINED INFORMAL AND FORMAL PROCESSING

- A youth is taken into custody or arrested; he or she juvenile is then booked, talked to, and released without further action.
- A youth is taken into custody or arrested and booked and then released with the firm warning that any further problems will be dealt with by arrest and prosecution.
- Once a youth is in custody, officers officially notify community agencies such as children and youth services that a youth needs their services and either send the youth to the agency or have the agency pick up the youth.

FORMAL PROCESSING: AT THE STATION

- The parents of arrested youths are called to the police station and, after booking, have their child released to their care and supervision. The case may end at that point or may be referred to juvenile court for further consideration.
- The youth is taken into custody, booked, fingerprinted, and then referred to juvenile intake, which has both informal and formal options. After evaluation by either the police or court intake personnel, youths may be placed in secure detention awaiting their preliminary hearing and trial. This secure detention may, in some cities, be in the local jail or a youth detention center.
- Police in states with legislative waiver will, after arresting and booking a youth, automatically waive the youth directly to adult court, which further evaluates the youth.

The further youths are processed into the system, the less discretionary authority the police have. On the street, the amount of discretion of police officers is considerable; in states with legislative waiver, police discretion is limited, especially with violent crimes. In addition, police discretion is governed to a considerable extent by departmental policy.[35]

WHAT LEGAL RIGHTS DO JUVENILES HAVE WITH THE POLICE?

Juveniles were at the mercy of the police for much of the twentieth century. Few or no laws protected juveniles in trouble because of the rehabilitative ideal in juvenile justice. Police officers, whose primary mission was to maintain law and order, used whatever tactics seemed appropriate to restore the peace. Friendliness, persuasion, threats, coercion, and force were all used to gain the compliance of juveniles. If these tactics failed, juveniles were taken into juvenile court or, depending on the laws of the state and the seriousness of the crimes, to adult court for prosecution. Few protections were granted juveniles in the areas of search and seizure, interrogation, fingerprinting, lineups, or other procedures.

In the 1960s, the U.S. Supreme Court's decisions began to change this relationship between the police and juveniles. Although not all police departments have endorsed or adhered to the guidelines laid down by the courts, most departments have made a conscientious effort to abide by the standards of justice and fairness implied by these decisions.[36]

SEARCH AND SEIZURE

The Fourth Amendment to the Constitution of the United States protects citizens from unauthorized **search and seizure.** This amendment states:

> The right of the people to be secure in their persons, houses, papers, and effects, against unreasonable searches and seizures, shall not be violated, and

These weapons were confiscated by mall security officers and police from Neo-Nazi gang members in the Washington, Pennsylvania, area. (Photo by Stuart Miller.)

Critical Thinking Question:
What procedures would police have to follow to legally search gang members for these weapons?

no Warrants shall issue, but upon probable cause, supported by Oath or affirmation, and particularly describing the place to be searched, and the persons or things to be seized.

The issue here is the right to privacy. All citizens are guaranteed the right by the Constitution to feel secure in their person and home. Law enforcement officers may not abridge that right without following very strict due process guidelines. In 1961, the Supreme Court decision in *Mapp v. Ohio* affirmed Fourth Amendment rights for adults. This decision stated that evidence gathered in an unreasonable search and seizure—that is, evidence seized without probable cause and without a proper search warrant—was inadmissible in court.[37] This inadmissibility of illegally obtained evidence is referred to as the *exclusionary rule*. In the 1967 *State v. Lowery* case, the Supreme Court applied the Fourth Amendment ban against unreasonable searches and seizures to juveniles:

> Is it not more outrageous for the police to treat children more harshly than adult offenders, especially when such is violative of due process and fair treatment? Can a court countenance a system, where, as here, an adult may suppress evidence with the usual effect of having the charges dropped for lack of proof, and, on the other hand, a juvenile can be institutionalized—lose the most sacred possession a human being has, his freedom—for "rehabilitative" purposes because the Fourth Amendment right is unavailable to him?[38]

Juveniles, therefore, are protected from unreasonable searches and seizures. Juveniles must be presented with a valid search warrant unless they have either waived that right, have consented to having their person or property searched, or have been caught in the act. If these conditions have not been met, courts have overturned rulings against the juveniles. For example, evidence was dismissed in one case when police entered a juvenile's apartment at 5:00 A.M. without a warrant to arrest him.[39] In another case, Houston police discovered marijuana on a youth five hours after he had been stopped for driving a car without lights and a driver's license. Confined to a Texas training school for this drug offense, the youth was ordered released by an appellate court because the search took place too late to be related to the arrest.[40] The least right to privacy is on the street, followed generally by the automobile and school; the greatest right to privacy is in the home.[41]

On the Streets

When a crime is committed in the community, the job of the police officer is to solve the crime and make an arrest. The officer must, however, follow legal rules that guarantee that the alleged offender is treated fairly. How do police proceed?

Using a police stop as an example, the police officer has the right to stop a youth on the streets and ask questions. Juveniles, however, do not have to stop or answer any questions if they do not want to answer. The officer does not pat them down, and they may leave if they desire.

A second example is that the police approach a youth and have a specific and articulable suspicion that the juvenile is armed and possibly dangerous. The law enforcement experience of the police officer, a high-drug-dealing area of town, an obvious bulge in clothing, or the presence of another officer who may have arrested the youth previously and found a weapon on the youth may all lead to reasonable suspicion justifying a pat down. In this case, the officer may do a *Terry* search; that is, pat down the youth's outer clothing in a search for weapons only.[42] Police may not do pat downs as part of their routine stops or in order to find contraband. The pat down is for weapons only.

However, in doing the pat down, if the police find an illegal weapon, they may take the weapon and arrest the youth for possessing it; then, they legally may search the youth for other contraband.[43]

A third scenario illustrates another type of concern. A police officer temporarily detains a youth on the street or takes the youth to the station. When is the juvenile actually under arrest? Some jurisdictions consider an arrest as occurring whenever the person stopped does not feel free to leave the presence of the police officer. Indeed, youths in any of the above examples could be taken or asked to come to the police station, be interviewed, and then leave; this would be perfectly legal and within the juveniles' rights in some states and jurisdictions. Other jurisdictions (and most courts), however, consider that an arrest occurs whenever the person is stopped by the police officer and does not feel free to leave; this stop could be on the street, in a car, or in the station. The clearest indicator, of course, is when an offender officially is charged with a crime and given notice to appear at further hearings. A juvenile may, in fact, ask the officer if it is permissible to leave. The options for the police officer here are to release the juvenile immediately, detain the juvenile longer and let him or her go after further questioning and satisfying their concerns, or arrest the youth.

In the Vehicle

Officers cannot pull over youths driving a vehicle and search the vehicle without a reason. The reason can be something simple, like a broken taillight or muffler, but an officer must have an articulable reason to stop the car. The juveniles being nervous or making nervous movements when stopped is not usually sufficient reason to search the car.[44]

Once the car is pulled over, officers may look into it from the outside for anything that is illegal and "in plain view," particularly weapons.[45] If nothing is visible, the officers may not search the car. But if the officers have information from reliable sources that the youths have contraband, they can search for the contraband. Also, if alcohol or marijuana can be smelled, the officers have a reasonable or articulable suspicion that a crime is occurring and can push their search to the next level, as they now have a reasonable suspicion or probable cause for doing so.

If a weapon or other contraband is visible from outside the car and within the reach of the juvenile, the officers will ask the youth to get out of the car and search the areas of the car in view, including the glove compartment, for other weapons and contraband. The police officers can search all areas in the interior of the car that the juvenile could reach into and possibly grab a weapon or attempt to dispose of contraband. Police may not, however, search the trunk of the car without a warrant because the trunk is out of reach of the juvenile.[46] If contraband is found, the police officers can then take the juvenile into custody or make an arrest and take the juvenile to the station; there the youth will be disposed of either formally or informally.

At Home

Police officers may come into a home without a warrant for a number of reasons. First, they may enter a home if a person authorized to let them in gives them permission or invites them in. They may even search a youth's room if they ask permission of the youth's parents, but many police officers still take the precaution of getting a warrant before going to the house. Police may also come into a home without a warrant if they have a reasonable or articulable reason or probable cause to suspect that a crime is being or will be committed. For example, if police are in "hot pursuit," believe that someone will be hurt or killed, or believe that contraband will be disposed of before they can get a warrant, then they may enter a home without a warrant.[47]

Officers may also go into a home if they are standing in the doorway and see illegal substances "in plain view." Now they may enter the house (or dorm room) and conduct a search relevant to only the contraband, as well as the possibility that weapons may be within reach of the offenders. Any further searches are contingent upon getting a warrant.

In the School

Juveniles' use of weapons and drugs is changing the nature of police–student relations in schools. The police are being called on in increasing numbers of communities to enforce drug-free school zone laws. Drug-free zones generally are defined as the school property and the area within a one-thousand-foot radius of the property's boundaries. The police are also called on to enforce the 1990 federal Gun-Free School Zones Act.

The use of dogs to sniff for drugs; the administration of breathalyzers; the installation of hidden video cameras; and the routine searches of students' purses, pockets, school lockers, desks, and vehicles on school grounds are increasing as school officials struggle to control crime in schools. In some cases, school officials conduct their own searches; in other cases, the police are brought in to conduct the searches.[48]

In *New Jersey v. T. L. O.* (1985), the U.S. Supreme Court examined whether the Fourth Amendment right against unreasonable searches and seizures applies to the school setting.[49] The facts of this case are the following: A teacher at Piscataway High School in Middlesex County, New Jersey, discovered on March 7, 1980, that two girls were smoking in a bathroom. He reported this violation of school rules to the principal's office, and the two students were summoned to meet with the assistant vice principal. T. L. O., one of the two, claimed that she had done no wrong, and the assistant principal demanded to see her purse. His examination discovered a pack of cigarettes and cigarette rolling papers, some marijuana, a pipe, a considerable amount of money, a list of students who owed T. L. O. money, and letters implicating her in marijuana dealing. T. L. O. confessed later at the police station to selling drugs on school grounds.[50]

The juvenile court found T. L. O. delinquent and sentenced her to probation for one year. She then appealed her case to the New Jersey Supreme Court on the grounds that the search of her purse was not justified in the circumstances of the case. When the court upheld her appeal, the state appealed to the U.S. Supreme Court, which ruled that school personnel have the right to search lockers, desks, and students as long as they believe that the law or the school rules have been violated. The importance of this case is that the Court defined that the legality of **school searches** need not be based on obtaining a warrant or on having probable cause that a crime has taken place. Instead, the legality of the search depends on its reasonableness, considering the scope of the search, the student's gender and age, and the student's behavior at the time.[51] See Focus on Law 4–2.

School officials' searches of students suspected of violating school rules, especially regarding drugs and guns, have continued to be upheld by the courts since the *T. L. O.* decision. Indeed, of the eighteen cases decided since 1985, state appellate decisions applied the *T. L. O.* decisions in fifteen.[52]

✓**Progress Check 4.2**
Review this section at
www.prenhall.com/bartollas

INTERROGATION AND CONFESSION

The Fifth and Fourteenth Amendments of the Constitution address standards of fairness and due process in obtaining confessions. The significant statement in the Fifth Amendment relevant to juvenile interrogations is that no person

shall be compelled in any criminal case to be a witness against himself, nor be deprived of life, liberty, or property, without due process of law. . . .

FOCUS ON LAW

SEARCH AND SEIZURE IN THE WISCONSIN SCHOOLS

4–2

The Wisconsin Department of Justice has summarized Fourth Amendment requirements for search and seizure rules as applicable to Wisconsin schools.[*] These rules are as follows:

School Officials

- The Fourth Amendment restricts public school officials, but to a lesser degree than the police. The Fourth Amendment does not apply to private or parochial school officials.
- School officials may search students and their belongings if they have reasonable suspicion.
- The police may also search with reasonable suspicion (as opposed to their usual probable cause standard) if they are working at the request of, and in conjunction with, school officials.

Consent Searches

- In order for consent to be valid, it must be voluntary and the person giving consent must have the authority to do so.
- Consent does not have to be in writing, but this form is preferable.
- A refusal to consent does not give a school official reasonable suspicion to believe that the student is hiding something.
- It is recommended that the student be advised what a school official is searching for prior to asking for consent to search.
- Consent to search a generalized area is consent to search any items found in that area.

Nonconsensual Searches of the Student's Person and Personal Belongings

- A school official may search a student or his or her belongings if the official has a reasonable suspicion that the area being searched contains contraband or evidence of a violation.
- School officials should balance the intrusion of the search with the severity of the violation involved.
- A school official of the same gender as the student should do any physical search of a student.
- School officials may not strip search students.

Locker Searches

- School officials may make random searches of lockers if the school has a written policy on this practice and the policy is widely disseminated to the student body.
- The Wisconsin legislature recently passed Wisconsin Statutes Section 118.325, which codifies the school's right to conduct random searches of lockers.

Vehicle Searches

- School officials may search a vehicle parked on school premises if they have a reasonable suspicion that the vehicle contains contraband or evidence of a violation.
- School officials may also search a vehicle with the consent of the student.

Drug-Detection Canines

- Random canine searches on school property are permissible, as they do not constitute a search within the meaning of the Fourth Amendment.
- If a properly trained canine alerts officials to the presence of drugs in an area, this constitutes probable cause to justify a search of the area.

Point of Entry/Exit Inspections

- Random inspection of student items at specific locations is permitted if the school has a clear policy on this practice, clearly marks the area involved, and performs these inspections in a fair and even-handed way.

Metal Detectors

- Metal detectors are considered minor intrusions; thus, their use can be justified without reasonable suspicion or consent.
- The wand metal detector is more intrusive than a stationary unit, and its use should be limited to those occasions when the school official has an articulable suspicion.

Surveillance Technology and Search Issues

- School officials may use visual surveillance in any area where a student does not have a reasonable expectation of privacy.
- School officials should refrain from visual surveillance in areas where it is likely that students could be observed in a partially nude state.
- Audio surveillance is a Fourth Amendment intrusion, and schools should not monitor telephone conversations without the consent of one of the participants in the conversation.

* Some of these requirements will vary by state.

Source: For the complete Search and Seizure statement by the Department of Justice for the state of Wisconsin, see http://www.doj.state.wi.us.

Critical Thinking Questions:
What is your evaluation of these search and seizure requirements?

Two concerns arise here. First, no one can be "compelled" to testify or incriminate himself or herself. Second, all persons must be afforded due process of law if they might lose their freedom. For the courts, the key issue is whether juveniles are in custody at the time they make any statements to the police.[53] If we look at some of the previous examples of police stops on the streets or brief detainments in the police station, the issue is whether the juvenile feels free to leave. Juveniles who are not in custody, that is, who feel free to leave, can and will have anything incriminating they say held against them; that is, they can and will be arrested and charged and their comments held against them in court.

If juveniles are in custody or arrested, their strongest option is not to say anything or answer any questions until their parents or a lawyer are present. At this point, the now familiar *Miranda* warnings are relevant. A typical *Miranda* warning is:

> You have the right to remain silent. If you give up that right, anything you say can and will be used against you in a court of law. You have the right to an attorney and to have an attorney present during questioning. If you cannot afford an attorney, one will be provided to you at no cost. During any questioning, you may decide at any time to exercise these rights, not answer any questions, or make any statements.[54]

At this stage of processing, the police have probable cause that the youth is a suspect and has information important to the case. Youths inadvertently can say something that ties them to a crime and results in their prosecution. For this reason, police are required to warn the juvenile against self-incrimination and, if the juvenile requests, make certain that a lawyer is present to discuss with the youth the answers to any questions the police might ask.

For police to use a confession by a youth in court, it must be obtained legally; that is, the youth must have been informed of his or her Miranda rights before giving the confession. Otherwise, the confession may not be used as evidence, as the youth's statements are inadmissible under the exclusionary rule.

At what age does a juvenile become capable of intellectually understanding the importance of the *Miranda* rights? Are juveniles under the influence of drugs or alcohol capable of legally waiving their rights? Should mentally ill or mentally handicapped youths be able to waive their rights? What about youths who do not understand English well?

These issues have been coming before various state courts for a number of years. In one case, the state of California upheld the confessions of two Spanish-speaking youths, one of whom had a mental age of slightly over ten years.[55] A North Carolina court upheld the confession of a twelve-year-old.[56] In another case, a Maryland appeals court upheld the confession of a sixteen-year-old high school dropout with an eighth-grade education.[57]

The questions raised by these court decisions require careful consideration. A study by T. Grisso found that almost all the juveniles questioned by St. Louis police in 1981 had waived their *Miranda* rights. Yet Grisso questioned whether these juveniles were able to understand the significance of the *Miranda* warnings. Grisso also concluded, after conducting a survey of juveniles, that almost all fourteen-year-olds and one-half of fifteen- and sixteen-year-olds were too young to understand the importance of their *Miranda* rights.[58] In addition, the police must stay within certain standards of fairness in their questioning.

The Supreme Court ruled in *Brown v. Mississippi* (1936) that force may not be used to obtain confessions.[59] In this case, police used physical force in extracting an admission of guilt from a suspect. Other confessions have been ruled invalid because the accused was too tired; was questioned too long; or was not permitted to talk to his wife, friends, or lawyer either while being interrogated or until he confessed.[60]

The *Haley v. Ohio* case (1948) is an early example of police **interrogation** excesses.[61] Haley, a fifteen-year-old juvenile, was arrested five days after a robbery and shooting of a store owner. The youth confessed after five hours of interrogation (i.e., formal questioning) by five or six police officers with neither parents nor a lawyer present. During the questioning, the officers showed him alleged confessions of two other youths. The Supreme Court responded by stating:

The age of the petitioner, the hours when he was grilled, the duration of his quizzing, the fact that he had no friend or counsel to advise him, the callous attitude of the police toward his rights combine to convince us that this was a confession wrung from a child by means which the law should not sanction. Neither man nor child can be allowed to stand condemned by methods which flout constitutional requirements of due process of law.[62]

The *Fare v. Michael C.* decision (1979) applies the "totality of the circumstances" approach to juveniles' interrogations. In this case, sixteen-year-old Michael C. was implicated in a murder that took place during a robbery. The police arrested the youth and brought him to the station. After he was advised of his *Miranda* rights, he asked to see his probation officer. When this request was denied, he proceeded to talk with the police officer, implicating himself in the murder. The Supreme Court ruled that Michael seemed to understand his rights, and even when his request to talk with his probation officer was denied, he still was willing to waive his rights and continue the interrogation.[63]

The states have passed statutes to force the police and the courts to comply with the standards of a constitutional interrogation of juveniles. Among these requirements are that parents or attorneys must be notified and present during questioning and that questioning should take place in an area other than the police station. In *Commonwealth v. Guyton* (1989), a Massachusetts motion appeals judge held that no other minor, not even a relative, can act as an interested adult.[64] Some states require that questioning occur at a juvenile detention facility, at the juvenile court, or at some other neutral place where the juvenile will not be intimidated by the surroundings.

FINGERPRINTING

The **fingerprinting** of juveniles is a controversial practice. The basic concern of critics is that the juveniles' records will not be destroyed when youths no longer fall under juvenile court jurisdiction. It they are labeled as criminals early in life, social analysts fear that juveniles will not be able to escape such a label as they mature.

Some states have passed statutes that prohibit the fingerprinting of juveniles without a judge's permission. Many of these states also require that judges control who has access to the fingerprints and further require that the fingerprints be destroyed after the juvenile becomes an adult.[65] In other states, the police control fingerprinting policy. Some police departments follow the courts' suggested guidelines, whereas others routinely fingerprint every juvenile taken into custody.

The most important fingerprinting case to reach the courts to date is *Davis v. Mississippi* (1969).[66] In that case, the Supreme Court ruled, among other things, that fingerprints taken by the police could not be used as evidence. The youth in question was detained by the police without authorization by a judicial officer, was interrogated at the time he was first fingerprinted, and was fingerprinted again at a later date. The Court ruled that the police should not have detained the youth without authorization by a judicial officer, that the youth was unnecessarily fingerprinted a second time, and that the youth should not have been interrogated at the first detention when he was fingerprinted.[67]

LINEUPS AND PHOTOGRAPHS

A **lineup** consists of the police placing a number of suspects in front of witnesses or victims, who try to identify the person who committed the crime against them. If no one can be identified, the suspects are released to the community. If one of the persons is identified as the perpetrator, the police then proceed with their prosecution. The courts have been careful to set standards for the police to follow, because innocent youths could end up labeled as delinquents and confined in an institution.

One important standard is that the offender must have an attorney at the initial identification lineup. This is to ensure that the identification of the offender is not tainted. For example, if a single suspect is shown to a victim with the suggestion by the police that they think "they got the offender," the victim might be pressured to identify the person even though the victim had never seen the accused before. Another concern is the possibility that simply showing a single suspect is "unnecessarily suggestive" and might bias the victim or witness.[68]

In *United States v. Wade* (1967), the Supreme Court ruled that the accused has the right to have counsel present at postindictment lineup procedures.[69] In *Kirby v. Illinois* (1972), the Court went on to say that the defendant's right to counsel at postindictment lineup procedures goes into effect as soon as the complaint or the indictment is issued.[70] In *In re Holley* (1970), a youth who was accused of rape had his conviction reversed by the appellate court because of the lack of counsel during the lineup identification procedure.[71]

Photographs also can play an important part in the identification of offenders. For example, in one case, a rape victim was shown a photograph of one suspect only. She could not identify the offender from the photograph but then later identified her attacker in a probation office. A California appellate court noted that permitting the identification of offenders on the basis of only one photograph was inappropriate because it could prejudice the victim.[72]

Another problem with photographs is their permanency and potential stigmatizing effect on youths in the community. A youth taken in for questioning who has his or her photograph taken is easily identified. Because photographs are filed and frequently reviewed by police officers, the police examine these photographs whenever something happens in the community. Innocent youths may never be able to escape the stigma of such labeling. For these reasons, some states require that judges give the police written consent to take photographs, that the photographs not be published in the media, and that the photographs be destroyed when the youths become adults.

HOW ARE POLICE DEPARTMENTS ORGANIZED TO FIGHT JUVENILE CRIME?

Police departments are organized much like the military in that the men and women are ranked in a hierarchy composed of captains (at the top), lieutenants, sergeants, detectives, and officers. Those at the top draw up the rules and make the decisions, and those at the bottom are expected to follow the rules. The officers and detectives at the bottom of this structure are responsible for the detection, investigation, and processing of juvenile offenders through the juvenile justice system. These officers also are responsible for any specialized programs that are set up to fight delinquency and other juvenile problems.

The major function of police in most communities is simply to maintain order and keep the peace, thereby keeping the streets free from crime and the residents of the community safe. This involves the peacekeeping details of running drunks, addicts, and prostitutes off the streets; supervising school crossings; appearing in court; working on traffic patrol; chasing juveniles off street corners; giving talks and demonstrations in schools; and participating in delinquency prevention programs.

When major crimes occur, the police vigorously attempt to solve them. This function is divided into two major roles, reactive and proactive. The reactive role focuses on solving crimes after they occur. Reactive policing involves a rapid response to the report of a crime on the part of the police. The officers try to get to the crime scene as soon as possible, investigate offenses, take suspects into custody, arrest offenders, and process them through the juvenile justice system. Historically, this approach is believed by many to be ineffective and slowly is giving way to a proactive or crime prevention role.

The preventive approach began early in the nineteenth century and involved putting females on police forces and setting up Police Athletic Leagues in many cities. This approach involves police officers in trying to prevent crimes. With today's large, complex cities and a national and very diverse population of about three hundred million, police departments are setting up different organizational structures to deal with juvenile problems. Some departments rely on regular police officers. Many larger departments may have specialized juvenile officers and different kinds of organizational structures within their departments, such as service bureaus, gang control units, gang details, and gang units.

DEPARTMENTS WITHOUT SPECIALIZED UNITS OF PERSONNEL

Smaller police departments usually do not have specialized individuals or units to deal with juvenile crime; and juvenile offenses are dealt with as a routine part of police work. Officers walking beats or assigned to traffic control, surveillance, detective work, vice squads, or other police activities come into contact with juveniles in the course of everyday work.

Officers whose major concern is adult crime often resist having to work on juvenile crime. These officers consider runaways, dependent/neglected youths, victimized/abused children, and status offenders to be nuisances. In addition, few if any of these patrol officers and detectives have had any specialized training in working with juveniles, and they are uncertain about how to recognize or approach juveniles in difficulty. Some treat all juveniles the same way and, in some cases, in a rude, forceful, insensitive, authoritarian, and coercive manner that intimidates the youths. Police critics charge that these approaches are all too likely to antagonize or alienate the youths and the public. Furthermore, some officers tend to view juvenile crime as "kiddie crime" and resent this "low-status" juvenile work. These officers are far more interested in making arrests for serious offenses that will earn them promotions and the reputation for being a good cop.

Police officers approach serious juvenile crimes in the same way as they do serious adult crimes. Because the age of an offender rarely is known at the time an offense is detected, officers and detectives often do not know whether the offender is an adult or a juvenile; nevertheless, officers may still be disappointed if the offender turns out to be a juvenile. Other officers and even prosecutors do not always consider juvenile arrests to be as important as those of adults.

DEPARTMENTS WITH SPECIALIZED UNITS OF PERSONNEL

Departments with specialized services for juveniles usually have trained juvenile officers, juvenile units, or gang control units.

Juvenile Officers

The size of the juvenile crime problem has led many police executives to assign individual officers solely to juvenile crime. These men and women are pulled from the ranks of patrol officers, and in smaller departments, they may be the only officers given this special assignment. Unfortunately, many of these men and women lack the specialized training that is believed necessary to work with juveniles. Unless they receive training, these officers will, in many cases, continue to deal with juveniles in much the same way as they deal with the adult offenders with whom they come into contact.

Larger departments often hire juvenile specialists. These officers may have backgrounds in the social sciences and specialized training in social work, sociology, psychology, public administration, and the administration of justice. They also may understand child development, the nature of juvenile–parent relationships, the problems of adolescence, identity formation, alcoholism and other addictions, and the consequences of living under poverty-stricken conditions. But unless a special department is set up to work with juvenile problems, these officers must operate alone in their departments and endure the low status that accompanies working with juveniles.

Juvenile Units

Juvenile units are found in many larger cities. These units have the normal crime-fighting tasks of detecting, investigating, and prosecuting offenders for everything from bicycle thefts to serious felonies. The units have the responsibility to investigate any crimes believed to have been committed by juveniles, to investigate complaints that children have been abused or victimized or are dependent or neglected, and to search for runaway youths. Juvenile unit members also refer juveniles to appropriate social service agencies in the community, counsel parents and children, supervise youth activities in the community, keep an eye on high-risk crime areas for juveniles, and develop and run antidelinquency programs. The intensive nature of these efforts requires that the juvenile officers in these units be highly trained, but even these officers cannot escape the low status that comes from dealing with juveniles.

Gang Control Units

The number of street gangs has been declining since the mid-1990s. The result has been a decline in the number of gang control units across the United States. The first type of unit is called the **Youth Service Program.** Although members of these gang programs may be regular officers pulled from any police unit, frequently they are from youth service bureaus who are sworn officers. This unit is formed to deal with a specific gang problem and is not a permanent unit within the police force. Officers continue to perform their regular duties and are not exclusively concerned with gang problems. Once a particular problem has been solved, the police officers involved return to their regular assignments. The **gang detail** is the second type of unit. The officers in these units generally are part of a traditional police unit assigned to gang problems. These officers do not routinely assist other members of their units with other types of problems. The **gang unit** is the third type of unit. These units are established to work solely on gang problems, and many will develop extensive intelligence networks with gang members in the community.[73]

HOW IS COMMUNITY-ORIENTED POLICING BEING USED TO TACKLE PROBLEMS IN TODAY'S COMMUNITIES?

The long-standing tradition in policing was for officers to enforce the law by trying to respond so rapidly to a report of crime that the offender was caught in the act; needless to say, this approach worked rarely. The traditional method also involved officers confronting offenders and suspects, conducting investigations, and making arrests. When these duties often were carried out in a demeaning, antagonistic, and authoritarian manner, the result was the alienation of youths and other community members from the police. Community members would then withhold information from the police, thereby making policing more difficult. The problems with this traditional method of policing have

Table 4–3   *Full-Time Community Policing Officers in Local Police Departments*

By Size of Population Served. United States, 2000

	Full-Time Community Policing Officers		
Population Served	*Percent of Agencies Using*	*Number of Officers*	*Average Number of Officers*[a]
All sizes	66	102,598	12
1,000,000 or more	100	33,214	2,208
500,000 to 999,999	85	8,617	297
250,000 to 499,999	95	6,866	180
150,000 to 249,999	94	8,580	53
50,000 to 149,999	93	7,167	20
25,000 to 49,999	83	7,854	12
10,000 to 24,999	72	9,184	7
2,500 to 9,999	63	12,745	5
Less than 2,500	60	8,370	3

Note: Community policing promotes organizational strategies to address the causes and reduce the fear of crime and social disorder through problem solving tactics and community partnerships. A fundamental shift from traditional reactive policing, community policing stresses the prevention of crime before it occurs. The implementation of a community policing plan supports and empowers front-line officers, decentralizes command, and encourages innovative problem solving (Source, p. 14). In some jurisdictions these officers may be known as community relations officers, community resource officers, or named for the community policing approach they employ (Source, p. 15).

[a]Excludes agencies that did not employ any full-time community policing officers.

Source: Matthew J. Hickman and Brian Reaves, *Local Police Departments 2000*, NCJ 196002 (Washington, DC: U.S. Department of Justice, 2003). p. 15. Table 32.

long been criticized and arguments made that police officers should be more intimately involved with the community.

Community-oriented policing (COP) is a policing philosophy reform originally proposed by Herman Goldstein in the late 1970s.[74] Goldstein believed that officers had to get involved personally with the local community in order to police effectively. The proposed reform slowly caught on and today is known by different names, including *community-oriented policing services* (COPS), *problem-oriented policing* (POP), and *situation-oriented policing*.[75]

By the year 2000, all cities of one million or more in population reported using full-time COP officers, with the percentages trailing off in the smaller communities (see Table 4–3). In total numbers, by the year 2000, 106,000, or roughly 16 percent of about 640,000 sworn full-time police officers in the United States, were involved in some form of community or problem-oriented policing practices. A common function of some of these personnel is to serve as full-time school resource officers. Also, some sheriffs' departments in U.S. cities also employ full-time community police officers. Overall, the data suggest that the COP philosophy is broader in philosophy than in practice.[76]

COP calls for collaboration among police and all members of the community, including businesses, schools, churches, neighborhood associations, improvement associations, watch groups, and members of various demographic groups. Police are encouraged to know and be on a first-name basis with as many members of the community as possible, stopping to chat and visit in homes, shops, schools, and churches. Police attend community meetings both as spectators and as participants. The idea is to gain the trust of community members, begin a collaborative effort, and improve information flow between the police and the community. When a problem is recognized, all of the parties relevant to and interested in solving it are brought together to share information, develop plans, and solve the problem. Police also initiate contacts with other agencies that can help address community problems, such as zoning boards, building inspectors, city ordinance enforcers, clinics, hospitals, schools, and public health departments.

Police who use this approach typically first go through their statistics and group all similar incidents together. They then determine whether the offenses share any common underlying features. Knowing that large numbers of robberies or burglaries occur in a specific area shortly after school is dismissed, for example, suggests to the police that students are responsible for the offenses. Second, the police then analyze the problem, collecting information from a variety of public and private sources, such as schools, transportation services, private police, businesses, and citizens. Using these data, police officers analyze the basic character of the problem, try to determine its causes, and develop a range of possible solutions. They wait for police to respond to the circumstances that create juvenile problems rather than to the incidents that result from the causes. The police officers further work with all involved parties to come up with a plan of action. Schools, businesses, service agencies, and citizens are approached to develop a workable plan to solve the problem. Finally, researchers and officers evaluate their results to determine whether the plan actually worked.[77]

Once a problem is identified by police or members of the community, the most directly affected members of these groups are pulled together and everyone's resources are used to focus on the problem. The result is the development of a wide range of activities, some simple and some complex, that are sometimes called *community* or *problem-oriented policing.*

Some of these activities include the following:

- Police facilitators mediate or negotiate agreements between victims and offenders (victim/offender mediation, or VOM). Victims are encouraged to express their anger and outrage, as well as stating the financial costs incurred as a result of the crime; the officer helps to negotiate a repayment program satisfactory to both the victim and the offender. The aim is to achieve juvenile accountability for the offense. (Some departments call this technique **restorative justice.**)
- Police community relations facilitators set up procedures and sites so that community members who have complaints against police officers have their concerns heard. These facilitators make certain that the sites and procedures are well publicized throughout the community.
- Police work with mall security personnel to deal with problems of juveniles in the malls. See Focus on Practice 4–3.
- Police and school officials work together to set up antidrug programs in the schools; an analysis of Project D.A.R.E. follows.
- The police and community members coordinate their forces to fight the presence of guns and gangs on the streets, in schools, and in neighborhoods; see the following discussion of antigun and antigang efforts.
- The police use restorative justice in a diversion program based upon sanctioning offenders and resolving disputes. Known as the *Wagga Wagga model,* this approach uses family group conferences to ad-

FOCUS ON PRACTICE

4–3

EXAMPLES OF COMMUNITY-ORIENTED OR PROBLEM-ORIENTED POLICING STRATEGIES

COP and Project D.A.R.E.

In the 1990s, the need for substance-abuse prevention programs demanded creativity and engagement on the part of the police. Project D.A.R.E. (Drug Abuse Resistance Education) is an innovative drug prevention program that has rapidly expanded across the United States. Developed in 1983 as a cooperative effort by the Los Angeles Police Department and the Los Angeles Unified School District, this program uses uniformed police officers to teach a formal curriculum to fifth- and sixth-grade students in a classroom.

In this program, the police officer teaches children in school to say "no" to drugs before they begin to experiment with them. The officer helps youths build their self-esteem and develop ways of saying "no." Youths are taught, for example, that real friends will not push them to use drugs and alcohol, that most of their friends do not use these substances, that being adult means that they can make positive and responsible decisions, and that they are able to resist peer pressure. The lectures presented in the classrooms also help children protect themselves, reduce stress, seek out alternatives to drug use, and generally take a stand against drugs.

An initial evaluation of the program suggested that the self-reported behavior of seventh-grade students who had received D.A.R.E. instruction in the sixth grade indicated significantly lower rates of substance abuse since graduation from sixth grade than those of seventh graders who had not received D.A.R.E. instruction. Furthermore, this evaluation indicated that D.A.R.E. students were more likely to use effective refusal strategies than were non-D.A.R.E. students when pressured by peers to use drugs or alcohol.

A 1994 analysis by the Research Triangle Institute in North Carolina was more critical of the program. It showed that the D.A.R.E. program was effective in increasing students' knowledge about substance abuse and enhancing their social skills but was less effective in developing negative attitudes toward drugs and improving self-esteem. The evaluation further found that D.A.R.E.'s short-term effects on deterring substance abuse by fifth and sixth graders were limited. The Institute recommended that D.A.R.E. revise its curriculum, using more interactive strategies and participatory learning and emphasizing social and general competencies. This recommendation was implemented nationwide in the fall of 1994. A 1999 report by David Partenheimer of the American Psychological Association also reported that the program had no long-term effect on drug use.

Problem-Oriented Policing in the Mall

Prior to 1987, Franklin Mall, a regional shopping mall in southwestern Pennsylvania that serves a population base of approximately fifty thousand people from Pennsylvania, West Virginia, and Ohio, had a low number of criminal incidents. But as the rates of retail theft, auto theft, disorderly conduct, and criminal mischief increased dramatically, mall management and security forces, merchants, and the elderly all became concerned. The elderly, particularly, became fearful that predatory juveniles would victimize them.

Mall management and local law enforcement officers were not prepared to deal with the problem. Traditional police methods of rapid response and incident-oriented policing simply did not work. Accordingly, the chief of police set out to develop a plan of action using problem-oriented policing.

Officer Richard Horner learned the basic concepts of problem-oriented policing and was assigned to the mall. His first task was to uncover the causes or factors behind the problem. Specifically, he looked at the nature of the surrounding community;

Female shoplifter being escorted from store in mall. The second officer follows to protect the first officer from being attacked from behind.
(Photo by Kathryn Miller.)

the attitudes of mall management; the practices and personnel of mall security; the attitudes and concerns of retail establishment managers; mall design; attitudes and concerns of mall patrons; and the problems of area schools.

The analysis of the juvenile arrests that had been made at the mall was another phase of the study. A profile of the juveniles indicated that eleven- to sixteen-year-old youths often drank alcohol, which led to general disorderly conduct and nuisance types of complaints. Seventeen- to nineteen-year-old youths also used alcohol and/or drugs but engaged in the more serious and violent types of incidents.

The area schools were approached next. School personnel were experiencing the same types of problems as the malls in that the schools also were faced with increased alcohol abuse and motor vehicle violations. The alcohol was, in addition, associated with fighting between so-called preppy and vo-tech student groups on school grounds and at the malls.

Once all the factors were understood, the police department developed a plan of action that included both traditional and innovative responses to the problem. These responses included some of the following:

1. The most violent crimes were identified as the first priority.
2. The police worked with mall management to decrease motor vehicle violations within the parking area.
3. Mall security personnel were trained to deal more appropriately with juveniles. Those unable to conform were removed from the mall security force.
4. The police initiated a campaign to reduce alcohol use. First of all, 118 juveniles were arrested in the first thirty days of the campaign, and their parents were brought in and told what the youths were doing, what they were saying at the time of their arrest, and the types of statements they were making during questioning.
5. The officer assigned to the mall traveled to the local school district to heighten student awareness of the alcohol problem, drinking and driving, domestic violence, problems at the mall, the law, and citizenship. The officer solicited students' help in changing the mall environment.
6. The mall management scheduled social activities at the mall that included juveniles of different age groups. This showed the juveniles that they were an important part of the mall community.
7. In 2006, local police and community members joined forces to pass an ordinance prohibiting the sale of theater tickets to youths under the age of eighteen if the film the youths wanted to view ended after the 1 A.M. curfew.

The initiation of problem-oriented policing produced a dramatic reduction in crime and relative peace at the mall and the surrounding area for the next three to four years. During this time, police continued to teach mall security officers how to spot potential problems and how to handle groups creating problems. They also encouraged mall security personnel to report incidents to a police officer assigned as a liaison to the mall.

Source: Information on the mall supplied by former North Franklin Police Chief Roger Cuccaro, current Police Chief Mark Kravakich, Lt. Kirk Hessler, Sgt. Richard Horner, and Mall Security Chief Richard Keys. References to the D.A.R.E. project are from William DeJong, "Project DARE: Teaching Kids to Say 'No' to Drugs," *NIJ Reports* (Washington, DC: U.S. Department of Justice, March 1986), 2–5; Bureau of Justice Assistance, *Program Brief Book I, An Invitation to Project DARE: Drug Abuse Resistance Education* (Washington, DC: U.S. Department of Justice, n.d.); National Institute of Justice, *The DARE Program: A Review of Prevalence, User Satisfaction, and Effectiveness* (Washington, DC: U.S. Department of Justice, 1994), 1–2; and David Partenheimer, "Project D.A.R.E.: No Effects at 10-year Follow-up," News Release, American Psychological Association, August 1, 1999 (online at http://www.druglibrary.org/think/~jnr/noeffect.htm).

Critical Thinking Questions:
How much of a problem are juvenile-related crimes in shopping malls? What is your evaluation of how this problem was handled in Franklin Mall? Why do you believe that D.A.R.E. has not been found to be more effective? Were you part of a D.A.R.E. program when you were in middle school or junior high? What was your evaluation of it?

dress a variety of offenses, including thefts, arson, minor assaults, drug offenses, vandalism, and, in some cases, child maltreatment.[78]

COP is useful in juvenile justice because:

1. It moves police officers from anonymity in the patrol car to *direct engagement* with a community that gives them more immediate information about neighborhood problems and insights into their solutions.
2. It frees officers from an emergency response system and permits them to engage more directly in *proactive crime prevention.*
3. It makes police operations more visible to the public, *increasing police accountability to the public.*
4. It *decentralizes* operations, allowing officers greater familiarity with the workings and needs of various neighborhoods.
5. It encourages officers to view *citizens as partners,* improving relations between the public and the police.
6. It moves decision making and discretion to police officers on the streets and therefore places more authority in the hands of those who best know the community's problems and experiences.[79]

One of the major problems in the evaluation of COP in the initial attempts is that violent crime has been dropping nationwide at the same time that the programs have come online. Therefore, it is impossible at this point to determine whether changes in crime rates are the result of police programs or broader societal changes. Another problem is identifying exactly which programs work best with which types of problems; drugs, guns, gangs, and teenage prostitutes may all have to be approached in a different manner. Furthermore, the organizational problems are daunting. Police departments and citizens have barriers of mistrust to overcome, turf battles to resolve, and philosophies to negotiate. In addition, some community groups do not want the problems solved. Absentee landlords make money from dilapidated buildings and houses out of which drug dealers operate; owners of properties

✓**Progress Check 4.3**
Review this section at
www.prenhall.com/bartollas

may not want the expense of cleaning up vacant lots; and drug dealers may attempt to intimidate citizens and police who are trying to chase them out of areas. Nevertheless, there is a strong belief that COP is the wave of the future (see Focus on Practice, 4–3).

SUMMARY

- The family and the local community were able to control wayward juveniles until the end of the 1700s.
- The increased urbanization and industrialization of the emerging society, however, called for a different response to juvenile crime.
- The public believed that the police were the answer to the problem during the first third of the 1800s. Social control moved from the community and the family to formal departments of police, courts, and correctional agencies.
- In spite of some initial efforts by the police to set up delinquency prevention programs in the early 1900s, reformers complained that the police were too often brutal, corrupt, and uncaring.
- The police exercised almost unlimited discretion in dealing with juveniles until the 1960s. At that time, court decisions began to limit police powers. Police were required to follow both court and statutory guidelines in the areas of search and seizure, detention, interrogation, confession, fingerprinting, photographing, and lineup.
- Police organization and culture undoubtedly were part of the early problems. Police departments were organized bureaucratically, and police culture called for rapid response and forceful control.
- Historically, few police departments had specialized units to deal with the community and juveniles on a cooperative basis. Today, that philosophy is changing slowly. Police departments are beginning to be more effective in police–juvenile relations and are attempting to organize effective antidrug, shoplifting, and gang programs.
- Currently, COP appears to be the wave of the future.

WEB SITES OF INTEREST

Information and links about the police and juvenile court processes can be found at

http://www.wiu.edu/library/govpubs/guides/p&cjuven.htm

Various links about the police and their interaction with juveniles can be found at

http://www.criminology.fsu.edu/jjclearinghouse/jj21.html

To see how the New Haven, Connecticut Police Department is working with the community to help curb juvenile justice, go to

http://www.cityofnewhaven.com/Police/YouthOrientedPolicing.asp

CRITICAL THINKING QUESTIONS

1. Summarize juveniles' attitudes toward the police.
2. How do departments without specialized personnel handle juvenile offenders?
3. How do departments with specialized personnel handle juvenile offenders?
4. Summarize the legal rights of juveniles taken into custody.

NOTES

1. Interview conducted in 1997 and published in Clemens Bartollas and Larry D. Hahn, *Policing in America* (Boston: Allyn & Bacon, 1999), 53.

2. David R. Johnson, *Policing the Urban Underworld: The Impact of Crime on the Development of the American Police, 1800–1887* (Philadelphia: Temple University Press, 1979), 78–89.

3. Robert M. Fogelson, *Big-City Police* (Cambridge, MA: Harvard University Press, 1977), 86–87.

4. Ibid.

5. Ibid.

6. Ibid.

7. Ibid.

8. Larry W. Fultz, *Public Relations and the Police: A Survey of Public Opinion* (Houston, TX: University of Houston Press, 1959).

9. Robert Portune, *Changing Adolescent Attitudes Toward Police* (Cincinnati: W. H. Anderson, 1971).

10. Donald H. Bouma, *Kids and Cops* (Grand Rapids, MI: William B. Eerdmans, 1969), 69–79. Other studies that examine juveniles' attitudes toward the police include Peggy Giordano, "The Sense of Injustice: An Analysis of Juveniles' Reactions to the Justice System," *Criminology* 14 (May 1976), 40; L. Thomas Winfree, Jr., and Curt T. Griffiths, "Adolescents' Attitudes Toward the Police: A Survey of High School Students," in *Juvenile Delinquency: Little Brother Grows Up*, edited by Theodore N. Ferdinand (Beverly Hills, CA: Sage Publications, 1977), 79–99; William T. Rusinko, W. Johnson Knowlton, and Carlton A. Hornung, "The Importance of Police Contact in the Formulation of Youths' Attitudes Toward Police," *Journal of Criminal Justice* 6 (Spring 1978), 65; J. P. Clark and E. P. Wenninger, "The Attitudes of Juveniles Toward the Legal Institution," *Journal of Criminal Law, Criminology and Police Science* 55 (1964), 482–89; V. I. Cizanckas and C. W. Pruviance, "Changing Attitudes of Black Youths," *Police Chief* 40 (1973), 42.

11. Winfree and Griffiths, "Adolescents' Attitudes Toward the Police," 79–99.

12. Rusinko et al., "The Importance of Police Contact in the Formulation of Youths' Attitudes Toward Police," 65.

13. Scott H. Decker, "Citizen Attitudes Toward the Police: A Review of Past Findings and Suggestions for Future Policy," *Journal of Police Science and Administration* 9 (1981), 80–87.

14. James R. Davis, "A Comparison of Attitudes Toward the New York City Police," *Journal of Police Science and Administration* 17 (1990), 233–42.

15. Komanduri S. Murty, Julian B. Roebuck, and Joann D. Smith, "The Image of Police in Black Atlanta Communities," *Journal of Police Science and Administration,* 17 (1990), 250–57.

16. Ibid., 256.

17. Michael J. Leiber, Mahesh K. Nalla, and Margaret Farnworth, "Explaining Juveniles' Attitudes Toward the Police," *Justice Quarterly* 15 (March 1998), 151–71.

18. These findings are taken from Kathleen Maguire and Ann Pastore, eds., *Sourcebook of Criminal Justice Statistics, 1994* (Washington, DC: U.S. Bureau of Justice Statistics, 1995), 206. Table in *Sourcebook* compiled from data provided by Lloyd D. Johnston, Jerald G. Bachman, and Patrick M. O'Malley, *Monitoring the Future Project* (Ann Arbor: Institute for Social Research, University of Michigan, 1982–1992).

19. Data for 2001 were provided by Johnston et al., *Monitoring the Future Project.*

20. Susan Guarino-Ghezzi and Bryan Carr, "Juvenile Offenders vs. the Police: A Community Dilemma," *Caribbean Journal of Criminology and Social Psychology* 1 (July 1996), 24–43.

21. Stephanie M. Myers, *Police Encounters with Juvenile Suspects: Explaining the Use of Authority and Provision of Support* (Washington, DC: National Institute of Justice, 2004).

22. See Donald J. Black and Albert J. Reiss, Jr., "Police Control of Juveniles," *American Sociological Review* 35 (February 1979), 63–77.

23. Robert M. Terry, "Discrimination in the Handling of Juvenile Offenders by Social Control Agencies," *Journal of Research in Crime and Delinquency* 4 (July 1967), 218–30; Nathan Goldman, *The Differential Selection of Juvenile Offenders for Court Appearances* (New York: National Council on Crime and Delinquency, 1963), 35–47; Black and Reiss, "Police Control of Juveniles," 63–77; Irving Piliavin and Scott Briar, "Police Encounters with Juveniles," *American Journal of Sociology* 70 (September 1964), 206–14.

24. Terry, "Discrimination in the Handling of Juvenile Offenders by Social Control Agencies"; Black and Reiss, "Police Control of Juveniles."

25. Gail Armstrong, "Females Under the Law—Protected but Unequal," *Crime and Delinquency* 23 (April 1977), 109–20; Meda Chesney-Lind, "Girls and Status Offenses: Is Juvenile Justice Still Sexist?" *Criminal Justice Abstracts* 20 (March 1988), 144–65; Meda Chesney-Lind and Randall G. Shelden, *Girls: Delinquency and Juvenile Justice* (Pacific Grove, CA: Brooks/Cole, 1992).

26. Studies that have found a racial bias in arresting juveniles include Theodore N. Ferdinand and Elmer C. Luchtenhand, "Inner-City Youths, the Police, the Juvenile Court and Justice," *Social Problems* 17 (Spring 1970), 510–27; Goldman, *The Differential Selection of Juvenile Offenders for Court Appearances*; Piliavin and Briar, "Police Encounters with Juveniles"; and Marvin E. Wolfgang, Robert M. Figlio, and Thorstein Sellin, *Delinquency in a Birth Cohort* (Chicago: University of Chicago Press, 1972), 252.

27. Philip W. Harris, "Race and Juvenile Justice: Examining the Impact of Structural and Policy Changes on Racial Disproportionality," paper presented at the annual meeting of the American Society of Criminology, Montreal (November 13, 1987).

28. James T. Carey et al., *The Handling of Juveniles from Offense to Disposition* (Washington, DC: Government Printing Office, 1976); A. W. McEachern and Riva Bauzer, "Factors Related to Disposition in Juvenile–Police Contacts," in *Juvenile Gangs in Context*, edited by Malcolm W. Klein (Upper Saddle River, NJ: Prentice Hall, 1967); Ferdinand and Luchterhand, "Inner-City Youths, the Police, the Juvenile Court and Justice," 510–17; Miriam D. Sealock and Sally S. Simpson, "Unraveling Bias in Arrest Decisions: The Role of Juvenile Offender Type-Scripts," *Justice Quarterly* 15 (September 1998), 427–57.

29. Merry Morash, "Establishment of Juvenile Police Record," *Criminology* 22 (February 1984), 97–111.

30. Piliavin and Briar, "Police Encounters with Juveniles," 206–14.

31. Carl Werthman and Irving Piliavin, "Gang Members and the Police," in *The Police*, edited by David J. Bordua (New York: Wiley, 1967), 56–98.

32. Richard J. Lundman, Richard E. Sykes, and John P. Clark, "Police Control of Juveniles: A Replication," in *Police Behavior: A Sociological Perspective*, edited by Richard J. Lundman (New York: Oxford University Press, 1980), 147–48.

33. Malcolm W. Klein, "Police Processing of Juvenile Offenders: Toward the Development of Juvenile System Rates" (Los Angeles County Sub-Regional Board, California Council on Juvenile Justice, Part III, 1970).

34. James Q. Wilson, "Dilemmas of Police Administration," *Public Administration Review* 28 (September–October 1968), 19.

35. John L. Worrall and Otwin Marenin, "Emerging Liability Issues in the Implementation and Adoption of Community Oriented Policing," *Policing: An International Journal of Police Strategies and Management* (MCB University Press), 21, No. 1 (1998), 121–36.

36. For a discussion of the Constitution and Supreme Court decisions relevant to the schools, see Reed B. Day, *Legal Issues Surrounding Safe Schools* (Topeka, KS: National Organization on Legal Problems of Education, 1994).

37. *Mapp v. Ohio,* 367 U.S. 643 (1961); Day, *Legal Issues Surrounding Safe Schools,* 25–38.

38. *State v. Lowery,* 230 A. 2d 907 (1967).

39. *In re Two Brothers and a Case of Liquor,* Juvenile Court of the District of Columbia, 1966, reported in *Washington Law Reporter* 95 (1967), 113.

40. *Ciulla v. State,* 434 S.W. 2d 948 (Tex. Civ. App. 1968).

41. For a good general discussion of search and seizure law see http://law.enotes.com/everyday-law-encyclopedia/search-and-seizure. Among the Supreme Court cases relevant to privacy are *Katz v. U.S.*, 389 U.S. 347, 88 S. Ct. 507. 19 L. Ed. 2d576 (1967) and *Hester v. U.S.*, 265 I.S. 57, 44 S. Ct. 445, 68 L. Ed. 898 (1924). See also Judge David Demers, "Search and Seizure Outline" (2002) at http://www.judges.com/Demers/page153-179.htm.

42. *Terry v. Ohio,* 392 U.S. 1, 20 L 2d 889, 911 (1968) at http://urban75.org/legal/rights.html.

43. Ibid.

44. For some examples of the use of reasonable suspicion in different types of cases, see Demers, "Search and Seizure Outline."

45. See, for example the plain view doctrine and search and seizure at http://dictionary.law.com/default2.asp?selected=1538 and http://dictionary.law.com/default2.asp?selected=1894.

46. Demers, "Search and Seizure Outline."

47. "Your Rights on Arrest: Legal Advice and Useful Information" at http://www.urban75.org/legal/rights.html.

48. For an extensive discussion of the relevant issues and court decisions related to police in the schools, see Samuel M. Davis, *Rights of Juveniles*, 2d ed. (New York: Clark Boardman Company, 1986), Sections 3–19 to 3–34.3.

49. *New Jersey v. T. L. O.,* 469 U.S. (1985).

50. Ibid.

51. Ibid.

52. J. M. Sanchez, "Expelling the Fourth Amendment from American Schools: Students' Rights Six Years After T. L. O.," *Education Journal* 21 (1992), 381–413; Day, *Legal Issues Surrounding Safe Schools,* 9–24.

53. *Wikipedia,* The Free Encyclopedia, at http://en.wikipedia.org/wiki/Miranda_Warning.

54. Ibid. Also, see Findlaw Lawyer Director at http://criminal.findlaw.com/articles/1387.html for a brief but good discussion of "Police Questioning Prior to Arrest."

55. *People v. Lara,* 62 Cal. Reporter, 586 (1967), cert. denied 392 U.S. 945 (1968).

56. *In re Mellot,* 217 S. E. 2d 745 (C.A.N. Calif., 1975).

57. *In re Dennis P. Fletcher,* 248 A.2d 364 (Md., 1968), cert. denied 396 U.S. 852 (1969).

58. T. Grisso, *Juveniles' Waiver of Rights: Legal and Psychological Competence* (New York: Plenum Press, 1981).

59. *Brown v. Mississippi*, 297 U.S. 278 (1936).

60. Davis, *Rights of Juveniles,* Section 3–45.

61. *Haley v. Ohio,* 332 U.S. 596 (1948).

62. Ibid.

63. *Fare v. Michael C.,* 442 U.S. 23, 99 S. Ct. 2560 (1979).

64. *Commonwealth v. Guyton,* 405 Mass. 497 (1989).

65. Elyce Z. Ferster and Thomas F. Courtless, "The Beginning of Juvenile Justice, Police Practices, and the Juvenile Offender," *Vanderbilt Law Review* 22 (April 1969), 598–601.

66. *Davis v. Mississippi,* 394 U.S. 721 (1969).

67. Ibid.

68. See Davis, *Rights of Juveniles,* Section 3–67.

69. *United States v. Wade,* 338 U.S. 218, 87 S. Ct. 1926 (1967).

70. *Kirby v. Illinois,* 406 U.S. 682, 92 S. Ct. 1877 (1972).

71. *In re Holley,* 107 R. I. 615, 268 A. 2d 723 (1970).

72. *In re Carl T.,* 81 Cal. Reporter 655 (2d C.A., 1969).

73. U.S. Department of Justice, "Community Policing," *National Institute of Justice* 225 (1992), 1–32.

74. Herman Goldstein, *Policing a Free Society,* (New York: Ballinger, 1977).

75. Different versions of COP exist, partly because community complexity is so great. As problems are analyzed by various researchers, it appears that names are assigned on the basis of the particular researcher's understanding of COP; thus, a brief review of the literature shows that the lines between the different types of programs are blurred and that no consensus yet exists. This conceptual and semantic problem will undoubtedly continue to exist for some time.

76. See Ann Pastore and Maguire, *Sourcebook of Criminal Justice Statistics—2003* (Washington, DC: Government Printing Office, 2005), see tables on law enforcement employment; see also Melissa Sickmund, "Juveniles in Corrections," Juvenile Offenders and Victims: National Reports Series, (Washington, D.C.: Office of Juvenile Programs, June 2004), 52–53.

77. William Spelman and John E. Eck, *Problem-Oriented Policing,* (Washington, DC: U.S. Department of Justice, 1997).

78. Pastore and Maguire, *Sourcebook of Criminal Justice Statistics—2003,* 36.

79. Paul McCold, "An Experiment in Police-Based Restorative Justice: The Bethlehem (Pa) Project," *Police Practice and Research* 4 (2003), 373–390.

5

THE JUVENILE COURT

To save a child from becoming a criminal, or from continuing in a career of crime, to end in maturer years in public punishment and disgrace, the legislature surely may provide for the salvation of such a child, if its parents or guardian be unable or unwilling to do so, by bringing it into one of the courts of the state without any process at all, for the purpose of subjecting it to the state's guardianship and protection.

The action is not for the trial of a child charged with a crime, but is mercifully to save it from such an ordeal, with the prison or penitentiary in its wake, if the child's own good and the best interests of the state justify such salvation. Whether the child deserves to be saved by the state is no more a question for a jury than whether the father, if able to save it, ought to save it. The act is but an exercise by the state of its supreme power over the welfare of its children, a power over which it can take a child from its father, and let it go where it will, without committing it to any guardianship or any institution, if the welfare of the child, taking its age into consideration, can be thus best promoted.

The design is not punishment, nor the restraint imprisonment, any more than is the wholesome restraint a parent exercises over his child. The severity in either case must necessarily be tempered to meet the necessities of the particular situation. There is no probability, in the proper administration of the law, of the child's liberty being unduly involved. Every statute which is designed to give protection, care, and training to children, as a needed substitute for parental authority, and performance of parental duty, is but a recognition of the duty of the state, as the legitimate guardian and protector of children where other guardianship fails. No constitutional right is violated.

—Julian W. Mack[1]

OUTLINE

OBJECTIVES

1. To present the development and legal norms of the juvenile court
2. To explore the main U.S. Supreme Court decisions that incorporated the due process movement into juvenile court proceedings
3. To discuss the intake stages of the juvenile court's proceedings
4. To examine social control of the status offender

KEY TERMS

bail
Breed v. Jones
constitutionalists
decriminalized status offenses
deinstitutionalization of status
   offenders
detention hearing
In re Barbara Burrus

ex parte Crouse
guardian *ad litem*
In re Gault
In re Terry
In re Winship
intake process
Kent v. United States
Juvenile Justice and Delinquency
   Prevention Act

McKeiver v. Pennsylvania
Missouri Plan
National Council of Juvenile
   and Family Court Judges
plea bargain
preventive detention
probation officers

The purpose of the court, as expressed in the chapter-opening quote from the *Commonwealth v. Fisher* decision in 1905, "is not for the punishment of offenders but for the salvation of children . . . whose salvation may become the duty of the state."[2] It is this type of statement that resulted in the juvenile court receiving fanatical support from its followers. Ever since the turn of the twentieth century, supporters have argued that the informal setting of the juvenile court, coupled with the fatherly demeanor of the juvenile judge, enables children to be treated, rather than punished, for their problems.[3] The state, the argument goes, rescues these youths from a life of trouble on the streets, rehabilitates them, protects them from placement with adult criminals in correctional facilities, and saves them from a life of crime. According to Judge Leonard P. Edwards, what is implicit in this position is that "children are different from adults, that they have developmental needs which they cannot satisfy without assistance and that care and supervision are critical to their upbringing." He then argues that "if children were no different from adults, the juvenile court would be unnecessary."[4]

Critics of the juvenile court sharply challenge these idealistic claims. They argue that the juvenile court has not succeeded in rehabilitating juvenile offenders, in reducing or even stemming the rise of youth crime, or in bringing justice and compassion to youthful offenders.[5] The juvenile court, they argue, acts in an arbitrary and whimsical fashion. It selects whom it "saves" on the basis of their sex and race, not on the basis of justice. The court harms children by processing them through its system, offering them inadequate programs, and labeling them as they return to the community.[6]

This chapter, the first of two on the juvenile court, presents those who are involved in the juvenile court process, its changing legal norms, the pretrial procedures of its proceedings, and the social control of status offenders.

HOW HAVE LEGAL NORMS CHANGED?

A group known as the **constitutionalists** argued that the juvenile court was unconstitutional because under its auspices the principles of a fair trial and individual rights were denied. This group primarily was concerned that children appearing before the juvenile court were denied their procedural rights as well as the rights to shelter, protection, and guardianship. The constitutionalists proposed that the procedures of the juvenile court be modified in three ways: (1) by the adoption of separate procedures for dealing with dependent and neglected children and those who are accused of criminal behavior; (2) by the use of informal adjustments to avoid official court actions as frequently as possible; and (3) by the provision of rigorous procedural safeguards and rights for children appearing before the court at the adjudicatory stage.[7]

A series of decisions by the U.S. Supreme Court in the 1960s and early 1970s rapidly accelerated the influence of the constitutionalists on the juvenile court. The five most important cases were *Kent v. United States* (1966), *In re Gault* (1967), *In re Winship* (1970), *McKeiver v. Pennsylvania* (1971), and *Breed v. Jones* (1975). See Figure 5–1, a time line for the most important court decisions concerning juveniles.

KENT V. UNITED STATES

The first major case was ***Kent v. United States.***[8] In this 1966 case, the juvenile court had disregarded all of Kent's due process rights in transferring the case to the adult court. The judge of the juvenile court did not rule on Kent's lawyer's motions. The judge also did not discuss the case with either Kent or Kent's parents, did not present any findings, did not offer any reason for waiving Kent to the adult court, and, in fact, made no reference to the motions filed by Kent's attorney. The judge also apparently ignored reports from juvenile court staff and the Juvenile Probation Section that indicated that Kent's mental condition was deteriorating. Rather, the judge entered an order waiving Kent to the adult court for trial. There, Kent was indicted by a grand jury on eight counts of housebreaking, robbery, and rape and was sentenced to a total of thirty to ninety years in prison. Focus on Law 5–1 describes the facts of this case.

Kent's counsel initiated a series of appeals that led to review of the case by the U.S. Supreme Court. The counsel argued throughout these appeals that Kent's parents had not been notified in time, that Kent's interrogation and detention were illegal because neither his parents nor his counsel were present, that probable cause for Kent's detention had not been established, that he had not been told of his right to remain silent or of his right to counsel, and that he was fingerprinted illegally.

The Supreme Court agreed that the procedures followed by the juvenile court were inadequate. In addition, the Court ruled that Kent had the right to a transfer hearing in which evidence was presented, that Kent had the right to be present at a waiver hearing, that Kent's attorney had the right to see the

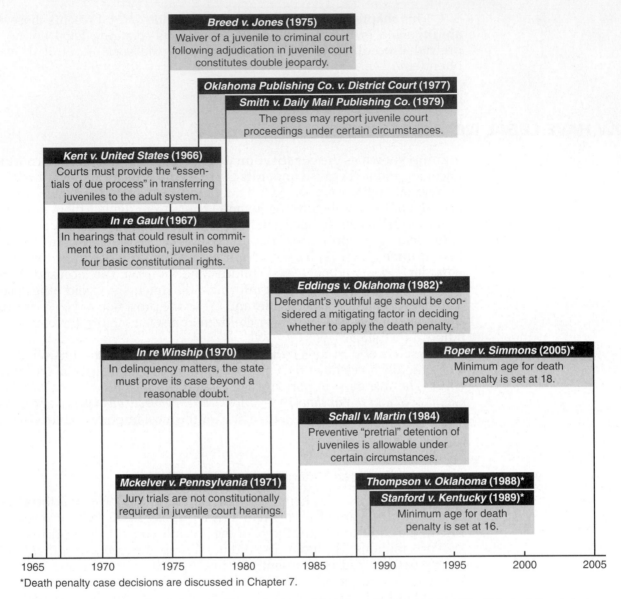

*Death penalty case decisions are discussed in Chapter 7.

Figure 5–1   *A Series of U.S. Supreme Court Decisions Made Juvenile Courts More Like Criminal Courts but Maintained Some Important Differences*

Source: Howard N. Snyder, and Melissa Sickmund, *Juvenile Offenders and Victims: 2006 National Report* (Washington, DC: U.S. Department of Justice, Office of Justice Programs, Office of Juvenile Justice and Delinquency Prevention, 2006), p. 101.

social service reports, and that the judge had to state the reasons for the transfer.[9] In this decision, Judge Abe Fortas stated:

> There is evidence, in fact, that there may be grounds for concern that the child receives the worst of both worlds; that he gets neither the protection accorded to adults nor the solicitous care and regenerative treatment postulated for children.[10]

IN RE GAULT

In May 1967, the U.S. Supreme Court reversed the conviction of a minor in the case of *In re Gault*.[11] This has been one of the most influential and far-reaching decisions to affect the juvenile court. In this case, the Court overruled the

FOCUS ON LAW   5–1
KENT V. UNITED STATES

Morris A. Kent Jr., a sixteen-year-old living in Washington, DC, was on juvenile probation when he broke into a house and raped and robbed a woman on September 2, 1961. His fingerprints were found in the woman's apartment, and he was taken into custody by the police on September 5, 1961. He was charged with three counts each of housebreaking and robbery and two counts of rape. Kent apparently admitted not only the offense for which he was taken into custody but other housebreaking, robbery, and rape offenses as well. He was interrogated by the police into the evening, was taken to the Receiving Home for Juveniles late that evening, and was returned to the police the next day for more questioning. No record exists as to when Kent's mother found out about his detention, but she retained counsel on the second day of Kent's detainment.

The social service director of the juvenile court discussed with Kent's counsel the possibility that Kent's case might be waived to adult court; Kent's counsel opposed the waiver and also arranged for Kent to undergo psychiatric evaluation. Kent's lawyer then filed a motion for a waiver hearing on the juvenile court's jurisdiction and provided a psychiatrist's affidavit certifying that Kent was "a victim of severe psychopathology" and recommending that he be hospitalized for psychiatric observation. The affidavit concluded that Kent could be rehabilitated if provided adequate treatment. Kent's counsel also requested a copy of Kent's social service file for use in his defense.

Source: Kent v. United States, 383 U.S. 541, 86 S.Ct. 1045, 16 L.Ed. 2d 84 (1966).

Critical Thinking Questions:
What did Supreme Court Justice Fortas mean when he said "that there may be grounds for concern that the child receives the worst of both worlds?" Do you agree with his criticism of the juvenile court?

Arizona Supreme Court for its dismissal of a writ of habeas corpus. This writ had sought the release of Gerald Gault, who had been adjudicated to the state industrial school by the Juvenile Court of Gila County, Arizona. Focus on Law 5–2 presents the facts of this case.

In reviewing the decision of the Arizona Supreme Court, which upheld the confinement of Gault, the U.S. Supreme Court considered which of the following rights should apply to juveniles:

1. Right to receive notice of the charges
2. Right to be represented by counsel
3. Right to confront and cross-examine witnesses
4. Right to avoid self-incrimination
5. Right to receive a transcript of the proceedings
6. Right to request appellate review[12]

Justice Fortas, in delivering the Court's opinion, recalled other cases that had provided juveniles with due process of law. In both *Haley v. Ohio* (1948) and *Gallegos v. Colorado* (1962), the U.S. Supreme Court had prohibited the use of confessions coerced from juveniles; in *Kent v. United States*, the Court had given the juvenile the right to be represented by counsel.[13] Justice Fortas concluded this review of legal precedent with the sweeping statement that juveniles have those fundamental rights incorporated in the due process clause of the Fourteenth Amendment of the Constitution.

FOCUS ON LAW   5–2
IN RE GAULT

Gerald Gault, a fifteen-year-old Arizona boy, and a friend, Ronald Lewis, were taken into custody on June 8, 1964, on a verbal complaint made by a neighbor. The neighbor had accused the boys of making lewd and indecent remarks to her over the phone. Gault's parents were not notified that he was taken into custody; he was not advised of his right to counsel; he was not advised that he could remain silent; and no notice of charges was made to either Gerald or his parents. Additionally, the complainant was not present at either of the hearings. In spite of considerable confusion about whether or not Gerald had made the alleged phone call, what he had said over the phone, and what he had said to the judge during the course of the two hearings, Judge McGhee committed him to the State Industrial School until he reached the age of twenty-one or until he was discharged by the law.

Source: In re Gault, 387 U.S. 1, 18, 1, 18 L. Ed. 2d 527, 87 S. Ct. 1428 (1967).

Critical Thinking Questions:
What due process rights did this case grant juveniles? What due process rights did juveniles still lack after the decision?

The *In re Gault* decision answered in the affirmative the question of whether a juvenile has the right to due process safeguards during confinement. But the Supreme Court did not rule that juveniles have the right to a transcript of the proceedings or the right to appellate review.

In rejecting the latter two rights, the Court clearly did not want to transform the informal juvenile hearing into an adversarial trial. The cautiousness of this decision was expressed in a footnote that indicated that the decision did not apply to preadjudication or postadjudication treatment of juveniles. Several other important issues were also left unanswered, such as the following:

1. May a judge consider hearsay in juvenile court?
2. Does the exclusionary evidence principle derived from the Fourth Amendment apply?
3. What is the constitutionally required burden of proof necessary to support a finding of delinquency?
4. Is a jury trial required?
5. Does the requirement of a "speedy and public trial" apply in juvenile court?[14]

IN RE WINSHIP

The Supreme Court ruled in the *In re Winship* case (1970) that juveniles are entitled to proof "beyond a reasonable doubt."[15] The *Winship* case involved a New York boy who was sent to a state training school at the age of twelve for taking $112 from a woman's purse. The commitment was based on a New York statute that permitted juvenile court decisions on the basis of a "preponderance of evidence." The Court reasoned that "preponderance of evidence," a standard much less strict than "beyond a reasonable doubt," is not a sufficient basis for a decision when youths are charged with acts that would be criminal if committed by adults.

The findings in the *Winship* case not only expanded the implications of *In re Gault* but also reflected other concerns of the U.S. Supreme Court. The Court desired both to protect juveniles at adjudicatory hearings and to maintain the confidentiality, informality, flexibility, and speed of the juvenile process in the prejudicial and postadjudicative states. The Court obviously did not want to bring too much rigidity and impersonality to the juvenile hearing.

MCKEIVER V. PENNSYLVANIA, *IN RE TERRY*, AND *IN RE BARBARA BURRUS*

The Supreme Court heard three cases together (*McKeiver v. Pennsylvania, In re Terry,* and *In re Barbara Burrus*) to determine whether the due process clause of the Fourteenth Amendment (guaranteeing the right to a jury trial) applied to juveniles.[16] The decision, which was issued in *McKeiver v. Pennsylvania* (1971), denied the right of juveniles to have jury trials. Focus on Law 5–3 reveals the facts of these three cases.

The Supreme Court explained its ruling that juveniles do not have the right to a jury trial as follows:

1. Not all rights that are constitutionally assured for adults are to be given to juveniles.
2. If a jury trial is required for juveniles, the juvenile proceedings may become a fully adversarial process, putting an end to what has been the idealistic prospect of an intimate, informal, protective proceeding.
3. A jury trial is not necessarily a part of every criminal process that is fair and equitable.
4. If the jury trial is injected into the juvenile court system, it could bring with it the traditional delays, the formality, and the clamor of the adversarial system.
5. There is nothing to prevent an individual juvenile judge from using an advisory jury when he or she feels the need. For that matter, there is nothing to prevent individual states from adopting jury trials.[17]

Although a number of states do permit jury trials for juveniles, most states adhere to this constitutional standard set by the Supreme Court. What is significant about this decision is that the Court indicated an unwillingness to apply further procedural safeguards to juvenile proceedings. This especially appears to be true concerning the preadjudicatory and postadjudicatory treatment of juveniles.

BREED V. JONES

The *Breed v. Jones* (1975) case was slightly different from the *Kent* case. Jones was taken into custody for committing a robbery and was detained for a hearing in juvenile court. At the juvenile court hearing, the allegations against Jones were found to be true. At the disposition hearing, the court determined that Jones could not be helped by the services of the juvenile court; Jones was waived to adult court, where he was found guilty of robbery.

FOCUS ON LAW

5–3

RIGHT OF A JURY TRIAL FOR JUVENILES

McKeiver v. Pennsylvania

Joseph McKeiver, who was sixteen years of age, was charged with robbery, larceny, and receiving stolen goods, all of which were felonies under Pennsylvania law. Found delinquent at an adjudication hearing, the youth was placed on probation after his request for a jury trial was denied.

In re Terry

Edward Terry, who was fifteen years of age, was charged with assault and battery on a police officer, which were misdemeanors under Pennsylvania law. His counsel requested a jury trial, which was denied, and he was adjudicated a delinquent on the charges.

In re Barbara Burrus

Barbara Burrus and approximately forty-five other youths, ranging in age from eleven to fifteen years, received juvenile court summonses in Hyde County, North Carolina. The charges arose out of a series of demonstrations in the county in late 1968 by African-American adults and children who were protesting school assignments and a school construction plan. The youths were charged with willfully impeding traffic. The several cases were consolidated into groups for hearing before the district judge, sitting as a juvenile court. A request for a jury trial in each case was denied. Each youth was found delinquent and placed on probation.

Source: McKeiver v. Pennsylvania, 403 U.S. 528, 535 (1971); *In re Terry,* 438 Pa., 339, 265A.2d 350 (1970); and *In re Barbara Burrus,* 275 N.C. 517, 169 Sk. E. 2d 879 (1969K).

Critical Thinking Questions:
What is the actual difference between "preponderance of the evidence" and "proof beyond a reasonable doubt"?
What was the importance of this difference in this case?

Jones's lawyer appealed the case, arguing that Jones had been subjected to double jeopardy; that is, this decision had violated the standard used in adult courts that prevents adults from being tried twice for the same crime. The Supreme Court concurred, stating that Jones's hearing in the juvenile court was an adjudicatory hearing and that his trial in adult court constituted double jeopardy.[18] For waiver to adult court to occur legally, according to the Supreme Court, juvenile courts must transfer youths to the adult court jurisdiction before any adjudicatory hearings are held on their cases.

In sum, the *In re Gault* and *In re Winship* decisions have unquestionably effected profound changes in the legal status of the juvenile justice system. The *McKeiver v. Pennsylvania* decision and the more conservative stance of the Supreme Court since 1971, however, have raised some question about whether or not this ultimate appellate court will be willing to change legal norms much more. These court decisions have, of course, received varying endorsements from juvenile courts across the United States. Some juvenile courts gave procedural rights to juveniles even before the Supreme Court decisions, but others have lagged far behind in implementing these decisions.

✓ **Progress Check 5.1**
Review this section at
www.prenhall.com/bartollas

HOW IS THE STATUS OFFENDER CONTROLLED?

Youths can be charged with at least three different categories of offenses. First, they can be charged with a felony or misdemeanor under federal, state, and local statutes. Second, they are subject to relatively specific statutes applying exclusively to juvenile behavior: truancy, consumption of alcoholic beverages, and running away from home are examples. Third, juveniles can be prosecuted under general omnibus statutes that include such offenses as acting beyond the control of parents, engaging in immoral conduct, and being ungovernable and incorrigible. Offenses under both the second and third categories are status offenses. The status offense statutes pertaining to behavior for which an adult could not be prosecuted have drawn increasing attention in recent years. Status offenders can be processed through the juvenile justice system along with youths who have committed criminal offenses, or they can be handled separately from felons and misdemeanants. States that pursue the latter course usually refer to status offenders as MINS (minors in need of supervision), CINS (children in need of supervision), PINS (persons in need of supervision), FINS (families in need of supervision), or JINS (juveniles in need of supervision). Some jurisdictions handle these youths in a different court; others will not place them in detention with delinquents or send them to a juvenile correctional institution.

The handling of status offenders, one of the most controversial issues in juvenile justice, has focused on two questions: should status offenders be placed with delinquents in correctional settings, and should the juvenile court retain jurisdiction over status offenders?

Deinstitutionalization of Status Offenders

There have been four positions expressed about the **deinstitutionalization of status offenders** (to no longer confine status offenders in secure detention facilities or secure correctional facilities with delinquents). First, researchers have raised real doubt about the policy of confining status offenders with delinquents. One study found that before their dispositional hearing, status offenders were more likely to be detained or treated more harshly than delinquents.[19] Examinations of juvenile institutionalization also revealed that status offenders stayed longer in training school than did delinquents, were vulnerable to victimization in these settings, and found institutionalization with delinquents to be a destructive experience.[20]

Second, other researchers have questioned whether status offenders are innocent youths who are significantly different from delinquents. That is, they have found that status offenders are more than incorrigible youths with family problems. Charles W. Thomas found that status offenders not only differ very little in offense behavior but also tend to progress from status to delinquent offenses.[21] P. Erickson also found that most adolescents who are brought to court for status offense behavior are mixed offenders who have, at one time or another, been involved in misdemeanors and felonies as well as status offenses.[22] Solomon Kobrin, Frank R. Hellum, and John W. Peterson's national study of status offenders found three groups of such offenders: The "heavies" committed serious offenses as well as some incidental status offenses; the "lightweights" committed misdemeanors as well as status offenses; and "conforming youths" were basically law-abiding but occasionally committed a status offense. Conforming youths would normally not be considered a problem by the courts, but the fact that the lightweights committed misdemeanors as well as status offenses suggests that it might be a mistake to keep them out of institutions.[23]

Third, juvenile judges have resisted this deinstitutionalization movement in some states, and they have found a way to continue the institutionalization of status offenders with delinquents (even in states that strongly support deinstitutionalization). What these juvenile judges do is redefine status offenders as delinquents.[24] A truant may be charged with a minor delinquent offense and be institutionalized for that reason; similarly, school attendance may be required as a condition of probation, and further truancy is then defined as a delinquent offense.[25]

Fourth, what served as the real impetus for a nationwide deinstitutionalization of status offenders was the passage of the 1974 **Juvenile Justice and Delinquency Prevention (JJDP) Act** and its various modifications.[26] In order for states to continue receiving federal funding for juvenile justice programs, the JJDP Act required that status offenders be kept separate from delinquents in secure detention and institutionalization. The act also limited the placement of juveniles in adult jail facilities. The effectiveness of this federal mandate could be seen in the dramatic decrease in the number of status offenders being held in secure facilities over several decades. For example, in 1975, an estimated 143,000 status offense cases involved detention; in 1992, the figure was 24,300.[27]

JURISDICTION OVER STATUS OFFENDERS

The juvenile court's long-standing jurisdiction over status offenders is an even more volatile issue. There are at least four distinct arguments for the removal of status offenders from the jurisdiction of the juvenile court. The legal argument states that the lack of clarity of the status offender statutes makes them unconstitutionally vague in their construction; that they often are blatantly discriminatory, especially in regard to sex; and that government bodies have no legitimate interest in many of these proscribed behaviors. Second, although status offenders have not committed a criminal act, they frequently are confined with chronic or hard-core offenders. Third, in keeping with the *parens patriae* philosophy of the juvenile court, the procedure of processing and confining the status offender is not in his or her best interests. Some theorists argue that the formal intervention of the juvenile court promotes rather than inhibits unlawful behavior. Fourth, many charge that status offenders are a special class of youth who must be treated differently from delinquents.[28]

Juvenile court judges, not surprisingly, challenge the movement to strip the court of jurisdiction over status offenders. They charge that status offenders will have no one to provide for them or to protect them if they are removed from the court's jurisdiction. The essence of this position is that other agencies will have to take over if the court relinquishes jurisdiction over these offenders and that few options are presently available for providing status offenders a nurturing environment in lieu of the home.

Maine, New York, and Washington are states that have **decriminalized status offenses**, thus removing from the juvenile court's jurisdiction youthful behavior that would not be a chargeable offense if committed by an adult.[29] The most broad-based movement to strip the juvenile court of jurisdiction over status offenders has taken place in New York State, heralded by the passage of the 1985 PINS Adjustment Services Act. A central purpose of this legislation was to displace the family court as the institution of first choice for minor family-related matters. The PINS legislation also has constructed an innovative system of its own that operates as formally as the juvenile court. Children whose families are receptive are referred to the Designated Assessment Service, which in turn refers these youths to a community-based agency for long-term services. The legal proceedings are suspended, as long as youths are responsive to the rehabilitative programs designed for them.[30]

The informality with which juvenile court cases are tried varies widely. Here, a Pennsylvania magistrate hears the case of an underage teenager caught drinking.
(Photo by Stuart Miller.)

It would appear unlikely that many more states will remove status offenders from the juvenile court's jurisdiction in the near future. In fact, between 1988 and 1992, the juvenile court's status offense caseload grew 18 percent.[31] The widespread resistance comes mainly from those who feel that status offenders need the control of the juvenile court over their lives or they will become involved in increasingly destructive behaviors. The juvenile court and its supporters also resist because they fear that loss of jurisdiction over serious offenders as well as status offenders may signal the beginning of the juvenile court's demise.

WHAT DOES THE JUVENILE COURT LOOK LIKE TODAY?

The structure of the juvenile court varies from jurisdiction to jurisdiction. Special and separate juvenile courts in certain urban areas devote their total effort to the legal problems of children. Juveniles in smaller cities and rural areas are often tried by judges of the adult courts. A separate statewide court exists in several states, and only juvenile judges sit on cases in the various districts of those states. In other parts of the country, juvenile offenders are handled exclusively by family court judges who hear both juvenile and domestic relations cases.

More typically, juvenile courts are part of a circuit, district, county, superior, common pleas, probate, or municipal court. This broad-based trial court may be either the highest court of general trial jurisdiction or the lower trial court in which lesser criminal and limited-claim civil matters are heard.

Nationally, juvenile courts today are affected by a movement toward a single trial court, inclusive of all courts in which initial trials take place. For example, in a massive court reorganization in Cook County, Illinois, 208 courts became the circuit court for Cook County. The juvenile court of the District of Columbia was absorbed into the new single trial court for the District.

A variety of personnel serve the juvenile court. These include the judge, who heads up the court; the defense attorney and the prosecutor, who, respectively, defends the client and tries the case; referees, who are assistants to the judge; probation officers, who investigate and supervise cases; and the nonjudicial support personnel, who do everything from providing client services to keeping the court running smoothly. The numbers and qualifications of these persons vary widely from court to court.[32]

THE JUDGE

Juvenile court judges have an enormously important and difficult job. The most traditional role of the juvenile court judge is to decide the legal issues that appear before the court. The judge must determine, according to Leonard P. Edwards, "whether certain facts are true, whether a child should be removed from a parent, what types of services should be offered to the family and whether the child should be returned to the family and the community or placed permanently in another setting."[33]

The juvenile court judge also has the following responsibilities:

1. To set juvenile justice standards within the community and within the criminal and juvenile justice systems
2. To make certain that juveniles appearing before the court receive the legal and constitutional rights to which they are entitled
3. To ensure that the systems that detect, investigate, resolve, and bring cases to court are working fairly and efficiently
4. To make certain that there are an adequate number of attorneys of satisfactory quality to represent juveniles in court
5. To know how cases that do not reach the juvenile court are being resolved
6. To monitor the progress of the child, the family, and the supervisory agency to make certain that each complies with the terms of the court's orders
7. To be an advocate within the community on behalf of children and their families
8. In some communities, to oversee the juvenile probation department and court staff[34]

Juvenile judges are chosen by a variety of methods. In some states, the governor appoints candidates chosen by a screening board. In other states, judges are chosen through partisan elections, and in still other states, judges run for office without party affiliation. The legislature appoints judges in a few states. A dozen states have adopted the **Missouri Plan,** which involves (1) a commission being appointed to nominate candidates for judge vacancies; (2) an elected official, generally the governor, making judicial appointments from the list submitted by the commission; and (3) nonpartisan and uncontested elections being held (usually every three years) to give incumbent judges an opportunity to run on their records.[35]

Juvenile judges wield considerable power and, not surprisingly, a few do abuse their power as they become despots or dictators in "their courts." But many juvenile judges rise to the challenge and do remarkable jobs. They scrupulously observe procedural safeguards and due process rights for juveniles. They are always seeking better means of detention and reserve the use of training schools as a last resort. They are extremely committed to the work of the juvenile court and sometimes even pass up promotions to more highly paid judgeships with greater prestige. The end result is that these judges change the quality of juvenile justice in their jurisdictions.

The **National Council of Juvenile and Family Court Judges,** located in Reno, Nevada, has done much to upgrade the juvenile court judiciary. This organization has sponsored research and continuing legal education efforts. It also maintains a research facility, the National Center for Juvenile Justice, in Pittsburgh, Pennsylvania. The council publishes quarterly the *Juvenile and Family Journal;* monthly, the *Juvenile and Family Law Digest;* and eight times per year, the *Juvenile and Family Court Newsletter.*

THE REFEREE

Juvenile courts frequently employ the services of a referee, who may or may not be a member of the bar. In the state of Washington, a referee is called a *commissioner;* in Maryland, a *master.* California uses both referees and commissioners. Although a number of states use only judges in the juvenile court, other states use referees, masters, and commissioners as the primary hearing officers. All perform similar functions for the courts.

Referees generally have a fundamental grasp of juvenile law, some basic understanding of psychology and sociology, and even some experience or training in social work. In some courts, referees hear cases at the fact-finding and detention hearings and may even adjudicate cases at the discretion of the judge. If a judicial disposition is necessary, it usually is left to the juvenile judge. The use of referees appears to be on the increase in some urban areas where the caseload pressures are great.

THE DEFENSE ATTORNEY

Defense attorneys, or *respondents,* have been part of the juvenile court structure ever since the *Gault* decision stated that juveniles have the right to be represented by an attorney. Whether they are public defenders, court-appointed attorneys, or privately retained attorneys, defense attorneys presently play an increasingly important role in juvenile trials.[36] Yet Barry C. Feld found that nearly half of the juveniles who appeared before the juvenile courts for delinquency and status offense referrals in Minnesota, Nebraska, and North Dakota were not represented by counsel. Equally serious, he found that many of the juveniles who were placed out of their homes in these states also did not have counsel.[37]

Defense attorneys typically have at least three roles from which to choose: (1) an adversarial advocate for the child, (2) a surrogate guardian or parent to the child, or (3) an assistant to the court with responsibilities to the children.[38] Defense attorneys from public defenders' offices tend to do a better job of representing the rights of youth than do private and court-appointed counsel, primarily because public defenders appear in juvenile court day after day, thereby gaining valuable experience, whereas private attorneys appear only occasionally.

Some evidence suggests that juveniles who had counsel received more severe dispositions than those who did not have counsel.[39] For example, juveniles with counsel seem more likely to receive an institutional disposition than do those without counsel.[40] Such a pattern could result if juvenile judges punished youths who chose to be represented by counsel. Other studies have not found juveniles to be penalized or to fare worse in juvenile courts because they were represented by counsel.[41]

Joseph B. Sanborn Jr.'s 1994 study of juvenile courts found that "judges never encouraged defendants to waive their right to counsel nor appointed any particular type of defense lawyer to represent children." He further found that there were a number of obstacles to fairness in the juvenile court. Representation by counsel was not always complete in the suburban and rural courts, and some counsel was not vigorous, effective, and competent. Sanborn determined that these obstacles to fairness were also found in adult courts in the counties studied. Finally, as with adult courts, these juvenile courts were pressured to hear a heavy volume of cases.[42]

A **guardian** *ad litem* is usually a lawyer who is appointed by the court to take care of youths who need help, especially in neglect, dependency, and abuse cases, but also occasionally in delinquency cases. In delinquency cases, a guardian *ad litem* may be appointed if there is a question of a need for a particular treatment intervention, such as placement in a mental health center, and the offender and her or his attorney are resisting placement.[43]

THE PROSECUTOR

The prosecutor, or *petitioner*, is expected to protect society and, at the same time, to ensure that children appearing before the court are provided with their basic constitutional rights. In urban courts, prosecutors typically are involved in every stage of the proceedings, from intake and detention through disposition. Prosecutors are particularly involved before the adjudication stage because witnesses must be interviewed, police investigations must be checked out, and court rules and case decisions must be researched. Prosecutors also play a role in detention decisions and represent the local or state government in all pretrial motions, probable cause hearings, and consent decrees. Prosecutors are especially involved in deciding whether juveniles should be waived to the adult court or kept in the juvenile court. In states in which certain offenses are excluded from juvenile court jurisdiction, prosecutors play send juveniles who commit those offenses to the adult court. Prosecutors further represent the county or state at the adjudication hearing and at the disposition of the case. In some urban courts, prosecutors may be involved in plea bargaining with the defense counsel. Prosecutors in some states are permitted to initiate appeals for the limited purpose of clarifying a given law or procedure. Moreover, prosecutors represent the state or county on appeals and in habeas corpus proceedings. Some critics contend that the prosecutor in some juvenile courts has come to dominate juvenile court proceedings.[44]

THE PROBATION OFFICERS

Probation officers have some of the most demanding jobs of any court personnel, as their functions involve developing interfaces between the probation department and community agencies that service children and managing cases from intake through aftercare. Probation officers act as intake officers, assess the needs of youths, write reports such as predisposition reports, and supervise youths in both probation and aftercare in some jurisdictions. The officer may be given an intensive probation caseload, may be responsible for youths who are on house arrest and are monitored with electronic equipment, or may be charged with intake or secure detention responsibilities. In addition, the probation officer is expected to be a treatment agent as well as an agent of social control.[45]

Probation officers appear to have four different orientations to their clients. First, probation officers oriented to the enforcer role perceive themselves as enforcement officers who are charged with regulating juvenile behavior. Second, probation officers oriented to the detector role attempt to identify problematic juveniles in advance on the basis of previous rule infractions. Third, probation officers oriented to the broker role refer juveniles to appropriate community services and programs—a common practice today. Finally, probation officers oriented to the educator, mediator, and enabler role are more likely to instruct and assist youthful offenders in dealing with the problems that impede their successful adjustment to the community.[46] Many of these probation officers have undergraduate backgrounds in sociology, psychology, and social work. Numerous other probation officers with these backgrounds go on to get master's degrees in social work or criminal justice to further their careers in the criminal justice system.

THE NONJUDICIAL SUPPORT PERSONNEL

Nonjudicial support personnel include volunteers, staff from agencies providing services to the court, and paid workers who perform routine administrative functions. Personnel from social service agencies also frequent the court as they make contact with youths and their families, but they have the job of writing reports to the courts summarizing the characteristics of youths as well as the progress youths are making. Finally, the court employs secretaries, clerks, bailiffs, legal researchers, and court administrators to perform the routine but necessary tasks of processing youths through the system.

WHAT ARE THE PRETRIAL PROCEDURES OF THE JUVENILE COURT?

The jurisdiction of the juvenile court, despite variations among and even within states, generally includes delinquency, neglect, and dependency cases. Children's courts may also deal with cases concerning adoption, termination of parental rights, appointment of guardians for minors, custody, contributing to delinquency or neglect, and nonsupport. The proceedings of the juvenile court can be divided into pretrial procedures and adjudicatory and dispositional hearings. This chapter considers pretrial procedures, and Chapter 6 examines the adjudicatory and dispositional stages of the court's proceedings.

The pretrial procedures consist of the detention hearing, the intake process, and the transfer procedure, which is discussed later. In 2002, 82 percent of delinquency cases were brought before the courts by law enforcement authorities, but there were variations across offense categories. Ninety percent of drug law violation cases, as well as 91 percent of property cases and 91 percent of person offense cases, were referred by law enforcement agencies. The remaining cases resulted from complaints by parents, citizens, probation officers, victims, school officials, and others.[47]

The reasons for referring youths to the courts vary. Of the delinquency offenses, police officers brought youths to the juvenile court for property and drug offenses more than any other category. Of the status offenses, liquor law and curfew violation headed the list for law enforcement officers. Conversely, sources other than law enforcement officers were most likely to refer youths for public order offenses and for status offenses, such as truancy, curfew violations, and ungovernability; the referral of runaways was about equally divided between law enforcement and other sources.

Between 1985 and 2002, the trends in case rates were generally similar across age groups. The person offense case rate for juveniles ages fourteen to seventeen rose from 1985 through 1995 and then dropped off. Youths ages twelve to thirteen had a similar pattern. For ten- to eleven-year-old youths, the person offense rate was highest in 2001. For all age groups, property case rates peaked in 1991 and then declined steadily thereafter. Drug offenses case rates were relatively stable for all age groups from the mid-1980s to the mid-1990s, when they began to rise sharply, but the rates flattened out again after 1996 for all ages.[48]

DETENTION HEARING

The use of detention has been a problem ever since the founding of the juvenile court. The original purpose of detention was to hold children securely until intake personnel reviewed the case and made a decision. The **detention hearing,** at which the decision to detain is made, must be held within a short period of time, generally forty-eight to seventy-two hours, excluding weekends and holidays. Those urban courts having intake units on duty twenty-four hours a day for detention hearings frequently act within a few hours.[49]

Detention hearings may occur at three points: (1) when the youth is taken in by the police, (2) during and after the time intake personnel review the case to decide whether to refer the case to juvenile court, and (3) after the adjudicatory hearing.

Police, as noted previously, make the first detention decision. Frequently, they must place the youth in a police lockup or local jail while they notify parents and decide what to do with the youth. The police usually exercise the option of simply releasing the youth to his or her parents. If police believe conditions warrant, as they often do with serious offenders and sometimes do with status offenders, they may hold these youths for their protection or for the protection of society. In other words, the police base their decision partly on how they classify the youth.[50]

The second point at which detention may occur is after the police take the youth to the intake personnel of the juvenile court. Intake personnel then review the case to determine whether the youth should be referred to the juvenile court. They, too, often make the decision to release the youth to his or her parents, but the intake personnel may decide that the youth needs to be detained either for his or her own protection or for the protection of society (**preventive detention**), or while awaiting the adjudicatory hearing.

The third point at which a detention hearing may be held is after the adjudicatory hearing. If the youth is adjudicated delinquent, the court may in some circumstances sentence the youth to a detention center, shelter care, or in-home detention for a period of time for punishment. Detention is then used as a *sanction*, in which juveniles serve their "sentence" in detention and are released afterwards. More commonly, the court sentences the youth to a private or public residential facility.

Youths who are held in detention are assigned to one of four types of placement. The detention home is the most physically restrictive. Shelter care is physically nonrestrictive and is available for those who lack home placements or who require juvenile court intervention. The jail or police lockup is juveniles' most undesirable detention placement and is not recommended for any juvenile. The final option available in many jurisdictions is in-home detention, which restricts a juvenile to his or her home, usually under the supervision of a paraprofessional staff member.

Five states have legislated a hearing on probable cause for detained youths, and appellate cases in other states have moved in the direction of mandating a probable-cause hearing to justify further detention. Georgia and Alaska courts have ruled that a juvenile is entitled to counsel at a detention hearing and to free counsel if indigent. The supreme courts in California and Alaska, as well as a Pennsylvania appellate court, have overturned cases in which no reason or an inadequate reason was stated for continuing detention. Furthermore, courts in the District of Columbia, Maryland, and Nevada have ruled that a youth in detention is entitled to humane care.

Bail for Children

Bail is *not* a form of punishment. Rather, its purpose is to ensure that the defendant will show up at his or her adjudicatory hearing. The court usually determines the amount of bail required at an early intake hearing, which reviews such factors as the youth's behavior, past history, and relationship with parents and school authorities. Once bail is set, the defendants and their families then have to come up with a percentage (usually 10 percent) of the required amount.

The controversies over bail are similar in adult and juvenile justice. The Eighth Amendment to the U.S. Constitution states that bail shall not be excessive, but determining what is excessive is difficult. In addition, the U.S. Supreme Court in *ex parte Crouse* stated that the Bill of Rights did not apply to children. This ruling therefore implied that the states and their courts may do as they please in setting bail. The result is that few can agree whether juveniles may be released on bail, and states and courts vary widely in their practices.

For example, some states prohibit bail altogether; Hawaii, Kentucky, Oregon, and Utah fall into this category. Other states allow bail, but not for juveniles. This practice is based on the assumption that normal juvenile court procedures and due process guarantees are sufficient to protect juveniles and allow their early release. In some of these states, it should be noted, judges occasionally require a juvenile to post bond. For the most part, however, requirements that juveniles are to be released to their parents as soon as possible are believed to be sufficient protection for juveniles.

Bail for juveniles is permitted in nine states: Arkansas, Colorado, Connecticut, Georgia, Massachusetts, Nebraska, Oklahoma, South Dakota, and West Virginia. Even though few juveniles are released on bail, most juvenile court statutes do limit the time that accused juveniles may be held in custody before their hearings.[51]

Alida V. Merlo and William D. Bennett's study of bail in Massachusetts indicated that bail was a factor in 72 percent of juvenile cases statewide in 1988. The trend for higher bail in Massachusetts is reflected in the detention admissions receiving from $101 to $500 bail (up 16 percent), $501 to $1,000 bail (up 70 percent), and more than $1,000 bail (up 48 percent). They conclude that these statewide trends indicate that juvenile judges may be starting to use bail as a means of ensuring the youth's detention and that judges, without actually using the term, may be engaging in the practice of preventive detention (confinement that is proactive, not punitive for a specific offense).[52]

The possibility of judges setting excessive bail has led some states to require higher courts to review the bail set by lower courts. In addition, some experts suggest releasing more youths on their own recognizance or under the supervision of third parties. Some recommend that states utilize citation programs; that is, police officers simply issue youths a "ticket," or summons, that requires the youth to appear in court on a certain date. Others suggest that police should require youths to report to the station house for a consultation with officers or members of the police youth bureau.

Preventive Detention

The 1984 *Schall v. Martin* decision of the U.S. Supreme Court represents a fundamental change that appears to be taking place in detention practices.[53] The plaintiffs originally filed a lawsuit in federal district court claiming that the New York Family Court Act was unconstitutional because it allowed for the preventive detention of juveniles:

The District Court struck down the statute as permitting detention without due process and ordered the release of all class members. The Court of

Appeals affirmed, holding . . . the statute is administered not for preventive purposes, but to impose punishment for unadjudicated criminal acts, and that therefore the statute is unconstitutional.[54]

In reversing the decision of the appeals court, Justice William Rehnquist declared that the "preventive detention under the statute serves the legitimate state objective held in common with every state, of protecting both the juvenile and the society from the hazards of pretrial crime."[55] Although the ultimate impact of this decision remains to be felt, there is reason to believe that the Court's ruling may encourage a significant expansion of preventive or secure detention for juveniles.

Preventive detention raises several controversial questions. First, laws are not supposed to be enforced against people unless some sort of overt act has occurred that violates the juvenile or criminal code. To put a youth in preventive detention under the assumption that he or she might commit an offense runs counter to the intent and, supposedly, the practice of the law. Second, preventive detention is experienced by the detainee as *punitive* confinement, regardless of the stated purpose of the practice. Finally, the propriety of incarceration before the determination of guilt and the procedural safeguards that must accompany such a practice is a major issue to be considered. Indeed, evaluations of the detention process indicate that the majority of juveniles who are preventively detained are not charged with serious offenses.[56]

INTAKE PROCESS

The **intake process** has several purposes: First, it screens cases to determine whether children need the help of the juvenile court. Second, it controls the use of detention, which is discussed later. Third, it reduces the courts' overwhelming caseloads. Fourth, it keeps inappropriate cases (e.g., minor cases) out of the juvenile court. Finally, it directs children to appropriate community agencies.[57]

Some probation departments have intake units, but in many departments, especially smaller ones, juvenile probation officers make intake decisions as part of their duties. When there are intake units, despite the similarity of their functions, they do not operate the same way. Juvenile court organization and available resources vary widely among the states. In addition, few states have attempted to spell out the criteria intake personnel should use to make their decisions. The result is that intake personnel exercise a great deal of discretion in deciding what to do with youths.

The first decision intake personnel must make is whether the case comes under their jurisdiction; for example, staff must determine whether the child or the child's offense falls under the appropriate age or offense category. If not, then the second decision of the staff will be either to dismiss the case or to refer it to an appropriate social agency or the adult court. Third, staff must decide whether the youth before them requires secure detention. Other options are to divert the case to a nonjudicial agency through an informal adjustment, put the youth on informal probation, issue a consent decree, or file a petition.

Case Dismissal

An intake officer reviews the cases of all youths brought to the court's attention. Often this review takes place with the police officer, the youths' parents, and perhaps the prosecutor and the youths' lawyers present. If the particular behavior in question is not an offense under the state's code, the charge will be dismissed. The case also will likely be dismissed if the case is too weak to bring before the court, if it is the youth's first offense, if the youth appears genuinely contrite, and if the parents appear concerned about the youth's behavior and promise to get the youth help. Youths whose cases are dismissed are sent home with their parents.

Informal Adjustment

This alternative, sometimes called *nonjudicial adjustment*, often is used for status and other minor offenders. One option of the intake official is simply to warn the child and to release him or her to parents. A more stringent option is to require the youth to pay restitution to the victim. A third option is to refer the youth to local diversion programs, which include youth service bureaus or other social agencies that are qualified to work with the problems of youth. The agencies to which the youth is referred are then responsible for supervising the youth and reporting back to the court.

Informal Probation

Informal probation means that the youth is released back to the community but must accept certain conditions that are spelled out by the court. The youth is usually supervised for a specified period of time by either a volunteer or a probation officer. If the youth is able to stay out of trouble in the community, a report is then sent back to the court, and the case is discontinued at that time. If the youth has difficulty, a petition may be filed with the court, and the youth may be held for further adjudication.

Consent Decree

Consent decrees are intermediate steps between informal handling and probation, and they are used to place the child under the jurisdiction of the court without a finding that the child is delinquent. Generally, a consent decree requires the child to agree to fulfill certain conditions in spite of the fact that he or she has not been found guilty. For informal sanctions, see Focus on Law 5–4.

FOCUS ON LAW
INFORMAL SANCTIONS

5–4

Informal processing usually is considered when the decision makers (such as the police, intake workers, probation officers, prosecutors, or other screening officers) believe that accountability and rehabilitation can be achieved without intervention from formal courts.

Informal sanctions are voluntary and, therefore, a juvenile cannot be forced to comply with an informal disposition. If a court decides to handle a matter informally (in lieu of formal prosecution), a youthful offender at that time has to agree to comply with one or more sanctions. These sanctions could include voluntary probation supervision, community service, and victim restitution. In some jurisdictions, the youth not only has to agree to sanctions but also has to agree that he or she committed the alleged act.

A case that is informally handled is usually held open pending the successful completion of the informal disposition. After the agreement on sanctions and the completion of this disposition, the charges against the offender are dismissed. But if the offender does not fulfill the court's conditions for informal handling, the case is likely to be reopened and formally prosecuted.

Informal handling has become less common but still occurs in a large number of cases. According to Juvenile Court Statistics 1996, 44 percent of delinquency cases disposed in 1996 were handled informally, compared with more than half in 1987.

Source: Howard N. Snyder and Melissa Sickmund, *Juvenile Offenders and Victims: A National Report* (Washington, DC: Office of Juvenile Justice and Delinquency Prevention, 1995), 159.

Critical Thinking Questions:
What is your evaluation of informal sanctions? What do you see as their strengths and weaknesses?

The intake officer can choose to file a petition if none of these options is satisfactory. There is some evidence that the broad discretionary power given to intake workers is sometimes abused. For example, Duran Bell, Jr., and Kevin Lang's study of intake in Los Angeles found that some extralegal factors, especially cooperative behavior, are important in reducing the length of detention.[58]

THE TRANSFER PROCEDURE

Some critics contend that the juvenile court should only work with youths who fall into the dependent/neglected and victimized/abused categories, not with those who violate the criminal code. These latter offenders, some critics believe, should be dealt with by adult courts.[59] They argue that the juvenile court not only has failed in its rehabilitative mission, but is relatively powerless to effect change in more seasoned and hard-core youthful offenders. Thus, the critics insist that offenders who commit felonies should be subject to the same punishments as adults. The popularity of this position led to an increase in the number of youths transferred to adult court in the past decade (see Chapter 7 for an expanded discussion and evaluation of transfer to adult court).

PLEA BARGAINING

Plea bargaining is increasingly emerging as an important issue in juvenile justice. One juvenile probation officer noted, "When I was a juvenile probation officer in a mid-sized urban county in Pennsylvania, many, if not most, of the cases were plea bargained."[60] Although little is known about how often or when it occurs, the increased trend toward "criminalization" of the juvenile court makes it likely that plea bargaining will come under increased scrutiny.[61]

A **plea bargain** is a deal made between the prosecutor and the defense attorney. The defense attorney, after consultation with his or her client, agrees that the client will admit to committing a lesser offense if the prosecutor will drop the more serious charges. The client receives a lighter sentence, and the necessity of having an adjudicatory hearing is avoided. The caseload of the court is thereby reduced.[62]

Critics of plea bargaining are concerned with its fairness. Their fear is that juveniles who are innocent of any wrongdoing may plead guilty to a lesser offense for fear that they will receive a harsh sentence if tried and found guilty of the more serious offense. This obviously is unfair to the innocent; even guilty youths may be subjected to inappropriate community referrals or placements if care is not taken to place them wisely. In addition, truly violent and dangerous youths may be able to negotiate a release back into the community when they should in all probability be placed in secure institutions. The problem at this time is that few guidelines exist to help direct prosecutors and defense attorneys in plea bargaining.

✓**Progress Check 5.2**
Review this section at
www.prenhall.com/bartollas

SUMMARY

- The philosophy of the juvenile court ever since it was founded in 1899 has been to help youths in need.
- The early reformers believed firmly that putting youths in facilities with adults was inappropriate and harmful.
- Reformers also believed that because youths were young and needed help, the juvenile court could not be modeled after the adult criminal courts.
- Their response was to staff the juvenile court with helping personnel and to develop procedures that protected youths from the more stigmatizing, and thus harmful, effects of adult trials and commitments to adult prisons.

- The procedures that were developed were made informal, court staff were given much discretion in how they handled cases, and any youth who came before the court was treated for his or her problems.
- The juvenile court was strongly criticized over the years because critics felt that it was overstepping its mission by attempting to address all youth crime.
- Critics further disparaged the informal procedures and discretion afforded court personnel and deplored the quality of the services offered by the court.
- Other critics simply contended that the juvenile court was ineffective and could not deal with the increasing number of hardened juvenile offenders.
- Two trends have resulted from these criticisms: The first trend has been to formalize the procedures of the juvenile court, which guarantees juveniles more due process rights in an effort to keep them from being unfairly and unjustly processed through the system.
- The second trend has been to waive juveniles to adult court through various legislative and judicial waiver provisions and through giving adult and juvenile courts concurrent jurisdiction. This trend is supported by those who want to subject juveniles to the same punishments as adults.
- The idea is to deter offenders from committing more crimes and to set an example for those who have not yet violated the law. The goal is to reduce the interventions of the juvenile court with minor offenders and perhaps with status offenders.
- Thus, while some today would prefer that the juvenile court retain its original mission, the juvenile court is in the midst of conflict and change.
- The resolutions of the current debate will have long-term repercussions for juvenile justice in the United States. It is hoped that the juvenile court will survive; the eternal optimism found in this nation that we can make a difference in the lives of children must remain a vital force in juvenile justice.

WEB SITES OF INTEREST

Information and links on the juvenile court process and related subjects can be found at

http://www.wiu.edu/library/govpubs/guides/p&cjuven.htm

To find general information as well as an overview of one juvenile court, go to

http://www.superiorcourt.maricopa.gov/juvenile/Court

CRITICAL THINKING QUESTIONS

1. Trace the development of the juvenile court.
2. What is preventive detention? What is your evaluation of this movement in juvenile justice?
3. What role does plea bargaining play in juvenile court proceedings? What is your evaluation of plea bargaining?
4. Do you think the juvenile court should be changed? Why? How?

NOTES

1. Quoted in Julian W. Mack, "The Juvenile Court," in *Readings in Juvenile Justice Administration*, edited by Barry C. Feld (New York: Oxford University Press, 1999), 15–16.

2. G. Larry Mays, "Transferring Juveniles to Adult Courts: Legal Guidelines and Constraints," paper presented at the annual meeting of the American Society of Criminology, Reno, Nevada (November 1989), 1.

3. *Commonwealth v. Fisher,* 213 P. 48, 62 A, 198–200.

4. Leonard P. Edwards, "The Juvenile Court and the Role of the Juvenile Court Judge," *National Council of Juvenile and Family Court Judges* 43 (1992), 4.

5. Barry Krisberg, *The Juvenile Court: Reclaiming the Vision* (San Francisco: National Council on Crime and Delinquency, 1988); Arnold Binder, "The Juvenile Court: The U.S. Constitution, and When the Twain Shall Meet," *Journal of Criminal Justice* 12 (1982), 355–66; and Charles E. Springer, *Justice for Children* (Washington, DC: U.S. Department of Justice, 1986).

6. Barry C. Feld, "The Transformation of the Juvenile Court," *Minnesota Law Review* 75 (February 1991), 711; Barry C. Feld, "The Juvenile Court Meets the Principle of the Offense: Legislative Changes in Juvenile Waiver Statutes," *Journal of Criminal Law and Criminology* 78 (1987), 571–73; and Barry C. Feld, "*In re Gault* Revisited: The Right to Counsel in the Juvenile Court," paper presented at the annual meeting of the American Society of Criminology, Montreal (November 1988).

7. Ellen Ryerson, *The Best Laid Plans: America's Juvenile Court Experiment* (New York: Hill and Wang, 1978), 574–575.

8. *Kent v. United States,* 383 U.S. 541, 86 S. Ct. 1045, 16 L. Ed. 2d 84 (1966).

9. Ibid.

10. Ibid.

11. *In re Gault,* 387 U.S. 1, 18 L. Ed. 527, 87 S. Ctg. 1428 (1967).

12. Ibid.

13. *Haley v. Ohio,* 332 U.S. 596 (1948); *Gallegos v. Colorado,* 370 U.S. 49, 82, S. Ct. 1209 (1962); and *Kent v. United States.*

14. Noah Weinstein, *Supreme Court Decisions and Juvenile Justice* (Reno, NV: National Council of Juvenile Court Judges, 1973).

15. *In re Winship,* 397 U.S. 358, 90 S. Ct. 1968, 25 L. Ed. 2d 368 (1970).

16. *McKeiver v. Pennsylvania,* 403 U.S. 528, 535 (1971). *In re Barbara Burrus,* 275 N.C. 517, 169 S.E. 2d 879 (1969).

17. Ibid.

18. 421 U.S. 519, 95 S. Ct. 1779 (1975).

19. See Chris E. Marshall, Ineke Haen Marshall, and Charles W. Thomas, "The Implementation of Formal Procedures in Juvenile Court Processing of Status Offenders," *Journal of Criminal Justice* 11 (1983), 195–211.

20. See Clemens Bartollas, Stuart J. Miller, and Simon Dinitz, *Juvenile Victimization: The Institutional Paradox* (New York: Halsted Press, 1976).

21. Charles W. Thomas, "Are Status Offenders Really So Different?: A Comparative and Longitudinal Assessment," *Crime and Delinquency* 22 (October 1976), 440–42.

22. P. Erickson, "Some Empirical Questions Concerning the Current Revolution in Juvenile Justice," in *The Future of Childhood and Juvenile Justice,* edited by LeMar Empey (Charlottesville: University of Virginia Press, 1979).

23. Solomon Kobrin, Frank R. Hellum, and John W. Peterson, "Offense Patterns of Status Offenders," in *Critical Issues in Juvenile Delinquency,* edited by David Shichor and Delos H. Kelley (Lexington, MA: D. C. Heath, 1980), 211.

24. Thomas C. Castellano, "The Justice Model in the Juvenile Justice System: Washington State's Experience," *Law and Policy* 8 (October 1986), 479–506.

25. Thomas J. Bernard, *The Cycle of Juvenile Justice* (New York: Oxford University Press, 1992), 28.

26. U.S. Congress, Senate Committee on the Judiciary, Subcommittee to Investigate Juvenile Delinquency, 1973, *The Juvenile Justice and Delinquency Prevention Act,* S.3148 and S.821. 92d Cong. 2d. sess.; 93d Cong., 1st sess.

27. National Council on Juvenile Justice, *National Juvenile Court Case Records 1975–1992* (Pittsburgh: National Center for Juvenile Justice, 1994).

28. Thomas, "Are Status Offenders Really So Different?," 440–42.

29. Martin Rouse, "The Diversion of Status Offenders, Criminalization, and the New York Family Court," paper presented at the annual meeting of the American Society of Criminology, Reno, Nevada (November 1989), 1, 2, 10–11.

30. Ibid.

31. Howard N. Snyder and Melissa Sickmund, *Juvenile Offenders and Victims: A National Report* (Pittsburgh: National Center for Juvenile Justice, 1995), 138.

32. For a more expansive examination of juvenile court personnel, especially the juvenile court judge, see Ted. H. Rubin, *Behind the Black Robes: Juvenile Court Judges and the Court* (Beverly Hills, CA: Sage Publications, 1985); Ted. H. Rubin, "The Juvenile Court Landscape," in *Juvenile Justice: Policies, Programs, and Services,* edited by Albert R. Roberts (Chicago: Dorsey Press, 1989); and Leonard P. Edwards, "The Juvenile Court and the Role of the Juvenile Court Judge," *National Council of Juvenile and Family Court Judges* 43 (1992), 4.

33. Edwards, "The Juvenile Court and the Role of the Juvenile Court Judge," 25.

34. Ibid., 25–28.

35. Larry J. Siegel and Joseph J. Senna, *Juvenile Delinquency: Theory, Practice, and Law,* 7th ed. (Belmont, CA: Wadsworth, 2000), 559.

36. See Floyd Feeney, "Defense Counsel for Delinquents: Does Quality Matter?," paper presented at the annual meeting of the American Society of Criminology, Montreal (November 1987).

37. Barry Feld, "Criminalizing Juvenile Justice: Rules of Procedure for Juvenile Court," *Minnesota Law Review* 69 (1984), 191, 199.

38. Ted H. Rubin, *Juvenile Justice: Policy, Practice, and the Law* (Santa Monica, CA: Goodyear, 1979), 194.

39. See Charles Thomas and Ineke Marshall, "The Effect of Legal Representation on Juvenile Court Disposition," paper presented at the annual meeting of the Southern Sociological Society, Louisville, Kentucky, 1981; and S. H. Clarke and G. G. Koch, "Juvenile Court: Therapy or Crime Control and Do Lawyers Make a Difference?," *Law and Society Review* 14 (1980), 263–308.

40. Ibid.

41. Joseph B. Sanborn, Jr., *Crime and Delinquency* 40, 4 ("Remnants of *Parens Patriae* in the Adjudication Hearing–Is a Fair Trial Possible in Juvenile Court?," 1994), 599–615.

42. Ibid., 157.

43. Siegel and Senna, *Juvenile Delinquency,* 561.

44. For other examinations of the prosecutor's role in the juvenile court, see John H. Laub and Bruce K. MacMurray, "Increasing the Prosecutor's Role in Juvenile Court: Expectation and Realities," *Justice System Journal* 12 (1987), 196–209; and Charles W. Thomas and Shay Bilchik, "Prosecuting Juveniles in Criminal Courts: Legal and Empirical Analysis," *Journal of Criminal Law and Criminology* 76 (1985), 438–79.

45. Lori L. Colley, Robert C. Culbertson, and Edward J. Latessa, "Juvenile Probation Officers: A Job Analysis," *Juvenile and Family Court Journal* 38 (1987), 1–12.

46. Ann Strong, *Case Classification Manual, Module One: Technical Aspects of Interviewing* (Austin: Texas Adult Probation Commission, 1981).

47. Charles Puzzanchera, Anne L. Stahl, Melissa Sickmund, Terrence A. Finnegan, Howard N. Snyder, Rowen S. Poole, and Nancy Tierney, *Juvenile Court Statistics* (Pittsburgh: National Center for Juvenile Justice, 2000), 6 (online at http://www.ncjrs.gov/html/ojjdp/jcs_1997/contents.html).

48. Howard N. Snyder and Melissa Sickmund, *Juvenile Offenders and Victims: 2006 National Report* (Washington, DC: National Center for Juvenile Justice, Office of Justice Programs, and Office of Juvenile Justice and Delinquency Prevention, 2006), 166.

49. Brenda R. McCarthy, "An Analysis of Detention," *Juvenile and Family Court Journal* 36 (1985), 49–50. For other discussions of detention, see Lydia Rosner, "Juvenile Secure Detention," *Journal of Offender Counseling, Services, and Rehabilitation* 12 (1988), 77–93; and Charles E. Frazier and Donna M. Bishop, "The Pretrial Detention of Juveniles and Its Impact on Case Dispositions," *Journal of Criminal Law and Criminology* 76 (1985), 1132–52.

50. Charles P. Smith, T. Edwin Black, and Fred R. Campbell, *A National Assessment of Case Disposition and Classification in the Juvenile Justice System: Inconsistent Labeling,* Vol. III, Reports of the National Juvenile Justice Assessment Centers (Washington, DC: Government Printing Office, April 1980), 97.

51. For a discussion of the use of bail for juveniles in Massachusetts, see Alida V. Merlo and William D. Bennett, "Criteria for Juvenile Detention: Who Gets Detained?," paper presented at the annual meeting of the American Society of Criminology, Reno, Nevada (November 1989).

52. Ibid.

53. *Schall v. Martin* (1984), *United States Law Review* 52 (47), 4681–96.

54. Ibid., 4681.

55. Ibid.

56. Barry C. Feld, "Criminalizing Juvenile Justice: Rules of Procedure for Juvenile Court," *Minnesota Law Review* 69 (1984), 191, 199. See also Deborah A. Lee, "The Constitutionality of Juvenile Preventive Detention: *Schall v. Martin:* Who Is Preventive Detention Protecting?" *New England Law Review* 38 (1987), 13–19.

57. See the section on intake in Patrick Griffin and Patricia Torget, *Desktop Guide to Good Juvenile Probation Practice* (Washington, DC: National Center for Juvenile Justice, 2002), 41–48.

58. Bell and Lang, "The Intake Dispositions of Juvenile Offenders," 309–28. See also Randall G. Sheldon and John A. Horvath, "Intake Processing in a Juvenile Court: A Comparison of Legal and Nonlegal Variables," *Juvenile and Family Court Journal* 38 (1987), 13–19.

59. Samuel M. Davis, *Rights of Juveniles: The Juvenile Justice System* (New York: Clark Boardman, 1984). Reprinted with Permission of West, a Thompson Business (St. Paul, MN: Updated March 2003), 4–26, 4–27. See also Barry C. Feld, "The Transformation of the Juvenile Court," *Minnesota Law Review* 75 (February 1991), 711; Barry C. Feld, "The Juvenile Court Meets the Principle of the Offense: Legislative Changes in Juvenile Waiver Statutes," *Journal of Criminal Law and Criminology* 78 (1987), 571–73.

60. Conversation with this officer in 1990.

61. For an excellent discussion of the "criminalization" of the juvenile court, see Feld, "Criminalizing Juvenile Justice," 141–276.

62. Joyce Dougherty, "Negotiating Justice in the Juvenile Justice System: A Comparison of Adult Plea Bargaining and Juvenile Intake," *Federal Probation* 52 (1988), 72–80.

6

THE JUVENILE COURT
Trial and Disposition

As the juvenile court approaches its 100th birthday . . . its future is less secure than at any point in its history. Recent increases in juvenile violent crime, including historic increases in juvenile homicides, have led politicians to "reform" the court by passing laws which minimize the court's jurisdiction, including a new wave of laws that transfer more juveniles, at younger ages, into the adult criminal court system. In most cases, these youthful offenders, once transferred, are treated no differently from adults. In fact, "reforms" in the sentencing of adult offenders, like mandatory minimum sentencing and "truth-in-sentencing," have made it increasingly common for youthful offenders to receive long incarcerative sentences in adult correctional facilities. In this rush to punish and incapacitate youthful offenders, policy makers have given less and less weight to the developmental perspective that led to the creation of separate courts and treatment interventions for juveniles and adults.[1]

OUTLINE

OBJECTIVES

1. To discuss the various stages of juvenile court proceedings
2. To consider judicial alternatives in the dispositional stage and the right to appeal
3. To evaluate the various sentencing structures for juveniles
4. To examine the feasibility of maintaining a separate court for juveniles

KEY TERMS

adjudicatory hearing

disposition hearing

National Council of Juvenile and
Family Court Judges

Thomas F. Geraghty and Steven A. Drizin, in the introduction to a symposium on the future of the juvenile court presented in the chapter-opening quote, suggest that the future of the juvenile court "is less secure than at any point in its history." They state that part of the problem relates to the perceived seriousness of juvenile crime, and part of the problem is found in a "get tough" attitude that is affecting the handling of juvenile as well as adult crime. In Donna Martin Hamparian and colleagues' study of dangerous juvenile offenders, they contend that another aspect of the problem is the need for an overhaul of the juvenile justice system:

> Troubled young people are responding to the troubles of our times. The overloaded juvenile justice system has responded erratically to them, mixing hostility with understanding, callous harshness with unreasoned lenience, and obsolete notions about human behavior with the insights of the latest research. In the most literal sense of the cliché, the juvenile justice system is much more a part of the problem than a part of the solution. The need for an overhaul is sensed everywhere, but prescriptions for change have not emerged from the incessant discussion of the issues.[2]

WHAT ARE OTHER STAGES OF JUVENILE COURT PROCEEDINGS?

After the pretrial procedures (discussed in Chapter 5), the adjudicatory hearing, or the fact-finding stage, and the disposition hearing are the two remaining stages of the juvenile proceedings.

ADJUDICATORY HEARING

The **adjudicatory hearing** for juveniles is equivalent to the trial in adult court. It is the point at which the judge reviews the charges as described in the petition, hears testimony from the parties involved, and decides whether the youth committed the offense.

Adjudicatory hearings today are a blend of the old and the new. First, the hearings are still somewhat less formal than the adult trial. Second, the hearings are closed in order to protect the juvenile's name and reputation in the community. Third, some juvenile courts, because they disagree strongly with the recent Supreme Court decisions, tend to ignore the new standards and operate much as in the past. Little change has occurred in these courts.

On the other side of the ledger, most states now spell out their procedural requirements very carefully. For example, all juveniles now have the right to a hearing, which is likely to be much more formal than in the past. Written petitions are required, and these may be amended if necessary. Hearsay is prohibited, and the case must be proved beyond a reasonable doubt. Youths have the right to protect themselves against self-incrimination, and they may cross-examine witnesses and victims. Attorneys and prosecutors are likely to be present. Finally, some state codes call for a separation of the adjudication and disposition hearings.

If an attorney has not been appointed or retained by the juvenile by this point in time, one will be appointed by the court and, hopefully, the date of the hearing reset to allow the attorney time to talk to the youth, review the case, and prepare the defense. Some courts may assign a public defender to the youth, allow the defender a couple of minutes to read the documents and talk with the youth, and go immediately into the adjudication hearing.

The **National Council of Juvenile and Family Court Judges** recommends that a script similar to that in Focus on Law 6–1 be used by the judge to ensure that the due process rights of the juvenile are maintained. These due process rights are given the juvenile as a result of the *Kent, Gault, Winship, Breed v. Jones*, and *McKeiver* cases (see Chapter 5 for a review of these cases).

If the youth's attorney and the prosecutor have agreed upon a plea bargain, the agreement is presented to the judge at this time. If the judge accepts the plea bargain, the judge will issue a predisposition at this time, a process called a *sequential hearing*, and immediately assign a disposition in the case that will likely parallel those the juvenile may already have experienced earlier in his or her career. If the judge rejects the plea bargain, the adjudicatory hearing continues.

FOCUS ON LAW   **6–1**
LEGAL RIGHTS OF THE JUVENILE

Juvenile Delinquency Court Judge: "I am now going to advise you of your legal rights:"

1. A petition has been filed against you, and it says that you (explain the offense).
2. Do you understand what you are charged with?
3. You have the right against self-incrimination. This means that you do not have to say anything about your part in the charges or even whether you were anywhere near where the charges happened if you do not want to. If you do choose to talk about it, what you say can be used against you. Do you have any question about what this means?
4. You have the opportunity to either admit to the charges if they are true or to deny the charges if they are not true. If you deny the charges, there will be a trial to determine whether or not the charges are true. At the trial, you have the right to:

   - Confront witnesses [who] testify against you, which means your attorney gets to ask them questions to try and show that the charges are not true. Do you have any questions about what this means?
   - Compel witnesses, which means the court can require a person who your attorney thinks can help you show [that] the charges are not true to come to court and tell what they know. However, you are not required to bring any witnesses. Do you have any questions about what this means?
   - You can choose to testify or not to testify at the trial. You can remain silent and not say anything if you want. If you decide not to testify, your choice will not be held against you. Do you have any questions about what this means?

- If you admit the charges, or if I find you are guilty at the trial, by law I can (explain what dispositions can be imposed). Do you have any questions about what this means?

5. Do you admit or deny the charges? Are the charges true or not true?

   If the youth denies the charge, proceed to set the trial date and deal with all pre-trial isues.

   If the youth admits the charges . . .

   - Do you understand that in saying the charges are true, you are giving up your right to a trial, which means you are also giving up your right to confront wit-ness[es], make witness[es] testify for you, and to remain silent about the charges?

   - Has anyone made any threats or promises to you to get you to do this?

   - Have you taken any drugs, medicine, or alcohol within the last 24 hours? (If the youth answer yes, the judge must explore further to determine if the drug currently impairs the youth, which would mean [that] the plea should not be accepted.)

   - Are you admitting these charges to benefit yourself and nobody else?

   - At the time you did this, you know those things were wrong?

     If the youth's answers support a plea of admit, the judge should ask the par-ent, custodian, or [person acting] *in loco parentis* whether they know of any rea-son that the judge should not accept the plea.

If the judge accepts the plea, the judge should call on the youth to explain what happened in detail. If the youth's explanation indicates that he or she is not really admitting to the offense, the judge should consider withdrawing the acceptance of the plea and setting the case for trial.

Source: National Council of Juvenile and Family Court Judges, *Juvenile Delinquency Guidelines* (Reno, NV: 2005), Appendix.

Critical Thinking Questions:

How are the juvenile's due process rights protected by such a script? Do you believe that most youthful offenders appearing before the court in an adjudicatory hearing have any understanding of what the script means?

The length of the hearings varies throughout the country from a "five-minute children's hour" to a full hour or more, possibly with continuances, if more evidence such as forensic data or social service agency data are needed. During the hearing, the prosecutor will present the facts of the case, the defense will present the youth's side of the story, and the parents will be asked for their input, as will the probation officer and the victim. In some jurisdic-tions today, the judge will render a verdict immediately after the conclusion of the trial. More and more jurisdictions, however, are setting a date for a dis-position hearing, often within ten days to two weeks after the adjudicatory hearing. The reason for this time frame is to keep all hearings as close to the time the offense was committed as possible in order to have the maximum impact on the juvenile.

In some jurisdictions, it is possible for juveniles to receive a jury trial. Twelve states presently mandate a jury trial for juveniles who request one dur-ing their adjudicatory hearings and who face the possibility of institutional confinement. But twenty-three states deny juveniles the right to a jury trial. South Dakota is the only state of the remaining ones that specifies whether ju-veniles are entitled to jury trial. In that state, a juvenile court order is required for a jury trial to be conducted in juvenile court.[3]

DISPOSITION HEARING

Disposition hearings, which are equivalent to sentencing in adult courts, are of two basic types. The first type, which is used less and less frequently in the United States, occurs at the same time as the adjudicatory hearing. The judge, after hearing the case and discussing it with the youth, the youth's parents, the prosecutor, and the defense attorney, reviews the social service report submitted by a probation officer and decides what disposition would be most effective for the youth.

The second type of disposition hearing occurs following the adjudicatory hearing. This *bifurcated system*, as it is sometimes called, has different evidentiary rules than are used in the single adjudicatory hearing. In the adjudicatory hearing, for example, the standard of "proof beyond a reasonable doubt" requires stringent rules and a limiting of the kinds of information that may be introduced. The dispositional hearing, however, calls for the judge to have as wide a range of information as possible concerning the youth; this often involves information that would be inadmissable or inappropriate in the adjudicatory hearing.[4]

The reason for separating the two hearings is to prevent judges from learning information that is prejudicial to the defendant. In a combined hearing, the judge may discover information that is not relevant to the case but nevertheless biases his or her finding of guilt or innocence. If the judge does not receive this extraneous information until after the finding of guilt, the defendant is protected from being found guilty on the basis of information unrelated to the specific allegation.

Predisposition Report

Another advantage of the bifurcated system is that it gives the probation department time to make a more comprehensive study of the youth's needs and background than is possible when presentencing reports are given at the time of the adjudicatory hearing. This, too, increases the amount of information available to the judge in making a disposition decision.

Predisposition reports are essential to defendants, defense attorneys, prosecutors, probation departments, and judges. California and Maryland Supreme Courts, in fact, have overturned lower court decisions because judges have not held dispositional hearings to consider relevant sentencing information.[5] This information is crucial because the reports contain background information on defendants that helps judges make individualized decisions.

The social work perspective has helped shape the way caseworkers and probation officers develop the predisposition reports. Since the 1920s, for example, the court has used psychiatric and psychological information obtained from existing school, social agency, and medical records. If such information is not available but is believed necessary, probation officers may refer juveniles for appropriate medical, psychological, or psychiatric evaluations to determine whether they are mentally ill or restricted. Other information is collected from law enforcement agencies, social service agencies that have dealt with the juvenile previously, the juvenile, and the juvenile's family, friends, and neighbors. The object is to collect any and all information that might be relevant to the case.[6]

The written report, then, contains a description of the referral incident as well as the youth's past conduct, prior contacts with the police and courts, and family environment and relationships. Information on the youth's employment history, school records, interests, and activities is also collected. If police officers have information on special problems of the youth or if special needs of the youth are discovered, these, too, are included in the report.

In this more formal courtroom setting, the judge is hearing testimony from a police officer and an offender who is accompanied by her parent. (Photo by Stuart Miller.)

Once the fact finding is completed, probation officers recommend a course of action to the court. The predisposition report draws up a plan for what the youth needs and how he or she can best be helped. The report is submitted to the judge, who reviews the report for the dispositional hearing and usually follows the advice given in the report. The juvenile has the right to be present at this hearing.

Both formal and informal factors influence decision making at the dispositional stage. The most important formal factors are the recommendation of the probation officer and the information contained in the social study investigation, or predisposition report; the seriousness of the delinquent offense; the juvenile's previous contact with the court; and the available options. Although the recommendation of the probation officer is usually followed by the juvenile judge, the seriousness of the delinquent behavior and the previous contacts with the court probably have the greatest impact on judicial decision making at this stage.[7] M. A. Bortner found from his examination of disposition decision making in a large midwestern county that age, prior referrals, and the detention decision were the most important influences.[8]

The informal factors that sometimes influence judicial decision making include the values and philosophy of the judge, the social and racial background of the youth, the youth's demeanor, the presence or absence of defense counsel, and political repercussions of the alleged delinquent acts. The most disturbing of these informal factors relate to the social and racial background of the youth. Ruth D. Peterson found that racial, ethnic, gender, and age disparities affected the disposition of older adolescents in New York State courts. Although race and ethnicity did not significantly influence disposition decisions in New York City, minority juveniles tended to be stereotyped and to receive harsh treatment outside the city.[9]

JUDICIAL ALTERNATIVES

Dispositions vary according to whether children are adjudicated delinquent, in need of supervision, abandoned/neglected, runaway, or abused/victimized. Some cases are dismissed. This may occur either as the adjudicatory hearing is beginning or as late as after the child has been found guilty of the charge. The judge may decide that the child's family environment, special circumstances, or other factors are such that the child may be sent home with his or her parents.

In other cases the child is assessed a fine or ordered to pay restitution to the victim. Parents, of course, usually end up paying the fine or restitution, but juveniles frequently are required to work for the victim or do community service in order to pay back the community.

Youths who are mentally restricted or mentally ill are sometimes required to undergo special training or therapy. Some larger courts in urban areas have their own clinics, but youths commonly are sent to community clinics, to private psychologists or psychiatrists, or to family services programs. Status offenders, minor delinquents, runaways, or youths who have been physically or sexually abused may be referred to these programs. Middle-class offenders appear to have greater access to these programs than do lower-class youths. One reason for this is the belief that middle-class offenders have more support at home. In this regard, the greater availability of programs to middle-class youths shows the biases of the system against lower-class youths.

Probation is used when youths are found guilty of an offense and in need of supervision but not secure confinement. The youths are released back to their parents and community under conditions stipulated by the court and are supervised by probation officers or court volunteers. A violation of the conditions laid down by the court may result in the youth being held in contempt of court and placed in a secure facility. For the most part, however, the courts direct the youths to any of a wide variety of community agencies for needed treatment. What is problematic about this approach is that communities vary widely in the quality and availability of services. For high-risk youths, some communities have intensive probation programs, in-house detention, and even electronic monitoring devices.

A much more severe disposition is to remove youths from their natural homes. This most often occurs when parents neglect or abuse their children or are in some other way unable to provide them with adequate care. These youngsters are placed in foster homes for short or extended periods of time, depending on their problems. A less extreme variation is to put the youths in day treatment programs. Youths are required to attend a structured program during the day but are allowed to return home in the evening.

Youths are removed from their homes in community-based correctional programs as well. These range from minimum-security facilities such as group homes and halfway houses to more secure homelike facilities. Whereas some of these homes are used simply for feeding and housing juveniles who need shelter, other homes offer specialized services for drug addicts, alcoholics, and mentally ill or mentally disturbed youths. Not surprisingly, people who live near such facilities often resist the placement of these homes in their local communities; they are afraid that the youths who live there will get into trouble and be a bad influence on their own children.

Judges occasionally use mental hospitals for placements. Some youths are confined in mental hospitals at the time of intake for evaluation, but these stays are fairly short, ranging from several to ninety days. After adjudication, youths may be confined until they either are ready for community living or, if necessary, reach the age of maturity.

Another kind of facility found in some parts of the country are county or city institutions. These are often fairly new facilities constructed because of the inadequacy of older county jails and detention centers. Youths who do not need placement in state training schools may be placed in these institutions for short periods of time.

The most secure juvenile facilities used by judges are state training schools. These range from minimum-security forestry camps and ranches to maximum-security training schools. In jurisdictions where juvenile judges have the authority to commit a youth to an institution rather than to the state correctional agency, judges will usually place the less serious of these offenders in medium- or minimum-security forestry camps and ranches. Maximum-security institutions are especially foreboding: They are often surrounded by high fences and barbed wire; steel bars and doors and heavy screens govern exits and entrances, and staff are extremely security conscious. The youths in these institutions typically have committed serious, repetitive, or violent offenses, but status and minor offenders also are occasionally placed in them.

Finally, some states permit juvenile judges to place youths in adult institutions. This practice has been used when youths presented a danger to themselves, other residents, or the staff or were serious escape risks. But this practice has basically ceased for two reasons. First, the "mutual compact theory of *parens patriae*" argues that juveniles give up due process rights in exchange for treatment by the juvenile court.[10] On this basis, the Vermont Supreme Court ruled in *In re Rich* that the state has to treat juveniles rather than transfer them to an adult facility because to do otherwise would subvert the mission of the juvenile court.[11]

Second, the Vermont Supreme Court also pointed out in *In re Rich* that transfer is unconstitutional if the juvenile has not received all of his or her due process rights at a legal hearing.[12] Thus, to the extent that juveniles today are not given all the rights accorded adults, their transfer to an adult institution would undoubtedly be ruled unconstitutional by the reviewing courts.

WHAT RIGHT DOES THE JUVENILE HAVE TO APPEAL?

Juveniles do not yet have a constitutional right to appeal. Nevertheless, practically all states grant them the right to appeal by statute for some of the following reasons. The states are following the lead of the U.S. Supreme Court. The Court pointed out in *Gault* that juveniles should have the same absolute right as adults have to appeal under the equal protection clause of the Constitution. Since that ruling, most state legislatures have passed laws granting juveniles the right to appeal. In addition, state courts have ruled that statutes granting the right to appeal for juveniles must be applied uniformly to all juveniles; this decision effectively undermines the tradition in some courts of giving judges the discretion to determine which juvenile cases could be appealed. The common practice today is to give juveniles the same rights to appeal as adults are given.[13]

The right to appeal is for the most part limited to juveniles and their parents. States may appeal in some circumstances, but this right is seldom exercised and few such cases have come before the courts. Some variation exists in the types of orders that may be appealed. States generally permit the appeal of "final" orders, although what is final varies from state to state. For example, some states authorize juvenile courts to order juveniles to be confined in secure facilities for a period of time. That is a final order. Nevertheless, certain states permit the youth or his or her parents to appeal that final order. States also vary in how they handle appeals. Most state statutes call for the case to be appealed to an appellate court, but a few states call for a completely new trial. Other common statutory rights of juveniles at appeal are the right to a transcript of the case and the right to counsel.[14]

WHAT IS THE JUVENILE SENTENCING STRUCTURE?

Determinate sentencing is a new form of sentencing in juvenile justice and is replacing in some jurisdictions the traditional form of indeterminate sentencing. In addition, increasing numbers of juvenile courts are using a "blended" form of sentencing.

Criticism of the decision making of the juvenile court has increased in the past twenty years. Early on, the criticism focused on the arbitrary nature of the decision making that violated the due process rights of juveniles; more recently, this criticism has been based on the belief that the juvenile court is too "soft" on crime. This latter criticism, especially, has led to a number of procedures that change sentencing and other juvenile procedures.

One of the first efforts at reform was the Juvenile Justice Standards Project, jointly sponsored by the Institute of Judicial Administration and the American Bar Association. Officially launched in 1971 by a national planning committee under the chairmanship of Judge Irving R. Kaufman, comprehensive guidelines for juvenile offenders were designed that would base sentences on the seriousness of the crime rather than on the needs of the youth. The proposed guidelines represented radical philosophical changes and still are used by proponents to attempt to standardize the handling of juvenile lawbreakers.

The belief that disparity in juvenile sentencing must end was one of the fundamental thrusts of the recommended standards. To accomplish this goal, the commission attempted to limit the discretion of juvenile judges and to make them accountable for their decisions, which would then be subject to judicial review. Also important in the standards was the provision that certain court procedures would be open to the public, although the names of juveniles still would remain confidential.

At the beginning of the twenty-first century, juvenile court judges remain quite concerned about these proposed standards. Their basic concern is that these standards attack the underlying philosophy and structure of the juvenile court. Judges also are concerned about how these standards would limit their authority. They see the influence of the hardliners behind this movement toward standardization and feel that the needs of children will be neglected in the long run. They also challenge the idea that it is possible, much less feasible, to treat all children alike.

Nevertheless, the standards are being adopted across the nation. New York State was the first to act on them through the Juvenile Justice Reform Act of 1976, which went into effect on February 1, 1977. The act orders a determinate sentence of five years for Class A felonies, which include murder, first-degree kidnapping, and first-degree arson. The initial term can be extended by at least one year. The juvenile, according to the act, should be placed in a residential facility after the first year. Then, if approved by the director of the division, the confined youth can be placed in a nonresidential program for the remainder of the five-year term. But the youth must remain under intensive supervision for the entire five-year term.

In 1977, the state of Washington also created a determinate sentencing system for juveniles in line with the recommendations of the Juvenile Justice Standards

Project. Moreover, in the 1980s, a number of states stiffened juvenile court penalties for serious juvenile offenders, either by mandating minimum terms of incarceration (Colorado, Kentucky, and Idaho) or by enacting a comprehensive system of sentencing guidelines (Arizona, Georgia, and Minnesota).[15]

In 1995, the Texas legislature introduced such get tough changes in the juvenile justice system as lowering the age at which waiver could occur to fourteen-year-olds for capital, first-degree, and aggravated controlled-substance felony offenses and greatly expanding the determinate sentence statute that was first enacted in 1987. Under determinate sentences, any juvenile, regardless of age, can be sentenced for up to forty years in the Texas Youth Commission, with possible transfer to the Texas Department of Corrections. Finally, prosecutors can choose to pursue determinate sentence proceedings rather than delinquency proceedings, but they first must obtain grand jury approval.[16]

Daniel P. Mears and Samuel F. Field's examination of the determinate sentencing statute for Texas found that increased proceduralization and criminalization of juvenile courts did not eliminate consideration of age, gender, or race/ethnicity in sentencing decisions.[17]

In the 1990s, nearly every state enacted mandatory sentences for violent and repetitive juvenile offenders. The development of graduated, or accountability-based, sanctions was another means in the 1990s that states used to ensure that juveniles who are adjudicated delinquent receive an appropriate disposition by the juvenile court. Several states have created a blended sentencing structure for cases involving repeat and serious juvenile offenders. Blended sentences are a mechanism for holding those juveniles accountable for their offenses. This expanded sentencing authority allows criminal and juvenile courts to impose either juvenile or adult sentences, or at times both, in cases involving juveniles.[18]

Critical Thinking Question:
Which sentencing standards could best be required for all states?

WHAT WOULD JUSTICE FOR JUVENILES LOOK LIKE?

The rationale for handling most delinquents within the juvenile court is that there is no evidence that the adult system works any better with these youths than does the juvenile system. But to make a persuasive case for maintaining a separate juvenile justice system, children must receive fairness and justice in the juvenile court.

Thomas F. Geraghty's article "Justice for Children: How Do We Get There?" makes a powerful case for the retention of the juvenile court.[19] He contributes two basic arguments for retaining and strengthening juvenile courts rather than abolishing them. First, "criminal courts will never adapt themselves to the distinct challenges of doing justice for children." Second, "procedural protections (including the right to jury trial) could be provided in 're-tooled' juvenile courts without destroying the distinctive mission of juvenile courts."[20]

In turning to the reasons why reliance on criminal courts to try children would be an exercise in futility, Geraghty makes the following points:

a. The operations of criminal courts, especially in urban areas, fall short.
b. Children will be second-class citizens in criminal court.
c. Children will be subjected to the influence of adults charged with crimes tried in criminal court.

d. Jury trials conducted in criminal courts will be incomprehensible and intimidating to children.
e. Jury trials held in juvenile court need not be frightening and incomprehensible.
f. The legal culture of criminal courts will damage children.
g. Plea bargaining in adult court will be unfair to children.
h. Sentences in adult court will be too harsh, and the focus on the development of youth-oriented correctional systems will be abandoned.
i. Adult court judges, prosecutors, and defenders will not be child specialists.[21]

Geraghty's general suggestion for reinvigorating juvenile courts is that they "must preserve individualized decision making with respect to the culpability and developmental needs of children, while insisting on appropriate imposition of responsibility."[22] His specific suggestions include more dedicated and "concerted efforts to create and support excellent juvenile courts," increased attention "to accurate fact-finding during adjudication hearings," less reliance on plea bargaining, and improvement in "the quality of judging, lawyering, and social work in juvenile courts."[23] What Geraghty is proposing is a court with a child-centered focus that, at the same time, provides "fair, impartial, and informed adjudications and dispositions of cases."[24]

Other suggestions that seem to be in order for juveniles to receive justice in the juvenile court are the following:

1. The juvenile court should no longer have jurisdiction over status offenders.
2. Policymakers must implement monitoring procedures to ensure that the nonjudicial agencies designated for status offenders are providing adequate care.
3. Juveniles accused of crimes should have the same due process rights and procedural safeguards accorded to adults, with the exception that juveniles should have a nonwaivable right to counsel.[25]
4. The quality of representation in juvenile court hearings must be raised.
5. Plea bargaining must be avoided if at all possible. Urban courts will have difficulty operating without plea bargaining, but too many opportunities for abuse are present in this practice.
6. The control of prosecutors over juvenile court must be minimized.
7. A youthful offender system between the juvenile and adult justice systems should be implemented, and the juvenile court should retain supervision over youths placed in this system.
8. Mandatory sentences of hard-core juveniles must replace indeterminate sentencing. The process of institutional release in indeterminate sentencing results in decision making that is too frequently unfair to the juvenile.
9. The lengths of mandatory sentences are to be designed by the National Council of Juvenile Court Judges rather than by state legislatures.

TOWARD EXCELLENCE IN THE JUVENILE DELINQUENCY COURT

The National Council of Juvenile and Family Court Judges takes a somewhat broader approach by identifying the functions of the court and its judges. The Council believes that the juvenile court should have exclusive jurisdiction in

FOCUS ON PRACTICE   6–2
KEY PRINCIPLES OF A JUVENILE DELINQUENCY COURT OF EXCELLENCE

1. Juvenile delinquency court judges should engage in judicial leadership and encourage system collaboration
2. Juvenile delinquency systems must have adequate staff, facilities, and program resources
3. Juvenile delinquency courts and juvenile abuse and neglect courts should have integrated one family–one judge case assignments
4. Juvenile delinquency judges should have the same status as the highest level of trial court in the state and should have multiple year or permanent assignments
5. All members of the juvenile delinquency court shall treat youth, families, crime victims, witnesses, and others with respect, dignity, courtesy, and cultural understanding
6. Juvenile delinquency court judges should ensure [that] their systems divert cases to alternative systems whenever possible and appropriate
7. Youth charged in the formal juvenile delinquency court must have qualified and adequately compensated legal representation
8. Juvenile delinquency court judges should ensure [that] crime victims have access to all phases of the juvenile delinquency court process and receive all services to which they are entitled by law
9. Juvenile delinquency courts should render timely and just decisions and trials should conclude without continuances
10. Juvenile delinquency system staff should engage parents and families at all stages of the juvenile delinquency court process to encourage family members to participate fully in the development and implementation of the youth's intervention plan
11. The juvenile delinquency court should engage the school and other community support systems as stakeholders in each individual youth's case
12. Juvenile delinquency court judges should ensure [that] court dispositions are individualized and include graduated responses, both sanctions and incentives
13. Juvenile delinquency court judges should ensure [that] effective post-disposition review is provided to each delinquent youth as long as the youth is involved in any component of the juvenile justice system
14. Juvenile delinquency court judges should hold their systems and the systems of other juvenile delinquency court stakeholders accountable
15. Juvenile delinquency court judges should ensure [that] the court has an information system that can generate the data necessary to evaluate performance
16. The juvenile delinquency court judge is responsible to ensure that the judiciary, court staff, and all system participants are both individually trained and trained across systems and roles

Source: National Council of Juvenile and Family Court Judges, *Juvenile Delinquency Guidelines: Improving Court Practice in Juvenile Delinquency Cases* (Reno, NV: Summer 2005).

Critical Thinking Questions:
How do you evaluate these recommendations? Are they likely to be implemented in most jurisdictions across the nation? Why or why not?

all matters affecting juveniles and families in delinquency cases, should have the same status as general trial courts, and should have the power and authority to "order, enforce, and review delivery of court ordered services and treatment for children and families."[26]

To overcome the many different forms and practices it has developed over the last one hundred years, the National Council on Juvenile and Family Court Judges made recommendations in 2005 to promote the best practices of the juvenile court and its personnel across the country.[27] The goals that the Council set forth for the nation's juvenile courts are to:

- Increase safety in communities by supporting and implementing effective delinquency prevention strategies, as well as a continuum of effective and least intrusive responses to reduce recidivism;[28]
- Hold juvenile offenders accountable to their victims and community by enforcing completion of restitution and community service requirements; and[29]
- Develop competent and productive citizens by increasing the responsible living skills of youth within the jurisdiction of the juvenile delinquency court.[30]

✓**Progress Check 6.1**
Review this section at
www.prenhall.com/bartollas

Because of the numbers and qualifications of its many staff vary so widely and because procedures used by juvenile courts vary so much from jurisdiction to jurisdiction, the National Council on Juvenile and Family Court Judges has set forth what it considers the key standards that the juvenile court and all of its personnel should follow. See Focus on Practice 6–2.

SUMMARY

- Juvenile courts have improved, especially in ensuring constitutional rights to juveniles, but there are many who believe that their improvements have been too slow and too limited.
- Critics also find fault with the dispositions of the juvenile court, claiming that the dispositions are too soft and too heavily based on the need of juveniles. Instead, the courts ought to be concerned with justice for society, and this involves punishing juveniles appropriately for the seriousness of their offenses.
- Others focus their attention on the prevention and amelioration of juvenile problems. Subsequently, even though individualized sentencing structures on one level are giving way to mandatory and determinate sentencing structures imposed on the courts, the actual practice of using diversion and informal and formal probation practices also appears to be growing.
- A number of measures are being suggested that would ensure more justice for juveniles, but these have not yet been consistently adopted.

WEB SITE OF INTEREST

For publications of the National Center for Juvenile Justice, including *Juvenile Court Statistics*, see

http://ncjj.servehttp.com/NCJJWebsite/main.htm

CRITICAL THINKING QUESTIONS

1. Who are the judges of the juvenile court and what are their roles?
2. Discuss the adjudicatory hearing and the procedures followed in it.
3. Describe the disposition hearing and the role of the disposition report in that hearing.
4. Discuss the range of dispositions available to judges in the disposition hearings.
5. What are the basic arguments in favor of and in opposition to the retention of the juvenile court?

NOTES

1. Thomas F. Geraghty and Steven A. Drizin, "The Debate Over the Future of Juvenile Courts: Can We Reach *Consensus*?" *Journal of Criminal Law and Criminology* 88 (1998), 2–3.
2. Donna Martin Hamparian, Richard Schuster, Simon Dinitz, and John P. Conrad, *The Violent Few: A Study of Dangerous Juvenile Offenders* (Lexington, MA: Lexington Books, 1978), 1.
3. Kathleen Maguire and Ann L. Pastore, *Bureau of Justice Statistics: Sourcebook of Criminal Justice Statistics—1994* (Washington, DC: Government Printing Office, 1995).
4. Patrick Griffin and Patricia Torbet, eds., *Desktop to Good Juvenile Probation Practice: Mission-Driven, Performance-Based, and Outcome-Focused* (Pittsburgh: National Center for Juvenile Justice, 2002), 64.
5. Ibid.
6. Ibid., 63–71.
7. Terence P. Thornberry, "Sentencing Disparities in the Juvenile Justice System," *Journal of Criminal Law and Criminology* 70 (Summer 1979), 164–71; M. A. Bortner, *Inside a Juvenile Court: The Tarnished Idea of Individualized Justice* (New York: New York University Press, 1982); Lawrence Cohen, "Delinquency Dispositions: An Empirical Analysis of Processing Decisions in Three Juvenile Courts, *Analytic Report* 9 (Washington, DC: Government Printing Office, 1975), 51.
8. Bortner, *Inside a Juvenile Court.*
9. Ruth D. Peterson, "Youthful Offender Designations and Sentencing in the New York Criminal Courts," *Social Problems* 35 (April 1988), 125–26.
10. Samuel M. Davis, *Rights of Juveniles: The Juvenile Justice System*, 2d ed. (New York: Clark Boardman, 1986), 6-7–6-8.
11. Ibid., 6–29.
12. Ibid.; see 125 Vt. 373, 216 A.2d 266 (1966).
13. Ibid.
14. Ibid., 6-34–6-37. See 408 U.S. 471 (1972) and 411 U.S. 778 (1973).
15. Martin L. Forst, Bruce A. Fisher, and Robert B. Coates, "Indeterminate and Determinate Sentencing of Juvenile Delinquents: A National Survey of Approaches to Commitment and Release Decision-Making," *Juvenile and Family Court Journal* 36 (Summer 1985), 1.
16. Daniel P. Mears and Samuel H. Field, "Theorizing Sanctioning in a Criminalized Juvenile Court," *Criminology* 38 (November 2000), 985–86.
17. Ibid., 983.
18. Barry C. Feld, "Violent Youth and Public Policy: Minnesota Juvenile Justice Task Force and 1994 Legislative Reform," paper presented at the annual

meeting of the American Society of Criminology, Miami (1994), 4. See also Feld, "Violent Youth and Public Policy: A Case Study of Juvenile Justice Law Reform," *Minnesota Law Review* 79 (May 1995), 965–1128.

19. Thomas F. Geraghty, "Justice for Children: How Do We Get There?" *Journal of Criminal Law and Criminology* 88 (1998), 190–241.

20. Ibid., 217.

21. Ibid., 217–28.

22. Ibid., 229.

23. Ibid., 230–33.

24. Ibid., 238.

25. Ira M. Schwartz, *(In)justice for Juveniles: Rethinking the Best Interests of the Child* (Lexington, MA: Lexington Books, 1989), 118.

26. National Council of Juvenile and Family Court Judges, *Juvenile Delinquency Guidelines: Improving Court Practice in Juvenile Delinquency Cases* (Reno, NV: Summer 1995), 37.

27. Ibid., 16.

28. Ibid., 17.

29. Ibid., 22.

30. Ibid., 22.

7

JUVENILES IN ADULT COURT

The body of Shirley Crook was found bound with electric cable and leather straps in the Meramec River in St. Louis County, Missouri, in 1993. Her head was wrapped in duct tape, her ribs were cracked and she had bruises on her body. The offender had thrown her, still alive, off a bridge and she drowned.

Christopher Simmons, aged seventeen, was arrested the next day at school and charged with the crime. He was interrogated for three hours without a parent or lawyer present and eventually confessed to the murder. Prior to the crime, Simmons had no previous criminal record.

On June 16, 1994, Christopher Simmons was convicted and sentenced to be executed for the crime.

Mr. Simmons is a product of dysfunctional family with intergenerational psychiatric disorders and is himself predisposed to mental illness. As a child, he was the victim of severe physical and psychological abuse by his alcoholic stepfather. For example, his stepfather took him to a bar at the age of four and got him drunk to entertain the bar's patrons; his stepfather beat him severely. Mr. Simmons continued to use drugs such a LSD, marijuana, and alcohol as an adolescent and was encouraged to commit crimes by a neighbor. He viewed himself as a helpless victim unable to change. Mr. Simmons exhibited low self-esteem, impulsivity, loneliness, hopelessness, and depression.

On August 26, 2003, the Missouri Supreme Court held that to execute Simmons would violate the Eighth Amendment to the Constitution the United States and vacated the execution of Mr. Simmons. That decision was appealed to the United States Supreme Court and was heard on October 13, 2004.

On March 1, 2005, the United States Supreme Court ruled that the execution of juveniles under the age of 18 was unconstitutional.[1]

OUTLINE

The Juvenile Death Penalty: Summary   Critical Thinking Questions
Three Decades of Change   Web Site of Interest   Notes
A Proposed Adult Court for
Juveniles

OBJECTIVES

1. To consider the differences in maturity between juveniles and adults
2. To describe and evaluate the policy of transferring juveniles to the adult court
3. To examine the possibility of developing an intermediate correctional system for juveniles
4. To examine the quality of life for a juvenile sentenced to an adult prison
5. To discuss the death penalty for juveniles
6. To evaluate the proposed adult court for juveniles

KEY TERMS

concurrent jurisdiction   life without parole sentence   statutorial exclusion
judicial waiver   prosecutorial discretion   youthful offender system

The mission of the juvenile court, as previously discussed, is hotly debated today. Proponents contend that its original mission was to deal with all juvenile crime, from minor misbehaviors to assault, robbery, and murder. The rise in violent youth crime over the past decades, however, has increased the public's fear of juvenile crime. In addition, the emergence of a "hard line" since the late 1970s has increased the willingness of others to question the juvenile court's original mission. The result of this get-tough policy is that numerous proposals are being made that increase the chances that juvenile lawbreakers, even very young ones, will be punished with the same severity as their adult counterparts.

This chapter examines some of the issues involved in ensuring justice for both juveniles and society. Beginning with the issue of immaturity and responsibility, this chapter considers the transfer to adult court, the recent *Roper v. Simmons* case that led to the abolishment of the juvenile death penalty, the sentence of a juvenile to a youthful offender system or to an adult prison, and a proposed adult court for juveniles.

CHILDREN OR ADULTS?

The point at which children become adults has varied from one period to another. An examination of the history of childhood suggests that in the Middle Ages, children became adults around the age of seven—when they could work in fields and begin to learn a trade. During the Renaissance, the children of the poor still became adults at the age of seven, but the children of the aristocracy became adults only after schooling that prepared them to help rule society.[2] One result of the Industrial Revolution was a demand for even more schooling for youths; society determined that childhood would not end, nor would adulthood begin, until children were out of school. Whether children were adults or not, in other words, depended partly on the socioeconomic conditions under which they lived and whether they had learned enough in school to hold down an adult job.

The age at which a juvenile becomes an adult is defined in much the same way even today. Youths are not adults until they graduate from high school or college or are able to hold down a job considered appropriate for an adult. Confusion is evident even here, for youths who achieve these milestones may be of widely different ages. When one considers further that theaters consider youths as adults at age twelve, the State Bureau of Transportation at age sixteen, the military and the Voting Commission at age eighteen, and the State Liquor Control Board at age twenty-one, it is clear why the criminal justice system has such a difficult time determining the age of responsibility.

In terms of wrongdoing, the elusive concept of responsibility has its roots in the notions that juveniles know right from wrong, have developed a social conscience, feel guilty or remorseful over their actions, are mentally sharp enough to know the rules, do not have any disease that reduces their ability to get along in society, fully understand that their actions are harming others, and are emotionally mature. None of these criteria are measurable; yet, for almost a century, the assumption of the juvenile court has been that juveniles are deficient in one or more of them. Proponents of the juvenile court also assume that it should have jurisdiction over the youths until their deficiencies are corrected and until they have developed the mental and emotional maturity of adults. What fuels the controversy over waiver to adult court is the disagreement over when youths reach this stage.

Stephen J. Morse has this to say about when individuals reach a state of minimal rationality in which they can be held responsible for their behavior:

> Law, unlike mechanistic explanation or the conflicted stance of the social sciences, views human action as almost entirely reason-governed. The law's concept of a person is a practical reasoning, rule-following being, most of whose legally relevant movements must be understood in terms of beliefs, desires and intentions. As a system of rules to guide and govern human interaction, the law presupposes that people use legal rules as premises in the practical syllogisms that guide much human action. No "instinct" governs how fast a person drives on the open highway. But among the various explanatory variables, the posted speed limit and the belief in the probability of paying the consequences for exceeding it surely play a large role in the driver's choice of speed. For the law, then, a person is a practical reasoner. The legal view of the person is not that all people behave consistently rationally according to some preordained, normative notion of rationality. It is simply that people are creatures who act for and consistently with their reasons for action and who are generally capable of minimal rationality according to most conventional, socially constructed standards.[3]

In examining the extent to which young people should be held responsible for their criminal activity, Morse contends that a "robust" theory of responsibility would result in most youths (in middle to late adolescence) being held responsible for their actions. He claims that there is empirical research to substantiate the position that it is often difficult to distinguish between the moral responsibility of children and young adults. Thus, he reasons, the responsibility of a juvenile should be no less than that of a similarly situated young adult. He does not believe that juveniles' susceptibility to peer pressure justifies differential allocation of responsibility.[4]

Elizabeth Scott and Thomas Grisso, in evaluating the differences between adults and youths, conclude that substantial differences exist between very young juveniles and adults in "moral, cognitive, and social development."[5] The differences between juvenile and adult decision making are more subtle as youths approach mid-adolescence, however. As Scott and Grisso express it: "A categorical presumption of adolescent nonresponsibility, such as that which was endorsed by the traditional juvenile justice system, is hard to defend on the grounds of immaturity alone."[6]

Scott and Grisso's developmental evidence does "support the argument of the post-Gault reformers of the 1970s and 1980s that a presumptive diminished responsibility standard be applied to juveniles."[7] They believe that this presumptive diminished responsibility is best applied in juvenile court systems, and they question whether the criminal justice system is able to respond to this developmental reality: "The ability or inclination of the criminal justice system to tailor its response to juvenile crime so as to utilize the lessons of developmental psychology is questionable. The evidence suggests that political pressure functions as a one-way ratchet, in the direction of ever stiffer penalties."[8]

They further question the assumption, proposed by Morse and others, that most juvenile offenders, even those in mid-adolescence, are as cognitively competent as adults are in decision-making capacity. They claim that the cognitive decision-making abilities of adolescents and adults are similar only when nondelinquent juveniles from middle-class backgrounds of above-average intelligence are compared with adults. But when children involved in the justice system, many of whom have emotional problems and learning disabilities that hinder their capacity for understanding, are compared with adults, there is real reason to question the cognitive competence of these youths.[9]

The fact of the matter is that some youths do commit brutal crimes, and the viciousness of their acts causes one to question the justice of their remaining in the juvenile system. Indeed, the media testify nearly daily to violent youth crime as they describe senseless killings and rapes committed by juveniles. Violent youth crime has contributed to the perception that something is seriously wrong with our society. Those who have been victims of youthful thugs feel especially vulnerable and call for stronger measures to deal with youthful predators.

One of the most vivid expressions of predatory and violent youth crime is the 1999 shooting at Columbine High School in Littleton, Colorado, described elsewhere. The attacks by juveniles on the homeless are even more recent examples. Mall security cameras in 2005 captured the beating of a homeless man in a Florida mall; the youths identified in that case also were responsible for the beatings and killings of other homeless men in and around the city of Ft. Lauderdale.[10]

HOW DOES TRANSFER TO ADULT COURT TAKE PLACE?

Today, all state legislatures have passed laws permitting juveniles to be transferred to adult court, but this is taking place less frequently than in the past. In 2002, courts had fever waivers of juveniles to adult court than in 1985, and 2001 had the fewest waivers of juveniles to adult court of any year since 1985.[11] Of course, states vary widely in the criteria they use in making the waiver decision. Some states focus on the age of the offender, and others consider both age

The formal setting of the adult court differs dramatically from the informal setting of the juvenile court and may be intimidating and scary to juveniles. (Photo by Kathryn Miller.)

and offense. Table 7–1 summarizes the broad age and offense provisions related to the transfer of juvenile offenders. Vermont (age ten), Georgia, Illinois, and Mississippi (age thirteen) transfer children at very young ages. More states transfer juveniles at fourteen than at any other age; seven states transfer juveniles at either fifteen or sixteen years of age.

The offenses juveniles commit are also important in the waiver decision. Some states permit waiver for any criminal offense, whereas others waive only those offenses specifically mentioned in the state's statutes. Many states permit waiver to the adult court if the juvenile previously has been adjudicated delinquent or has a prior criminal conviction. Depending on the state, three major mechanisms are used to waive juveniles: judicial waiver, prosecutorial discretion, and statutorial exclusion.

JUDICIAL WAIVER

Except where state laws mandate that a youth be tried in adult court, someone has to make the decision to waive a youth. **Judicial waiver,** the most widely used transfer mechanism, involves the actual decision-making process that begins when the juvenile is brought to intake. Predictably, the mechanisms used vary by state. In some states, intake personnel, juvenile prosecutors, or judges make the decision based, in part, on the age or offense criteria spelled out in Table 7–1. In other states, a court other than the juvenile court makes the decision. For example, the prosecutor or judge in the adult court may decide where a juvenile is to be tried.[12] The decision is determined by the requirements of the state and the way the intake officer, prosecutor, or judge interprets the youth's background. Typically, the criteria used include the age and maturity of the child; the child's relationship with parents, school, and community; whether the child is considered dangerous; and whether court officials believe that the child may be helped by juvenile court services.

Table 7–1 *Age and Offense Provisions for Judicial Waiver*

In most states, juvenile court judges may waive jurisdiction over certain cases and transfer them to criminal court

State	Minimum Age for Judicial Waiver	*Judicial Waiver Offense and Minimum Age Criteria, 2004*							
		Any Criminal Offenses	Certain Felonies	Capital Crimes	Murder	Certain Person Offenses	Certain Property Offenses	Certain Drug Offenses	Certain Weapon Offenses
Alabama	14	14							
Alaska	NS	NS				NS			
California	14	16			14	14	14	14	
Colorado	12		12		12	12			
Dist. of Columbia	NS	16	15		15	15	15		NS
Florida	14	14							
Idaho	NS	14	NS		NS	NS	NS	NS	
Illinois	13	13	15						
Kansas	10	10	14			14		14	
Kentucky	14		14	14					
Maryland	NS	15		NS					
Michigan	14		14						
Missouri	12		12						
Nevada	14	14	14			14			
North Carolina	13		13	13					
North Dakota	14	16	14		14	14		14	
Oregon	NS		15		NS	NS	15		
Pennsylvania	14		14			14	14		
South Dakota	NS		NS						
Tennessee	NS	16			NS	NS			
Vermont	10				10	10	10		
Virginia	14		14		14	14			
Wisconsin	14	15	14		14	14	14	14	
Wyoming	13	13							

Note: Ages in the minimum age column may not apply to all offense restrictions, but represent the youngest possible age at which a juvenile may be judicially waived to criminal court. "NS" indicates that in at least one of the offense restrictions indicated, no minimum age is specified.

Source: Howard N. Snyder and Melissa Sickmund, *Juvenile Offenders and Victims: 2006 National Report* (Washington, DC: U.S. Department of Justice, Office of Justice Programs, Office of Juvenile Justice and Delinquency Prevention, 2006), p. 112.

PROSECUTORIAL DISCRETION

Prosecutorial discretion occurs in states with **concurrent jurisdiction** statutes. These laws give prosecutors the authority to decide whether to try juveniles in either juvenile or adult courts. Table 7–2 illustrates which states utilize concurrent jurisdiction statutes and the statutory conditions that prosecutors must use in making their decisions. Table 7–2 demonstrates that age is one factor taken into consideration by the states in setting up these statutes. It also indicates that three states, Nevada, Vermont, and Wyoming, permit charges to be filed in either juvenile or adult court for any criminal offense, but most states specifically mention in their juvenile codes precisely which offenses may be tried in either court.

STATUTORIAL EXCLUSION

Some states have a **statutorial exclusion** of certain offenses from juvenile court, thereby automatically transferring perpetrators of those offenses to adult court.

Table 7–2 *States That Permit Prosecutorial Discretion*

In states with concurrent jurisdiction, the prosecutor has discretion to file certain cases, in either criminal court or juvenile court

Concurrent Jurisdiction Offense and Minimum Age Criteria, 2004

State	Minimum Age for Concurrent Jurisdiction	Any Criminal Offense	Certain Felonies	Capital Crimes	Murder	Certain Person Offenses	Certain Property Offenses	Certain Drug Offenses	Certain Weapon Offenses
Arizona	14		14						
Arkansas	14		16	14	14	14			
California	14		14	14	14	14	14	14	
Colorado	14		14		14	14	14		
Dist. of Columbia	16				16	16	16		
Florida	NS	16	16	NS	14	14	14		14
Georgia	NS			NS					
Louisiana	15				15	15	15	15	
Michigan	14		14		14	14	14	14	
Montana	12				12	12	16	16	16
Nebraska	NS	16	NS						
Oklahoma	15		16		15	15	15	16	15
Vermont	16	16							
Virginia	14				14	14			
Wyoming	13		14		14	14	14		

Note: Ages in the minimum age column may not apply to all offense restrictions, but represent the youngest possible age at which a juvenile's case may be directly filed in criminal court. "NS" indicates that in at least one of the offense restrictions indicated, no minimum age is specified.

Source: Howard N. Snyder and Melissa Sickmund, *Juvenile Offenders and Victims: 2006 National Report* (Washington, DC: U.S. Department of Justice, Office of Justice Programs, Office of Juvenile Justice and Delinquency Prevention, 2006), p. 113.

Table 7–3 shows that the states that exclude offenses from juvenile court primarily focus on "safety" crimes such as murder and other offenses against a person. The statutes also, however, spell out the minimum age that youths must reach before they may be transferred to adult court.

Other variations on waiver also exist, some very subtle. One such variation is a state legislature lowering the age over which the juvenile court has jurisdiction. For example, if a state's age of juvenile court jurisdiction is eighteen, the legislature may lower the age to sixteen. This approach focuses entirely on the age of the juvenile but ignores the offenses committed.

Yet other state legislatures have specified that juveniles of specific ages who commit specific crimes are to be tried in adult court. For example, until recently, Indiana statutes stated that any child age ten or older who committed murder would be tried as an adult. This method of legislative waiver focuses as much on the offense as it does on the age of the offender.

Another method of waiver is one in which the statutes simply state that anyone who commits a specific crime may be tried in adult court. No reference is made to the age of the offender. This approach is attractive to those who believe that any youth who violates the law should receive an appropriate punishment.

REVERSE WAIVER AND BLENDED SENTENCING

In *reverse waiver*, some state laws permit youths who are over the maximum age of jurisdiction to be sent back to the juvenile court if the adult court believes the case is more appropriate for juvenile court jurisdiction. For a reverse waiver, defense counsel and prosecutors attempt to make their case for their

Table 7–3 *States with Statutorial Exclusion*

In states with statutory exclusion provisions, certain cases involving juveniles originate in criminal court rather than in juvenile court

State	Minimum Age for Statutory Exclusion	Statutory Exclusion Offense and Minimum Age Criteria, 2004							
		Any Criminal Offense	Certain Felonies	Capital Offense	Murder	Certain Person Offenses	Certain Property Offenses	Certain Drug Offenses	Certain Weapon Offenses
Alabama	16		16	16				16	
Alaska	16					16	16		
Delaware	15		15						
Florida	NS				16	NS	16	16	
Illinois	13		15		13	15		15	15
Indiana	16		16		16	16		16	16
Maryland	14			14	16	16			16
Massachusetts	14				14				
Montana	17				17	17	17	17	17
Nevada	NS	16[a]	NS		NS	16			
Oklahoma	13				13				
Oregon	NS				15	15			
South Dakota	16		16						
Utah	16		16						
Washington	16				16				
Wisconsin	NS				10	NS			

Note: Ages in the minimum age column may not apply to all offense restrictions, but represent the youngest possible age at which a juvenile may be excluded from juvenile court. "NS" indicates that in at least one of the offense restrictions indicated, no minimum age is specified.

[a]In Nevada, the exclusion applies to any juvenile with a previous felony adjudication, regardless of the current offense charged, if the current offense involves the use or threalened use of firearm.

Source: Howard N. Snyder and Melissa Sickmund, *Juvenile Offenders and Victims: 2006 National Report* (Washington, DC: U.S. Department of Justice, Office of Justice Programs, Office of Juvenile Justice and Delinquency Prevention, 2006), p. 114.

desired action. Some evidence and testimony are allowed, and arguments are presented. When each side has had a chance to present its case and to rebut the opponents' arguments, the judge makes the decision.[13]

In *blended sentencing*, some states permit juvenile court judges at the disposition hearing in the delinquency court to impose both an adult and a juvenile sentence concurrently. This option may be given to juveniles who have received a direct file, mandatory or a prosecutorial waiver to the adult court. In these cases, the juvenile is given both sentences but is first given the juvenile disposition. If the juvenile fulfills the requirements of this disposition satisfactorily, the adult disposition is suspended. If the juvenile does not fulfill the conditions of the juvenile disposition, the juvenile is then required to fulfill conditions of the adult disposition. In some states, the juvenile may be required to fulfill the juvenile disposition until he or she reaches the age of majority; at this point, the juvenile must begin to fulfill the adult sentence minus the time already spent fulfilling the juvenile disposition.

CHANGING CRITERIA FOR WAIVER

In the past, youths were waived to adult court without hearings, without sufficient fact-finding on the part of the court, without reasons being given for the waiver, and without the youth having the benefit of an attorney. Critics fought these procedures. Their essential argument was that the decision to waive juveniles to adult court was a serious matter and that youths should be entitled to due process rights. On reviewing two cases in particular, *Kent v. United States* and *Breed v. Jones* (see Chapter 5), the U.S. Supreme Court ruled that traditional juvenile court procedures for waiver were inadequate and that juveniles were guaranteed many of the same due process rights as adults. Since *Kent* and *Jones,* most states now require that waiver hearings be held before transferring juveniles to adult court. Yet these hearings are not required in all states, as some permit prosecutors to make the waiver decision. In addition, states that provide for mandatory legislative waiver do not have to hold such hearings.

Where juvenile courts are responsible for making the waiver decision, the Supreme Court stated in *Kent* that they must use the following criteria:

1. The seriousness of the alleged offense to the community and whether the protection of the community requires waiver
2. Whether the alleged offense was committed in an aggressive, violent, premeditated, or willful manner
3. Whether the alleged offense was against persons or against property, greater weight being given to offenses against persons, especially if personal injury resulted
4. The prosecutorial merit of the complaint, that is, whether there is evidence on which a grand jury may be expected to return an indictment
5. The desirability of trial and disposition of the entire offense in one court when the juvenile's associates in the alleged offense are adults who will be charged with a crime in the [criminal court]
6. The sophistication and maturity of the juvenile as determined by consideration of his home, environment, emotional attitude, and pattern of living
7. The record and previous history of the juvenile
8. The prospects for adequate protection of the public and the likelihood of reasonable rehabilitation of the juvenile (if he [or she] is found to have committed the alleged offense) by the use of procedures, services, and facilities currently available to the juvenile court[14]

WHAT GOES ON IN THE TRANSFER OR WAIVER HEARING?

Once a prosecutor has decided that a juvenile is beyond the help of the juvenile court and has reviewed the legal sufficiency of the case, the prosecutor files a motion to send the youth to adult court; this motion requires a probable cause hearing by juvenile judge. These hearings are required for both a mandatory judicial waiver and a discretionary judicial waiver. The judge begins either hearing by explaining the nature of the hearing and making certain that the youth and his or her parents understand the youth's rights and the consequences of the outcome. All interested parties should be at this hearing.[15]

In the probable cause hearing, everything said should be under oath. The prosecutor presents the state's case against the juvenile, affirming the identity of the juvenile and reviewing the affidavit, petition, and jurisdiction requirements—both of the age of the offender and the geographical region from which the offender comes—and of witnesses. The defense attorney then challenges the evidence of the prosecutor and may present witnesses; both the prosecutor and the defense attorney cross-examine the witnesses on the legal facts of the case. Both attorneys then summarize their cases at the conclusion of testimony.[16]

If the judge believes that probable cause has been established, he or she then determines whether the case satisfies the state's legally sufficient requirements for mandatory judicial waiver. If it does, the youth is transferred to criminal court. If probable cause is not established and the prosecutor's motion is denied, the National Council of Juvenile and Family Court Judges recommends the dismissal of the case. Some courts, in practice, refer the youth back to the probation department.[17]

In the judge's review of the case, the youth's dangerousness to self and others, the youth's sophistication and maturity in understanding the nature and consequences of his or her behavior, and the youth's amenability to further treatment are all evaluated. Whether to waive or retain also is based on whether the youth had a history of violent crimes, was a gang member, tested antisocial, had co-offenders, engaged in premeditated offenses, and had experienced trauma in childhood and adolescence. Very important is the availability of alternative treatments, including out-of-state placements. The youth's attorney plays a critical role in helping to evaluate the youth and in presenting alternatives that can benefit the youth. The judge must decide, if the youth is in detention, whether to continue detention or release the youth. The decision the judge finally makes should be based on clear and convincing evidence.[18]

WAIVER TO CRIMINAL COURT

Once the waiver decision is made, the juvenile's case is transferred to the adult court prosecutor. Prosecutors in some states may decide to send the case back to the juvenile court because the case does not meet the standards of legal sufficiency, such as probable cause. The prosecutor may confer with a judge about any legal questions the prosecutor believes the judge might have about the case before making a decision. In some states, the prosecutor takes the case to a grand jury; in other states, the prosecutor sets a date for an arraignment. There, the legal process starts all over again with the same people present, with some juveniles put on informal or formal probation and with others tried in adult court. The case now usually is tried in front of a jury, and the youth has the potential of receiving the same sentence as an adult.[19]

EVALUATION OF WAIVER

Although waivers are still relatively infrequent and have recently decreased in number, they are an important issue in juvenile justice.[20] Significantly, juveniles waived to adult court are not always the most serious and violent offenders. Donna Bishop and colleagues' examination of 583 prosecutorial waivers of sixteen- and seventeen-year-old youths in Florida from 1981 to 1984 revealed that most transferred juveniles were property and low-risk offenders.[21] Examinations of waiver have found that little consensus exists today on which criteria should be used in making the waiver decision.[22] Furthermore, although remanded youth are receiving severe penalties, waiver generally does not result in more severe penalties than juvenile offenders would have received in juvenile court. Several states have attempted to develop a process that would identify those juveniles unfit for retention in juvenile court. For example, using such criteria as age, offense, and prior record, Minnesota has codified the transfer procedures to be followed by judges and prosecutors. But Lee Ann Osburn and Peter A. Rose's evaluation concluded that Minnesota's procedures were inadequate for making acceptable transfer decisions.[23] With adult courts' massive caseload and their limited judicial experience with sentencing youths, little evidence exists that adult judges know what to do with juveniles appearing before them. Finally, even when waiver does occur, some evidence exists that waiver may have the effect not of deterring crime by juveniles, but of increasing it.[24]

✓**Progress Check 7.1**
Review this section at
www.prenhall.com/bartollas

HOW DOES A YOUTHFUL OFFENDER SYSTEM WORK?

Juveniles sentenced in adult courts are subject to the same range of dispositions as are adults. Cases may be dismissed or offenders may be found guilty. If found guilty, youths may be released to the care of their parents, placed on probation, fined, ordered to pay restitution, or referred to a social agency qualified to deal with their problem. But a very controversial disposition is the placement of youths in adult correctional facilities.

The crowding, violence, and exploitative relationships found in adult prisons make this disposition extremely questionable. Furthermore, although some states have attempted to develop special institutions for juveniles, even these appear to have the same characteristics as adult prisons. Youths who are placed in them can no better protect themselves than they can in adult facilities. Given the young age of even the most violent of these offenders, society has the task of deciding whether any type of adult institutional placement is appropriate for these youths.

At the time of the Hamparian study, only two states, Delaware and Kentucky, prohibited the placement of juveniles in state correctional institutions.[25] Some variations on the practice of confining a juvenile in an adult institution do exist among the states. In some jurisdictions, states have no alternative but to place juveniles in adult institutions if the courts require incarceration. Some states can, under special circumstances, place youths in either juvenile or adult institutions, yet other states can refer juveniles back to juvenile court for their disposition. In some instances, very young juveniles are sent to juvenile facilities but then are transferred to adult institutions when they become of age. Recognizing the dangers and inadequacies of placing juveniles with adults, some jurisdictions have developed special institutions for these younger adult offenders.

Hamparian and colleagues propose that a **youthful offender system** be developed for young adults (sixteen to nineteen years of age). In these institutions, programs would emphasize work readiness, job training, and work experience. They would also attempt to establish close ties to the community to which the youth would return; employ flexible staff who would act as positive role models; enforce the rules strictly; provide opportunities for decision making, with consequences clearly and fully related to the choices made; provide opportunities to enhance self-esteem; create a continuity of care between the program or treatment sequence and integration into the community to which the youth is returning; and offer supportive services in the community after completion of the program or treatment sequence as long as the youth needs them.[26]

The California Youth Authority has long extended its jurisdiction over youthful offenders to those up to twenty-three years of age. North Carolina was one of the first states to develop Youthful Offender Camps for sixteen- to eighteen-year-old males. In the 1990s, Colorado, New Mexico, and Minnesota also developed transitional, or intermediate, systems between the juvenile and adult systems. The Minnesota Juvenile Justice Task Force recommended the following:

> a more graduated juvenile justice system that establishes a new *transitional component between the juvenile and adult systems*. . . . [T]his new [Serious Youthful Offender] category will create viable new dispositional options for juvenile court judges facing juveniles who have committed serious or repeat offenses. It will give the juvenile *one last chance* at success in the juvenile system, with the threat of adult sanctions as an incentive not to re-offend.[27]

In 1994, the Minnesota legislature adopted the task force's recommendation but relabeled the category "Extended Jurisdiction Juvenile" (EJJ) to make the label less attractive to delinquent "wannabes." For juveniles who are designated as EJJs, final legislation extended the juvenile court's jurisdiction until age twenty-one. The Department of Corrections was also required to license and regulate regional secure treatment facilities for EJJs.[28]

Intermediate sentencing for youthful offenders that bridges the juvenile and adult systems certainly appears to be a positive means to keep some juveniles out of adult correctional facilities. It is hoped that the 1994 legislation in Minnesota, as well as the youthful offender systems in Colorado and New Mexico, will encourage the development of such legislation in more states.

The current get-tough mood of society does not seem to be one in which the development of youthful offender systems will be viewed as an attractive option to policymakers in many states. Yet, if the juvenile population explosion occurs in the next two decades, as predicted by some experts, and increasing numbers of juveniles are referred to the adult systems, perhaps there will be greater receptivity toward an intermediate correctional system for youthful offenders.

WHAT IS LIFE LIKE FOR A JUVENILE SENT TO PRISON?

Adult prisons are a world apart from most training schools. Prisons are much larger, sometimes containing several thousand inmates and covering many acres of ground. Life on the inside is generally austere, crowded, and dangerous and institutionalized juveniles are particularly subject to sexual victimization and sexual assault. Richard E. Redding concluded from his review of the programming that juveniles receive in adult correctional facilities: "Once incarcerated in adult facilities, juveniles typically receive fewer age-appropriate rehabilitative, medical, mental health and educational services, and are at greater risk of physical and sexual abuse and suicide."[29]

In 2002, an estimated 4,100 new court commitments were admitted to state adult prison systems involving juveniles younger than age eighteen. Between 1997 and 2004, while the population of prisons rose, the number of inmates under age eighteen fell 54 percent. However, this decline of the youth proportion of prison populations was primarily the result of the large increase in the total prison population during this period. For example, between 1985 and 2002, the annual number of new court commitments to state prison involving juveniles younger than eighteen increased 22 percent, but the overall new commitments increased 114 percent.[30]

From 1994 to 2001, almost 3,000 juveniles were committed to the custody of the Federal Bureau of Prisons (BOP) for offenses committed under eighteen years of age. Of these, 1,639 were committed to the BOP as delinquents and 1,346 as adults. The vast majority of these juveniles committed as delinquents (about 70 percent) were American Indians.[31]

In some states, judges opt for the **life without parole sentence** to incarcerate juveniles for the rest of their natural lives. See Focus on Law 7–1 for an Iowa case in which a fifteen-year-old received a life without parole sentence.

Providing for the care and special needs of juvenile offenders in adult facilities is proving to be a real problem. The youthful offender may be as young as thirteen and feel overwhelmed by older and more aggressive offenders. Indeed, most juvenile offenders placed in adult prisons are not violent offenders. A gang culture may be present in the prison, in which gang members pressure youthful offenders to become part of their gang, usually to exploit them. Furthermore, with their need to be part of something, youthful offenders tend to be highly impressionable and easily used or manipulated.[32]

The state of Washington has attempted to manage imprisoned youthful offenders more effectively. In 1997, the state enacted Senate bill 3900 defining the jurisdiction, custody, and management requirements for juvenile offenders. This legislation requires juvenile offenders to be placed in adult prisons for serious offenses such as aggravated murder. In addition, it dictates the

FOCUS ON LAW   7–1
YOU WILL SPEND THE REMAINDER OF YOUR NATURAL LIFE IN PRISON

In 1994, four Midwestern teenagers decided to take a Ford Bronco belonging to one of their parents and run away to Canada. The Bronco broke down in a neighboring state, and they realized that they would need to steal another car. They stopped a woman, who thought that the Bronco with lights on top was a police vehicle. One of the teenagers approached the woman and pretended to be a police officer. She demanded to see identification. He returned to the Bronco and instructed one of his companions to take the .22 rifle they had brought along and shoot her. The fifteen-year-old youth, who had committed no more serious acts than vandalism, complied. He shot her once, broke the window of her vehicle on the driver's side when she locked the door, and stabbed her thirty-one times.

The four youths called their parents after they left the crime scene. Later that night, one of their parents arrived and took them home. Within a couple of days, all four were arrested and charged with this crime. Tried in the jurisdiction where the crime was committed, the four juveniles were quickly transferred to the adult court.

During the trial of the youth who had committed the stabbing, his defense attorney attempted to explain the youth's ruthless behavior: The jury was informed that he came from a totally inadequate family background. He had been sexually abused by his natural father at the age of two and had been physically assaulted by an adopted father at the age of fifteen. His mother had been married eight times, and she failed to supply his emotional needs in a number of ways. He also did poorly in school and had failed twice. He had been charged with using marijuana on a couple of occasions but had not been involved in any serious personal or property offenses. He was particularly fearful of the youth who had instructed him to shoot the woman. In summary, the defense attorney claimed that what had taken place that night emerged from the totality of the youth's experiences, frustrations, inadequacies, and unmet needs. The child deserved punishment, the attorney admitted, but not to the extent of spending the rest of his life in prison.

Upon being sentenced to prison for life without parole, the youth admitted that he was fearful of being sexually assaulted. As a small white youth, his fears were not unreasonable. He said that he had made up his mind to be placed in the prison population (with other inmates). He did not want to be locked up twenty-four hours a day for the rest of his life. Whatever it took, he vowed, he would keep the other inmates off him. He was briefly placed in a diagnostic facility. Later, when he was transferred to an adult reformatory, it did not take him long to attack a pressuring inmate with a shank. He was charged with attempted murder and placed in administrative segregation.

Source: One of the authors was involved with this defense as an expert witness.

Critical Thinking Questions:
How much time do you believe this offender should spend in prison for a crime he committed when he was fifteen? If you were this inmate, would you want to be locked up in protective custody or try to make it in the prison population? If you chose the prison population, what would you be willing to do to protect yourself?

housing and educational requirements for youthful offenders within the Department of Corrections (DOC) as follows:

- An offender under the age of eighteen who is convicted in adult criminal court and sentenced to the DOC must be placed in a housing unit, or a portion of a housing unit, separated from adult inmates;

- The offender may be housed in an intensive management unit or administrative segregation unit, if necessary, for the safety or security of the offender or the staff; and
- The DOC must provide an educational program to an offender under the age of eighteen who is incarcerated at a DOC facility. The program must enable the offender to obtain a high school diploma or general equivalency diploma (GED).[33]

Female youthful offenders are placed at the Washington Corrections Center for Women (WCCW), and males are confined at the Clallam Bay Corrections Center. A multidisciplinary team was formed in September 1997 in order to meet the challenge of accommodating juveniles in adult prisons. This team has been concerned with providing a safe and secure environment; an environment distant from adult offenders' contact and influences; programs and services similar to those available to the general population; and an educational program offering credit for a high school diploma or GED.[34]

THE JUVENILE DEATH PENALTY: THREE DECADES OF CHANGE

The most severe sentence in the adult courts is, of course, the death penalty. Much debate has centered on this issue, and in June 1989, the U.S. Supreme Court ruled that sixteen- and seventeen-year-old juveniles could be executed for their crimes.[35]

This decision generated an outburst of debate. It was applauded by conservatives, who contended that society needs the death penalty for its retributive and deterrent effects on violent crime. Conservatives also believe that juveniles are mollycoddled by the juvenile court and that juveniles who break the law deserve the same punishments as adults. Liberals, however, decried the decision. Their objections reflect, in part, the disdain that many have for the death penalty in a "civilized" society. These modern progressives also believe that youthful offenders should be rehabilitated because they are young and still in the formative years of their lives.

Victor L. Strieb traces the development of the current debate.[36] The constitutionality of the death penalty was decided in *Gregg v. Georgia* in 1976.[37] In that decision, the U.S. Supreme Court ruled that the death penalty did not violate the Eighth Amendment's prohibition against cruel and unusual punishment. The Court did stipulate that before lower courts handed down the death penalty, the special characteristics of the offender, such as his or her age, as well as the circumstances of the crime, had to be considered.[38] In later decisions considering statutes in Ohio and other states, the Court ruled that mitigating circumstances had to be considered in any death penalty case.[39] Accordingly, states that have handed down the death penalty without considering mitigating circumstances have had their cases overturned.[40] States that permit the death penalty today, in other words, must statutorily require that mitigating circumstances be considered.

In some ways, the debate over the death penalty for juveniles is a curious one. Strieb points out that historically, few juveniles were ever executed for their crimes. Indeed, even when juveniles were sentenced to death, few if any executions were carried out.[41] In the United States, for example, youths under the age of eighteen were executed at the rate of twenty to twenty-seven per decade, or about 1.6 to 2.3 percent of all executions from the 1880s to the 1920s.[42] The peak in the United States occurred in the 1940s, when fifty-three, or 4.1 percent of all those executed, were juveniles.[43]

Of the thirty-eight states that permitted capital punishment, twenty-four allowed it for individuals who were under the age of eighteen when they committed the crime. Fourteen states have never executed juveniles, but Georgia leads all states with forty-one juvenile executions, followed by North Carolina and Ohio, with nineteen each.

In 1982, in the case of *Eddings v. Oklahoma*, the Supreme Court was able to avoid directly addressing the constitutionality of the juvenile death penalty by ruling that "the chronological age of a minor is itself a relevant mitigating factor of great weight."[44] Monty Lee Eddings was sixteen when he shot and killed an Oklahoma State Highway Patrol officer, but his execution sentence was reversed in 1982 because of his age.[45]

In *Wilkins v. Missouri*, sixteen-year-old Heath A. Wilkins of Missouri stabbed Nancy Allen Moore to death on July 27, 1985, as she worked behind the counter of a convenience store. The jury found him guilty of first-degree murder, armed criminal action, and carrying a concealed weapon. During the sentencing hearing, both the prosecution and Wilkins himself urged the court to apply the death penalty. The aggravating circumstances of the case led the court to decide that the death penalty was appropriate and sentenced Wilkins to die. The Missouri Supreme Court later upheld this decision.[46] Wilkins had not been executed by the time the *Roper v. Simmons* decision was made to eliminate the juvenile death penalty.

In 1988, the U.S. Supreme Court heard the case of *Thompson v. Oklahoma*.[47] Wayne Thompson was fifteen when he was arrested, along with his twenty-seven-year-old half-brother and two other older men, for the shooting and stabbing death of Charles Keene, Thompson's former brother-in-law. The Court ruled by a five-to-three vote that "the Eighth and Fourteenth Amendment[s] prohibit the execution of a person who was under sixteen years of age at the time of his or her offense."[48]

The Supreme Court upheld the constitutionality of the death penalty for juveniles in two 1989 cases. In the case of *Stanford v. Kentucky*, Kevin Stanford, a seventeen-year-old African-American youth, repeatedly raped and sodomized his victim during a robbery.[49] He then drove her to a secluded area, where he shot her point blank in the face and in the back of the head. A jury convicted Stanford of first-degree murder, first-degree sodomy, first-degree robbery, and receiving stolen property. Stanford was sentenced to death on September 28, 1989, and was transferred to death row.[50] He was not executed.

The important *Atkins v. Virginia* decision, rendered on June 20, 2002, emphasized very clearly the importance of mental retardation as a mitigating factor to be considered in sentencing juveniles. Atkins was convicted of abduction and armed robbery with a semiautomatic handgun. After the robbery, he drove the victim to a remote location and murdered him. Atkins was convicted of capital murder and sentenced to death. However, he was mentally deficient, and the Supreme Court ruled that mentally retarded juveniles could not be executed for their offenses.[51]

Individuals who were given capital sentences for crimes committed while they were juveniles continued to be executed until 2005. For example, on April 3, 2003, Scott Allen Hain was executed in Oklahoma for a murder he committed at age seventeen. Nevertheless, the juvenile death penalty has many vocal opponents. The human rights organization Amnesty International, the United Nations General Assembly, and other influential organizations continued to opt for the elimination of the juvenile death penalty in the United States. On March 1, 2005, in the case of *Roper v. Simmons* [(03-633) 112 SW 3d 397], the Supreme Court ruled, in a five-to-four decision, that no juveniles who committed their crimes under the age of eighteen could be executed. Focus on Policy 7–2 examines the arguments for and against the juvenile death penalty.

FOCUS ON POLICY   7–2
WHAT WERE THE ARGUMENTS OVER THE JUVENILE DEATH PENALTY?

The contentious issues that have fueled the debate over the death penalty for juveniles since the 1970s were highlighted in the arguments of both the advocates and opponents of the death penalty on the U.S. Supreme Court. The proponents of the death penalty were Justices Rehnquist, Scalia, Thomas, and O'Connor; the opponents were Justices Stevens, Kennedy, Souter, Breyer, and Ginsberg.

The Proponents of the Juvenile Death Penalty

Most of the proponents are considered conservatives or hardliners, who framed the following positions in their support of the juvenile death penalty:

- At the time the U.S. Constitution was written, common law permitted the execution of anyone age seven or over who committed a crime. Age, mental illness, and mental retardation were not then considered mitigating factors and were irrelevant from a strictly constitutional point of view. The argument of the proponents for juvenile executions today is simple—nothing in the Constitution forbids the execution of juveniles over the age of seven or those who are mentally retarded or mentally ill.

- Constitutionalists today will accept a movement away from the strict wording of the Constitution, but only very reluctantly and with deep consternation. Only if a very strong consensus emerges in society that supports a change not mandated explicitly by the Constitution can the laws be changed. Conservatives on the Rehnquist Court argued that it was very unlikely that a national consensus for change of the laws regulating the death penalty had come into existence since the issue was last ruled upon.

- Proponents of the juvenile death penalty also argue that, while it might be true that immaturity should be a bar to execution, juries today have been willing to distinguish between the immature and mature in capital cases; for that matter, juries in capital cases also appear to be quite capable of assessing the other mitigating factors of mental illness and mental retardation in their decision making.

- Many proponents of the juvenile death penalty go on to argue that some youths ages sixteen and seventeen are more mature than those in their late teens and twenties. Setting an arbitrary age of eighteen is untenable given the wide range of ages at which juveniles are recognized to be mature; nothing magical exists about the ages of eighteen and below, and these youths should be punished for their crimes.

- One very important argument of the conservative bloc of the Supreme Court emphasizes the need for proportionality in punishment; that is, that the punishment should fit the crime and not be cruel or unusual. Neoclassical theory argues that by ensuring that the punishment matches the crime in severity, the state and the law will have the respect of those the law governs.

The Opponents of the Juvenile Death Penalty

The opponents of the juvenile death penalty were for the most part justices considered part of a liberal bloc. These justices focused on the findings of modern science more than on classical and neoclassical thought and the importance of punishment.

The opponents agree with neoclassical assumptions about how individuals differ, but their emphasis is less on punishment than on individuals and the maturity level of juveniles.

- Opponents of the juvenile death penalty argue that society considers individuals under the age of eighteen not responsible enough to drink, vote, serve on juries, or even see certain movies; youths of about this age often are viewed as impetuous, impulsive, and reckless. These youths also have less control over their surroundings and are more vulnerable to outside influences. Consensus has long existed in society, in other words, that not until the age of eighteen do youths have a fully developed character.

- Opponents of the juvenile death penalty utilize their knowledge of research on childhood development today that recognizes the effects of family background on later personality development. They note that Mr. Simmons's early family life was very difficult. His father beat him and introduced him to drugs and alcohol at an early age; in his later adolescence, drugs and alcohol became staples of his life. He was impulsive, susceptible to being influenced and manipulated by others, and away from home for long periods of time. These characteristics, along with a subnormal intelligence, reflected the influences of his home life that resulted in his not being mature or cognitively aware to the extent that he could control his behavior.

- The opponents of the juvenile death penalty focus on the inability of an immature youth to understand, benefit, or be deterred from further offending. To the extent that the youth has "diminished responsibility," both cognitively and emotionally, because of youthfulness, immaturity, mental illness, or mental defectiveness, the impact of any punishment or "knowledge of the consequences" on his or her behavior is also diminished. Youths either will not or cannot understand the consequences of their actions or the punishments they receive to the same degree as adults.

- The opponents of the juvenile death penalty further maintain that a national consensus has developed against the juvenile death penalty. Some thirty states do not permit the execution of juveniles; no state has lowered the age at which juveniles may receive the death penalty in recent years; and five states have raised or established the age at eighteen.

- The opponents of the juvenile death penalty also point out that the execution of juveniles is a very rare event in recent years—an argument that may be important in future considerations of the adult death penalty.

- Finally, the juvenile death penalty opponents argue that "evolving standards of decency" and the mark of a "civilized society" call for the abolition of the juvenile death penalty. They point out that the 1994 Federal Death Penalty Act prohibited giving the death penalty to juveniles and that the United States was one of only two countries that officially permitted the execution of juveniles.

Critical Thinking Questions:
What do you believe ultimately influenced the U.S. Supreme Court to rule against the death penalty for any juvenile under eighteen? In your mind, which of these two groups of arguments make the most sense?

A PROPOSED ADULT COURT FOR JUVENILES

Whereas Thomas Geraghty and others advocate retaining the juvenile court, Barry C. Feld recommends abolishing it altogether. In one of the most highly respected articles on juvenile justice, Feld's "Criminalizing the American Juvenile Court" argues that youthful offenders should be tried in criminal court:

> If the child is a criminal and the primary purpose of formal intervention is social control, then young offenders could be tried in criminal courts alongside their adult counterparts. Before returning young offenders to criminal courts, however, there are preliminary issues of substance and procedure that a legislature should address. Issues of substantive justice include developing a rationale for sentencing young offenders differently, and more leniently, than older defendants. Issues of procedural justice include affording youths alternative safeguards *in addition* to full procedural parity with adult defendants. Taken in combination, legislation can avoid the worst of both worlds, provide more than the protections accorded to adults, and do justice in sentencing.[52]

Feld is quick to admit that "juveniles deserve less severe punishment than adults for comparable crimes."[53] Reasons for this, he adds, are that "juveniles are less able to understand the consequences of their acts" and that a juvenile's "removal from home is a more severe punishment than it would be for adults."[54]

The basis of Feld's argument for handling juveniles in the adult system is that "shorter sentences for reduced responsibility is a more modest rationale for treating young people differently than [are] the rehabilitative justifications advanced by the Progressive child savers."[55] He acknowledges that adult courts would be able to "impose shorter sentences for reduced culpability on a discretionary basis," but he thinks it would make more sense for legislatures "to provide youths with categorical fractional reductions of adult sentences." This could take the form of a formal "youth discount of adult sentences."[56] For example, he suggests that "a fourteen-year-old might receive 33 percent of the adult penalty, a sixteen-year-old 66 percent, and an eighteen-year-old the full penalty."[57]

He goes on to state that this "graduated age/culpability sentencing scheme" in adult court provides more justice than is typically found in juvenile waiver proceedings, such as ensuring similar consequences to similar youthful offenders, and that it saves considerable resources, especially eliminating the need for transfer hearings. It also ensures that juvenile offenders receive the same due process protections accorded adult offenders. Indeed, he says that "differentials in age and competency suggest that youths should receive more protection than adults, rather than less."[58]

In a number of other articles, Feld renews his previous call for the abolition of the juvenile court and, at the same time, recognizes youthfulness as a mitigating factor in sentencing juveniles in criminal court. He charges that the abolition of the juvenile court is necessary because changes in this court's jurisdiction, purpose, and procedures since its inception have transformed the court from its "original model as a social service agency into a deficient second-rate criminal court that provides people with neither positive treatment nor criminal procedural justice."[59]

Feld's solution is an integrated criminal court that has a separate sentencing policy for younger offenders, or a "youth discount." This discount is only fair because juveniles are more likely, due to their age, impulsiveness, and grandiosity, to be greater risk-takers than adults are. They also have limited ability to think about the long-term consequences of their actions and are more susceptible than adults are to negative peer influences. Feld also suggests that "[s]tates should maintain separate age-segregated youth correctional facilities to protect both younger offenders and older inmates."[60]

Feld is mindful of the dangers of his approach. He states:

> [A]lthough abolition of the juvenile court, enhanced procedural protections and a "youth discount" constitute essential components of a youth sentencing policy, nothing can prevent legislators from selectively choosing only those elements that serve their "get tough" agenda, even though doing so unravels the threads that make coherent a proposal for an integrated court.[61]

Irene Merker Rosenberg concurs with Feld's fear that legislatures' get tough agendas will corrupt this proposal for an integrated court. She charges that this proposal has two other serious flaws. First, she questions whether "the disparity in procedural and constitutional protection between the adult and juvenile courts [is] significant enough to justify opting out of the juvenile justice system."[62] She does not believe that these differences are as substantial as Feld and others claim. Second, she questions: "If children are tried in the criminal courts, will their immaturity and vulnerability be taken into account adequately in assessing culpability and determining sentencing?"[63] She argues that states are likely to conclude that "bringing children within the criminal jurisdiction is an assertion by the state that minors do not deserve specialized treatment."[64] Rosenberg then describes what perhaps is the fatal flaw of abolishing the juvenile court:

> Initially, perhaps there would be a burst of concern for the kiddie defendants. But once the glow wore off, and that would not take long, it would be back to business as usual: treadmill processing for adults both over and under the age of eighteen. Let us face it: As bad as the juvenile courts are, the adult criminal courts are worse. Adding a new class of defendants to an already overburdened system can only exacerbate the situation, all to the detriment of children.[65]

✓**Progress Check 7.2**
Review this section at
www.prenhall.com/bartollas

SUMMARY

- Justice for juveniles is decided within the context of society grappling with ways to solve the juvenile crime problem.
- Defining when childhood ends and adulthood begins is a worrisome problem; unfortunately, no objective tests are available to help society draw the line. The result is much confusion from state to state over the ways in which youths and adults are defined.
- Concern about status offenders persists, but the real debate focuses on the handling of serious juvenile crime.
- An increasingly popular trend is toward harsher treatment of younger violent and repetitive offenders. Punishments are being called for with increasing stridency, and state legislatures have developed mechanisms to ensure that punishment occurs.
- One such mechanism is to transfer juveniles to adult court through various types of waiver. Proponents of this practice believe that if juveniles are processed by adult courts, punishment is ensured and society will become safer as a result.
- Up to the *Roper v. Simmons* decision, which outlawed the death penalty for acts committed under the age of eighteen, the most serious consequence for juveniles was the possibility of being sentenced to the death penalty.

WEB SITE OF INTEREST

Various links about juveniles and the death penalty can be found at
http://www.abanet.org/crimjust/juvjus/links.html#death

CRITICAL THINKING QUESTIONS

1. What are the main types of waiver to the adult court?
2. Why is waiver such a controversial matter in juvenile justice?
3. What is your stand on the death penalty for juveniles? Do you support it or oppose it? Why?
4. When is treatment in the juvenile system no longer desirable for a juvenile?

NOTES

1. Compiled from the International Justice Project, "Juveniles: Christopher Simmons," http://www.internationaljusticeproject.org/juvCsimmons.cfm; Death Penalty Information Center, "U.S. Supreme Court; *Roper v. Simmons*," http://www.deathpenaltyinfo.org/(May 5, 2006); American Bar Association, "Christopher Simmons," http://www.abanet.org/crimjust/juvjus/simmons.html (May 5, 2006).

2. John P. Conrad, "Crime and the Child," in *Major Issues in Juvenile Justice Information and Training*, edited by Donna Hamparian et al. (Columbus, OH: Academy for Contemporary Problems, 1981), 179–82.

3. Stephen J. Morse, "Immaturity and Responsibility," *Journal of Criminal Law and Criminology* 88 (1998), 19–20.

4. Thomas F. Geraghty and Steven A. Drizin, "Foreword—The Debate Over the Future of Juvenile Courts: Can We Reach Consensus?" *Journal of Criminal Law and Criminology* 88 (1998), 6.

5. Elizabeth S. Scott and Thomas Grisso, "The Evolution of Adolescence: A Developmental Perspective on Juvenile Justice Reform," *Journal of Criminology and Criminal Justice* 88 (1998), 137, 174.

6. Ibid.

7. Ibid., 174–75.

8. Ibid., 189.

9. Ibid., 174–75.

10. Compiled by various news media.

11. Howard N. Snyder and Melissa Sickmund, *Juvenile Offenders and Victims: 2006 National Report* (Washington, DC: U.S. Department of Justice, Office of Justice Programs, Office of Juvenile Justice and Delinquency Prevention, 2006), 186.

12. Samuel M. Davis, *Rights of Juveniles: The Juvenile Justice System,* 2d ed. (New York: Clark Boardman, 1986), Section 4-2; see also Melissa Sickmund, *How Juveniles Get to Juvenile Court* (Washington, DC: Juvenile Justice Bulletin, 1994).

13. Davis, *Rights of Juveniles,* 24–26.

14. See the National Council of Juvenile and Family Court Judges, *Juvenile Delinquency Guidelines: Improving Court Practice in Juvenile Delinquency Cases,* (Reno, NV: Summer, 2005), 51.

15. Ibid, 106.

16. Ibid.

17. Ibid., 107.

18. Ibid., 108.

19. Ibid., 110.

20. Snyder and Sickmund, *Juvenile Offender and Victims: 2006 National Report*, 1986.

21. Donna Bishop, Charles E. Frazier, and John C. Henretta, "Prosecutorial Waiver: Case Study of a Questionable Reform," *Crime and Delinquency* 35 (1989), 179–201.

22. Marcy R. Podkopacz and Barry C. Feld, "The End of the Line: An Empirical Study of Judicial Waiver," *Journal of Criminal Law and Criminology* 86 (1996), 449–92.

23. Lee Ann Osburn and Peter A. Rose, "Prosecuting Juveniles as Adults: The Quest for 'Objective' Decisions," *Criminology* 22 (1984), 187–202.

24. Donna M. Bishop, Charles E. Frazier, Lonn Lanza-Kaduce, and Lawrence Winner, "The Transfer of Juveniles to Criminal Court: Does It Makes a Difference?" *Crime and Delinquency* 42 (1996), 171–91.

25. Donna Hamparian et al., " Youth in Adult Court: Between Two Worlds," major issues in *Juvenile Justice Information and Training* (Columbus, OH: Academy for Contemporary Problems, 1981).

26. Donna Martin Hamparian et al., *The Violent Few: A Study of Dangerous Juvenile Offenders* (Lexington, MA: Lexington Books, 1980), 33–34

27. Quoted in Barry C. Feld, "Violent Youth and Public Policy: Minnesota Juvenile Justice Task Force and 1994 Legislative Reform," paper presented at the annual meeting of the American Society of Criminology, Miami (1994), 9.

28. Ibid. See also Barry C. Feld, "Violent Youth and Public Policy: A Case Study of Juvenile Justice Law Reform," *Minnesota Law Review* 79 (May 1995), 965–1128.

29. Richard E. Redding, "Juvenile Offenders in Criminal Court and Adult Prison: Legal, Psychological, and Behavioral Outcomes," *Juvenile and Family Court Journal* 50 (1999), 1–20.

30. Snyder and Sickmund, *Juvenile Offenders and Victims: 2006 National Report*, 237.

31. Ibid., 117.

32. Salvador A. Godinez, "Managing Juveniles in Adult Facilities," *Corrections Today* 61 (April 1999), 86–87.

33. Gary Fleming and Gerald Winkler, "Sending Them to Prison: Washington State Learns to Accommodate Female Youthful Offenders in Prison," *Corrections Today* 61 (April 1999), 132–33.

34. Ibid., 133.

35. The decision was rendered in two cases. One was *Stanford v. Kentucky,* No. 87–5765. See Linda Greenhouse, "Death Sentences Against Retarded and Young Upheld," *New York Times,* June 27, 1989, A1, A18.

36. Much of the current section on the development of the death penalty comes from Victor L. Strieb, *Death Penalty for Juveniles* (Bloomington: Indiana University Press, 1987), 21–40.

37. *Gregg v. Georgia,* 48 U.S. 153 (1976).

38. Ibid., 197.

39. Lockett v. Ohio, 438 U.S. 536 (1978).

40. Strieb, *Death Penalty for Juveniles,* 22.

41. Ibid., 24–25.

42. Ibid.

43. Ibid.

44. *Eddings v. Oklahoma,* 102 S. Ct. (1982).

45. Ibid.

46. *Stanford v. Kentucky; Wilkins v. Missouri,* 109 S. Ct. 2969 (1989).

47. *Thompson v. Oklahoma,* 102 S. Ct. (1988).

48. Ibid.

49. *Stanford v. Kentucky,* 492 U.S. 361 (1989).

50. Ibid.

51. *Atkins v. Virginia,* 536 U.S. 304 (2002).

52. Barry C. Feld, "Criminalizing the American Juvenile Court," in *Readings in Juvenile Justice Administration,* edited by Barry C. Feld (New York: Oxford University Press, 1999), 361.

53. Ibid., 364.

54. Ibid.

55. Ibid.

56. Ibid.

57. Ibid., 336.

58. Barry C. Feld, "The Transformation of the Juvenile Court," *Minnesota Law Review* 75 (1991), 691–725; Barry C. Feld, "Abolish the Juvenile Court: Youthfulness, Criminal Responsibility, and Sentencing Policy," *Journal of Criminal Law and Criminology* 88 (1997), 115–33.

59. Feld, "Abolish the Juvenile Court," 90.

60. Ibid., 130.

61. Ibid., 133.

62. Irene Merker Rosenberg, "Leaving Bad Enough Alone: A Response to the Juvenile Court Abolitionists," in *Readings in Juvenile Justice Administration,* 368.

63. Ibid.

64. Ibid., 370.

65. Ibid.

8

JUVENILE PROBATION

One success story I remember is a seventeen-year-old black girl who had been arrested on first-degree robbery and prostitution. She had never been referred before. What it came down to was there were two juvenile girls with two adult males who were their boyfriends, and they were in a bar trying to shake down this white guy. The girls got him up to their apartment, and they were going to get it on with him. Then their boyfriends came up and were real mad because he was with their women. The white guy said, "Take anything," and they took some money he had in his car. The robbery charge was dropped, but there was a finding of fact on prostitution charge. She was placed on supervision until her eighteenth birthday. When I got her, the first thing we did was go out to the hospital's family practice center to have her checked and placed on birth control. But she was already pregnant. The majority of time we spent together was concentrated on job, education, getting ready for the baby, and independent living skills. It wasn't a traditional probation case. We spent a lot of time together, getting ready for her future. Her mother was dead and her father was in the Mental Health Institute. Several older sisters were already on ADC [Aid to Dependent Children], weren't married, and were not models by any means. So I felt like I'm the one she counted on. I took her to the hospital when she had her baby and was with her during delivery. It was a neat experience. She asked me to be the godmother for her baby. She's now very motivated to make something out of herself. She is now nineteen, has her own car, and keeps an apartment fairly well. She has either gone to school or worked since before she had the baby. With what she has had to work with, it's amazing she is doing so well.

—Probation officer[1]

OUTLINE

OBJECTIVES

1. To define juvenile probation and discuss its operations
2. To discuss the history of probation services
3. To reveal the problems and challenges of probation services
4. To evaluate the effectiveness of juvenile probation

KEY TERMS

balanced approach to juvenile
   probation
electronic monitoring
house arrest
intake
intensive supervision programs
   (ISPs)

investigation
justice model
probation
probation subsidy programs
restitution
restorative justice model
social study report

supervision
Wisconsin system

Probation is a judicial disposition under which youthful offenders are subject to certain conditions imposed by the juvenile court and are permitted to remain in the community under the supervision of a probation officer. The probation officer assists offenders in their efforts to meet the conditions of the court. As expressed vividly in this chapter's opening quote, the basic goal of probation, over and above giving troublesome youths a second chance, is to provide services that will help offenders stay out of trouble with the law. Probation is the most widely used judicial disposition of the juvenile court.

In 2000, the juvenile court ordered probation in 20 percent of the more than one million cases that received a juvenile court sanction. Probation was ordered in 23 percent of the cases involving person offenses, 40 percent involving property offenses, 13 percent involving drug law violations, and 24 percent involving public order offenses.[2]

The word *probation* is used in at least four ways in the juvenile justice system. It can refer to (1) a disposition of the juvenile court in lieu of institutionalization, (2) the status of an adjudicated offender, (3) a subsystem of the juvenile justice system (the term's most common use), and (4) the activities, functions, and services that characterize this subsystem's transactions with the juvenile court, the youthful offender, and the community. The probation process includes the intake phase of the juvenile court's proceedings, preparation of the social investigation for the disposition stage, supervision of probationers, and obtaining or providing services for youths on probation.

Probation is considered a desirable alternative to institutionalization for several reasons: First, it allows offenders to retain their liberty but provides society with some protection against continued disregard for the law. Second, it promotes the rehabilitation of offenders because they can maintain normal community contacts by living at home, attending school, and participating in community activities. Third, it avoids the negative impact of institutional confinement, and furthermore, it costs less than incarceration.

HOW IS PROBATION ADMINISTERED?

In fifteen states and the District of Columbia, probation is under the control of the juvenile court and is funded by city or county government, as shown in Table 8–1. In the other thirty-five states, a variety of means to organize and administer juvenile probation are found. The most effective strategy is probably placing juvenile probation under the control of the juvenile court and funding it through local government agencies. This is particularly true in states that provide revenue support of staff to local systems that meet state standards.

Private contractors are increasingly being used in juvenile probation, especially in providing intensive probation and aftercare services. To encourage the expansion of privatization in juvenile probation, the Office of Juvenile Justice and Delinquency Prevention funded a $1.7 million three-year project, the Private Sector Probation Initiative. The selected experimental sites were the Third Judicial District of Utah (Salt Lake City); Cuyahoga County (Cleveland), Ohio; Kenosha County, Wisconsin; Oklahoma County (Oklahoma City), Oklahoma; and the city and county of San Francisco.[3]

In order to bring about greater uniformity in administration of local probation, several states offer rewards of either revenue support or manpower to local systems if they comply with state standards. Michigan, for example, assigns state-paid probation officers to work with local probation officers. Usually, though, states make direct payments to local governments to defray part of the costs of probation services. In New York State, for example, a local community that is willing to meet state staffing patterns is reimbursed for up to 50 percent of its operating costs for probation services.

Other states, such as California, Nevada, Oregon, and Washington, have developed **probation subsidy programs** that encourage a decreased rate of commitment of offenders by counties to state institutions. The money saved by the state is returned to the counties. California initiated this program after a study indicated that many offenders committed to state correctional institutions could safely remain in the community under good probation supervision.

The California Probation Subsidy Program was set up in 1966 by the state's youth authority, which was authorized to pay up to $4,000 to each

Table 8–1   *National Summary of the Organization and Administration of Juvenile Probation*

Organizational and Administration of Probation	Number of States	States
Local/judicial	15	Alabama, Arizona, Arkansas, Colorado, District of Columbia, Illinois, Indiana, Kansas, Michigan, Missouri, Montana, Nevada, New Jersey, Pennsylvania, Texas
State/judicial	10	Connecticut, Hawaii, Maine, Maryland, New Hampshire, New Mexico, North Carolina, Rhode Island, South Carolina, Vermont
State/executive	11	Alaska, Delaware, Florida, Maine, Maryland, New Hampshire, New Mexico, North Carolina, Rhode Island, South Carolina, Vermont
Local/executive	3	Idaho, New York, Oregon
combination	4	California, Kentucky, Washington, Wisconsin

Source: National Center for Juvenile Justice 2000, "National Overviews." State Juvenile Justice Profiles (Pittsburgh, PA: NCJJ). Online: http://www.ncjj.org/stateprofiles.

county for every adult and juvenile offender not committed to a state correctional institution. In turn, the counties were required to improve probation services by employing additional probation officers and reducing caseloads. Additionally, it was required that each county demonstrate innovative approaches to probation, such as intensive supervision of hard-core adult offenders and certain types of juvenile offenders.

Washington's juvenile probation subsidy is modeled on the one in California. It has been instrumental in reducing commitment rates to juvenile institutions and in improving the quality of probation services because 90 percent of Washington's thirty-nine counties participate in the program.

WHAT ARE THE FUNCTIONS OF PROBATION SERVICES?

The three basic functions of juvenile probation are intake, investigation, and supervision. At the intake stage of the court proceedings, the probation officer decides whether or not to file a petition on a child referred to the court. Investigation involves compiling a social history or study of a child judged delinquent to assist the judge in making the wisest disposition. Supervision, initiated when the judge places a youth on probation, focuses primarily on risk control and crime reduction.

INTAKE

During the intake stage of the court proceedings (which was discussed in Chapter 5), the probation officer carefully screens the referrals to the court. Both the statutes of the state and the office of the state's prosecutor are helpful in determining whether or not any case referred to the court actually falls under its jurisdiction. At **intake**, the probation officer also conducts a preliminary investigation, which includes an interview during which the youth is advised of his or her legal rights. If parents or guardians have not already been contacted, the probation department gets in touch with them to discuss the status of the child and to advise them of their right to have an attorney. The intake probation officer may need to interview the family, witnesses, victims, arresting officers, peers, or neighbors to obtain sufficient information with which to make a sound determination on the necessity of filing a court petition for detention of the child. The probation officer also may need to contact the school and other agencies that have worked with the child. If the youth has been in court before or is already on probation, the intake officer must also familiarize himself or herself with the previous reports. Table 8–2 lists the

Table 8–2   *Some Programs Utilized by Local Probation Departments*

4-H programs	Self-improvement classes	Day school
Social skills development	Youth courts	Evening care
School-based probation	Teen courts	Community service
Truancy programs	Drug courts	Volunteer work
After-school study program	Positive peer group	Big Brothers/Big Sisters
Sports programs	Reintegration programs	Volunteers in probation
After-school counseling	Faith-based initiatives	Drug counseling
Writing a paper	Treatment court	Sex offender programs
Curfew requirements	Job training	Aggression replacement training
Restorative programs	Alcohol counseling	Runaway programs
Restitution programs	Intensive supervision	House arrest

types of programs to which probation officers can refer youths at the intake stage or later in the juvenile court process. Some jurisdictions, of course, have more of these programs than others.

INVESTIGATION

If a juvenile court uses the bifurcated hearing (separation of adjudicatory and disposition stages), a **social study report** is ordered by the judge when a youth is found delinquent at the fact-finding stage of the court proceedings. Probation officers usually are given up to sixty days to make their **investigation**, but if the court combines the adjudicatory and disposition stages, the social study must be completed before a youth appears in front of the judge. The judge is not supposed to read this social study *until* the child is found to be delinquent.

The social study report details the minor's personal background, family, educational progress present offense, previous violations of the law, and employment. Also included are a description of the offender's neighborhood; the family's ability to pay court and institutionalization costs; the minor's physical and mental health; the attitude of the family, the police, the neighbors, and the community toward the minor; and the attitude of the minor toward the offense in question and toward himself or herself. The social study concludes with the probation officer's diagnosis and treatment plan for the youth. An important part of this treatment plan is the probation officer's recommended course of action. In this report the officer determines whether the youth should remain in the community; if so, the conditions of probation are stated. For a social study report, see Focus on Practice 8–1.

SUPERVISION

The length of time a juvenile must spend on probation varies among states. The maximum length in some states is until the juvenile reaches the age of majority, which is usually age sixteen or seventeen. Other states limit juvenile probation to a specific duration. In Illinois, it is limited to five years; in New York, two years; in Washington, DC, one year; and in California, six months.

Once a youth has been placed on probation, the probation officer is required to provide the best possible **supervision**, which includes surveillance, casework services, and counseling or guidance. Surveillance involves careful monitoring of the minor's adjustment to the community. To accomplish this, the officer must establish personal contact with the minor and must learn whether the youth is attending school or is working each day, whether adequate guidance is being received from parents, and whether the child is obeying the terms of probation. At the same time, the probation officer must determine if the youth is continuing to break the law.

In 1973, the job responsibilities of the probation officer changed when the National Advisory Commission on Criminal Justice Standards and Goals recommended that a community resource manager could meet the goals of probation and parole more effectively than could a caseworker. Fulfilling the community resource manager, or broker, role required probation officers to refer clients to the community resources needed for their rehabilitation. This role requires the probation officer to mesh a probationer's identified needs with the range of available services. In helping probationers to obtain needed services, the probation officer must assess the situation, contact the appropriate available resource providers, assist the probationer in obtaining needed services, and follow up on the case. The probation officer, in this new role, should take the responsibility for ensuring that the needed services are delivered, and then should monitor and evaluate the services.[4]

As the reintegration model came under increased attack in the mid-1970s, a number of juvenile probation departments adopted the concept of the Community

FOCUS ON PRACTICE 8–1
JUVENILE COURT RECOMMENDATIONS

I. Juvenile Under Consideration

Name: (juvenile)
D.O.B.: 00-00-0000
Court Docket No. JVJV00—XXXXX

A. Intake Information

On mm/dd/yy, the juvenile was charged with Disorderly Conduct by the Waterloo Police Department. This incident centered around a neighborhood conflict that led to (juvenile) throwing rocks and yelling out profanities.

On mm/dd/yy, the juvenile was charged with two counts of Third Degree Burglary and Possession of Burglar Tools by the Waterloo Police Department. These charges were in reference to car burglaries that occurred in a parking ramp in downtown Waterloo.

On mm/dd/yy, a delinquency petition was filed in the Black Hawk County Juvenile Court alleging the juvenile to be a delinquent child regarding three counts of delinquency.

II. Victim Impact Information

(Juvenile) has been Court ordered to pay $417.82 as his share of restitution regarding the Third Degree Burglary charge that was dismissed.

B. Referral and Court History

The juvenile was first referred to this office on mm/dd/yy by the Waterloo Police Department in regard to the delinquent act of Criminal Mischief in the Third Degree. The juvenile was placed on an Informal Adjustment Agreement on mm/dd/yy, that he successfully completed, warranting the case to be dismissed in month 1997.

The juvenile was referred to the Department of Juvenile Court Services on mm/dd/yy, regarding the delinquent act of Theft in the Fifth Degree. The juvenile was once again placed on an Informal Adjustment Agreement; however, the family moved to Cedar Rapids, Iowa, three months after that agreement was entered into. He remained on an Informal Adjustment Agreement and the matter was closed in month 1998.

Between month, 1998, and month, 1998, the juvenile was referred to the Department of Juvenile Court Services on the delinquent acts of Third Degree Burglary, Theft Fourth Degree, and Disorderly Conduct. On mm/dd/yy, the juvenile admitted to the Third Degree Burglary charge and a formal adjudication of delinquency was withheld of Theft in the Fourth Degree and Disorderly Conduct.

On mm/dd/yy, a Pre-Trial Conference was held in the interest of Juvenile Case No. JVJV009053 in front of [an] Associate Juvenile Court Judge. The parties were unable to come to an agreement in this matter, so a contested Adjudication Hearing was scheduled.

An Adjudication Hearing was held on mm/dd/yy, in the interest of (juvenile) in front of an Associate Juvenile Court Judge. At the time of the hearing, the Court was informed that the juvenile would be admitting to the charges of Disorderly Conduct and Theft Fifth. In return for this admission, the State would agree to dismiss paragraph 3(b) alleging the delinquent act of Third Degree Burglary as long as the juvenile agreed to pay restitution. The Court accepted the plea agreement and entered formal adjudications of delinquency on the charges of Disorderly Conduct and Theft Fifth and ordered the juvenile to pay the restitution in regards to the dismissed charge of Third Degree Burglary. The juvenile was also Court ordered to complete twenty hours of community service in regards to the Disorderly Conduct charge. The matter was then scheduled for a Dispositional Hearing.

C. Personal History

(Juvenile) was born mm/dd, 1986, in Chicago, Illinois. (Please see Certificate of Birth attached to this document for verification.)

a. *Health History* The juvenile and his mother are unable to report any significant health concerns that would prohibit this juvenile from successfully complying with the terms of his probation.

b. *Parental Concerns Regarding Juvenile's Behavior* The parent reports that the juvenile has always been respectful toward her and his grandparent. She reports that her biggest concerns regarding her son are the struggles he has academically in school and his tendency to be a follower.

c. *Juvenile's Attitude toward Parents* (Juvenile) readily admits that he respects and loves his mother and that he wants to reside in her home. However, he is also quick to admit that he is somewhat confused and not real comfortable with the current situation. (Juvenile), his younger siblings, and his mother were just recently evicted from their home.

d. *Juvenile's Attitude Regarding Offense* (Juvenile) claims he does not like breaking the law and wants to get off of probation as soon as possible. He understands that the acts of delinquency he did commit were wrong and that if he continues to behave in that manner he will find himself deeper and deeper into the system, which is something he wants to avoid. He has agreed to comply with the Juvenile Court and up until this time he has for the most part.

D. Education

Other than attending preschool through third grade in Chicago, Illinois, and a brief portion of his sixth-grade year in Cedar Rapids, the juvenile has attended school in the Waterloo Public School System for the majority of his educational needs. He is currently a ninth-grade student at the high school. He does receive special education services through Area Educational Agency VII for mental and learning disabilities and has been involved with these services since 1993.

(Juvenile) is performing at an unacceptable level currently academically. His third-quarter grades consisted of five F's and two C's. His teachers feel that he can do better, as does (juvenile). His school progress will continue to be monitored and it is hoped that this officer can arrange for some tutorial assistance this summer through an agency like University of Northern Iowa—Center for Urban Education (UNI-CUE)—in an effort to assist (juvenile) with achieving some high school credits or at least enhancing his academic ability.

III. The Family

A. Father

(Parent) is (juvenile's) biological father. (Parent) is thirty-six years of age and resides in the Chicago area. (Juvenile) has not had any significant contact with his father in almost ten years.

B. Mother

(Parent) is (juvenile's) biological mother. (Parent) was born mm/dd, 1968, in the State of Illinois. (Parent) has earned her GED since moving to Waterloo, Iowa, in 1992. She reports no criminal or military history.

(Parent) is currently unemployed. Her previous work experience includes working for a telephone company and in the housekeeping department through a local hotel.

C. Siblings

(Sibling), fifteen, is (juvenile's) half-brother. (Sibling) recently moved back to the area after living with his grandfather briefly in Cincinnati, Ohio. (Sibling) has a history with the Department of Juvenile Court Services that included his participation in day/evening treatment programming.

(Sibling), thirteen, is (juvenile's) half-sister. (Sibling) is residing at [the] current time with her grandmother in Waterloo and is attending school. She does have a history regarding a misdemeanor charge with this office and was supervised by a Volunteer Juvenile Court.

(Sibling), nine, is (juvenile's) half-brother. He is currently residing with his mother.

D. Child Abuse Information

There was a registered child abuse complaint regarding (parent). This involved denial of critical care due to the conditions of her home. There were services offered to the family through the Department of Human Services at that time.

IV. Conclusions

A. Recommendation to the Court

It is the recommendation of the First Judicial District Department of Juvenile Court Services that the custody of (juvenile) remain with his mother while he is placed under the formal supervision of the Department of Juvenile Court Services, and ordered to abide by the conditions of a probation contract that will be submitted to the Court the day of the hearing.

B. Reasons Supporting Recommendations

a. The juvenile has been adjudicated delinquent on the charges of Disorderly Conduct and Theft in the Fifth Degree, as well as ordered to pay restitution in the amount of $417.82 in regard to a Third Degree Burglary charge that was dismissed.

b. (Juvenile) has demonstrated some compliance with the expectations laid upon him by the Juvenile Court since the time of his Adjudication Hearing. Examples of this compliance are no unexcused absences from school and repayment of approximately $100.00 toward his restitution obligation.

c. The Juvenile Court can add some structure and guidance, as well as supervision, to this juvenile's life during this chaotic period with his family.

d. If (juvenile's) family situation does not stabilize or if he experiences further behavior problems, more restrictive dispositional alternatives may have to be considered.

Source: Provided by Juvenile Court Services, Blackhawk County (Iowa), 2001.

Critical Thinking Questions:
What were your impressions of this juvenile after reading his social study report? Why do you think he became involved in juvenile crime? Are his law-violating behaviors likely to continue?

Resource Management Team (CRMT). Under this approach to probation services, officers are divided into teams, and each team takes responsibility for a caseload and makes decisions on what community resources are needed by clients. New probationers are interviewed by a member of the team, and their needs are plotted on a needs assessment scale. The members of the teams are usually specialists in "needs subsystems" dealing with such problems as drug abuse, alcoholism, mental illness, or runaway behavior, and the specialist links the probationer with the necessary services in the community.[5] A director of court services in a midwestern state indicates why she supports such a team approach:

> For probation to really be effective, the credibility of the probation officer would have to be enhanced and caseloads would have to be [limited to] fifteen. If we took all the resources we're putting into institutions, group homes, and psychiatric resources, we would have the necessary resources for probation. I would go with the team approach; we need a case manager so that we could use different treatment for different kids.[6]

In the 1980s, supervision in juvenile probation was influenced by the Wisconsin system, the justice model, the balanced approach to probation, and the reduced risk and increased surveillance models.

Concerns for public safety in the 1980s persuaded many probation departments to develop classification systems or to use the Wisconsin system or community assessment centers to place probationers under intensive, medium, or minimum supervision. Under the **Wisconsin system**, a risk/needs assessment is conducted for each probationer at regular intervals. The risk scale was derived from empirical studies that showed certain factors to be good predictors of recidivism—prior arrest record, age at first conviction, the nature of the offense for which the probationer was convicted, school or employment patterns, and so forth. The needs assessment focuses on such indicators as emotional stability, financial management, family relationships, and health. The scores derived from the risk/needs assessment are used to classify probationers by required level of supervision—intensive, medium, or minimum. Reassessment of cases takes place at regular intervals, and the level of supervision may be increased or reduced.[7]

The most widely used risk/needs assessment of human behavior is the Problem Severity Index, a screening tool that gives intake officers and others clues about the types of problems the offenders might have. Once a problem area(s) is identified, the juvenile is assessed using diagnostic tools in an attempt to identify the problem more specifically. Clinicians then can combine various diagnostic measures to develop protocols for treatment. Risk assessment today is used to classify offenders, to predict future behavior for reducing recidivism, and for intervention planning.[8] An examination of risk assessment distinguishes between risk assessments that are developed to *predict* behavior and those developed to enable workers to *manage* behavior.[9]

The use of risk/needs assessments in juvenile probation raises the issue of how effective they are in predicting juveniles' behaviors. The fact of the matter is that it is very difficult to predict behavior, especially for juveniles. Thus, whatever predictive techniques or classification systems are used in juvenile justice, the results are far less than desirable in forecasting juvenile behavior.[10]

The **justice model** influenced the reduction of discretion in juvenile probation in the 1980s and early 1990s. David Fogel, in advocating the reduction of the discretionary authority of probation officers, recommended that the standard of proof for the revocation of probation be as strong as the original finding that resulted in the sentence of probation (i.e., beyond a reasonable doubt). Proponents of the justice model contend that the social study report should be regarded as a legal document, and defendants have the right to know the

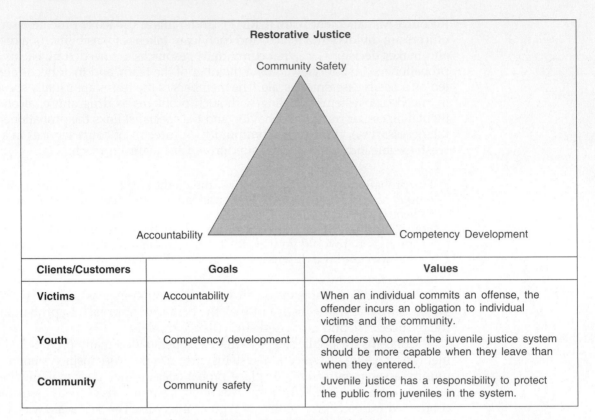

Figure 8–1 *Graphic Representation of the Balanced Approach Mission*

Source: Adapted from D. Maloney, D. Romig, and T. Armstrong, *Juvenile Probation! The Balanced Approach* (Reno, NV: National Council of Juvenile and Family Court Judges, 1998).

contents of this report. Fogel and other advocates of the justice model have recommended increasing restitution programs, because they believe it is only fair for offenders to pay for the social harm they have inflicted.[11] Not everyone would agree; for example, a female juvenile probation officer in the Midwest described this legal movement in juvenile probation: "It was a lot easier for us to get things done five years ago when the law was more flexible."[12]

Accountability models began to be formulated in the 1980s for supervising juvenile probationers. For example, Dennis Maloney, Dennis Romig, and Troy Armstrong developed what they called the **balanced approach to juvenile probation.** Its purpose is "to protect the community from delinquency, to impose accountability for offenses committed, and to equip juvenile offenders with the required competencies to live productively and responsibly in the community."[13] One of the popular features of this balanced approach is the equal attention it gives to the community, the victim, and the juvenile offender (see Figure 8–1). Juvenile probation departments in Oregon, Texas, and Wisconsin have implemented this accountability model in supervising juvenile probationers.[14]

The formulation of the balanced approach to juvenile probation has led to the development of the **restorative justice model.** This model, as suggested in Chapter 1, gained impetus in the 1970s and 1980s from the victim's movement, from youthful offenders' experiences with reparative sanctions, and from the rise of informal neighborhood programs and dispute resolution programs in the community.[15] The purpose of this integrated, balanced, and restorative justice model is to reconcile "the interests of victims, offenders, and the community through common programs and supervision practices that meet mutual needs."[16] For a restorative justice yardstick, see Focus on Practice 8–2.

✓**Progress Check 8.1**
Review this section at
www.prenhall.com/bartollas

FOCUS ON PRACTICE
A RESTORATIVE JUSTICE YARDSTICK

8–2

1. Do victims experience justice?
   - Do victims have sufficient opportunities to tell their truth to relevant listeners?
   - Do victims receive needed compensation or restitution?
   - Is the injustice adequately acknowledged?
   - Are victims sufficiently protected against further violation?
   - Does the outcome adequately reflect the severity of the offense?
   - Do victims receive adequate information about the crime, the offender, and the legal process?
   - Do victims have a voice in the legal process?
   - Is the experience of justice adequately public?
   - Do victims receive adequate support from others?
   - Do victims' families receive adequate assistance and support?
   - Are other needs—material, psychological, and spiritual—being addressed?
2. Do offenders experience justice?
   - Are offenders encouraged to understand and take responsibility for what they have done?
   - Are misattributions challenged?
   - Are offenders given encouragement and opportunities to make things right?
   - Are offenders given opportunities to participate in the process?
   - Are offenders encouraged to change their behavior?
   - Is there a mechanism for monitoring or verifying changes?
   - Are offenders' needs being addressed?
   - Do offenders' families receive support and assistance?
3. Is the victim–offender relationship addressed?
   - Is there an opportunity for victims and offenders to meet, if appropriate?
   - Is there an opportunity for victims and offenders to exchange information about the event and about one another?
4. Are community concerns being taken into account?
   - Are the process and the outcome sufficiently public?
   - Is community protection being addressed?
   - Is there a need for restitution or a symbolic action for the community?
   - Is the community represented in some way in the legal process?
5. Is the future addressed?
   - Is there provision for solving the problems that led to this event?
   - Is there provision for solving problems caused by this event?
   - Have future intentions been addressed?
   - Are there provisions for monitoring and verifying outcomes and for problem solving?

Source: Howard Zehr, *Changing Lenses* (Scottdale, PA: Pennsylvania Herald Press, 1990).

Critical Thinking Questions:
What is your evaluation of this restorative justice yardstick? Do you believe that restorative justice is a good direction for juvenile justice to go? Why or why not?

HOW ABOUT RISK CONTROL AND CRIME REDUCTION?

In the 1990s, as juvenile probation continued to face the criticism that it allowed probationers to escape punishment, reduced risk and increased surveillance models received major emphasis. Restitution and intensive supervision were the most widely used of these short-term behavior control models, but house arrest, electronic monitoring, and shock probation also gained some attention.

RESTITUTION

Restitution, a disposition that requires offenders to repay their victims or the community for their crime, began to be used widely in probation during the 1970s and 1980s. Indeed, by 1985, formal programs were known to exist in more than four hundred jurisdictions; more than thirty-five states now have statutory authority to order monetary or community service restitution.[17] Part of the reason for the skyrocketing growth of restitution programs is that the Office of Juvenile Justice and Delinquency Prevention (OJJDP) has spent some $30 million promoting the use of restitution in eighty-five juvenile courts across the nation.[18] OJJDP followed this initiative with the National Restitution Training Program in 1983 and the Restitution Education, Specialized Training, and Technical Assistance (RESTTA) Project in 1985. These initiatives are directly responsible for most of the growth of restitution programs.[19] Figure 8–2 shows the growth of restitution programs.

Three broad types of restitution obligation can be ordered by the juvenile court: straight financial restitution, community service, and direct service to victims. Community service is the most common type, probably because it is the easiest to administer. Direct service is the most rare, largely because of victims' reluctance to have contact with offenders. However, the three program

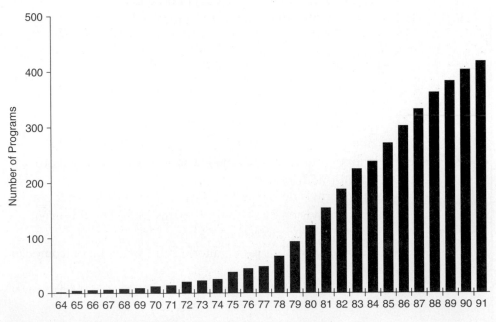

Figure 8–2   *Dramatic Rise of Restitution Programs (Average)*

Source: Peter R. Schneider and Matthew C. Finkelstein, *New Trends in Restitution Programming Results from the 1991 RESTTA Survey* (Washington, DC: Office of Juvenile Justice and Delinquency Prevention, 2000), p. 15.

types frequently blend together. For example, a local jurisdiction may organize work crews and even enter into recycling, janitorial, and other service contacts with public or private agencies in order to provide youthful offenders with jobs so that they can pay restitution. The most common goals of restitution programs are holding juveniles accountable, providing reparation to victims, treating and rehabilitating juveniles, and punishing juveniles.[20]

When it comes to making restitution and community service work, probation officers are key players, and in many jurisdictions it is up to a juvenile probation officer to do some or all of the following:

- Determining eligibility for participation
- Calculating appropriate amounts
- Assessing the offender's ability to pay
- Developing a payment/work schedule
- Monitoring performance
- Closing the case[21]

Juvenile courts have instituted job skills preparation classes to help juveniles with ordered restitution to find and hold jobs. The private and public sectors sometimes provide jobs in which youths required to make restitution can earn money and compensate victims. Juveniles failing to complete their restitution payments may have their probation term extended.

With community work restitution, probationers generally are required to work for a certain number of hours at a private nonprofit or government agency. Sites where the work may be performed include public libraries, parks, nursing homes, animal shelters, community centers, day-care centers, youth agencies, YMCAs and YWCAs, and local streets. In large departments, restitution programs provide supervised work crews in which juveniles go to a site and work under the supervision of an adult.

A juvenile probation officer tells why he supports the restitution program in his department:

> The restitution program deals with kids who damage property and harm others. The kids who go into the C.R.P. [Community Restitution Program] aren't hard-core offenders; they are less serious—simple assaults, theft in fifth-degree. Actually, they don't need supervision of a PO [probation officer]. Things at home are okay; school and peer relationships are also okay. So there's no real service we can provide. But we feel they need some kind of consequence for the action they've taken and that's why they're placed in the program. POs also use our program for those who won't comply with supervision. For example, if they have a kid who is missing appointments, they'll ask the judge to assign him so many hours to work in the C.R.P.[22]

In Hennepin County, Minnesota (Minneapolis), youthful offenders quickly discover themselves placed by the juvenile judge on a Saturday work squad for a specified amount of community service. First-time offenders usually find that they are sentenced to forty hours. Every Saturday, these youths are required to be at the downtown meeting place at 8:00 A.M. From there, five trucks are sent out with ten youths and two staff members in each truck. The coordinator of the program, who is on the staff of the probation department, then assigns each youth to a specific work detail. These details include recycling bottles and cans, visiting patients at a nursing home, doing janitorial work, cleaning bus stops, planting trees or removing barbed wire fences at a city park, and working at a park reserve.[23]

INTENSIVE SUPERVISION

In the early 1980s, **intensive supervision programs (ISPs)** began to be used in adult probation as a response to the emerging issues of prison crowding, cost escalation, and society's hardline response to crime. It was called *intensive probation supervision* (IPS) because it was operated or administered by probation, because it involved increased contacts, and because it generally emphasized external controls and surveillance.[24]

Juvenile justice soon followed adult justice, as so frequently happens, in implementing ISPs in juvenile probation. Georgia, New Jersey, Oregon, and Pennsylvania have experimented with or have instituted statewide ISPs for juveniles.[25] Indeed, by the end of the 1980s, juvenile judges across the nation were commonly placing high-risk offenders on small caseloads and assigning them frequent contact with a probation officer.

For example, the Juvenile Court Judges' Commission in the Commonwealth of Pennsylvania developed such a project in the 1980s because of its concern with increased commitments to training schools.[26] The standard adopted for this project included a caseload size of no more than fifteen, a minimum of three contacts per week with the youth, a minimum of one contact per week with the family or guardian, and a minimum of six months and a maximum of twelve months of intensive services.[27] Thirty-two counties in Pennsylvania had established ISPs with these standards by the end of 1989.[28]

An Integrated Social Control (ISC) model of intensive supervision recently has been developed to address the major causal factors identified in delinquency theory and research. This proposed model integrates the central components of strain, control, and social learning theories. It contends that the combined forces of inadequate socialization, strains between educational and occupational aspirations and expectations, and social disorganization in the neighborhood lead to weak bonding to conventional values and to activities in the family, school, and community. Weak bonding, in turn, can lead juveniles to delinquent behavior through negative peer influence.[29] See Figure 8–3 for this model.

The evaluation of adult ISPs in adult probation has received encouraging results in prevention of recidivism.[30] Two national evaluations of these programs in juvenile probation, however, have discovered that "neither the possible effectiveness nor the possible ineffectiveness of these programs had been carefully examined. As a result, their status in this regard, including their impact on recidivism, was essentially unknown."[31]

HOUSE ARREST AND ELECTRONIC MONITORING

House arrest, or home confinement, is a program of intermediate punishment whereby youths are ordered to remain confined in their own residences during evening hours after curfew and on weekends.[32] Those receiving house arrest may be allowed to leave during the day for doctors' appointments, school, employment, or approved religious services. Electronic monitoring equipment may be used to verify probationers' presence in the residence in which they are required to remain. Electronic monitoring methods include:

- Continuous signaling devices, which use a transmitter attached to the probationer that emits a continuous radio signal.
- Programmed contact devices, which call the juvenile probationer at scheduled or random times and use various technologies to determine the identity of the person who answers (voice verification or a device worn by the probationer to insert in a verifier box attached to the phone, or a camera for visual verification).

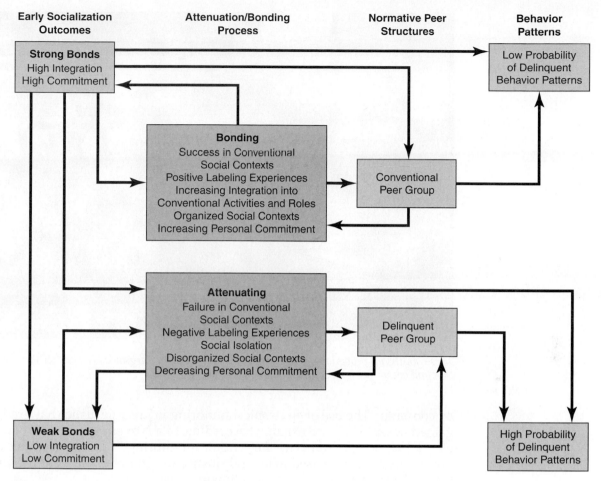

Figure 8–3 *Integrated Strain-Control Paradigm*

Source: Barry Krisberg et al., *Juvenile Intensive Supervision: Planning guide* (Washington, DC: Office of Juvenile Justice and Delinquency Prevention, 1994), p. 7.

- Global positioning systems, in which the juvenile probationer wears a transmitter that sends signals to a satellite and back to a computer monitor, pinpointing the offender's whereabouts at all times.
- Remote alcohol testing devices, which may be used alone or with other devices listed above. The probationer is required to blow into a device (alcosensor), which transmits the results to a computer that records the amount of alcohol consumed. These devices may be attached to automobile ignitions in order to prevent driving after consuming alcohol.[33]

Electronic monitoring was developed when a New Mexico district court judge read a comic strip in which the character Spiderman was tracked by a transmitter affixed to his wrist. At the judge's request, an engineer designed an electronic bracelet to emit a signal picked up by a receiver placed in a home telephone. The design of the bracelet was such that if an offender moved more than 150 feet from his or her home telephone, the transmission signal would be broken. Authorities then would know that the offender had left his or her residence.[34]

In 1997, an estimated 89,095 adults—3.5 percent of all probationers—were on electronic monitoring surveillance. Nearly every state has adults on electronic surveillance, although the courts in some states limited its use by banning certain types of monitoring equipment and allowing monitoring only

These youths on probation are working to clean up county fairgrounds as part of their restitution and community service. (Photo by Stuart Miller.)

by consent.[35] The use of electronic monitoring in juvenile justice has gradually gained acceptance. For example, according to a November 1988 survey, only eleven juvenile programs used electronic monitoring.[36] Today, electronic monitoring programs are used in juvenile justice programs throughout the United States. These programs have the following goals:

- To increase the number of juveniles safely released into existing home-confinement programs
- To reduce the number of juveniles returned to juvenile detention for violating home-confinement restrictions
- To reduce the number of field contacts required of home-confinement officers
- To provide a reasonably safe alternative for lower-risk offenders
- To provide for early reunification with the juvenile's family
- To allow the juvenile to return to school[37]

HOW DO PROBATION OFFICERS DO THEIR JOBS?

The probation officer does not have an easy job. He or she is sometimes asked to supervise youths on aftercare as well as those on probation. The officer may be given a large caseload, may be responsible for youths who are on house arrest and are monitored with electronic equipment, or may be charged with intake or secure detention responsibilities. In addition, the probation officer is expected to be a treatment agent as well as an agent of social control.[38]

ROLE CONFLICT

The nearly opposite roles of law enforcement and treatment create problems for the probation officer. The police and citizens of the community are constantly challenging the treatment role of probation officers, berating them for leaving dangerous and hard-core youths in the community. But, at the same time, probation officers encounter hostility from probationers because of their law enforcement role. The wide use of urinalysis to test for alcohol and drug use is evidence of this law enforcement role. Probation officers must convince the juvenile judge that they are properly filling both roles and are doling out proper portions of treatment and control.

The roles of probation officers today also are more complex than at any time in the past. The increased knowledge developed in fields that study human behavior demands that probation officers continually upgrade their knowledge and skills about child and adolescent development. In addition, schools and other community agencies that share clients with probation departments are being inundated with the same new knowledge. As their professionals become aware of cutting edge research about potential causes of problems and their solutions, they too, are scrambling to incorporate the findings into their programs and to seek out those in their communities who can assist them. Probation officers, particularly those in the larger urban departments, often find themselves as the brokers between these organizations and the juvenile court.

CONFLICTING PRESSURES

Probation officers not only encounter role dilemmas, but also must satisfy three needs—the juvenile justice system's needs, their own ego needs, and the human needs of the client. That the system comes first is a reality that probation officers face early in their careers. If the juvenile judge wants a youth's social study completed by next Tuesday, it must be done, regardless of the needs and problems of other probationers during that week. Similarly, probation officers know that the system will not tolerate too much adverse publicity; consequently, it is wise for them to be conservative in terms of taking chances on troublesome youths.

Probation officers, too, are human. They have ego needs and want to feel important. They want approval and acceptance from the juvenile judge; from the director of probation, or court, services; from other probation officers; and from clients. Even though interest in others brought many of them to their jobs, few probation officers can function effectively or happily if their own needs are not met. If an adolescent female fails to respect her probation officer, she is not likely to receive much tolerance from that officer. If an adolescent male is constantly arguing with or harassing his officer, he can expect the full weight of justice if he violates his probation terms.

The client, all too often, is considered long after the needs of the system and the officer have been satisfied. If the officer's initial job enthusiasm and involvement have waned and he or she regards the job only as one that demands much, pays little, and offers slight opportunity for advancement, his or her client may indeed be shortchanged. The endless paperwork, the hours spent on the road trying to locate clients, the broken appointments, the intractable and undependable probationers, and the hostility directed toward the probation officer also make it difficult for the officer to maintain close involvement with clients.

COMMUNICATION WITH CLIENTS

Probation officers who relate well and do an effective job with clients tend to have certain characteristics in common:

1.　They are genuine in their relationships with probationers and do not hide behind a professional role; that is, they attempt to avoid barriers that would isolate them from their clients. Furthermore, they try to be honest with their clients and expect the juveniles to be honest in return.

2. They respond to others with respect, kindness, and compassion. Because they are caring persons, they are able to listen and reach out to others.

3. They are not gullible or easily hoodwinked by probationers, because they know what life on the streets is like.

4. They are able to encourage others to pursue positive experiences; they also have an uncanny knack of knowing what to say and do when others fail.

5. They have a good understanding of themselves and have a reasonable idea of their own problems, shortcomings, and needs. They know, in addition, their biases, prejudices, and pet peeves.

6. They are very committed to their jobs, for the job to them is much more than a paycheck. Moreover, their enthusiasm does not wane following the first few weeks or months as probation officers.

Probation officers who continually have problems with clients also have certain characteristics in common:

1. They do not keep their word. Either they promise more than they are capable of delivering or they simply fail to follow through on what they have said they would do.

2. They become bored with their jobs, chiefly because they see little meaning in working with youths whom they regard as losers who will always be marginal citizens.

3. They either have unreal expectations for probationers or are inflexible in interpreting the terms of probation.

4. They permit their personality problems to affect their performance on the job, which often results in a lack of warmth, a preoccupation with self, or a sharp, biting response to others. Not surprisingly, these personality traits alienate them from both probationers and other probation staff.

5. They seem to be unable to respond to lower-class youths who do not share their own middle-class values, so they become judgmental and moralistic in dealing with clients.

6. They are unwilling to pay the price of changing their own lives in order to influence or alter the lives of juvenile offenders.

A basic problem for the conscientious probation officer is disciplining the violator without alienating him or her. For example, one probation officer, in describing the problems he had working with a boy, lamented the fact that just as he began to get close to him, he would be forced to discipline him: "I can't let him go too far or you'll have to snap him back. And this destroys any kind of relationship. . . . He just clams up. . . . Underneath it all, I think he's an angry boy."[39]

But regardless of how effective and committed the probation officer may be, a number of troublesome youths will flagrantly violate their probation terms and will have to be returned to the juvenile court, which may lead to probation revocation. Before punishing a youngster who has violated the terms of his or her probation, the probation officer should make every effort to gain the compliance of the youth. An understanding of the negative impact of institutionalization should compel the probation officer to return a youth to the court only as an extreme last resort.

WHAT ARE THE RIGHTS OF PROBATIONERS?

The U.S. Supreme Court has ruled on two cases concerning probation revocation: *Mempa v. Rhay*[40] and *Gagnon v. Scarpelli*.[41] The Court held in the *Mempa* case that the Sixth Amendment's right to counsel applies to the sentencing hearing because it is an important step in criminal prosecution. The Court then extended this right to deferred sentencing and probation revocation hearings, and it reversed the decision of the lower courts because Mempa did not have counsel at his revocation hearing.

Gagnon v. Scarpelli involved an offender whose probation was revoked in Wisconsin without a hearing. Scarpelli, who had been sentenced to fifteen years of imprisonment for armed robbery, had his sentence suspended and was placed on probation for seven years. He was given permission to reside in Illinois, where he was subsequently arrested for burglary. His probation at that point was revoked without a hearing. Scarpelli appealed this revocation, claiming that his failure to receive a hearing and to have counsel violated his due process rights. Although the Supreme Court held that the right to counsel should be decided on a case-by-case basis, the Court did indicate that counsel should be provided on request when the probationer denies that he or she committed the violation or when the reasons for the violation are complex.[42]

These two adult cases have influenced what takes place during probation revocation in juvenile court, because in many jurisdictions the juvenile probationer has the same basic rights as an adult. The juvenile has the right to a hearing, the right to five-day notification of the probation revocation hearing, the right to be represented by an attorney, the right to confrontation, and the right to see the reports citing his or her violations.

"Reasonable efforts" is the standard that most juvenile judges adhere to at the probation revocation hearing. According to this standard, the probation officer must show that reasonable efforts have been made to provide different services and programs to the probationer. It, therefore, provides clear and convincing evidence that the youth's refusal or inability to profit from these services and programs show that he or she cannot be kept in the community.[43]

WHAT IS THE ROLE OF VOLUNTEERS IN PROBATION?

As mentioned earlier, throughout the second half of the nineteenth century, volunteers were used widely to provide probation services, but they largely disappeared at the beginning of the twentieth century and did not reappear until the late 1950s. Indeed, only four courts were using volunteers in 1961; but today more than two thousand court-sponsored volunteer programs are in operation in this country. The use of volunteers has become one of the most valuable ways to help offenders adjust to community life.

The National Information Center on Volunteers in Court has identified several areas in which volunteers can work effectively with juvenile offenders. A volunteer can provide a one-to-one support relationship for the youth with a trustworthy adult; can function as a child advocate with teachers, employers, and the police; can be a good role model; can set limits and teach prosocial values; can teach skills or academic subjects; and can help the youth to develop a realistic response to the environment.

In addition to these areas of direct contact, volunteers can assist in administrative work. They can help recruit, train, and supervise other volunteers; can serve as consultants to the regular staff; can become advisers to the court, especially in the policymaking area; can develop good public relations with the community; and can contribute money, materials, or facilities.

Volunteers can improve the morale of the regular probation staff, because they are usually positive and enthusiastic about the services they provide. Because many volunteers are professionals (physicians, psychiatrists, psychologists, and dentists), they can provide services that the probation department may not have the financial resources to obtain. Finally, their contributions can reduce the caseload of the regular staff.

Several criticisms have been leveled at volunteer programs: The programs tend to attract a high ratio of middle-class persons, and they often create more work than they return in service. Volunteers cannot handle serious problems and sometimes in fact can harm their clients. Parents may resist the volunteer as an untrained worker. Although inappropriate volunteers clearly can do a great deal of damage, proper screening, training, and supervision can do much to ensure high-quality probation services from volunteers. See Focus on Practice 8–3 for a list of guidelines for working with juveniles.

IS PROBATION EFFECTIVE?

The evaluative studies of probation in the 1960s and 1970s indicated that probation was more effective than any other method for rehabilitating youthful offenders. For example, Douglas Lipton and colleagues' work reviewed the studies of adult and juvenile probation and arrived at the following conclusions: (1) evidence exists that a large proportion of offenders now incarcerated could be placed on probation instead without any change in the recidivism rates; (2) probationers have a significantly lower violation rate than do parolees; and (3) intensive probation supervision (a fifteen-ward caseload) is associated with lower recidivism rates for youths under age eighteen.[44]

But a major problem in evaluating the effectiveness of probation today is that probation has changed so much since these early evaluation studies. The risk-reduction programs, such as restitution, intensive supervision, and house arrest, are still in the early stages of evaluation. Evidence suggests that restitution and intensive supervision studies are experiencing some positive results, but it is much too early to draw any conclusions about the present effectiveness of juvenile probation from these studies.

✓**Progress Check 8.2**
Review this section at
www.prenhall.com/bartollas

SUMMARY

- Juvenile probation continues to have more supporters than does any other disposition within the justice system.
- Traditionally, it alone has demonstrated a positive impact on youthful and adult offenders.
- Yet juvenile probation has experienced a major change in focus during the past three decades—from rehabilitation to crime control—and the new methods of crime control are currently being evaluated.
- Probation is primarily under the control of the juvenile court and too frequently is poorly funded by local government agencies.
- Probation officers often feel overworked and underpaid; they sometimes are young, inexperienced, and inadequately trained.
- Some states and many localities have underdeveloped probation services, and probationers tend to perceive the law enforcement role or probation rather than its counseling or supportive role.

FOCUS ON PRACTICE   **8–3**
CONSIDERATIONS WHEN WORKING WITH JUVENILES

1. Keep in contact with the child. We recommend one visit a week as a minimum.
2. Patience. Don't expect overnight success. When things have been going wrong for years, they don't get corrected in a few weeks, or months, or even years.
3. Be ready for setbacks. Although we all like to achieve success with a child, remember [that] he or she does not owe it to us; the youth owes it only to himself or herself.
4. Give attention and affection. The child you are working with may never have known really sustained attention and affection and (at least at first) may not know how to handle it in a normal way.
5. Be prepared to listen and to understand what your child says. Too much talking on your part is more likely to break communication than enhance it.
6. Be a discerning listener. But listening does not mean you have to believe everything you hear.
7. Don't prejudge. Avoid forming fixed and premature opinions until you have gathered all the background information you can.
8. Know your youngster. Get all the information you can on him or her.
9. Respect confidentiality, utterly and completely. Whatever you know about a youngster is under no circumstances to be divulged to or discussed with anyone but a person fully authorized by the court to receive this information.
10. Report violations. Confidentiality does not include keeping known violations a secret from the probation officer in charge of the youngster.
11. Be supportive, encouraging, friendly, but also firm. Although you have to report infractions, you can still be supportive, encouraging, and friendly, to the limit possible.
12. Present your ideas clearly, firmly, and simply. Always mean what you say, be consistent, and keep your promises.
13. Be a good role model. Before accepting court volunteer work, you must decide to live up to this special condition.
14. Avoid being caught in the middle. Be careful not to get caught between the child and his or her parents, the child and his or her teachers, or the child and the court.
15. Be yourself and care sincerely about the child. The more you are yourself, the easier it will be to communicate with the child.

Source: "Manual for Volunteer Probation Officer Aides" (Waterloo, IA: Black Hawk County Juvenile Court Services, 1981), pp. 35–39.

Critical Thinking Questions:
Is this a good list of considerations for working with juveniles? Would you like to be a volunteer probation officer? Which of these considerations would be most difficult for you to follow?

- Difficult challenges for probation services include the continuing get-tough mood of society and the increased use of drugs and guns by juvenile offenders.
- The ability of probation to become an even more effective vehicle of juvenile justice depends on whether it can resolve creatively these and other problems and challenges.

WEB SITES OF INTEREST

To view a report on juvenile probation by the OJP, go to
  http://www.ojp.usdoj.gov/probation/rethink.pdf
The Probation Model Report by the OJJDP can be found at
  http://www.ncjrs.org/txtfiles/d0010.txt
To see how one juvenile probation department is set up, go to the Superior Court of Arizona Web site:
  http://www.superiorcourt.maricopa.gov/juvenileprob/

CRITICAL THINKING QUESTIONS

1. What do you feel is the most effective way to administer probation?
2. Do you believe that probation and parole should be administered together?
3. How can probation officers establish better relations with probationers?
4. Would you like to be a probation officer? Why or why not? What major problems would you face? How would you attempt to solve them?

NOTES

1. Probation officer interviewed in 1985 in the Midwest.
2. Charles Puzzanchera, Anne L. Stahl, Terrence A. Finnegan, Nancy Tierney, and Howard N. Snyder, *Juvenile Court Statistics* (Washington, DC: Office of Juvenile Justice and Delinquency Prevention, 2003), 48.
3. "Privatizing Juvenile Probation Services: Five Local Experiments," *OJJDP Update on Programs* (Washington, DC: Office of Juvenile Justice and Delinquency Prevention, 1989), 1.
4. National Advisory Commission on Criminal Justice Standards and Goals, *Corrections* (Washington, DC: Government Printing Office, 1973), 313–16.
5. Rob Wilson, "Probation/Parole Officers as 'Resource Brokers,'" *Corrections Magazine* 5 (June 1978), 48.
6. Interviewed in July 1984.
7. Joan Petersilia, *The Influence of Criminal Justice Research* (Santa Monica, CA: Rand, 1987), 72.
8. K. Heilbrun, C. Cottle, and R. Lee, "Risk Assessment for Adolescents," *Juvenile Justice Fact Sheet* (Charlottesville: Institute of Law, Psychiatry, and Public Policy, University of Virginia, 2000).
9. Ibid.
10. C. Cottle, R. Lee, and K. Heilbrun, "The Prediction of Criminal Recidivism in Juveniles: A Meta-Analysis," *Criminal Justice & Behavior*, vol. 28 No. 3, June 2001, p. 367–394.
11. For Fogel's thoughts on probation, see the interview in Clemens Bartollas, *Correctional Treatment: Theory and Practice* (Upper Saddle River, NJ: Prentice Hall, 1985), 45–46.
12. Interviewed in April 1983.
13. See Dennis Maloney, Dennis Romig, and Troy Armstrong, "The Balanced Approach to Juvenile Probation," *Juvenile and Family Court Journal* 39 (1989), 1–49.
14. Ibid., 10. See also Gordon Bazemore and Mark S. Umbreit, *Balanced and Restorative Justice: Program Summary* (Washington, DC: Office of Juvenile Justice and Delinquency Prevention, 1994).

15. Bazemore and Umbreit, *Balanced and Restorative Justice*, 5.

16. Ibid., 7.

17. Anne L. Schneider, "Restitution and Recidivism Rates of Juvenile Offenders: Results from Four Experimental Studies," *Criminology* 24 (1986), 533.

18. William G. Staples, "Restitution as a Sanction in Juvenile Court," *Crime and Delinquency* 32 (April 1986), 177.

19. OJJDP Model Program Guide, *Restitution/Community Service* (online at http://www.dsgonline.com/mpg_non_flash/restitution?community?service.htm).

20. Patrick Griffin and Patricia Torbet, eds., *Desktop Guide to Good Juvenile Probation Practice: Mission-Driven, Performance-Based, and Outcome-Focused* (Pittsburgh: National Center for Juvenile Justice, 2002), 85.

21. Ibid., 85–86.

22. Interviewed in August 1985.

23. Information gained during an on-site visit and updated in a phone call to a staff member in September 2001.

24. Ted Palmer, *The Re-Emergence of Correctional Intervention* (Newbury Park, CA: Sage Publications, 1992), 80.

25. Emily Walker, "The Community Intensive Treatment for Youth Program: A Specialized Community-Based Program for High-Risk Youth in Alabama," *Law and Psychiatry Review* 13 (1989), 175–99.

26. Cecil Marshall and Keith Snyder, "Intensive and Aftercare Probation Services in Pennsylvania," paper presented at the annual meeting of the American Society of Criminology, Baltimore, Maryland (November 7, 1990), 3.

27. Bernadette Jones, "Intensive Probation, Philadelphia County, November 1986–February 1989," paper presented at the annual meeting of the American Society of Criminology, Baltimore, Maryland (November 1990), p. 1 of Appendix.

28. Marshall and Snyder, "Intensive and Aftercare Probation Services in Pennsylvania," 3.

29. Barry Krisberg et al., *Juvenile Intensive Supervision: Planning Guide* (Washington, DC: Office of Juvenile Justice and Delinquency Prevention, 1994), 7.

30. For a review of these studies in intensive supervision programs for adults, see Clemens Bartollas and John P. Conrad, *Introduction to Corrections*, 2d ed. (New York: HarperCollins, 1992).

31. Palmer, *The Re-Emergence of Correctional Intervention*, 82.

32. J. Robert Lilly and Richard A. Ball, "A Brief History of House Arrest and Electronic Monitoring," *Northern Kentucky Law Review* 13 (1987), 343–74.

33. Griffin and Torbet, eds., *Desktop Guide to Good Juvenile Probation Practice: Mission-Driven, Performance-Based, and Outcome-Focused*, 79.

34. Richard A. Ball, Ronald Huff, and Robert Lilly, *House Arrest and Correctional Policy: Doing Time at Home* (Newbury Park, CA: Sage Publications, 1988), 35–36.

35. TDCI/Community Justice Assistance Division, *Electronic Monitoring Agency Brief* (Austin, TX: Texas Department of Criminal Justice, 1997), 1.

36. Joseph B. Vaughn, "A Survey of Juvenile Electronic Monitoring and Home Confinement Program," *Juvenile and Family Court Journal* 40 (1989), 4, 22. For a description of another program, see Michael T. Charles, "The Development of a Juvenile Electronic Monitoring Program," *Federal Probation* 53 (1989), 3–12.

37. Vaughn, "A Survey of Juvenile Electronic Monitoring and Home Confinement Program."

38. See Lori L. Colley, Robert C. Culbertson, and Edward J. Latessa, "Juvenile Probation Officers: A Job Analysis," *Juvenile and Family Court Journal* 38 (1987), 1–12.

39. Robert Emerson, *Judging Delinquents: Context and Process in the Juvenile Court* (Chicago: Aldine, 1969), 253.

40. *Mempa v. Rhay*, 339 U.S. 128 Cir. 3023 (1968).

41. *Gagnon v. Scarpelli*, 411 U.S. 778 (1973).

42. Ibid.

43. Information gained from a September 1992 interview with a juvenile probation officer in Iowa.

44. Douglas Lipton et al., *The Effectiveness of Correctional Treatment: A Survey of Evaluation Studies* (New York: Praeger, 1975), 59–61.

9

COMMUNITY-BASED PROGRAMS

I was a real terror as a kid. I was into gangs, violence, and drugs and was in and out of training school. I was also in and out of a number of foster placements. Then I met Mr. Sullivan, and he turned my life around. I gave him a run for his money, but he wouldn't give up on me. If it wouldn't have been for Mr. Sullivan, I don't know what would have become of me, but I can tell you this, that I wouldn't be talking with you today.

—Director of Court Services[1]

OUTLINE

OBJECTIVES

1. To discuss the operations of the main types of community-based programs
2. To evaluate the effectiveness of these programs
3. To examine the main issues in community-based programming

KEY TERMS

community corrections acts   diversion programs   reintegration philosophy
day treatment programs   group home   wilderness programs
delinquency prevention

In the chapter-opening quote, a director of court services in a midwestern state tells of the impact a foster parent had on him. An impressive array of programs for juvenile offenders exists in the community. These programs include delinquency prevention, runaway facilities, foster care, diversion, day treatment, group homes, and wilderness learning experiences. The ongoing search for a panacea to the problem of youth crime, the popularity of deinstitutionalization in juvenile justice, and the emphasis in the 1980s and 1990s on short-term behavior control probably best explain why there are so many programs for juvenile offenders. These community-based programs range from those focusing on prevention and diversion from the juvenile justice system to those designed for short-term residential care.

WHAT HAS BEEN THE COMMUNITY'S ACCEPTANCE OF COMMUNITY-BASED PROGRAMS?

Community-based programs rest on a **reintegration philosophy** that assumes that both the offender and the receiving community must be changed. The community is as important as the client and plays a vital role in facilitating the reabsorption of offenders into its life. The task of corrections, according to this philosophy, involves the reconstruction, or construction, of ties between offenders and the community through maintenance of family bonds, employment and education, and placement in the mainstream of social life. Youths should be directed to community resources, and the community should be acquainted with the skills and needs of youthful lawbreakers.

Critics of community-based programs challenge several assumptions of reintegrative philosophy. They hold that the community deserves protection from predatory youths who intimidate and hurt the young, rape women of all ages, and victimize the elderly. They further contend that youths sent to juvenile institutions are those who have failed to benefit from a number of community placements. It is also argued that keeping youths in the community only reinforces their antisocial behavior; institutional confinement provides the punishment they deserve.

Communities often have resisted the charge that they must assume responsibility for the problems they generate. It is much easier (and more comforting) for the community to blame the crime problem on the failure of training schools, the inefficiency of the juvenile justice system, or the personalities of offenders themselves than to accept responsibility for its social problems. Instead of coordination between the justice system and the community, all too frequently an adversarial we–they relationship exists. Citizens often believe that the youth commission is trying to foist a group home or a day treatment facility on their community; correctional administrators, in turn, often tend to perceive negativism or outright hostility on the part of many citizens.

On-the-job training is one way youths are reintegrated into their local communities. (Photo courtesy of Ohio Department of Youth Services.)

HOW ARE COMMUNITY-BASED PROGRAMS ADMINISTERED?

Comprehensive state-sponsored, locally sponsored, and privately administered programs are the three basic types of organizational structures in community-based programs.

In California, Indiana, Kansas, Michigan, Minnesota, and Oregon, the state sponsors residential and day treatment programs under **community corrections acts.** The Minnesota Community Corrections Act, which has become a model for other community corrections acts, provides a state subsidy to any county or group of counties that chooses to develop its own community corrections system. The costs for juvenile offenders who are adjudicated to a training school are charged back to the county, and these costs are subtracted from the county's subsidy. Counties in Minnesota have been understandably reluctant to commit youths to a training school because of the prohibitive costs and therefore have established and encouraged a wide variety of residential and day treatment programs.

The deinstitutionalization movement in Maryland, Massachusetts, North Dakota, South Dakota, and Utah also has led to the development of a wide network of residential and day treatment programs for youths. In Massachusetts, the Department of Youth Services administers some of these programs, but more often the juvenile court sponsors these programs, or state or local agencies contract services for those youths from private vendors in the community. Whoever administers these community programs, the most innovative and effective ones attempt to provide a continuum of care for youthful offenders.

Private delivery of correctional services to youthful offenders originated in the early days of juvenile justice in this nation. Most of these programs were religious or business backed. In 1972, the private sector reentered the field of juvenile corrections in an unprecedented manner. Privatization, or placing control of facilities in the hands of the private sector, has expanded significantly in the past few decades. Privately run programs are emerging as a result of budget problems that prevent local or state agencies from supplying the services in an efficient manner. Privatization has become big business and has sparked the interests of investors from all walks of life. Those operating in the private sector receive payment for their programs through federal, state, or local funding, from insurance plans, or from the juvenile's parents.[2]

Federal grants are the basis of the funding of many community programs. SafeFutures is a new program funded by the OJJDP that appears to be a model worth replicating in communities across the nation. SafeFutures urban sites are located in Boston, Massachusetts; Contra Costa County, California; Seattle, Washington; and St. Louis, Missouri. The other two sites are Imperial County, California (rural), and Fort Belknap Indian Community, Harlem, Montana (tribal government). SafeFutures seeks to improve the service delivery system by creating a continuum of care responsive to the needs of youths and their families at any point along the path toward juvenile offending. This coordinated approach of prevention, intervention, and treatment is designed both to serve the juveniles of a community and to encompass the human service and the juvenile justice systems. A national evaluation is being conducted to determine the success of the continuum of services in all six sites.[3]

Project CRAFT (community restitution and apprenticeship-focused training program), a vocational training program for high-risk youths, is sponsored by the Home Builders Institute (HBI), the educational arm of the National Association of Home Builders (NAHB). Project CRAFT offers preapprenticeship training and job training for adjudicated juveniles who are referred to the program. It was started in 1994 by HBI in Bismarck, North Dakota; Nashville, Tennessee; and Sabillasville, Maryland. It has been replicated in five sites in Florida (Avon Park, Daytona Beach, Fort Lauderdale, Lantana, and Orlando) and in Texas. This program works in partnership with private facilities, juvenile judges, juvenile justice system personnel, educational agencies, and other human service agencies.[4]

WHAT IS THE ROLE OF DELINQUENCY PREVENTION?

Delinquency prevention is defined as any attempt to thwart youths' illegal behavior before it occurs. The Juvenile Justice and Delinquency Prevention Act of 1974 and the Juvenile Justice Amendments of 1977, 1980, and 1984 established the prevention of delinquency as a national priority.[5] Anne Newton has identified three levels of delinquency prevention:

Primary prevention is directed at modifying conditions in the physical and social environment at large.

Secondary prevention is directed at early identification and intervention in the lives of individuals or groups in criminogenic circumstances.

Tertiary prevention is directed at the prevention of recidivism (after delinquent acts have been committed and detected).[6]

An example of primary prevention is the Mobilization for Youth program, which took place in a 67-block area of Manhattan's Lower East Side in New York City. This project was designed to improve educational and work opportunities for area youth, to make a variety of services available to individuals and families, and to provide assistance in community organization.[7] DARE, a drug prevention program conducted by the police for elementary

Numerous cities across the United States support programs to help youths before they get into difficulty. (Photo by Allison Bartosh.)

school students, is an expression of secondary prevention. Tertiary prevention is aptly illustrated by "Scared Straight," a label derived from the title of an award-winning documentary film about the Juvenile Awareness Project at New Jersey's Rahway State Prison. The Scared Straight programs conducted at Rahway and other prisons across the nation used the horrors of prison life, as well as intensive confrontation sessions between adult prisoners and juveniles, to deter youths from committing any or additional delinquent acts (see Focus on Programs 9–1 for background information on the Straight Life program, an example of a recent Scared Straight-type program.[8]

A number of primary and secondary prevention programs have been conducted since the beginning of the twentieth century, using neighborhood groups, the family and school environment, youth gangs, and social and mental health agencies as points of intervention.[9] Unfortunately, the results of most of these programs have been disappointing.[10] The Chicago Area Projects is one program that achieved some success in the fifty years or so that it was conducted. More recently, a number of programs have been developed that promise to be more effective in preventing juvenile crime, including juvenile violence and drug abuse.

CHICAGO AREA PROJECTS

Clifford Shaw and Henry McKay, the founders in 1934 of the Chicago Area Projects (CAP), were committed to creating community consciousness directed at solving social problems on the local level. The first projects were initiated in three areas: South Chicago, the Near West Side, and the Near North Side. Shaw and his colleagues recruited local leaders to promote youth welfare because they had lost confidence in official agencies. These local leaders supported indigenous community organizations and made a special effort to involve those who played important formal and informal roles in community life. Shaw was also able to get men with criminal records to agree to work in the program because he made no moral judgment about what they had done

FOCUS ON PROGRAMS 9–1
TEENS TASTE PRISON

Inmates Help Turn Young Lives Around

TRACY [CALIF.]—Angel couldn't stop the tears from clouding his 14-year-old eyes as he faced, then embraced, the smiling man clad in prison blue.

They hugged, saying nothing, the convict and the boy he helped save.

A few months before, Angel had been running with the wrong crowd, a Hispanic gang based in southern San Joaquin County. Drinking, drugs, crime, F-riddled report cards—it was a way of life, one Angel knew was wrong but couldn't escape.

"I felt no reason to live anymore," he said.

Enter a school counselor who convinced him, and some of his home boys, to attend the Straight Life youth-diversion program run by inmates at Deuel Vocational Institution.

Sessions are right in the prison, where youths get a feel for what life is like when they don't play by society's rules.

Inmates, almost all of them sentenced to life terms, confronted the young toughs in Angel's group. One handed him a pen, explained how to use it as a weapon, then ordered him to kill another prisoner.

"I just stood there," Angel recalled. "It freaked the hell out of me."

"When they brought me here, I decided this was where I did not want to be," Angel said.

Except for last week, when he returned one more time for the seventh annual Straight Life banquet, it was a chance to say thanks to men he credits with changing his life, men who were buoyed by the obvious turnaround in the boy.

"Through this program, our lives' worth increases," inmate Tony Young said.

Straight Life, which has brought nearly 3,000 at-risk youth from Sacramento to Fresno to within the walls of Deuel, is the best program inmate Michael de Vries has ever been involved in, he said. For the youths, and for the convicts.

"It makes us look at what got us here," said de Vries, convicted of murder in Berkeley in 1984. "If this were happening everywhere, we might not have the problems we're having."

Source: Garth Stapley, "Teens Taste Prison," *Modesto Bee,* Summer 1996, A1, A10.

Critical Thinking Questions:
What is your evaluation of this program? How does this program appear to be different from the critically evaluated Scared Straight program?

previously. He regarded youth crime as a normal response to the situation of the inner city, believing that individuals did what they had to do to survive, but that this illegal behavior was no indication of an offender's true beliefs and commitments.[11]

Each project area has a committee that operates as an independent unit under the guidance of a board of directors chosen by the local community residents. CAP has also received support from the state of Illinois—at first, from the Illinois Department of Welfare through the Institute of Juvenile Research, then from the Illinois Youth Commission, and most recently from the Department of Corrections. Twenty such projects are now functioning in Chicago, and others have formed throughout the state. In addition, other groups in Illinois have taken the projects as the model for their own delinquency control programs.[12]

The projects have three basic goals: First, they provide a forum for local residents to become acquainted with new scientific perspectives on child rearing, child welfare, and juvenile delinquency. Second, they initiate new channels of communication between local residents and the institutional representatives of the larger community, those influencing the life chances of local youth. Third, they bring adults into contact with local youths, especially those having difficulties with the law.

The philosophy of CAP is based on the belief that instead of turning over youth so quickly to the justice system, the community should deal with its own problems and intervene on behalf of its youth. Citizens of the community show up in juvenile court to speak on behalf of the youths; they organize social and recreational programs so that youths have constructive activities in which to participate. The leaders of the local groups, often individuals who were once in CAP programs, know how to relate to and deal with youths who are having problems at school or with the law.

CAP has several noteworthy strengths: they have had far-reaching impacts on youths who have participated in their activities; they have encouraged communities to deal with their own social problems; and, depending primarily on volunteers, they have been excellent sources of leadership development within local communities.[13] Steven Schlossman's fifty-year assessment of CAP concluded: "All of our data consistently suggest that the CAP has long been effective in organizing local communities and reducing juvenile delinquency."[14]

Yet critics contend that CAP has been ineffective in dealing with youth crime in its most serious forms in the areas of the city with the highest crime rates.[15] Jon Snodgrass adds that their neglect of the realities of politics and economics made CAP a basically conservative response to the radical changes needed in disorganized communities.[16]

More than fifty years ago, Saul Alinsky stated, "It's impossible to overemphasize the enormous importance of people doing things for themselves."[17] What is ultimately significant about CAP is that this philosophy was its basic approach to delinquency prevention. CAP advocated grassroots leadership, neighborhood revitalization, the community's role in policing itself, and the importance of community dispute resolution. These same emphases were incorporated into most community crime prevention strategies in the late 1990s.[18]

PROMISING PREVENTION PROGRAMS

The Blueprint for Violence Prevention, which was developed by the Center for the Study and Prevention of Violence at the University of Colorado-Boulder and supported by the Office of Juvenile Justice and Delinquency Prevention, identified eleven model programs as well as twenty-one promising violence prevention and drug-abuse programs that have received rigorous evaluation.[19] Table 9–1 presents the complete list of the model and promising programs the researchers identified; the following discussion briefly describes the eleven model programs.

Big Brothers Big Sisters of America (BBBSA)

With a network of more than 500 local agencies throughout the United States that maintains more than 145,000 one-to-one relationships between youth and volunteer adults, BBBSA is the best-known and largest mentoring program in the nation. The program serves youths ages six to eighteen, a significant number of whom are from disadvantaged and single-parent households. Mentors meet with their matches for three to five hours at least three times a month and participate in a variety of activities.[20] An eighteen-month evaluation found that compared with a control group waiting for a match, youths in this

Table 9–1 *Model and Promising Programs and Age Groups of Juveniles Targeted*

Blueprints Program	Age Group				
	Pregnancy/ Infancy	Early Childhood	Elementary School	Junior High School	High School
MODEL PROGRAMS					
Big Brothers Big Sisters of America (BBBSA)			x	x	x
Bullying Prevention Program			x	x	
Functional Family Therapy (FFT)				x	x
Incredible Years		x	x		
Life Skills Training (LST)				x	
Midwestern Prevention Project (MPP)				x	
Multidimensional Treatment Foster Care (MTFC)				x	x
Multisystemic Therapy (MST)				x	x
Nurse-Family Partnership	x				
Project Toward No Drug Abuse (Project TND)					x
Promoting Alternative Thinking Strategies (PATHS)			x		
PROMISING PROGRAMS					
Athletes Training and Learning to Avoid Steroids					x
Brief Strategic Family Therapy			x	x	x
CASASTART			x	x	
Fast Track			x		
Good Behavior Game			x		
Guiding Good Choices			x	x	
High/Scope Perry Preschool		x			
Houston Child Development Center	x	x			
I Can Problem Solve		x	x		
Intensive Protective Supervision				x	x
Linking the Interests of Families and Teachers			x		
Preventive Intervention				x	
Preventive Treatment Program			x		
Project Northland				x	
Promoting Action through Holistic Education				x	x
School Transitional Environmental Program				x	x
Seattle Social Development Project			x	x	
Strengthening Families Program: Parents and Children 10–14			x	x	
Student Training through Urban Strategies				x	x
Syracuse Family Development Program	x	x			
Yale Child Welfare Project	x	x			

Source: Sharon Mihoulic, Abigail Fagan, Katherine Irwin, Diane Ballard, and Delbert Elliott, *Blueprints for Violence Prevention* (Washington, DC: Office of Juvenile Justice and Delinquency Prevention, 2004), Table 1–1.

mentoring program were 46 percent less likely to start using drugs, 27 percent less likely to start drinking, and 32 percent less likely to hit or assault someone. They also were less likely to skip school and more likely to have improved family relationships.[21]

Bully Prevention Program

The primary purpose of the Bully Prevention Program is to restructure the social environment and secondary schools in order to provide fewer opportunities for bullying and to reduce the peer approval and support that reward bullying behavior. This program seeks to ensure that adults in the school are aware of bullying problems and are actively involved in their prevention.[22] In a large sample evaluated in Norway and South Carolina, the Bully Prevention Program has proved effective. For example, children in thirty-nine schools in South Carolina in grades four through six reported that they experienced a 25 percent decrease in bullying by other children.[23]

Functional Family Therapy (FFT)

A short-term family-based prevention and intervention program, FFT has been successfully applied in a variety of contexts to treat high-risk youths and their families. Specifically designed to help underserved and at-risk youth ages eleven to eighteen, this multisystemic clinical program provides twelve one-hour family therapy sessions spread over three months. More difficult cases receive up to twenty-six to thirty hours of therapy.[24] The success of this program has been demonstrated and replicated for more than twenty-five years. Using controlled follow-up periods of one, three, and five years, evaluations have demonstrated significant and long-term reductions in the reoffending of youth, ranging from 25 to 60 percent.[25]

Incredible Years: Parent, Teacher, and Child Training Series

The Incredible Years model program has a comprehensive set of curricula designed to promote social competence and to prevent, reduce, and treat conduct problems in children ages two to eight who exhibit or are at risk for conduct problems. In the parent, teacher, and child training programs, trained facilitators use videotaped scenes to encourage problem solving and sharing of ideas. The parent program teaches parents interactive play and reinforcement skills, local and natural consequences, and problem-solving strategies. The teacher training component is designed to strengthen teachers' skills in classroom management. The child training component emphasizes building empathy with others, developing emotional competency, solving interpersonal difficulties, managing anger, and succeeding at school.[26] All three series of this program have received positive evaluations as meeting their original goals.[27]

Life Skills Training (LST)

LST is a three-year intervention curriculum designed to prevent or reduce the use of "gateway" drugs such as tobacco, alcohol, and marijuana. The lessons emphasize social resistance skills training to help students identify pressures to use drugs. Although this intervention is meant to be implemented in school classrooms by teachers, it also has been taught successfully by health professionals and peer leaders. LST targets all middle/junior high school students, using an initial fifteen-lesson intervention in grade six or seven and booster sessions over the following two years.[28] Using outcomes from more than a dozen studies, evaluators have found LST to reduce tobacco, alcohol, and marijuana use by 50 to 75 percent in intervention students compared to control students.[29]

Midwestern Prevention Project (MPP)

MPP includes school normative environment change as one of the components of a comprehensive three- to five-year community-based prevention program that targets gateway use of alcohol, tobacco, and marijuana. The school-based intervention is the central component of the program. The program begins in either sixth or seventh grade and includes ten to thirteen classroom sessions taught by teachers trained in the curriculum. Five booster sessions are offered in the second year of the program. A parent component follows the school sessions and is designed to develop family norms that discourage drug use. The community component takes place during the last stages of this prevention effort and involves the support of community leaders.[30] Researchers followed students from eight schools who were randomly assigned to treatment or control groups for three years and found that the program brought net reductions of up to 40 percent in adolescent smoking and marijuana use, with results maintained through high school graduation.[31]

Multidimensional Treatment Foster Care (MTFC)

MTFC has been found to be a cost-effective alternative to group or residential treatment, confinement, or hospitalization. This program provides short-term (usually about seven months), highly structured therapeutic care in foster families. Its goal is to decrease negative behaviors, including delinquency, and to increase youths' participation in appropriate prosocial activities, including school, hobbies, and sports.[32] Evaluations of MTFC demonstrated that youths who participated in the program had significantly fewer arrests (an average of 2.6 versus 5.4 offenses) and spent fewer days in lockup than youths placed in other community-based programs.[33]

Multisystemic Therapy (MST)

MST provides cost-effective community-based clinical treatment of chronic and violent juvenile offenders who are at high risk of out-of-home placement. The overarching goal of the intervention is to help parents understand and help their children overcome the multiple problems contributing to antisocial behavior. MST uses the strengths of each youth's social network to promote positive change in his or her behavior. Treatment generally lasts for about four months, which includes about sixty hours of therapist–family contact.[34] Program evaluations have revealed 25 to 70 percent reductions in long-term rates of rearrest and 47 to 64 percent reductions in out-of-home placements. These and other positive results were maintained for nearly four years after treatment ended.[35]

Nurse–Family Partnership

Formerly called Prenatal and Infancy Home Visitation by Nurses, the Nurse–Family Partnership sends nurses to the homes of lower-income, unmarried mothers, beginning during pregnancy and continuing for two years following the birth of the child. Tested with both white and African-American families in rural and urban settings, this program is designed to help women improve their prenatal health and outcomes of pregnancy by encouraging good health habits, giving mothers the skills they need to care for their infants and toddlers, and improving women's personal development.[36] Follow-up showed that this program had long-term positive effects on both mothers and children. During the first fifteen years after delivery of their first child, unmarried women who received nurse visits had 31 percent fewer subsequent births, longer intervals between births, fewer months on welfare, 44 percent fewer behavioral problems due to alcohol and drug abuse, 69 percent fewer arrests, and 81 percent fewer criminal convictions than those in the control group. Youths whose mothers had received nurse home visits more than a decade earlier were 60 percent less likely to have run away, 56 percent less likely to have been arrested, and 89 percent less likely to have been convicted of a criminal violation than youths whose mothers had not received visits.[37]

Project Toward No Drug Abuse (PROJECT TND)

This project targets high school youth ages fourteen to nineteen who are at risk for drug abuse. Over a four- or five-week period, twelve classroom-based lessons offer students cognitive motivation enhancement activities, information about the social and health consequences of drug use, correction of cognitive misperceptions, help with stress management, training in self-control, and instruction in active listening.[38] At a one-year follow-up, participants in forty-two schools revealed reduced use of cigarettes, alcohol, marijuana, and hard drugs.[39]

Promoting Alternative Thinking Strategies (PATHS)

A comprehensive program for promoting social and emotional competencies, PATHS focuses on the understanding, expression, and regulation of emotions. The year-long curriculum is designed to be used by teachers and counselors with classrooms of children in kindergarten through fifth grade. The basic outcome goals are to provide youths with tools to achieve academically as well as to enhance the classroom atmosphere and the learning process. Evaluations have found positive behavioral changes related to hyperactivity, peer aggression, and conduct problems.[40]

THE VIOLENT JUVENILE AND DELINQUENCY PREVENTION

Funded and spearheaded by the OJJDP, the belief emerged in the 1990s that the most effective strategy for juvenile corrections is to place the thrust of the prevention and diversion emphases on high-risk juveniles who commit violent acts. These juveniles are the ones that commit the more serious and most frequent delinquent acts and are the ones that officials are quick to place into the adult system. At the same time that the seriousness of their behaviors have effected changes in juvenile codes across the country, research is beginning to find that these high-risk youths can be impacted by well-equipped and well-implemented prevention and treatment programs.[41]

These programs are based on the assumption that the juvenile justice system does not see most serious offenders until it is too late to effectively intervene.[42] It also presumes that in order to reduce the overall level of violence in American society, it is necessary to successfully intervene in the lives of high-risk youth offenders, who commit about 75 percent of all violent juvenile offenses.[43]

The general characteristics of these programs is that they: (1) address key areas of risk in youths' lives, (2) seek to strengthen the personal and institutional factors that contribute to the development of a healthy adolescent, (3) provide adequate supervision and support, and (4) offer youths a long-term stage in the community.[44] It is emphasized that these prevention programs must be integrated with local police, child welfare, social services, school, and family-preservation programs. Comprehensive approaches to delinquency prevention and intervention require a strong collaborative effort between the juvenile justice system and other service provision systems, such as health, mental health, child welfare, and education. An important component of a community's comprehensive plan is to develop mechanisms that effectively link these service providers at the program level.[45]

The comprehensive, or multisystemic, aspects of these programs are designed to deal simultaneously with many aspects of youths' lives. The intent is that they are intensive, often involving multiple contacts weekly, or possibly daily, with at-risk youth. They build on the strength of these youths, rather than dwell on their deficiencies. These programs operate mostly, although not exclusively, outside of the formal justice system under a variety of public, non-profit, or university auspices. Finally, they combine accountability and sanctions with increasingly intensive treatment and rehabilitation services which are achieved through a system of graduated sanctions, in which an integrated

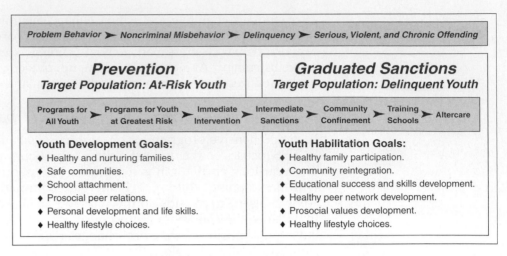

Figure 9–1   *Overview of Comprehensive Strategy*

Source: Mark A. Matese and John A. Tuell, *Update on the Comprehensive Strategy for Serious Violent, and Chronic Juvenile Offenders* (Washington, DC: Office of Justice Programs; Office of Juvenile Justice and Delinquency Prevention, 1998), p. 1.

approach is employed to stop the penetration of youthful offenders into the system.[46] See Figure 9–1 for an overview of this comprehensive prevention strategy.

In 1996, three communities—Lee and Duval Counties in Florida and San Diego County in California—collaborated with the OJJDP to apply the processes and principles that were described in *Comprehensive Strategy*. Initial evaluations of the three pilot projects found that each of the sites has benefited significantly from the comprehensive planning process. Although it was deemed premature to assess any long-term impact on juvenile delinquency, there are several short-term indicators of success.[47] The following are among the pilot programs' accomplishments:

- Enhanced community-wide understanding of prevention services and sanctions options for juveniles
- Expanded networking capacity and better coordination among agencies and service providers
- Institution of performance measurement systems
- Hiring of staff to spearhead the ongoing Comprehensive Strategy planning and implementation efforts
- Development of comprehensive five-year strategic action plans[48]

✓**Progress Check 9.1**
Review this section at
www.prenhall.com/bartollas

WHAT IS THE ROLE OF DIVERSION?

In the late 1960s and early 1970s, **diversion programs** sprouted across the nation. *Diversion*, which refers to keeping juveniles outside the formal justice system, can be attempted either through the police and the courts or through agencies outside the juvenile justice system. The main characteristic of diversion initiated by the courts or police is that the justice subsystems retain control over youthful offenders. A youth who fails to respond to such a program usually will be returned to the juvenile court for continued processing within the system.

In the 1970s, youth service bureaus (YSBs) and runaway centers were the most widely used diversion programs outside the juvenile justice system.

More recently, family counseling, substance abuse, teen courts, the juvenile drug court movement, and juvenile mediation programs have been used by juvenile courts and probation departments to divert juveniles from the formal justice system. Gang intervention programs have been implemented in some communities across the nation to divert gang youths from the justice system.

THE YOUTH SERVICE BUREAU

The major impetus to YSBs came in 1967 when the President's Commission on Law Enforcement and Administration of Justice recommended that such agencies be established to work with youths outside the juvenile justice system. Although *youth service bureau* was the name most frequently used, other names used include *youth resource bureau, youth assistance program,* the *Listening Post,* or the *Focus on Youth.*

Sherwood Norman, who was highly influential in the development of YSBs, identified the basic objectives of this diversion agency:

> The Youth Service Bureau is a noncoercive, independent, public [some are private] agency established to divert children and youth from the justice system by (1) mobilizing community resources to solve youth problems, (2) strengthening existing youth resources and developing new ones, and (3) promoting positive programs to remedy delinquency-breeding conditions.[49]

From 1967 to 1973, 150 YSBs were established throughout the nation. More YSBs were created in California than in any other state; Illinois had the second largest number. But the decline of federal funding in the late 1970s and early 1980s reduced the number of YSBs. In 1981, the director of a YSB in Illinois noted, "There are now 54 YSBs in Illinois; there were 78 two years ago."[50] Before the end of the 1980s, nearly all of the YSBs across the nation had closed their doors.

At the peak of their popularity, YSBs offered a variety of programs. Drop-in centers, hot lines, truancy and school outreach programs, and twenty-four-hour crisis programs were common services. Some large YSBs also arranged temporary care for runaways, conducted programs for pregnant teenagers, and provided school dropouts with employment, for which they were paid a minimum wage. YSBs under one name or another are still found across the country today.

RUNAWAY CENTERS

An estimated one million youths run away from home each year. Some of them have been thrown out of their homes, but the majority choose to leave because of child abuse, unmanageable conflicts with parents, the influence of peers, or the thrill of being on their own. Youths who are absent from home for a period of time must deal with survival, and about 50 percent of these runaways become involved in delinquent acts such as stealing, prostitution, and drug abuse.[51] Although the 1983 Missing Persons Act allows parents to list missing children with the FBI, runaway centers remain one of the few services that exist for runaway youths.

Under the Runaway and Homeless Youth Act, Title III of the 1974 Juvenile Justice and Delinquency Prevention Act, assistance was given to states, localities, and nonprofit private agencies in order to operate temporary shelters for runaway youths, resulting in the creation of such centers throughout the nation. A staff member of Covenant House, a twenty-four-hour drop-in crisis center located in New York City, explains why these programs are needed:

> Thousands of runaway and nomadic adolescents are drawn to the Times Square area each year. These young people survive by panhandling, stealing, by exploiting and being exploited. Many, perhaps most, must touch at least temporarily the life of prostitution. . . . There is a total lack of service available to them in the Times Square area. There are no public or private agencies meeting the immediate and urgent needs of the runaway and delinquency-prone youth, hundreds of whom can be seen in Times Square at literally any hour of the day and night, drifting and wandering.[52]

The Door—A Center of Alternatives, also in New York City, was cited as a model program by the Department of Health, Education, and Welfare (now Health and Human Services) and is frequently mentioned at national conferences. The heart of this program is the S.O.S. Service, which provides emergency shelter, food, and clothing for desperate youths. It is one of the largest runaway programs in the United States, and four hundred or more youths are involved at any one time in such activities as drug-abuse counseling, job advising, prenatal counseling, dance or theater workshops, and martial arts classes. A number of other New York City programs have been established. Group-Live-In Experience (GLIE), located in the Bronx, has expanded from a storefront location to an operation including three temporary care shelters, where thirty homeless youths can stay from three to eight months; two crash pads are found where nineteen youths can stay up to two weeks; and a reentry program, called Last Stop, is present in which fourteen youngsters can prepare for as much as a year for independent living. Hot Line Cares, located in Spanish Harlem, operates a telephone crisis line and referral agency; after screening callers carefully, hot line workers place them in seven temporary safe houses, where youths can stay for seven weeks.[53]

A number of safe houses in St. Paul and Minneapolis, Minnesota, provide temporary placement for runaway youths with no place to go. The high rate of female and male prostitution in the Twin Cities, which are known as a national pipeline of prostitution, was a factor in the establishment of these houses. In addition to food and shelter, these programs provide group and individual counseling.

Runaway centers contribute a great deal to youths who are receptive to these temporary placements. The centers provide runaways with food and shelter. Staff members furnish support and crisis counseling, and the larger runaway centers offer many helpful programs. Nevertheless, the impact of such centers on runaway youths is still minimal because they are considered undesirable places by most runaways and because the few centers in existence generally are located in large urban areas. To lessen the involvement of runaways in crime, increased family and community services are clearly needed for them.

ÉLAN

Élan, a therapeutic community for juveniles in Poland Springs, Maine, is a treatment program for substance abusers and predelinquents. Started in 1971 by Dr. Gerald Davidson, a psychiatrist, and Joe Ricci, a former drug addict, Élan has grown into a finely tuned million-dollar operation with twenty-five therapeutic staff members, seventeen educational staff members, forty support staff members, five houses, an accredited school, and 140 residents.[54]

The program involves self-responsibility, intense peer pressure, self-disclosure, hard physical and emotional work, and often humiliating punishments. Staff claim that the treatment is not as intense or encapsulated in negativity as it was in the past. The 160 residents stay an average of 27 months, and the annual fees for a 12-month stay are $49,071. A high percentage of those who are admitted to the program receive diplomas. Of this number, according to an in-house evaluation, about 80 percent stay out of trouble. Supporters claim that Élan is an exemplary therapeutic experience for youth; foes, including many former residents, regard it as coercive and brutal.[55]

Although there is little evidence that the majority of substance abuse programs for juveniles are any more successful than those for adults, it is clear that Élan is several notches above the average. Other noteworthy youth substance abuse programs are Rocky Mountain in Colorado; Provo Canyon in Utah; and Cascade, Cedu, and Hilltop in California.[56]

Yet critics regard these programs' confrontive environments with intense pressure from peers and staff members as degrading and harmful. Other shortcomings are that few individuals can afford the cost of such programs and that the programs do not have the necessary beds available for the juveniles who need such a therapeutic experience.

TEEN COURTS

Teen courts, also known as *youth courts*, have become a widely used form of intervention for young, usually first-time, offenders. An evaluation of teen courts, with 335 teen courts responding, which is more than 70 percent of the programs contacted, was performed in 1998.[57]

More than two-thirds of the court programs that were surveyed indicated that they had existed for less than five years. Twenty percent had been operating for less than one year. Most of the courts had a small caseload, with 48 percent indicating that they received fewer than one hundred referrals per year. Survey findings also revealed that U.S. teen courts handled about sixty-five thousand cases in 1998.[58]

Four possible case-processing models are used by these courts:

- *Adult judge.* An adult serves as judge and rules on legal terminology and courtroom procedures. Youths serve as attorneys, jurors, clerks, bailiffs, and so forth.
- *Youth judge.* This is similar to the adult judge model, except that a youth serves as the judge.
- *Tribunal.* Youth attorneys present the case to a panel of three youth judges, who decide the appropriate disposition for the defendant. A jury is not used.
- *Peer jury.* This model does not use youth attorneys: the case is presented to a youth jury by a youth or adult. The youth jury then questions the defendant directly.[59]

Most courts surveyed indicated that they used only one of these case-processing models. Forty-seven percent used the adult judge model, 12 percent used the peer jury model, 10 percent used the tribunal model, and 9 percent used the youth judge model. The remaining 22 percent used more than one case-processing model.[60]

Teen courts usually handle first-time offenders who are charged with offenses such as theft, misdemeanor assault, disorderly conduct, and possession of alcohol. The majority of these teen courts (87 percent) reported that they rarely or never accepted any juveniles with prior arrest records. The most common disposition used by these courts is community service. Following this disposition in level of use are victim apology letters (86 percent), apology essays (79 percent), teen court jury duty (75 percent), drug/alcohol classes (59 percent), and monetary

FOCUS ON OUTCOME 9–2

Early research on the effectiveness of teen courts suggests that they might well be more effective than traditional juvenile courts, at least in the short term. Figure 9–2 shows that juveniles who go before teen courts have a recidivism rate less than half that of youths who are processed traditionally. Only further longitudinal research will demonstrate whether the effects of teen courts are long-term.

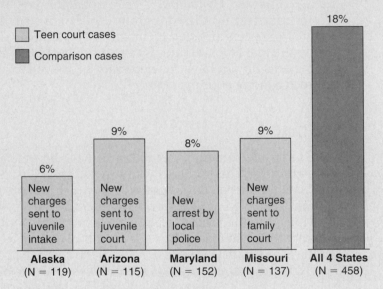

Figure 9–2   What Happened to Youth Six Months Later?

Source: Jeffrey A. Butts, Janeen Buck, and Mark B. Coggeshall, "The Impact of Teen Court on Young Offenders," *Research Report*, The Urban Institute Justice Policy Center (Washington, DC: OJJDP, April 2002), Front Matter, Online under Teen Courts.

restitution (34 percent).[61] See Figure 9–2 for the offenses handled in teen court in 2000. See Focus on Outcome 9–2 for the results of some teen court programs.

THE JUVENILE DRUG COURT MOVEMENT

By 2003, approximately three hundred juvenile drug courts had opened and another one hundred were being planned. The juvenile drug court movement is dedicated to juveniles. It is part of an expanding adult drug court movement that has been stimulated by Title V of the Violent Crime Control and Law Enforcement Act of 1994, an act that authorizes the Attorney General to make grants to various agencies to establish drug courts. These agencies include states, state, and local courts, units of local government, and Indian tribal governments.[62]

A number of strategies are common to juvenile drug courts compared with traditional juvenile courts:

- Much earlier and much more comprehensive intake assessments
- Much greater focus on the functioning of the juvenile and the family throughout the juvenile court system

- Much closer integration of the information obtained during the assessment process as it relates to the juvenile and the family
- Much greater coordination among the court, the treatment community, the school system, and other community agencies in responding to the needs of the juvenile and the court
- Much more active and continuous judicial supervision of the juvenile's case and treatment process
- Increased use of immediate sanctions for noncompliance and incentives for progress for both the juvenile and the family[63]

Currently six states operate juvenile drug courts, with the greatest activity in California (two programs) and Florida (four programs). For example, the Escambia County Juvenile Drug Court in Pensacola, Florida, began operating in April 1996. It is a twelve-month, three-phase approach to treating substance use and abuse. Phase I lasts about two months, Phase II lasts four months, and Phase III lasts six months. The drug court judge supervises treatment of up to forty offenders by reviewing reports from treatment personnel to determine the need for either positive or negative incentives to encourage participation and involvement.[64]

JUVENILE MEDIATION PROGRAM

The purpose of the Juvenile Mediation Program is for all involved parties to join together to resolve differences without court involvement. It began in Brooke County and then spread to Hancock, Marshall, Ohio, Tyler, and Wetzel counties in West Virginia. The program works with school-age children and adolescents, ages six to eighteen, and their families or guardians.[65]

Status and nonviolent offenders from the aforementioned five counties are eligible to participate in this program. There is a mediator whose responsibilities include determining the sincerity of remorse of the accused juvenile, deciding a fair and just penalty for his or her wrongdoing, and concluding whether any services are necessary. Before proceeding to the mediation hearing, the juvenile has admitted that he or she is guilty of a crime and signs a waiver of rights. This waiver relinquishes the rights of having witnesses or lawyers present.[66]

The program is designed to last no more than ninety days and is terminated under one of the following conditions: (1) successful: juveniles completed the required contractual agreement in ninety days; (2) unsuccessful: juveniles failed to meet the required agreement and are referred to the probation department for formal proceedings; and (3) dismissal: the mediator recommends dismissal prior to disposition. As of September 30, 2000, the rate of successful contract resolutions was 93 percent, or 625 of the first 670 participants. As of July 1, 2001, all 625 juveniles have remained delinquent and status offense-free.[67]

GANG INTERVENTION PROGRAMS

Communities have a tendency to deny that they have gangs even when gang youths are causing considerable problems at school and in the neighborhood.[68] But when a dramatic incident takes place, such as the killing of an innocent victim or a drive-by shooting, this initial denial may give way to the use of all available means to repress gangs.

Some communities have attempted a variety of means to divert gang youth from the juvenile and adult justice systems. For example, Paramount, California, developed the highly regarded Alternative to Gang Membership Program. In six years, only fifteen of the three thousand youths who participated in the antigang curriculum in school joined gangs. Moreover, more than 250 neighborhood meetings on gang awareness attracted twenty-five hundred parents. The city is proud of the fact that the $75,000 cost of the program is much *less* than the cost of putting one patrol car on the streets. Twelve other California communities have also adopted the Paramount plan.[69]

The fact of the matter is that although such approaches are promising, only an integrated, multidimensional, community-organized model is likely to have any long-term effect in preventing and diverting gang participation in the United States.

In sum, excited by the original vision of diversion, reformers promised that it would bring far-reaching changes in juvenile justice. But by the end of the 1970s, it became clear that the lack of funding, the hard-line mood toward crime, and the problems with implementation of the programs would make it difficult for diversion to survive, much less thrive. Although diversion has made some comeback in recent years, inadequate funding plagues diversion efforts; the political mood of the nation is still not overly receptive to diversion, and implementation problems have not been resolved.[70]

HOW DO DAY TREATMENT PROGRAMS OPERATE?

Day treatment programs, in which youngsters spend each day in the program and return home in the evenings, have been widely used in community-based juvenile corrections. These court-mandated programs are popular because they are more economical than residential placements. They do not need to provide living and sleeping quarters; they make parental participation easier; they require fewer staff members; and they are less coercive and punishment-oriented.

Nonresidential programs generally serve male juveniles, although California has operated two programs for girls and several coeducational ones. Nonresidential programs have been used widely by the California Treatment Project, the New York Division for Youth, and the Florida Division of Youth Services. Nonresidential programs in New York, which are called STAY, are similar to many other nonresidential programs in that they expose youths to a guided-group interaction experience.

Day treatment programs, similar to diversion programs, were used less in the 1980s and early 1990s than they were in the 1970s, but two of the most promising programs—the Associated Marine Institute (AMI) and Project New Pride—continue to thrive.

Camp counselors for the Washington, Pennsylvania, Leader Program prepare to take their youths on a rafting trip as part of their day treatment assignment. (Photo by Tony Hood.)

ASSOCIATED MARINE INSTITUTE

The Associated Marine Institute (AMI) is a privately operated program funded jointly by state and private donations. It tailors its programs to the geographical strengths of each community, using the ocean, wilderness, rivers, and lakes to stimulate productive behavior in youths referred by the courts or by the Division of Youth Services. Of the forty schools and institutes of the AMI, twenty-five are nonresidential. The fourteen- to eighteen-year-old male and female trainees in the nonresidential programs live at home or in foster homes.[71]

The Marine Institutes, which constitute most of the schools, set individual goals for the training period in a dozen categories, including diving, ship-handling skills, ocean science, lifesaving, first aid, and such electives as photography and marine maintenance. The most popular incentive for the youths is to earn official certification as a scuba diver. Other incentives designed to maintain enthusiasm are certificates awarded for short-term achievement in first aid, ship-handling skills, and diving; trophies for trainees of the month; and field trips to the Bahamas or the Florida Keys.[72]

The AMI has three main ingredients. First, it has a strong commitment to meaningful work. Regarding work as one of the most beneficial forms of therapy, it teaches that nothing worthwhile is achieved without hard work. Second, academic success is emphasized. The intent of the AMI programs is to motivate students and to give them the right tools and opportunities to succeed in school. Students are encouraged to take their GED exam and then attend vocational school, community college, or a four-year college. Third, modeling is emphasized throughout this experience because it is believed that what staff do is more important than what they say. An apt expression of the AMI's philosophy on modeling is this: Tell me, I'll forget. Show me, I may remember. Involve me, I'll be committed.[73] Focus on Practice 9–3 communicates the basic values of the AMI.

In September 1993, Attorney General Janet Reno and President Bill Clinton visited the Pinellas Marine Institute in St. Petersburg, Florida. In a nationally broadcast television program in which he announced his crime bill, the president said, "These [AMI] programs are giving young people a chance to take their future back, a chance to understand that there is good inside them."[74]

Clearly, the AMI programs provide interesting activities and teach worthwhile skills to youths. For those who can qualify, these programs certainly are preferable to placements in residential settings in the community or in long-term juvenile correctional institutions. Yet such programs are expensive, tend to be limited to certain parts of the country, and appear to be more suited to minor than serious offenders.

PROJECT NEW PRIDE

A community program that offers services to youths who have committed serious offenses is Project New Pride in Denver, Colorado. Most of the youngsters involved in the project, which had been designated as an exemplary project by Law Enforcement Assistance Administration (LEAA), are African Americans or Mexican Americans. Each youth receives intensive services in the program for the first three months and then continues treatment geared to individual needs and interests for a nine-month follow-up period. Academic education, counseling, employment, and cultural education are the four main areas of service provided in Project New Pride. For education, youths are assigned to classes in either the New Pride Alternative School or the Learning Disabilities

---

FOCUS ON PRACTICE   **9-3**

AMI VALUES

Integrity:	Doing what we say, when we said we would do it, or notifying the other party in advance.
Safety:	Creation of the environment where staff and students can function free from hazard and injury.
Honesty:	Dealing with everyone who comes in contact with us in an upright and truthful fashion.
Enthusiasm:	Operating with a strong inspirational display of excitement and commitment to the mission and goals of AMI.
Leadership:	Using others in pursuit of common goals.
"Kids First":	All key decisions are made on the basis of what's best for the students in the program. All other priorities relate to this value.
Excellence:	Our goal is to be the best. Our promise is to pursue any strategy that might improve service.
Loyalty:	Our company is operated in such a way that no one should be asked to compromise on ethical issues. On all other issues, each employee has two obligations: (1) to make every effort to communicate pertinent facts and opinions, and (2) to implement the final decision with enthusiasm and commitment.
Dedication:	A commitment to making all decisions in the best interest of the youths we serve.
Creativity:	Each employee strives to create an environment which fosters new ideas and champions them to make those ideas reality, with the goal of providing the safest, most effective service possible.
Family:	Creation of an environment that provides warmth, discipline, and empowerment for student and staff.
Goal Orientation:	We are a result-oriented organization that believes in setting goals and pursuing the most direct and effective paths to achieving those goals.

Source: Memo circulated throughout the schools and institutes of the AMI.

Critical Thinking Questions:
What is your evaluation of these goals? How difficult would it be to actually achieve these goals?

Center. The goal of the counseling, which tries to match specific counselors and clients, is to enhance a youth's self-image and to help him or her cope with the environment. Job preparation is heavily emphasized; youths attend a job-skills workshop and then receive on-the-job training. The purpose of cultural education is to expose youths to a range of experiences and activities in the Denver area.[75]

Project New Pride has established four primary goals in working with its difficult clientele: (1) reduction of recidivism, (2) job placement, (3) school reintegration, and (4) remediation of academic and learning disabilities. The project has had some success in achieving the first three of these goals but less success on educational remediation. The success of this project also has been demonstrated by its replication in Boston; Chicago; Fresno, California; Haddonfield, New Jersey; Kansas City, Missouri; Los Angeles; San Francisco; Pensacola, Florida; Providence, Rhode Island, and Washington, DC.[76]

The New Pride Replication Program, which examined the recidivism of the ten replication programs, was conducted from 1980 to 1984. It began with a six-month intensive phase involving daily or nearly daily contacts with each program participant, followed by six months of decreasing involvement. The study found that "essentially no significant recidivism differences (e.g., new petitions and readjudications) existed between New Pride youths and their fairly well-matched site-by-site comparisons, after an average of 2.6 years follow-up from program entry."[77]

In sum, although there is no question that nonresidential programs play a much smaller role in community-based corrections than they did a decade or two ago, these programs appear to be a preferred way of handling minor youthful offenders. They are more economical, more humane (as they permit the juvenile to live at home), and less coercive and punishment oriented than are residential facilities. But the conflicting findings on their success with hardcore offenders make them a somewhat questionable placement for the serious juvenile delinquent. Some juvenile recidivists seem to require more secure placements to gain control over themselves and their antisocial behaviors.

HOW DO GROUP HOMES OPERATE?

The group home, the group residence, and the group foster home are all used in juvenile corrections in this country. The term **group home** generally refers to a single dwelling owned or rented by an organization or agency for the purpose of housing offenders. Although it is not part of an institutional campus, this facility provides care for a group of about four to twelve children, and staff are viewed as houseparents or counselors rather than as foster parents. The administrative, supervisory, and service responsibility for the group home rests with the parent agency or organization. Usually indistinguishable from nearby homes or apartments, the group home reaches out to the community for resources and service.

The terms *group residence* or *halfway house* are used in some parts of the country to identify a small facility serving about thirteen to thirty-five youths. It usually houses two or more groups of youths, each with its own child-care staff. This residence tends to use agency rather than community services, and its architecture and large size differentiate it from nearby homes and apartments.

Group homes fulfill several purposes in juvenile corrections. First, they provide an alternative to institutionalization. Dependent, neglected, and other noncriminal youths, especially, are referred to them. Second, group homes may be used as short-term residences. The communities in which they are located provide the youths with the resources to deal with such problems as family conflict, school difficulties, and peer interactions. Third, group homes can be used either as a "halfway-in" setting for offenders who are having difficulty keeping to the conditions of probation or as a "halfway-out" setting for juvenile offenders who are returning to the community but do not have adequate home placement.

Group home programs tend to vary from home to home because they have been developed to meet varying needs for different populations and communities, and standard guidelines do not exist. Consequently, group homes often reflect the personal philosophies of their founders or directors. Intake criteria, length of stay, treatment goals, target population serviced, quantity and quality of staffing, services offered, physical facilities, location in relation to the rest of the city, and house rules are extremely diverse in group homes in this country. This diversity need not be a problem, however, if additional support services are available. One of the most important studies of juvenile justice found a significant reduction in recidivisim in Massachusetts when community-based programs had an integrated network of services.[78]

Many group homes are treatment oriented. Group therapy often is used as a treatment modality. These group sessions are largely supportive; they do not probe very deeply, and discussion usually is limited to problems as they arise. Guided Group Interaction (GGI) is probably the most popular treatment method; the members of the group are expected to support, confront, and be honest with one another so that they may be helped in dealing with their own problems. The role of the therapist in GGI is to help the members develop a more positive and prosocial group culture. Some group homes deliberately avoid a comfortable climate, and staff may even try to arouse anxiety. The treatment philosophy behind this is that without a relaxed atmosphere, youths are more likely to become unsettled and thereby more receptive to personality change.

The teaching-family group home concept was developed in 1967 with the establishment of the Achievement Place group home in Lawrence, Kansas. In the 1970s, the teaching-family model was used in more than forty homes in twelve states.[79] Group foster homes also shelter youthful offenders. These homes sometimes are effective for youngsters who are unable to tolerate a close one-on-one relationship with foster parents. Group-care foster homes have become increasingly popular in the Midwest, chiefly in Iowa, Michigan, Minnesota, Ohio, and Wisconsin.

Florida has developed a fairly extensive network of group homes. Of the seventeen community-based treatment centers serving four hundred youngsters, nine are halfway houses, or group homes, developed on the Criswell House model. The first Criswell House in Florida was established in 1958; it housed twenty-five youths on probation and parole and used guided group interaction.[80] In addition to these larger halfway houses, Florida has three START centers—small group homes located in rural settings with their own schools on the grounds—and five group homes for emotionally disturbed children, administered by husband-and-wife teams.

The House of Umoja (HOU) was founded in 1968 and was officially organized in 1970 as a youth development agency. When she became aware that one of her six sons had joined a gang, Sister Falaka and her husband, David Fattah, took the bold step of inviting the gang to become a part of their family. Sister Falaka saw possible solutions to the violence of gangs in "the strength of the family, tribal concepts, and African value systems." She and her husband created an African-style extended family in which members of the gang could find alternative values to those of their street-life culture. Residents are required to be drug-free and are encouraged to maintain good grades. Since its establishment, three thousand adolescents belonging to seventy-three different street gangs have passed through the HOU doors. The success of the Umoja concept has led to its duplication in Bridgeport, Connecticut, and Portland, Oregon. The principles of this resident program are part of the National Center for Neighborhood Enterprise's highly successful Violence-Free Zone initiative that has been instituted in five cities.[81]

Yet innovative programs still are not typical of group homes across the nation. In too many group homes, vacancies are hard to find and there may even be a long waiting list. Staff are notoriously underpaid, believe that they have not been properly trained, and have high rates of turnover.[82] Residents also typically have longer stays than they would have in training schools, and this raises real questions about whether group homes are a less punitive placement than juvenile institutions are. The evaluations of residential programs further make it difficult to support the conclusion that residential programs in the community result in lower rates of recidivism than do institutional programs. Nevertheless, a convincing case can be made that residential programs are at least as successful as training schools, with far less trauma to youths and usually at less cost to the state. In Focus on Offender 9–4, a former resident

FOCUS ON OFFENDER

WHAT QUAKERDALE MEANT TO ME

9–4

I spent an entire day thinking about what Quakerdale really means to me. I didn't want to just write a bunch of meaningful praise—I wanted to capture the truth of Quakerdale's impact on my life. As I was thinking, [I] realized that I could probably write an entire novel about my experiences there and what it has done for me. Quakerdale taught me tolerance, patience, respect, self-restraint, and communication.

When I was admitted to Quakerdale, I was a lost, hopeless, self-serving 17 year old. I had recently attempted suicide, run away from home, dropped out of high school, gotten into marijuana, was a self-mutilator, and didn't understand the meaning of "impulse control." Throughout my six months there, I worked intensively with staff and participated whole-heartedly in groups and peer activities, as well as actively "working my program."

I learned patience when dealing with others and when working through my own problems. I learned that sometimes, I will not get what I want or expect, but that it's still okay.

I learned respect. I did not need to learn to respect others so much as to respect myself. I came to realize that my behavior was hurting no one worse than it was hurting me. It was destroying me physically and, especially, emotionally. And I deserved a lot better than that. I opened my eyes to the ways in which I was treating myself. I realized that I would hope to never allow another person to treat me the way I was treating myself. I saw that the worst relationship I had in my life was my relationship with me. For example, I would never dream of murdering someone, but that's exactly what I tried to do to myself. I realized that I could not hope to be happy if I continued my present, self-hating relationship.

If I was to ever learn to love myself, I needed to learn self-restraint. Quakerdale taught me this, as well. Sometimes, it's better to delay gratification for a more permanent, safer sense of gratification. Impulse control is still something that I work on daily, but I think it is obvious from my present life-circumstances versus my "pre-Quakerdale" life-circumstances that I learned a great deal about self-control. I think that a big part of what helped me learn self-control was Quakerdale's "open door" policy. I had the option to run away, but every day that I chose to remain, I gained more responsibility and privileges. After only four months at Quakerdale, I was allowed to walk to and from East High School every day by myself. This showed me that staff trusted me, which made me *want* to be trustworthy. I received positive reinforcement for acting and reasoning appropriately, which built up my confidence in myself and [the] staff's ability to help me.

I learned communication. I had family sessions once a week, and I had group [sessions] many times a week. We were always encouraged to hold others accountable, hold ourselves accountable, and be honest. I learned that telling the truth can be much more rewarding than trying to "stay out of trouble" by lying. If I did something wrong or lied to staff, I was positively reinforced if I confessed on my own. I learned that it is my responsibility to be honest, and *others'* responsibility to react to my honesty in an appropriate way. It is not my responsibility to keep everyone happy, especially if it ruins me inside. However, I also learned to "pick my battles."

What it all comes down to is that: before Quakerdale, I was literally taking my life in my hands and not even caring if I dropped it. Since Quakerdale, I have gone on to graduate from Dowling High School with a 3.89 cumulative grade point average, made [the] National Honor Society, received the Aquinas Key, [and] received an

Academic medal, and [a] letter in academics. I was accepted to all three colleges to which I applied, and I now attend the University of Minnesota, where I have a cumulative grade point average of 3.48, made the Dean's List second semester, and am majoring in English and taking a minor in psychology. I am by no means completely "cured" of the emotional difficulties that I had before Quakerdale, but I can honestly say that I have learned how to live a wonderful life, despite, and sometimes due to, my trials and difficulties. Thank you, Quakerdale, for helping me grow into the woman I have become [italics included in the original].

Sincerely,

Source: Letter received from Rita Fernau, Director of the Quakerdale program, and used with permission of the author.

Critical Thinking Questions:
What does this letter say to the "nothing works" thesis of Robert Martinson? Why do you think this program was so successful with this young woman? What would it take for us to have more House of Umoja and Quakedale programs?

writes a letter to the director of Quakerdale, a residential program for girls, expressing her appreciation for what the program has meant to her life.

WHAT ARE WILDERNESS PROGRAMS?

Outward Bound and VisionQuest are the two best-known wilderness, or survival, programs. All of these outdoor **wilderness programs,** whether they take place in the mountains, the canoe country, the forest, the sea, or the desert, conclude that the completion of a seemingly impossible task is one of the best means to gain self-reliance, to prove one's worth, and to define oneself as a person.

OUTWARD BOUND

Outward Bound programs were first used in England during World War II. The first Outward Bound school in the United States was the Colorado Outward Bound School, which was established in 1962 and accepted its first delinquents in 1964. This program, situated in the Rocky Mountains at an altitude of eighty-eight hundred feet, consists of mountain walking, backpacking, high-altitude camping, solo survival, rappelling, and rock climbing. Other Outward Bound programs soon followed in Maine, Minnesota, North Carolina, Oregon, and Texas. A similar program, a Homeward Bound school, was opened in 1970 in Massachusetts. Several community-based wilderness programs that begin and end in the community but include sessions in a nearby wilderness area are also in operation.[83]

Today, Outward Bound offers 750 wilderness courses serving adults, teens, and youths. Courses include rock climbing, kayaking, dogsledding, sailing, rappelling, backpacking, and more. Over ten thousand students participate in wilderness courses. Outward Bound also offers multiyear partnership with 125 schools across the United States. It encourages over thirty thousand students and four thousand teachers to reach high levels of achievement and to discover their potential. Outward Bound also has urban programs in New York, Boston, Philadelphia, Baltimore, and Atlanta.[84]

The most important staff members in Outward Bound are the persons who work directly with youths. These counselors literally have the lives of youths in their hands; several youths, in fact, have lost their lives in Outward Bound programs. Enrollees may be experts on how to survive in the streets, but they are usually experiencing a new and frightening world in the wilderness. Participants must be motivated to do their best, supported while they are struggling with the difficulty and fear of the tasks, and responded to with praise and reinforcement when they successfully complete each experience. The job of the counselor is to make certain that the program is a successful experience for as many participants as possible. He or she has to be a master psychologist, knowing how to push and when to quit. He or she must be able to encourage those who are ready to drop out and to alert those whose carelessness may cost them their own lives or the lives of others.

John Calhoun, former commissioner of youth services in Massachusetts, is positive about this wilderness experience, which is called Homeward Bound in his state:

> That's done well; we love it. It probably is the single most consistently effective program we have. The problem is a kid comes back on his twenty-seventh day on a high, having battered the elements for his last solo. Then, he hits the hard streets. It's a magnificent temporary program, but where we have failed in that program is in the aftercare. These kids feel they're world beaters when they [get] back to the grim reality of the projects. What we have to figure out is how to support that wondrous high.[85]

Francis J. Kelly and Daniel J. Baer presented the results of a two-year demonstration project conducted by the Massachusetts Department of Youth Services that involved sixty boys who attended Outward Bound schools and sixty boys who were treated routinely by juvenile corrections authorities. Effectiveness was measured primarily by comparing the recidivism rates between the two matched groups twelve months after parole. Recidivism among the experimental group was much lower after the first year: 42 percent of the control group had failed compared to 20 percent of the experimental group. But the differences between the two groups had nearly disappeared after five years.[86]

Kelly and Baer's evaluation of the Outward Bound program, along with Calhoun's statement, appears to evaluate accurately the effectiveness of wilderness survival programs; the programs have an initial positive impact on youths, which wears off as youths return to their home environments. Effective aftercare services for those youths who have participated in Outward Bound programs are clearly needed.

VISIONQUEST

Started by Robert Ledger Burton and Stan Rogers in Tucson, Arizona, in 1973, the VisionQuest survival program seeks to provide adjudicated youth the opportunity to succeed in meeting challenges, to see a new future for themselves, and to give them skills to achieve their goals and reach their highest potential. Other key components of the VisionQuest approach, which has been accused of abusive treatment of youths, include the emphasis on staff as parents rather than counselors, the use of rigorous outdoor activity (such as wilderness training, a sea survival experience, or the mule and horse wagon train), the use of living history to connect youths to their heritage and culture, and the blending of military influences with education and treatment.[87]

Peter W. Greenwood and Susan Turner's examination of the effectiveness of VisionQuest on youths assigned to it by the San Diego Juvenile Court found that the probation department strongly opposed placement to this program. Among the probation department's criticisms were that VisionQuest placed youths in potentially dangerous activities; that it resisted interference by probation staff; that it insisted on determining when youths would be released from the program; and that it handled youths in abusive ways. Indeed, probation staff filed child abuse charges, none of which led to further legal action.[88]

ARE COMMUNITY-BASED PROGRAMS EFFECTIVE?

It would appear that improving the effectiveness of community-based corrections ultimately requires some positive gains in breaking down community resistance, in obtaining greater citizen involvement in community-based programs, and in developing a broader continuum of services in the community for juveniles who need such services.

First, to break down community resistance and to obtain greater citizen involvement in community-based programs, departments of juvenile corrections must develop and implement a certain plan of action. This plan needs to include a well-developed plan for the establishment of programs and for deciding who will be placed in community facilities. Unfortunately, no agreement has been reached on how to implement either of these strategies.

Careful planning is obviously necessary to gain greater public support for community-based programs. A department should mount a massive public education effort through the communications media, should seek support for the project from the various subcommunities of the community—ethnic, racial, and special interest groups—and should develop a sophisticated understanding of the decision-making processes in society. But should this be done before or after a program has been initiated in the community?

Advocates of keeping the community informed as soon as a site for a program is chosen claim that to do otherwise is dishonest. Opponents of this approach argue that advance information will permit the community to mobilize resistance against the proposed community program. They claim that the community is more likely to accept an already established and successful program than one that exists only on the drawing board.

Widespread controversy also exists over the selection of youths to be placed in community-based programs. One approach is conservative: If the wrong youth is put in the wrong place at the wrong time and commits a serious or violent crime, such as rape or murder, the adverse publicity may destroy the best-planned and implemented program. Therefore, to preserve the viability of community-based programs, only juveniles most likely to be helped should be kept in the community. The opposite approach argues that all but the hard-core recidivist should be retained in the community, for it is there that the youth's problems began in the first place. Advocates of this position believe that institutionalization will only make more serious criminals out of confined youths. Some of these supporters even propose leaving many of the hard-core or difficult-to-handle youths in the community.

Second, improving the continuum of services for juveniles in a community usually requires a strong deinstitutionalization emphasis. The programs that have this integration of services are more likely to have positive effects on youthful offenders assigned to them. Another advantage of these continuum-of-service programs is that they are not as likely to experience the fragmentation and duplication of services that are found so frequently in other programs in the juvenile justice system.

✓**Progress Check 9.2**
Review this section at
www.prenhall.com/bartollas

SUMMARY

- Advocated by national commissions, supported by reintegrative philosophy, and funded largely by federal grants, community programs for juveniles expanded to include an impressive variety of situations during the 1970s and 1980s.

- Some proponents of community-based programs for juveniles even advocated dealing with all youthful offenders within the community and closing all juvenile schools.

- The effectiveness of community-based programs is controversial. Even in studies that have found lower recidivism rates for youths left in the community, the criticism is often made that juveniles who were more likely to succeed were selected for the experimental group and the authorities altered the results by giving the experimentals more chances than the controls before returning them to the juvenile court.

- Even though it is difficult to substantiate the widespread conclusion that community-based programs lower the recidivism rate, a good case can be made for the assumption that community-based corrections programs are at least as successful as institutional confinement is, with far less trauma to youngsters and less cost to the state.

- Community-based programs continue to face several challenges, especially those posed by the reduction of federal funding and the public's preference for getting tough on youth crime. Yet the cost effectiveness of these programs, as opposed to the prohibitive expense of long-term institutions, should continue to lead to an increased use of alternative programs in the community.

WEB SITES OF INTEREST

To find many links on various kinds of prevention programs, go to
http://www.criminology.fsu.edu/jjclearinghouse/jj19.html
Links to community-based programs can be found at
http://www.criminology.fsu.edu/jjclearinghouse/jj27.html
VisionQuest 2006:
http://www.vqconference.com
Outward Bound:
http://www.outwardbound.org
Associated Marine Institutes:
http://www.amikids.org

CRITICAL THINKING QUESTIONS

1. Why have delinquency prevention programs generally been so ineffective?
2. Why is the widening criticism of many of these programs a serious indictment?
3. Of the programs discussed in this chapter, which do you feel is the best for helping offenders reintegrate into the community?
4. What specific strategies can departments of juvenile corrections pursue to enlist greater support from the community for community programs?

5. What are the main types of residential and nonresidential programs for juvenile delinquents?
6. How effective are community-based corrections? What is the essential link in increasing the effectiveness of community-based corrections?

NOTES

1. Interview with a director of court services in 1978.
2. Willie T. Barney contributed this material on privatization to this volume. He is a high school principal who has worked in the private sector with youthful offenders.
3. Kristgen Krackle, *SafeFutures: Partnership to Reduce Youth Violence and Delinquency* (Washington, DC: Office of Juvenile Justice and Delinquency Prevention, 1996), 1.
4. Robin Hamilton and Kay McKinney, "Job Training for Juveniles: Project CRAFT," *OJJDP Fact Sheet* (Washington DC.: Office of Juvenile Justice and Delinquency Prevention, 1999), 1.
5. For an expanded treatment of delinquency prevention, see Clemens Bartollas, *Juvenile Delinquency*, 4th ed. (Boston: Allyn & Bacon, 1997), 524–51.
6. Anne M. Newton, "Prevention of Crime and Delinquency," *Criminal Justice Abstracts* (June 1978), 4.
7. Marylyn Bibb, "Gang-Related Services of Mobilization for Youth," in *Juvenile Gangs in Context: Theory, Research, and Action*, edited by Malcolm W. Klein (Upper Saddle River, NJ: Prentice Hall, 1967), 175–82.
8. For a description and evaluation of "Scared Straight," see James O. Finckenauer, *Scared Straight! and the Panacea Phenomenon* (Upper Saddle River, NJ: Prentice Hall, 1982).
9. For a description of the various prevention programs, see Bartollas, *Juvenile Delinquency*, 521–51.
10. For a review of these studies examining the effectiveness of prevention programs, see ibid., 524.
11. The following description of CAP is largely derived from Harold Finestone, *Victims of Change: Juvenile Delinquents in American Society* (Westport, CT: Greenwood Press, 1976), 125–30. For more recent evaluations of CAP, see Steven Schlossman and Michael Sedlak, "The Chicago Area Projects Revisited," *Crime and Delinquency* 26 (July 1983), 398–460; and Steven Schlossman, Gail Zellman, and Richard Shavelson, *Delinquency Prevention in South Chicago: A Fifty-Year Assessment of the Chicago Area Project* (Santa Monica, CA: Rand, 1984).
12. A book describing the organization and goals of CAP on the Near West Side by one of these local leaders is Anthony Sorrentino's *Organizing Against Crime* (New York: Human Sciences Press, 1977).
13. For the best evaluation of CAP, see Solomon Kobrin, "The Chicago Area Projects—A Twenty-Five-Year Assessment," *Annals of the American Academy of Political and Social Sciences* 322 (March 1959), 20–29.
14. Schlossman et al., *Delinquency Prevention in South Chicago*, v.
15. Kobrin, "The Chicago Area Projects—A Twenty-Five-Year Assessment," 23.
16. Jon Snodgrass, "Clifford Shaw and Henry D. McKay," in *Delinquency, Crime, and Society*, edited by James F. Short, Jr. (Chicago: University of Chicago Press, 1976), 16. See also Jon Snodgrass, *The American Criminological Tradition: Portraits of the Men and Ideology in a Discipline.* Ph.D. dissertation, University of Pennsylvania, 1972.

17. Cited in Jeremy Travis, "Communities and Criminal Justice: A Powerful Alignment," *National Institute of Justice Journal*, Issue 254 (August 1996), 2.

18. For these same emphases, see ibid., table of contents.

19. Sharon Mihalic, Katherine Irwin, Abigail Fagan, Diane Ballard, and Delbert Elliott, *Successful Implementation: Lessons from Blueprints* (Washington, DC: Office of Juvenile Justice and Delinquency Prevention, 2004), p. 1.

20. Sharon Mihalic, Katherine Irwin, Abigail Fagan, Diane Ballard, and Delbert Elliott, *Blueprints for Violence Prevention* (Washington, DC: Office of Juvenile Justice and Delinquency Prevention, 2004), p. 55.

21. D. E. McGill, S. Mihalic, and J. K. Grotpeter, "Big Brothers Big Sisters of America," in *Blueprints for Violence Prevention*: Book 2, edited by D. S. Elliott (Boulder: University of Colorado, Institute of Behavioral Science, Center for the Study and Prevention of Violence, 1997).

22. Mihalic et al., *Blueprints for Violence Prevention*, pp. 30–31.

23. M. A. Pentz, S. Mihalic, and J. K. Grotpeter, "The Midwestern Prevention Project," in *Blueprints for Violence Prevention*: Book 1, edited by D. S. Elliott (Boulder: University of Colorado, Institute of Behavioral Science, Center for the Study and Prevention of Violence, 1997).

24. Mihalic et al., *Blueprints for Violence Prevention*, pp. 26–27.

25. J. E. Alexander et al., "Functional Family Therapy," in *Blueprints for Violence Prevention: Juvenile Justice Bulletin*, edited by D. S. Elliott (Boulder: University of Colorado, Institute of Behavioral Science, Center for the Study and Prevention of Violence, 2000).

26. Mihalic et al., *Blueprints for Violence Prevention*, pp. 22–23.

27. C. Webster-Stratton et al., "The Incredible Years: Parents, Teachers and Child Training Series," in *Blueprints for Violence Prevention*: Book 11, edited by D. S. Elliott (Boulder: University of Colorado, Institute of Behavioral Science, Center for the Study and Prevention of Violence, 2001).

28. Mihalic et al., *Blueprints for Violence Prevention*, p. 47.

29. G. Botvin, S. Mihalic, and J. K. Grotpeter, "Life Skills Training," in *Blueprints for Violence Prevention*: Book 5, edited by D. S. Elliott (Boulder: University of Colorado, Institute of Behavioral Science, Center for the Study and Prevention of Violence, 1998).

30. Mihalic et al., *Blueprints for Violence Prevention*, pp. 31–33.

31. Pentz et al., "The Midwestern Prevention Project."

32. Mihalic et al., *Blueprints for Violence Prevention*, pp. 56–58.

33. P. Chamberlain and S. Mihalic, "Multidimensional Treatment Foster Care," in *Blueprints for Violence Prevention*: Book 8, edited by D. S. Elliott (Boulder: University of Colorado, Institute of Behavioral Science, Center for the Study and Prevention of Violence, 1998).

34. Mihalic et al., *Blueprints for Violence Prevention*, pp. 27–28.

35. S. W. Henggeler et al., "Multisystemic Therapy, in *Blueprints for Violence Prevention*: Book 6, edited by D. S. Elliott (Boulder: University of Colorado, Institute of Behavioral Science, Center for the Study and Prevention of Violence, 2001).

36. Mihalic et al., *Blueprints for Violence Prevention*, pp. 18–20.

37. D. Olds et al., "Prenatal and Infancy Home Visitation by Nurses," in *Blueprints for Violence Prevention*: Book 7, edited by D. S. Elliott (Boulder: University of Colorado, Institute of Behavioral Science, Center for the Study and Prevention of Violence, 1998).

38. Mihalic et al., *Blueprints for Violence Prevention*, pp. 47–48.

39. Ibid., p. 48.

40. Ibid., p. 46.

41. James C. Howell, ed., *Guide for Implementing the Comprehensive Strategy for Serious, Violent, and Chronic Juvenile Offenders* (Washington, DC: Office of Juvenile Justice and Delinquency Prevention, 1995), 10.

42. Ibid., 3.

43. Ibid., 5.

44. Ibid.

45. Ibid., 9–10.

46. Ibid., 11.

47. Kathleen Coolbaugh and Cynthia J. Hansel, "The Comprehensive Strategy: Lessons Learned from the Pilot Sites," *Juvenile Justice Bulletin* 2000, 1.

48. Ibid., 10.

49. Sherwood Norman, *Youth Service Bureau: A Key to Prevention* (Paramus, NJ: National Council on Crime and Delinquency, 1972), 12–13.

50. Interviewed in October 1981.

51. Tim Brennan, David Huizinga, and Delbert S. Elliott, *The Social Psychology of Runaways* (Lexington, MA: D. C. Heath, 1978).

52. U.S. Senate Subcommittee on the Constitution of the Committee on the Judiciary, *Homeless Youth: The Saga of "Pushouts" and "Throwaways" in America*, 96th Cong., 1980, 36.

53. Ibid., 35–44.

54. For the early history of Élan, see Philip B. Taft Jr., "Élan: Does Its Bizarre Regimen Transform Troubled Youth or Abuse Them?" *Corrections Magazine* 5 (March 1979), 18–28. The recent materials on Élan were contributed by Deanna Atkinson, an administrator in the Élan program, in a September 1995 phone conversation.

55. For this information on Élan, see its Web page: http://www.elanschool.com/. This Web citation also includes several statements from former residents testifying to the brutal methods used at Élan and its negative effect on them.

56. This information was contributed by Deanna Atkinson, an administrator in the Élan program, in a September 1995 phone conversation.

57. Survey results are found in Jeffrey Butts, Dean Hoffman, and Jancen Buck, "Teen Courts in the United States: A Profile of Current Programs," *OJJDP Fact Sheet* (Washington, DC: Office of Juvenile Justice and Delinquency Prevention, 1999).

58. Ibid., 1.

59. T. M. Godwin, *Peer Justice and Youth Empowerment: An Implementation Guide for Teen Court Programs* (Lexington, KY: American Probation and Parole Association, 1998).

60. Butts et al., "Teen Courts in the United States," 1.

61. Ibid., 2.

62. Marilyn Roberts, Jennifer Brophy, and Caroline Cooper, *The Juvenile Drug Court Movement* (Washington, DC: Office of the Juvenile Justice and Delinquency Prevention, 1997), 1.

63. Ibid., 1–2.

64. Ibid., 2.

65. Robert R. Smith and Victor S. Lombardo, "Evaluation Report of the Juvenile Mediation Program *Corrections and Comprendium*" (Laurel, MD: American Correctional Association, 2001), 1.

66. Ibid., 2.

67. Ibid., 2.

68. See C. Ronald Huff, "Youth Gangs and Public Policy," *Crime and Delinquency* 35 (October 1989), 524–37.

69. Elaine S. Knapp, *Embattled Youth: Kids, Gangs, and Drugs* (Chicago: Council of State Governments, 1988), 14.

70. Stanley Cohen, *Vision of Social Control: Crime, Punishment and Classification* (Cambridge, England: Policy Press, 1985), 93.

71. Information on the Associated Marine Institute was supplied in a 1995 phone conversation with Magie Valdés.

72. Ibid. See also Ronald H. Bailey, "Can Delinquents Be Saved by the Sea?" *Corrections Magazine* 1 (September 1974), 77–84.

73. "The Programs of the Associated Marine Institute," mimeograph, n.d.

74. Unpublished mimeographed statement circulated by AMI, n.d.

75. S. E. Lawrence and B. R. West, *National Evaluation of the New Pride Replication Program: Final Report,* Vol. 1 (Lafayette, CA: Pacific Institute for Research and Evaluation, 1985).

76. Ibid.

77. Ted Palmer, *The Re-Emergence of Correctional Intervention* (Newbury Park, CA: Sage Publications, 1992), 84.

78. B. Krisberg, J. Austin, and P. Steele, *Unlocking Juvenile Corrections* (San Francisco: National Council on Crime and Delinquency, 1991).

79. D. L. Fixsen, E. L. Phillips, and M. M. Wolf, "The Teaching Family Model of Group Home Treatment," in *Closing Correctional Institutions,* edited by Yitzhak Bakal (Lexington, MA: D. C. Heath, 1973).

80. For the early history of Criswell House, see Ronald H. Bailey, "Florida," *Corrections Magazine* 1 (September 1974), 66.

81. For the House of Umoja, see http://www.volunteersolutions.org/volunteer-way/org/1236595.

82. One of the authors has had a number of former students who were employed in group homes, and they consistently make these criticisms.

83. Joshua L. Miner and Joe Boldt, *Outward Bound USA: Learning Through Experience* (New York: Morrow, 1981).

84. For Outward Bound USA, see http://www.outwardbound.org/.

85. Interviewed in June 1978.

86. Cited in Joseph Nold and Mary Wilpers, "Wilderness Training as an Alternative to Incarceration," in *A Nation without Prisons,* edited by Calvert R. Dodge (Lexington, MA: D. C. Heath, 1975), 157–58.

87. VisionQuest Changes Lives, accessed online at http://www.vq.com/overview.htm.

88. Peter W. Greenwood and Susan Turner, *The VisionQuest Program: An Evaluation* (Santa Monica, CA: Rand, 1987).

10

JUVENILE INSTITUTIONALIZATION AND AFTERCARE

The staff here do not emphasize enough what is going on in a student's life and how the student can better himself. Students come in with one mentality, and they leave with the same mentality.

On the outs, I had a driver's license, used to drive around, had all the girls liking me, and used to deal drugs. I come in here and see people who I knew out there. It's just like a family reunion, or a party, or a vacation. You go back out there with the same mentality, only you're worse because you know better ways. You've used your experience from being locked up, from talking to other people who've been caught. You find better ways to do what you've done before.

The staff don't make you go to school or show you that schooling is important. They're more concerned with keeping you controlled, keeping your aggression on tap. They don't offer programs that will help you control your anger. They don't attempt to persuade you to go to AA or NA [Alcoholics Anonymous or Narcotics Anonymous] groups. So, if I like to sit in the cottage and do nothing, staff are happy. That keeps me quiet. I am an aggressive person, and they're happy so long as I'm not bothering nobody. They want me to make their job easy. All they are concerned about is putting in their eight hours.

—Institutionalized Youth[1]

OUTLINE

OBJECTIVES

1. To examine the rhetoric and reality of juvenile institutionalization
2. To evaluate the quality of juvenile institutionalization
3. To portray how juveniles respond to institutionalization
4. To reveal the rights that juveniles have in juvenile institutions
5. To examine the current procedures of juvenile aftercare

KEY TERMS

attention homes
boot camps
detention centers
intensive supervision programs
jails

kinship social structure
ranch/wilderness camps
reception and diagnostic centers
shelter care facilities
social roles

training schools
victimization

The confined youth speaking in the chapter-opening quote makes three devastating critiques of juvenile institutionalization. First, he charges that institutional staff do not care. Second, he claims that the needed programs are not available to residents of training schools. Third, he views training schools as schools of crime, in which youths learn more about a life of crime than they knew when they were first confined. As part of this negative impact of juvenile institutionalization, this training school resident believes that confinement increases the will to commit crime in the future. One of the purposes of this chapter is to evaluate the charges made by this Ohio youth.

The juvenile justice system often is accused of being too lenient, yet youths who are believed to be dangerous or who show little sign of mending their ways frequently find themselves locked up behind walls. The facilities in which these youths are placed are divided into two general categories: temporary care facilities and correctional facilities. Detention homes, shelters, reception centers, and jails are temporary care facilities; boot camps, ranches, forestry camps, and training schools are long-term correctional facilities. The primary differences between these two categories of facilities are the absence of correctional programs and the shorter length of stay in temporary care facilities. Temporary care facilities frequently house both males and females in the same general location, whereas correctional facilities often separate them. Juveniles to the adult court can also be sentenced to adult prisons, or they can be transferred to mental health placements. This chapter focuses on the training school because of the length of time it holds youths and because of the special role it has played in juvenile justice.

This chapter further examines juvenile aftercare or parole, which is concerned with the release of a juvenile from an institution when he or she can best from release and can make an optimal adjustment to community living. The importance of aftercare services is that they provide the supervision and release that are necessary for juveniles to make a successful reentry to society.

WHAT ARE THE SHORT-TERM CONFINEMENTS OF JUVENILES?

Juvenile offenders are placed in jails, detention centers, and shelter care facilities for short-term confinement.

JAILS

The degrading conditions of nineteenth-century **jails**, as previously suggested, were one of the reasons motivating reformers to establish houses of refuge. It was commonly agreed that the jails were no place for a juvenile. Overcrowded conditions and idleness fostered a lawless society, one in which the juvenile was frequently a sexual victim. Juveniles also had alarming rates of suicide in jail.[2]

Still, partly because so few alternatives were available, large numbers of juveniles continued to be confined in county jails and police lockups. Estimates varied, but between five hundred thousand and one million youths each year were locked up in jails during the 1970s.[3]

The numbers appeared to decline in the 1980s and 1990s, chiefly because of the Juvenile Justice and Delinquency Prevention Act (JJDPA) of 1974. This act provided restrictive criteria governing the confinement of juveniles in adult facilities. Congress amended the JJDPA in 1980, requiring participating states to remove all juveniles from adult jails and lockups by the end of 1985 if they wanted to receive federal funding for juvenile justice. The 1985 deadline was extended to 1988 and then again was amended in 1989 because so few states had achieved full compliance.[4]

According to the data published in 2006, an estimated 7,083 youth younger than eighteen were held in adult jails on June 30, 2004. These inmates

Juveniles arrested for serious offenses occasionally had to spend at least short periods of time in the "hole" in the Old Washington, Pennsylvania, County Jail. The facility was open until approximately April, 1996. Many crime control advocates argue that the use of such cells for juveniles is appropriate. (Photo by Stuart Miller.)

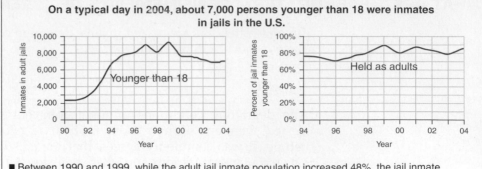

On a typical day in 2004, about 7,000 persons younger than 18 were inmates in jails in the U.S.

■ Between 1990 and 1999, while the adult jail inmate population increased 48%, the jail inmate population under age 18 increased more than 300%.

■ Between 1999 and 2004, the adult jail inmate population increased 19%, while the jail inmate population under age 18 decreased 25%.

■ The number of jail inmates younger than 18 held as adults was 6,159 in 2004—up 21% from 1994.

■ The number of jail inmates younger than 18 held as juveniles in 2004 was 924—down 42% from 1994.

Figure 10–1   *Juveniles in Adult Jails by Year and Percent*

Source: Howard N. Snyder and Melissa Sickmund, *Juvenile Offenders and Victims: 2006 National Report* (Washington, DC: National Center for Juvenile Justice and Office of Juvenile Justice and Delinquency Prevention, 2006), p. 236; adapted from Beck's *Prison and Jail Inmates at Midyear 1999,* Beck and Karberg's *Prison and Jail Inmates at Midyear 2000,* Harrison and Karberg's *Prison and Jail Inmates at Midyear 2002,* and Harrison and Beck's *Prison and Jail Inmates at Midyear 2004.*

accounted for 1 percent of the total jail population, as in 2003. In 2004, 87 percent of the jail inmates younger than eighteen were held as adults; this proportion was greater than the 80 percent in 2000 and the 76 percent in 1994.[5] Figure 10–1 contains the data related to the confinement of juveniles in adult jails.

Several reasons exist why jail removal of juveniles continues to remain a distant goal. First, juveniles who are transferred to adult court and are waiting for criminal trials make up an increasingly large category of youths confined in jail. Second, at least forty states continue to resist full compliance with the JJDPA jail-removal mandate. The claim is frequently made that the states lack the necessary resources and alternatives to implement the jail-removal mandate.[6] Third, the belief is widely held that separating juveniles from adult inmates is sufficient to protect the juveniles against the harmful effects of jail confinement.

What is hopeful is that a number of states have taken a strong stand against the jailing of juveniles. California and Utah have made it unlawful to jail a youthful offender.[7] Illinois, Missouri, North Carolina, Tennessee, and Virginia have enacted legislation either prohibiting the jailing of minors or restricting the number of admissions.[8]

DETENTION CENTERS

Established at the end of the nineteenth century as an alternative to jail for juveniles, **detention centers**, also called *juvenile halls*, are intended to be temporary holding centers. The court administers the majority of juvenile detention centers, although state agencies, city or county governments, welfare departments, and juvenile courts also manage these facilities. The state governments of Connecticut, Delaware, Vermont, and Puerto Rico assume responsibility for

A detention center is often the first stop for youths who have committed serious offenses or are in need of protection. (Photo by Kathryn Miller.)

administering juvenile detention centers. Georgia, Maryland, Massachusetts, New Hampshire, and Rhode Island operate regional detention facilities.

The traditional detention center has sparked many horror stories, and on more than one occasion, former residents have described to the authors the toxic environment of these facilities. Fortunately, detention in the United States has experienced marked improvement in the past two decades. A nationwide movement to develop standards for detention and more innovative detention programs have provided the impetus to improve detention practices in the United States.

Attention homes were initiated in Boulder, Colorado, and have spread to other jurisdictions. Their stated purpose is to give juveniles *attention* rather than *detention*. These facilities have no fences, locked doors, or other physical restraints. They also provide more extensive programming and involvement between residents and staff. Home detention, as previously discussed, is a nonresidential approach to confinement. It was first used in St. Louis, Newport News, Norfolk, and Washington, DC, and is now being used throughout the nation.

In spite of the overall improvement, detention practices still exhibit many disturbing features in the United States. The most serious concerns are that over half offer no treatment program and that increasing numbers of detention centers have turned to mechanical restraints and isolation to control their populations.[9]

SHELTER CARE FACILITIES

Shelter care facilities were developed in the early 1970s to provide short-term care for status offenders and for dependent or neglected children. Although only 23 public shelters existed in 1975, they quickly increased in number because of the funding mandate of the JJDPA, which requires that noncriminal youths be placed in such facilities. In 1991, there were 309 private and 439 public shelters in operation.[10]

The length of stay in these nonsecure facilities with no locked doors varies from overnight to a few days. Occasionally, a juvenile must stay several weeks because of difficulty in scheduling court-required family therapy sessions or because of hearing delays in the juvenile court. Delinquent youths may be placed in shelter care facilities if the county has no detention center and the juvenile judge is reluctant to detain the youth in the county jail or if a judge decides to reward a delinquent youth's positive behavior in detention by transferring him or her to the more open shelter care.

Shelter care facilities do permit residents to enjoy home visits on weekends and field trips into the community during the week. However, as an associate director of a midwestern shelter care facility clearly states, these facilities do not offer treatment programs:

> There is no other place that will take all the kids we do. We're not here to punish kids; nor are we here to treat them. We're like a bus stop. You get into serious problems when you try to offer treatment programs. Referral sources, such as social workers and probation officers, want to have a place that is safe for children, and they want them here when they're ready to go to whatever placement they're going.[11]

The openness of these settings, not surprisingly, creates problems with runaways and makes it difficult to control contraband drugs among residents. Another problem for staff is that these facilities have their share of disciplinary problems among residents, who often have difficulty controlling their attitudes and actions.

WHAT ARE THE LONG-TERM CONFINEMENTS OF JUVENILES?

Boot camps, reception and diagnostic centers, ranches and forestry camps, and training schools are the main forms of long-term juvenile correctional institutions. Juveniles also may be transferred to mental health placements or sentenced to youthful offender facilities and adult prisons.

BOOT CAMPS

Boot camps received increased attention in juvenile justice in the late 1980s and 1990s. Emphasizing military discipline, physical training, and regimented activity for periods that typically range from 30 to 120 days, the intent of these programs is to shock youthful offenders to prevent them from committing further crimes. Boot camp programs generally are designed for offenders who have failed with lesser sanctions such as probation. The Orleans Parish program, established in 1985, was the first boot camp for juveniles in the country. This program accepts anyone who is sentenced by the juvenile judge, but most programs generally exclude sex offenders, armed robbers, and violent offenders.[12]

The rationale for juvenile boot camps is consistent with the juvenile justice system's historical emphasis on rehabilitation, usually incorporating explicit assumptions about the needs of delinquent youths and providing remedial, counseling, and aftercare programs necessary to address these needs.[13] All the programs employ military customs and courtesies, including uniformed drill instructors, a platoon structure, and summary punishment of participants, including group punishment under some circumstances. Although there are differences in emphasis, with Denver creating the most militaristic environment, juvenile boot camp programs have generally discovered that they must tailor their environment to participants' maturity levels.[14]

Boot camps for juveniles are generally reserved for midrange offenders; those who have failed with lesser sanctions such as probation but who are not yet hardened delinquents. The shock aspect of the boot camp experience includes incarceration as the environment within which the program takes place.[15] These programs typically focus on youths in the mid- to late teens and exclude sex offenders, armed robbers, and violent offenders. Only a few programs limit themselves to youths who are nonviolent, have committed their first serious offense, or are being confined for the first time.[16]

Three programs—located in Cleveland, Denver, and Mobile—were funded through the OJJDP, which launched a three-site study of boot camps for youthful offenders in 1991. The program guidelines of these three experimental programs identified six key components to maximize their effectiveness: education and job training and placement, community service, substance abuse counseling and treatment, health and mental health care, individualized and continuous case management, and intensive aftercare services. The 1994 evaluation of the three sites found that the sites were unable to implement the program guidelines fully. Each program "experienced considerable instability and staff turnover" and was unable to "implement and sustain stable, well-developed aftercare services."[17]

Boot camps for juveniles included some type of work detail; most allocate more than half the day to educational and counseling activities, and most include some form of drug and alcohol counseling. In addition, most of the boot camp programs assign graduates to a period of intensive community supervision.[18]

A fair assessment may be that the quality of boot camps depends largely on how much they tailor their programs to participants' maturity levels and how effective they are in implementing and sustaining effective aftercare services. Doris McKenzie and colleagues completed a study of twenty-six juvenile boot camps, comparing them with traditional facilities (the experiences of 2,668 juveniles in twenty-six boot camps were compared to 1,848 juveniles in twenty-two traditional facilities).[19] They found that overall, juveniles in boot camps perceived their environments as more positive or therapeutic, less hostile or dangerous, and more structured than juveniles in traditional facilities perceived their environments. Moreover, this study revealed that, over time, youths in boot camps became less antisocial and less depressed than did youths in traditional facilities.[20]

Other follow-ups on juvenile boot camps have almost all found recidivism rates of boot camps to be slightly higher or about the same as those of traditional juvenile facilities.[21] Charges of abuse in boot camps have taken place in almost all states with boot camps. In the summer of 1999, a fourteen-year-old girl in South Dakota died from dehydration during a long-distance run.[22] In July 1, 2001, Anthony Haynes, a fourteen-year-old boy from Arizona, died at a boot camp, where troubled juveniles were allegedly kicked and forced to eat mud. In this camp, the regimen includes forced marches, in-your-face discipline, and a daily diet of an apple, a carrot, and a bowl of beans.[23]

The combined disappointing recidivism results, as well as the charges of abuse, have prompted Georgia, Maryland, Arizona, Florida, and South Dakota to shut down or reevaluate the get tough with juveniles approach popularized in the early 1990s. Arizona removed fifty juveniles from the boot camp in which Haynes died. Maryland shut down one boot camp and suspended the military regimens at its other two facilities after reports of systematic assaults. In Maryland, the charges of abuse led to the ouster of the state's top five juvenile justice officials.[24] In March 2006, Florida closed all of its boot camps after charges of abuse and the beating death of a juvenile by boot camp staff.

Panaceas die hard in juvenile corrections, and this highly acclaimed approach of the past two decades will continue to be used across the nation. Its recent criticisms and disappointing recidivism data probably will result in fewer new programs being established and more scrutiny of the existing programs.

Critical Thinking Questions:
On the basis of everything you have read and heard about boot camps, would you continue their use? Why or why not?

RECEPTION AND DIAGNOSTIC CENTERS

The purpose of **reception and diagnostic centers**—which are both publicly and privately administered—is to determine which treatment plan suits each adjudicated juvenile and which training school is the best placement.

A few of the larger states have reception and diagnostic centers, but for most states, this diagnostic process takes place in one of the training schools. Although staff are more concerned about short-term diagnosis than long-term treatment, youths frequently receive more attention during this period than at any other time during their confinement. A psychiatrist usually will evaluate the youth and will see him or her several times if the youth is confined for a violent crime. A clinical psychologist, or a person with skills in administering psychological tests, frequently will subject the youth to a battery of tests to determine intelligence, attitudes, maturity, and emotional problems. A social worker, meanwhile, completes a case study of each youth. Equipped with background material from the court, which sometimes takes a week or two to arrive at the reception center, the social worker primarily investigates the youth's family background. Academic staff identify any learning problems and determine the proper school placement. A physical and dental examination also is frequently administered. Finally, cottage or dormitory supervisors evaluate the youth's institutional adjustment and peer relationships. A case conference on each resident is held once all the reports are prepared, the needs and attitudes of the youth are summarized, and recommendations are made as to the best cottage or institutional placement.

Although staff previously have evaluated residents over a period of four to six weeks, this process has been condensed today to an average length of stay of thirty-four days.[25] The youth is then transferred to the approved institutional placement, and the diagnostic report goes with him or her. It is not uncommon for this report to receive little attention, so the youth often must repeat a similar process in the admitting institution.

RANCHES AND WILDERNESS CAMPS

Ranches and wilderness camps are minimum-security institutional placements that are normally reserved for youths who have committed minor offenses or who have been committed to the department of youth services or private corrections for the first time. Of the 157 **ranch/wilderness camps** in the United States in 2002, thirty-nine were publicly owned and sixty-one were privately owned. Of the public facilities, sixteen were run by the states and twenty-three were run by local agencies.[26]

In these camps, residents typically do conservation work in a state park, cutting grass and weeds, cleaning up, and doing general maintenance. Treatment programs generally consist of individual contacts with social workers and the child-care staff, group therapy, and an occasional home visit. Residents may be taken to nearby towns on a regular or weekly basis to make purchases and to attend community events.

In 2002, ranches and camps held about 4 percent of all committed offenders. These facilities generally have minimum security, and only about 20 percent have one or more confinement features other than locked sleeping rooms. They contrast with detention homes and long-term secure facilities, roughly 90 percent of which have one or more confinement features beyond locked sleeping rooms. Unlike the past, when ranches and camps tended to be populated by white youths, today's ranch and camp residents are 76 percent minority offenders; 12 percent of the residents are female. Also, in keeping with today's concerns, it is important to note that 68 percent of secure facilities screen incoming youth on their first day for suicide risk, and another 17 percent screen some youths.[27]

The Hennepin County Home School, one of the most innovative juvenile institutions in the nation, combines features of camps and ranches. Except for a fourteen-bed security unit, it is an open facility, located in a beautiful 160-acre wooded site approximately seventeen miles from downtown Minneapolis. The 164-bed facility is coeducational and holds youths who range in age from thirteen to seventeen, with an average age of fifteen. The school receives no status offenders; instead, the population is made up of those who have committed a variety of property and personal offenses. The typical resident has had at least five prior court involvements, and far more than half the residents have been involved in some type of out-of-home placement before their commitment to the Hennepin County Home School.[28]

The institution is divided into three Juvenile Male Offender cottages, two Juvenile Sex Offender cottages, one cottage for female offenders, and one Beta cottage for short-term restitution offenders. The residents remain in the Beta program for three to eight weeks and in other cottages as long as a year. Each resident of the Juvenile Sex Offender cottages has received an indeterminate sentence, while residents of the other cottages have received a determinate sentence. The institution's sophisticated treatment program uses such modalities as an educational program that focuses on the learning disabled, family therapy, transactional analysis, behavior modification, and reality therapy. Horseback riding and canoeing are favorite recreational activities.[29]

Residents are typically more positive about a placement at a wilderness camp or ranch than about placement in a training school. They like the more relaxed security, the more frequent community contacts, the shorter stays, and the better relations with staff. Yet some youths cannot handle these settings. They may be too homesick or too victimized by peers, so they repeatedly run away until they are transferred to more secure facilities.

✓**Progress Check 10.1**
Review this section at
www.prenhall.com/bartollas

TRAINING SCHOOLS

In 2003, 307 juvenile offenders were in custody for every 100,000 juveniles in the U.S. population. Table 10–1 lists the numbers of juveniles detained and in custody in each state. The total number of youthful offenders in residential placement facilities rose 41 percent from 1991 to 1999 and then declined 10 percent from 1999 to 2003. The result was an overall increase of 27 percent between 1991 and 2003. The number of status offenders in juvenile facilities peaked in 1995, but between 1995 and 2003, the number dropped 36 percent.[30]

The 2006 report *Implementing Reform in California* reveals the average cost of skyrocketing juvenile institutional care and the average length of stay in months. It costs California $115,129 per year to institutionalize a resident, which is greater than the cost in five other states for which data were available (see Figure 10–2). California's 2004's length of stay was 25.9 months, which was nearly three times as long as the average of the nineteen states that participated in a nationwide-survey (see Figure 10–3). It should be noted that California is one of only six states that has an extended age of jurisdiction that goes beyond the age of twenty. California's length of stay for a juvenile offender

Table 10–1   *Juvenile Detention and Commitment Rates by State*

In 2003, the national commitment rate was 2.6 times the detention rate, but rates varied by state

State of offense	Juveniles in custody	Custody rate per 100,000			State of offense	Juveniles in custody	Custody rate per 100,000		
		Total	Detained	Committed			Total	Detained	Committed
U.S. Total	96,665	307	83	219	**Upper age 17 (continued)**				
Upper Age 17					Oklahoma	1,059	265	74	190
Alabama	1,794	351	76	267	Oregon	1,275	323	63	259
Alaska	336	370	158	208	Pennsylvania	4,341	317	67	224
Arizona	1,890	284	124	144	Rhode Island	342	295	5*	284
Arkansas	675	217	30	186	South Dakota	522	564	117	444
California	16,782	392	128	263	Tennessee	1,434	226	38	185
Colorado	1,776	344	99	244	Utah	954	307	56	251
Delaware	333	364	187	177	Vermont	51	72	43	30
District of Columbia	285	625	381	230	Virginia	2,376	289	110	178
Florida	8,208	452	94	352	Washington	1,656	236	63	170
Hawaii	129	97	34	63	West Virginia	498	269	83	185
Idaho	489	287	65	222	Wyoming	357	606	97	509
Indiana	3,045	415	98	313	**Upper age 16**				
Iowa	975	299	63	232	Georgia	2,451	273	84	155
Kansas	1,071	336	78	255	Illinois	2,715	212	56	151
Kentucky	837	185	50	131	Louisiana	1,821	387	136	246
Maine	222	153	33	116	Massachusetts	1,302	216	84	128
Maryland	1,167	181	75	106	Michigan	2,706	257	63	191
Minnesota	1,527	259	47	208	Missouri	1,413	246	59	185
Mississippi	528	152	33	118	New Hampshire	198	150	20	127
Montana	261	245	37	200	South Carolina	1,443	346	110	236
Nebraska	672	331	111	220	Texas	7,662	318	73	243
Nevada	921	362	157	204	Wisconsin	1,524	274	58	216
New Jersey	1,941	199	100	98	**Upper age 15**				
New Mexico	606	258	83	175	Connecticut	627	210	49	161
North Dakota	246	347	25	317	New York	4,308	272	48	223
Ohio	4,176	318	93	224	North Carolina	1,203	169	57	109

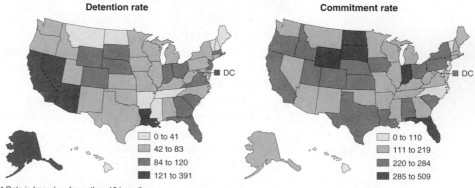

Detention rate   **Commitment rate**

Detention rate legend: 0 to 41 | 42 to 83 | 84 to 120 | 121 to 391

Commitment rate legend: 0 to 110 | 111 to 219 | 220 to 284 | 285 to 509

* Rate is based on fewer than 10 juveniles.

Note: Custody rate is the count of juvenile offenders in custody per 100,000 youth ages 10 through the upper age of juvenile court jurisdiction in each state. U.S. totals include 1,398 youth in private facilities for whom state of offense was not reported and 124 youth in tribal facilities.

Source: Howard N. Snyder and Melissa Sickmund, *Juvenile Offenders and Victims: 2006 National Report* (Washington, DC: National Center for Juvenile Justice and Office of Juvenile Justice and Delinquency Prevention, 2006), p. 198.

goes to twenty-four years old, and this has contributed to the lengthy stay for those sentenced to juvenile facilities in California.[31]

California, Illinois, Michigan, New York, and Ohio have several **training schools** each. Smaller states have one training school for boys and another for girls, and Massachusetts and Vermont have no training schools. Although coeducational institutions gained some acceptance in the 1970s and North Carolina even converted all its training schools into coeducational institutions, that trend seems to have passed.

Organizational Goals and Security Levels

Several organizational goals exist in training schools. David Street, Robert D. Vinter, and Charles Perrow's classic study of several public and private training

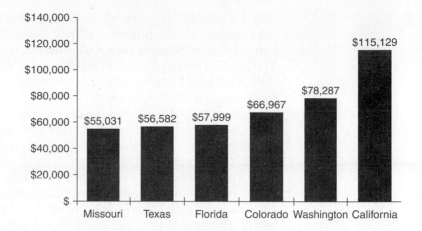

Figure 10–2 *Cost per Youth per Year in Comparison States*

Source: Christopher Murray, Chris Baird, Ned Loughran, Fred Mills, and John Platt, *Safety and Welfare Plan: Implementing Reform in California* (Sacramento: California Department of Corrections and Rehabilitation, Division of Juvenile Justice, 2006), 5.

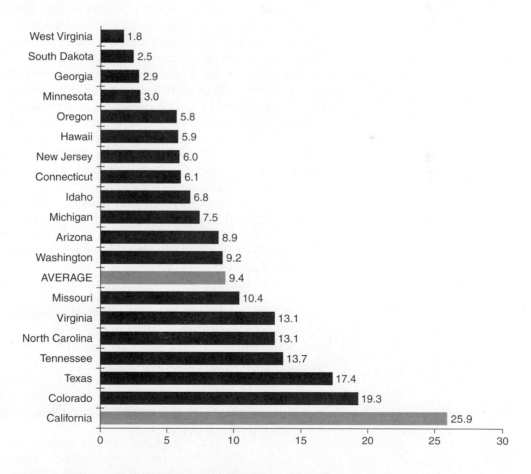

Figure 10–3 *Average Length of Stay in Months 2004—Males*

Source: Christopher Murray, Chris Baird, Ned Loughran, Fred Mills, and John Platt, *Safety and Welfare Plan: Implementing Reform in California* (Sacramento: California Department of Corrections and Rehabilitation, Division of Juvenile Justice, 2006), 2.

schools identified three basic organizational goals: obedience/conformity, reeducation/development, and treatment. They found that staff in obedience/conformity institutions kept residents under surveillance and emphasized rules. They were also punitive with residents and did not become involved with them. Although staff in reeducation/development institutions demanded conformity, hard work, and intellectual growth, they were more willing to give additional rewards for conformity to positive behavior and to develop closer relationships with residents. Staff in treatment-oriented training schools were much more involved with residents as they worked with, helped, and permitted residents to become more emotionally involved with them.[32]

The philosophy of *parens patriae* has encouraged training schools' administrators to claim rehabilitation as their official goal, but the overall objective for most training schools is to provide a safe, secure, and humane environment. The actual goal depends on the security level of the training school. States that have only one training school for boys and one for girls must enforce all security levels in the one facility, but states with several training schools have the option of developing minimum-, medium-, and maximum-security institutions.

Paint Creek Youth Center (PCYC) in southern Ohio is one of the most widely hailed minimum-security institutions in the nation. This privately operated facility has the capacity to hold thirty-three residents but generally has a population of twenty-six or twenty-seven. Juveniles who have committed serious offenses from the southern counties of the state are typically committed to PCYC. The facility features a comprehensive and integrated therapeutic approach emphasizing accountability, social learning, and positive peer culture. The PCYC treatment approach operates on three levels. A youth begins on level one and achieves level two when he or she has been problem-free for a period of time. When staff determine that a youth is ready to return to the community, this youth is granted prerelease status, or level three. Increased responsibilities and privileges are then granted to residents, contingent on positive behavior within the institution. Security is maintained by staff and peers rather than by fences and locked doors. Furthermore, PCYC has successfully implemented a family therapy program along with intensive aftercare services to those residents returning to the community.[33]

Peter W. Greenwood, Susan Turner, and Kathy Rosenblatt evaluated PCYC using a control group of youths who were randomly assigned to either PCYC, Training Institution Central Ohio (TICO), or another Department of Youth Services (DYS) institution. These researchers found that juveniles who had been assigned to PCYC were less likely than those from TICO to be rearrested upon their return to the community and much less likely to be recommitted to a correctional facility on new charges.[34]

The physical design of medium- and maximum-security training schools varies from fortresslike facilities with individual cells to open dormitories with little privacy to the homelike atmosphere of small cottages. Maximum-security training schools usually have one or two fairly high fences and sometimes even a wall. The interiors in maximum-security schools are characterized by bleak hallways, locked doors, and individual cells covered by heavy screens or bars; the youths' daily lives are constrained by rules (see Focus on Practice 10-1).

Medium-security training schools usually are designed as dormitories or cottages. Similar to maximum-security institutions, medium-security training schools usually have the perimeter security of a six- or seven-foot-high fence. The atmosphere in medium-security institutions is more relaxed, and residents can move around more freely than is true in maximum-security training schools.

Security is a primary feature of medium- and maximum-security facilities. (Photo by Kathryn Miller.)

Institutional security is the primary emphasis in medium- and maximum-security training schools. Administrators' jobs typically depend on their success in avoiding running away. The account of a runaway incident from a maximum-security facility, for example, may receive statewide media coverage. If a runaway commits a violent crime, then even more pressure is placed on institutional administrators and their staffs. Fortunately, the federal courts' recent involvement in juvenile institutions has eliminated some of the past abuses that sometimes took place to punish those who attempted to run away and those who actually did but were caught and returned.

Programs

The programs in medium- and maximum-security training schools are much more adequate than those in jails or detention homes and more varied than those in camps and ranches. Most larger training schools have a full-time nurse on duty and a physician who visits one or more days a week. Such services as the removal of tattoos are sometimes available if residents desire them.

Most medium- and maximum-security training schools provide educational programs for residents. These may be accredited by the state for granting high school diplomas, and most offer classes to prepare for a GED test. In addition to the regular academic courses, training schools usually offer basic skills classes consisting of a review of the necessary techniques for reading, writing, and arithmetic; some programs have laboratories and programmed instruction as well. Classes are usually small, and pupils are permitted to progress according to their own rate of learning. The Indiana Boys School is an example of one training school that focuses on the learning disabilities of residents, for Indiana correctional officials believe that learning disabilities are closely linked to delinquent behavior.

FOCUS ON PRACTICE   10–1
RULES OF YOUTH CONDUCT

1. You will not be allowed to fight with peers or staff.
2. You will follow the direct orders of staff.
3. You will treat others with courtesy by avoiding the use of profanity, disrespectful language, or physical gestures.
4. You will avoid sexually inappropriate language or gestures towards staff and other youth.
5. You will avoid horseplay, rowdy-rough play, body punching, shadow boxing, verbal taunting, running, [and] wrestling, which could lead to more serious behavior.
6. You will avoid destroying, defacing, or altering state property or the property of others.
7. You will avoid the use of and/or passing of any form of tobacco, alcohol, and drugs.
8. You will avoid the use of and/or possession of contraband.
9. You will avoid leaving trash on tables, chairs, or floors by placing it in proper receptacles.
10. You will maintain personal grooming, hygiene, and clothing at all times throughout the institution. Appropriate dress includes shirttails in pants, pants zipped and uncuffed (not pegged), belt fastened, shoes tied, and socks on.
11. You will refrain from borrowing, lending, buying, trading, betting, selling, and gambling with peers, staff, or visitors.
12. You will play radios only in acceptable areas and at acceptable times.
13. You will not enter any office or restricted areas without staff permission.
14. You will avoid interfering with staff members' duties.
15. You will report any injury or any change in a medical condition to a staff member immediately.
16. You will not steal.
17. You will adhere to all movement instructions.
18. You will not spit.
19. You will not use any phone without staff supervision.
20. You will not use the restroom without permission.

Source: The Ohio Department of Youth Services, Training Institution, Central Ohio, 1990.

Critical Thinking Questions:
Do you believe all these rules are necessary? What rules would you substitute? How would you feel if restricted by these rules?

Well-equipped male training schools offer vocational training in automobile repair, printing, welding, carpentry, woodworking, barbering, machine shop skills, drafting, and food service. Training schools for girls generally are more limited, as they offer training programs in sewing, food service, secretarial skills, and beauty care.

As a rule, this vocational training does not help residents secure jobs after release for several reasons: They have difficulty gaining admission to the necessary labor unions; they lack the necessary credentials, such as a high school education; or they simply choose not to pursue the skills they learned. Yet some residents leave the institution and acquire excellent jobs with their acquired skills.

Recreation has always been popular in training schools. Some staff emphasize it because they believe that a tired youth is a well-behaved one, or, in the words of one recreation leader, "If we wear them out during the day, they won't fool around at night." Other staff advocate a heavy dosage of recreation because they believe that teaching residents a competitive sport builds self-respect and self-confidence. Still other staff know that juveniles like to play, and recreation is simply a good way for them to entertain themselves and to work off excessive energy. Male residents can compete in softball, volleyball, flag football, basketball, and sometimes even boxing. Cottages usually compete against one another, and the institution may even have a team that competes with other institutions or with teams in the surrounding community. Nonathletic recreational activities include movies, building model cars, painting, decorating the cottages (especially at Christmas), and playing ping-pong, pool, checkers, and chess. Female residents also have recreational possibilities such as softball, volleyball, and basketball. In addition to the nonathletic recreational activities that the boys have, girls perform in talent shows or dramatic productions, and occasionally, they have dances with boys from nearby training schools.

Religious instruction and services are always provided in state training schools. Larger training schools usually have a full-time Protestant chaplain and a part- or full-time Roman Catholic chaplain. Smaller training schools contract services of clergy from a nearby community. Religious services generally include attending Sunday mass and morning worship, confession, baptism, instruction for church membership, choir, and the participation of community groups. Yet, few residents have much interest in organized religion, and they are usually quite resistant to compulsory attendance at these religious services.

The most widely used treatment modalities are transactional analysis, reality therapy, psychotherapy, behavior modification, guided group interaction, positive peer culture, and drug and alcohol treatment. The errors-in-thinking modality, models to deactivate gangs, and law enforcement education are new forms of treatment recently implemented in a number of private and public training schools across the nation (see Chapter 11 for an examination of these modalities).

Volunteers are an important adjunct to institutional programs, and an institution that has an active volunteer program can greatly enrich the stay of its residents. Some states have better developed volunteer programs than others and have volunteer coordinators in their major institutions. Confined offenders frequently are receptive to services rendered by unpaid volunteers who do not represent authority figures, but who can present the needs of youth and become their advocates in the community. Among the many services that volunteers provide for institutionalized youths are the following:

1. Education—tutoring and supplying books
2. Entertainment—arranging choral programs and other means of entertainment provided by community groups
3. Chaperones—escorting selected youths to community events
4. Counseling—providing one-to-one contact with offenders
5. Family service—contacting and reassuring parents on the progress of their children
6. Financial aid—providing money for youths' canteen accounts

7. Gifts—supplying Christmas and birthday remembrances
8. Job-finding—assisting youths in locating community jobs while they wait to be released or in securing permanent jobs after release
9. Letter writing—helping youths to correspond with family and friends
10. Recreation—playing basketball, softball, and other sports with residents

Finally, prerelease programs are a desired component of institutional activities. These programs typically occur more in minimum- than in medium- or maximum-security facilities. In some training schools, residents are transferred to another cottage or to another location to begin a formal program of community reintegration, including exposure to experiences designed to prepare them for a full return to the community. Techniques of interviewing for a job, instruction in reading the help-wanted section of a newspaper, and assistance in money management are important elements of these programs.

Home furloughs, afternoon trips off campus, and permission to work in the community are typical of the privileges given to residents of prerelease cottages or to those who are just a step or two away from release. Home furloughs are probably the most widely used. Some staff believe that reintegrating youths gradually to the community after a long absence of perhaps several years will help ease the shock of release. Home visits also provide opportunities for residents to interview for jobs and visit with family members. Trips off campus for several hours with parents are sometimes permitted by some training schools. This enables parents and children to spend time together away from the institution and possibly to shop for clothing or to eat in a restaurant. Community jobs generally are reserved for those youths who are only two or three months from release and who need financial resources before they return to community living. Staff members are very careful in choosing the residents who are permitted to work in the community. Prerelease programs usually have a positive impact on residents, but home visits, especially, result in a high percentage of runaways.

Social Control of Institutional Residents

Until the last ten years or so, most training schools still employed cottage parents. These individuals often were a retired couple who were attracted to this work because of their interest in young people. Cottage parents sometimes provided a strong parental model for the youth placed in their care. The cottage parents system was continued so long simply because institutional administrators felt that cottage parents created more of a homelike atmosphere for confined delinquents than did staff members who worked eight-hour shifts and lived in the nearby community. But the appearance of increasingly difficult-to-handle delinquents and efforts to develop more efficient institutional management techniques resulted in the replacement of cottage parents with those staff members commonly called *youth supervisors*, *youth leaders*, *cottage supervisors*, *group supervisors*, or *group-care workers*. The emerging nature of this role has left a number of questions unanswered: How much of a homelike atmosphere should these supervisors establish in the cottages? How involved should they become with residents? Are they to be only custodial agents, or do they also have treatment responsibilities? What are they to do if residents refuse to cooperate? What personal fulfillment can they expect to achieve in their jobs? Although encumbered by these and other questions, the role of youth supervisor is slowly being established in juvenile correctional settings in this country.

The youth supervisors wake residents in the morning, see to it that their charges wash and dress for breakfast, supervise the serving of breakfast in the cottage or escort residents to a central dining facility, and conduct a brief room inspection. They also ensure that those youths enrolled in the academic and vocational programs go to school and that those who work on the grounds, in the kitchen, or in the community go to their jobs. In medium- and maximum-security training schools, residents are usually escorted to their particular assignments, but on many honor farms, and in conservation camps and ranches, they are permitted movement without staff supervision.[35]

Cottage parents typically remained in the cottage to prepare lunch and to take care of other cottage tasks, but youth supervisors are generally assigned duties that keep them occupied until they pick up their residents for lunch. These duties may include school patrol, inspection of the rooms of residents on restriction, and outside patrol of the recreation field.

Residents are met at the academic area and escorted back to the cottage for lunch, after which they are returned to school or to other assigned duties. The afternoon shift of supervisors picks up the youths in school and brings them back at the end of the day. If the institution has an active group program and youth supervisors are involved, they usually hold several group meetings a week after school. Guided group interaction, positive peer culture, and transactional analysis are the most popular group modalities used in these sessions. Time generally is structured after school because many administrators believe that problems arise when youths have a great deal of free time, but in some institutions the period from the end of school until the evening meal is a free one.

After the evening meal, especially during warmer weather, residents are permitted to engage in outside recreational activities. They may participate in organized activities or may choose to throw a football, shoot a basketball, pitch a softball, or talk with a friend. Staff must at this time be particularly alert, because runaways often take place during these outside activities. Following a shower and a little television, residents are usually sent to their rooms and lights are out around 10 P.M.

The night shift, normally consisting of one person, takes over at 11 or 11:30 P.M. This person's job basically is to make certain that youths do not escape from the cottage during the nights and to be available if a problem such as an illness or escape attempt occurs. The youth supervisor generally spends the greater part of the eight-hour shift sitting at a desk in the staff office and responding to a periodic phone check on cottage security.

As part of their daily tasks, youth supervisors also intervene in conflicts among residents, respond to emergency situations, search residents and residents' living quarters, orient new residents, advise residents concerning personal or institutional progress, and assign tasks to residents and monitor their performance. For an effective youth supervisor, see Focus on Careers 10-2.

Differences Between Public and Private Training Schools

Six in ten juvenile facilities holding offenders in 2003 were private, but public facilities held more than six in ten juvenile offenders. Compared with public facilities, private facilities hold a smaller share of delinquents and a larger share of status offenders.[36] Table 10-2 compares the various types of juvenile custody facilities and shows how the numbers and profiles of these facilities have changed. Public facilities hold more than three-quarters of those confined for homicide, robbery, aggravated assault, weapons possession, and technical violations of probation or aftercare. Nevertheless, as noted in the

FOCUS ON CAREERS

JIM ROBERTS: PROFILE OF AN EFFECTIVE YOUTH SUPERVISOR

10–2

One of the authors of this book had the privilege of working with an individual who was a youth supervisor par excellence. Jim, a soft-spoken, middle-aged African American, possessed a high school education and had no formal training in working with delinquent youth. However, it did not take long to recognize that this man was ideally suited for working with juveniles.

Jim was perceptive. He knew his "boys" and could always identify their needs and concerns. A keen listener and observer, he was able to see when a youth was hurting and knew what to do about it. It did not take a new resident long to learn that Mr. Roberts cared deeply about his charges and therefore they would flock around his office, waiting to talk with him.

Jim was trusting. He believed in adolescents. He was always willing to help residents and never seemed to burn out. When the cottage social worker objected to sending a youth on a home visit because the social worker considered him to be a poor risk, Jim quietly responded, "You've got to take a chance on kids. If we don't believe in them, how can we expect them to believe in themselves?" Of course, he had some failures, but he also had many successes.

Jim was an excellent role model. He was street-wise and could not be manipulated. He was fair, consistent, and nonprejudiced; he was mature and healthy himself and did not take his problems out on the residents. Although he was strong physically, he never struck his residents or raised his voice at them. Significantly, he had as much control over residents as any other youth supervisor in the institution.

Few residents ever left his cottage without a profound admiration for Jim Roberts. Some referred to him as "father"; others looked upon him as a big brother or a wise uncle. Youths developed such strong emotional ties with him that they did not want to let him down. They continued to write and call after they were released; many traveled across the state to visit this man who had had such a significant impact upon their lives.

Jim was a splendid teacher to all who came in contact with him. He knew what to say when a youth failed or received sad news from home. When a youth had given up and saw no more reason to go on living, Jim Roberts was usually the one person who could touch him and give him a renewed lease on life. He had a quiet but effective way of driving a painful point home to another staff member who had engaged in inappropriate behavior. He was also skillful in persuading cottage staff to reinforce youths at their three-month cottage review. Finally, he helped social worker after social worker to translate book knowledge and theory into practice.

Source: Clemens Bartollas, Stuart J. Miller, and Paul B. Wice, *Participants in American Criminal Justice: The Promise and the Performance* (Upper Saddle River, NJ: Prentice Hall, 1983), pp. 292–293.

Critical Thinking Questions:

Do you believe there are many like Jim Roberts working as staff members in juvenile institutions? What do you think might have motivated this remarkable youth supervisor?

2006 Juvenile Offenders in Correctional Facilities, "public and private facilities had fairly similar offense profiles in 2003."[37]

David Shichor and Clemens Bartollas's examination of the patterns of public and private juvenile placements in one of the larger probation departments in southern California, however, revealed that few offense differences existed between juveniles sent to public and private facilities. Although juveniles

Table 10–2 *Juveniles in Private and Public Facilities by Year, Number, and Percent*

Six in 10 juvenile facilities holding offenders were private; public
facilities held more than 6 in 10 juvenile offenders

Residential placement facilities

Type of facility	Number				Percent	
	1997	*1999*	*2001*	*2003*	*1997*	*2003*
All	2,842	2,838	2,980	2,861	100%	100%
Public	1,106	1,134	1,197	1,170	39	41
State	508	533	533	501	18	18
Local	598	601	664	669	21	23
Private	1,736	1,795	1,774	1,682	61	59
Tribal		9	9	9	0	0

Juvenile offenders in residential placement

Population held	Number				Percent	
	1997	*1999*	*2001*	*2003*	*1997*	*2003*
All facilities						
All residents	116,701	120,996	118,008	109,225	100%	100%
Juvenile offenders	105,055	107,856	104,413	96,655	90	88
Other residents	11,646	18,140	13,595	12,570	10	12
Public facilities						
All residents	77,798	78,519	75,461	67,917	67	62
Juvenile offenders	75,600	76,379	73,328	66,210	65	61
Other residents	9,354	11,082	11,509	10,862	8	10
State facilities						
All residents	48,185	49,011	45,224	38,470	41	35
Juvenile offenders	46,516	47,504	43,669	37,335	40	34
Other residents	2,586	2,293	2,376	1,855	2	2
Local facilities						
All residents	29,613	29,508	30,237	29,447	25	27
Juvenile offenders	29,084	28,875	29,659	28,875	25	26
Other residents	9,354	10,908	11,315	10,738	8	10
Private facilities						
All residents	38,903	42,298	42,353	41,177	33	38
Juvenile offenders	29,455	31,303	30,891	30,321	25	28
Other residents	1,669	1,507	1,555	1,135	1	1
Tribal facilities		179	194	131	0	0
Juvenile offenders		174	194	124	0	0
Other residents		5	0	7	0	0

Note: Other residents include youth age 21 or older and those held in the facility but not charged
with or adjudicated for an offense. Detail may not total 100% because of rounding.

Source: Howard N. Snyder and Melissa Sickmund, *Juvenile Offenders and Victims: 2006 National Report*
(Washington, DC: National Center for Juvenile Justice and Office of Juvenile Justice and
Delinquency Prevention, 2006), p. 197.

Juveniles in all facilities have recreational opportunities. (Photo published with permission of the Ohio Youth Commission.)

placed in private facilities had more personal problems and those in public institutions were somewhat more delinquent, placements in private facilities included delinquents with serious offenses.[38]

Second, privately administered training schools are probably better known to the public than are state facilities because of their public solicitation of funds. Boys' Town in Nebraska and Glen Mills School in Pennsylvania (near Philadelphia) are two private institutions that are well known to the public.[39] Private training schools also have avoided most of the scathing critiques faced by public training schools during the past two decades.

Third, proponents of private training schools claim that they are more effective than public training schools because they have a limited intake policy that allows them to choose whom they want to admit, they have more professional staff, they have better staff-client ratios, they are smaller, and they are more flexible and innovative.

Gaylene Style Armstrong and Doris Layton MacKenzie examined forty-eight residential juvenile correctional facilities in nineteen states (sixteen private and thirty-two public facilities). Using both self-report surveys and data from facility records, they found that private facilities had a more extensive admission process, had a higher percentage of juvenile delinquents incarcerated for property offenses, were smaller, and held a higher percentage of males than female offenders. Yet they found that there were no significant differences between private and public juvenile facilities in terms of the quality of their environments.[40]

The advantage of private over public rehabilitation programs may have been more true in the past than in the present. The increased use of interstate commerce of children has resulted in some private schools taking as many children as they can get. Indeed, some private institutions exploit the inadequate licensing procedures of the states to warehouse youths as cheaply as possible and thereby reap good profits.[41] It is also true that private training schools are smaller than public ones, but even so, one-half of private institutions hold 100 or more children; these are still too large to effectively rehabilitate juveniles.

The greater flexibility of programs is probably accurate because private institutions are relatively free from political processes and bureaucratic inertia. Yet Bartollas and Shichor's comparison of the attitudes of staff and residents at a state training school for adolescent males in the Midwest and at a private facility in the same state found that the enforcement of excessive rules in the private placement created a rigid cottage structure and living environment.[42] Moreover, Shichor and Bartollas found that private placements in southern California do not always provide the services of professional treatment personnel that they purport to provide.[43] Perhaps the old adage is true after all: The best institutions are private ones and the worst institutions are also private ones.

WHAT ARE THE TROUBLING ASPECTS OF JUVENILE INSTITUTIONALIZATION?

Institutionalization is a painful process for most youthful offenders, though it is clearly more painful for some than for others. The residential social system and juvenile victimization are two of the most troubling aspects of juvenile institutionalization. Together, they call into question the quality of long-term institutional care that this nation provides for juveniles in trouble.

RESIDENTIAL SOCIAL SYSTEM

The social structure of the training school has a variety of social networks: (1) subgroups of residents based on race, age, criminal conduct, locale, or gang affiliation; (2) informal primary groupings of friends; (3) networks of instrumental relationships revolving around the production or supply of illicit goods and services; (4) social hierarchies in the living unit with expected role behavior of residents who occupy these social positions; and (5) official positions allocated by staff, such as honor unit members.[44] The more custodially oriented or coercive the training school, the more likely it is that a power-oriented social hierarchy will dominate the other social relationships.

Social Roles in Training Schools for Boys

The **social roles** in most training schools for boys are divided into aggressive, manipulative, and passive groups.[45] Youths who pursue aggressive roles are usually cottage leaders, their lieutenants, and sexual exploiters. The cottage leader is given argot names such as "wheel," "bruiser," "heavy," "El Presidente," and "duke." The leader controls physical attack, exploitation, agitation, and patronage. This leader's lieutenants may be called "vice-president," "tough," "tough boy," "all right guy," "hard rock," "thug," "bad dude," "redneck," and "wise guy." Sexual exploiters are often referred to as "daddy" and "booty bandits."

Youths who adopt manipulative roles generally do whatever is necessary to make their institutional stay easier. Residents who do whatever staff want them to do simply to reduce the length of confinement are called "slick," "cool," "con man," and "con artist." The "peddler" or "merchant" is the role occupant who trades stolen, illegal, or exploited goods from one resident to another.

Passive roles are adopted by youths who for one reason or another are uninvolved in the social structure of the cottage. Residents who are prostaff and are not embroiled in the delinquent subculture are called "straight," "straight kid," "quiet type," and "bushboy." Occupants receiving deprecation from peers are called "mess-up," "pain freak," "weak-minded," "stone-out," and "lame." Sexual victims, the social pariahs of the peer culture, are given such names as "scapegoats," "punk," "sweet boy," "girl," and "tag."

Family Social Structure

The social roles in training schools for girls are generally based on a family or **kinship social structure.** Rose Giallombardo's examination of three training schools for girls in various parts of the United States found that aggressive girls tended to adopt the male sexual roles ("butches") and put pressure on new residents to adopt the female sexual roles ("fems"). Giallombardo identified the following social types in one institution for females: "true fems," "trust-to-be-butches," "trust-to-be-fems," "jive time butches," "jive time fems," "straights," "squealers," "pimps," "foxes," "popcorns," and "cops."[46] Christopher M. Sieverdes and Bartollas's study of six southeastern coeducational training schools also revealed the presence of the family social structure in the girls' cottages. This study further divided the seven social roles found in these living units into aggressive, manipulative, and passive roles: "bruiser" and "bitch" (aggressive roles), "lady" and "bulldagger" (manipulative roles), and "child," "girlfriend," and "asskisser" (passive roles).[47] Alice Propper examined three coeducational and four girls' training schools scattered through the East, Midwest, and South, five of which were public and two of which were private Catholic facilities. In contrast to previously held assumptions, she found little overlap between pseudo-family roles and homosexual behavior; participation in homosexuality and make-believe families was just as prevalent in coeducational as in single-sex institutions, and homosexuality was as prevalent in treatment- as in custody-oriented facilities.[48]

JUVENILE VICTIMIZATION

Those who lack the credentials to impress peers are often forced into lowly social positions. Although they are aware that they must avoid **victimization,** these youths may not be able to protect themselves against predatory peers. Staff generally offer little help and may even inform potential victims, "If you are a man, you'll protect yourself." In institutions for older males, there may be a respected resident who is willing to protect weaker peers, but the price of protection is often steep—the protégé must become his "boy" or "sweet boy." A sexual victim finds himself on the last rung of the social hierarchy, engulfed in a social role from which escape is very difficult.

The degradation of victim status presents nearly overwhelming stress to a youth. In a revealing incident, a resident was making fun of a scapegoat one day when the scapegoat, much to the surprise of everyone, attacked the supposedly more aggressive youth. In the fight that ensued, the scapegoat clearly got the better of the other youth. Staff locked both youths in their rooms until a disciplinary meeting could be held. The youth who had had a higher position in the cottage until the fight tried to commit suicide by setting his room on fire; he clearly preferred to die rather than take on the role of the scapegoat. This youth did become the cottage scapegoat and later confessed to a staff member that he was committing oral sodomy on half of the twenty-four youths in the cottage.[49]

Bartollas and colleagues' examination of an end-of-the-line training school in Ohio concluded that 90 percent of the 150 residents were involved in an exploitation matrix and that they created an extremely brutal system. If anything, the environment of this institution was less fair, less just, less humane, and less decent than the worst aspects of the social worlds from which residents came. Brute force, manipulation, and institutional sophistication carried the day and set the standards that ultimately prevailed. In this process, many of the most dangerous and toughest delinquents in the outside community became the meek, doubly and triply stigmatized victims within the institution.[50]

Miller, Bartollas, and Simon Dinitz have reexamined the degree of victimization in this maximum-security training school. In this follow-up of the 1976 study, their preliminary findings include the following:

1. The youth culture described in the 1976 study still thrives, and the strong still victimize the weak, but mostly for food, clothing, and toiletries rather than sex.
2. Consensual sexual behavior appears to be more widespread than in the earlier study.
3. Instead of the violent population found in the 1976 study, most of the training school's present residents are relatively minor drug dealers, addicts, and users but do include a few extremely violent and dangerous youths.
4. Gang members from the community are confined, but, unlike in some training schools, gang organization is not present, nor is it providing an intimidating factor in institutional life.
5. Treatment has all but disappeared from this training school. The only treatment still existing is a drug abuse program. A social worker summed this up when he said, "We don't do anything in here for kids." A cottage staff member added, "This place is a warehouse for children."
6. Staff members are more disillusioned than they were at the time of the first study. They also are more fearful of victimization from residents.[51]

DO INSTITUTIONALIZED YOUTHS HAVE RIGHTS?

The rights of juveniles is a major issue in juvenile justice. The Children's Rights Movement, as well as proponents of due process rights of children within the juvenile justice system, challenge whether institutionalized youths have sufficient legal protection. They argue that confined juveniles ought to receive three basic rights: the right to treatment, the right not to be treated, and the right to be free from cruel and unusual punishment. The rights of confined offenders have been examined by the federal courts and the Civil Rights of Institutionalized Persons Act (CRIPA).

RIGHT TO TREATMENT

Several court rulings have found that a juvenile committed to a training school has a right to treatment. In the *White v. Reid* (1954) case, the court ruled that juveniles could not be held in institutions that did not provide for their rehabilitation.[52] The *Inmates of the Boys' Training School v. Affleck* (1972) decision also stated that juveniles have a right to treatment because rehabilitation is the true purpose of the juvenile court.[53] In *Nelson v. Heyne* (1973), Indiana's Seventh Circuit agreed with the district court that inmates of the Indiana Boys' School have a right to rehabilitative treatment.[54]

Moreover, in the 1973 *Morales v. Turman* decision, the U.S. District Court for the Eastern District of Texas held that a number of criteria had to be followed by the state of Texas in order to ensure that proper treatment would be provided to confined juveniles. These criteria included minimum standards for assessing and testing children committed to the state; minimum standards for assessing educational skills and handicaps and for providing programs aimed at advancing a child's education; minimum standards for delivering vocational education and medical and psychiatric care; and minimum standards for providing a humane institutional environment.[55] This finding was overruled by the Fifth Circuit Appeals Court on the grounds that a three-judge court should have been convened to hear the case. On *certiorari* to the U.S. Supreme Court, that Court reversed the Court of Appeals and remanded the case. What may affect future considerations of confined juveniles' right to treatment is whether the order of the District Court can withstand the assault against it.

RIGHT NOT TO BE TREATED

Advocates argue that treatment should be voluntary; should not be related to the length of institutional confinement; and should not degrade, dehumanize, punish, or humiliate residents. The standards of the Institute of Judicial Administration of the American Bar Association (IJA-ABA), for example, propose that children may voluntarily refuse services except in three cases: "services juveniles are legally obliged to accept (as school attendance), services required to prevent clear harm to physical health, and services mandated by the court as a condition to a nonresidential disposition."[56]

RIGHT TO BE FREE FROM CRUEL AND UNUSUAL PUNISHMENT

Some courts have applied the Eighth Amendment, barring cruel and unusual punishment, to juvenile institutions to forbid the use of corporal punishment in any form, the use of Thorazine and other medications for the purpose of control, and the use of extended periods of solitary confinement.[57] The *Pena v. New York State Division for Youth* decision held that the use of isolation, hand restraints, and tranquilizing drugs at Goshen Annex Center was punitive and antitherapeutic and, therefore, violated the Eighth Amendment.[58] In the case of *Inmates of the Boys' Training School v. Affleck,* the court also condemned such practices as solitary confinement and strip cells, and it established minimum standards for youths confined at the training school.[59] In the *Morales v. Turman* decision in Texas, the court found instances of physical brutality and abuse, including staff-administered beatings and tear gassings, homosexual assaults, excessive use of solitary confinement, and the lack of clinical services.[60] In *Morgan v. Sproat,* a Mississippi case, the court found that youths were confined in padded cells with no windows or furnishings and only flush holes for toilets and were denied access to all programs or services except a Bible.[61] Finally, in *State v. Werner,* the court found that residents were locked in solitary confinement; were beaten, kicked, slapped, and sprayed with mace by staff; were required to scrub floors with a toothbrush; and were forced to stand or sit for prolonged periods without changing position.[62] In each of these cases, the courts condemned these cruel practices.

CRIPA AND JUVENILE CORRECTIONAL FACILITIES

As of November, 1997 the Civil Rights Division had investigated three hundred institutions under CRIPA. Of these, seventy-three institutions, or about 25 percent, were juvenile detention and correctional facilities. The Civil Rights Division is monitoring conditions in thirty-four juvenile correctional facilities through consent decrees in Kentucky, New Jersey, and Puerto Rico. The consent decree filed in Kentucky covers all thirteen juvenile facilities in the state; the decree in New Jersey is for one facility, and in Puerto Rico for twenty facilities.[63]

HOW DOES JUVENILE AFTERCARE OPERATE?

The purpose of aftercare or entry services is to help ensure juveniles' successful transition from residential placement to life in the community. Too frequently, juveniles are simply released from residential care and returned, with little or no preparation, monitoring, or services. Aftercare approaches vary across the nation, but any well-designed aftercare strategy will impose concrete expectations for returning juveniles, with a reliable means of ascertaining compliance and well-developed incentives and sanctions for noncompliance. It will provide some level of intensive surveillance and enhanced services to those at serious risk of failure or recidivism and will use formal risk-eligibility assessment to target those interventions carefully.[64]

Juveniles released from training school are placed on aftercare or parole status. The bases on which they are released from these schools vary, and so do the individuals responsible for making the release decision. In some states, such as Illinois, juvenile judges have the authority to remove juveniles from training schools, but in the majority of states the decision is made by probation or aftercare officers.

States that use determinate or mandatory sentencing for juveniles usually have determined the time of institutional release when the youth is committed to training school. A variation of this approach is for the length of confinement to be determined within the department responsible for institutional care, using such guidelines as offense severity, previous offense history, and perhaps other criteria. For example, the Ohio Department of Youth Services established an Office of Release Review in order to provide a structured, centralized, objective release decision-making process. The goal of this office has been to set a length of institutional stay for each juvenile felony offender proportionate to the severity of his or her offenses and the impact on the victims. A parole hearing officer scores each youth using a specialized worksheet. In most cases, the score establishes the length of stay unless overriding conditions are present, as determined by an administrative committee within the office (see Figure 10–4 for an example of the release guideline worksheet).[65]

In Minnesota, the release of a juvenile from a training school is the responsibility of a juvenile aftercare hearing officer who uses a scale incorporating the severity of the offense and the offense history (see Table 10-3). For example, a youthful offender who committed first-degree burglary would have a severity level of 3. If his or her delinquent history factors equaled 3, this offender would normally be paroled somewhere between the ninth and thirteen months of confinement.

RISK CONTROL AND CRIME REDUCTION

The current emphasis in aftercare, as in juvenile probation, is on short-term behavior control. Consequently, we can assume that even if more states adopt determinate sentencing statutes for juveniles, mandatory aftercare services will probably continue to be provided for those released from public and private placements. Similar to juvenile probation, **intensive supervision programs** are increasingly being used, but in-house detention and electronic monitoring programs still have not received the attention that they have in juvenile probation. Juvenile aftercare also emphasizes drug and alcohol urinalysis (sometimes called *drug drops*) and is turning to boot camp programs as a means of releasing juveniles early from training school.[66]

There appear to be more than eighty intensive aftercare supervision programs in the United States today.[67] The most noteworthy of these intensive

STATE OF OHIO
DEPARTMENT OF YOUTH SERVICES

RELEASE GUIDELINE WORKSHEET

Youth's Name _JOHN SMITH_   DYS # _999999_
County _SUMMIT_   Institution _IRS_
Adm. Date _03/13/90_   MSED _03/12/91_   Region _AKRON_

1. This Commitment

List most serious committing offense:
Offense ORC# _2907.02_ F _1_   Offense _RAPE_

A. Score committing offense
☒ Class 1 = 12   ☐ Class 2 = 10
☐ Class 3 = 6   ☐ Class 4 = 4   A [12]

B. Score enhancements (6 point maximum)
☐ Death of victim   = 6
☐ Firearm/dangerous ordnance   = 3   List other felonies heard:
☐ Other deadly weapon   = 2   1. ORC#_____
☐ Vulnerable victim   = 2   2. ORC#_____   B [2]
☒ Serious injury to victim   = 2   3. ORC#_____
☐ Multiple felony offenses   = 2
    or victims [#]

COMMITMENT TOTAL   (A + B) =   1 [14]

2. Previous Offense History

Score number of prior endangering offenses
☐ None (0) = 1.00
☒ One   (1) = 1.25   ORC #   Disposition Date
☐ Two   (2) = 1.50   1. _2907.05_ _09/14/89_   2 [1.25]
☐ Three (3) or more = 1.75   2. _____ _____
                             3. _____ _____

3. Determine Base Guideline Score (#1 X #2) =   3 [17.50]

4. Guideline Override: Add [ ]   Sub [ ]
(If used, provide additional written justification)

5. Total Guideline Score (#3 + #4)   5 [18]

6. Recommendation For Release

Early Release Eligibility: Yes ☐   Conditional ☐   No ☒

For those youth Early Release eligible, submit request by:	For those youth not Early Release eligible, revised sentence expiration date:
__/__/__	09 / 12 / 91

prepared by _Edwin Heller_   date _03/13/90_

Figure 10–4 *Release Guideline Worksheet*
Source: State of Ohio, Department of Youth Services.

programs are the ones in the thirty counties in Pennsylvania; "Lifeskills 95"; the Violent Juvenile Offender Research and Development Program in Boston, Memphis, and Detroit; juvenile aftercare in a Maryland drug treatment program; the Skillman Intensive Aftercare Project; the Michigan Nokomis Challenge program; the PARJO program in New York; and the Office of Juvenile Justice and Delinquency Prevention IAP Project.

Table 10–3 *Juvenile Commitment to the Minnesota Department of Corrections*

		Projected Institution Length of Stay in Months			
Severity Level	Most Serious Current Offense*	Delinquent History Factors			
		0	1	2	3
I	Violation of Probation Contempt of Court Prostitution Assault—4th & 5th Degree Driving Under Influence of Alcohol Negligent Fires Burglary—3rd & 4th Degree Damage to Property—$2,500 or less Forgery—$2,500 or less Possession of Controlled Substance Receiving Stolen Goods—$2,500 or less Theft—$2,500 or less Unauthorized Use of Motor Vehicle Dangerous Weapons (not including firearms) Trespass All Other Misdemeanors and Gross Misdemeanors	4–3	5–3	6–4	7–5
II	Assault—2nd & 3rd Degree Burglary—2nd Degree Damage to Property—Over $2,500 Forgery—Over $2,500 False Imprisonment Receiving Stolen Goods—$2,500 Felony Possession/Sale of Controlled Substance Theft from Person Theft—Over $2,500 Arson—3rd Degree Criminal Sexual Conduct—3rd & 4th Degree Simple Robbery Terroristic Threats Criminal Vehicular Homicide Dangerous Weapons—Firearms	6–3	7–4	8–5	9–6
III	Burglary—1st Degree Criminal Negligence Resulting in Death Aggravated Robbery Arson—1st & 2nd Degree Criminal Sexual Conduct—1st & 2nd Degree Kidnapping Manslaughter Assault—1st Degree	10–6	11–7	12–8	13–9
IV	Murder (all degrees)	**	**	**	**

*Commitment offenses not specifically listed shall be placed on the grid at the discretion of the hearing officer at the time of the initial institution review.

**Murder shall be dealt with on an individual basis.

Source: Minnesota Department of Corrections.

The IAP project, which is a combination of social control, strain, and social learning theories and focuses on the reintegrative process, has been implemented in four pilot programs: in Colorado (Arapahoe and Jefferson Counties), Nevada (Clark County), New Jersey (Camden and Essex Counties), and Virginia (Norfolk County). The participation of the New Jersey counties ended in 1997, but the other three programs carried through on preparing high-risk offenders for progressively increased responsibility and freedom in the community. The well-developed transition components that began shortly after a youth was adjudicated to an institution and continued through the early months of community adjustments are particularly strict in these programs. The results of the first five years of implementation (1995–2000) reveal a dramatically improved level of communication and coordination between institutional and aftercare staff, as well as the ability to involve parolees in community services almost immediately after institutional release.[68]

✓**Progress Check 10.2**
Review this section at
www.prenhall.com/bartollas

SUMMARY

- Over seven thousand juveniles continue to be placed in the problematic settings of adult jails. Detention centers that are temporary holding centers for juveniles vary from the traditional detention center to model facilities for youth. The attention homes that started in Colorado and have spread to other jurisdictions are one example of positive experiences provided for juveniles in confinement.

- Shelter care facilities are more open settings in which youths in trouble, often status offenders, are placed for a short period of time.

- Boot camps were widely regarded in the early 1990s, and supporters often viewed them as a panacea for juvenile corrections.

- More recently, high recidivism rates, as well as charges of abuse, have persuaded states, including Georgia, Maryland, Arizona, Florida, and South Dakota, to shut these programs down or to reevaluate them.

- Reception and diagnostic centers found in larger states are used to determine the best treatment plan for delinquents adjudicated to long-term institutional care.

- Ranches and forestry camps are minimum-security institutional placements that are normally reserved for youths who have committed minor offenses.

- Disagreements on social policy for training schools range from arguing for an increase in the number of these facilities to arguing for closing all training schools.

- There are those who believe that with proper staff–resident ratios and improved programs, these facilities can provide well for juveniles in trouble.

- Others assert that training schools are violent, inhumane, and damaging to all children.

- Some believe that these facilities should be located in the community, and still others recommend isolating them in rural areas.

- Beyond these disagreements is the reality that the number of youthful offenders confined in residential facilities increased 27 percent between 1991 and 2002.

- Private training schools were usually reserved for status offenders, while delinquents were adjudicated to public training schools, but the offense backgrounds of those placed in private and public training schools are now quite similar.

- In implementing a confinement policy for juveniles, a number of factors should be taken into consideration:

  1. If at all possible, youths should be kept in their home communities.
  2. If confinement is necessary, the detention home or training school (jails should never be used for children) should be in or very near the home community.
  3. The facilities should remain small, with detention home populations not exceeding thirty and training school populations not exceeding fifty.
  4. The facilities should be pleasantly furnished and security features provided only after adequate staffing, programming, and a satisfactory, safe physical plan have been developed. If such facilities are absolutely necessary, they should be completely committed to full use of community resources and, wherever possible, should integrate residents into community programs.

- Aftercare, or parole, is the least-developed segment of juvenile corrections.
- The current emphasis in aftercare, as in juvenile probation, is on short-term behavior control.
- It is reasonable to assume that if juveniles were provided with comprehensive and integrated complements to institutional programs, their chances of failure while on aftercare would be greatly reduced.

WEB SITES OF INTEREST

Information and links on the various types of boot camps can be found at OJJDP Boot Camps for Juveniles

> http://ojjdp.ncjrs.org

To view sources on Juvenile Correctional Facilities, simply type into your search engine:

> Juvenile Correctional Facilities

General information and links about juvenile aftercare can be found at

> http://www.criminology.fsu.edu/jjclearinghouse/jj30.html

CRITICAL THINKING QUESTIONS

1. How would you describe the social structure of residents in training schools?
2. Why are training schools damaging to some youths?
3. How can training schools be improved?
4. What are the major shocks a juvenile faces upon release to the community?
5. What is the purpose of aftercare?
6. What programs appear to have the most promise for juvenile aftercare?
7. Using the information in this chapter, draw up a set of rules that juveniles on aftercare would consider reasonable and that would contribute to reducing recidivism.

NOTES

1. Confined youth interviewed in 1989 in an Ohio training school for boys.
2. The safety of juveniles in jail has become a major issue. See Dale G. Parent, Valerie Lieter, Stephen Kennedy, Lisa Livens, Daniel Wentworth, and Sarah Wilcox, *Conditions of Confinement: Juvenile Detention and Corrections Facilities* (Washington, DC: Office of Juvenile Justice and Delinquency Prevention, 1994), 102–3.

3. According to Rosemary C. Sarri, the number of youths confined in jails each year during the 1970s ranged from ninety thousand (Children's Defense Fund) to one hundred thousand (National Council on Crime and Delinquency). See Sarri, "Gender Issues in Juvenile Justice," *Crime and Delinquency* 29 (1983), 390.

4. Howard N. Snyder and Melissa Sickmund, *Juvenile Offenders and Victims: A National Report* (Pittsburgh: National Center for Juvenile Justice, 1995), 72.

5. Howard N. Snyder and Melissa Sickmund, *Juvenile Offenders and Victims: 2006 National Report* (Washington, DC: National Center for Juvenile Justice and Office of Juvenile Justice and Delinquency Prevention, 2006), 236.

6. Charles E. Frazier and Donna M. Bishop, "Jailing Juveniles in Florida: The Dynamics of Compliance to a Sluggish Federal Referral Initiative," paper presented at the annual meeting of the American Society of Criminology, Baltimore (November 1990), 4.

7. Ira M. Schwartz, Linda Harris, and Laurie Levi, "The Jailing of Juveniles in Minnesota: A Case Study," *Crime and Delinquency* 34 (1988), 146; David Steinhart, "California's Legislature Ends the Jailing of Children: The Story of a Policy Reversal," *Crime and Delinquency* 34 (1988), 169–70.

8. David Steinhart and Barry Krisberg, "Children in Jail," *State Legislature* 13 (1987), 12–16.

9. Parent et al., *Conditions of Confinement,* 180–81. For other criticisms of detention practices, see Ira M. Schwartz and William H. Barton, eds., *Reforming Juvenile Detention: No More Hidden Closets* (Columbus: Ohio State University Press, 1994).

10. Melissa Sickmund, *Juvenile Offenders and Victims National Report Series Bulletin Juvenile Residential Facility Census, 2002: Selected Findings* (Washington, DC: National Center for Juvenile Justice and Office of Juvenile Justice and Delinquency Prevention, 2006), 2.

11. Interviewed in August 1996.

12. Roberta C. Cronin, *Boot Camps for Adult and Juvenile Offenders: Overview and Update,* Final Summary Report (Washington, DC: National Institute of Justice, 1994), 37. See also Mark Jones and Steven Cuvelier, "Are Boot Camp Graduates Better Probation Risks?" paper presented at the annual meeting of the American Society of Criminology, New Orleans (November 1992); and Thomas W. Waldron, "Boot Camps Offer Second Chance to Young Felons," *Corrections Today* 52 (1990), 144–69.

13. Jean Bottcher, "Evaluating the Youth Authority's Boot Camp: The First Five Months," paper delivered to Western Society of Criminology, Monterey, California, February 1993; Institute for Criminological Research and American Institute for Research, *Boot Camp for Juvenile Offenders: Constructive Intervention and Early Support—Implementation Evaluation Final Report* (New Brunswick, NJ: Rutgers University Press, 1992).

14. Roberta C. Cronin, *Boot Camps for Adults and Juvenile Offenders: Overview and Update,* a final summary report presented to the National Institute of Justice, 1994, 37.

15. Anthony W. Salerno, "Boot Camps: A Critique and a Proposed Alternative," *Journal of Offender Rehabilitation* 20 (1994), 149.

16. Ibid., 37.

17. Michael Peters, David Thomas, Christopher Zamberlan, and Caliber Associates, *Boot Camps for Juvenile Offenders: Program Summary* (Washington, DC: Office of Juvenile Justice and Delinquency Prevention, 1997), 3, 35.

18. Ibid.

19. Doris Layton MacKenzie, David B. Wilson, Gaylene Styve Armstrong, and Angela R. Glover, "The Impact of Boot Camps on Traditional Institutions of Juvenile Residents: Perceptions, Adjustment, and Change," *Journal of Research in Crime and Delinquency* 38 (August 2000), 279–313.

20. Ibid., 279.

21. Brent Zaehringer, *Koch Crime Institute White Paper Report Juvenile Boot Camps: Cost and Effectiveness vs. Residential Facilities,* http://www.hrf.uni-koeln.de/sitenew/content/e/filejuvbootcamps.pdf

22. Alexandra Marks, "States Fall Out of (Tough) Love with Boot Camps," *The Christian Science Monitor,* December 27, 1999, p. 1.

23. Associated Press, "Teen Dies at Boot Camp for Troubled Teens," *Milwaukee Times,* 4 July, 2001. For an article that suggests that what takes place at boot camps may be considered cruel and unusual and gives rise to costly inmate litigation, see Faith E. Lutze and David C. Brody, "Mental Abuse as Cruel and Unusual Punishment: Do Boot Camp Prisons Violate the Eighth Amendment," *Crime and Delinquency* 45 (April 1999) 242–55.

24. Alexandra Marks, "States Fall Out of (Tough) Love with Boot Camps," *The Christian Science Monitor,* December 27, 1999, p. 1.

25. For the classification system in California, the most highly developed in the nation, see Christopher Murray, Chris Baird, Ned Loughran, Fred Mills, and John Platt, *Safety and Welfare Plan: Implementing Reform in California* (Sacramento: California Department of Corrections and Rehabilitation, Division of Juvenile Justice, 2006), 12–18.

26. Melissa Sickmund, "Juvenile Residential Facility Census, 2002: Selected Findings" (Washington, DC: Office of Juvenile Justice and Delinquency Prevention, June 2006), 10.

27. For the most recent data on ranches and camps, see Howard N. Snyder and Melissa Sickmund, *Juvenile Offenders and Victims: 2006 National Report* (Washington, DC: National Center for Juvenile Justice and Office of Juvenile Justice and Delinquency Prevention, 2006), 208, 221–227; Melissa Sickmund, *Juvenile Residential Facility Census, 2002: Selected Findings* (Washington, DC: June 2006), OJJDP Publications online at http://www.ojjdp.ncjrs.gov/publications/index.html

28. A basic description of this program is included in a brochure developed by the Hennepin County Home School (n.d.). See also the Web page of the Hennepin County Home School.

29. Refer to Selection 20, authored by Terry Wise, Superintendent of the Hennepin County Home School, in the *Voices of the Juvenile Justice System.*

30. Howard N. Synder and Melissa Sickmund, *Juvenile Offenders and Victims: 2006 National Report* (Washington, DC: National Center for Juvenile Justice and Office of Juvenile Justice and Delinquency Prevention, 2006), 198.

31. Murray, Baird, Loughran, Mills, and Platt, *Safety and Welfare Plan: Implementing Reform in California, 2.*

32. David Street, Robert D. Vinter, and Charles Perrow, *Organization for Treatment: A Comparative Study of Institutions* (New York: Free Press, 1966).

33. Peter W. Greenwood, Susan Turner, and Kathy Rosenblatt, *Evaluation of Paint Creek Youth Center: Preliminary Results* (Santa Monica, CA: Rand, 1989).

34. Ibid., 58.

35. One of the author's experiences in several juvenile institutional systems revealed these activities of youth supervision.

36. Howard N. Synder and Melissa Sickmund, *Juvenile Offenders and Victims: 2006 National Report* (Washington, DC: National Center for Juvenile Justice and Office of Juvenile Justice and Delinquency Prevention, 2006), 197.

37. Ibid.

38. David Shichor and Clemens Bartollas, "Private and Public Juvenile Placements: Is There a Difference?" *Crime and Delinquency* 36 (April 1990), 286–99.

39. Glen Mills, for example, was featured in Bill Howard, "Florida Tries to Clone Preppy Glen Mills," *Youth Today: The Newspaper on Youth Work* 5 (July–August, 1996), 1, 12, 13.

40. Gaylene Styve Armstrong and Doris Layton MacKenzie, "Private versus Public Juvenile Correctional Facilities: Do Differences in Environmental Quality Exist?" *Crime and Delinquency* 49 (October 2003), 542–63.

41. Shichor and Bartollas, "Private and Public Juvenile Placements."

42. Clemens Bartollas and David Shichor, "Juvenile Privatization: The Expected and the Unexpected," paper presented at the annual meeting of the American Society of Criminology, Baltimore, Maryland (November 1990).

43. Shichor and Bartollas, "Private and Public Juvenile Placements," 286–99.

44. C. A. McEwen, *Designing Correctional Organizations for Youths: Dilemmas of Subcultural Development* (Cambridge, MA: Ballinger, 1978), 151–52.

45. Clemens Bartollas, Stuart J. Miller, and Simon Dinitz, *Juvenile Victimization: The Institutional Paradox* (New York: Halsted Press, 1976); Barry Feld, *Neutralizing Inmate Violence: Juvenile Offenders in Institutions* (Cambridge, MA: Ballinger, 1977); H. W. Polsky, *Cottage Six: The Social System of Delinquent Boys in Residential Treatment* (New York: Russell Sage, 1963); Sethard Fisher, "Social Organization in a Correction Residence," *Pacific Sociological Review* 5 (Fall 1961), 89.

46. Rose Giallombardo, *The Social World of Imprisoned Girls: A Comparative Study of Institutions for Juvenile Delinquents* (New York: Wiley, 1974).

47. Christopher M. Sieverdes and Clemens Bartollas, "Social Roles, Sex, and Racial Differences," *Deviant Behavior* 5 (1982), 203–18.

48. Alice Propper, *Prison Homosexuality: Myth and Reality* (Lexington, MA: D. C. Heath, 1981).

49. Interviewed in 1973.

50. Bartollas, Miller, and Dinitz, *Juvenile Victimization.*

51. Stuart J. Miller, Clemens Bartollas, and Simon Dinitz, "Juvenile Victimization Revisited: A Fifteen-Year Follow-Up at TICO" (unpublished manuscript).

52. *White v. Reid,* 125 F. Supp. 647 (D.D.C.) 1954.

53. *Inmates of the Boys' Training School v. Affleck,* 346 F. Supp. 1354 (D.R.I. 1972).

54. *Nelson v. Heyne,* 355 F. Supp. 451 (N.D. Ind. 1973).

55. *Morales v. Turman,* 364 F. Supp. 166 (E.D. Tex. 1973).

56. H. Swanger, "Juvenile Institutional Litigation," *Clearinghouse Review* 11 (1977), 22.

57. See *Lollis v. N.Y. State Department of Social Services* (1970) and N. N. Kittie, *The Right to Be Different: Deviance and Enforced Therapy* (Baltimore: Johns Hopkins University Press, 1971), for more information on this subject.

58. *Pena v. New York State Division for Youth,* 419 F. Supp. 203 (S.D.N.Y. 1976).

59. *Inmates of the Boys' Training School v. Affleck.*

60. *Morales v. Turman,* 364 F. Supp. 166 (E.D. Tex. 1973).

61. *Morgan v. Sproat*, 432 F. Supp. 1130 (S.D. Miss. 1977).

62. *State v. Werner*, 242 S.E.2d 907 (W. Va. 1978).

63. Patricia Puritz and Mary Ann Scali, *Beyond the Walls: Improving Conditions of Confinement for Youth in Custody Report* (Washington, DC: Office of Juvenile Justice and Delinquency Prevention, 1998), 4–7.

64. Murray, Baird, Loughran, Mills, and Platt, *Safety and Welfare Plan: Implementing Reform in California, 98.*

65. Department of Youth Services, *Mission Statement, Office of Release Review* (Columbus, OH: Department of Youth Services, n.d.), 1.

66. David M. Altschuler, Troy L. Armstrong, and Doris Layton MacKenzie, "Reintegration, Supervision Release, and Intensive Aftercare," *OJJDP: Juvenile Justice Bulletin* (Washington, DC: Office of Juvenile Justice and Delinquency Prevention, 1999).

67. Ted Palmer, *The Re-emergence of Correctional Intervention* (Newbury Park, CA: Sage Publications, 1992), 86.

68. Richard G. Wiebush, Betsie McNulty, and Thalo Le, *Implementation of the Intensive Community-Based Aftercare Program* (Washington, DC: Office of Juvenile Justice and Delinquency Prevention, 2000).

11

TREATMENT TECHNOLOGIES

We have a gym that has a basketball court and a weight room, but the cottages don't get down there very often. We are lucky if it is once a week. We are scheduled to go outside [fenced-in recreational area] every now and then, but then they usually cancel it right before it happens. All this stuff looks real good on paper, but when you come right down to it, the administration ain't really doing a lot for us back here.

They came out with this new level system. It goes from one to four—one being the lowest and four being the highest. Level fours are supposed to have a possibility of off-ground jobs, and there is a big list of things we are supposed to be able to do. But the only thing we've gotten so far is that we went off grounds once to see a movie. They run a lot of stuff down, and it looks real good for Central Office. But when you come right down to it, you are here to do your time. That's it!

We got some vocational classes, and they got their Mickey Mouse high school over there. If you don't go to school, you get a write-up and locked up. . . . We ain't even being educated to a point where we see we have a need for education. A lot of guys are illiterate. They can't even write their name or can write very little.

And these guys are taught no self-worth, except maybe a couple of staff will say something to them. There is no programs to teach them. They ain't getting a lot of help brought to them. All this place is doing is setting them for a letdown when they get back out in society. This place is setting them up for prison.

They can't get a job. They ain't even got a GED. Where are they going to get money? The first place is that they are going to go to Sam Smith's house, take his stereo, and there they go. That's really sad! There could be more help, but there is just a lot of people who don't care. It is a political game. The guys in charge don't care. It's sad that all these people are crying out for help, and there is no help for them. That's why we got to build seven new prisons in this state every year. They cry about all this money they got to spend on a prison. They should spend the money on the guys who are sixteen and seventeen in this institution.

—Institutionalized Male Delinquent[1]

OUTLINE

OBJECTIVES

1. To identify different camps or positions concerning treatment in juvenile justice
2. To explain the treatment modalities that are used most frequently in juvenile justice
3. To evaluate these treatment modalities
4. To present suggestions for improving treatment in juvenile justice agencies

KEY TERMS

behavior modification
cognitive-behavioral interventions
drug and alcohol abuse interventions
family therapy

gang deactivation
Guided Group Interaction (GGI)
Integrated treatment model
Interpersonal Maturity Level (I-Level) Classification System
law-related education (LRE)

positive peer culture (PPC)
psychotherapy
Quay classification system
reality therapy
skill development
transactional analysis (TA)

The training school resident speaking in the chapter-opening quote claims that no positive programs are being used in this institution for boys. Indeed, he argues that he is likely to leave in worse shape than when he was first confined by the "kindly parent, the state." In spite of the perceptions of this youth, juvenile offenders are confronted and almost overwhelmed by the various methods used to treat, save, rehabilitate, remodel, remake, or otherwise "recycle" them. Juvenile corrections, far more than adult corrections, has as its guiding premise the rehabilitation of youths before they become hardened criminals. To that end, researchers from every discipline have looked for the key that will modify the behavior of offenders.

Punishment was believed to be the answer for a long period of time. But in the 1700s, the founding fathers of our country substituted a religious orientation as the proper approach to working with wayward children. This moral and religious emphasis slowly gave way by the second half of the nineteenth century to firm discipline and rigorous work training. The study of the character and mental condition of individual lawbreakers was the accepted treatment during the first four decades of the twentieth century. Sociology began to dominate treatment efforts in the 1950s and 1960s with the use of predelinquency community programs, detached workers (social workers whose jobs are on the streets with juvenile gangs), group interaction, job training, and community reorganization. Indeed, during this period, a new idea sprang up nearly every day, each one heralded as the panacea for youth crime. In the

1970s, as discussed in the next section, correctional treatment was bombarded with criticism from all sides and still has not fully regained its former popularity.

Approaches to treatment range from individual to group methods. This chapter presents a general discussion of treatment in juvenile justice, and describes and evaluates the treatment modalities that are most popular today.

WHAT IS THE TREATMENT DEBATE?

Correctional treatment came under increased criticism in the late 1960s and early 1970s. In 1966, reporting on the results of one hundred empirical evaluations of treatment, Walter C. Bailey concluded that there seemed to be little evidence that correctional treatment was effective.[2] In 1971, J. Robison and G. Smith added that "there [was] no evidence to support any program's claim to superior rehabilitative strategy."[3] Then, in 1974, the late Robert Martinson startled both correctional personnel and the public with the pronouncement that "with few and isolated exceptions, the rehabilitative efforts that have been reported so far have had no appreciable effect on recidivism."[4] The media quickly simplified Martinson's statement to the idea that "nothing works" in correctional treatment. In 1975, Douglas Lipton, Robert Martinson, and Judith Wilks published *The Effectiveness of Correctional Treatment*, which critically evaluated the effectiveness of correctional treatment programs.[5] In that same year, Martinson announced on *60 Minutes* that "there [was] no evidence that correctional rehabilitation reduces recidivism."[6] A spirited debate on the "nothing works" thesis has continued to rage since the late 1970s.

Ted Palmer, a correctional researcher in California, challenged Lipton and his colleagues' research by tabulating eighty-two studies mentioned in the book and showing that thirty-nine of them, or 48 percent, had positive or partly positive results on recidivism.[7] Palmer used Martinson's own words to reject the "nothing works" thesis:

> These programs seem to work best when they are new, when their subjects are amenable to treatment in the first place, and when the counselors are not only trained people, but "good people" as well.[8]

Robert R. Ross and Paul Gendreau reviewed the literature published between 1973 and 1978 and found that 86 percent of the ninety-five intervention programs studied reported success.[9] According to Gendreau and Ross, this success rate was "convincing evidence that some treatment programs, when they are applied with integrity by competent practitioners in appropriate target populations, can be effective in preventing crime or reducing recidivism."[10] In the late 1970s, Martinson conceded that "contrary to [his] previous position, some treatment programs *do* have an appreciable effect on recidivism. Some programs are indeed beneficial."[11] But, despite Martinson's recantation of his "nothing works" thesis and Palmer's and Gendreau and Ross's defense of correctional treatment, the general mood regarding offender rehabilitation in the late 1970s and early 1980s was one of pessimism and discouragement.

In the late 1980s, Gendreau and Ross reviewed the offender rehabilitation literature for the period between 1981 and 1987 and again found that the number and variety of successful reported attempts at reducing delinquent behavior contradicted the "nothing works" hypothesis.[12] Moreover, the rehabilitative evidence in the 1980s grew at a much greater rate than it did during the 1970s and suggested several strategies for developing more effective programs.[13]

Several meta-analyses have evaluated the effectiveness of correctional treatment. The statistical tool of meta-analysis has been developed to enable reviewers to combine findings from different experiments. Meta-analysis undertakes the "aggregation and side-by-side analysis of large numbers of experimental studies."[14] One of the advantages of meta-analysis is that it can "incorporate adjustments for the fact that studies vary considerably in the degree of rigour of their experimental design."[15] Focus on Programs 11–1 summarizes the findings of the most widely studied meta-analyses of correctional treatment.

Ted Palmer's 1992 publication, *The Re-Emergence of Correctional Intervention,* contends that during the 1980s, both juvenile and adult corrections struggled with institutional crowding, rising costs, and behavioral control of offenders. But interest in and commitment to rehabilitation or habilitation, increased steadily throughout the 1980s. By the end of the decade, according to Palmer:

> Growth-centered intervention had gained still more strength in terms of focus, direction, and perceived legitimacy. This change, especially intervention's relegitimization, is a major development in American corrections, particularly considering rehabilitation's and habilitation's low status and quasi-banishment from 1975 to 1981.[16]

FOCUS ON PROGRAMS   **11–1**

META-ANALYSIS OF CORRECTIONAL TREATMENT

- Garrett (1985) surveyed 111 papers and found a significant overall effect of treatment on a variety of outcomes, including reoffending.
- Gottschalk and colleagues (1987) examined community-based interventions and found a weaker effect.
- Lab and Whitehead (1988, 1989) reported predominantly negative findings in their meta-analyses and described only a few promising results.
- Izzo and Ross (1990) compared programs that contained a cognitive component with those that did not, and they found a marked superiority in terms of reduced recidivism among programs with a cognitive component.
- Andrews and colleagues (1990) incorporated findings from 150 research reports and included studies undertaken with adult offenders; they found overall positive effects of correctional treatment.
- Lipsey examined 397 outcome studies of offenders between the ages of twelve and twenty-one, which produced a sample in excess of forty thousand clients. A principal finding of this survey was that a total of 64.5 percent of the experiments showed positive effects of treatment in reducing recidivism.

Thus, taking all these meta-analyses together, the net effect of treatment is an average reduction in recidivism rates of between 10 and 12 percent.

Source: James McGuire and Philip Priestley, "Reviewing 'What Works': Past, Present, and Future," in *What Works: Reducing Reoffending—Guidelines from Research and Practice,* edited by James McGuire (New York: Wiley, 1995), pp. 8–9.

Critical Thinking Questions:

Do these meta-analyses suggest that "nothing works" in correctional treatment? What types of youthful offenders do you think would be more receptive to rehabilitative services?

Intervention's new direction or emphasis, according to Palmer, resulted from the fact that many skeptics and most supporters of correctional intervention by the 1990s largely agreed on the following principles for working with serious offenders: (1) programs with multiple modalities must be used; (2) intensity of contact must be increased in most programs; and (3) greater attention must be paid to offenders' needs and characteristics so that they can be matched with particular program elements.[17]

HOW ARE YOUTHFUL OFFENDERS CLASSIFIED?

Throughout the twentieth century, classification was considered the first step of treatment in juvenile correction. Psychiatric evaluations and psychological workups of juvenile delinquents were conducted in child guidance clinics by the second decade of the twentieth century. A number of reception and diagnostic centers were built in the 1930s and 1940s so that delinquents could be assigned to programs compatible with their psychological, educational, and vocational needs. Classifying youths in terms of their personality dynamics, worldview, and behavior were the three most popular schemes in the 1960s and 1970s. But in the past decade, classification systems for treatment purposes in juvenile corrections have lost much of their former popularity.

Most juvenile delinquents are involved in psychiatric interviews and psychological workups on one or more occasions. Psychiatric interviews may be used to determine the psychological problems of a youth, and the therapist may use such terms as *psychoneurotic, antisocial, passive-aggressive, passive dependent, adjustment reaction to adolescence, group delinquent,* and *unsocialized* in describing the problems of a youth. Psychiatric interviews also are frequently conducted before releasing from training school a delinquent who has committed violent offenses in order to provide corrections officials with assurance that the youth is no longer dangerous. Various psychological tests, such as the Jesness Personality Inventory, categorize youthful offenders according to such concepts as social maladjustment, value orientation, immaturity, autism, alienation, manifest aggression, withdrawal-depression, social anxiety, repression, denial, and asocial index.

The **Interpersonal Maturity Level (I-Level) Classification System,** developed by J. Grant and M. Grant in the late 1950s in California, assumes that personality development follows a normal sequence and attempts to identify the developmental stage of offenders by focusing on their perception of themselves, others, and the world. A seven-point classification scheme ranges from I_1 (infantile in interpersonal maturity) to I_7 (ideal social maturity). Researchers have found that most delinquents are fixated at one of the lower levels of social maturity and, therefore, can be classified at the I_2, I_3, and I_4 levels; these levels are further divided into nine delinquent subtypes.[18] Proponents of the I-Level system contend that the impact of treatment varies from one youth to another according to his or her developmental stage; accordingly, what works with one youth may have no effect or even a negative impact on another. The I-Level system was rigorously evaluated at California's Community Treatment Project (CTP) and at the Preston Boys' School in California during the 1960s and has been widely used, especially in training schools, throughout the nation.

Herbert C. Quay developed a classification system that evaluates delinquents in terms of their behavior rather than their worldview.[19] The **Quay classification system** is based on five personality types: inadequate-immature, neurotic-conflicted, unsocialized aggressive or psychopathic, socialized or subcultural delinquent, and subcultural-immature delinquents. Inadequate-immature offenders behave childishly or irresponsibly. Neurotic-conflicted delinquents are anxious, insecure youths whose internal conflicts create problems for themselves and others. Unsocialized delinquents adhere to the values of their delinquent peer group. Offenders in the subcultural classification are usually involved in gang delinquency. Subcultural-immature delinquents are youths who violate the law but feel alienated from delinquent peer groups. The Quay classification and treatment model continues to be used but has lost much of its popularity.

WHAT ARE THE MAIN TREATMENT MODALITIES?

Various treatment modalities are widely used in community-based corrections and have been established in nearly every training school in the United States. Psychotherapy, transactional analysis, reality therapy, behavior modification, family therapy, guided group interaction, and positive peer culture are the traditional treatment modalities most widely used in juvenile justice. Drug and alcohol abuse interventions, law-related education, skill development programs, and gang deactivation groups are also increasingly used.[20]

PSYCHOTHERAPY

Various adaptations of Freudian **psychotherapy** have been used by psychiatrists, clinical psychologists, and psychiatric social workers since the early twentieth century. Either in a one-to-one relationship with a therapist or in a group context, juvenile offenders are encouraged to talk about past conflicts causing them to express emotional problems through aggressive or antisocial behavior. The insight that offenders gain from this individual or from group psychotherapy supposedly helps them resolve the conflicts and unconscious needs that drive them to crime. As a final step of psychotherapy, youthful offenders become responsible for their own behavior.

Acceptance of the therapist is a key to successful psychotherapy, for youths must discover that all adults are not like their rejecting parents. A trusting therapeutic relationship, coupled with firmness and justice on the part of the therapist, is intended to help offenders acquire a new sense of dignity and self-worth.

Within the community, psychotherapy has been used recently much more with middle- and upper-class youthful offenders than with lower-class youngsters. Middle- and upper-class youths who abuse drugs or alcohol or who have conflicts at home are likely to be referred for psychotherapy. Other than in a few private institutions, little psychotherapy takes place in institutional contexts. The few psychiatrists and clinical psychologists available in these settings spend most of their time doing intake evaluations for classification purposes and crisis intervention with acting-out youths. Crisis intervention generally consists of one interview in which the therapist recommends a treatment plan for the resident's cottage; psychiatrists may also prescribe medication to calm a youth.

One of the fundamental problems with psychotherapy is that youthful offenders usually do not see themselves as having emotional problems and, furthermore, are reluctant to share their thoughts with a therapist. This is particularly true of lower-class youths, most of whom can relate a bad experience with a psychiatrist or psychologist. But it is also true of middle- and upper-class youths, who frequently have authority problems and view these "treaters" as part of the establishment against which they are rebelling. It is not surprising that there is no recent evidence of the effectiveness of psychotherapy with youthful offenders.

TRANSACTIONAL ANALYSIS

Transactional analysis (TA) focuses on interpreting and evaluating interpersonal relationships. This treatment modality tries to teach youthful lawbreakers to relate to others in an adult, mature way. Eric Berne, founder of TA, believes that it can overcome the typical resistance to psychotherapy:

> . . . as most kids are forced into therapy and must maintain a subservient status vis-à-vis the therapist. In TA, youths learn to interact with the therapist on an adult-to-adult basis. The youths learn the procedure of TA and are free to implement the therapy for themselves as they see fit.[21]

In applying this modality, the TA leader usually first does a script analysis, which is an attempt to understand how the "tapes" of the past are influencing the behavior of the juvenile in the present. This concept of script analysis is based on the premise that human memory acts as a three-track tape that records the events individuals experienced during their first years of life, the meaning attached to those events, and the emotions they experienced when those events occurred. Each person often replays his or her tape when similar situations are encountered later in life. The consequence of negative script replay is that many individuals become "losers," failing to attain their goals and becoming involved in self-defeating behavior. The TA leader seeks to discover the youth's script by diagnosing his or her voice, vocabulary, demeanor, gestures, and answers to questions. TA is based on the belief that persons can change their scripts, and the function of the TA leader is to help individuals make this change. For example, if a mother has told her daughter that she will never succeed at anything and if this has become a self-fulfilling prophecy, the therapist tries to communicate to the daughter that she *can* succeed in achieving her goals.

One of the hopeful outcomes of the life-script interview is that offenders are willing to negotiate a treatment contract; that is, the youths will state how they wish to change. This treatment contract normally has both short- and long-range goals, project group goals, academic goals, and social behavior goals. Once goals are set, the youth is considered to be in treatment. Throughout the treatment period, these goals and progress toward them are constantly reviewed by staff.

As soon as offenders are placed in groups, they learn that one of the first objects of TA is to make them become aware of the different kinds of social interaction they use in dealing with others. TA conceptualizes three ego states—the "Child" (relic of one's past), the "Parent" (internalization of the teaching and values of one's parental figures), and the "Adult" (the mature and responsible adult). The TA therapist then tries to help the residents recognize when they are emerging from each state so that they are able to function more often in the Adult ego state. Since the Adult can turn off the not-OK feelings of the Child tape, the TA leader tries to free the Adult state so that it can deal objectively with the other two states.

The youthful offender also is taught the four life positions that constitute the relationship perceived between the self and others:

1. I'm OK—You're OK: This is the position of the normal, healthy individual who starts on the assumption that he or she and others are emotionally well adjusted to life.
2. I'm not OK—You're OK: This position reflects a neurotic, depressed outlook on life; others are emotionally healthy, but the individual is not.

3. I'm not OK—You're not OK: This position, which is that of autistic children and schizophrenics, produces severe individual problems in relating to the world and to the people in it.

4. I'm OK—You're not OK: This position, often observed in the delinquent and the sociopath, means that individual believes that he or she is justified in gratifying his or her own immediate impulses, regardless of the consequences.[22]

A further function of TA is to teach the games that group members play in their interactions. According to TA, a *game* is a series of transactions that moves toward a predictable, well-defined outcome. Berne describes game behavior as "a series of moves with a snare or 'gimmick.'"[23] Games serve to keep a person from establishing intimacy with others, and they usually involve offenders who are "coming out" of their impulsive, immature Child states. These games are the means by which youthful offenders keep their emotional distance from staff. Such game behavior no doubt began with juveniles' feeling of powerlessness at the hands of the police and judges and continued throughout their stint in the system.

Thus, the TA leader, whether psychotherapist, psychiatric social worker, or paraprofessional, not only dispenses information about the basic tenets of TA, but also helps offenders become more aware of their social interactions. In addition to helping offenders individually, the TA leader observes group interactions among offenders and, when these interactions are taped on audiovisual equipment, studies in greater depth each youth's interpersonal relationships. Focus on Programs 11–2 relates the success of TA with one youthful offender.

Using TA for treating juveniles has several advantages. The first is that TA is easy to learn. Offenders, for instance, readily understand gaming behavior. One TA leader altered TA terminology further to make it even more comprehensible to offenders. The Parent ego state became "the man"; the Adult was changed to "cool head"; and the Child was altered to "the kid."[24]

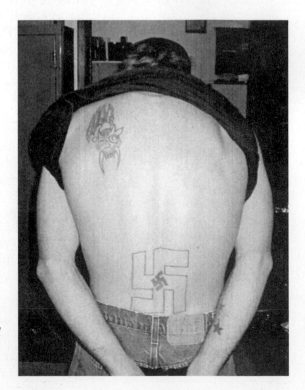

Which approach in this chapter would you use on this skinhead? Would you use any of them? Why or why not?
(Photo by Jerry Cavanaugh.)

FOCUS ON PROGRAMS   11–2
A TA SUCCESS STORY

Bill, a sixteen-year-old African-American youth, had spent several years in juvenile institutions before he arrived at the training school. Although his home was intact, he felt a great deal of rejection from his mother. His offenses were incorrigibility at home and in school and two charges of assault and battery toward peers (fighting in school). His average to above-average intelligence was not apparent from his school performance. Psychiatric reports diagnosed him as withdrawn and as having schizoid tendencies.

His first adjustment report stated: "The prognosis is poor. Extremely depressed about his home life, especially his relationship with mother, Bill is experiencing conflict with peers and staff alike. Bill is resistant to his placement and refuses to become involved in any institutional program."

Then, Bill was persuaded by a TA leader to join a group. TA fascinated Bill, who took an active part in the group and never missed a meeting; he also read all he could find on this therapy. More important, he used the concepts of TA to change his behavior and his perception of himself. He frequently informed staff, "I changed from the Child to the Adult state on that one, didn't I?" Bill decided he would finish his last three years of high school, which he did at the institutional high school in the next year and a half. He was granted a home visit to resolve his conflict with his mother, but when she blatantly rejected him on the visit, he used TA to work through the pain of rejection. He applied to Ohio State University, was accepted, and, on his release, became a college student. Four years later, the youth who had been given such a poor prognosis received his college diploma.

Source: Case study of a youth with whom one of the authors worked.

Critical Thinking Questions:
Why do you believe this youth was receptive to TA? Did rehabilitation work for him?

Another advantage of TA, according to the only major study that examined its effectiveness, is that it appears to have positive impact on some offenders. This study of a training school in California further revealed that residents exposed to TA tend to have higher morale, develop more positive attitudes toward staff members, become more hopeful and optimistic about the future, and establish greater feelings of self-esteem and well-being. Finally, subjects paroled from this training school did significantly better during their first twelve months following release than had offenders released in prior years. The parole violation rates were also significantly lower than those of juveniles in comparable age groups released from other California juvenile institutions.[25]

In spite of the popularity and success of TA, especially in the 1960s and 1970s, its most glaring limitation is the difficulty in applying the technique to youths who are evading personal change, who have gross behavior problems, and/or who are not motivated to examine their own problems. The mature are the most likely to profit; the immature and sociopathic usually withdraw, and the manipulator tries to "game" staff and the other inmates. Youthful offenders with borderline intelligence are also limited in their ability to examine their behavior through such an intellectual exercise.

REALITY THERAPY

Reality therapy, a very popular treatment modality, was developed by two Los Angeles psychiatrists, William Glasser and G. L. Harrington. This modality assumes that irresponsible behavior arises when a person is unable to fulfill his or her basic needs. According to this approach, the basic human needs are relatedness and respect, and one satisfies these needs by doing what is realistic, responsible, and right.[26]

The three Rs of reality therapy are reality, responsibility, and right and wrong. In using this approach with older delinquent girls at the Ventura School in California, Glasser always made each adolescent face the reality of her behavior in the present, he refused to accept any reason for irresponsible behavior, and he expected the girls to maintain a satisfactory standard of behavior.

Glasser defines the major differences between conventional and reality therapy as follows:

1. Because we do not accept the concept of mental illness, the patient cannot become involved with us as a mentally ill person who has no responsibility for his behavior.
2. Working in the present and toward the future, we do not get involved with the patient's history because we can neither change what happened to him nor accept the fact that he is limited by his past.
3. We relate to patients as ourselves, not as transference figures.
4. We do not look for unconscious conflicts or the reasons for them. A patient cannot become involved with us by excusing his or her behavior on the basis of unconscious motivations.
5. We emphasize the morality of behavior. We face the issue of right and wrong which we believe solidifies the involvement, in contrast to conventional psychiatrists who do not make the distinction between right and wrong, feeling it would be detrimental to attaining the transference relationship they seek.
6. We teach patients better ways to fulfill their needs. The proper involvement will not be maintained unless the patient is helped to find more satisfactory patterns of behavior as part of therapy.[27]

Reality therapy involves three phases: first, the offender forms an honest personal relationship with the therapist; second, the therapist always accepts the youth but, at the same time, rejects the negative behavior; third, the therapist teaches offenders better ways to fulfill their needs within their social reality.

Glasser emphasizes consistent discipline and warm acceptance and believes that offenders should be given increased responsibilities:

We firmly believe that an institutional training school, or a mental hospital, can produce better results when warm relationships along with increasing responsibilities are stressed by an undivided staff. The girl who comes to Ventura has spent her life excusing her behavior in a world where people were not consistent, where one person told her one thing, someone else told her another, and most told her different things from day to day. Every effort must be maintained to provide a unified philosophy of treatment where the staff provides both consistent discipline and warmth and affection. But warmth never supersedes discipline, nor discipline warmth.[28]

Reality therapy has not been sufficiently studied with juvenile offenders to permit any definite statements about its effectiveness. Glasser estimates that it has succeeded with about 80 percent of the girls at Ventura School. He cites as proof of his case the statistic that only 43 out of 370 girls at the school were returnees while he was a therapist there.

Using this modality with juveniles has several advantages. The first is that paraprofessionals can play a major role in working with clients because the basic tenets are easily learned. Second, paraprofessionals are much more attracted to the basic assumptions of reality therapy than to other treatment modalities. For example, they like its emphasis on responsibility, its negation of extenuating circumstances, and its focus on the present. Third, it seems to be easier to achieve consistent treatment with this modality.

Criticisms of this modality center on its oversimplification of the dynamics of the human personality. Critics believe, in this regard, that insight is helpful to certain offenders in dealing with their antisocial behavior and that an exploration of the past is sometimes necessary to deal adequately with the present. Reality therapy is further criticized for its tendency to encourage paternalistic and authoritarian attitudes in therapeutic interaction. Similarly, others suggest that this modality attracts rigid and inflexible persons who use it as a shield to hide their own authoritarian attitudes. The proponents of reality therapy are also accused of moralism and of oversimplifying the definitions of right and wrong.

Despite these criticisms, reality therapy is pervasive and influential in juvenile justice. Because so many of its assumptions are agreeable to line staff, the popularity of this modality will endure long after most of the other treatment technologies have been forgotten.

BEHAVIOR MODIFICATION

Behavior modification refers to the application of instrumental learning theory to problems of human behavior. This modality is based on the assumption that all behavior is under the control of its consequences in the external environment. If a behavior is reinforced immediately and systematically in a positive way, the frequency and rate of that behavior should increase, but if a behavior does not receive positive reinforcement, the frequency should decrease. Attention, praise, money, food, and privileges are positive reinforcers; threats, confinement, punishment, and ridicule are negative reinforcers. Positive reinforcers produce more effective and enduring behavior changes. A wide variety of techniques are used to reinforce positive and extinguish negative behavior. They include systematic desensitization, extinction of undesirable responses, training in assertiveness, counterconditioning, conditioning against avoidance responses, and the use of tokens. Behavior modification uses environmental contingencies to alter the offender's response.[29]

Behavior modification does not employ such terms as *repressed desires, self-concept, unconscious needs,* and *superego,* because they refer unnecessarily to internal psychological characteristics. Actions, rather than self-awareness or self-knowledge, are important in behavior modification. Attending primarily to the observable stimulus and the observable response, the behavior modification therapist tries to change a person's conduct by determining the desired result, the stimuli that can control it, and the reinforcements that are contingent on the response. The behavior modification therapist attempts to reduce gradually the antisocial behavior of youthful offenders. The expectation is that each reduction will lead to greater accomplishments and that eventually the youth will be able to live within the law. Consistency is a crucial component of behavior modification therapy; therefore, each staff member must systematically provide the positive and negative reinforcers.

Behavior modification therapy also cautions against the use of punishment unless youths are dangerous to themselves or to others. When punishment is needed, swift and consistent action should follow the undesirable behavior. Instead of punishment, behavioral therapy recommends the use of brief time-out periods during which no reinforcement of any kind is available.

One of the great strengths of behavior modification therapy is that it appears to have a greater impact on the sociopathic offender than do other treatment modalities. A major reason for this is that behavior modification techniques can immediately reinforce target behaviors. A study by J. L. Bernard and R. Eisenman reported that sociopathic offenders are easier to condition than are normal subjects by either social or monetary reinforcement once the behavior therapist discovers what is rewarding for the youth who is undergoing treatment.[30] Behavior modification also appears to have a greater impact on the manipulator than do more traditional therapies. Furthermore, behavior modification is specific and often is effective in short-term intervention. Finally, behavior modification is one of the most flexible treatment modalities.

Opponents of behavior modification have leveled several major criticisms against it. One of the most frequent ones is that treating only the offender's overt symptoms is too superficial to be effective. Many critics also charge that this treatment method is not lasting. Humanists believe that human beings are too unique and complicated to be treated only according to their overt behavior. It is also feared that behavior denoting even greater disturbance may take the place of the eliminated symptom. Another criticism is that the principles of behavior modification require considerable consistency and continuity, if not sophistication, which is atypical of correctional treatment. Finally, critics argue that it is very difficult to apply behavior modification to youths who do not manifest overt behavioral problems.

R. Schwitzgebel and D. A. Kolb's study of behavior modification is one of the most frequently cited. Their study involved twenty delinquent boys in Boston in a nine-month project, in which the youths were paid for talking into a tape recorder about their life experiences. The boys came to their appointments on an individual basis two to three times a week. The measured result of the program was that attendance became more prompt. After three years, follow-up data showed significantly fewer arrests and fewer months incarcerated among those in the program than among those in a matched control group. But there was no significant difference in recidivism, as measured by those youths who went on to the reformatory or prison. The authors attributed the success that was achieved to the fact that individualized rewards were used and that the experimenters were empathetic, direct, and unorthodox in their relationships with the youths.[31]

Dennis A. Romig, in reviewing fourteen studies of behavior modification involving almost two thousand juvenile offenders in programs across the United States, found that behavior modification was effective in changing certain behaviors, such as those related to school attendance, test scores, promptness, and classroom behavior. Yet it has had less impact on such global factors as delinquency or arrest rates. Romig concludes that the more the youthful offenders are involved in the process of behavior modification and the more specific and behaviorally simple the behaviors to be changed are, the more likely it is that the results will be positive.[32]

FAMILY THERAPY

Treating the entire family has become a widely used method of dealing with a youthful offender's socially unacceptable behavior. The Sacramento 601 Diversion Project is one of the most successful examples of **family therapy.**

This project was designed to determine whether youths in need of supervision (status offenders) could more effectively be diverted from delinquency through short-term family crisis counseling involving the entire family than through involvement in traditional juvenile court intake procedures. The evaluation of the 601 Diversion Project indicated that it has successfully achieved its four major goals: (1) to reduce the number of cases ending in juvenile court; (2) to reduce the number of repeat offenders; (3) to decrease overnight detentions; and (4) to accomplish these goals without increasing the cost required for regular processing of cases. Romig postulates that the positive results of the 601 Diversion Project "can be attributed to the involvement of the youths' families at the crisis points and the subsequent attempts by the project staff to improve the communication patterns of the family."[33]

Romig evaluated twenty studies involving 2,180 youths and concluded that family therapy did not reduce delinquent behavior. When such therapy focused on the positive goal of improving communication among family members, however, significant decreases of youth offenses occurred. Further, crisis intervention counseling, especially when used to teach systematic problem solving, was successful.[34]

In sum, family therapy appears likely to be more effective when it is focused on teaching parents communication, problem-solving, and disciplinary skills. Accordingly, status offenders and their families are more likely than youthful offenders and their families to benefit from effective family therapy.

✓ **Progress Check 11.1**
Review this section at
www.prenhall.com/bartollas

GUIDED GROUP INTERACTION

Guided Group Interaction (GGI) is probably the most widely used treatment modality. It has been used in at least eleven states: Florida, Georgia, Illinois, Kentucky, Maryland, Michigan, Minnesota, New Hampshire, New Jersey, South Dakota, and West Virginia. Since the 1950s, when this modality was first used, it has been based on the assumption that youths could confront their peers and force them to face the reality of their behavior more effectively than could staff.

The GGI approach is characterized by a nonauthoritarian atmosphere, intensity of interaction, group homogeneity, and an emphasis on group structure. The most important characteristic is the nonauthoritarian atmosphere. Residents in many residential GGI programs, for example, are given considerable say in when a group member will be released, granted a home furlough, or approved for off-campus visits; in how a group will be punished; and in whether the outside door will be locked or left open at night.

Giving residents responsibility for decision making, of course, is a different approach to child care from that followed in most correctional settings. The adult leader constantly refers the decision making back to the group. When informed by a youth that a group member planned to run away, for example, one staff member retorted: "So what do you want me to do? He's your buddy; he's part of your group. You can talk to him if you have to; but it's up to all of you to help one another."[35]

Youthful offenders usually go through several stages in becoming involved in guided group interaction. Youths initially are guarded in their responses, but as their defenses begin to weaken, they learn to give up their games and defenses because of the encouragement received from peers and the group leader. In the second stage, the residents' interpersonal problems are brought into the open. They are encouraged to talk about themselves and to have their values scrutinized and challenged by the group. In the third stage, the offenders begin to examine the difficulties they have had with their environment. The group members, who begin to develop real trust among one another, probe the problems of institutional and street living. The fourth stage is that in which the offenders feel secure and accept reeducation. When they see that their problems are not unique and that dealing with them is possible, they feel less antagonistic toward the group and become more receptive to what is said. In the final stage, the residents set up an outline of a plan for change. Using his or her own self-evaluation, as well as that of the group, each youth makes a conscious decision about the way he or she wants to behave in the future.[36]

GGI was first used with juvenile offenders in the Highfields Project in New Jersey in the early 1950s. The success of this project led other agencies to adopt this approach to treating youthful offenders. Joseph W. Scott and Jerry B. Hissong describe the way GGI was implemented in a juvenile institution in Kentucky. In this setting, groups met five times a week for ninety-minute sessions. Every attempt was made to form groups that were homogeneous in sex, delinquent sophistication, and physical and emotional maturity. The group therapist checked daily with cottage parents, work supervisors, and other staff to determine the problems that were being manifested by various group members. Each meeting focused on the problems of a single youth. Residents were encouraged to disclose their problems as long as their acting out did not harm others. In return for their commitment to the prosocial values of the group process, group members had some say about when they were ready for release.[37]

A great strength of GGI is its determination to circumvent the values of the delinquent-peer subculture. This modality, in urging residents to be honest and open with one another, attempts to move group participants to a more positive, prosocial stance. Another advantage is that it represents a comprehensive strategy for dealing with troubled youth. In effect, it is a total system for mitigating the impact of a delinquent subculture. A third advantage is that GGI seems to have gained acceptance on the state level. Also important is the fact that GGI can be led by line staff, thereby increasing staff involvement in the treatment process. A final advantage is that responsibility is given to offenders; thus, in interacting with peers, offenders become aware of their problems and are directed toward resolutions.

A major problem in using GGI is the shortage of trained group leaders. Also, since this approach to group work lacks a single spokesman, a number of versions and designs of the basic principles have emerged. As a consequence, no clear and consistent philosophy guides the process of working with offenders in groups. The emphasis of GGI on peer group norms and values further tends to slight the importance of individualism. Extreme care must be taken to ensure that peer group norms established and monitored by institutional staff do not repress the youthful offenders' needs for self-identity and autonomy. Finally, peer group norms created by GGI may not always be transferable to actual life situations that will be encountered upon release.

Although the research findings on GGI have been mixed, the general picture that emerges is that a GGI experience in a nonresidential program is at least as effective as and much less costly than confinement in a state facility and that a GGI experience in an institutional program seems to have more positive impact on less delinquent youngsters.[38]

Positive Peer Culture

The concept of **positive peer culture (PPC)** generated considerable excitement in juvenile corrections, especially in the 1970s. Developed by Harry Vorrath and associates as an outgrowth of GGI, PPC has been implemented in all of the juvenile state institutions in West Virginia, Michigan, and Missouri.[39]

Vorrath believes that PPC "is a total system for building positive youth subcultures."[40] The main philosophy of PPC is to "turn around" the negative peer culture and to mobilize the power of the peer group in a positive way. PPC does this by teaching group members to care for one another; caring is defined as wanting what is best for a person. Vorrath believes that once caring becomes "fashionable" and is accepted by the group, "hurting goes out of style."[41]

PPC involves the same stages as GGI, but it places more emphasis on positive behavior. Group members learn to speak of positive behaviors as "great," "intelligent," "independent," "improving," and "winning." In contrast, negative behaviors are described as "childish," "unintelligent," "helpless," "destructive," "copping out," and "losing."

Vorrath acknowledges the pervasiveness of peer influence and feels that winning over its subculture is necessary if its influence is to be positively rechanneled. Young people, according to Vorrath, can become experts in dealing with the problems of other young people. The group meetings sponsored by PPC, however, must break through the antisocial values of young offenders if such meetings are to be positive.

PPC is developed through ninety-minute meetings five times per week. Characterized by trust and openness, PPC focuses on the direct and immediate problems of the lawbreaking youth. Believing that groups function most effectively when they are homogeneous, leaders try to include youths who are similar in age, sex, maturity, and delinquency sophistication. Coeducational groups are believed to be counterproductive.

Groups are made up of nine youths who sit in a circle; the leader is part of the circle but sits at a desk. The meeting is usually opened by each youth in turn talking about the particular problems encountered that day. Then the group decides, largely based on what has been said, who will "have" the meeting. Instead of this person being on the "hot seat," as might be the case in some encounter groups, PPC provides a context in which help is received from other group members. The group leader, a line staff member who works directly with residents, concludes the meeting with an eight- or ten-minute summary of what has taken place.

The group leader in this modality is not a therapist in the traditional sense, but instead is a special teacher or coach who instructs, guides, redirects, and motivates the group to work on problems. The leader, who must be both an effective limit setter and a sympathetic listener, also needs to have a kind of mystique. Since part of the leader's responsibility is to build a degree of anxiety into the group, group members must be prevented from understanding and predicting the leader's behavior. But the primary basis of this mystique rests in the leader's knowledge of what is taking place in the group. All interactions and the functioning of each group member must be understood. The leader can keep the group off balance by perceiving what takes place "backstage." To fulfill this demanding leadership role, the leader must be able to detect rigged meetings, read nonverbal behavior, protect weaker members from being hurt by the group process, discover each resident's basic problem, and neutralize negative or controlling leadership in the group.

The negative indigenous leader (NIL) poses a significant challenge to this group process. Usually operating with assistants, this strong peer leader generally is adept at handling staff and skilled in playing roles. Because the NIL assesses the situation, plans moves in advance, and keeps cool under stress, he or she is a real threat to a positive, caring group. To thwart this negative leader, Vorrath suggests that the most effective strategy is to undercut any foundations of peer support, which can be accomplished by capturing the lieutenants. But, according to PPC, the lieutenants must be captured outside of the group so that the NIL cannot come to their defense. This capture can be effected by making the lieutenants responsible for both their own behavior and that of the NIL. The group leader is advised to push this a step further and to accuse the lieutenants of disloyalty to the NIL. If they really cared, the rationale states, they would want to help their leader. Once the lieutenants are captured, Vorrath recommends that new roles be given to them so that they can use their strength positively.

Vorrath also believes that the group has to be involved in decision-making processes, such as whether to give a youth a home visit or when to release a resident. Although he acknowledges that institutional staff ultimately must make these decisions, he states that the recommendations initially should come from the group members. The group, in discussing the possibility of releasing a member, concerns itself with both the member's present problems and those he or she will experience in the community.

Certain problems are implicit in the use of PPC. First, where does PPC expect to find these "ideal" leaders? The authors have met relatively few staff in juvenile corrections who come anywhere near to filling these high expectations. Also, Vorrath seems to underestimate the ingenuity and resourcefulness of peer subcultures. This modality suggests, for example, that staff must remain beyond the understanding and predictability of their charges. When it is remembered how intensively residents study staff, this presents an almost impossible obstacle to the average person. And, even if staff members could build a high enough wall around themselves to avoid disclosing "where they are coming from," this wall might be so high that their care and love could not break through. Is it possible, too, to teach caring relationships to youths who have experienced exploitation and deprivation all their lives and who, in fact, see life as a total survival experience? An additional problem is neutralizing lieutenants and, ultimately, the NIL, for it is not likely that this youth will give up as easily as Vorrath suggests. Finally, although Vorrath believes that the basic assumptions of these youths can be changed, few people change many of their background assumptions over the period of a lifetime—much less when they are stripped of their freedom and are in therapy.

For this modality to be properly evaluated and for these and other questions to be answered, more research is needed. But its present successes should remind both followers and critics that PPC remains one of the most promising ways to treat, change, correct, and rehabilitate juvenile offenders.

DRUG AND ALCOHOL ABUSE INTERVENTIONS

Drug and alcohol abuse by juveniles, as well as their drug trafficking in the community, constitutes a serious social problem today. A director of guidance in a training school acknowledged the seriousness of the problem when he said, "Rarely do we get a boy who doesn't have some history of drug or alcohol abuse in his background."[42]

Drug and alcohol abuse interventions increasingly are being developed in community-based and institutional settings to assist those who need help with such problems. These groups are being conducted in training schools in at least three ways. First, institutionalized juveniles assessed to have a problem with alcohol and/or drugs are placed in a separate cottage or in a chemical-abuse group. Specialized staff are hired to work in these cottages or lead these groups. Second, in other training schools, the social worker or another cottage staff member conducts ongoing drug and alcohol abuse groups. Third, outside groups, such as Alcoholics Anonymous (AA) or Narcotics Anonymous (NA), come into the institution and hold sessions for interested residents.

In considering the extensiveness of the problem of drug use and trafficking among juvenile offenders, there are still too few programs being offered in juvenile placements. The programs that are offered tend to be relatively unsophisticated, lacking adequate theoretical design, treatment integrity, and evaluation

Twelve-step programs for addicted youths are popular in institutions as well as in community-based programs. (Photo courtesy of Ohio Department of Youth Services.)

follow-up. Unquestionably, effective alcohol and drug abuse programs represent one of the most important challenges of juvenile justice today.

COGNITIVE-BEHAVIORAL INTERVENTIONS

S. Yochelson and S. E. Samenow's research at St. Elizabeth Hospital in Washington, DC, with the criminally insane concluded that there exists a criminal personality that incorporates some fifty-two errors in thinking.[43] In the 1980s, this notion that offenders have certain personality characteristics leading to basic errors in thinking became popular as society's need to control and reform serious habitual offenders increased. During the 1980s, the Ohio Department of Youth Services used this approach in some of its institutions, and the Paint Creek Youth Center also incorporated Yochelson and Samenow's principles into the facility's token economy or point system. During the 1990s, the "thinking errors," or criminal orientation, approach was widely adopted throughout the nation (see Focus on Programs 11–3 for the list of errors in thinking used by staff members of Four Oaks, Inc., an eighteen-day treatment and residential center for conduct disorder youths in Iowa).

The basic rationale of the **cognitive-behavioral interventions** is to identify the errors characteristic of a youthful offender's thinking. These errors include the blaming of others, the attempt to control or manipulate, the inability to empathize, the desire to play a victim role, the failure to accept obligations, and the attempt to lie or confuse.[44] The therapist attempts to determine the sequence of thoughts, feelings, events, and other factors that make up the *offense syndrome* and then to get the offender to "own" his or her behaviors. Once the offender takes responsibility for his or her actions, he or she is then taught how to intervene in the illegal behavior when it first starts in order to bring it under control. After a prolonged period of treatment, the offender is moved into residential aftercare, joins a support group, and is given continuing access to treatment.[45]

What is involved here is a cognitive restructuring strategy that is specifically targeted at the dysfunctional cognitive patterns of offenders. These

FOCUS ON PROGRAMS   **11–3**
DEFINITION OF THINKING ERRORS

1. Closed Channel—The criminal communicates from a closed position.

   a. When he talks, he controls what others know about him.
   b. When he listens, he lacks receptivity.
   c. When he evaluates, it is from a position of self-righteousness, faulting or blaming others.

2. Fragmentation—Fluctuation in interests, attitudes and goals . . . result in the criminal making good starts and poor finishes.

3. Uniqueness—The criminal tends to think about himself as different than others, usually superior.

4. Superoptimism—The criminal tends to think that he will be successful in all he undertakes because of his uniqueness; therefore, preparation and effort are not needed. Superoptimism is absolutely essential prior to and during criminal activity.

5. Pride—The criminal takes pride in his ability to live by his wits, to do what others are fearful of doing and [in] his "tough guy" view of himself.

6. Pretentiousness—[There is] a component of power and control whereby the criminal displays his inflated, "big shot" image in an effort to impress the world.

7. Failure to Assume Obligations—The criminal views an obligation as something that controls him. Failing to assume an obligation results in hardship for people who depend on him, i.e., child, spouse, employer.

8. Ownership—[There is] an attitude whereby the criminal assumes possession of other people's property and domination over other people.

9. Failure to Make an Effort or Endure Adversity—Because of his uniqueness thinking, and superoptimism thinking, the criminal doesn't believe he should have to put forth effort or endure hardship to accomplish a goal.

10. Lack of Time Perspective—The criminal's time frame is mainly in the present. There is little learning from the past or using the present to prepare for the future.

11. Poor Decision Making—[This is] the outcome of poor reasoning, failure to find out facts or consider the future from a responsible perspective.

12. Lack of Trust—The criminal demands [that] others trust him but objects to trusting others.

13. Anger—The criminal [uses] anger to control and regain control of others.

14. I Can't—The criminal [says] "I can't" when he really means "I don't want to" or "I am not going to," [which] results in rejecting responsible behavior.

15. Victimstance—The criminal uses this thinking pattern when being held accountable for wrongdoing in an attempt to avoid punishment.

Source: Materials used as part of staff training at Four Oaks, Inc., in Iowa.

Critical Thinking Questions:
Do you think it would be difficult to identify these thinking errors in youthful offenders? Would it be difficult for a youth to change his or her thinking errors?

dysfunctional cognitive patterns, or thinking errors, serve to support, excuse, and even reinforce criminal behavior. This approach presumes that the use of such errors releases inhibitions toward committing a crime, which "frees one" to behave in a criminal or delinquent manner. The job of the counselor is to correct these thinking errors, and the task of the facility is to provide an environment in which such errors can be corrected by treatment, by custody staff, and also by residents in group sessions or day-to-day institutional living.[46]

In sum, this modality is being used increasingly across the nation, largely because of the popularity of the get tough approach. Still, little evidence suggests that it has any short- or long-term benefits to juveniles who receive such a treatment intervention.

INTERVENTION WITH JUVENILE SEX OFFENDERS

Violent sex crimes often shape the public's perception of sex offenders and sex offending. The view that immediately comes to mind is that of an adult male who by force, guile, or cunning persuades a young person to perform sexual acts deemed inappropriate or illegal by society.[47] These image of adult offenders are assumed to be true of all youthful sex offenders as well; the result is pressure is put on legislators to "pass a law" that somehow will punish youthful sex offenders severely and that will deter others from committing sex offenses (see Focus on the Law 11–4) Adolescents who are growing up, learning how to develop age-appropriate relationships, and assimilating the rules of society often become surprised victims of overzealous citizens, legislators, and prosecutors. Given this perspective, just what is the reality of juvenile sex offending, and how accurate is the imagery?

The *Uniform Crime Reports* indicate that of 17,914 arrests for forcible rape committed in the year 2000, 1,142, or 6 percent, were youths under the age of fifteen and 2,937, or 16 percent, were under the age of eighteen. Of the arrests for other sex offenses, 5,933, or 9.7 percent, involved youths under the age of fifteen, and 11,399, or 18.6 percent, involved youths eighteen years of age or younger.[48] But do these figures account for all types of juvenile sex offending?

An accurate answer to this question is unknown. Much juvenile sexual behavior is concealed in the confines of family, community, and school and remains hidden. Even if it is discovered, children, parents, and teachers may be confused as to what really happened and are often ashamed or embarrassed by their own behavior and by that of their own children, relations, and family friends. Many victims will not report sexual victimization because they believe they deserved what happened, feel guilty, do not want to get others in trouble, or somehow believe that what happened was normal. Yet, the victims often end up psychologically distraught and damaged; sleeplessness, anxiety, depression, sexual dysfunction, and suicide can result. Damaged emotions and fear destroy their ability to form lasting relationships, and many victims' marriages are filled with violence or do not last. The cost to individuals and society often is perpetuated because many imprisoned adolescent and adult sex offenders report having been abused as youths. The cost of a sex offense early in life often extends into adulthood.

Are all sex offenders alike? No. Their relationships with each other and their personal motives vary widely, making them a diverse lot. The offending behaviors range from noncontact offenses such as voyeurism and exhibitionism to contact offenses such as touching and fondling to sexual penetration with body parts or foreign objects. Most sex offenders also commit nonsexual offenses at rates similar to those of other juvenile offenders. For example, children who experience neglect and physical abuse and who witness family violence are more likely to commit sexual offenses than

FOCUS ON THE LAW   11–4
THE TEEN SEX OFFENDER

The victims of sex offenders frequently are scarred for life. Coercive or violent rape by family members, friends, serial offenders, or members of the same sex devastates victims emotionally. In addition to the physical pain and suffering they experience, these victims wrestle with depression, sleepless nights, and fear of others; many are never able to form normal emotional relationships with others they love. These reasons alone are sufficient to incur society's wrath, but when murder accompanies the act, members of society become particularly incensed, and legislators succumb willingly to public pressures to take up the charge for action. Often knee-jerk reactions take the place of reason, and the laws that are passed have unintended consequences.

Teenage boys often are the unwitting victims of legislators' zeal. Not that what the boys do is right, but consider the following: sixteen- and seventeen-year-old boys frequently have sex with their fourteen- and fifteen-year-old girlfriends—both of whom intend to marry each other. Some youths engage in "heavy" petting and sexual experimentation with members of the opposite sex on dates. In one case, a boy was dared by his friends at a football game to touch a girl's breast. He did, and he, along with the other youths noted above, are now registered as sex offenders by their state.

The consequences of this registration are enormous. Some of these youths may be tried in juvenile or adult courts and remanded to juvenile or adult institutions. They are placed on extended supervision when they get out. Their names are kept on police "watch" lists. People living in their neighborhoods or parents who have children in schools will not want them anywhere near them. The "offenders'" names may be published on informal sex offender lists on the Internet and be available to all. Many states publish formal lists and may require youths to register for periods of time ranging from ten to twenty-five years to life. These youths will be unable to get into the military or obtain private security jobs; they cannot become doctors, nurses, school teachers, scout masters, or band directors or coach youth sports teams; some companies will not hire them. The youths are labeled for life.

Source: Prepared for this volume by the authors.

Critical Thinking Questions:
In your opinion, is justice served concerning sex offenders? What should be done with boys responding to dares or having sex with their girlfriends? Develop a system of classification for sex offenders.

those who do not, although at an only modestly higher rate.[49] Also, sex offenders who have had prior consensual sexual experiences have higher rates of offending than those without such experiences.

In addition to early sexual experience, offenders tend to come from families that are either unstable or dysfunctional, that is, families with problems of neglect or physical, emotional, or sexual abuse.[50] These backgrounds appear to be related to juvenile sex offenders having deficient social skills, poor relationships with their peers, and being socially isolated. Ferrara and McDonald, in a review of the literature, estimated that one-quarter to one-third of sex offenders have some form of neurological impairment.[51] Other studies document conduct disorder and antisocial traits in juvenile sex offenders. A limited number of studies suggest that pornography plays some role in juvenile offending.[52]

More important, a study by Ryan et al. determined that only one-third of juvenile offenders perceive sex as a way to show love and support to another person; 24 percent perceive that sex is a way to feel power and control; 9.4 percent, as a way to get rid of anger; and 8.4 percent, as a means to hurt, degrade, or punish others.[53]

How Do We Treat Sex Offenders?

The *sexual abuse cycle* is referred to frequently throughout the sex offender literature. The assumption behind the concept is that sex offenders engage in a pattern of emotional and thinking processes that lead them to sex offending and that must be broken if offenders are to be helped with their problems. Righthand and Welch describe the cycle as follows:

> The concept is based on the premise that offending is preceded by a negative self-image that contributes to negative coping strategies when the juvenile anticipates negative responses from others, perceives such responses, or both. To avoid such negative anticipated or perceived reactions, the juvenile withdraws, becomes socially isolated, and fantasizes to compensate for resulting feelings of powerlessness and a lack of control. This process culminates in the sex offense, which results in more negative experiences, more feelings of rejection, and an increasingly negative self-image; and the cycle continues.[54]

This model is not empirically based and has several limitations. Much abusive behavior, such as that committed by "naive experimenters," nonrecidivists, group offenders, and youths who suffer from psychopathological or deviant sexual arousal, does not fit easily into the stages of this cycle.

The treatment goals of many programs for sex offenders include breaking the sex offense cycle. Youths are encouraged to assume responsibility for their abusive behavior and to increase their positive and constructive behaviors in both thinking and relations to others. These goals are designed to prevent further sexual misconduct and the emergence of psychosexual problems and, conversely, to help youths develop appropriate relationships with peers of their own age. Therapists attempt to achieve these goals through individual, group and family interventions. For more extensive examination of the treatment of juvenile sex offenders, see the statement by Domenick A. Lombardo in the *Voices* (of offenders and professionals) *in the Juvenile Justice System* supplement.

LAW-RELATED EDUCATION

Law-related education (LRE) is an educational program designed to promote the development of characteristics that lead to healthy behavior. LRE is designed to teach students the fundamental principles and skills needed to become responsible citizens in a constitutional democracy. Programs are characterized by high-interest course material; wide use of volunteer resource persons from the justice system; field experiences (court tours, internships, and police ride-alongs); student-involved teaching methods (group discussions and poster making); and cocurricular activities (mock trials and other public performances).[55]

LRE has experienced remarkable growth since 1975. A 1985 national survey revealed that LRE has been added to the curriculum in more than half of the forty-six states involved in the study.[56] In 1992, fifty-six programs in training schools, diversion, detention, and community-based settings used law-related education.[57]

An instructor of LRE in a midwestern training school for boys had this to say about the program:

> Our program is based on teaching aspects of the law as it relates to everyday life. A lot of these kids haven't been habilitated in the first place, and what we try to do is to teach them such skills as problem solving and critical thinking, conflict resolution, communication skills and empathy, and avoidance of triggers or verbal and nonverbal cues that elicit negative emotions. We do this by dealing with social issues and by discussing the legal system, including the attorney's role and rights of offenders. We have had this program for the [past] eleven years and are very happy with it. Kids are interested in it, and we hope that they apply it to their own lives when they are released.[58]

One of the few studies evaluating LRE programs found that, when properly conducted, these programs can reduce tendencies toward delinquent behavior and improve a range of attitudes related to responsible citizenship. Successful students, this study found, were also less likely to associate with delinquent peers and to use violence as a means of resolving conflict.[59] Although it is unreasonable to believe that such a knowledge-based course would have much impact on hard-core youthful offenders, it could very well be that LRE is a valuable delinquent prevention program.

GANG DEACTIVATION GROUPS

Gangs, as noted in previous chapters, constitute one of the most serious problems facing juvenile justice today. One of the pioneer projects for working with gangs was the previously discussed House of Umoja. A number of other community projects have been developed to work with youth gangs. The most widely known of these projects are the Youth-in-Action (Chester, Pennsylvania), El Control del Puebo (New York City), the Inner City Roundtable of Youth (New York City), the Youth Identity Program, Inc. (New York City), the South Arsenal Neighborhood Development Corporation (Hartford, Connecticut), and SEY Yes, Inc. (Los Angeles). The basic purpose of these treatment interventions is to defuse the violence of youth gangs within urban communities and to involve gang members in more constructive activities.

In the 1990s, with the spread of gangs throughout the nation, the Maclaren Training School in Portland, Oregon; the Ethan Allen School in Wales, Wisconsin; and the School for Boys in Eldora, Iowa found it necessary to develop specialized groups for their increasingly large numbers of gang members.[60] Usually required and perhaps even court mandated, these sessions generally consist of twelve or thirteen sessions focusing on **gang deactivation**—that is, removing youths from gang involvements. In the training school in Eldora, Iowa, which probably includes the most sophisticated model of gang deactivation, the groups were led for years by Samuel Dillon, a former gang leader in the Blackstone Rangers.

WHY IS TREATMENT EFFECTIVENESS SO DIFFICULT TO ATTAIN?

The overall quality of treatment in juvenile justice is not impressive. Enforced offender rehabilitation has sometimes resulted in making delinquents worse rather than better through treatment. The frequent criticism that offender rehabilitation is defective in theory and a disaster in practice has been true on too many occasions. Program designs have often given little consideration to what a particular program can realistically accomplish with a particular group of offenders and have frequently relied on a single cure for a variety of complex problems. In addition, programs generally have lacked integrity, because they have not delivered the services they claimed with sufficient strength to accomplish the goals of treatment. Furthermore, the research on offender rehabilitation has generally been inadequate, with many projects and reports on rehabilitation almost totally lacking in well-developed research designs.[61]

Still, enough progress has been made that the various meta-analyses and literature reviews from the 1980s indicated that treatment programs had somewhat greater success in reducing recidivism than earlier studies had revealed.[62] The emerging picture that has received increased support in the past decade is that "'something' apparently works though no generic method or approach, as distinct from individual programs, especially shines." Or, to state this differently, several methods appear promising, but none has produced major reductions in recidivism.[63]

To improve the quality of institutional treatment even further, three basic steps appear to be necessary: (1) more programs must include the ingredients of effective interventions; (2) more programs must be based on better program design, ensure higher program integrity, and be evaluated by more rigorous research methods; and (3) research must provide more information on what works for whom and in what context.

INGREDIENTS OF EFFECTIVE PROGRAMS

Effective programs usually have a number of ingredients in common. They usually are set up by an inspired individual or group of individuals, have developed a unified-team approach among staff, have a transmittable philosophy of life, trust offenders with decision-making responsibilities, help offenders develop needed skills, are regarded as unique and different by offenders, and provide an integration treatment model.[64]

The Inspired Leader Who Means Business

The inspired individual or group of individuals who has serious dedication in setting up a program has been found time after time to be one of the chief ingredients of effective programs. In Outward Bound, Kurt Hahn was able to generate enthusiasm and support among those who contacted him.[65] Sister Falaka Fattah and her husband also set up the House of Umoja in Philadelphia, committed to deal with the gang problem in that urban community.[66] The inspiration of Clifford Shaw continues to influence the Chicago Area Projects long after his death.

Unified Treatment Team

A program is more likely to have an impact on offenders if the treatment team is unified. In a unified treatment team, all staff members become treatment agents as they design the program, develop short- and long-range goals for the program, and involve themselves with offenders.

Philosophy of Life That is Transmittable

Effective programs also generate a sense of mission or purpose among offenders by transmitting a philosophy of life. Martin Groder has noted, "It's not that the guy has to adopt the philosophy of the program, but he's got to learn it well enough to integrate it with his own life experience and come out with his own version."[67] Bartollas, Miller, and Dinitz reported that having a mission or purpose in life is one characteristic of hard-core offenders who are later successful in the community.[68]

Involvement of Offenders in the Decision-Making Process

Effective programs also frequently provide decision-making responsibilities for juvenile offenders. Although many correctional interventions treat these offenders as helpless children incapable of making decisions for themselves, the more noteworthy programs encourage decision making and then make participants responsible for their choices. The more offenders are permitted to make choices concerning what happens to them, the more likely they are to be involved in a treatment program and to seek to benefit from it.

Skill Development

Effective programs include **skill development,** which helps offenders learn new tasks that prepare them for adjustment in the community. These range from educational and vocational to interpersonal and problem-solving skills. Such abilities make offenders believe that they can accomplish something or that they have acquired important insights about themselves or about life.

Uniqueness

The most distinguishing characteristic of effective interventions is sometimes their uniqueness. That is, the components of these programs that make them different from other correctional interventions are sometimes the most important factors in grabbing the attention of youthful offenders and getting them involved in these interventions.

Integrated Treatment Model

The states of Washington, Texas, and Colorado have developed integrated treatment models, and California is in the process of developing such a model. These programs based their treatment philosophy and intervention on cognitive-behavioral treatment. The **integrated treatment model** provides the central guiding vision that unites screening, assessment, case planning, treatment, transition, and aftercare. These concepts are used across all parts of the juvenile correctional system, including the core treatment program, special treatment programs, work, education, recreation, mental health, and parole. All staff members, including administrators, treatment providers, support staff, and line staff, receive training in the model. This not only helps structure the environment to promote success in changing behavior but also creates a common treatment vocabulary for all parts of the agency. Another advantage of this integrated model is that it provides adequate community follow-up in order for offenders to sustain positive changes in their lives.[69]

STRATEGY FOR IMPROVING THE EFFECTIVENESS OF CORRECTIONAL PROGRAMS

Improving program effectiveness requires that program designs be based on theoretical premises, that programs be implemented with integrity, and that programs be evaluated with rigorous research methods.

Program Design

The theoretical premises, or constructs, of programs must be examined in order to determine whether they are appropriate for particular groups of offenders. The processes by which any set of interventions will change antisocial behavior must also be examined in order to determine whether the treatment has sufficient strength to produce the desired behavior or attitudinal change. Finally, the theoretical constructs must be meshed with the setting in which treatment takes place to ensure that programs are implemented in appropriate settings.[70]

Program Implementation

Juvenile offenders must be placed in the right program at the optimal time for them to benefit from treatment. Effective interventions must actually deliver the services they claim to deliver, with sufficient strength to accomplish the goals of treatment. In addition, program integrity requires that personnel be equipped to deliver the specified services; thus, treatment personnel must have some degree of expertise in what they are doing, must have sufficient training to do it, and must receive adequate supervision. Finally, it must be possible to modify interventions according to changing interests and needs of offenders.[71]

Program Evaluation

The Panel on Research on Rehabilitative Techniques concluded after nearly two years of examining offender rehabilitation that "the research methodology that has been brought to bear on the problem of finding ways to rehabilitate criminal offenders has been generally so inadequate that only a relatively few studies warrant any unequivocal interpretations.[72] Sample sizes must be large enough to measure subtle effects, such as changes in interactions. True randomized experiments must be conducted whenever feasible because they permit some certainty about causal relationships. Researchers need to identify the common elements of effective programs and to determine how these elements affect success with particular groups of offenders. In addition, researchers need to determine how effective programs can be replicated in other settings. Finally, more empirical work must be done on measuring the outcomes of correctional treatment.[73]

WHAT WORKS FOR WHOM AND IN WHAT CONTEXT

Correctional treatment must discover what works for which offenders in what context. In other words, correctional treatment could work if amenable offenders were offered appropriate treatments by matched workers in environments conducive to producing positive effects.[74]

To match individual offenders with the treatments most likely to benefit them will be no easy task. Only through well-planned and soundly executed research will the necessary information be gained. The Panel of Rehabilitative Techniques recommends the use of the "template-matching technique."[75] This technique creates a set of descriptors, or a *template*, of the kinds of people who are most likely to benefit from a particular treatment according to the theory or basic assumptions underlying it.[76] Because of the scarcity of treatment resources, matching programs to those offenders most likely to profit from them is only sensible.

Palmer's approach is somewhat different in determining what works for which offenders in what contexts. He suggests that effective intervention for each offender must take seriously internal difficulties, skill deficits, and external pressures and disadvantages:

1. Skill/Capacity Deficits. Various, often major, developmental challenges—frequently including life and social skills deficits in such areas as educational and vocational abilities

2. External Pressures/Disadvantages. Major environmental pressures and/or major social disadvantages, including comparatively limited or reduced family, community, and other supports or social assistance.

3. Internal Difficulties. Long-standing or situational feelings, attitudes, and defenses; ambivalence regarding change; particular motivations, desires, and personal and interpersonal commitments.[77]

✓**Progress Check 11.2**
Review this section at
www.prenhall.com/bartollas

SUMMARY

This chapter discusses and evaluates the basic treatment modalities in juvenile justice.

- These therapies can be grouped under insight (psychotherapy, transactional analysis, law-related education, and errors in thinking approach).
- They can be grouped in terms of behavior treatment (reality therapy and behavioral modification).
- They can be grouped in terms of group therapy (guided group interaction, positive peer culture, drug and alcohol interventions, and gang deactivation groups. See Table 11–1 for the relationship of these modalities to one another.
- One of the contentions of this chapter is that we may have expected too much from correctional treatment.
- Long-term training schools are among the least promising places for treatment to take place.
- But even in community-based programs, the lack of resources for overworked staff, clients' histories of failure, and drug and alcohol addictions result in far more failures than successes.
- The danger, however, is to expect too little from correctional treatment.
- Some youthful offenders do benefit from treatment in community-based or institutional settings. The programs may simply make their present confinement or restrictions more bearable, or they may provide a purpose for offenders so that they can go on to live free from crime.
- Thus, some programs are effective, and some treatment agents do have positive impacts on youthful offenders.
- The future effectiveness of correctional treatment in juvenile justice may be contingent on three conditions:

1. Funding research so that more effective technologies can be developed.
2. Identifying what works for which group of offenders so that youthful offenders interested in treatment can be given the interventions most compatible with their needs and interests.
3. Creating more humane environments, where residents are treated with dignity and respect, so that environmental conditions will not interfere with the treatment process.

Table 11–1 Treatment Technologies

Type	Treatment Goal	Qualifications of Therapist	Length of Treatment	Frequency of Treatment	Expected Offender Response
Individual or group psychotherapy	Lead youths to insight	Psychiatrist, psychologist, psychiatric social worker	Frequently extensive or long term	Several times per week if possible	Will examine individual problems with therapist
Transactional analysis	Lead youths to insight	Psychiatrist, psychologist, trained nonprofessional staff	Usually several months	Once or more per week	Will examine individual problems in a group context and will learn a new approach to interpersonal relationships
Reality therapy	Help youths to fulfill basic needs	Psychiatrist, psychologist, trained nonprofessional staff	Short period of time	Once or more per week	To learn reality responsible behavior, and right from wrong
Behavior modification	Help youths to react positively	Anyone who can assume role of therapist	Usually long term	Continuous rather than interwoven with nontreatment	To continue their reinforced, positive behavior
Guided group interaction	Develop prosocial norms and values	Anyone trained in GGI	Several months	Four or five times per week	Will become responsible for others in the group
Positive peer culture	Develop prosocial norms and values	Anyone trained in PPC	Several months	Four or five times per week	Will genuinely care for other group members
Drug and alcohol abuse programs	Help youths to overcome addiction	Anyone who has understanding of problem	Extensive or long term	Once or more per week	Will gain skills and knowledge to overcome substance abuse
Errors in thinking approach	Insight into individual behavior	Psychiatrist, psychologist, psychiatric social worker	Extensive or long term	Once or more per week	To learn responsible and prosocial behavior
Skill development programs	Personal empowerment	Anyone who can assume role of staff member	Short or long term	Daily	Will gain skills and knowledge to pursue positive behavior
Family therapy	Insight into family dynamics	Psychiatrist, psychologist, psychiatric social worker	Usually several months	Once or more per week	Will examine family problems with therapist
Law-related education	Help youths to react positively	Anyone trained in LRE	Usually long term	Once or more per week	To learn responsibility and prosocial behavior
Gang deactivation groups	Help youths to withdraw from gangs	Anyone with understanding of gangs	Several months	Once or more per week	To empower youths so they no longer need the gang

WEB SITE OF INTEREST

Information on criminal and juvenile justice treatment networks can be found at
http://www.maine.gov/dhns/osa/cj/juvenile/jtn.htm

CRITICAL THINKING QUESTIONS

1. Do you agree that no treatment is effective for juvenile offenders?
2. If you were superintendent of a training school, which treatment methods would you use? Why? What treatment technologies would you use in a residential program for juvenile probationers?
3. What type of staff member would be effective in carrying out the treatment method you have chosen? Why?
4. Would you hire ex-offenders to work in your community-based or institutional facility? Why or why not?
5. Do you feel that the goals of PPC are realistic?
6. How would you treat youths who do not respond to the rules of your prescribed treatment method?

NOTES

1. Interviewed in 1989.
2. Walter C. Bailey, "Correctional Outcome: An Evaluation of 100 Reports," *Journal of Criminal Law, Criminology, and Police Science* 57 (June 1957), 153–60.
3. J. Robison and G. Smith, "The Effectiveness of Correctional Programs," *Crime and Delinquency* 17 (1971), 67–70.
4. Robert Martinson, "What Works?—Questions and Answers about Prison Reform," *Public Interest* 35 (Spring 1974), 22–54.
5. Douglas Lipton, Robert Martinson, and Judith Wilks, *The Effectiveness of Correctional Treatment* (New York: Praeger, 1975).
6. CBS Television Network. Excerpted from *60 Minutes* segment, "It Doesn't Work" (August 24, 1975).
7. Ted Palmer, "Martinson Revisited," *Journal of Research in Crime and Delinquency* 12 (July 1975), 133–52.
8. Ibid., 137.
9. Paul Gendreau and Robert Ross, "Effective Correctional Treatment: Bibliotherapy for Cynics," *Crime and Delinquency* 27 (October 1979), 463–89.
10. Robert R. Ross and Paul Gendreau, eds., *Effective Correctional Treatment* (Toronto: Butterworth, 1980), viii.
11. Robert Martinson, "New Findings, New Views: A Note of Caution Regarding Sentencing Reform," *Hofstra Law Review* 7 (Winter 1979), 244.
12. Paul Gendreau and Robert R. Ross, "Revivification of Rehabilitative Evidence," *Justice Quarterly* 4 (September 1987), 349–407.
13. Ibid. For a review of the meta-analyses of correctional treatment in the 1980s, see Ted Palmer, *The Re-Emergence of Correctional Intervention* (Newbury Park, CA: Sage Publications, 1992), 50–76.
14. James McGuire and Philip Priestley, "Reviewing 'What Works': Past, Present, and Future," in *What Works: Reducing Reoffending—Guidelines from Research and Practice*, edited by James McGuire (New York: Wiley, 1995), 7–8.

15. Ibid.

16. Palmer, *The Re-Emergence of Correctional Intervention*, xiii.

17. Ibid., 4.

18. Marguerite Q. Warren, "The Community Treatment Project: History and Prospects," in *Law Enforcement Science and Technology*, edited by S. A. Yefsky (Washington, DC: Thompson Book Company, 1972), 193–95.

19. Roy Gerard, "Institutional Innovations in Juvenile Corrections," *Federal Probation* 34 (December 1970), 38–40.

20. Rhena L. Izzo and Robert R. Ross, "Meta-Analysis of Rehabilitation Programs for Juvenile Delinquents: A Brief Report," *Criminal Justice and Behavior* 17 (March 1990), 139. See also McGuire and Priestley, "Reviewing 'What Works,'" 9–10.

21. Eric Berne, *Transactional Analysis in Psychotherapy* (New York: Grove Press), 355.

22. Thomas A. Harris, *I'm OK—You're OK* (New York: Harper & Row, 1967), 37–53.

23. Eric Berne, *Games People Play,* (New York: Grove Press, 1964), 48.

24. Lois Johnson, "TA with Juvenile Delinquents," *Transactional Analysis Bulletin* 3 (1969), 31.

25. Carl F. Jesness, "The Fricot Ranch Study: Outcomes with Small versus Large Living Groups in the Rehabilitation of Delinquents," Research Report No. 47 Processed (Sacramento: California Youth Authority, October 1965), 89, 90, 313.

26. William Glasser, *Reality Therapy* (New York: Harper & Row, 1965), xii.

27. Ibid., excerpts from 44–45.

28. Ibid., 70.

29. Jesness, "Fricot Ranch Study," 7.

30. J. L. Bernard and R. Eisenman, "Verbal Conditioning in Sociopaths with Spiral and Monetary Reinforcement," *Journal of Personality and Social Psychology* 6 (1976), 203–6.

31. R. Schwitzgebel and D. A. Kolb, "Inducing Behavior Change to Adolescent Delinquents," *Behavior Research Therapy* 1 (1964), 297–304.

32. See Dennis A. Romig, *Justice for Our Children: An Examination of Juvenile Delinquent Rehabilitation Programs* (Lexington, MA: D. C. Heath, 1978), 20–21.

33. Ibid., 87.

34. Ibid., 92–93.

35. Interview with Harry Vorrath quoted in Oliver J. Keller, Jr., and Benedict S. Alper, *Halfway Houses: Community Centered Correction and Treatment* (Lexington, MA: D.C. Heath, 1970), 55.

36. Robert J. Wicks, *Correctional Psychology: Themes and Problems in Correcting the Offender* (San Francisco: Canfield Press, 1974), 50–51.

37. Joseph W. Scott and Jerry B. Hissong, "Changing the Delinquent Subculture: A Sociological Approach," in *Readings in Juvenile Delinquency*, edited by Ruth Shonle Cavan (Philadelphia: J. B. Lippincott, 1975), 486–88.

38. Ibid.

39. The following materials are adapted from Harry H. Vorrath and Larry K. Brendtro, *Positive Peer Culture* (Chicago: Aldine, 1974).

40. Ibid.

41. Ibid.

42. Interviewed in 1986 in a midwestern training school.

43. S. Yochelson and S. E. Samenow, *The Criminal Personality*, 2 vols. (New York: J. Aronson, 1976, 1977).

44. David Berenson, *Ohio Department of Youth Services Sex Offender Project: Preliminary Report on a Treatment Program for Adolescent Sex Offenders* (Columbus, OH: Department of Youth Services, 1989).

45. Ibid., 6–8.

46. David Lester and Patricia Van Voorhis, "Cognitive Therapies," in *Correctional Counseling and Rehabilitation,* 3d ed., edited by Patricia Van Voorhis, Michael Braswell, and David Lester (Cincinnati: Anderson Publishing, 1997), 172.

47. Materials from this section are drawn largely from Sue Righthand and Carlann Welch, *Juveniles Who Have Sexually Offended: A Review of the Professional Literature* (Washington, DC: OJJDP, 2001). Wherever appropriate, the authors of this text refer the reader to the original sources from which Righthand and Welch have drawn their materials.

48. Federal Bureau of Investigation, *Crime in the United States 2000: Uniform Crime Reports* (Washington, DC: U.S. Department of Justice 2001), 226.

49. C. Bagley and D. Shewchuk-Dann, "Characteristics of 60 Children and Adolescents Who Have a History of Sexual Assault Against Others: Evidence from a Controlled Study," *Journal of Child and Youth Care* (Fall Special Issue) (1991), 43–52.

50. Sue Righthand and Carlann Welch, "Juveniles Who Have Sexually Offended: A Review of the Professional Literature" (Washington, DC: OJJDP, March, 2001), *Executive Summary,* xi–xiii.

51. M. L. Ferrara and S. McDonald, *Treatment of the Sex Offender: Neurological and Psychiatric Impairments."* (Northvale, NJ: Jason Aronson, 1996.)

52. Righthand and Welch, "Juveniles Who Have Sexually Offended," 8.

53. G. Ryan, T. J. Miyoshi, J. L. Metzner, R. D. Krugman, and G. E. Fryer, "Trends in a National Sample of Sexually Abusive Youths," *Journal of the American Academy of Child and Adolescent Psychiatry* 35(1) (1996), 17–25.

54. Righthand and Welch, *Juveniles Who Have Sexually Offended.*

55. Norma D. Wright, "From Risk to Resiliency: The Role of Law-Related Education," pamphlet Des Moines, IA: Institute on Law and Civic Education, June 20–21, 1995).

56. Carole L. Hahn, "The Status of the Social Studies in Public Schools of the United States: Another Look," *Social Education* 49 (March 1985), 220–23.

57. National Law-Related Education Resource Center, *Law-Related Education Programs in Juvenile Justice Settings* (Chicago: American Bar Association, September 1992).

58. Interviewed in August 1996.

59. Judith Warren Little and Frances Haley, *Implementing Effective LRE Programs* (Boulder, CO: Social Science Education Consortium, 1982).

60. Catherine H. Conley, *Street Gangs: Current Knowledge and Strategies* (Washington, DC: U.S. Department of Justice, 1993), 55.

61. Lee Sechrest, Susan O. White, and Elizabeth D. Brown, eds., *The Rehabilitation of Criminal Offenders* (Washington, DC: National Academy of Sciences, 1979); and Susan Martin, Lee Sechrest, and Robin Redner, eds., *Rehabilitation of Criminal Offenders: Directions for Research* (Washington, DC: National Academy of Sciences, 1981).

62. For an examination of the various meta-analyses, see Palmer, *Re-Emergence of Intervention,* 50–76. See also Izzo and Ross, "Meta-Analyses of Rehabilitation Programs for Juvenile Delinquents," 134–42.

63. Ibid., 48.

64. These elements of effective programs are suggested by the work of Martin Groder and of Alden D. Miller, Lloyd E. Ohlin, and Robert B. Coates. See

"Dr. Martin Groder: An Angry Resignation," *Corrections Magazine* 1 (July–August 1975), 3; and Alden D. Miller, Lloyd E. Ohlin, and Robert B. Coates, *A Theory of Social Reform: Correctional Change Processes in Two States* (Cambridge, MA: Ballinger, 1977).

65. Joshua L. Miner and Joe Boldt, *Outward Bound USA: Learning Through Experience in Adventure-Based Education* (New York: William Morrow, 1981).

66. Robert L. Woodson, *A Summons to Life: Mediating Structure and the Prevention of Youth Crime* (Cambridge, MA: Ballinger, 1981).

67. "Dr. Martin Groder," 33.

68. Clemens Bartollas, Stuart J. Miller, and Simon Dinitz, "Boys Who Profit: The Limits of Institutional Success," in *Reform in Corrections: Problems and Issues*, edited by Harry E. Allen and Nancy J. Beran (New York: Praeger, 1977), 18–19.

69. Christopher Murray, Chris Baird, Ned Loughran, Fred Mills, and John Platt, *Safety and Welfare Plan: Implementing Reform in California* (Sacramento, CA.: Safety and Welfare Planning Team, 2006), 42.

70. Sechrest et al., eds., *The Rehabilitation of Criminal Offenders*, 35–37.

71. For the development of these various aspects of intervention, see Palmer, *The Re-Emergence of Correctional Intervention*, 151–57.

72. Sechrest et al., eds., *The Rehabilitation of Criminal Offenders*, 3–4.

73. Martin et al., eds., *The Rehabilitation of Criminal Offenders*, 6.

74. Sechrest et al., eds., *The Rehabilitation of Criminal Offenders*, 45.

75. The template-matching technique was originally proposed in D. Bem and D. Funder, "Predicting More of the People More of the Time: Assessing the Personality of Situations," *Psychological Review* 85 (1978), 485–501.

76. Martin et al., *Rehabilitation of Criminal Offenders*, 82.

77. Palmer, *The Re-Emergence of Correctional Intervention*, 113.

12

JUVENILE GANGS

The road to success is a hard one. It begins in the family unit. It is in the family that parents plant the seeds for a young person to succeed. This young person is taught morals and ethics and learns behavior patterns.

By the age of seven or eight, this young person has learned whether he will be loved, whether his needs will be met, and how fair life is. What he thinks will have an effect on his behavior. If he feels he is on the short end of the stick, he may wake up angry as hell in the morning. He will seek elsewhere to have his needs met. He is not in a good place to compete with peer pressure.

It is not long before he is in gangs, doing drugs, and hurting people. It is also not long before he is serving time in the "joint." When he comes out, it is even harder to achieve success. It is a lot easier to go back to crime than to stay away from it.

For those of us who are determined not to go back to a life of crime, we may make it. It takes determination. It takes the opportunity to stand on your own feet. It takes support from others. It takes luck. But we are never out of the woods because it is real easy to go back.

What I am saying is that if we want to deal with youth crime, adult crime, and street gangs, we must go back to the family unit, must improve our schools, must make our neighborhoods more desirable, and must [provide] other alternatives to gangs and drugs.

—Fred "Bobby" Gore[1]

OUTLINE

OBJECTIVES

1. To view how gangs have evolved in the United States
2. To examine the scope of gang activity
3. To investigate how toxic gang activity is to communities
4. To present the seven stages of emergent gang development
5. To discuss why youths join gangs
6. To evaluate how gangs can be prevented and controlled

KEY TERMS

crack	emergent gangs	urban gangs
emerging youth gangs	representing	

"The lure of gang life quickly faded for Fred Gore. He turned away from his early gang membership and committed himself to improving the lives of youths and the quality of Chicago communities. His empathy for the young men and women growing up in Chicago's rough and tumble streets led him to his life work. Mr. Gore's exceptional acumen into social conditions made him an advocate for social change. He has long been one of the city's most insightful community leaders. He is widely recognized as a peace-maker and expert on gangs and he continues to lecture frequently at universities and colleges across the country."

This chapter focuses on youths who are involved in a gang. A gang is usually identified as a group with some sense of identity and permanence and with some involvement in illegal activities.[2] Many youths, especially in urban areas, are involved in adult street gangs.[3] Other youths form gangs or become part of gangs made up of adolescents.

Beginning in 1988 and continuing through the early 1990s, an upsurge of youth gangs suddenly appeared throughout the United States. Some of these youth gangs used names of the national urban gangs, such as the Bloods and Crips from Los Angeles or the Gangster Disciplines, Vice Lords, or Latin Kings from Chicago. Other gangs made up their own names, based on neighborhoods or images they wanted to depict to other peers and the community. By the mid-1990s, nearly every city, many suburban areas, and even some rural areas across the United States experienced the reality of youths who have banded together to form a youth gang.

The good news is that from 1996 to 2003, the estimated number of youth gangs and youth gang members in the United States decreased. According to the 2002 National Youth Gang Survey, an estimated 731,500 gang members and 21,500 gangs were active in the United States in 2002. The estimated number of gang members decreased 14 percent between 1996 and 2002, and the estimated number of jurisdictions that experienced gang problems decreased by 32 percent. One explanation for this decline is that smaller cities and rural counties have been reporting comparatively fewer gang members over the survey years. Approximately 85 percent of the estimated number of gang members in 2002 came from larger cities and suburban counties.[4] Figure 12–1 shows the percentage of law enforcement agencies that reported youth gang problems from 1996 to 2002.

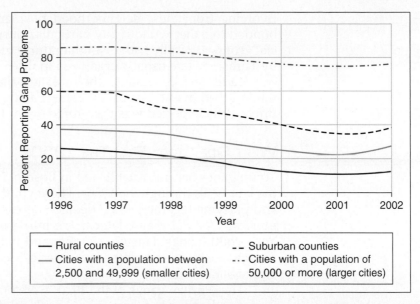

Figure 12–1 *Law Enforcement Agency Reports of Gang Problems, 1996–2002*

Note: For the random-sample groups, the observed variation in the percentage of agencies reporting gang problems from 2000 to 2002 is within the range attributable to sampling error; therefore, it does not represent a definitive change in the estimated number of jurisdictions with gang problems.

Source: Arlen Egley, Jr., and Aline K. Major, *Highlights of the 2002 National Youth Gang Survey* (Washington, DC: Office of Juvenile Justice and Delinquency Prevention, 2004), p. 1.

The bad news is that too many juveniles, especially at-risk youths, are involved in gangs; that gang involvement is likely to lead to further involvement in delinquency and drug use; that gang involvement increases the likelihood of the carrying and use of weapons; and that gang involvement increases the probability of going on to adult crime and of spending time in prison.[5]

HOW HAVE GANGS EVOLVED IN THE UNITED STATES?

Youth gangs may have existed as early as the American Revolution.[6] Others have suggested that they first emerged in the Southwest following the Mexican Revolution in 1813.[7] In the early 1800s, youth gangs seemed to have spread in New England, with the shifts from agrarian to industrial society. Youth gangs began to flourish in Chicago, New York, and other large cities in the nineteenth century as immigration and population shifts reached record levels. Youth gangs were primarily Irish, Jewish, and Italian, but this would change in the twentieth century.

GANGS AND PLAY ACTIVITY: THE 1920S THROUGH THE 1940S

A pioneering work on youth gangs was Frederick Thrasher's *The Gang: A Study of 1,313 Gangs in Chicago.*[8] Thrasher viewed these gangs as a normal part of growing up in ethnic neighborhoods. He found that youths who went to school together and played together in the neighborhood naturally developed a strong sense of identity leading to their forming close-knit groups.

Evolving from these neighborhood play groups, Thrasher found that they bonded together without any particular purpose or goal. These transitory social groups typically had fewer than thirty members. The youth gangs studied by Thrasher were usually organized in three concentric circles: a core made up of a leader and lieutenants, the rank-and-file membership, and a few youths who drifted in and out of the gang. Each gang was different, but what was universally expected was the protection of turf.[9]

WEST SIDE STORY ERA: THE 1950S

Youth gangs became established in Boston, New York, and Philadelphia from the late 1940s through the 1950s. These youth gangs spent time "hanging out" and partying together; when deemed necessary, they fought other gangs. The musical *West Side Story,* later made into a movie, presented two 1950s New York youth gangs dancing, singing, and battling over turf. It focused on the Sharks, recent immigrants from Puerto Rico, defending their neighborhood ethnic boundaries.

These **urban gangs** of the 1950s were not the lethal weapons they became in recent decades, but they were capable of violent behavior. In 1960–1961, one of the authors was hired to work with a white gang in Newark, New Jersey. This job became available because his predecessor, who had been on the job for two weeks, had a knife held to his chest, cutting his shirt and drawing a little blood. Warned that bad things would happen if he did not quit, he chose to resign.

The 1950s gangs attracted considerable attention among researchers and policymakers. Millions of dollars in federal, state, and local money were spent on projects and programs designed to prevent and control their behaviors. One of the most widely funded efforts was the detached workers program. This program sent professional workers into the community to work with gang youths, but this effort proved to have little or no positive effect on reducing their rates of delinquent activities. Indeed, one of the most consistent findings of these detached workers' programs was that workers' efforts ended up increasing the size of the youth gang, as well as the commitment of participants.[10]

DEVELOPMENT OF THE MODERN GANG: THE 1960S

The 1960s are known as a decade of rapidly changing social and political climates. The development of *supergangs* in Chicago and Los Angeles, the involvement of gangs in social betterment programs, and their participation in political activism were the most significant changes in youth gangs during the 1960s.

The major supergangs developed when neighborhood gangs became larger and more powerful than other gangs in surrounding neighborhoods, and they forced the small groups to become part of their gang organization. Eventually, a few gangs controlled the entire city of Chicago. During this decade, three African-American supergangs, the Vice Lords, the Blackstone Rangers, and the Disciples, either had their beginnings or developed into supergangs. In the 1960s, the Crips, an African-American supergang, began as a small clique in a section of Los Angeles.[11] It was not long before the Bloods, another African-American supergang in Los Angeles, arose to challenge the Crips. See Social World of the Offender 12–1 for the development of these supergangs.

During the late 1960s, the Vice Lords and the Blackstone Rangers, two of the Chicago supergangs, became involved in programs of community betterment. Their social action involvement began in the summer of 1967 when the Vice Lord leaders attended meetings at Western Electric and Sears and Roebuck. Operation Bootstrap, which resulted from these meetings, formed committees for education, recreation, and law, order, and justice. A grant from

SOCIAL WORLD OF THE OFFENDER   12–1
ORIGINS OF THE CHICAGO "SUPERGANGS"

The Vice Lord Nation

In the late 1950s, Peppilow was a fifteen-year-old youth who was sent to the St. Charles reformatory for boys. He persuaded Leonard Calloway, Maurice Miller, and four others to form a new gang when they got out. They played with names. It was Calloway who thought of lords, and vice came to mind. He looked both words up in the dictionary and found vice to mean "having a tight hold." He knew he had it. They would be called "Vice Lords."

It was not until 1964 that the name "Conservative Vice Lords" became well known. Maurice Miller was a conservative type, and he wanted *conservative* added to the name. They did that for him, ending up with Conservative Vice Lords.

As the Conservative Vice Lords grew in number and power, they began to take over other youth gangs in their neighborhood and in surrounding neighborhoods. One of the reasons for the success of this gang's development is that while it was annexing groups to the Conservative Vice Lords, this gang allowed other groups to retain their own identity and to become part of the Vice Lord Nation.

For example, Willie Lloyd became a member of the Vice Lords in the mid-1960s and was put in charge of the Peewees, a junior division of the Conservative Vice Lords. But when the Peewees evolved into another youth gang, Willie was not selected as an officer, nor was his suggested group name accepted. He was able to persuade two friends at that point to begin a new youth gang, which they called the "Unknown Conservative Vice Lords." This new gang, in spite of the opposition it initially received from established Vice Lord groups, eventually was accepted as a major division of the Vice Lord Nation.

Alfonso Alforde became chief of the Lords in the mid-1960s. Tired of humbugging, he began to search for meaning in a world where fighting was the only honor known. Too old to go back to school and with few jobs available, Al suggested the Lords try to open a business, moving toward construction rather than destruction. The Lords just shook their heads. It just didn't sound right. They enjoyed the partying, the drinking, and the fights. But Al kept insisting that together they could make it happen. They had to try.

Between 1965 and 1967, they stopped the gang wars. They opened businesses and ran community programs for the hungry, the unemployed, the homeless, and the young with nothing to do. They reached out to show the people on the streets that there was a thing called hope. For a moment in time they made a difference, but the forces working against them do not remember the moment. They are all dead now. All but Bobby Gore, who continues to have hope and to fight for his brothers and sisters on the streets.

As the decade came to an end, the Vice Lords contained twenty-nine branches. In addition to the Conservatives, the largest groups included the Unknown, Four Corner Hustlers, Mafia Insane, 21st Street Executioners, the Travelers, and the Maniac Vice Lords, but they were still all Lords.

Blackstone Rangers

Jeff Fort was a scrawny young man who lived in Woodlawn on the west side of Chicago. He and a few friends began to steal hubcaps and groceries, dividing the proceeds among themselves. As others were attracted to this group, they were named the Blackstone Rangers. Fort selected twenty-one leaders, giving them responsibility and power. They became known as the Main 21, and their major role was to enforce the rules of the Blackstone Rangers.

The Reverend John Fry, minister of the First Presbyterian Church in Chicago, permitted this gang to hold its meetings in the gymnasium of the church. The meetings captured the emotions of a religious revival. The Blackstones filled the gym, and the Main 21 were seated in a semicircle across the stage at the end of the gym.

Jeff Fort appeared out of nowhere, going to the microphone and podium. He raised his fist, jerking it back hard, with power they all knew him to have. He yelled, "Blackstone," and together the thunderous roar resounded back, "Blackstone."

Fort whipped the Blackstones into a frenzy. In a deep, booming voice that sent static flying across the gym, he demanded, "Stones run it!" Thousands of bodies extended their right fists like banners hammering the winds and responded, "Stones run it!" Over and over the thunder filled the gym, "Blackstones, Blackstones, Blackstones."

The Stones soon spread beyond their neighborhoods throughout Chicago. It was not long before they were known as America's most powerful gang. Some drug sales took place in the 1960s, but gang arrests were typically for crimes ranging from resisting arrest to armed robbery and murder.

The Disciples

David Barksdale was a self-directed leader who defied anyone, accustomed to reaching out and taking what he wanted. During his frequent trips as a teenager to the Illinois Youth Commission, he recruited youths from the south, west, and east sides, organizing a domain that was to extend his field of influence beyond that of just the south side. The movement spread.

He was stocky at age fifteen, standing about 5' 10" tall. He was stoic, quiet, and always serious, with a charisma that instilled fear and awe at the same time. Well mannered with few words, he dressed to perfection, looking fine with processed hair. But above all else he was an excellent boxer. One of the very best.

It was Barksdale's boxing skill that led to the development of the Disciples gang. Champ Harris was the nineteen-year-old leader of the Devil Disciples, which had a membership of about four hundred youths. Champ's girlfriend, Linda Samuels, was pursued by Barksdale, and Champ challenged the boy to a boxing match. By the time Harris hit the floor, he had lost his girlfriend and control over his gang.

Barksdale surrounded himself with leaders he could trust. They fought the Egyptian Cobras, led by Charlie Adkins, and the Supreme Gangsters, led by Martin Givens and Larry Hoover. Barksdale looked around for the small, unknown groups just coming up and recruited them easily most of the time; at other times they had little choice, if any.

With Barksdale on the run a couple of years later, Robert Allen, known to most as Old Timer, assumed responsibility for the leadership of the Devil Disciples. He made the decision to offer Larry Hoover an opportunity to coexist with him as leader of this gang. They would coexist together in one land, two kings ruling one nation, each with equal power. David would be king of the Devil Disciples, and Larry would be king of the Gangster Disciples. They were allies, six thousand strong.

In the early 1970s, David Barksdale was wounded and then died a couple of years later. His side of the kingdom was taken over by Jerome Freeman and became known as the Black Disciples. Imprisoned Larry Hoover used the magic of the name "Gangster Disciple" to become a legend and to build one of the largest gang organizations in the United States. Known as the King and Chairman of the Board, he is the head of the vast Gangster Disciples nation.

Source: Linda Dippold Bartollas researched and wrote this material. She was assisted by Nehemiah Russell and Samuel Dillon.

the Rockefeller Foundation in February 1967 enabled the Vice Lords to fund a host of economic and social ventures. The Vice Lords also worked with Jesse Jackson on Operation Breadbasket and, in the summer of 1969, joined with the Coalition for United Community Action to protest the lack of African American employees on construction sites in African-American neighborhoods.

The supergangs in Chicago became involved in political activism when they joined together to work against the reelection of Mayor Richard Daley's Democratic machine. This activism brought increased strain to their relationship with the Democratic Party organization. With Daley's reelection, gangs in Chicago began to experience what they perceived as harassment from the police. As soon as he began a new term, Daley announced a crackdown on gang violence, and State's Attorney Edward Hanrahan followed by appraising the gang situation as the most serious crime problem in Chicago. The courts complied with this crackdown on gangs by increasing dramatically the number of gang members sent to prison in Illinois.

EXPANSION, VIOLENCE, AND CRIMINAL OPERATIONS: THE 1970S, 1980S, AND 1990S

A number of changes took place with gangs in the past three decades. The most important of these changes were that gangs became increasingly made up of adults; that street gangs became responsible for a larger portion of crime, including violent crime; that urban gangs grew in the 1970s and expanded dramatically throughout the nation in the late 1980s and early 1990s; and that crack cocaine hit the streets in the mid-1980s.

What became evident by the late 1960s was that juveniles were not leaving the urban gangs to which they belonged when they became adults. One of the major reasons for this is that these gangs supplied certain needs that were not being met in other social groups or traditional rites of passage into adulthood. Another reason was that the increased imprisonment of gang members fostered the development of prison gangs and kept their allegiance to these gangs while in and subsequent to being released from prison.

In the 1970s and 1980s, urban gangs became responsible for a major portion of muggings, robberies, extortions, and drug-trafficking operations in the United States. With leadership increasingly assumed by adults, gangs were more intent on making money from crime. With legal weapons available more so than in the past, gangs became much more violent. Walter B. Miller's research found that in the mid-1970s the rate of murder by firearms or other weapons was higher than ever before; the five cities that had the most serious gang problems averaged at least 175 gang-related killings a year between 1972 and 1974.[12]

Both youth gangs and street gangs made up largely of adults have expanded dramatically over the past thirty years. In a 1982 study, Miller expanded the original study to twenty-six localities in the United States, including twenty-four of the largest cities and two counties. According to Miller's 1982 study, 2,300 youth gangs, with 100,000 members, were found in three hundred cities.[13] An estimated 26,700 street gangs and 780,200 members were active in the United States in 1998. This was a decline from an estimated 30,500 street gangs and 816,000 gang members in 1997 and 31,000 gangs and 846,000 gang members in 1996.[14]

The mid-1980s were a turning point for many ghetto-based gangs, for crack cocaine had hit the streets. These urban street gangs competed with each other for the drug trade. Several Los Angeles gangs established direct connections to major Colombian smugglers, which ensured a continuous supply of top-quality cocaine. In some Chicago neighborhoods, heavily armed teams sold drugs openly on the street corners, using gang "pewees" (youngsters) as police lookouts.

WHAT IS IMPORTANT TO KNOW ABOUT URBAN STREET GANGS?

Important features of urban street gangs include their types, organizational features, participation in drug trafficking, their behavior in school, and the degree of law-violating behaviors for juveniles involved in these groups. Juveniles may be in a minority in urban street gangs, but they have certain role expectations (usually drug "runners" and lookouts for crack houses) and frequently remain in the gang even after they become adults.

TYPES OF URBAN GANGS

Detroit urban gangs, according to Carl S. Taylor, can be classified as scavenger, territorial, and corporate. Scavenger gangs lack goals, purpose, and consistent leadership and prey on those who are unable to defend themselves. Territorial gangs define an area as belonging exclusively to them and attempt to defend this space from outsiders. They become the controllers of the streets and defend their territory to protect their narcotics business. Organized or corporate gangs, which Taylor views as organized crime groups, have as their main purpose the participation in illegal money-making ventures, especially trafficking **crack** cocaine. Different divisions of the gang handle sales, distribution, marketing, and enforcement.[15]

    C. Ronald Huff's examination of gangs in Cleveland and Columbus, Ohio, identified informal hedonistic gangs, instrumental gangs, and predatory gangs. The basic concerns of informal hedonistic gangs were to get high (usually on alcohol, marijuana, or other drugs) and to have a good time. These gangs were more involved in property crimes than in violent personal crimes. The main focus of instrumental gangs was economic gain, and they committed a large number of property crimes. Most of these gang members used drugs, including crack cocaine; some members also sold drugs, but doing so was not an organized gang activity. Predatory gangs committed robberies, street muggings, and other crimes of opportunity. Members of these gangs were likely to use crack cocaine and to sell drugs to finance the purchase of more sophisticated weapons.[16]

    Jeffrey Fagan identified four types of gangs in his analysis of the crime–drug relationships in three cities. Type 1 gangs were involved in a few delinquent activities and only alcohol and marijuana use. These gangs had low involvement in drug sales and appeared to be social gangs. Type 2 gangs were heavily involved in several kinds of drug sales, primarily to support their own drug habits. They were also heavily involved in vandalism. Type 3 gangs had the highest levels of member participation, including extensive involvement in both serious and nonserious offenses. Another feature of this type was less involvement in both drug sales and the use of such substances as cocaine, heroin, PCP, and amphetamines. Type 4 gangs were extensively involved in both serious drug use and serious and nonserious offenses and had higher rates of drug sales. This cohesive and organized type, according to Fagan, "is probably at the highest risk for becoming a more formal criminal organization."[17]

ORGANIZATIONAL FEATURES OF URBAN GANGS

Martin Sánchez Jankowski, who spent more than ten years studying thirty-seven gangs in Los Angeles, New York, and Boston, suggested that the most important organizational features of urban gangs are structure, leadership, recruitment, initiation rites, role expectations and sanctions, and migration patterns.[18] Jankowski observed three varieties of gang organizational structure:

1. The *vertical/hierarchical* structure divides leadership hierarchically into several different levels. Power and authority are related to one's position in the line of command.

2. The *horizontal/commission* structure consists of several officeholders who share about equal authority over members. The leaders share the duties as well as the power and authority.

3. The *influential* structure assigns no written duties or titles to the leadership positions. This type of system has two to four members who are regarded as the leaders of the gang. The authority of the influential leaders is derived from charisma.[19]

The most conspicious example of the vertical/hierarchical type of leadership is found in the Gangster Disciples, the Vice Lords, the Black Disciples, and the El Rukns, whose leaders have become legends.

The Bloods and the Crips, the most notorious Los Angeles gangs, are representative of the horizontal/commission type. In a real sense, they are not gangs at all but confederations among hundreds of subgroups or sets. Sets are established along neighborhood lines, and most sets have twenty to thirty members.[20]

Gangs regularly go on recruiting parties, and the recruitment of young members, or soldiers, is easy because the life of a gang member looks glamorous. The methods of initiation into some gangs include some or all of the following: (1) must be "jumped in" or fight the other members; (2) must participate in illegal acts; (3) must assist in trafficking drugs; and (4) must participate in "walk-up" or "drive-by" shootings.[21] Recently, there has been a movement away from jumped in initiations in urban gangs, unless there is some question about the initiate's courage.[22]

A street gang's clothing, colors, and hand signs are held sacred by gang members. Each gang has its own secret handshakes and hand signs, known as **representing.** Prayers are also rituals of many gangs; they are often said

A Texas youth gangs' members representing involves the demonstrating of gang signals that are recognized by other gang members and that distinguish it from other gangs.
(Photo by Hector Mata, Getty Images, Inc.—Agence France Presse.)

before going into battle against rivals or are chanted before wounded members die. A chief value of gangs is loyalty, and members are charged to give up everything, including their lives, to defend the gang.

A final organizational feature of urban gangs is migration. Gang migration can occur in the establishment of satellite gangs in another location, in the relocation of gang members with their families, and in the expansion of drug markets. Cheryl L. Maxson, Malcolm W. Klein, and Lea C. Cunningham surveyed law enforcement agencies in more than 1,100 cities nationwide. Of these, 713 reported some gang migration. The most frequent pattern of gang migration was the relocation of gang members with their families (39 percent); the next most common pattern was the expansion of drug markets (20 percent). But their survey failed to offer much support for gangs attempting to establish satellites in other communities across the nation.[23]

In 1994 and 1995, one of the authors asked the gang chiefs of the largest Chicago gangs whether there had been an attempt to establish satellites in other communities. These chiefs all responded that they did not have the desire or the organizational capacity to form nationwide satellite gangs. They even questioned how much control they had over gangs in other locations that use their gang name.[24]

DRUG TRAFFICKING AND GANGS

Beginning in the mid-1980s, street gangs with origins in the urban centers of Los Angeles, Chicago, New York, Miami, and Detroit became criminal entrepreneurs in supplying drugs, especially crack cocaine, to urban communities. They had begun by the late 1980s and early 1990s to develop intrastate and interstate networks to expand their illegal drug market sales.

The Crips and Bloods of Los Angeles have been the most active in drug trafficking nationwide. In a 1988 report, the Drug Enforcement Administration claimed that Los Angeles street gangs were identified with drug sales in forty-six states.[25] The Miami Boys of south Florida, the Jamaican Posses of New York and Florida, and the Vice Lords and Gangster Disciples in Chicago are also among the street gangs that have entered the field in the largest scale.[26]

The depth of gang involvement in drugs is documented in the *1997 National Youth Gang Survey*. Respondents to the survey estimate, on the average, that 42 percent of the drug sales across jurisdictions are conducted by gangs. Gangs are responsible for 43 percent of drug sales in suburbs, 35 percent in rural areas, 31 percent in small cities, but 49 percent in large cities.[27]

When ranking gangs according to their involvement in drug sales at low, moderate, or high levels, data indicate that more than half (53 percent) of gang members were reported to be involved at the low level of drug sales, 18 percent at the moderate level, and 29 percent at the high level.[28] The highest proportion of youth gangs involved in drug sales was in large cities, and the lowest was in small cities. Larger cities apparently have more opportunities for the individual entrepreneur.

✓**Progress Check 12.1**
Review this section at
www.prenhall.com/bartollas

GANGS IN SCHOOL

Urban schools have also become fertile soil for the violence of youth gangs. The percentage of high school students that reported the presence of street gangs at school varied by the type of school and whether the school was public or private. Urban schools had a significantly larger percentage of students who reported the presence of gangs at school than did suburban or rural schools. Indeed, more than twice as many students in urban schools compared with students in rural schools reported the presence of gangs. This same pattern was true of public

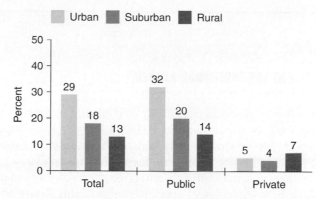

Figure 12–2 *Percentage of Students Ages Twelve through Eighteen Who Reported That Street Gangs Were Present at School during the Previous Six Months of 2001*

Note: "At school" means in the school building, on school property, on a school bus, or going to and from school.

Source: U.S. Department of Justice, Bureau of Justice Statistics, "School Crime Supplement to the National Crime Victimization Survey, January–June 2001." Reproduced in Arlen Egley Jr. and Aline K. Major, *Highlights of the 2002 National Youth Gang Survey* (Washington, DC: Office of Juvenile Justice and Delinquency Prevention, 2004), p. 1.

schools, but it was less true of private schools. Figure 12–2 shows the percentage of students ages twelve through eighteen who reported the presence of street gangs at school during the previous six months in 2001.[29] C. R. Huff and K. S. Trump's examination of youth gangs in Cleveland, Ohio; Denver, Colorado; and south Florida revealed that 50 percent of their respondents reported that members of their gangs had assaulted teachers, more than 80 percent said gang members took guns and knives to school, and more than 60 percent claimed that gang members sold drugs at school.[30]

Gangs perpetrate school violence in a number of ways. They are likely to bring concealed weapons into the school. They are constantly recruiting new members, and nongang youths who refuse to join may be assaulted. Also, when more than one gang is present in a school, conflict among these gangs takes place on a regular basis. Furthermore, conflict among rival gangs in different schools perpetrates violence.

Youths involved in gangs also are known to be disruptive in the classroom, to do poorly in their academic work, to intimidate nongang youth on the way to and from school, to frequently be absent, to be suspended or even expelled from school, and to drop out of school. When an urban high school has a large percentage of gang youths, the culture of that school tends to be chaotic, out of control, and dangerous. A visitor to a typical urban high school is likely to feel very uncomfortable.

Nehemiah Russell, a former Assistant Principal of Englewood Technical Preparatory Academy in Chicago, explains the grim situation of urban schools:

As educators, legislators, public officials, and the concerned public approach the twenty-first century, the prevalence of students' violence and disruptive behavior in the public education system impede the academic and social performance of students. Certain public school districts spend millions of dollars to implement traditional strategies to decrease students' inappropriate behavior to no avail.[31]

See Focus on Policy 12–2 for an alternative approach to reducing the chaos and violence of urban schools. While this program was eventually disbanded, largely because of the controversy it created, it resulted in a dramatically different quality of life in an urban school dominated by two rival street gangs.[32]

FOCUS ON POLICY

A NEW CULTURE AT THE ENGLEWOOD ACADEMY

12–2

When the Englewood community led the nation in violence in 1991, community leaders turned to gangs to help improve the neighborhood. One of the programs that was developed was the Community Liaison Program in Englewood Academy. Larry Hoover and Jerome "Shorty" Freeman, the leaders of the Gangster Disciples and the Black Disciples, joined school officials and community leaders to develop this program.

In a 1995 interview, Larry Hoover had this to say about the Englewood program:

Other methods of decreasing negative school behavior of students have failed. This unorthodox approach to classroom management will meet resistance by certain educational authority figures, but those who adopt this approach will reap the benefits of this non-traditional program.

What is positive about this program is that it provides a constructive learning environment for students that is rarely found in an urban setting. In visiting this school on several occasions, one of the authors witnessed no drugs being sold, no conflict among gang members, no victimization of nongang members, no turmoil in the hallway or on school grounds, no disrespect of teachers. Nor did students or faculty appear to be afraid.

What is questionable about Englewood's gang deactivation program is that control that school officials permitted gangs to have. Another troubling aspect of this gang deactivation program is the corporal punishment that misbehaving gang members receive from the gangs. In a time when corporal punishment is widely forbidden in schools across the nation, a school violation at Englewood is likely to mean that a student who is a gang member will be fined or beaten, perhaps severely.

This cooperative effort with gangs certainly had its critics, and it was not long before the principal and assistant principal were terminated and the program was disbanded. Yet this program represents one of the more innovative attempts across the nation to promote a positive learning experience in an urban school. The renewal of urban education is one of the most serious challenges facing education today, and perhaps it will take such radical proposals as the one being used at Englewood to regain control of urban schools.

Source: Based on participant observation and interviews conducted by one of the authors.

Critical Thinking Questions:
What is your reaction to such a proposal? Could urban gangs that have created a problem be part of the answer to the problem? What is the danger of such a proposal?

LAW-VIOLATING BEHAVIORS AND GANG ACTIVITIES

Despite the fluidity and diversity of gang roles and affiliations, it is commonly agreed that core members are involved in more serious delinquent acts than are situational or fringe members.

The follow-up of a sample of Cohort I to the age of thirty by Wolfgang and colleagues provided insights into the influence of gangs on delinquency in Philadelphia. They found that one-sixth of the whites belonged to gangs and were responsible for one-third of the offenses committed by whites; 44 percent of the nonwhites were gang members and were responsible for 60 percent of the offenses committed by nonwhites. Gang youths, who represented

29 percent of the total offender sample, were responsible for 50 percent of the offenses.[33]

This study also found that boys who belonged to gangs persisted in delinquent behavior nearly three years longer than did those who never joined. But when racial aspects are examined, it became clear that the persistence of delinquent behavior was traceable primarily to the nonwhite gang members. Moreover, Wolfgang and colleagues found that 81 percent of the boys (90 percent of the nonwhites and 60 percent of the whites) became delinquent after joining a gang. Another indicator of the relationship between gang membership and delinquency is that 90 percent of the whites committed no further offenses after leaving the gang; however, for nonwhites, no clear effect of leaving the gang was evident.[34]

More recently, studies in Aurora, Colorado; Broward County, Florida; and Cleveland, Ohio, found some major differences between the behavior of gang members and that of at-risk youths.[35] Individual gang members in these studies reported that they had stolen more cars, that they had participated in more drive-by shootings, that they were far more likely to own guns, that they owned guns of larger caliber, and that they were more involved in selling drugs than was the sample of at-risk youths.[36] Of those youths selling drugs, "gang members reported doing so more frequently, having fewer customers, making more money from the sales, and relying more on out-of-state suppliers than nongang youths who sold drugs." This study added that "both gang members and at-risk youths reported that gangs do not control drug trafficking in their communities."[37]

Studies of large urban samples found that gang members are responsible for a large proportion of violent offenses. In Rochester, gang members, who made up 30 percent of the sample, self-reported committing 68 percent of all adolescent violent offenses, which was about seven times as many serious and violent acts as committed by nongang youths.[38] In Seattle, gang members, who made up 15 percent of the sample, self-reported committing 85 percent of adolescent robberies.[39] In Denver, gang members, who made up 14 percent of the sample, self-reported committing 89 percent of all serious violent adolescent offenses. Gang members committed about three times as many serious and violent offenses as did nongang youth.[40]

A further study in Columbus, Ohio, analyzed the arrest records of eighty-three gang leaders in the years 1980 to 1994. During these fifteen years, the gang leaders accumulated 834 arrests, 37 percent of which were for violent crimes (ranging from domestic violence to murder). In this project, researchers theorized that violent crimes tended to increase as the gangs began engaging in drug activity and may have been connected to the establishment of a drug market.[41]

Gang membership appears to contribute to this pattern of violent behavior. Studies in Rochester, Denver, and Seattle showed that the influence of gang membership on levels of youth violence is greater than the influence of other delinquent peers.[42] Youths commit more serious and violent acts while they belong to a gang than they do after they leave the gang.[43] In addition, the effects of gang membership on a propensity toward violence seems to be long-lasting. In all three sites, even though gang members' offense rates dropped after leaving the gang, they still remained fairly high.[44]

The overall number of youth gang homicides declined during the 1990s, but trends varied by city. The 1996, 1997, and 1998 National Youth Gang Surveys revealed that 237 cities reported both a gang problem and a gang homicide statistic in all three years. Forty-nine percent of these cities indicated a decrease in gang homicide over the three-year period, 36 percent indicated an increase, and 15 percent indicated no change. The total number of gang homicides for these cities was 1,294 in 1996, 1,260 in 1997, and 1,061 in 1998. Los Angeles and Chicago stand out among the cities with the highest rates of gang homicides.[45]

Gang norms seem to contribute to the elevated rates of violence in youth gangs.[46] Most gangs have norms that support the expressive use of violence to settle disputes. The gang's sanctioning of violence is also dictated by a code of honor that stresses the importance of violence in demonstrating toughness and fighting ability and in establishing status in the gang. Levels of violence, as James C. Howell summarized it, do vary "from one city to another, from one community to another, from one gang to another, and even within cliques within the same gang."[47]

S. H. Decker describes a seven-step process that accounts for the peaks and valleys in the levels of gang violence.[48] The process begins with a gang that is loosely organized:

1. Loose bonds to gang
2. Collective identification of threat from a rival gang (through rumors, symbolic shows of force, cruising, and mythic violence), reinforcing the centrality of violence that expands the number of participants and increases cohesion
3. A mobilizing event, possibly, but not necessarily, violent
4. Escalation of activity
5. Violent events
6. Rapid deescalation
7. Retaliation[49]

Juveniles' propensity for gun ownership and violence are known to be closely related. One study found that juvenile males who "own guns for protection rather than for sport are six times more likely to carry guns, eight times more likely to commit a crime with a gun, four times more likely to be in a gang, and three times more likely to commit serious and violent crimes than youth who do not own guns for protection."[50] In addition, gangs are more likely to recruit youths who own firearms, and gang members are more than twice as likely as those who do not belong to a gang to own a gun for protection, more likely to have peers who own guns for protection, and more likely to carry their guns outside their home.[51]

Other researchers have also discovered a "significant connection among gang involvement, gang violence, and firearms."[52] For example, one study based on the responses of 835 institutionalized male residents of six juvenile correctional facilities in four states found that "gang membership brought increases in most forms of gun-involved conduct." Indeed, 45 percent of the respondents in this study reported that gun theft is a regular gang activity, 68 percent indicated that their gang bought and sold guns on a regular basis, and 61 percent said that "driving around shooting at people you don't like" is a regular gang activity.[53]

A final dimension of law-violating behaviors of urban street gangs is an examination of the extent to which they are becoming organized crime groups. Decker, Tim Bynum, and Deborah Weisel interviewed members of African-American and Hispanic gangs in San Diego and Chicago and found that only the Gangster Disciples in Chicago are assuming the attributes of organized crime groups.[54] Several commentaries have spelled out the organizational features of the Gangster Disciples, including a chairman of the board, two boards of directors (one for the streets and one for prisons), governors who control drug trafficking on the streets, regents who supply the drugs, area coordinators who collect revenues from drug-selling spots, enforcers who punish those who violate the rules, and "shorties" who staff drug-selling spots and execute drug deals.[55]

It can be argued that aspects of organized crime groups are found in such drug-trafficking gangs as the Bloods and Crips in Los Angeles, the Miami Boys of south Florida, and the Jamaican Posses of New York and Florida. Beginning in the mid-1980s, these street gangs appeared to become criminal entrepreneurs in supplying illicit drugs. In a brief period of several years, many of these street gangs developed intrastate and interstate networks for the purpose of expanding their illegal drug market sales. The Crips and Bloods of Los Angeles have been the most active in drug trafficking across the United States. A study by the U.S. Congress concluded that during the latter part of the 1980s the Crips and Bloods controlled 30 percent of the crack cocaine market across the nation.[56] The Drug Enforcement Administration claimed in a 1988 report that Los Angeles street gangs were identified with drug sales in forty-six states.[57]

RACIAL AND ETHNIC GANGS

African-American gangs, such as the Bloods and Crips from Los Angeles and the Chicago supergangs, are widely recognized because they are the ones that have established drug-trafficking networks across the nation. Jamaican and Cuban gangs also have gone into many cities to sell and supply narcotics. Hispanic street gangs are found primarily in the Southwest and Southeast. These gangs usually divide themselves into groupings called *cliques* and are distinguished by the loyalty members show to the gang. White gangs, which began on the West Coast and were known as Stoners, frequently abuse drugs and alcohol and listen to heavy metal rock music. Some evidence suggests that white gangs are increasingly becoming involved in satanic cults. Asian gangs, including Chinese, Vietnamese, Filipino, Japanese, and Korean gangs, began in California and have spread to other major American cities. These gangs are often more organized and have more identifiable leadership than do other street gangs.[58]

WHAT ARE EMERGENT STREET GANGS?

In the late 1980s and early 1990s, gangs began to appear in most communities of this nation. In G. David Curry and colleagues' 1992 survey of law enforcement departments in the 79 largest U.S. cities, 91 percent of respondents reported the presence of gang problems. These researchers estimated that there were 4,881 gangs with 249,324 gang members. Forty cities also reported a total of 7,205 gang members. Twenty-seven cities reported that there were 83 independent female gangs. Significantly, these cities with emerging gangs reported that juveniles made up 90 percent of the gangs.

Emergent gangs have been examined in Denver, Colorado;[59] Kansas City, Missouri; Rochester, New York; and Seattle, Washington. These studies generally found that gang members were involved in levels of delinquent activity that were much greater than those of nongang members, that the participation in gangs increased each year from the late 1980s to the early 1990s, and that these emerging gangs brought new levels of violence to a community.[60]

This nationwide expansion, which began in the late 1980s, appeared to occur in four different ways. First, it took place in some communities when urban gangs sent ranking gang members to persuade local youths to sell crack cocaine. Second, gang-related individuals expanded their established drug-trafficking operations among community youths. Third, youth members of urban gangs whose families had moved to these new communities were instrumental in developing local chapters of urban gangs. Fourth, youths in communities with little or no intervention from outsiders developed their own version of gangs. The first two scenarios were more likely to involve drug trafficking than were the last two.

Many communities across the nation have experienced the first form of gang expansion. Although the gangs appear to be somewhat different in each community, the degree and seriousness of gang activity in a community depend on its stage of development. Five stages of gang development could be identified by the end of 1999, with the possibility of two additional stages.

Stage 1

Gang leaders are aware of the ripe drug markets outside the major urban areas throughout the nation. They are also aware that crack cocaine in these new markets would bring a higher price than it does in the saturated urban areas. A plan is developed—which varies little from one drug-trafficking urban gang to another—for a gang member to go to a city without gangs. When he arrives, either by plane or auto, he goes to a low-income minority neighborhood and recruits several juveniles to sell crack cocaine. As part of his sales pitch, this ghetto-based gang member assures these juveniles that the mother gang intends to develop a connection, or satellite, in their community. The recruited juveniles are promised a percentage of the money they make from the drug sales. The adult gang member agrees to return on a regular basis to supply more drugs, to pick up the money, and to check on operations. It is not long before a second and sometimes a third representative of urban-based gangs arrives to recruit youths to sell crack cocaine.

Stage 2

By stage 2, the adult gang member has informed the youths selling drugs enough about the gang that they are able to identify with it. They can wear the proper clothing, can represent the gang signs, and can come together as a group. But their basic activity remains that of selling crack cocaine. One midwestern youth claimed that he was making $40,000 a month selling crack cocaine for the Almighty Unknown Vice Lords when he was arrested and institutionalized. Competition between these youths who claim to be part of the rival street gangs inevitably results in conflict and sometimes violence. Fights are likely to break out during school functions, at athletic events, and in parks. Weapons may be discharged at this time. Police also become aware that increasing numbers of weapons are being brought into the community.

Stage 3

The organization of the gangs develops during stage 3. Gang membership increases as more youths are brought into the core group. Leadership of the gang is usually assumed by a member of the initial core group, as well as by young adult members of the community. Gang members become more visible at school and at school functions, usually by the colors or clothing they wear and by the gang signs they represent. It is not long before a sizable number of "wannabes" are considering themselves gang members. The process of initiation begins at this time, and pressure is placed especially on African-American males to join a gang. White youths also frequently are accepted as part of these developing gangs.

Stage 4

The competition between rival gangs erupts in open conflict in school, at school dances, at athletic events, and in shopping centers. Drugs also are increasingly sold in the school environment. White gangs often appear at this time, and African-American gangs are more likely to wear their colors and to demonstrate gang affiliation.

Stage 5

Drugs are openly sold in the school, on street corners, and in shopping centers. Extortion of students and victimization of both teachers and students occurs widely in the public schools. Moreover, the gangs are led by adults who remain in the community, and the organizational structure and numbers of gang members show a significant increase.

Stage 6

The gangs are clearly in control in minority neighborhoods, in the school, at school events, and in shopping centers. The criminal operations of the rival gangs also become more varied during stage 6, including robberies, burglaries, aggravated assaults, and rapes. Citizens' fear of gangs dramatically increases, and the police express the inability to control drug trafficking and violence.

Stage 7

The final stage is characterized by the deterioration of the city as a result of gang control. Citizens move out of the city, stay away from shopping centers, and keep their children home from school.

HOW IS GANG INVOLVEMENT TOXIC?

Youths involved in emergent gangs are sounding more and more like those who are members of urban gangs. They both talk about justice. Justice means that honor is revenged. "I feel that what we did that night wasn't enough. Justice, to me, would have been killing seven or eight of them. Even though only one guy shot my brother, there were three guys there."[61]

They both talk about how gang "bangin'" becomes a way of showing that a youth is "bad." "Shootin' guns and stabbin' people" is how a gang youth shows heart and courage, and killing to many gang youths "ain't nothing." The violence of this substitute family makes a youth feel powerful and connected to something worthwhile. To youths who must deal with hopelessness in so many areas of their lives, the fear of dying makes them feel alive.

They both talk about the violence of the 1990s street gangs and how this violence far exceeds that of the past:

> It's more tense now than ever before. Because back then, if you saw somebody from an enemy set, chances are you'd just fight with 'em. You know, you'd come at them from the shoulder. Whereas now—it's gunplay. Back then not as many sets were fightin' with each other. It was much simpler: Crips versus Bloods. Now, it seems as if every other Crip set is fightin' with each other, killin' each other. And everything is high-tech now. Weapons, surveillance, communications, everything. Makes you wonder what would happen if some "banger" with a hate on got his hands on a nuclear device, doesn't it?[62]

Beyond gang youths attempting to make sense of their social world is the reality that gangs are destructive to their members. First, gang youths become involved in dangerous, even deadly, games. As one former gang leader put it, "I've gone to more gang funerals than I can even count."[63] Second, although joining a gang may be a normal rite of passage for a youth, gangs minister

FOCUS ON THE OFFENDER   **12–3**

INSTITUTIONALIZED JUVENILE WHO WENT HOME AND KILLED

One of the authors was doing a research project comparing a state and private facility when he was approached by staff members who inquired whether he would like to talk to all the gang kids. It quickly got around that this coauthor knew Willie Lloyd, the leader of the Unknown Vice Lords, and so all the gang youths wanted to talk to him, especially the Vice Lords. One young man came into the office to talk when this researcher was interviewing staff youth leaders. They were having a good talk, when suddenly the gang youth announced that he had to go home and kill the Crip who had recently killed his nephew. He would be released the next week and planned to take care of business.

The researcher tried to talk him out of it, with a variety of reasoning ploys. Nothing worked. He went home the next week, and was soon involved in the killing of a Crip on a drive-by shooting. He is presently doing life without parole for this crime.

Critical Thinking Question:

If you were this researcher, what would you have said to this young man?

poorly to such basic adolescent needs as preparation for marriage and employment and learning to adapt to the adult world. Third, juvenile males who join gangs for protection are exposed to dangers that most nongang juveniles are able to avoid. Fourth, gang youth frequently are victimized by both juvenile and adult members of street gangs.[64] Adolescent females who often are exploited sexually by male gang members aptly show how gangs victimize younger members. Finally, although joining a gang may provide status and esteem in the present, it also increases the likelihood of incarceration in juvenile and adult facilities.[65] See Focus on the Offender 12–3.

Juveniles who belong to urban street gangs or **emerging youth gangs** are involved in more serious delinquent acts than are youths who do not belong to gangs. The influence of gang participation on violent behavior has been documented by a number of studies. The studies of gangs in Rochester, New York; Denver, Colorado; and Pittsburgh, Pennsylvania, all found that gang youths committed more violent behaviors than did nongang delinquents and that youths commit more serious and more violent acts when they are gang members than they do after leaving the gang.[66] James C. Howell's examination of youth gang homicides found that the recent growth in youth gang homicides has been driven by increased access to firearms. Yet it appears that gang-related homicides are generally not about drugs but are personal, vendetta-like, and motivated primarily by self-protection.[67]

WHAT CAN COMMUNITIES DO TO PREVENT AND CONTROL YOUTH GANGS?

Communities across the United States have had a tendency to deny that they have gangs even when gang youths are causing serious problems at schools and in the neighborhoods. When an incident takes place, such as the killing of an innocent victim or a shootout, and one or more youths are killed, communities tend to substitute repression for denial. The problem is turned over to the police with the directive to make gangs invisible. Gang units are sometimes established in police departments to focus on getting rid of the gang problem.

Irving Spergel and colleagues' 1989 survey of forty-five cities with gang problems identified five strategies of intervention: (1) community organization, including community mobilization and networking; (2) social intervention, focusing on individual behavioral and value change; (3) opportunity provision, emphasizing the improvement of basic education, training, and job opportunities for youth; (4) suppression, focusing on arrest, incarceration, monitoring, and supervision of gang members; and (5) organizational development and change, or the creation of special organizational units as well as procedures.[68]

In examining the implementation of these strategies, Spergel and colleagues found that suppression (44 percent) was most frequently used, followed by social intervention (31.5 percent), organizational development (10.9 percent), community organization (8.9 percent), and opportunity provision (4.8 percent).[69] Community organization was more likely to be used with gang programs in emerging gang cities, whereas social intervention and opportunity provision tended to be primarily strategies of programs in cities with chronic gang problems. But in only seventeen of the forty-five cities was there any evidence of improvement in the gang situation.[70]

Spergel and colleagues, in developing a model for predicting general effectiveness in dealing with gang problems, stated:

A final set of analyses across all cities indicate that the primary strategies of community organization and provision of opportunity along with maximum participation by key community actors is predictive of successful efforts at reducing the gang problems.[71]

What this research by Spergel and colleagues has demonstrated is that only an integrated, multidimensional, community-oriented effort is likely to have any long-term effect in preventing and controlling gangs in the United States. This gang prevention and control model must have several components: (1) the community must take responsibility for developing and implementing this model; (2) this structural model must take seriously the hopelessness arising from the unmet needs of underclass children; (3) prevention programs, especially in the first six years of school, must receive a major emphasis; (4) those who support this model must coordinate all the gang intervention efforts taking place in a community; and (5) sufficient financial resources must be available for implementing the model.

✓**Progress Check 12.2**
Review this section at
www.prenhall.com/bartollas

SUMMARY

- Adolescents finding that their needs are not met in social contacts with family members, teachers, and leaders and participants in churches, school activities, and community organizations are more likely to be attracted to street gangs and youth gangs.
- These gangs become quasi-families offering acceptance, status, and esteem.
- The number of gang members, as well as the number of youth gangs, decreased from the late 1990s to the present.
- Youth gangs remain a problem throughout the United States; even small towns and rural areas often must contend with the presence of youth gangs.
- Much is the same and much is new about youth gangs.

What is new is the widespread use of gun violence, particularly involving automatic and semiautomatic handguns; the juvenile drug trafficking that takes place now much more than in the past; and the frequency with which youth gangs become street gangs with adults as leaders. Juveniles are often a minority in these urban street gangs.

- Gangs have thrived because of the poverty in urban neighborhoods.
- The hopelessness of these environments makes drug trafficking attractive and gang membership desirable even with the high possibility of being injured, killed, or imprisoned.
- Grassroots community groups seem to make the most sense in reducing the spread of gangs, but gang reduction actually depends on providing at-risk children with more positive options than they have today.

WEB SITES OF INTEREST

The National Youth Gang Center can be found at
http://www.iir.com/nygc
Learn more about street gangs from the Streetgangs Web site
http://www.streetgangs.com

CRITICAL THINKING QUESTIONS

1. Why are adolescents likely to become involved in youth gangs?
2. How have youth gangs changed throughout the years?
3. If you had the opportunity to teach a class of high school students, most of whom were in youth gangs, what would you say to them?
4. Why is community participation the most effective means of gang prevention and control?
5. Why do you believe gang participation and membership decreased in the final years of the twentieth century?

NOTES

1. Interviewed in 1995.
2. See Finn-Aage Esbensen, "Preventing Adolescent Gang Involvement," *Juvenile Justice Bulletin* (Washington, DC: Office of Juvenile Justice and Delinquency Prevention, 2000), 2.
3. Arlen Egley, Jr., *Highlights of the 2002–2003 National Youth Gang Surveys* (Washington, DC: Government Printing Office, 2005), 2.
4. Arlen Egley, Jr., and Aline K. Major, *Highlights of the 2002 National Youth Gang Surveys* (Washington, DC: Government Printing Office, 2004), 1.
5. See the section on law-violating behaviors of juveniles for studies supporting these conclusions.
6. Luc Sante, *Low Life: Lures and Snares of Old New York* (New York: Vintage Books, 1991).
7. Robert Redfield, *Folk Culture of Yucatan* (Chicago: University of Chicago Press, 1941).
8. Frederick Thrasher, *The Gang: A Study of 1,313 Gangs in Chicago* (Chicago: University of Chicago Press, 1927).
9. Ibid.

10. See Walter B. Miller, "The Impact of a Total Community Delinquency Control Project," *Social Problems* 10 (Fall 1962), 168–91.

11. John C. Quicker and Akil S. Batani-Khalfani, "Clique Succession among South Los Angeles Street Gangs, the Case of the Crips," paper presented at the annual meeting of the American Society of Criminology, Reno, Nevada (November 1989).

12. Walter B. Miller, *Violence by Youth Gangs and Youth Groups as a Crime Problem in Major American Cities* (Washington, DC: Government Printing Office, 1975).

13. Walter B. Miller, *Crime by Youth Gangs and Groups in the United States,* a report prepared for the National Institute of Juvenile Justice and Delinquency Prevention, February 1982.

14. See James Howell, *OJJDP Fact Sheet* (Washington, DC: Office of Juvenile Justice and Delinquency Prevention, 1997).

15. Carl S. Taylor, *Dangerous Society* (East Lansing: Michigan State University Press, 1990), 4–7.

16. C. Ronald Huff, "Youth Gangs and Public Policy," *Crime and Delinquency* 35 (October 1989), 528–29.

17. Jeffrey Fagan, "The Social Organization of Drug Use and Drug Dealing Among Urban Gangs," *Criminology* 27 (1989), 633–64.

18. Martin Sánchez Jankowski, *Islands in the Streets: Gangs and American Urban Society* (Berkeley: University of California Press, 1991), 5.

19. Ibid., 64–67.

20. Joan Moore, Diego Vigil, and Robert Garcia, "Residence and Territoriality in Chicago Gangs," *Social Problems* 31 (December 1985), 182–94.

21. For more information about drive-by shootings, see William B. Sanders, *Gangbangs and Drive-Bys: Grounded Culture and Juvenile Gang Violence* (New York: Aldine De Gruyter, 1994).

22. Conversations with urban gang chiefs in 1996.

23. Cheryl Maxson, Malcolm W. Klein, and Lea C. Cunningham, "Street Gangs and Drug Sales," Report to the National Institute of Justice (1993).

24. These conversations took place in 1994 and 1995 during prison visits.

25. Drug Enforcement Administration, *Crack Cocaine Availability and Trafficking in the United States* (Washington, DC: U.S. Department of Justice, 1988).

26. Shay Bilchik, *1997 National Youth Gang Survey* (Washington, DC: Office of Juvenile Justice and Delinquency Prevention, December 1999), 25.

27. Ibid., 24.

28. Ibid., 40.

29. Egley, *Highlights of the 2002 National Youth Gang Surveys,* 1.

30. C. Ronald Huff and K. S. Trump, "Youth Violence and Gang: School Safety Initiatives in Urban and Suburban School Districts," *Education and Urban Safety* 28 (1996), 5592–5603.

31. Interviewed in 1996.

32. Jeffery Fagan, "Social Processes of Delinquency and Drug Use Among Urban Gangs," in *Gangs in America,* edited by C. Ronald Huff (Newbury Park, CA: Sage Publications, 1990), 199–200.

33. Marvin E. Wolfgang, Terence P. Thornberry, and Robert M. Figlio, *From Boy to Man: From Delinquency to Crime* (Chicago: University of Chicago Press, 1987), 155–56.

34. Ibid., 156–58.

35. See C. Ronald Huff, *Criminal Behavior of Gang Members and At-Risk Youths: Research Preview* (Washington, DC: National Institute of Research, 1998), 1,

36. Ibid., 1–2.

37. Ibid., 1.

38. Terence P. Thornberry, "Membership in Youth Gangs and Involvement in Serious and Violent Offending," in *Serious and Violent Juvenile Offenders: Risk Factors and Successful Intervention*, edited by R. Loeber and D. P. Farrington (Thousand Oaks, CA: Sage Publications, 1998), 147–66.

39. Sara R. Battin-Pearson, Terence P. Thornberry, J. David Hawkins, and Marvin D. Krohn, "Gang Membership, Delinquent Peers, and Delinquent Behavior," Juvenile Justice Bulletin (Washington, DC: Office of Justice Programs, Office of Juvenile Justice and Delinquency Prevention, 1998).

40. David Huizinga, "Gangs and the Volume of Crime," paper presented at the annual meeting of the Western Society of Criminology, Honolulu (1997).

41. Huff, *Criminal Behavior of Gang Members and At-Risk Youths*, 2.

42. Sara K. Battin, et al., "The Contribution of Gang Membership to Delinquency: Beyond Delinquent Friends," *Criminology* 36 (February 1998), 93–115.

43. Finn-Aage Esbensen and David Huizinga, "Gangs, Drugs, and Delinquency in a Survey of Urban Youth," *Criminology* 31 (1993), 565–89.

44. James C. Howell, "Youth Gangs: An Overview," *Juvenile Justice Bulletin* (Washington, DC: Office of Justice Programs, Office of Juvenile Justice and Delinquency Prevention, 1998).

45. David Curry, Cheryl L. Maxson, and James C. Howell, "Youth Gang Homicides in the 1990s," *OJJDP Fact Sheet* (Washington, DC: Office of Juvenile Justice and Delinquency Prevention, 2001), 1.

46. Howell, "Youth Gangs: An Overview."

47. Ibid.

48. Scott H. Decker, "Collective and Normative Features of Gang Violence," *Justice Quarterly* 13 (1996), 262.

49. Ibid.

50. Howell, "Youth Gangs: An Overview."

51. Beth Bjerregaard and Alan J. Lizotte, "Gun Ownership and Gang Membership," *Journal of Criminal Law and Criminology* 86 (1995), 37–53.

52. Coordinating Council on Juvenile Justice and Delinquency Prevention, *Combating Violence and Delinquency: The National Juvenile Justice Action Plan* (Washington, DC: Office of Juvenile Justice and Delinquency Prevention, 1996), 35.

53. Joseph F. Sheley and James D. Wright, "Youth, Guns and Violence in Urban America," paper presented at the National Conference on Prevention Strategies against Armed Criminal and Gang Violence: Federal, State, and Local Coordination, San Diego, CA (Washington, DC: National Institute of Justice, 1992).

54. Scott H. Decker, Tim Bynum, and Deborah Weisel, "A Tale of Two Cities: Gangs as Organized Crime Reports," *Justice Quarterly* 15 (September 1998), 395–425.

55. James McCormick, "The 'Disciples' of Drugs and Death," *Newsweek* (February 5, 1996), 56–57.

56. U.S. General Accounting Office, *Nontraditional Organized Crime* (Washington, DC: Government Printing Office, 1989).

57. Drug Enforcement Administration, *Crack Availability and Trafficking in the United States* (Washington, DC: U.S. Department of Justice, 1988).

58. Robert K. Jackson and Wesley D. McBride, *Understanding Street Gangs* (Costa Mesa, CA: Custom Publishing, 1985), 31–51.

59. G. David Curry, Robert J. Fox, Richard A. Ball, and Darryl Stone, "National Assessment of Law Enforcement Anti-Gang Information Resources," report to the U.S. Department of Justice, National Institute of Justice (1993).

60. For a review of gang research, including that of emergent gangs, see James C. Howell, "Recent Gang Research: Program and Policy Implications," *Crime and Delinquency* 40 (October 1994), 491–515. For the study in Denver, see Finn-Aage Esbensen and David Huizinga, "Gangs, Drugs, and Delinquency in a Survey of Urban Youth," *Criminology* 31 (1993), 565–89. For the study in Kansas City, Missouri, and Seattle, Washington, see Mark S. Fleisher, "Youth Gangs and Social Networks: Observations from a Long-Term Ethnographic Study," paper presented at the annual meeting of the American Society of Criminology, Miami (November 1994). For the study in Rochester, New York, see Terence P. Thornberry, Marvin D. Krohn, Alan J. Lizotte, and Deborah Chard-Wierschem, "The Role of Juvenile Gangs in Facilitating Delinquent Behavior," *Journal of Research in Crime and Delinquency* 30 (1993), 55–87.

61. Howell, "Recent Gang Research."

62. Leon Bing, *Do or Die* (New York: HarperCollins, 1991), 257.

63. Ibid.

64. Interviewed in 1996.

65. For example, see Felix Padilla's *The Gang as an Ethnic Enterprise* (New Brunswick, NJ: Rutgers University Press, 1992) for the way that youths who traffick drugs for the gang are victimized. For a discussion of the destructiveness of gangs to their members, see James F. Short, Jr., "Gangs, Neighborhood, and Youth Crime," *Criminal Justice Research Bulletin* 3 (1990), 3.

66. T. P. Thornberry, "Membership in Youth Gangs and Involvement in Serious and Violent Offending," in *Serious and Violent Offenders: Risk Factors and Successful Interventions,* edited by R. Loeber and D. P. Farrington (Thousand Oaks, CA: Sage Publications, 1998), 147–166.

67. James C. Howell, "Youth Gang Homicides: A Literature Review," *Crime and Delinquency* 45 (April 1999), 208–41.

68. I. A. Spergel, G. D. Curry, R. A. Ross, and R. Chance, *Survey of Youth Gang Problems and Programs in 45 Cities and 6 Sites.* Tech. report No. 2, National Youth Gang Suppression and Intervention Project (Chicago: University of Chicago, School of Social Service Administration, 1989), 211.

69. Ibid., 212.

70. Ibid., 216.

71. Ibid., 218.

13

DRUGS AND YOUTHFUL OFFENDING

I started using drugs when I was eight years old. It makes you feel like you can beat anything that comes along. I thought, "Wow, this is great!" When I was nine, some-one asked me if I wanted to take some acid. I figured, sure, why not? This was really great because I could sit around and watch the walls melt. My English teacher deteri-orated in her chair one time at school. As the years went by, I started to peddle a lot of speed and acid. Pretty soon, I was drug dependent. I needed speed in the morning, and I had to take speed in school to make it through the day. I got to the point that I couldn't handle speed anymore. I was too juiced up. Now I regret doing so many drugs because I can't remember simple things that I should remember, like talking with someone over the phone the night before. I became spacey; in fact, people have called me spacey for two years now.[1]

OUTLINE

OBJECTIVES

1. To illustrate the relationship between social attitudes and drug use
2. To examine how much drug use there is among adolescents in the United States
3. To describe the main types of drugs used by adolescents

333

4. To identify the theoretical explanations related to the onset of drug use

5. To propose what can be done to prevent and control drug use among adolescents in the United States

KEY TERMS

addicts	cocaine	high-risk
alcohol	crack	inhalants
anabolic steroids	Ecstasy	marijuana
amphetamines	heroin	sedatives

Drug and alcohol use and juvenile crime have long been identified as the most serious problem behaviors of adolescents. According to self-report surveys, more than half of high school seniors have tried drugs and more than 75 percent use alcohol.[2] As the adolescent male realized in the chapter-opening quotation, drug use affected the way that he lived his life as he got older. As articulated by the majority of the individuals whose stories appeared in the *Voices*, the use of drugs and alcohol became an important part of their lives. Even for those from small towns who would not have considered smoking marijuana or taking other drugs, drinking became an important rite of passage from adolescence to adulthood.

Life-time illicit drug use by juveniles increased from the 1960s until the early 1980s, dropped until the early 1990s, rose until the late 1990s, and then diminished slightly until today; the trends fluctuate by age groups and drugs used. Recently, however, drug use has increased among **high-risk** juveniles and is linked strongly to juvenile crime. Other problems are increased drug selling by juveniles and the spread of acquired immunodeficiency syndrome (HIV) by intravenous drug users and their sex partners.[3]

A difference does exist between drug use and drug abuse. Drug use can be viewed as a continuum that begins with nonuse and includes experimental use, culturally endorsed use, recreational use, and compulsive use.[4] An example of a culturally endorsed use is the sacramental use of peyote in the Native American churches for centuries. Twenty-three states presently exempt this sacramental use of peyote from criminal penalties.[5]

Adolescent drug use becomes abusive only when the user becomes dysfunctional, such as being unable to attend or perform in school; pursuing dangerous, aggressive, or reckless behavior; or endangering his or her health. Such dysfunctional drug use generally results in focusing one's life on obtaining, maintaining, and using drugs.[6] It can also result in early death or arrest, prosecution, and incarceration in correctional facilities.

WHAT ARE THE MAIN TYPES OF DRUGS?

The licit and illicit drugs that are used by adolescents, in decreasing order of frequency, are alcohol, tobacco, marijuana, cocaine, methamphetamine, inhalants, sedatives, stimulants (amphetamines and hallucinogens), and heroin. The licit drugs are permitted to users who are of age (eighteen and older for tobacco and twenty-one and older for alcohol). The illicit drugs are forbidden by law. Drugs that are an exception to this pattern are those prescribed by a physician or marijuana in jurisdictions that permit the use of this drug.

ALCOHOL AND TOBACCO

What makes **alcohol** so dangerous is that it relaxes inhibitions, and adolescents participate in risky behavior while under its influence. Adolescents' alcohol use is further linked to fights, property damage, academic failure, occupational problems, and conflicts with law enforcement officials.[7] Juveniles who are under the influence of alcohol may commit unlawful acts that they otherwise would not.

Tobacco is often neglected in a discussion of drugs. Even though nicotine is not considered a mind-altering drug, considerable evidence exists that tobacco users suffer severe health consequences from prolonged use and subject others to the same consequences. A 2000 analysis quantified the major factors contributing to death in the United States and found that tobacco contributed to 435,000 deaths annually, whereas alcohol contributed to 85,000 deaths, and all illicit drugs combined contributed to 20,000 deaths.[8]

MARIJUANA AND HASHISH

Marijuana is produced from the leaves of *Cannabis sativa*. Hashish (hash) is a concentrated form of cannabis made from unadulterated resin from the female plant. The main active ingredient in both marijuana and hashish is tetrahydrocannabinol (THC), which is a mild hallucinogen. One indication of the popularity of **marijuana** is the many names given to it, including *Acapulco Gold, A-bomb, aunt mary, baby, ashes, African black bammy, California red, birchwood, Columbian gold, gigglewood, golden leaf, dope, grass, hay joints, Mexican green, pot, reefer, Panama gold, reefer weed, shit stinkweed, seaweed, weed,* and *Texas tea.*[9]

Debates have existed for some time concerning the hazards of using marijuana. In the short run, smoking small amounts produces an early excitement ("high") that can lead to drowsiness. In the long run, smoking large amounts of

Many communities are posting drug-free school zone signs as warnings to those who might try to sell drugs to youths on their way to or from school. (Photo by Kathryn Miller.)

pot can cause distortions in visual and auditory perception. Research in the 1980s documented more ill effects of long-term marijuana use than had been recognized before. For example, several studies concluded that marijuana smoking combines the hazardous features of alcohol and tobacco, as well as containing a number of pitfalls of its own. These studies further suggest that long-term marijuana use can have harmful effects on the vital systems of the body, on the brain, on immunity and resistance, and on sex organs and reproduction.[10]

COCAINE

Cocaine is the powder derivative of the South American coca plant. When it was introduced in 1860, it was considered a medical breakthrough that could relieve depression and fatigue, and it quickly became a staple of patent medicines. When its addictive qualities and dangerousness became apparent, its use was controlled by the Pure Food and Drug Act of 1906.

Street names for cocaine include *coke, lady, snow, nose candy, toot,* and *Super Fly.* The main source of cocaine is Columbia, and its distribution has become a diplomatic issue in many Central and South American countries. At one time, cocaine was believed to be less addicting than other illegal drugs. However, users crave the extreme mood elevation, elation, grandiose feelings, and heightened physical prowess that cocaine induces. When these begin to wane, a corresponding deep depression is experienced. Users feel strongly motivated to use the drug again to restore the euphoria.

Snorting (inhaling) is the most common method of using cocaine. Freebasing became popular in the 1980s. Freebase cocaine is derived from a chemical process in which the purified cocaine is crystallized. The crystals are crushed and smoked in a special heated glass pipe. Smoking freebase cocaine provides a quicker, more potent rush and a more powerful high than does regular cocaine. The intravenous use of cocaine produces a powerful high, generally within fifteen to twenty seconds. A related method is the intravenous use of cocaine along with another drug, which is known as *speedballing.* Speedballing intensifies the effect but can be extremely dangerous. It was speedballing that killed actor-comedian John Belushi in 1982.[11]

Crack is processed street cocaine. Its manufacture involves using baking soda (sodium bicarbonate) or ammonia to remove the hydrochlorides and create a crystalline form of cocaine that can be smoked. Crack gets its name from the fact that the sodium bicarbonate frequently emits a crackling sound when it is smoked. It is known by users as *bricks, boulders, eight-ball* (large rocks), *doowap* (two rocks), and *crumbs.* Crack is generally smoked in special glass pipes or makeshift smoking devices. It is also smoked with marijuana in cigarettes, which are called *pin joints, geek joints,* or *lack joints.* A *shotgun,* which is secondary smoke exhaled from one crack user into the mouth of another also can provide the desired high.

METHAMPHETAMINE

Methamphetamine is a synthetic drug otherwise known by its street names: *meth, crank, ice, chalk, glass,* and *crystal meth* (to name a few). This highly addictive stimulant can be snorted, smoked, or injected. Its effects last for up to eight hours (with an initial rush at the beginning and a less intensive high for the duration). Use of this drug makes an individual feel awake, aware, and happy, but also agitated and paranoid.

According to the 2002 National Household Survey on Drug Abuse, 12.3 million, or 5.3 percent, of Americans over the age of twelve had used methamphetamine in their lifetime. About 1.5 million, or 0.7 percent, had used it in the

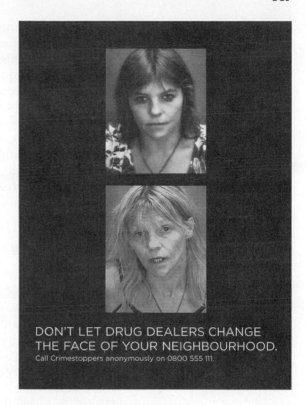

Youths seldom realize the serious internal and external damage drugs can do to one's body. This woman's before and after photos illustrate the effects of methamphetamine well.
(Photo by National Picture/Topham, The Image Works.)

DON'T LET DRUG DEALERS CHANGE THE FACE OF YOUR NEIGHBOURHOOD.
Call Crimestoppers anonymously on 0800 555 111.

past year (2001–2002). And 597,000, or 0.3 percent, had used it in the past month.[12] The use of meth is growing. It was formerly concentrated in California (especially in the San Diego area) but has spread to other states in the West and to states in the South and the Midwest.

In *Voices in the Juvenile Justice System*, Daniel Block, a juvenile court judge, reports that meth users are increasingly appearing in his courtroom and that meth labs are found in a variety of locations in his jurisdiction. Judge Block believes that meth is replacing crack cocaine as a drug of choice for many adolescent drug users. White adolescent drug users are not only the users of meth but also the ones who have learned how to cook and deal meth.

INHALANTS

Adolescents use many types of **inhalants,** but what these drugs have in common is that youths have to inhale the vapors to receive the high that they seek. Butyl nitrite, commonly called *RUSH*, is one frequently used inhalant. It is packaged in small bottles and can often be found in adult bookstores, as well as on the street. Chlorohydrocarbons and hydrocarbons—which can be inhaled directly from gasoline, paint thinner, glue, or aerosol cans—are other inhalants that are easier for youthful drug users to obtain.

The use of these drugs can bring a feeling of excitement that is frequently followed by a disorientation accompanied by slurred speech and a feeling of sleepiness. The use of inhalants can also be followed by mild to severe headaches as well as nosebleeds. Chronic use of some inhalants is associated with injury to the liver and kidneys and other neurological damage.[13]

SEDATIVES

Many different forms of **sedatives,** or barbiturates, are used by youth. What is common to all these barbiturates is that they are taken orally and affect the user by depressing the nervous system and inducing a drowsy condition. On the street, barbiturates are known by the color of their capsule. Seconal pills are known as *reds*, Amytas are called *blue devils,* and Tuinals are known as *rainbows.* Methaqualone, another popular sedative, is known as *Quaaludes* or *Ludes* on the street.

Adolescents frequently abuse prescription drugs. Benzodiazepines (minor tranquilizers or sedatives) are among the most widely prescribed drugs. Librium, Valium, and Eqyabuk are commonly prescribed for anxiety or sleep disorders, and adolescents can obtain them by simply raiding their parents' medicine cabinets. When used in combination with other controlled substances, these prescription drugs produce effects similar to those of alcohol and barbiturates.[14]

AMPHETAMINES

Amphetamines were first made in Germany in the 1880s, but it was not until the Second World War that they were first used in the United States. All the military branches issued Benzedrine, Dexedrine, and other amphetamines to relieve fatigue and anxiety, especially in battle conditions. Amphetamines became more readily available after the war and were used widely by truck drivers who had to stay alert for extended periods of time, by people attempting to lose weight, by students studying for examinations, and by people seeking relief from nasal congestion. Street names for the amphetamines included *bennies, black beauties, King Kong pills, pinks,* and *purple hearts.*[15]

By the early 1990s, MDMA and methamphetamine arrived on the drug scene in the United States. MDMA, which had been used by psychiatrists and other therapists because of its therapeutic benefits, had become a Schedule I drug by 1986, which meant that its manufacture, distribution, and sale violated federal law. Yet it maintained some popularity among undergraduate populations across the nation. **Ecstasy,** the common name for MDMA, became popular on college campuses and with adolescents; it was widely used at parties, sometimes called *raves* in the United States but more often in the United Kingdom. Ecstasy usually is ingested orally in tablet or capsule form, sometimes snorted, and occasionally smoked. MDMA is reported to produce profound pleasurable effects, such as acute euphoria and positive changes in self-confidence and attitude.[16] Ecstasy and various other substances are often called *club drugs.*

HALLUCINOGENS

A variety of hallucinogens have been available over the years to adolescents interested in embracing mind-expanding experiences. Leading the parade has been D-lysergic acid diethylamide, usually known as LSD. Public reaction in the late 1960s against LSD and other psychedelic substances resulted in a dramatic decline in their use in the 1970s.

PCP, or phencyclidine, a nervous system excitant that has analgesic, anesthetic, and hallucinogenic properties, was introduced in the late 1960s and became popular during the 1970s. First marketed as the Peace Pill, PCP was also known as *angel dust, animal tank, aurora borealis, buzz, devil dust, DOA, dummy dust, elephant, elephant juice, goon, THC,* and *rocket fuel.* The use of PCP began to decline in 1979, as it became apparent how dangerous this drug was, and has continued to decline until 2004, when it reached its lowest prevalence point to data at 0.7 percent.[17]

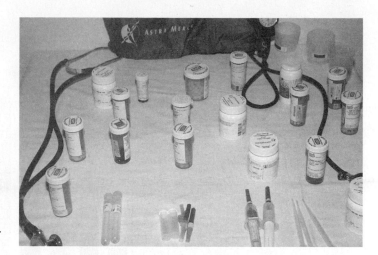

Modern biological and medical research is changing our conceptions of what causes delinquency and thus, how to treat it. (Photo by Kathryn Miller.)

HEROIN

Opium, which is derived from certain species of poppy, is the source of **heroin,** morphine, pargonic, and codeine, some of which are used medically. Heroin, a refined form of morphine, was introduced about the turn of the twentieth century and has such street names as *horse, shit, smack, H, harry, henry, boy, brown,* and *black tar.*[18]

The danger of heroin overdose has for several decades marked heroin as a very dangerous drug. Although chronic heroin use, unlike the use of most other drugs, appears to produce relatively minor direct or permanent physiological damage, street heroin users typically neglect themselves and, consequently, report such disorders as heart and lung abnormalities, scarred veins, weight loss, malnutrition, endocarditis (a disease of the heart valves), strokes, gynecological problems, hepatic problems, local skin infections, and abscesses.[19]

STEROIDS

Adolescents, college athletes, and professional athletes use highly dangerous **anabolic steroids** to gain muscle bulk and strength. Baseball players, such as Mark McGuire, Sammy Sosa, and Barry Bonds, all of whom have become the greatest homerun hitters, have been accused of steroid use. Black-market sales of these drugs approach $1 billion annually. Long-term users may spend up to $400 a week on steroids. Steroids have a number of health problems associated with their long-term use: liver ailments, tumors, kidney problems, sexual dysfunction, hypertension, and such mental problems as depression. Also, steroid users frequently share needles, which puts them at high risk for contracting human immunodeficiency virus (HIV), the virus that causes AIDS.[20]

✓**Progress Check 13.1**
Review this section at
www.prenhall.com/bartollas

HOW MUCH DRUG USE IS THERE AMONG JUVENILES?

The abuse of alcohol and other drugs are identified, along with juvenile unlawful behavior, as two of the most serious problems of adolescents. Figure 13–1 shows, for a one-month period, the illicit use of drugs of any kind in a national household sample of juveniles and adults. Young people are clearly

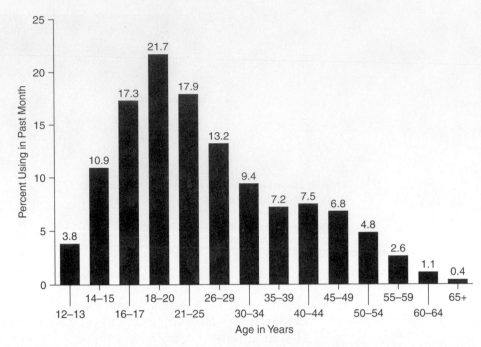

Figure 13–1   *Past Month Illicit Drug Use Among Persons Aged 12 or Older, by Age: 2004*

Source: Substance Abuse and Mental Health Services Administration, *Results from the 2004 National Survey on Drug Use and Health: National Findings* (Rockville, MD: Office of Applied Studies, NSDUH Series H-28, DHHS Publication No. SMA 05-4062), 2005.

the leaders in illicit drug use in the United States. After age eighteen, drug use tends to drop off, with only 2.6 percent of persons over age fifty using illicit drugs of any kind. Somewhat surprising to some, a few studies are now beginning to focus on the long-known fact that elementary students are using various types of drugs. Most research today, unfortunately, focuses on youths ages twelve and older. Our attention here, of course, is focused on the use of alcohol and other drugs by juveniles.

One of the most important subjects studied by the *Monitoring the Future Project* is drug use by middle school students. Data for 2004 indicate that the upturn in drug use that started in the early 1980s has reversed modestly and has been dropping in recent years. For example, the proportion of eighth graders taking any illicit drug increased somewhat between 1994 and 1996, from 25.7 to 31.2 percent. By 2004, the proportion of eighth graders who had used any illicit drug in the previous year dropped to 15 percent, while drug use by tenth graders and twelfth graders had stabilized. Nevertheless, in 2004, the annual prevalence for using any drug by tenth and twelfth graders was 14 and 39 percent, respectively. Alcohol and marijuana remain the drugs of choice for middle and high school students, with alcohol use remaining stable through 2004 and a slight decrease in past-month marijuana use by males ages twelve to seventeen. Time will tell whether the decrease will continue, remain stable, or rise in this century.[21]

Even with this recent drop, rates of drug use are higher than anyone would like. It is somewhat sobering that approximately 39 percent of all high school seniors have tried illicit drugs in the past year, followed by 31 percent of tenth graders and 15 percent of eighth graders. Of some interest, a significant proportion of these students used marijuana only, but the data also indicate that many students used other, more potent drugs as well. In addition to alcohol and marijuana, rather large percentages of youths over their lifetimes used inhalants, hallucinogens, stimulants, and sedatives. Disconcerting is the extent to which youths experimented with cocaine, heroin, and other opiates as early as the eighth grade and below.

WHAT IS THE RELATIONSHIP BETWEEN DRUG USE AND DELINQUENCY?

One of the important issues in the juvenile delinquency/juvenile justice field is whether drugs cause delinquency or delinquency leads to drug use, or whether the use of other drugs precedes both delinquency and the onset of drug use.[22] Research has found that delinquency tends to precede the use of drugs.[23] Other research proposes that what might appear to be a causal association is actually a product of shared antecedents.[24] A common factor may underlay both the frequency and type of drug use.[25] Furthermore, a number of researchers have found that substance abuse is just one of an interrelated and overlapping group of adolescent problem behaviors, including delinquency, teen pregnancy, school failure, and dropping out of school.[26] According to this position, substance abuse is one of the problem behaviors developed by adolescents during their early life course.

Consensus has been increasing on three findings that explain the onset and continuing use of illicit drugs. First, widespread agreement exists that a sequential pattern of involvement in drug use takes place during adolescence.[27] Denise B. Kandel and colleagues, using cross-sectional research and longitudinal data, proposed a developmental model for drug-use involvement. This model suggests that alcohol use follows a pattern of minor delinquency and exposure to friends and parents who drink. The use of marijuana follows participation in minor delinquency and adoption of beliefs and values that are consistent with those held by peers but who are opposed to parental standards. Finally, an adolescent's use proceeds to other illicit drugs if relationships with parents are poor and there is increased exposure to peers who use a variety of illegal drugs.[28]

Second, a number of risk factors seem to be related to delinquency and drug use. Preperinatal risk factors consist of in-the-womb difficulties, minor physical abnormalities, and brain damage. Early developmental risk factors are found in the family environment, including a family history of alcoholism, family conflict, and poor family management practices. Other risk factors are related to early antisocial behavior and academic failure. Community risk factors include living in disorganized neighborhoods. According to J. David Hawkins, Richard E. Catalano, and Devon D. Brewer, the more of these risk factors a child has, the more likely it is that he or she will become involved in drug abuse.[29]

Finally, youths who use hard drugs are more likely to engage in chronic delinquent behavior.[30] Elliott and Huizinga found that nearly 50 percent of serious youthful offenders were also multiple-drug users. Eighty-two percent of these offenders reported use, beyond experimentation, of at least one illicit drug.[31] David M. Altschuler and Paul J. Brounstein's examination of drug use and drug trafficking among inner-city adolescent males in Washington, DC, found that the use and sale of drugs affected the frequency and seriousness of delinquent behavior. The heaviest users were significantly more likely than nonusers to commit property offenses; those who trafficked in drugs were significantly more likely to commit crimes against people than youths who did not sell drugs; and juveniles who both used and sold drugs were the most likely to commit offenses against property and persons.[32]

WHAT CATEGORIES MAKE UP DRUG AND ALCOHOL USERS?

As indicated by the statistics in this chapter, drug use is pervasive and increasing among some young people, especially those involved in antisocial behaviors. One group of juveniles includes experimental users; they are curious about drugs and occasionally use them to test the effects. Another group consists of social or recreational users who occasionally take drugs to socialize with friends. In a third group are youths who spend considerable time and money obtaining drugs, and these substances play an important role in the users' lives. Despite heavy and regular use, however, adolescents in this group are still functional and able to meet social and academic responsibilities. The lives of juveniles in a fourth group are dominated by drugs, and the process of securing and using drugs interferes with their everyday functioning. These four groups fit into two clusters: (1) social or recreational users and (2) those whose lives are dominated by drugs—**addicts.** Some of these users are plagued by internal demons.

SOCIAL OR RECREATIONAL USERS

Adolescents generally prefer substances that are not too costly. Beer and marijuana meet this criterion better than hard drugs do. Availability and potency are also important in drug use, for these substances are likely to be used as means to other ends, especially for achieving excitement. For example, marijuana, alcohol, and other drugs used at football games, rock concerts, parties, outings, dances, and similar activities provide additional excitement already inherent in such activities or, in some cases, produce excitement when it seems to be lacking. In addition to excitement, experience-enhancing substances serve the purpose of exploration. They enable the youth to experience new social orbits, mating relations, and unfamiliar places. Narcotic substances are further used to escape or retreat from the external world into a private inner self.

The fact is that drug and alcohol use among American adolescents is increasing, with no good news on the horizon. Alcohol use is continuing to rise among *all* American adolescents, rich as well as poor, nonoffenders as well as offenders. It constitutes a serious social problem that currently is attracting national attention. More bad news is that the use of marijuana has experienced a major increase among American adolescents in the past decade.[33]

ADDICTS

Too many adolescents' lives are dominated by drugs. Many of these drug-dependent youths need speed in the morning, and they require speed in school to make it through the day. Others become intoxicated several evenings a week and may even drink at school. Still others use so much marijuana that they become known to their peers as *pot heads.* Even sadder, other youths, especially high-risk ones, become addicted to crack cocaine. They are likely to be unable to give up this addiction even if they become pregnant. Further, drug-dependent youths typically are multiple-drug users.

The factors that make a youth a high risk for later substance abuse include the following:

1. Early initiation: use of any substance by the age of ten or twelve
2. School problems: low expectation that school will be a positive experience, low grades, disruptive behavior in school, and truancy
3. Family problems: lack of parental support and guidance

4. Peer influences: relationships with peers who use substances and an inability to resist their influences

5. Personality: nonconformism, rebellion, or a strong sense of independence[34]

Those who work with juvenile offenders argue that rarely is a youth institutionalized or placed on probation who does not have some history of alcohol or narcotic abuse.[35] As one director of guidance noted, "We only have one or two youths a year admitted to this institution who don't have a problem with substance abuse."[36]

The use of drugs, especially on a daily basis, increases the likelihood that a youth will be arrested and referred to the juvenile justice system. Other short-term consequences are vulnerability to other drugs, loss of interest in school, and impaired psychological functioning. Long-term consequences include respiratory problems, drug dependence, chronic depression and fatigue, and social and financial problems. A long-term risk of taking intravenous drugs today is AIDS.[37]

One of the many sad stories of addiction is that of Amanda Peterson, who was introduced to meth by her father and who became completly hooked on the drug:

Following the classic pattern of addiction, she ate or smoked more and more of the drug, getting less and less effect.

She willingly recounts the facts behind the drug charges and assault arrests that littered her teenage years. She speaks more reluctantly about an earlier incident, for which court papers listed her as "victim." Authorities referred to her then as "Jane Doe," because the 1998 crime was so awful. And after all, she was just a kid. In the "defendant" space, the court papers list a man's name. Peterson barely recognizes it, because she only knew him by his nickname, Satan.

Satan threw drug parties at his house, and he let kids participate. When Peterson was wasted, he would have sex with her on a couch. Police found out about it, and they arrested him on charges of sex abuse and running a drug house. Peterson didn't understand, at first, what was wrong. She thought he loved her. She was thirteen. He was thirty-two. She sees the truth now. "He didn't love me," she said. "He was just a damned pedophile."[38]

WHAT ABOUT DRUG-TRAFFICKING JUVENILES?

Some evidence exists that independents sell drugs as frequently as, or even more frequently than, drug-trafficking gangs do. Malcolm W. Klein, Cheryl L. Maxson, and Lea C. Cunningham's 1991 study found that "crack distribution, while including many individual gang members, was not primarily a street gang phenomenon."[39] Some adolescents also sell drugs independently of any gang affiliation, particularly in suburban settings.

Our understanding of juveniles and drug trafficking is enriched by Felix M. Padilla's 1992 book, *The Gang as an American Enterprise,* and Daniel M. Monti's 1994 book, *Wannabe Gangs in Suburbs and Schools.*[40] Padilla, in studying a Hispanic drug-dealing gang in Chicago, found that the drug enterprise had an occupational hierarchy in which the cocaine and marijuana suppliers were on top, followed by "older guys," "chiefs," and "mainheads." The street-level dealers, or mainheads, were juveniles who barely made enough money to survive and who generally had to supplement their income by stealing. Yet they never got ahead, because they were inevitably arrested, and it was necessary for the distributor's attorney to bail them out. It took them months to repay the distributor.[41]

Monti's examination of gangs in suburbs and schools focused on juveniles selling drugs in the schools he studied. He found that the Gangster Disciples had real control in the suburbs. The Crips and Bloods were also represented in the gangs that sold drugs. The drugs they sold included marijuana, crack cocaine, and different kinds of pills. Girls' involvement in drug trafficking usually consisted of holding drugs for boys, generally their boyfriends, when they thought that the boys might be searched by the police or school officials. Monti contends that the youths who sold drugs kept the profits for themselves and did not pool the money with the gang.[42]

Personal interview data add to this portrait of juveniles involved in trafficking. In urban settings, juveniles are members of drug-trafficking gangs, and as part of their membership, they are supposed to assist in selling drugs. As young as eleven or twelve, they may be given a firearm and told to stand watch at a crack house. If anyone tries to enter who is not supposed to be there, they are told to shoot and kill. As they get a little older, they are given the job of what is usually called a *mule*, delivering drugs to specific locations. Older juveniles are placed on streetcorners where they sell drugs, usually crack cocaine, to regular customers and people driving by. As Padilla's study found in other urban settings, juveniles do not get rich from selling drugs. If they are no longer going to school, they usually must supplement their income through other criminal pursuits.

In the cities and in settings made up of what in Chapter 12 is called *emerging gangs*, those juveniles selling crack cocaine may be working for someone from an urban setting who may or may not be a representative of an organized gang in that setting. They usually get a percentage of the profits from the sale of these drugs. Interviewees have reported that this is up to 10 percent and that they make a fair amount of money selling drugs. They like to talk about how much money they have made selling drugs throughout the years; a couple of the stories in the *Voices* address this issue.

Typically, those who made considerable money from selling drugs have trafficked in other drugs besides crack cocaine. Those juveniles selling marijuana sometimes make a lot of money. They are able to purchase several cars and have a closet full of expensive clothing. They also buy all kinds of presents for their girlfriends, and always have money to purchase "toys" and any entertainment they want for themselves.

In Focus on the Offender 13–1, the brief career of a youth who spent his life trafficking drugs and having authority over others who were trafficking drugs is reviewed. In this account, the tragic consequences of drug trafficking are revealed, both to those who traffic in drugs and to those who get caught up in this victim and addict cycle of buying drugs. Juveniles, especially those who sell drugs, are inevitably caught by the police, quickly processed by the courts, and sent to prison. Sometimes, they end up in training school first, but at other times they are sent directly to prison.

WHAT EXPLAINS THE ONSET OF DRUG USE?

A number of theories have attempted to explain the onset and escalation of juveniles' drug use. One of the most popular ones is that the bleak economic situation of the inner cities encourages the poor to find ways to seek solace and relief from their pain. Drug and alcohol abuse provides an immediate fix for their hopelessness but, of course, creates other problems in the long run.

FOCUS ON THE OFFENDER 13–1
THE DRUG-TRAFFICKING JUVENILE GANG MEMBER

Shorty Four is "... the tragedy of a young Black man who is indoctrinated into the well-organized and violent world of a Chicago west side street gang.... The subject of this collaborative autobiography is a victim even if he does not fully grasp the reason why. For like many young Black men who are being programmed to participate in the game of Russian Roulette, Albert Kinnard becomes a victim even though he [is] also a victimizer. Albert receive[s] his indoctrination into a street gang (a.k.a. organization) when he is just eleven years old and is adopted as a son of the chief of one of Chicago's most notorious street gangs. For the uninformed and misinformed, Albert describes the hierarchy of their gang, which may rival a major corporation or small nation. However, one may challenge their perception, which bears little compatibility to the political realities that characterize sovereign nations. Nonetheless, it gives their leaders and members a sense of power and ownership that may compensate for some of the social equities which have been denied to many of them. Albert has limited contact with his father and is raised by his mother, who does her best to keep him straight. But she is no rival to the attraction of the street gang where Albert begins his passage to adulthood.

As the son of a chief, Albert becomes a prince and immediately acquires status. After proving his loyalty to the gang in a shooting, he is put in charge of one drug operation. In this capacity he has authority over all the drug pushers in the demonstration (operation, activity). If he does well, the chief promises him three additional operations; thus the name Shorty Four. Albert lives up his chief's confidence in him and runs his operations with audacity, authority, and muscle. As the result of his propensity to take care of business, at any risk, he is given responsibility to run three more demonstrations. Until his incarceration [for life], Albert's life is filled with violence, killings, sporting women (hoes), and surviving each hour so he can live and see the next day."

Source: Albert Kinnard and Marlon Wilson, *Shorty Four* (Bloomington IN: Authorhouse, 2000). If you are interested in this publication, see http://www.authorhouse.com.

Critical Thinking Questions:
Why would drug trafficking be so attractive to a young, impoverished African-American youth? Unlike the experience of so many other youths selling drugs, why did it turn out to be so profitable for Shorty Four? If you had an opportunity to talk with him in prison (and he is still there), what would you say?

Another strong predictor is the drug use of peers. Some argue that drug use begins and continues chiefly because juveniles or adults have contact with peers who use drugs. Peers then provide role models, as well as social support, for drug use. Peers appear particularly influential for beginning marijuana use (see several of the stories in the *Voices*) but seem to be less important for starting the use of hard drugs. Of course, once peers persuade a person to begin using drugs, a pattern of use can be established that may lead eventually to addiction and continued use.[43]

A third explanation for the onset and continued use of drugs is that the typical addict has an addiction-prone personality and suffers from some deep-rooted personality disorder. Isidor Chein and colleagues' study, *The Road to H*, argues that youthful heroin addicts suffer from such personality disorders as "defective superego," "weak ego functioning," and "inadequate masculine identification."[44]

A further explanation for the appeal of substance abuse is that it provides a high or a peak experience. Anthropologist Philippe Bourgois puts it this way: "Substance abuse in general, and crack in particular, offers the equivalent of a born-again metamorphosis. Instantaneously," he says, "the user is transformed from an unemployed, depressed high school dropout, despised by the world—and secretly convinced that his failure is due to his own inherent stupidity and disorganization." Bourgois explains why it is such a sensate experience: "There is a rush of heart-palpitating pleasure, followed by a jaw-gnashing crash and wide-eyed alertness that provides his life with concrete purpose: Get more crack—fast."[45]

✓**Progress Check 13.2**
Review this section at
www.prenhall.com/bartollas

SUMMARY

- Drug and alcohol abuse is a problem behavior for many juveniles in the United States.
- Its onset, duration, and offset are determined by the dynamics of the interchange between the environment and the youth, which vary over developmental periods.
- Drug use appears to have increased considerably since the late 1970s, and today appears to be declining.
- The bad news is that high-risk children are becoming increasingly involved in substance abuse.
- Although the use of crack cocaine may be declining across the nation, it remains the drug of choice for disadvantaged youth.
- It is disconcerting that adolescents have increased their use of marijuana; indeed, some evidence exists that marijuana use among young people ages twelve to seventeen has nearly doubled since 1992.
- The use of meth has also increased, especially in the Midwest and the West. Meth, unlike crack cocaine, is more popular among white youths.
- Those who become involved in drug trafficking are usually caught up in the juvenile and criminal justice systems, sometimes with long periods of confinement.

WEB SITES OF INTEREST

Read more about marijuana at the National Institute on Drug Abuse Web site
http://www.nida.nih.gov/drugpages/marijuana.html
Learn more about drug-trafficking juveniles on this National Criminal Justice Reference Service site
http://www.ncjrs.gov/app/topics/topic.aspx?topicid=61

CRITICAL THINKING QUESTIONS

1. What explains the popularity of drug use in the United States?
2. "Just say no" is a common saying when it comes to drugs. Will that approach work? Why or why not? Under what conditions will it work or not work? If the user is a friend, what would you say to him or her? Would you turn in a friend if you believed you could help this person? Where would you go for help?

3. What do you think is the relationship between drug use and delinquency?

4. Why do college students drink as much as they do? How is their drinking related to the subject matter of this chapter?

NOTES

1. Interviewed in June 1981.

2. Lloyd D. Johnson, Patrick M. O'Malley, Jerald G. Bachman, and John D. Schulenberg, *Monitoring the Future: National Results on Adolescent Drug Use. Overview of Key Findings, 2003* (Bethesda, MD: National Institute on Drug Use, 2004), Table 1.

3. Rand Drug Policy Research Center, *Newsletter* (June 1995), 1; Lloyd D. Johnston, Patrick M. O'Malley, Jerald G. Bachman, and John D. Schulenberg, *Monitoring the Future: National Survey Results on Drug Use, 1975–2004:* Vol. 1, secondary school students, NIH Pub. Bi 05-5727 (Bethesda, MD: National Institute on Drug Abuse, Executive Summary); U.S. Department of Health and Human Services, *Youth Drug Use Continues to Decline*, SAMHSA Advisory, Press Release, September 2005. For high risk and crime, see Rand Drug Police Research Center, A Joint Endeavor of Rand Health and Rand Infrastructure, Safety, and Environment (http://www.rand.org/multi/dprc).

4. Howard Abadinsky, *Drugs: An Introduction*, 4th ed. (Belmont, CA: Wadsworth/Thompson Learning, 2001), 4.

5. In 1990, the U.S. Supreme Court ruled six to three in an Oregon case that states can prohibit the use of peyote by members of the Native American churches. However, Congress enacted a law providing a defense for those who use the substance "with good faith practice of a religious belief."

6. Abadinsky, *Drugs: An Introduction*, 4.

7. U.S. Public Health Service, *Healthy People 2000: National Health Promotion and Disease Prevention Objectives—Full Report with Commentary* (Washington, DC: Department of Health and Human Services, 2001).

8. Ali H. Mokdad, James S. Marks, Donna F. Stroup, and Julie L. Gerberding, "Actual Causes of Death in the United States, 2000," *Journal of the American Medical Association* 291 (March 2004), 1238, 1241.

9. For many other names, see James A. Inciardi, *The War on Drugs II* (Mountain View, CA: Mayfield, 1992), 62.

10. For a review of these studies, see Joseph M. Rey, Andres Martin, and Peter Krabman, "Is the Party Over? Cannabis and Juvenile Psychiatric Disorder: The Past Ten Years," *Journal of the American Academy of Child and Adolescent Psychiatry* 43 (October 2004), 1194–1208.

11. Inciardi, *The War on Drugs II*, 94.

12. U.S. Department of Health and Human Services, *2002 National Household Survey on Drug Abuse* (Washington, DC: U.S. Department of Health and Human Services, 2003).

13. T. M. McSherry, "Program Experiences with the Solvent Abuser in Philadelphia," in *Epidemiology of Inhalant Abuse: An Update*, edited by R. A. Crider and B. A. Rouse (Washington, DC: National Institute on Drug Abuse Research Monograph 85, 1989), 106–20.

14. Abadinsky, *Drugs: An Introduction*, 82.

15. Inciardi, *The War on Drugs II*, 39.

16. Abadinsky, *Drugs: An Introduction*, 143–44.

17. Lloyd D. Johnson, Patrick M. O'Malley, Jerald G. Bachman, and John E. Schulenberg, *Monitoring the Future: National Survey Results on Drug Use, 2004* (Bethesda, MD: National Institute on Drug Abuse, 2005), 148.

18. Inciardi, *The War on Drugs II,* 63.

19. For the medical complications associated with heroin addiction, see Jerome J. Platt, *Heroin Addiction: Theory, Research, and Treatment* (Malabar, FL: Robert E. Krieger, 1986), 80–101.

20. Paul Goldstein, "Anabolic Steroids: An Ethnographic Approach," unpublished paper (New York: Narcotics and Drug Research, Inc., March, 1989).

21. Lloyd D. Johnson, Patrick M. O'Malley, Jerald G. Bachman, and John E. Schulenberg, *Monitoring the Future: National Results on Adolescent Drug Use: Overview of Key Findings, 2003* (Bethesda, MD: National Institute on Drug Abuse, 2004).

22. David M. Altschuler and Paul J. Brounstein, "Patterns of Drug Use: Drug Trafficking and Other Delinquency Among Inner-City Adolescent Males in Washington, DC," *Criminology* 29 (1991), 590.

23. Lloyd D. Johnson et al., "Drugs and Delinquency: A Search for Causal Connections," in *Longitudinal Research on Drug Use: Empirical Finds and Methodological Issues,* edited by Denis B. Kandel, Ronald C. Kessler, and Rebecca Z. Margulies (Washington DC: Hemisphere, 1978), 137–56.

24. Altschuler and Brounstein, "Patterns of Drug Use."

25. Marc Le Blanc and Nathalie Kaspy, "Trajectories of Delinquency and Problem Behavior: Comparison of Social and Personal Control Characteristics of Adjudicated Boys on Synchronous and Nonsynchronous Paths," *Journal of Quantitative Criminology* 14 (1998), 181–214.

26. Richard Jessor and Shirley L. Jessor, *Problem Behavior and Psychosocial Development: A Longitudinal Study of Youth* (New York: Academic Press, 1977).

27. U.S. Bureau of Justice Statistics, *Drugs, Crime, and the Justice System* (Washington, DC: Government Printing Office, 1993), 23.

28. Kandel et al., eds., *Longitudinal Research on Drug Use.*

29. J. David Hawkins, Richard F. Catalano, and Devon D. Brewer, "Preventing Serious, Violent, and Chronic Juvenile Offending," in *A Sourcebook: Serious, Violent and Chronic Juvenile Offenders,* edited by James C. Howell, Barry Krisberg, J. David Hawkins, and John L. Wilson (Thousand Oaks, CA: Sage Publications, 1995), 48–49.

30. Delbert S. Elliott, David Huizinga, and Suzanne S. Ageton, *Explaining Delinquency and Drug Use* (Beverly Hills, CA: Sage Publications, 1985).

31. D. S. Elliott and D. Huizinga, "The Relationship between Delinquent Behavior and ADM Problem Behaviors," paper prepared for the ADAMHA/OJJDP State of the Art Research Conference on Juvenile Offenders with Serious Drug/Alcohol and Mental Health Problems, Bethesda, Maryland (April 17–18, 1984).

32. Altschuler and Brounstein, "Patterns of Drug Use," 587.

33. See the statistics on the rise of marijuana earlier in this chapter.

34. Joy G. Dryfoos, *Adolescents at Risk: Prevalence and Prevention* (New York: Oxford University Press, 1990), 54.

35. A statement made to one of the authors by several training school staff in the early 1990s.

36. Interviewed during the early 1990s.

37. Dryfoos, *Adolescents at Risk,* 48.

38. T. Leys, "Addicts Battle Back," *Des Moines Register,* November 26, 2003 (online at http://www.desmoinesregister.com).

39. Malcolm Klein, Cheryl Maxson, and Lea C. Cunningham, "Crack, Street Gangs, and Violence," *Criminology* 29 (November 1991), 623–50.

40. Felix M. Padilla, *The Gang as an American Enterprise* (New Brunswick, NJ: Rutgers University Press, 1992).

41. Ibid.

42. Daniel L. Monti, *Wannabe Gangs in Suburbs and Schools* (Cambridge, England: Blackwell, 1994).

43. For the positive relationship between peers and drug use, see T. J. Dishion and R. Loeber, "Adolescent Marijuana and Alcohol Use: The Role of Parents and Peers Revisited," *American Journal of Drug and Alcohol Abuse* 11 (1985), 11–25.

44. Isidor Chein, Donald L. Gerard, Robert S. Lee, and Eva Rosenfeld, *The Road to H: Narcotics, Juvenile Delinquency and Social Policy* (New York: Basic Books, 1964), 14.

45. Philippe Bourgois, "Just Another Night on Crack Street," *New York Times* (November 12, 1989), 52–53, 60–65, 94.

14

GENDER, RACE/ETHNICITY, AND CLASS

Last year Mia, a 17-year-old girl who lived with her boyfriend with parental consent, was kidnapped and raped by another man. When she reported it to the police, they arrested her as a runaway and shipped her off to juvenile hall instead of going after the rapist. Wilma had a similar experience on the East Coast, when she went back for a visit. Raped and dumped by a man who gave her a ride, she made her way to the nearest police station, where she was promptly arrested. The judge, seeing her past record, said he would sentence her to a state reformatory until she was 21—unless the social worker put her on a plane to California within 24 hours.[1]

OUTLINE

OBJECTIVES

1. To present the various explanations for why adolescent females become involved in offending
2. To present a feminist theory of delinquency
3. To examine the relationship between adolescent male and female offending

4. To examine how gender affects the processing of adolescent females in the juvenile justice system

5. To explore how race/ethnicity affects the handling of juveniles in the juvenile justice system

KEY TERMS

adolescence-limited (AL)
  delinquents
class oppression
cognitive transformation
disproportionate minority
  confinement

disproportionate minority
  contact (DMC)
DMC Relative Rate Index
early-onset, persistent offenders
  (life course persistent [LCP])

feminist theory of delinquency
gender-neutral

In addition to these accounts, countless other examples demonstrate how female adolescents face discriminatory treatment from the juvenile justice system. Female delinquency, like all other social behaviors, takes place in a world where gender still shapes the lives of adolescents in powerful ways. Feminist theory starts with the assumption that juvenile females are positioned in society in ways that produce vulnerability to victimization by males, including abuse and the negative effects of poverty.[2] Nor can the variable of class be ignored in understanding the behavior of juveniles. In all dimensions of their lives, class is important in determining how juveniles perceive themselves, are responded to by others, and are treated by the juvenile justice system. The middle-class male youthful offender typically is treated very differently by the police and court officials than is his lower-class counterpart. Finally, one of the most serious indictments of the juvenile justice system is the mounting evidence of unfair treatment of African-American, Native-American, and Hispanic adolescent males and females by the juvenile justice system.

This chapter initially compares the explanations of why males and females become involved in antisocial behaviors and presents a feminist theory of delinquency. The next section considers the various types of female delinquent offending following an examination of how gender, along with race/ethnicity and class, affects the processing of the female delinquent. The final two sections investigate the influence of race/ethnicity on the handling of male and female youthful offenders and explore how the categories of gender, class, and race are interlocked and influence both delinquent behavior and how this behavior is handled by the juvenile justice system.

WHAT ARE EXPLANATIONS OF FEMALE CRIME?

One of the research questions frequently raised is whether adolescent females have different explanations of why they become involved in delinquency than adolescent males do. There is little disagreement that adolescent females have different experiences than adolescent males. It is commonly agreed that females are more controlled than males, enjoy more social support, are less disposed to crime, and have fewer opportunities to commit certain types of crimes.[3]

There are three different opinions concerning how the commonly accepted male–female approach to delinquency should be handled. One approach focuses on the question of generalizability. Those who support this

gender-neutral position usually have examined such subjects as social learning, delinquent peer relationships, social bonding, the family, and deterrence and strain.[4] They claim to see no reason for separate theories to account for female and male delinquency and criminality because female delinquents and women in crime operate through the same factors as male delinquents and criminals.[5]

In contrast, another approach argues that new theories are needed to account for female delinquency and criminality. Eileen Leonard, for example, questions whether differential association, anomie, labeling, subculture, and Marxist theories can be used to explain the crime patterns of adolescent females and adult women.[6] Meda Chesney-Lind further suggests that existing theories of delinquency are inadequate for explaining female delinquency. Instead, she proposes a **feminist theory of delinquency,** which examines adolescent females' sexual and physical victimization at home and the relationship between these experiences and their crimes.[7] This position argues that the structural categories of gender, class, and race are more helpful than individual or sociopsychological explanations in understanding women's involvement in crime.

In the face of these divergent positions—one seeking to explain away gender gaps and to be gender neutral and the other focusing on the importance of gender in understanding delinquency and crime—Darrell Steffensmeier and Emilie Allen have attempted to put the two approaches together. They contend that there "is no need for general-specific theories," although they acknowledge that "qualitative studies reveal major general differences in the context and nature of offending."[8] These researchers are developing what they consider to be a "middle-road position."

WHAT IS A FEMINIST THEORY OF DELINQUENCY?

The feminist theory of delinquency argues that girls' victimization and the relationship between that experience and girls' crime have been continually ignored. Meda Chesney-Lind, one of the main proponents of this position, states that it has long been understood that a major reason for girls' presence in juvenile court is their parents' insistence on their arrest. Those who study female offending, as well as those who work with female offenders, have discovered that a substantial number are victims of both physical and sexual abuse.[9]

Chesney-Lind developed a number of propositions on the causes of female delinquency. First, girls are often the victims of violence and sexual abuse (estimates are that up to three-quarters of sexual-abuse victims are girls); but, unlike those of boys, girls' victimization and their response to that victimization are shaped by their status as young women. Second, their victimizers (generally male caretakers) have the ability to invoke official agencies of social control to keep daughters or stepdaughters at home and vulnerable. Third, as girls run away from abusive homes characterized by sexual abuse and parental neglect, they are forced into the life of an escaped prisoner. Unable to enroll in school or take a job to support themselves because they fear detection, female runaways are forced to engage in panhandling, petty theft, and, often, prostitution to survive. Finally, it is no accident that girls on the run from abusive homes or on the streets because of impoverished homes become involved in criminal activities that exploit their sexuality. Apart from their sexuality, they have little of value to trade and feel compelled to utilize their resource.[10]

Emily Gaarder and Joanne Belknap interviewed twenty-two girls convicted and sentenced as adults in a large midwestern state. They examined their lives before they were incarcerated and their perceptions of being tried and convicted as adults. These girls described lives filled with victimization and violence, racism, sexism, and economic marginalization. Significantly, the offending pattern of these girls was found to be similar to that of girls who remained in the juvenile justice system. Status offenses played a major role in this group of offenders tried as adults.[11]

Mary E. Gilfus's analysis of life history interviews with incarcerated female offenders further found that women's childhood and adolescence were plagued with neglect and abuse. Many responded by running away from home. Once they were on the streets, they became involved in drug use and stealing, after which many became involved in prostitution as a survival strategy. These offenders became prostitutes simply as a survival strategy, but it further enmeshed them in criminal networks. As they moved into adulthood, the majority of these offenders experienced additional victimization and many developed drug addictions.[12]

Furthermore, Mimi Silbert and Ayula M. Pina found that 60 percent of the street prostitutes they interviewed had been sexually victimized as juveniles.[13] Chesney-Lind and Rodriguez's investigation of the backgrounds of adult women in prison underscored the links between their victimization as children and their later criminal careers. Virtually all of these interviewed women were victims of physical and/or sexual abuse as youngsters; more than 60 percent had been sexually abused, and about half had been raped.[14]

WHAT ARE THE MOST IMPORTANT DIMENSIONS OF FEMALE DELINQUENT BEHAVIOR?

The studies of female delinquents have examined several dimensions of delinquent behavior: females' involvement in offenses, their use of drugs and alcohol, their participation in illegal behaviors, including gangs and prostitution; adolescent females' experiences across the life course; and their desistance and persistence as offenders. A feminist theory of delinquency addresses childhood victimization and the ways that discrimination and oppression, based on a juvenile's race or sex, can shape her experiences, options, and identity.

RELATIONSHIP BETWEEN MALE AND FEMALE PATTERNS OF ADOLESCENT OFFENDING

Early cohort studies provide some evidence of the relationship between male and female patterns of delinquency. Delinquency cohort studies generally include all people born in a particular year in a city or county and follow this group, or cohort, through part or all of their lives. The second Philadelphia cohort study examined all males and females born in 1958 in that city. It found that males were two and a half times more likely than females to become involved in delinquent acts. Law-violating females were much more likely to be one-time offenders and less likely to become chronic offenders.[15] The Columbus cohort study found that males outnumbered females by almost six to one in the delinquent population. The violent cohort consisted of 84.6 percent boys and 15.7 percent girls.[16]

Moffitt, Lynam, and Silva's examination of the neuropsychological status of several hundred New Zealand males between the ages of thirteen and eighteen revealed that poor neuropsychological scores "were associated with early onset of delinquency" but were "unrelated to delinquency that began in adolescence."[17] Moffitt's developmental theory views delinquency as proceeding along two developmental paths. On one path, the **early-onset, persistent offenders (life course persistent [LCP])** develop a lifelong course of delinquency and crime at an early age. On the other path, that of the **adolescence-limited (AL) delinquents,** the majority of male delinquents begin offending during the adolescent years and desist from delinquent behaviors around their eighteenth birthday. The early and persistent problems found in members of the LCP group are not found in the AL delinquents.[18] In Focus on Research 14–1, Moffitt and her colleagues follow a New Zealand sample of one thousand males and females from age three to age twenty-one, identifying how male and female delinquents differed in their behavior over this span of their life course.

FOCUS ON RESEARCH   14–1

GENDER DIFFERENCES IN THE DUNEDIN LONGITUDINAL STUDY

In *Sex Differences in Antisocial Behavior,* Terrie Moffitt and her colleagues reported on the findings of the Dunedin Longitudinal Study. The basic findings indicate that youths develop antisocial behavior for two reasons. One form of antisocial behavior may be understood as a disorder with neurodevelopmental origins—a disorder that, like hyperactivity, autism, and dyslexia, shows a strong male preponderance and low prevalence in the population. Extreme gender differences are apparent in this form of antisocial behavior. The other form of antisocial behavior represents the bulk of such behavior, especially by females. This form is best understood as a social phenomenon originating in the context of social relationships, with onset in adolescence and high prevalence across the population. Gender differences in antisocial behaviors, according to this study, are negligible. Males' and females' antisocial behaviors are particularly alike when alcohol and drugs are involved, near the time of female puberty, and when females are yoked with males in intimate relationships. Other important insights were:

- Increasing numbers of symptoms of conduct disorder predict increasingly poor outcomes in juveniles, regardless of gender.
- Antisocial behavior has disruptive effects on both females and males as they make the transition from adolescence to adulthood.
- The LCP antisocial female is extremely rare; approximately one in one hundred females in a birth cohort seem to be on the LCP path.
- Females and males on the LCP path share similar risk factors of family adversity, poor discipline, cognitive deficits, hyperactivity, undercontrolled temperament, and rejection by peers.
- Almost all females who engage in antisocial behavior best fit the AL type. In AL delinquency, the gender ratio is 1.5 males to 1 female.
- Males on the LCP path suffer from multiple poor outcomes as young adults, and youth on the AL path also have some poor outcomes.

Source: Terrie E. Moffitt, Avshalom Caspi, Michael Rutter, and Phil A. Silva, *Sex Differences in Antisocial Behavior* (Cambridge: Cambridge University Press, 2001).

Critical Thinking Questions:

Why do you think so few females in this study became LCP offenders? What predicted offending among male and female offenders? Were you surprised by any of the findings of this study?

FEMALE USE OF DRUGS AND ALCOHOL

According to the National Survey on Drug Use and Health, 11.6 percent of juveniles ages twelve to seventeen reported current use of illicit drugs n 2002. In the same survey, approximately 30 percent of juveniles reported having used an illicit drug at least once during their lifetime, and 22.2 percent reported having used an illicit drug within the past year. The major illicit drug used by this age group was marijuana, with 8.2 percent of juveniles being current users.[19] The results of this survey were quite similar to those of the *Monitoring the Future* survey, which found that 24.1 percent of twelfth graders reported drug using during 2003.

These studies and others have revealed a marked decrease in gender differences among adolescent drug users. Female high school students are slightly more likely than male high school students to smoke cigarettes and to use some illicit drugs, including amphetamines; they use alcohol and marijuana at about the same rates as male high school seniors. Yet male adolescents are more likely to be involved in heavy, or binge, drinking than female adolescents.[20]

GANG BEHAVIOR AMONG FEMALE ADOLESCENTS

The involvement of girls in gangs has become an increased interest of social researchers. Lee Bowker and Malcolm Klein's examination of a group of female African-American gang members in Los Angeles in 1980 reported that they never planned a gang activity. The planning was done by the males, who usually excluded the females; nevertheless, the female gang members would participate in violent crimes and drug-related activities.[21] J. C. Quicker's study of Mexican-American adolescent female gangs in East Los Angeles in 1983 found that the gangs always had a connection with a male gang and that they often derived their name from that of their male counterparts. The females were not coerced into the gang, but had to prove their loyalty and undergo an initiation procedure.[22]

M. G. Harris's study of a Latina gang in California's San Fernando Valley in the 1980s revealed that these adolescent females were becoming more independent of male gangs. This gang rejected the traditional image of the Latina as wife and mother and substituted a more "macha" homegirl role. Gang affiliation also supported members in their estrangement from organized religion, acting as a form of familism serving to "provide a strong substitute for weak family and conventional school ties."[23]

Esbensen, Deschenes, and Winfree, Jr.'s examination of the Denver Youth Survey revealed that girl gang participants committed a wide variety of offenses and at only a slightly lower frequency than boys involved in this survey. Their findings also failed to support the notion that girls involved in gangs were mere sex objects and ancillary members. In addition, this study showed that girls aged out of gangs before boys and that girls received more emotional fulfillment from their involvement with gang activity.[24]

Beth Bjerregaard and Carolyn Smith, using data from the Rochester Youth Development Study, found that involvement in gangs for both females and males was associated with increased levels of delinquency and substance abuse. Female gang members, for example, reported a delinquency prevalence of 66.8 percent, compared to 6.6 percent for nongang members. One of the most important factors associated with gang membership for both males and females was lack of school success.[25]

Jody Miller found from her research conducted in Columbus, Ohio, and St. Louis, Missouri, that a female in a mixed-gender gang must learn to negotiate to survive in the gang milieu.[26] Gang membership exposes young women to risks of victimization. Young women can choose to be "one of the guys" and expose themselves to higher risks of being arrested, injured, or even killed in conflicts with rival gangs. Or they can use gender to decrease their risk of being harmed by not participating in "masculine" activities such as fighting and committing crime. Females who opt out of violence and crime are then viewed as lesser members and, accordingly, are more likely to be victimized within their gangs.[27]

In sum, most studies have found that female gangs continue to serve as adjuncts to male gangs. Yet an increasing number of studies show that female gangs provide girls with the necessary skills to survive in their harsh communities while allowing them a temporary escape from the dismal future awaiting them. These studies reveal that girls join gangs for the same reasons that boys do and share with boys in their neighborhood the hopelessness and powerlessness of the urban underclass.

ADOLESCENT FEMALES AND PROSTITUTION

In contrast to the ever-increasing number of studies on adolescent females and gang behavior, much less research has been done on the adolescent female and prostitution. Eleanor M. Miller's *Street Women* is the classic study, based on intensive interviews with sixty-four Milwaukee prostitutes. Miller found that prostitution evolves out of the profound social and economic problems confronting adolescent females, especially those of color.[28] For African-American women, who made up more than half of Miller's sample, movement into prostitution was a consequence of exposure to deviant street networks. Generally recruited by older African-American males, these women organized themselves into "pseudofamilies" and engaged chiefly, though not exclusively, in prostitution. These women viewed prostitution as an alternative to boring, low-paying jobs and as a means to relieve the burdens of pregnancy and single motherhood.[29]

For whites, Miller found that street prostitution was not a hustle into which one drifted but rather a survival strategy. For this group, a direct link existed between prostitution and difficulties with parents, runaway behavior, and contact with the juvenile justice system. Interviewees described family lives characterized by disorganization and extremely high levels of violence and abuse. Yet running away from these chaotic settings resulted in the girls' arrest and lengthy detention as status offenders.[30]

Silbert and Pines's study, previously cited, found that a high percentage of street prostitutes had been abused sexually as juveniles.[31] Chesney-Lind and Rodriquez's investigation of the backgrounds of adult women in prison underscored the links between victimization as children and later careers as prostitutes.[32] Furthermore, R. J. Phelps and colleagues' survey of 192 female youths in the Wisconsin juvenile justice system revealed that 79 percent of them had been subjected to physical abuse that resulted in some form of injury.[33]

ADOLESCENT FEMALES AND VIOLENT BEHAVIOR

Since the late 1960s, the media have been quick to identify the violent female criminal, a type not previously supported by research on females and crime.[34] In the late 1980s, the media focused on the rise of violence among juvenile girls when reporting increased arrest trends. Between 1992 and 2003, juvenile females' arrests increased by 6.4 percent, while arrests of adolescent boys decreased by 16.4 percent. While decreases were present across many crimes of violence for both juvenile males and females, the period saw a 7 percent increase in girls' arrests for aggravated assault and a 29.1 percent decrease in boys' arrests for this offense. Similarly, arrests of juvenile girls for simple assaults climbed 40.9 percent while arrests of juvenile males rose only 4.3 percent.[35]

Brown, Chesney-Lind, and Stein's article, "Patriarchy Matters: Toward a Gendered Theory of Teen Violence and Victimization," challenges this notion of a rise of violence among juvenile females. They claim that self-report data sources reveal that juvenile girls' and boys' violence *decreased* dramatically in the late 1990s. They also cite the findings of the Youth Risk Behavior Survey, the biennial survey of the Centers for Disease Control (CDC). In this survey, while 34.4 percent of girls surveyed in 1991 said that they had been in a physical fight the previous year, this figure had dropped to 23.9 percent in 2001, a 30.5 percent decrease in girls' fighting. Furthermore, these researchers are skeptical of arrest data reporting rises in violence among young women, because studies of other systems that monitor injury and mortality do not show dramatic increases in violent victimization. Finally, in considering other forms of violence, such as robbery and murder, no data show that girls are becoming more violent. Instead, arrests of juvenile girls for other crimes of violence, including the most lethal, have shown decreases rather than increases.[36]

Brown, Chesney-Lind, and Stein conclude that "someone's behavior has been changing, but it is likely not the behavior of girls, but rather that of police and those who monitor youthful behavior, including the behavior of girls."[37] They believe that three factors are at work in this social construction of crime data on juvenile females' increased rates of violence. The first is *relabeling*, often called *bootstrapping*, of female girls' status offense behavior from noncriminal charges like incorrigibility to assaultive charges. The second factor involves a rediscovery of girls' violence," especially in the arrests of both girls and women for domestic violence. These researchers have found that a closer reading of the available studies reveals that most of these juvenile female assaults are "the result of nonserious, mutual combat, situations with parents."[38] The third factor is the *upcriming* of minor forms of youth violence (including juvenile females' physical aggression). Upcriming refers to policies, such as "zero tolerance policies," which have the effect of increasing the severity of criminal penalties associated with particular offenses, such as minor forms of fighting and school bullying.[39]

✓**Progress Check 14.1**
Review this section at
www.prenhall.com/bartollas

GENDER ACROSS THE LIFE COURSE

Longitudinal studies usually reveal that delinquent careers differ by gender. Male careers usually begin earlier and extend longer into the adult years. Studies of youth gangs reveal that female members are more likely than male members to leave the gang if they have a child. Also, conventional life patterns—particularly marriage, parenting, and work—draw both males and females away from gangs and offending behaviors, but do so more completely and quickly for females.[40]

Amy C. D'Unger and colleagues' follow-up of the second Philadelphia cohort study found the presence of both LCP and AL delinquents (see Moffitt's classification scheme earlier in the chapter) among the males. There was a higher and lower category for each group. Among the females were comparable AL groups as with the boys, though with lower overall offending levels. The high-rate AL female offenders did share marked similarities with low-rate chronic male offenders. Yet the chronic or persistent category of offenders was less prominent among the females.[41]

Rebecca K. Katz, using waves one and seven of the National Longitudinal Study of Youth, found that similar to other studies, childhood victimization, sexual discrimination, adult racial discrimination, and the experience of domestic violence largely explained women's involvement in crime and deviance.[42] John Hagan and Holly Foster, based on their analysis of data from the first two waves of the National Longitudinal Study of Adolescent Health, found that the life course consequences of experiences with violence, especially violence in intimate adolescent relationships, results in special difficulties for female juveniles, including depression and teenage pregnancy.[43]

DESISTANCE FROM CRIME

Three studies have examined the desistance process among women. Ira Sommers, Deborah R. Baskin, and John Fagan found that quality marriages led women to desist from crime, with some variation depending on the class and race of the women studied.[44] A later study by Sommers and Baskin revealed that the desistance process was quite different for inner-city women of color. These women were more likely to desist as the result of receiving alcohol and drug treatment or because they grew tired or fearful of repeated imprisonment.[45]

Peggy C. Giordano and her colleagues developed a theory of cognitive transformation to explain desistance, or the dropping out of cirme, in their follow-up of a sample of serious adolescent female delinquents. They found that neither marital attachment nor job stability was strongly related to female desistance. Instead, desisters underwent a **cognitive transformation.** These researchers found that four types of cognitive transformation take place as an integral part of the desistance process: (1) a shift takes place in the actor's openness to change; (2) the individual is exposed to a hook or set of hooks for change; (3) the individual begins to envision and fashion an appealing and conventional "replacement self"; and (4) a transformation takes place in the way the actor views the former deviant lifestyle. These cognitive transformations or shifts not only influence receptivity to one or more hooks of change but also inspire and direct behavior. These hooks "facilitated the development of an alternative view of self that was seen as fundamentally incompatible with criminal behavior."[46]

HOW DOES GENDER BIAS AFFECT THE PROCESSING OF THE FEMALE DELINQUENT?

The oppressive effect of gender in the processing of adolescent females in the juvenile justice system is illustrated in several ways. First, adolescent females frequently receive discriminatory treatment because of society's disapproval of their sexual activity. Krohn, Curry, and Nelson-Ilger's analysis of ten thousand police contacts in a midwestern city over a thirty-year period found that adolescent females who were suspected of status offenses were more likely than their male counterparts to be referred to juvenile court for such offenses during all three decades.[47]

Second, adolescent females who are victims of violence and sexual abuse at home have few or no rights. Parents have the power to invoke official agencies of social control to keep their daughters at home. If the girls run away from these abusive environments, as previously noted, they are defined as status offenders.[48] Christine Adler's analysis of referral patterns in evaluations of diversion programs across the nation found that adolescent females constituted 40 percent of the population in these programs and that more adolescent females than males were in these programs because of "noncriminal" behavior.[49] Randall R. Beger and Harry Hoffman's study of case files of juveniles ordered into detention by an Illinois juvenile court for technical probation violations found that females were confined in detention longer than males for disobeying probation rules.[50] Five basic factors were cited as responsible for this disparity: (1) probation officers perceived female offenders to be more difficult to work with than males; (2) female offenders had more severe family dysfunctions than males; (3) conflicts with parents were an issue, because parents reacted more negatively to minor deviations by daughters; (4) community-based resources were inadequate; and (5) more females than males had had multiple social service interventions before probation.[51]

Third, the early studies, especially, found that police officers, intake personnel, and judges supported a sexual double standard. Female status offenders were more likely than their male counterparts to be petitioned to formal court proceedings, to be placed in preadjudicatory detention confinement, and to be confined in juvenile institutions. But at the same time, males who committed delinquent acts frequently received harsher treatment than their female counterparts.[52] See Focus on Policy 14–2 for the lack of gender-specific services in the juvenile justice system.

Finally, in an attempt to continue institutionalizing status offenders, some juvenile judges across the nation have been bootstrapping status offenders into delinquents by issuing criminal contempt citations, referring or committing status offenders to secure mental health facilities, and referring them to "semi-secure" facilities.[53] A Florida study of these contempt proceedings found them to be disadvantageous to female status offenders. Girls who were referred for contempt were more likely to be petititioned to the juvenile court than boys referred for contempt. Females also were far more likely than males to be sentenced to detention.[54] This study concluded the following:

> The traditional double standard is still operative. Clearly, neither the cultural changes associated with the feminist movement nor the legal changes illustrated in the JJDP [Juvenile Justice and Delinquency Prevention] Act's mandate to deinstitutionalize status offenders have brought about equality under the law for young men and women.[55]

WHAT IS THE INFLUENCE OF CLASS ON THE HANDLING OF JUVENILE OFFENDERS?

Decades of debate still have not produced consensus on the true relationship between social class and youthful offending behavior. The early studies of the 1950s and 1960s found that middle- and upper-class juveniles were as delinquent as their lower-class peers. Then, Richard Johnson in 1980, in redefining social class as "underclass" and "earning class," concluded: "The data provides no firm evidence that social class, no matter how it is measured, is a salient factor in generating delinquent involvement."[56] Charles Tittle and colleagues' 1978 review of thirty-five studies examining the relationship between class and crime concluded that little support existed for the contention that delinquency is basically a lower-class phenomenon.[57]

Critics charged that self-report studies tended to overload their questionnaires with trivial offenses. Thus, when middle- and upper-class youths recorded their participation in such offenses as swearing or curfew violations, they were found to be as delinquent as lower-class youths. However, Ageton and Elliott's 1978 national study found that a different pattern emerged when juveniles were asked how many times they had violated the law during the previous year. They found that the average number of delinquent acts reported by lower-class youths exceeded the average number reported by working-class youths. The average number of crimes against person reported by lower-class juveniles was one and one-half times greater than that reported by the working-class group and nearly four times greater than that reported by the middle-class group. The average number of reported crimes against property was also slightly higher for lower-class than for working-class or middle-class youth.[58]

FOCUS ON POLICY   14–2
SARA GOODKIND: GENDER-SPECIFIC SERVICES IN THE JUVENILE JUSTICE SYSTEM: A CRITICAL EXAMINATION

Goodkind refers to the 1992 Juvenile Justice and Delinquency Prevention Appropriations Authorizations (JJDPA) that states that "the term 'gender-specific services' means services designed to address needs unique to the gender of the individual to whom such services are provided." She adds that "the term *gender specific* has been interpreted to mean 'for girls' and that gender-specific programming refers to a comprehensive approach to female delinquency rooted in the experience of girls."

Goodkind found four fundamental critiques of the literature of gender-specific programming for female delinquency.

1. The need for gender-specific services is demonstrated and justified by frequent citations of increased rates of arrest and confinements for girls. However, Goodkind concludes that self-report and other sources have indicated that girls' delinquent behavior may not be on the rise.

2. An essentialized notion of gender is used that services to reify socially constructed categories and ignore intersections of gender with race, ethnicity, class, sexuality, and other axes of difference.

3. Her third critique is that there is too great a focus on the individual. Interventions focus primarily on changing individuals, with few efforts geared toward institutional or structural change.

4. Her final critique is that girls' delinquency is frequently tied to their victimization, especially physical and sexual abuse. This approach ignores girls' agency and neglects the fact that girls continue to be punished for behavior that is considered to be acceptable among boys.

Goodkind's concern is to shift the way treatment agents, such as social workers, think about and engage gender. She is proposing an understanding of gender that is part of a framework for designing services for boys and girls that address their differential social locations without reifying socially constructed gender differences. This framework is based on the following seven principles, which she developed through her critical review:

- Deconstruct and move beyond false dichotomies;
- Adopt an interpretivist or constructionist epistemology that recognizes categories as socially constructed and presents a vision for social change;
- Uncover assumptions and identify interests and goals;
- Attend to the importance of context;
- Balance structure and agency and think in terms of interdependence;
- Focus on progress;
- and rethink difference.

Source: Sara Goodkind, "Gender-Specific Services in the Juvenile Justice System: A Critical Examination," *Affifia 20* (Spring 2005), pp. 52–70.

Critical Thinking Questions:
What is your evaluation of Goodkind's article? Do you believe that her recommendations would improve the services for adolescent females involved in the juvenile justice system?

Margaret Farnworth and colleagues' examination of the first four waves of data from the Rochester Youth Development Study found that the "strongest and most consistent class–crime associations are found between measures of continuing underclass status and sustained involvement in street crimes."[59] Their 1994 article further explored the possibility that "inadequate measurement may explain past findings indicating no relationship between class and delinquency."[60]

CLASS OPPRESSION

As part of the female delinquent's "multiple marginality," **class oppression** is another form of exploitation experienced by an adolescent female.[61] In a number of ways, serious problems of childhood and adolescence related to poverty set the stage for the young person's entry into homelessness, unemployment, drug use, survival sex and prostitution, and, ultimately, even more serious delinquent and criminal acts. Even adolescents from middle-class homes may be thrust into dire situations for economic survival if they choose to run away from abusive environments.

Traditional theories fail to address the life situations of girls on the economic and political margins, because researchers fail to examine the situations or talk with these girls. For example, nearly all urban females identified by police as gang members have been drawn from low-income groups.[62] Lee Bowker and Malcolm Klein's examination of girls in gangs in Los Angeles revealed the importance of class as well as racism:

> We conclude that the overwhelming impact of racism, sexism, poverty and limited opportunity structure is likely to be so important in determining the gang membership and juvenile delinquency of women and girls in urban ghettos that personality variables, relations with parents and problems associated with heterosexual behavior play a relatively minor role in determining gang membership and juvenile delinquency.[63]

Class becomes important in shaping the lives of adolescent females in a number of ways. Lower-class adolescent females tend to confront higher risks

Middle-class teenagers often find themselves under suspicion of alcohol or drug-related offenses.
(Photo by Stuart Miller.)

than middle- and upper-class adolescent females. They tend to have more unsatisfactory experiences at school, to lack educational goals beyond high school, to experience higher rates of physical and sexual abuse, to deal with pregnancy and motherhood more frequently, to be involved in higher rates of drug and alcohol dependency, and to lack supportive networks at home.[64] Not all adolescent females at risk end up in the juvenile justice system, but the likelihood of such a placement is greater for lower-class girls.

WHAT IS THE INFLUENCE OF RACE ON JUVENILE JUSTICE?

Race has been examined in terms of discrimination and gender and the effect of race/ethnicity and the processing of minorities in the juvenile justice system. The latter has become one of the most serious indictments of juvenile justice policy and has led to the enforcement of federal law to attain more fair treatment of minorities by the justice system.

GENDER AND RACIAL DISCRIMINATION

Young women of color, as well as other minority girls, frequently grow up in contexts very different from those of their white counterparts. Signithia Fordham's "Those Loud Black Girls" showed that young African-American women resisted the norms of femininity of white culture as they became loud or asserted themselves vocally. Yet this behavior led to negative school experiences, and it did not take long for these juvenile females to discover that the quiet ones were those who did well in school. Some of these young women decided to "pass for white" or to adopt more acceptable norms of femininity in order to succeed in school. Others refused to adopt this survival strategy, and their tool for liberation contributed to their lack of school success.[65]

The fact that racism and poverty often go hand in hand means that girls are forced by their minority status and poverty to deal early and on a regular basis with problems of abuse, drugs, and violence.[66] Minority girls' strategies for coping with these problems, as well as their gang membership, increases the likelihood that they will come to the attention of the juvenile justice system.[67]

Finally, there is the belief that girls of color enjoy the benefits of chivalry much less than white girls do. Middle- and upper-class white girls, especially those who have committed minor offenses, not sexual ones, may be given greater latitude by the police, court intake, and juvenile court workers than their minority counterparts. Like male minority offenders, female minority offenders are likely to be viewed as more dangerous to society and more likely to require long-term confinement.

RACIAL INFLUENCE ON JUVENILE JUSTICE PROCESSING

When racial/ethnic disparities do occur, they take place at any stage of processing within the conviction and incarceration rates with respect to their population base. A serious issue, of course, is whether this disproportionate representation in the juvenile justice system is due to a pattern of racist decision making.

Janet L. Lauritsen, in examining what is know about racial and ethnic differences in juvenile offending, offers the following conclusions which have wide support in the literature:

- Rates of juvenile homicide are higher for minorities than for white youthful offenders. Variations do exist in rates of lethal violence among minority groups.

- Official data suggest disproportionate involvement in nonlethal violence on the part of African-American youth. When arrest data are restricted to specific forms of nonlethal violence, African-American youth appear to be disproportionately involved in robbery, aggravated assault, and rape.

- Juvenile property crime data show that African-American youths are slightly more involved than white youths, although the level of disproportionate involvement varies by type of property crime.

- Arrest data show that white youths are disproportionately involved in alcohol offenses, and that American Indian youths are slightly more likely than African-American or Asian youths to be arrested for these crimes.

- African-American youths are disproportionately arrested for drug abuse violations and drug use, but data from juveniles on their own drug use and selling do not confirm the differences between African-American and white youths suggested by the arrest data. Indeed, white youths are somewhat more likely to report using marijuana (ever and in the past thirty days), selling any drugs, and selling marijuana.

- The arrest data for weapons violations indicate that African-American youths are disproportionately likely to be arrested for weapon violations.[68]

Lauritsen contends that the empirical evidence suggests that the relationship between race and ethnicity and juvenile involvement in delinquency is complex and contingent on the type of offense. Although the most commonly occurring crimes exhibited few group differences, the less frequent and serious crimes of violence showed generally higher levels of African-American and Latino youth involvements.[69]

Donna Bishop, in what will likely become a definitive article on race and ethnicity in juvenile justice, concludes that minority overrepresentation is attributable to inequities in the juvenile justice process rather than the incidence, seriousness, and persistence of their offending. Minorities are overrepresented among youths held in secure detention, petitioned to juvenile court, and adjudicated delinquent. Among those who are adjudicated delinquent, minorities are more often committed to the "deep end" of the justice system. When confined, they are more likely to be housed in large public institutions rather than privately run, specialized treatment facilities or group homes. Furthermore, at "the end of the line," prosecutors and judges are quicker to relinquish jurisdiction over minorities, transferring them to criminal court for prosecution and punishment as adults.[70]

Carl E. Pope and William H. Feyerherm's highly regarded assessment of the issue of discrimination against minorities reveals that two-thirds of the studies they reviewed found "both direct and indirect race effects or a mixed pattern (being present at some stages and not at others)."[71] They add that selection bias can take place at any stage and that small racial differences may accumulate and become more pronounced as minority youth are processed into the juvenile justice system.[72]

The Coalition for Juvenile Justice (then the National Coalition of State Juvenile Justice Advisory Groups) brought national attention to this problem of **disproportionate minority confinement** in their 1988 annual report to Congress. In that same year, Congress responded to this evidence of disproportionate confinement of minority juveniles in secure facilities by amending the Juvenile Justice and Delinquency Prevention Act (JJDPA) of 1974 by mandating that

[s]tates participating in the Formula Grants Program must address efforts to reduce the proportion of the youth detained or confined in secure detention facilities, secure correctional facilities, jails, and lockups, who are members of minority groups if such proportion exceeds the proportion such groups represent in the general population.[73]

During the 1992 reauthorization of the JJDPA, Congress substantially strengthened the effort to address disproportionate confinement of minority youth in secure facilities. Disproportionate minority confinement was elevated to the status of a "core requirement" alongside deinstitutionalization of status offenders, removal of juveniles from adult jails and lockups, and separation of youthful offenders from adults in secure institutions.[74]

The JJDPA was reauthorized in late 2002 and took effect in October 2003. The first three mandates, for the most part, stayed the same. The fourth mandate was changed from disproportionate minority confinement to **disproportionate minority contact (DMC).** The focus presently is on efforts to reduce minority contact with the system. Programs geared to delinquency prevention, as well as a multipronged approach to DMC, are encouraged.[75] See Figure 14–1 for a summary of state compliance with the DMC Core Requirement as of December 2002.

The status reported in this summary is current as of December 31, 2003. DSO, separation, and jail/lockup removal compliance is based on 2001 state monitoring reports (2002 reports for Oregon, Puerto Rico, and South Carolina). DMC compliance is based on FY 2003 Formula Grants program comprehensive plans. Wyoming did not participate in the FY 2003 Formula Grants program. As of December 31, 2003, South Dakota's application was pending review and approval.

Section 223(a)(12)(A): Deinstitutionalization of Status and Nonoffenders (DSO)

Full compliance—zero violations: American Samoa, Guam, Maine, Northern Mariana Islands, Puerto Rico.

Full compliance—de minimis exceptions:[a] Alabama, Alaska, Arizona, Arkansas, California, Colorado, Connecticut, Delaware, District of Columbia, Florida, Georgia, Hawaii, Idaho, Illinois, Indiana, Iowa, Kansas, Kentucky, Louisiana, Maryland, Massachusetts, Michigan, Minnesota, Mississippi, Missouri, Montana, Nebraska, Nevada, New Hampshire, New Jersey, New Mexico, New York, North Carolina, North Dakota, Ohio, Oklahoma, Oregon, Pennsylvania, Rhode Island, Tennessee, Texas, Utah, Vermont, Virginia, West Virginia, Wisconsin.

Not in compliance: South Carolina, Virgin Islands, Washington.

Section 223(a)(13): Separation of Juveniles and Adult Offenders

Full compliance—zero violations: Alabama, Alaska, American Samoa, Arkansas, California, Connecticut, Delaware, District of Columbia, Florida, Guam, Hawaii, Idaho, Illinois, Indiana, Kansas, Kentucky, Maine, Michigan, Minnesota, Mississippi, Missouri, Montana, Nebraska, Nevada, New Hampshire, New Mexico, New York, North Carolina, North Dakota, Northern Mariana Islands, Ohio, Oklahoma, Pennsylvania, Rhode Island, South Carolina, Utah, Vermont, Virginia, Washington, West Virginia, Wisconsin.

Full compliance—exception provision:[b] Arizona, Colorado, Georgia, Iowa, Louisiana, Maryland, New Jersey, Oregon (provisional),[c] Tennessee, Texas.

Not in compliance: Massachusetts, Puerto Rico, Virgin Islands.

Section 223(a)(14): Jail and Lockup Removal

Full compliance—zero violations: Alabama, American Samoa, District of Columbia, Guam, Nevada, New Mexico, North Carolina, Northern Mariana Islands, South Carolina.

Full compliance—de minimis exceptions: [d] Alaska, Arizona, Arkansas, California, Colorado, Connecticut, Delaware, Florida, Georgia, Hawaii, Idaho, Illinois, Indiana, Iowa, Kansas, Kentucky, Louisiana, Maine, Maryland, Massachusetts, Michigan, Minnesota, Mississippi, Missouri, Montana, Nebraska, New Hampshire, New Jersey, New York, North Dakota, Ohio, Oklahoma, Oregon, Pennsylvania, Rhode Island, Tennessee, Texas, Utah, Vermont, Virginia, Washington, West Virginia, Wisconsin.

Not in compliance: Puerto Rico, Virgin Islands.

(Continued)

Figure 14–1   *State Compliance with Core Protections of the Juvenile Justice and Delinquency Prevention Act*

Figure 14–1 *(Continued)*

Section 223(1)(23): Disproportionate Minority Confinement (DMC)

Completed identification and assessment/updated assessment/implementing intervention, monitoring, and evaluation: Colorado, Pennsylvania, Washington.

Completed identification and assessment/implementing intervention/submitted updated data (evidencing ongoing monitoring): Alabama, Alaska,[e] Arizona, California,[e] Connecticut, Delaware,[f] Georgia, Hawaii, Idaho, Illinois, Iowa, Michigan, Missouri, Montana, Nevada, New Jersey, New Mexico,[g] New York, North Dakota, Oklahoma, Oregon, South Carolina,[g] Tennessee,[e] Texas, Virginia.

Completed identification/implementing intervention/planning to update identification and/or conduct formal assessment: Indiana, North Carolina, Ohio, West Virginia.

Completed identification and assessment/implementing intervention: Florida, Maryland, Massachusetts,[g] Nebraska, Utah, Wisconsin.

Updated identification/planning or conducting assessment: American Samoa, Guam, Northern Marianas.

Completed identification/planning or conducting assessment: Maine, Vermont.

Exempt from DMC requirement (racially homogeneous population): Puerto Rico.

Drawdown restriction:[h] Arkansas, Kansas, Kentucky, Louisiana, Minnesota, Mississippi, New Hampshire, Rhode Island, Virgin Islands.

DMC status under review: District of Columbia.

---

[a]Fewer than 29.4 violations per 100,000 persons under age 18 in the state.

[b]OJJDP regulatory criteria set forth in Section 31.303(f)(6)(ii) of the OJJDP Formula Grants Regulations (28 C.F.R. 31), published in the May 31, 1995, *Federal Register,* allow states reporting noncompliant incidents to continue in the program provided the incidents are not in violation of state law and no pattern or practice exists.

[c]State currently allows commingling of juveniles and young adult inmates in juvenile correctional facilities and training schools and must submit an acceptable plan to eliminate noncompliant incidents. OJJDP is working with the state on the plan.

[d]State was found in compliance based on the numerical or substantive *de minimis* standard criteria set forth in Section 31.303(f)(6)(iii)(B) of the OJJDP Formula Grants Regulations (28 C.F.R. 31) and published in the May 31, 1995, *Federal Register.*

[e]State began to receive intensive DMC technical assistance in January 2002 to further enhance its DMC efforts.

[f]State received intensive DMC technical assistance from November 2000 to July 2001 to further enhance its DMC efforts.

[g]State has received intensive DMC technical assistance since November 2000 to further enhance its DMC efforts.

[h]Drawdown restriction (25 percent of FY 2003 Formula Grant allocation) pending submission of required information.

Source: Office of Juvenile Justice and Delinquency Prevention, *OJJDP Annual Report: 2003–2004* (Washington, DC: OJJDP, December 2004), pp. 37–38.

When racial/ethnic disparities do occur, they take place at any stage of processing within the juvenile justice system. Research suggests that disparity is typically most pronounced at arrest and that when racial/ethnic differences do exist, their effects accumulate as youths are processed through the juvenile justice system.[76]

In understanding overrepresentation, one factor to consider is that outcomes often depend on the jurisdiction in which the youth is processed. For example, juveniles processed in urban jurisdictions are more likely to receive severe outcomes, such as detention prior to adjudication or out-of-home placement following adjudication, than are those in nonurban areas.[77]

Prior to 2002, the JJDPA required states to assess their level of disproportionate minority confinement (DMC) by using a statistic dividing the proportion of a given minority group of youths who were detained or confined in a state's secure detention facilities, secure correctional facilities, jails, and lockups by the proportion that group represented in the general population. If this DMC Index was significantly greater than 1.0, the state was required to develop and implement a plan to reduce the disproportionality.[78]

However, it was soon evident that problems existed in interpreting the DMC Index. First, comparing one jurisdiction's Index to another was difficult. The value of the DMC Index was related in part to the proportion of minority youths in the general population. Those communities with low minority proportions could have very high DMC Indexes, in contrast with communities with high proportions. Another problem, even more critical, was that the Index provided limited guidance on where to look for the source(s) of disparity. Was disparity introduced at all stages of the system? Or did it accumulate from beginning to end? Or was it introduced only at the earliest stage and then remain through the end stages?[79]

Measuring the disparity at each decision point gives a better understanding of where disparity is introduced and/or magnified in the handling of cases by the juvenile justice system. To address problems with the DMC Index, the Office of Juvenile Justice and Delinquency Prevenetion developed a tool, called the **DMC Relative Rate Index,** to measure the level of disparity at each decision point.[80] Table 14–1, using the Relative Rate Index, examines at what stages racial disparity takes place among decision-making points in the juvenile justice system.

✓**Progress Check 14.2**
Review this section at
www.prenhall.com/bartollas

Table 14–1   *Rates of Racial Disparity by Arrest, Detention, and at Other Decision Points, 2002*

The national Relative Rate Index matrix for 2002 finds more racial disparity at arrest and detention than at other decision points

Decision Points	White	Black	Relative Rate Index
Juvenile arrests	1,576,400	625,500	
Cases referred to juvenile court	1,086,700	473,100	
Cases detained	199,700	118,600	
Cases petitioned	596,800	306,000	
Cases judicially waived to criminal court	4,400	2,500	
Cases adjudicated delinquent	421,400	179,000	
Adjudicated cases resulting in placement	90,400	47,500	
Rates (per 100)			
Juvenile arrests to population*	6.1	11.5	1.9
Cases referred to juvenile arrests	68.9	75.6	1.1
Cases detained to cases referred	18.4	25.1	1.4
Cases petitioned to cases referred	54.9	64.7	1.2
Cases waived to cases petitioned	0.7	0.8	1.1
Cases adjudicated to cases petitioned	70.6	58.5	0.8
Placements to cases adjudicated	21.5	26.5	1.2

- For every 100 white youth ages 10–17 in the U.S. population, there were 6.1 arrests of white youth under age 18. The rate for black youth was 11.5, yielding an RRI for the arrest decision of 1.9. The black rate was almost double the white rate.
- Except for the adjudication decision point, the RRI shows a degree of racial disparity for black youth. This disparity accumulates throughout the process, so that in the end, while black youth were 16% of the youth population and were involved in 28% of the arrests of youth in 2002, they accounted for 33% of the juvenile court cases that resulted in an out-of-home placement.

*Population ages 10–17 = 25,994,400 (white) and 5,431,300 (black).

Source: Howard N. Snyder and Melissa Sickmund, *Juvenile Offenders and Victims: 2006 National Report* (Washington, DC: National Center for Juvenile Justice, Office of Justice Programs, and Office of Juvenile Justice and Delinquency Prevention, 2006), 189.

SUMMARY

- Female offending, like all other social behavior, takes place in a world where gender still shapes the lives of adolescents in powerful ways.
- The value of feminist theory is ultimately based on accepting the notion that juvenile females are positioned in society in ways that produce vulnerability to victimization by males, including abuse and the negative effects of poverty.
- The problems of sexism, racism, and class and their influence on female adolescent offending generally have been ignored by criminologists.
- An examination of how the categories of gender, class, and race are interlocked and influence delinquency across the life course will lead to needed insights into the problems female delinquents face in the United States.
- One of the major tasks facing juvenile justice is to develop a more just and humane juvenile justice system.
- The influence of class cannot be ignored in the handling of youthful offenders by police officers and officials of the juvenile justice system.

WEB SITES OF INTEREST

Check out Meda Chesney-Lind's homepage at this site:
> http://home.hawaii.rr.com/chesneylind

On girls and gangs, see
> http://gangresearch.net/gangresearch/seminars/female%20gangs/female.html

For the Texas Youth Commission on adolescent girls with co-occurring disorders, see
> http://www.tyc.state.tx.us/prevention/adolescent_girls.html

CRITICAL THINKING QUESTIONS

1. How has the social context affected the legal context in terms of female delinquency?
2. Why is the interlocking nature of gender, class, and race so important in understanding female delinquency?
3. Has your experience led to the conclusion that social class matters in the way individuals are perceived and handled in this society?
4. Why is racial disparity such a serious issue for the juvenile justice system?

NOTES

1. C. Macleod, "Street Girls of the 70s," *The Nation* (April 20, 1974), 486. Cited in Meda Chesney-Lind and Randall G. Shelden, *Girls, Delinquency, and Juvenile Justice*, 3rd ed. (Belmont, CA: Wadsworth, 2004), 194.
2. Donald J. Shoemaker, *Theories of Delinquency: An Examination of Delinquent Behavior*, 5th ed. (New York: Oxford University Press, 2005), 266.
3. *Juvenile Female Offenders: A Status of the States Report* (Washington, DC: Office of Juvenile Justice and Delinquency Prevention, 1998).
4. Jody Miller, *One of The Guys: Girls, Gangs, and Gender* (New York: Oxford University Press, 2001), 3–4.

5. Kathleen Daly, "Looking Back, Looking Forward: The Promise of Feminist Transformation," in *The Criminal Justice System and Women: Offenders, Victims, and Workers,* edited by B. R. Price and N. J. Sokoloff (New York: McGraw-Hill, 1995), 447–48.

6. Eileen Leonard, "Theoretical Criminology and Gender," in *The Criminal Justice System and Women: Offenders, Victims, and Workers,* 54–70.

7. Meda Chesney-Lind, *The Female Offender: Girls, Women, and Crime* (Thousand Oaks, CA: Sage Publications, 1997).

8. D. Steffensmeier and E. Allen, "Gender and Crime: Toward a Gendered Theory of Female Offending," *Annual Review of Sociology* 22 (1996), 459–87.

9. Chesney-Lind, *The Female Offender.*

10. See Clemens Bartollas, *Juvenile Delinquency,* 7th ed. (Boston: Allyn & Bacon, 2006), 211–12.

11. E. Gaarder and J. Belknap, "Tenuous Borders: Girls Transferred to Adult Court," *Criminology* 40 (2004), 481–517.

12. M. E. Gilfus, "From Victims to Survivors to Offenders: Women's Routes of Entry and Immersion into Street Crime," *Women and Criminal Justice* 4 (1992), 63–89.

13. M. Silbert and A. M. Pines, "Entrance into Prostitution," *Youth and Society* 13 (1982), 471–500.

14. Cited in Meda Chesney-Lind, "Girls, Crime, and Women's Place," *Crime and Delinquency* 35 (1988), 5–29.

15. M. Wolfgang, R. M. Figlio, and T. Sellin, *Delinquency in a Birth Cohort* (Chicago: University of Chicago Press, 1972).

16. D. Hamparian, R. Schuster, S. Dinitz, and J. P. Conrad, *A Violent Few: A Study of Dangerous Juveniles* (Lexington, MA: D. C. Heath, 1980).

17. T. E. Moffitt, M. Rutter, and P. A. Silva, *Sex Differences in Antisocial Behavior: Conduct Disorder, Delinquency, and Violence in the Dunedin Longitudinal Study* (Cambridge: Cambridge University Press, 2001).

18. T. E. Moffitt, "Adolescent-Limited and Life-Course Persistent Antisocial Behavior: A Developmental Taxonomy," *Psychological Review* 100 (1993), 674–701.

19. Office of National Drug Control Policy, *National Drug Control Strategy* (Washington, DC: Office of National Drug Control Policy, 2003).

20. U.S. Department of Health and Human Services, *2002 National Household Survey of Drug Abuse* (Washington, DC: U.S. Department of Health and Human Services.

21. L. Bowker and M. Klein, "Female Participation in Delinquent Gang Activities," *Adolescence* 13 (1983), 750–51.

22. J. C. Quicker, *Home Girls: Characterizing Chicano Gangs* (San Pedro, CA: International University Press, 1983).

23. M. G. Harris, *Cholas: Latino Girls and Gangs* (New York: AMS Press, 1979).

24. F. A. Esbensen, E. P. Dechenes, and L. T. Winfree, Jr., "Differences Between Gang Girls and Gang Boys: Results from a Multi-site Survey," paper presented at the annual meeting of the Academy of Criminal Justice Sciences in Albuquerque, New Mexico (1998).

25. B. Bjerregaard and C. Smith, "Gender Differences in Gang Participation, Delinquency, and Substance Abuse," *Journal of Quantitative Criminology* 9 (1993), 329–48.

26. J. Miller and R. K. Brunson, "Gender Dynamics in Youth Gangs: A Comparison of Males' and Females' Accounts," *Justice Quarterly* 17 (2000), 419–49.

27. J. Miller, *One of The Guys: Girls, Gangs, and Gender* (New York: Oxford University Press, 2001).

28. Eleanor M. Miller, *Street Woman* (Philadelphia: Temple University Press, 1986).

29. Ibid.

30. Ibid.

31. Silbert and Pines, "Entrance into Prostitution."

32. Cited in Chesney-Lind, "Girls, Crime, and Women's Place."

33. Ibid.

34. Federal Bureau of Investigation, *Uniform Crime Reports* (Washington, DC: Government Printing Office, 2003).

35. L. Brown, M. Chesney-Lind, and N. Stein, "*Patriarchy Matters: Toward a Gendered Theory of Teen Violence and Victimization,*" Wellesley Centers for Women, Working Paper No. 417 (Wellesley, MA: Center for Research on Women, Wellesley College, 2004), 5.

36. Ibid., 6.

37. Ibid.

38. Ibid., 8.

39. Ibid.

40. J. Bottcher, "Social Practices of Gender: How Gender Relates to Delinquency in the Everyday Lives of High-Risk Youths," *Criminology* 39 (2001), 899.

41. A. V. D'Unger, K. C. Land, and P. L. McCall, "Sex Differences in Age Patterns of Delinquent Criminal Careers: Results from Poisson Latent Class Analysis of the Philadelphia Cohort Study," *Journal of Quantitative Criminology* 18 (2002), 371–73.

42. R. S. Katz, "Explaining Girls' and Women's Crime and Desistance in the Context of Their Victimization Experiences," *Violence against Women* 6 (2000), 633–60.

43. J. Hagan and H. Foster, "Youth Violence and the End of Adolescence," *American Sociological Review* 66 (2001), 874–900.

44. I. Sommers, D. R. Baskin, and J. Fagan, "Gettng Out of the Life: Crime Desistance by Female Street Offenders," *Deviant Behavior* 15 (1994), 125–49.

45. I. Sommers and D. R. Baskin, "Situational or Generalized Violence in Drug Dealing Networks," *Journal of Drug Issues* 27 (1997), 833–49.

46. P. C. Giordano, S. A. Cernkovich, and J. L. Rudolph, "Gender, Crime, and Desistance: Toward a Theory of Cognitive Transformation," *American Journal of Sociology* 107 (2002), 990–1064.

47. Marvin D. Krohn, James P. Curry, and Shirley Nelson-Kilger, "Is Chivalry Dead?" *Criminology* 21 (1983), 417–39.

48. Meda Chesney-Lind and Randall G. Sheldon, *Girls, Delinquency and Juvenile Justice* (Pacific Grove, CA: Brooks/Cole, 1992).

49. Christine Alder, "Gender Bias in Juvenile Diversion," *Crime and Delinquency* 30 (1984), 400–14.

50. Randall R. Beger and Harry Hoffman, "The Role of Gender in Detention Dispositioning of Juvenile Probation Violators," *Journal of Crime and Justice* 21 (1998), 173.

51. Ibid., 183–84.

52. Donna M. Bishop and Charles E. Frazier, "Gender Bias in Juvenile Justice Processing: Implications of the JJDP Act," *Journal of Criminal Law and Criminology* 82 (1992), 1165.

53. Chesney-Lind, "Girls, Crime, and Women's Place," 116.

54. Bishop and Frazier, "Gender Bias in Juvenile Justice Processing: Implications of the JJDP Act."

55. Ibid.

56. Richard E. Johnson, "Social Class and Delinquent Behavior: A New Test," *Criminology* 18 (1980), 91.

57. Charles Tittle, Wayne Villemez, and Douglas Smith, "The Myth of Social Class and Criminality: An Empirical Assessment of the Empirical Evidence," *American Sociological Review* 43 (1978), 643–56.

58. Suzanne S. Ageton and Delbert S. Elliott, *The Incidence of Delinquent Behavior in a National Probability Sample of Adolescents* (Boulder, CO: Behavioral Research Institute, 1978).

59. Margaret Farnworth, Terence P. Thornberry, Marvin D. Krohn, and Alan J. Lizotte, "Measurement in the Study of Class and Delinquency: Integrating Theory and Research," *Journal of Research in Crime and Delinquency* 31 (1994), 32.

60. Ibid.

61. Chesney-Lind, *The Female Offender: Girls, Women, and Crime.*

62. Bowker and Klein, "Female Participation in Delinquent Gang Activities," 750–51.

63. Ibid.

64. J. G.. Dryfoos, *Adolescents at Risk: Prevalence and Prevention* (New York: Oxford University Press, 1990).

65. Signithia Fordham, "'Those Loud Black Girls': (Black) Women, Silence and Gender 'Passing' in the Academy," in *Beyond Black and White: New Faces and Voices in U.S. Schools,* edited by Maxine Seller and Lois Weis (Albany: State University of New York Press, 1997), 81–111.

66. Chesney-Lind, *The Female Offender,* 23.

67. Ibid.

68. Janet L. Laurtsen, "Racial and Ethnic Differences in Judicial Offending," in *Our Children, Their Children: Confronting Racial and Ethnic Differences in American Juvenile Justice,* edited by Darrell F. Hawkins and Kimberly Kempf-Leonard (Chicago: University of Chicago Press, 2005), 91–95.

69. Ibid., 99.

70. Donna M. Bishop, "The Role of Race and Ethnicity in Juvenile Justice Processing," in *Our Children,* 23.

71. Carl E. Pope and William H. Feyerherm, "Minority Status and Juvenile Justice Processing: An Assessment of the Research Literature," *Criminal Justice Abstract* (June 1990), 333–34. See also Donna Bishop and Charles E. Frazier, "The Influence of Race in Juvenile Justice Processing," *Journal of Research in Crime and Delinquency* 25 (August 1988), 242.

72. Pope and Feyerherm, "Minority Status and Juvenile Justice Processing."

73. Donna Hamparian and Michael J. Leiber, *Disproportionate Confinement of Minority Juveniles in Secure Facilities: 1996 National Report* (Champaign, IL: Community Research Associates, 1997), p. 1.

74. Ibid.

75. Howard N. Snyder and Melissa Sickmun, *Juvenile Offenders and Victims: 2006 National Report* (Washington, DC: National Center for Juvenile Justice, Office of Justice Programs, and Office of Juvenile Justice and Delinquency Prevention, 2006), 189.

76. Ibid.

77. Ibid., 189.

78. Ibid.

79. Ibid., 190.

80. Ibid.

15

INTERNATIONAL JUVENILE JUSTICE

In Sweden the responsibility for handling young people is shared by the social authorities and the judicial system. In the Swedish language there is no equivalent concept for "juvenile delinquent." Instead they speak of juvenile criminality. This system does not formally recognize status offenses. Such behaviors are dealt with through social welfare measures. All juvenile crime falls under the Swedish Penal Code of 1990. By law juveniles receive special consideration when found committing a crime. Youth[s] under the age of 15 are handled by social authorities rather than the police. Criminal responsibility begins at age 15. [More than] 80 percent of all juvenile crimes are not prosecuted but dealt with informally. Nearly 50 percent are resolved through the use of day fines without a trial procedure being used. Fewer than 10 percent of delinquent youth[s] are placed on probation. The Swedish model is more treatment oriented than [those of] most Western countries. But, in recent years the model has been subjected to substantial criticism as youth crime in Sweden has been on the increase and there does not appear to be any empirical support for the treatment oriented programs.

—John A. Winterdyk[1]

OUTLINE

OBJECTIVES

1. To introduce the *Beijing Rules*, their content, and their proposed model rules for juveniles for all nations
2. To describe the basic approach to administering juvenile justice in three industrialized countries—Canada, England, and Australia

3. To examine how four emerging countries—South Africa, China, India, and Brazil—deal with problem youths

4. To illustrate how some countries with extreme population, social, and/or economic difficulties—South Africa, China, India, and Brazil—deal with problem juveniles

KEY TERMS

apartheid
Beijing Rules
capital punishment
common law
corporal punishment
crime control model
developing countries

family conferences
indigenous populations
industrialized countries
jati
nongovernmental organizations
    (NGOs)
Panchayats

statutory law
traditional cultures
welfare model
Young Offenders Act (YOA)

One of the most exciting developments in juvenile justice over the past two decades has been a growing international awareness of the problems faced by youths. The world's media, child-care experts, national governments, and international organizations are for the first time looking at the problems of children in a broader context. Their findings, as illustrated by the comments in the chapter-opening quote on juvenile justice in Sweden, are both illuminating and sobering. Stark contrasts exist in how countries in different parts of the world and in different stages of economic development treat children. Industrialized and democratized countries, so often held up as models of rational and responsible systems of justice, often fall far short not only of their own ideals but also of those of the international community.

Arguments about what to do about juveniles and juvenile crime in countries around the world are similar to those found in the United States, Canada, and England. Discussed throughout the industrialized world, particularly, are the age of criminal culpability, diversion from the system, due process, the role of the police in dealing with juveniles, the separation of the dependent and neglected from the delinquent and criminal, the severity of sanctions, the efficacy of community-based programs and institutionalization, probation and parole, and the death penalty. Countries vary widely in how they handle these issues. Some governments ignore juveniles totally, while others engage in serious debate and study over what works best. This diversity has a number of sources.

Some of the variation is related to each country's stage of economic, social, and political development. Democratized and **industrialized countries** usually base their criminal and juvenile law on constitutionally derived formal rules and procedures. Well-developed educational systems provide them with trained police, judges, and professional child care workers capable of giving juveniles needed help. **Developing countries** with **indigenous populations,** however, frequently rely on the internalized and long-standing folkways and mores of **traditional cultures.** Rules in these countries are enforced by parents and by religious and community leaders and very likely are more effective than the formalized methods of democratic nations. Sometimes the two systems collide. Nations colonized by western countries even centuries ago often still experience social strains as traditional ways conflict with modern methods, thereby setting the stage for mistrust, acrimony, and sometimes violent conflict between the governing and the governed.

Attitudes of governmental leaders toward citizens also contribute to the diversity. More than a few countries are governed by political, religious, or ideological despots who care only about wealth, power, and control. Indeed, police, military, and civilian authorities in these countries often engage in beatings, torture, sexual assault, and murder. The methods of suppression used are so horrific that worldwide condemnation is directed at the guilty police, paramilitary security forces, and others. International media, United Nations White Papers, U.S. Department of State reports, and **nongovernmental organizations (NGOs)** such as Amnesty International constantly urge those responsible to cease their human rights violations. Yet the leaders of these countries continue to ignore even the most fundamental rights of their citizens. Nevertheless, momentum is building, pushing leaders everywhere to carefully consider their actions and the consequences of their actions before they condone violence against their citizens.

This chapter briefly addresses the first major effort by the United Nations to set standards for the treatment of children—the *Beijing Rules*. Then the focus of the chapter turns to its primary emphasis: justice systems in several other countries. These countries were chosen either for their similarity to the United States or because their population, culture, or state of socioeconomic development makes them unique. First examined are three postindustrial countries: Canada, England, and Australia. The modern, statutory legal systems of these English-speaking countries evolved from English common law; Canada and Australia, like the United States, disenfranchised their indigenous populations several centuries ago. Four countries, Brazil, China, India, and South Africa, are developing or emerging economically. These include three of the world's largest nations in terms of population; all are extremely poor and represent different areas of the world with diverse cultural traditions. In India, South Africa, and Brazil, the laws of colonial nations replaced traditional native laws of indigenous peoples, usually with **common law.**

Children throughout Africa and other Third World countries are often conscripted by adults to be soldiers, slaves, and prostitutes. (Photo by Patrick Robert, Corbis/Sygma.)

These common laws were, in turn, replaced by formal **statutory law.** Today, years after the end of colonization, the formal statutory laws remain in place, but long-discarded indigenous practices of native populations are reemerging as challenges to the statutory laws. Brazil has the largest population in South America and a colonial history that includes the disenfranchisement of native populations; its problems are characteristic of many South American countries. China has a huge population, numerous ethnic groups, ideological conflicts, and problems that accompany a changing socioeconomic structure. India's population matches that of China. India faces abject poverty and has fewer resources. South Africa is still reeling from the consequences of its former apartheid policies.

WHAT ARE THE *BEIJING RULES*?

One outcome of the emerging world order is the setting of international standards for the administration of juvenile justice. The earliest standards, which were developed in 1955 as the United Nations Minimum Rules for the Treatment of Prisoners, did not directly address the issue of children.[2] The *Beijing Rules* were the first to do this but should be placed alongside two other sets of rules adopted in 1990, the *United Nations Guidelines for the Prevention of Juvenile Delinquency* (the Riyadh Guidelines) and the *United Nations Rules for the Protection of Juveniles Deprived of Their Liberty* (the JDL Rules). These three sets of rules cover the prevention of delinquency, the due process required for processing offenders through justice systems, and the reintegration of offenders into their communities after confinement and/or rehabilitation. The *Beijing Rules* set standards for all countries (see Focus on Policy 15 –1).

The fundamental perspective of the *Beijing Rules* is based on the broader human rights movement. The actual rules state "musts" and "shoulds" that sound much like the modern due process requirements of the United States, Canada, England, and Australia. For example, the framers of the *Beijing Rules* emphasize the well-being of all youths as the fundamental principle behind the rules. "Juveniles" include all youths from seven to eighteen, although the age may vary according to local customs. The rules mandate that authorities not overreact to either the offender or the offense and that all youths are presumed innocent until fair hearings are held. Rule 7.1, for example, states:

> Basic procedural safeguards such as the presumption of innocence, the right to be notified of the charges, the right to remain silent, the right to legal representation, the right to the presence of a parent or guardian, the right to call and cross-examine witnesses and the right of appeal to a higher authority shall be guaranteed at all stages of the proceedings.[3]

The rules call for training juvenile justice officials to exercise proper discretion when working with youths. "No intervention" is considered the best policy for many children, and authorities should divert youths from the system at all stages of the proceedings. Youthful offenders should be placed with local families, schools, or agencies capable of providing the youths with appropriate care and protection. If juveniles are taken into custody, authorities must notify their parents at the earliest possible moment. Youths have the right to privacy when in custody, and their identities must be kept confidential at all stages of the proceedings. A youth should not be confined unless absolutely necessary, and no juvenile should ever be harmed.

FOCUS ON POLICY   **15–1**
THE BEIJING RULES: FUNDAMENTAL PERSPECTIVES

1. Member States shall seek, in conformity with their respective general interests, to further the well-being of the juvenile and her or his family.

2. Member States shall endeavour to develop conditions that will ensure for the juvenile a meaningful life in the community, which, during that period in life when she or he is most susceptible to deviant behaviour, will foster a process of personal development and education that is as free from crime and delinquency as possible.

3. Sufficient attention shall be given to positive measures that involve the full mobilization of all possible resources, including the family, volunteers and other community groups, as well as schools and other community institutions, for the purpose of promoting the well-being of the juvenile, with a view to reducing the need for intervention under the law, and of effectively, fairly and humanely, dealing with the juvenile in conflict with the law.

4. Juvenile justice shall be conceived as an integral part of the national development process of each country, within a comprehensive framework of social justice for all juveniles, thus, at the same time, contributing to the protection of the young and the maintenance of a peaceful order in society.

5. These Rules shall be implemented in the context of economic, social and cultural conditions prevailing in each Member State.

6. Juvenile justice services shall be systematically developed and coordinated with a view to improving and sustaining the competence of personnel involved in the services, including their methods, approaches, and attitudes.

Source: United Nations, "United Nations Standard Minimum Rules for the Administration of Juvenile Justice: The *Beijing Rules*" (New York: United Nations Department of Public Information, 1986), pp. 1–15.

Critical Thinking Questions:
How does the operation of juvenile justice in the United States fare in terms of the *Beijing Rules?* What changes do you think should be made in terms of juvenile justice in the United States to make it more humane, just, and efficient?

The rules go on to state that youths must be permitted to express themselves freely and without fear of recrimination. Juveniles have the right to an attorney and free legal aid; they should have confidence that the courts are informed accurately of their special social, educational, and emotional backgrounds through preadjudicatory and presentencing reports by trained court officers. The courts, additionally, should have access to a wide range of dispositional alternatives including "various care orders, probation, community service orders, compensation to the victim or financial penalties, group counseling and foster care or other educational establishments."[4] Confinement is the last resort, and confined youths must be released as soon as possible and must be placed in programs for reintegrating them back into the community. Corporal punishments are prohibited, and no youth under the age of eighteen should be put to death.

Importantly, the laws of all nations "shall be applied to juvenile offenders impartially, without distinction of any kind, for example as to race, colour, sex, language, religion, political or other opinions, national or social origin, property, birth or other status."[5] Few if any nations in the world today meet the standards set by the *Beijing Rules.*

HOW DO INDUSTRIALIZED NATIONS HANDLE JUVENILE CRIME?

This section focuses on three industrialized, English-speaking countries: Canada, England, and Australia. All share common social, cultural, and legal backgrounds.

CANADA

The development of Canadian juvenile justice parallels that of the United States in that juveniles in colonial Canada were tried in the same courts and held in the same prisons as adults. Then, in the early 1800s, some houses of refuge were built, and a few reformatories were constructed in the mid-1800s. Most juveniles were tried in adult courts and confined in adult prisons throughout the nineteenth century. Whether youths had the mental capacity to understand their actions, however, was debated as much then as it is today. Child savers of the late 1800s maintained that youthful offenders were misdirected children who required assistance more than punishment. Reformers of this era further believed that juveniles needed to be tried in separate juvenile courts and confined in facilities separate from those for adults, a clear shift in thinking from the past.[6]

The consequence was that a Juvenile Delinquents Act (JDA) was passed in 1908 at the federal level, calling for Canada's provinces and territories to implement a new approach to juvenile justice. This law called for a **welfare model** approach to juvenile justice similar to that of the 1899 act that created the juvenile court in Chicago.[7] Provinces and territories developed their own facilities and set the age of jurisdiction at sixteen, seventeen, or eighteen, depending on the prevailing philosophy in the particular political jurisdiction. The system that was developed called for informal practices with officials free to exercise great discretion. This approach dominated Canadian juvenile justice until the 1960s, when reformers questioned whether juveniles actually were being rehabilitated.

A 1965 report on juvenile delinquency in Canada criticized the informal and often arbitrary procedures of the 1908 act, but it continued to accept the ideals of the welfare model. After a number of unsuccessful tries, a new reform act, the **Young Offenders Act (YOA),** was passed in 1982. This act set the age of eighteen as the upper limit of jurisdiction across Canada and called for a modified justice model approach to juvenile crime.[8] Youths began to be held accountable for their crimes, to be provided with many of the same due process rights as adults, and to receive sentences proportionate to their offenses. Nevertheless, the YOA principles calling for welfare services for youths in need remained strong, but they emphasized that these needs should not be addressed in the criminal justice system.[9] Thus, the YOA was a compromise between the welfare and justice models, although the C.19 Bill of 1995 removes some of the treatment objectives of the YOA and strengthens justice and due process responses to serious and violent offenders.[10] These last two changes move Canadian juvenile justice toward a **crime control model** and have implications for all components of the juvenile justice system. See Focus on Practice 15-2 for the get tough approach in Canada.

The Police

The police function in Canada is to respond to and investigate youth crime. Upon apprehending a juvenile, police must inform the youth of his or her rights, which include consulting parents or counsel and remaining silent. In the event that the juvenile is willing to talk to the police, police must obtain a written statement that the youth agrees to waive these rights before the police are permitted to take a

FOCUS ON PRACTICE   **15–2**
PRESENT CONTROVERSY ON JUVENILE JUSTICE IN CANADA

There is evidence that juvenile justice in Canada is more controversial now than it has ever been in its century-old existence. This controversy has focused on the issue of youth violence.

Politicians at the municipal, provincial, and federal levels of government are responding in earnest to the growing public and media clamor to "get tough" with youthful offenders in general and violent juveniles in particular. Daily, the media tell of accounts of largely unprecedented horrific and senseless violent acts committed by youthful offenders; of youth gangs operating in suburbs; of drive-by shootings; of home invasions by juveniles in wealthy neighborhoods; of crimes involving "smash and grabs" in large shopping mall jewelry stores in which semiautomatic guns are fired into the ceiling and shoppers are terrorized; of children under 12 years of age committing serious crimes who can be neither arrested nor charged; and of vicious murders by youthful offenders that often result in failed efforts to transfer these cases to adult courts and therefore result in a maximum three-year youth detention sentence. While the homicide rate by youthful offenders in Canada has remained stable over the past 20 years, the charges for violent offenses have more than doubled since 1986.

Some Canadian scholars charge that the fear of youth crime is the unwarranted result of a media-induced "moral panic." They argue that the media sensationalize the few violent acts by a handful of youthful offenders, which greatly exaggerates the (minimal) real threat to the public. Furthermore, they maintain that due to the tremendous spillover of news and entertainment media from the United States, the public projects media images of endemic youth violence in major American cities into the Canadian context. This results in erroneous views of Canadian juvenile offenders who have only superficial parallels with their American counterparts.

Source: Raymond R. Corrado and Alan Markwart, "Canada," in *International Handbook on Juvenile Justice*, edited by Donald J. Shoemaker (Westport, CT: Greenwood Press, 1996), pp. 34–35.

Critical Thinking Questions:
Besides the similarity of the politicians' "get tough" approach on violent youth crime, what other comparisons have you found between juvenile justice in Canada and that in the United States? How much has the media contributed to a "moral panic" against youthful offenders in the United States?

statement or conduct an interview. In some provinces, Crown counsel must approve the police charge before information is sworn. If a youth is put on probation, the police enter his or her status on a national law enforcement computer information network and check the network on a regular basis when investigating juveniles considered suspicious. Police share information with probation officers to facilitate the filing of new charges in the event that a youth violates probation.[11]

Prosecution

The prosecution's role is most comprehensive in British Columbia, Quebec, and New Brunswick, where prosecutors make all decisions relating to intake, diversion, and filing charges; the prosecutor may divert the youth from the system if he or she desires.[12] In other provinces, police still are responsible for filing charges, although their charges, the evidence, and the possibility of conviction are reviewed by Crown counsel before the youth is taken to court. In all provinces, Crown counsel must "show cause" before remanding a youth to a juvenile facility before trial.

In addition, Crown counsel decides whether to transfer violent youths to adult court for trial. This decision usually is made on the grounds that youths cannot benefit from the treatment services offered by the juvenile justice system. This area of transfer is pervaded with ambiguous standards because of the conflict between the rehabilitative and crime control models of justice; the ambiguities force Crown counsel into many arguments and appeals over whether transfers should occur.[13] Beyond these roles, the prosecuting attorneys are deeply involved in recommendations to the courts concerning the proper dispositions for youths. Generally, Canada's Supreme Court relies on the "special needs" principle when evaluating appeals concerning the transfer of youths to adult court, and relatively few youths are transferred to adult court as a consequence.

Probation Officers

The probation officer's role has changed considerably since the implementation of the YOA. Probation officers now work closely with prosecution counsel in preparing background reports on youths. In addition, probation officers interview police in preparing their reports and again in supervising youths on probation. Judges, too, expect probation officers to play more of a law enforcement role than under the JDA, where probation officers were expected to employ the welfare model and seek treatment for youths in need. Instead of playing a youth advocacy role, as in the past, judges now prefer probation officers to be neutral in the courtroom and in the community. Also, many youths in the past were remanded to hospitals or clinics under "treatment orders recommended by the probation officers." These orders are no longer available to the courts today unless requested by the youth. Indeed, the current emphasis on law enforcement and due process makes it difficult for probation officers to develop comprehensive and integrated case plans for juveniles.[14]

The Courts

Judges' roles also changed with the implementation of the YOA. Whereas judges' discretion was extremely broad and informally administered under the JDA, judge's roles today are restricted in that judges cannot remand younger juveniles to child care agencies, nor can they transfer older offenders directly to adult court. Yet judges now may impose determinate sentences, assess whether youths should be placed in open or secure custodial facilities, and release youths from custody early. Judges today may also sentence young offenders to extended terms for murder; offenders now have the responsibility of demonstrating to judges why they should remain in the juvenile system.[15]

Juvenile Facilities

In spite of some changes, the traditions initiated by the JDA and the philosophy of the juvenile court at its beginning continue to influence Canadian juvenile justice today. Community-based corrections are found in all provinces and include community service, intensive supervision, and counseling services. Also used are private-sector programs such as wilderness camps and public-sector initiatives such as foster care, alternative schools, drug and alcohol abuse centers, and counseling centers. With the exception of Quebec and, to a certain degree, Ontario and Saskatchewan, these are not full-service programs, and probation officers remain somewhat frustrated with their inability to implement the welfare model.[16]

Juvenile institutions vary by security level and by province as much as juvenile facilities do in the United States. Some open facilities tend to lack fences and walls, while others, depending on the province, have all the security features of a U.S. maximum-security juvenile facility. Facilities focus on security, health, education, and recreation, with treatment provided when requested by youths. Most treatment is delivered by outside contractors, with the exception of facilities in Quebec, which offer treatment in institutions. Ontario and Quebec try to keep both minor offenders and criminal youths in the juvenile system because the legislators from these provinces believe that both types of offenders face the same fundamental problems.[17] Reports of physical and sexual assault by peers and staff continue to filter out of Canada's juvenile facilities.

Current Concerns

Canada today is experiencing basic tension among the welfare, due process, and crime control models of justice. Its juvenile justice code is an amalgam of the three, with the welfare model remaining strong but with the crime control and due process models gaining strength. Police particularly resent tenets of the welfare model that call for helping youths. Police further believe their hands are tied when arresting or working with street children and juvenile gangs. In addition, the amount of paperwork has increased as authorities attempt to guarantee fairness to youths. Tensions also exist within the courts as defense attorneys, prosecutors, and judges must perform a balancing act between the principles of the three models.

Many critics of Canada's juvenile justice system question whether the police and courts discriminate against minority youths. Police and court activity does vary from province to province, but evidence exists that Native Indians are prosecuted four times as often as nonnatives in British Columbia. In other provinces, more than half of the confined youths are Native Indians. Government reports state that the discrepancy between natives and nonnatives is the result of widespread discrimination, but some studies find no evidence of such discriminatory practices.

ENGLAND AND WALES

As noted in earlier chapters, English common law helped set the stage for criminal and juvenile law in the United States. The concept of *parens patriae* was of particular importance as it justified the intervention of the king in the lives of, first, all citizens and their families and, later, children. To review, children under the age of seven seldom faced any legal sanctions for misbehavior; children between the ages of seven and fourteen could face criminal sanctions, depending on the seriousness of the crime, their intent, and their ability to determine right from wrong.

Children who met one or more of these latter criteria faced the possibility of being punished as adults—often by imprisonment or **corporal punishment** such as whipping and branding. English law also called for **capital punishment** (the death penalty) for close to two hundred offenses as well as for the transportation of youthful offenders to British colonies in Australia, New Zealand, and North America. Many of those sentenced to death were pardoned or transported, but according to Leon Radzinowicz, eighteen of twenty people executed in London in 1785 were under the age of eighteen.[18]

In the late 1700s, the English and U.S. methods for handling juveniles roughly paralleled each other. The English initiated the use of private homes to house minor offenders, and lower courts were set up to adjudicate minor offenses. In 1847, the Juvenile Offenders Act permitted summary trials of youths under the age of fourteen. Then, in 1854, the first Reformatory Schools Act was passed; this act called for placing youths in reformatories separate from adult prisons. In 1879, summary trials for youths under the age of sixteen were permitted for most offenses, and in a significant reform, the number of juveniles imprisoned with adults was reduced.

The first juvenile court was established in England under the Children Act of 1908.[19] This court's jurisdiction was over criminal matters for *children* under age fourteen, for *young persons* between fourteen and sixteen, and for civil jurisdiction over youths in need of welfare services.[20] The Children Act called for abolishing the imprisonment of youths with adults and for placing juveniles in reformatories for treatment.[21]

The early acts did not emphasize special training for judges, nor did they focus on the special needs of youths—unless the youth's needs were exceptional. In the Children and Young Persons Act of 1933, the principle that the court "should always act in the best interests of the welfare of the child was affirmed as was the principle of *in loco parentis*."[22] The philosophy behind this act clearly was based on positivism and a welfare model rather than a punishment model of justice. Also established were changes in the ages of youths under the jurisdiction of the courts; "the age of criminal responsibility was raised from seven to eight (Sec. 50) and sixteen-year-olds were placed under the criminal jurisdiction of the juvenile court."[23] Thus, the court had both criminal and civil jurisdiction.

The Children and Young Persons Act of 1969 reemphasized the importance of treating delinquents the same way as any other youths in need. The age of minimum responsibility was raised from eight to ten, and juveniles who formerly were treated as criminals were handled through civil proceedings. Police were required to consult social work personnel about decisions concerning youths, and children under the age of seventeen were not to be confined in Borstals or detention centers.[24] Nevertheless, the ideals of the welfare model were not met, and the juvenile court took on the form of a criminal court that emphasized punishment.[25] A hard line emerged in England at this time paralleling the development of a similar hard line in the United States. Even so, the Criminal Justice Act of 1982 empowered magistrates to place delinquent youths in custody, issue care orders with residential requirements, and require community service; this act reflected a blend of treatment and punishment.[26] In 1989, the Children Act affirmed an existing philosophy that youths should be prosecuted only as a last resort; care cases were transferred to the civil courts.

The Criminal Justice Act of 1991 renamed the juvenile court the youth court, broadened the court's jurisdiction to include youths as old as seventeen, emphasized individualized sentencing based on the maturity of youths, placed more responsibility on parental responsibility, called for more interagency cooperation in dealing with youths, and developed new procedural guidelines for the police and courts. The 1994 Criminal Justice and Public Order Act was passed. It called for longer custodial sentences and a "secure training order" for juveniles.[27] The hard line was now in place.

The Police

The police departments in England are usually the first formal agencies to make contact with juveniles. Depending on the behavior of youths and the evidence, English Bobbies (police officers) are expected to exercise discretion in determining whether to hold youths for further action. If further action is believed necessary, youths and their parents must go to the police station, where most juveniles are released to their parents. Information about the children is collected by the juvenile bureau and is used by the Chief Inspector to determine whether to prosecute, issue a formal caution, or drop the case. If a formal reprimand is decided on, the juveniles are warned about their behavior and informed that further offenses will result in court action. According to David

Farrington and Trevor Bennett, "A caution can only be administered if the juvenile admits the offence, if the parents agree that the juvenile should be cautioned, and if the complainant or victim is willing to leave the decision to the police."[28] Cautions are used widely to minimize the penetration of youths into the system.

The ability to issue cautions has resulted in "net widening" in that officers are now bringing increasing numbers of youths into stations to reprimand them. At the court level, the number of youths diverted from the juvenile court increased and the number of youths sentenced to confinement declined.[29]

Police make arrests in England for the following types of offenses: in 1994, some 60 percent of males ages ten to fourteen were arrested for theft and handling stolen goods, 18 percent were arrested for burglary, 10 percent for crimes against the person, and 1 percent for drug violations. Females followed the same pattern, although the male-to-female arrest ratio was roughly three to one. Also, the youthful crime rate in England is slowly decreasing, as it is in the United States.[30]

Juvenile Courts

Juvenile courts in England usually are presided over by three lay magistrates or, less frequently, one magistrate. These magistrates are citizens who are believed to be well-qualified for working with juveniles and who undergo twelve months of special training in courtrooms, in juvenile institutions, and with juvenile probation and parole officers.[31] The court sessions are more informal than adult trials and are conducted by the magistrates at different times and places than the adult courts when possible; court proceedings are closed to the public. As in the United States, juveniles have no right to jury trials. The media may be present but must keep all information about the juveniles confidential. In England, unlike in the United States, juveniles have the right to bail.

Whereas only police officers prosecuted cases in the past, today either a representative from the Crown Prosecution Service or a police officer may try cases. Whereas in the past the courts relied on the presumed fairness of the police in presenting cases, the system today is moving toward the representation of juveniles by lawyers.

Once in the courtroom, juveniles and their parents must be present as the charges are read. If the magistrate is not convinced that the parent or child understands the charges, the magistrate may enter a "not admit" (not guilty) plea on behalf of the family and throw the burden of proof on the prosecution.[32] The prosecution then presents the information available about the case to the magistrate(s), who asks the youth and his or her parents if the information is accurate. The child's parents or counsel may cross-examine the police officer and any available witnesses.[33] If the youth is found guilty, a predisposition report is prepared, and, once completed, the juvenile and his or her parents are called back before the magistrate for sentencing.

Magistrates, depending on the seriousness of the offense, have a range of sentences available to them. They may discharge cases, issue fines, require offenders to pay recognizance (which is refunded if the offenders complete their "binding over" successfully), place juveniles under supervision (probation), require community service or the payment of compensation to the victim(s), or defer sentences for six months to see how well the youths behave during that time.[34] Magistrates attempt to avoid imposing the maximum custodial sentence of six months on offenders, although two consecutive sentences of six months each may be handed out if necessary. For more serious offenses, juveniles over the age of fifteen may be tried in Crown court, where longer sentences, including life sentences for murder, may be handed down.

Juvenile Institutions

Juveniles were housed with adults in local jails, prisons, and galleys in the late 1700s and early 1800s. The violence and disease in these facilities attracted the attention of reformers, who began to look for safer alternative placements for juveniles. One of the first reforms involved putting some juveniles with minor problems into private homes. Then the Juvenile Offenders Act of 1847 was passed, and the first reformatories for juveniles under the age of sixteen were built. Not until the early 1900s did the Borstal system develop, with a heavy emphasis on aftercare. Borstals lasted until the 1980s, when they were turned into youth custody centers in which sentences were determinate and youths received shorter confinements. The other institutions used for juveniles are junior detention centers for youths fourteen to seventeen years of age and senior detention centers for youths seventeen to twenty-one years old. These centers emphasize cleanliness, order, discipline, and hard work.[35] See Focus on Practice 15-3.

FOCUS ON PRACTICE   15–3
THE BORSTAL SYSTEM

The principles of the Borstal system are important to outline because they became influential in setting up similar programs in the United States and in the British overseas dominions. Briefly, the Borstal system called for the lad's reform by "individualization," mentally, morally, and physically. There would be physical drills, gymnastics, and technical literacy training. Good conduct would be rewarded. The staff were selected for characteristics that were likely to influence youths of the kind that a Borstal had to work with. Soon after the beginning of the program, it was decided that the minimum period of exposure to the Borstal should be at least a year.

The Borstal system proceeded on this fairly austere plan until 1921, when the remarkable personality of Alexander Paterson (1884–1947) was added to the Prison Commission. He was one of a kind. The son of an affluent family, he attended a public school and went on to Oxford University like hundreds of others headed for conventional careers in the civil service or politics. At the age of 21, he graduated from Oxford and settled in Bermondsey, one of London's worst slums, as a member of the staff of the Oxford Medical Mission. He lived in Bermondsey for 20 years, organizing boys' clubs and recruiting Oxford students to work with him in the clubs and, later, when he became a prison commissioner, to take on assignments in the Borstal system.

Paterson's work in the Borstal system was notable for at least four achievements. First, so far as possible, he removed the appearances and the procedures of the British prisons from the Borstals. The governor was still called the governor, but the assistant governors were housemasters serving, as far as possible, the roles of housemasters in an English public school. The prison officials were taken out of uniform, and so were the lads, who were allowed to wear civilian clothes instead of the convicts' demeaning uniform.

Second, having removed as many of the earmarks of prison as he could, he went on to bring in young university men to fill the posts of governors and housemasters. To induce scions of the upper and middle classes to choose a career in penology was an astonishing innovation. The governor in one of the largest prisons in England tells how he was recruited to work in the Borstal system. He had worked in Paterson's settlement house in Bermondsey during a university vacation. Shortly after his return to Oxford, there was a knock on the door of his college room, and there was

Paterson. He said, "I need you as a housemaster at a new Borstal. I want you to report to my office in London next Monday." The startled young student protested that he was only in his second year at Oxford but perhaps could work during the next vacation. "That's not soon enough," Paterson replied. "I need you full time, beginning next Monday." To the mystification of the college authorities and the dismay of his parents, he left Oxford, reported the following Monday, and continued in the Borstal system and later in the Prison Commission for the succeeding 40 years.

Paterson's third innovation was a training school for prison and Borstal staff at Wakefield in the north of England. The prison staff college was opened in 1935 to train likely candidates for promotion—not a popular new departure among prison officers accustomed to promotion by seniority. Eventually, the training program was expanded to include a six-week curriculum for all new recruits for prisons and Borstals and a six-month course for new assistant governors and housemasters.

Paterson's fourth and surely his most significant contribution was the Borstal mystique. He had a flair for aphorisms: "You cannot train a man for freedom in conditions of captivity." He added:

> The Borstal System has no merit apart from the Borstal Staff. It is men and not buildings who will change the hearts and ways of misguided lads. Better an institution that consists of two log huts in swamp or desert, with a staff devoted to their task, than a model block of buildings . . . whose staff is solely concerned with thoughts of pay and promotion.

American prison reformers took a considerable interest in the Borstal model. In 1940 the American Law Institute made a long and comprehensive study of the problem of delinquency that culminated in a model Youth Correction Authority Act, recommended for adoption by each state; it also called specifically for new institutions patterned on the Borstal system. The system was adopted in California and in modified form by several other states.

Source: Sir Evelyn Ruggles-Brise, *The English Prison System* (London: Macmillan, 1921), pp. 85–87.

Critical Thinking Questions:
Do we have such charismatic and dedicated leaders as Paterson today in juvenile justice in the United States? Can such a person still make a real difference? Do you believe that you can make a difference in juvenile justice in this nation? How?

Current Concerns

A hard-line consensus appears to dominate the thinking of both the Conservative and Labour Parties in England. Nevertheless, critics of the English system continue to argue that detention and other custodial facilities are "schools of crime" and that a return to treatment and the welfare model is in order. On another level, more specific issues are of concern. The murder of a two-year-old boy by two ten-year-old youths in 1993 generated national soul-searching and debate similar to that resulting from the Columbine High School massacres in Colorado in the United States. The emergence of a "rave culture" and the fact that one-half of all males and one-third of all females have tried drugs suggests to many that drug use is increasing among British youths.[36] Particularly disturbing to the middle class is that it is middle-class children, not lower-class children, who are involved with drugs, particularly Ecstasy. Finally, extreme reservations are being expressed about the increased use of guns by disadvantaged youths. Whether a lack of jobs in England will result in problems of violence becoming more endemic and comparable to that in the United States is in the back of many minds. Concern, too, is expressed about reports that British police are using unjustified violence among the immigrant minority populations that make up an increasingly large part of the British population.

AUSTRALIA

European settlers arrived in New South Wales in 1788. The age of responsibility was seven, and older youths were tried in the same courts and often confined in the same institutions as adults. Most early attention was directed to neglected or vagrant youths, and institutions were developed to handle the needs of these children. Later, these same institutions held juvenile offenders. In the latter half of the 1800s, industrial schools were established for neglected youths, and reformatories were created for young offenders, an early effort to distinguish youths in need from criminal or delinquent youths. Magistrates often confined youths in these institutions for indefinite periods of time as well as in institutions for adults.[37] The early efforts to treat juveniles separately from adults set the stage for what was to become a welfare model in Australian juvenile justice.

In the late 1800s and early 1900s, children's courts modeled after the English juvenile courts were adopted throughout Australia.[38] These children's courts were influenced by both U.S. and English philosophy and were based on the *parens patriae* principle. The age of responsibility for youths in these courts ranged from seven in Tasmania and eight in the Australian Capital Territory to seventeen in three states and one territory; the remaining Australian territories and states used the age of eighteen as the minimum age of responsibility.

Panels

Major mechanisms of dealing with juveniles until recently were Children's Aid Panels, mechanisms that reflected Australian thinking that most young offenders should be handled outside the courts. Troublesome youths were diverted to a panel consisting of a social worker and a police officer, who had the options of dropping the case, sending the child to the police for a caution, referring the youth to a Children's Aid Panel, or recommending prosecution.[39] The Children's Aid Panels were heavily criticized for their net-widening effect as well as for arbitrariness, coerciveness, and lack of concern for due process. Children's Aid Panels are now being disbanded in favor of a restorative model of juvenile justice as a consequence of 1993 legislation in South Australia. The panels are being replaced by a system of community or family conferences that initially was developed in New Zealand.[40]

Family Conferences

The **family conferences** vary in form but are designed to overcome the problems of the Children's Aid Panels and to facilitate implementation of the restorative model of justice. These goals are accomplished by police bringing together all members of the community who are affected by an offense to determine the best method of repairing the damage and restoring the victim. People close to both the offender and the offended are invited to the conferences and are called on to help minimize the damage done to the community.[41] Family conference members include a police officer, the offender, and a youth justice coordinator who chairs the hearing. Parents, relatives, or others who know the offender well also may attend, and lawyers are permitted to represent the youth.[42] Youths are required to do anything the conference members believe will benefit them. Options include requiring the youth to pay restitution, perform community service, or apologize to the victim; conference members may also issue a formal caution. A youth who fails to attend a conference hearing as requested is charged and prosecuted for the offense.

The restorative model currently in effect has several premises: (1) the victim is of central importance, (2) offenders must face consequences for their actions, (3) more sanctions should be developed with which to punish offenders more quickly, (4) the offender's family is partly responsible for the youth's actions, and (5) the police should actively participate in the process. The restorative model's goal is to promote concern for the victim, the payment of restitution by the offender, the facilitation of the healing process, and the restoration of calm to the community.[43] Furthermore, it is important to note that many crime control strategies are called for that focus on a quick response by the police, protection of the community, and more involvement of the police in the juvenile justice process.

The Police

The general philosophy of the Australian police is to arrest only when necessary. The organization of police departments varies considerably by state and territory, and only a few of the state and territorial police forces have special juvenile units. Police are encouraged to use extensively both formal and informal cautioning processes, particularly for first and minor offenders. Informal cautions are given on the streets, and formal cautions are administered in police stations.[44] The cautioning process available to the police today is fairly flexible. Cautions given on the streets typically consist of police warning offenders, telling them to avoid certain individuals, and encouraging youths to find better ways to spend their free time. Nevertheless, a major criticism of the Australian police is that they traditionally have been overzealous in their contacts with Aboriginal youths. See Focus on the Police and the Offender 15–4.

FOCUS ON THE POLICE AND THE OFFENDER

15–4

AUSTRALIA

"Edith" is a fourteen-year-old Aboriginal girl living in the Northern Territory, Australia. In 1997, when she was twelve years old, she was arrested for stealing to get food for herself and for other hungry and neglected children she was caring for, including a baby. She was kept overnight in an adult cell in the local police station and then released but ordered to stay with relatives. When she broke the order several times by running away, including to visit the baby in the hospital and to see her family, she was rearrested and detained in Don Dale, the only juvenile detention center in the Northern Territory, which is located some fifteen hundred kilometers away from Edith's home. Her case did prompt the welfare authorities to start supplying emergency food to her family.

Since July 1998, Edith has repeatedly been detained for up to three weeks at Don Dale, usually for minor offenses such as stealing and repeatedly breaching court orders. In August 1998 short-term juvenile holding cells for children awaiting court hearings were opened at her home town's Aboriginal Youth refuge. However, earlier this year, Edith was detained for six more weeks at Don Dale for new offences and breaches of court orders. On one occasion, she reportedly ran away to visit a critically ill relative in the hospital. She was arrested and detained for two weeks. Aboriginal children make up only about one-third of the child population of the Northern Territory, but account for about 90 percent of its juvenile detainees.

Source: http://amnesty.org/ailib/intcam/children/kids99/kidreport.htm. Accessed July 24, 2003.

Australia further limits the role of the police through guidelines and rules governing assistance, cautions, arrest, interrogation, searches, the issuance of summons, pretrial detention, photographing, and fingerprinting.[45] The offending juvenile is supposed to be interviewed by the police in the presence of a parent or independent adult, but the courts have almost unlimited discretion to use evidence gathered in violation of the rules. The police are encouraged to issue summonses, and in two states, a "court attendance notice" is given to the suspect at the police station. Serious offenders occasionally are held in police cells until their court hearing, although a few offenders in need of detention are held in remand centers run by departments of welfare.

The Courts

Children's courts are presided over by magistrates or judges who can try juveniles for all but the most serious indictable offenses such as murder. The states and territories vary considerably according to whether specific offenses are excluded from the jurisdiction of these courts by legislative, judicial, or prosecutorial exclusion. Only Western Australia and Queensland children's courts may try all offenses. Not all states or territories prohibit bystanders in the courtroom, although all do prohibit the publishing of youths' names or relevant identifying information in the media.

Judges select dispositions from a wide range of options once a youth is found guilty of an offense. Cases may be conditionally or unconditionally discharged and youths reprimanded or placed on regular or intensive probation. In addition, judges may require youths to perform community service such as working alongside members of community organizations. Judges also send youths to community centers in the evenings or on weekends, where the youths receive further education, participate in recreational opportunities, undergo counseling, receive vocational training, or acquire assistance in finding jobs. The most serious offenders in all states and territories may be placed in detention centers.[46] Courts in three jurisdictions have the power to transfer juveniles over age sixteen to adult prisons if offenders have been sentenced to detention centers; courts in Tasmania, Western Australia, and the Northern Territory have the power to imprison juveniles in adult facilities.

Juvenile Institutions

Training schools are used less frequently than in the past. The programming in these facilities is not particularly rigorous, and youths are held for fairly short periods of time. The institutions of choice are detention centers, which are found in every state and territory. These facilities, like training schools, are primarily for less serious offenders with maximum sentences of two to three years, depending on the age of the juvenile and the political jurisdiction; a parole board determines a juvenile's release date.

Debate is ongoing over the use of the facilities. Although all provide educational and recreational programs as well as trade and vocational training, many serve primarily as warehouses for youths and employ staff who are repressive, brutal, and discipline oriented.[47] Some detention homes, however, pride themselves on the ability of their staff to meet their charges' social and personal needs. Finally, youths convicted of murder or other extremely serious offenses often serve part of their sentences in detention centers and the remainder in adult prisons.

Current Concerns

The direction of juvenile justice in Australia is under considerable debate, and some changes have occurred over the past two decades. While Australia remains committed to a restorative model of juvenile justice, violent crimes in the early 1990s generated a movement to take serious and dangerous offenders off the streets and to give them longer and harsher sentences than in the past, often in adult prisons. Some concern also exists over the role of juvenile institutions. The debate is whether these institutions should be primarily custodial and pay little attention to the needs of their inmates, or should dedicate themselves to a welfare model that tries to meet the personal needs of their residents. Finally, a major issue is the way the juvenile justice system treats Aboriginal children. Evidence exists that in some jurisdictions, these youths are arrested, referred to court, convicted, and confined at much higher rates than the dominant, largely white Australian population. Police in South Australia, for example, appear to favor the use of arrest over the use of cautions when dealing with Aboriginal youths, and Aboriginal juveniles are considerably overrepresented in correctional facilities.[48] These charges of racism are troubling to many in the Australian society.

✓**Progress Check 15.1**
Review this section at
www.prenhall.com/bartollas

HOW DO EMERGING NATIONS HANDLE JUVENILE CRIME?

Most nations around the world either have economies based on agriculture or are just beginning to industrialize. Their per capita incomes are extremely low, most citizens are impoverished, and life is a desperate struggle for survival. The four countries discussed here were chosen in part because of the regions of the world they represent; combined, their populations constitute close to one-half of the world's population.

SOUTH AFRICA

The first Europeans in South Africa found stable tribal societies with well-integrated family, religious, and community life. Youths were socialized to accept traditional tribal, social, and other customary laws, and social control was immediate, firm, and harsh when deemed necessary. As Europeans began to achieve dominance over populations and institutions they considered inferior, Western law and legal institutions were substituted for traditional tribal practices.

Europeans treated both youths and adults in trouble quite harshly. Not until 1856 were magistrates allowed to place youths under the care of responsible persons. In 1882, the first reformatory was chartered for the detention and rehabilitation of youths under the age of sixteen. In 1911, an act was passed that permitted the construction of nine different types of reformatories as well as the development of programs for the education of confined youths. These facilities ranged from child-care schools to reformatories with very strict regimens but with considerable emphasis on rehabilitation.[49] Reformatories generally were (and are) the last stop before prison. Throughout the 1900s, whites continued to increase their dominance over the black population.

With the formalization of **apartheid** in 1950, whites completed the formation of a segregated society. Separate societies were set up with strict social, legal, economic, and political barriers between whites and suppressed minorities. This separation of whites and minorities in South Africa continues even today—a decade after the dismantling of the apartheid system in the late 1980s and the implementation of a new constitution in 1993. The result is that, from a native African's perspective, the law remains a "white man's" law that is applied in a racially discriminatory manner. Also, although modernization has resulted in the call for more formal procedures of the type found in industrialized countries, South Africa is only now setting up a juvenile justice system separate from that for adults.[50] The consequence is, in part, that no statistical data are available on juvenile crime.

Even today, nevertheless, many nonwhite South Africans consider the family the primary political unit and rely on traditional law and custom as tools of social control. In addition, the *people* are considered the first and final source of all power, and community elders make decisions on behalf of the community at large.[51] At this level, traditional law and custom often emerge as more important than the formal rules of the modern state when dealing with juveniles in need. Indeed, neither formal rules nor magistrates are respected or trusted by native Africans.

The Police

Police in South Africa are a paramilitary force, many of whose white officers had served as counterinsurgency personnel in the military. This background, combined in the past with the apartheid policies of the white government, resulted in widespread abuses by the police. Confessions extracted by torture and beatings and unjustified shootings of suspects by police death squads undermined public confidence in law enforcement officers. Today, more than 50 percent of the police officers are black, and the government is attempting to develop standards to bring South Africa in line with recommendations of the *Beijing Rules.*[52] Efforts are being made to extend formal training of officers, to limit police powers, to increase the community's role in law enforcement, and to reduce police corruption.[53] Nevertheless, police practices are far from ideal. Most juveniles arrested are street youths who are taken into custody for petty crimes such as loitering, shoplifting, drunkenness, and marijuana use. Even in these minor cases, police often do not follow through on their responsibility to notify the parents of the children of the arrest and/or trial date and some youths may be held for three years in prisons and may not begin serving their sentences until four years after their arrest. Nevertheless, One-Stop Child Justice Centers are processing many youths quickly and using restorative justice methods to attack the youthful crime problem.[54]

The Courts

By law, all persons under eighteen in South Africa are considered children, and those under the age of seven are not considered criminally culpable.[55] Youths between the ages of seven and fourteen may be held culpable, but only if prosecutors can prove beyond reasonable doubt that the child comprehends the nature and consequences of his or her actions, understands that the actions were wrong, and intended to commit the offenses for which he or she was charged. How courts respond to juveniles depends on both the maturity of children and the type of offense when deciding whether and at what level the child should be tried.

Two basic forms of juvenile courts are found in South Africa. Children's courts hear the cases of youths determined to be in need of care. Youths who are abandoned, have no parents, are out of control, keep bad company, beg, engage in street trading, or are in undesirable home conditions come under the jurisdiction of these courts. These courts usually send juveniles to child-care schools. Youths who commit offenses under South African law are, however, tried by criminal courts. Only in larger urban areas are some criminal courts set aside for the trying of delinquent juveniles, although separate children's courts are available for youths in need.[56] Conviction in these courts classifies the offending youth as a criminal and may result in the youth being sent to reform school or prison. Juvenile courts may sentence a youth to corporal punishment (some thirty-five thousand youths were caned annually until 1995). Courts also fine them; place them under the supervision of probation officers, parents, or other suitable persons designated by the courts; or sentence them to reform schools or imprisonment. Youths may not be given the death penalty.[57] These adult courts may convert themselves into a "Children's Court Inquiry" if the court's members decide that a juvenile needs care rather than punishment.[58]

Institutions

Facilities for youths include clinic schools, child-care schools, reform schools, and prisons. The *clinic schools* cater to youths who are unable to perform well, have behavioral problems, do not respond to counseling, live in dysfunctional families, or are caught breaking the law. The *child-care* schools formerly were called *industrial schools*. These are residential facilities that attempt to reintegrate secondary school students into their communities through psychological and educational services. The *reform schools* accept youths who continue to have difficulty in other placements such as private custody, clinics, children's homes, and child-care schools. The juvenile courts also send to reform schools youths who have previous convictions for less serious offenses but who are then arrested for a more serious offense such as a serious assault, rape, robbery, or murder. South Africa's two *juvenile prisons* are reserved for youths who either are troublemakers in the reform schools or are sent directly to prison from the juvenile court.[59] Youths also may be assigned to prison farms for juveniles.[60] Unfortunately, large numbers of youths end up in jails and prisons which, even though the youths are sometimes segregated by age, are extremely dangerous and degrading.[61]

Current Concerns

The South African government is working continually to bring its justice system in line with those of other countries. Tradition dictates that the people, their elders, and the informal courts and councils of the communities are primarily responsible for maintaining order in the community.[62] But the formal law puts more emphasis on governmental control and the courts in judicial decision making than it does on the people. The result is that people lack confidence in the formal system of law, and a gap is widening between the government and the people that could result in future conflict. Another concern is the approximately nine thousand children wandering the streets throughout South Africa as a result of parental alcoholism, abuse, and poverty. The overwhelming majority of these youths are males of African origin who average thirteen years of age.[63]

Importantly, the hold of the local family, religion, and community over youths is weakening as the poverty level remains high and families continue to move to urban areas in the hope of finding work and a better life. The problems of children also are heightening as the number of AIDS cases increases the frequency of children losing parents and relatives to the epidemic. The South African government is setting up a variety of social programs to combat these various problems as well as to implement the juvenile justice standards of the *Beijing Rules*.

CHINA

The People's Republic of China is the world's most populous nation today, with approximately 1.2 billion people crowded into a land area roughly the size of the United States. Slightly more than 43 percent of China's population is under the age of thirty-four, with 25 percent under the age of eighteen.[64] Whereas China relied historically on traditional family, school, and community structures and processes to control its youths, China today is attempting to shift the responsibility for the social control of juveniles to the state. This shift accompanies a general weakening of local family, neighborhood, and factory controls as China is permitting some horizontal mobility of its citizens and more individual entrepreneurism in its quest for an economically productive and competitive society.

Historical Periods

Children in feudal China were ranked by family, sex, and age. Males were ranked higher than the females, who were raised as child bearers and servants. Children were expected to serve their families by working on the farms and rice paddies, and their role was one of subservience and helpfulness. The family's responsibility was to ensure the conformity of its children, and when the family failed in its mission, the school and the community intervened. In addition, most eras in Chinese history were characterized by such desperate living conditions that social upheaval, unrest, and wars resulted; thousands of children were neglected, abused, and wandering the streets in need of care as a consequence.[65] Not until after World War II did the first serious efforts to aid juveniles occur.

The first era in modern Chinese juvenile justice extends from 1949 to 1965. Following the seizure of control by Mao Zedong and the Communist Party in 1949, the government cracked down on "criminals" left over from pre-Mao days. The government also initiated efforts to improve the welfare of dependent and neglected children by setting up welfare services and institutions for juveniles and to eliminate the thousand-year-old practice of child labor.[66] The purpose was to rescue millions of children from the sex trade and to provide youths in need with proper care and attention. Emergency shelters, educational facilities, orphanages, and child welfare houses were set up to get children back to their families, adopted, or in foster homes.[67] The primary concern of governmental agencies was with children's needs, their susceptibility to abusive upbringing, and their dependence on others. Particular attention was paid to holding parents responsible for the way they raised their children.

The second era, 1966 to 1976, was a period of social chaos as China underwent a "cultural revolution." In this process, Chinese rulers attempted to rid the nation of all enemies of the proletariat class. During this time, the operations of all criminal justice institutions, including those directed toward juveniles, were suspended.

The third era extends from shortly after Mao's death in 1976 to the present. Authorities wrote a new constitution in 1982 and took appropriate steps for strengthening the legal system.[68] Authorities also recognized that its justice institutions were flawed and that crime rates among the young were increasing. Steps were taken to deal with the problem. Youths who are guilty of minor behavioral problems such as incorrigibility or who commit minor offenses are sometimes required by parents, schoolteachers, or community leaders to go to work-study schools called *gongdu* schools.[69] Youths guilty of more serious offenses most frequently are confined, without trial, in reformatories or penal institutions that focus on Education through Labor and Reform through Labor.[70] Both types of youths, in other words, are dealt with administratively rather than processed through the system. Although no national statistics are published, available data suggest that 75 percent of all crime in China is committed by individuals under age twenty-five.[71] Chinese youths' problem behaviors cover the spectrum from major to minor, yet the number of major offenses in China appears to be low compared with those in more industrialized nations.

The Police

Youths receive four chances. The first chance is when the neighborhood faction of the Communist Party comes to the child's home, discusses potential or real problems with his or her parents, and asks the parents for their help;

neighbors and neighborhood organizations also may be approached. The second chance is when assistance is sought from schoolteachers and other authorities such as the police. The third chance is when the youth is sent to a work-study school, and the fourth comes when the youth is sent to a reformatory, with or without court action.[72]

On the negative side, police are permitted to use coercion, torture, beatings, and violence against citizens, depending on the situation.[73] On the positive side, the police role is to provide service and order maintenance to communities. Thus, police actually may become aware of a youth's problems at any of the above times and, in fact, counsel, mediate, and negotiate with juveniles and work with the community to help children solve their problems. In this regard, police act more like social workers than crime fighters. When the rare juvenile who does commit a serious crime comes to the attention of the police, he or she is taken into police custody, where interrogation must be undertaken within twenty-four hours; remand to the prosecutor's office must occur within four days. By law, police may detain the youth only in juvenile facilities or an adult facility if no juvenile facility is available. As in other countries, police may not release a child's name, address, or photo to the media. See Focus on Practice 15-5.

FOCUS ON PRACTICE   **15–5**
INFORMAL JUSTICE IN CHINA

China is much more oriented toward informal juvenile justice than most industrialized nations. In China, the police's role with juveniles primarily involves either order maintenance or service activities, rather than law enforcement.

The informal role of the police, especially, is oriented toward crime prevention and services. Police precincts assign their officers to different neighborhoods or large dwelling complexes to work closely with the neighborhood committees and schools to oversee the safety and welfare of those neighborhoods. The behavioral problems of children are quickly identified at the first sign of trouble by an informally organized coalition consisting of parents, school teachers, neighborhood committee volunteers, and police officers. The lower expectation for family privacy in the Chinese cultural tradition permits police officers to penetrate the community and family lives. It is not at all unusual for police officers to make casual visits to members to whom children have been adjudicated by the court and have been placed under parents' custody or in which juveniles have been released from juvenile institutions for postrelease supervision.

Most police officers in China carry neither a gun or a baton, therefore they appear more like social workers than police officers. In fact, the police generally devote about 90 to 95 percent of their time and resources to serving the community's various social and human needs. Exercising police discretion to arrest juvenile offenders is rare and considered as a last resort. Only when a juvenile commits a serious crime would he or she be taken into police custody and be adjudicated by the court. Otherwise, police usually work with parents, schools, or neighborhood committees to counsel children in trouble.

Source: Xin Ren, "People's Republic of China," in *International Handbook on Juvenile Justice*, edited by Donald J. Shoemaker (Westport, CT: Greenwood Press, 1996), pp. 63–64.

Critical Thinking Questions:

What would trouble you if the powers of the U.S. police were expanded with children in trouble? What would be the advantages of increasing police control over children? What should the police be doing in the United States that they are not doing to prevent and control juvenile crime?

The Courts

Most juveniles with problems are dealt with by parents, local citizens, and neighborhood groups, but China's central government today is attempting to expand the more formal methods of handling juvenile offenders. The *Beijing Rules* standard of defining a juvenile as anyone under age eighteen is now accepted as the age of majority for Chinese youth, although for some purposes the age of majority is twenty-five. Age, in other words, is a mitigating factor in Chinese juvenile justice. For example, serious offenders under the age of eighteen actually are tried in adult courts, but these trials are closed to the public in deference to the youth's age. Youths between the ages of fourteen and sixteen may be held criminally liable for crimes, but no youth under the age of eighteen may be executed for a crime unless the crime is extremely serious. Juveniles ages sixteen or seventeen who commit a capital crime and who are given the death penalty are held until the age of eighteen before execution.

Crimes in China are classified according to whether they are intentional or negligent and whether the offender violated a criminal law or committed minor violations not deemed criminal.[74] Once juveniles' cases are turned over to the procurator, the courts must either render a decision or dismiss the cases within thirty days. Typically, the courts decide on the adequacy of police evidence, but juveniles have no rights in the proceedings and are assumed to be guilty. The state's responsibility, under the inquisitory system, is to prove the guilt of the offenders by presenting the facts of the cases to the judges, one of whom is from the formal court system and two of whom are lay judges from the community. Typically, the courts decide whether the juveniles should be dealt with in the community by their parents or a community agency, given criminal detention in a jail or another facility, placed in Institutions of Juvenile Management and Education for Juvenile Offenders, or given a fixed-term imprisonment, life imprisonment, or the death penalty.[75] In recent years, more and more youths have been placed on probation in community organizations than confined in institutions, as the Chinese prefer that all youths under the age of fourteen are worked with intensively by parents, neighborhood organizations, local police, and schools.

Institutionalization

Some youngsters are not placed with families or treated by community organizations or schools. These youths are likely to be between the ages of fourteen and sixteen and guilty of serious criminal law violations, or to have parents who are deemed incapable of taking care of them; this latter group includes youths up to the age of twenty-five. Both of these groups of youths are subject to confinement in juvenile facilities such as the *gongdu* schools; some are placed in adult institutions. Yet another classification of youths is sometimes confined; these are juveniles sentenced by local police, schools, and neighborhood committees for up to three years in educational camps through the Labor Department under what is called "administrative commitment."[76] Educational camps are reformatories guarded by armed guards who march uniformed youths from one assignment to the next in double time.

Two basic types of institutions designated for juveniles exist: community-based facilities and Institutions of Management and Education for Juvenile Offenders. Sixty percent of juveniles are placed in institutions for five years or less. Regardless of the length of stay, the emphasis in institutions is on "persuasion and salvation," with reintegration of the youth into their family with a better education and newly developed values.[77]

Current Concerns

China's massive population, limited resources, increasing inflation, and rapidly increasing unemployment rate pose significant problems to all Chinese who want a higher standard of living. Chinese rulers, in an effort to improve productivity and increase the number of jobs, are encouraging individual entrepreneurial activity as well as industrial growth.[78] The consequence is that parents work harder for longer hours and spend less time socializing with their children. In addition, only one-third of today's Chinese high school students are accepted into college, thereby shaming their parents and guaranteeing themselves a bleak economic future; considering these trends, the reasons for juvenile offending become clear.[79] With weakening family, neighborhood, and social controls, youths are freer today than at any time in recent history. All of these factors together result in an increase in delinquency that must be brought under control.

Furthermore, the Chinese central government has stated that it desires to bring the country into compliance with the *Beijing Rules*. Thus, for juveniles at least, it would appear that China is moving slowly away from traditional methods of social control to a more formal system of justice. Still, tradition is strong, and the Chinese place heavy emphasis on informal community services and organizations to keep youths in line. Parents, schoolteachers, trade union representatives, neighborhood committees, Juvenile Scouts, police officers, special schools, and many others try to rehabilitate youths both in the community and in juvenile institutions. Of considerable interest is the fact that while China seems slowly to be moving *away* from these informal methods of control, many countries in other parts of the world are moving *toward* such methods.[80] Given that much of the industrialized world is trying to reintegrate youths into their families and communities, some question exists as to whether China is going in the right direction.

Another important consideration is that China is notorious for its human rights violations. Police apparently are permitted to use certain types of torture; charges of abuse are not condemned; investigations of rights violations are not investigated; and youths are tried without being indicted, not permitted effective legal representation, or given fair trials. If the Chinese government is to win the respect of other countries, due process of justice must be developed in all thirty of China's administrative units.

INDIA

India's population is projected to surpass that of China's by the year 2025.[81] Birth rates now hover around 3.2 children per woman of childbearing age. Of the projected population of more than 1.4 billion (in 2025), more than three hundred million will be juveniles. Still, even with more than several hundred million youths, only a tiny fraction of these youths are arrested each year for all national Indian Penal Code violations and local codes combined. The low arrest rates are explained by a combination of factors, including that the crime rate is, in fact, low and that most offenders are handled informally; a major factor, however, is the extensive police corruption found throughout India.[82]

The first major Indian acts identifying juveniles as a special category of offenders began with the Apprentice Act of 1850 that granted special protection to young people. An 1860s act established the age of responsibility as seven. An 1861 act called for separate trials for youths under age fifteen, and an 1897 act permitted the confinement of males under age fifteen in reformatories in place of exile or confinement in adult prisons.[83] Separate judicial and confinement systems were established for juveniles and adults in the early 1920s.[84] In 1960, a national Children's Act was passed for use by all nationally governed territories and as a model for India's states, a goal that is only partially met.

The most recent major change in Indian juvenile justice law is based on the 1960s national Children's Act. In 1986, some fifty-five political jurisdictions passed laws facilitating the treatment and rehabilitation of neglected and delinquent youths.[85] *Delinquent* and *neglected* were defined in this act, as were the procedures to be used in processing each through the system. In India, a juvenile is any male under the age of sixteen and any female under the age of eighteen. A delinquent, as might be expected, is anyone who violates one of India's codes, and a neglected youth is any youth who might be classified as a status offender in the United States. The act also describes the types of residential and correctional facilities each type of youthful offender is to be confined in and the qualifications of correctional staff. Within the formal system, the first stop for youths is either the welfare boards or courts, although a semiofficial agency, the *Panchayat,* recently has reemerged as an agent of social control in Indian society.[86]

An important consideration relates to the traditional methods of social control in Indian society. Custom and tradition enforced by the family long were used to maintain order. Equally important as a social control factor was the fact that the family's position in the caste or subcaste (or *jati*) was based on its reputation in that *jati.* Youths who engaged in deviancy of any type threatened the reputation of their families and therefore also threatened the family's ability to obtain jobs, the family's ability to arrange good marriages for their daughters, and the family's overall socioeconomic status. Also important is that a deep distrust still is directed at the police and courts as a result of British rule. Indians today still prefer traditional methods of social control, with the consequence that few youths ever come to the attention of the police and courts.[87]

Panchayats

Panchayats are quasi-governmental organizations at the community level. These groups have their roots in ancient India but were eliminated at the time of British colonization. With the return of the nation to Indian rule, the *Panchayats* have again emerged. They consist of elected members of the community, usually village elders, who understand community traditions and who are able to deal with all aspects of youthful misbehavior. *Panchayats* hear cases, levy fines, order youths to stop associating with others, and, in extreme cases, compel youths to undergo corporal punishment.[88]

The Police

Police in India generally are viewed with suspicion because of the way the British used them to maintain control. Police today continue to control, but often in the name of the upper classes or whoever happens to have power. Thus, child labor and bondage and female and child prostitution are often overlooked by the police in deference to the ruling parties. Police are also known to engage in extralegal beatings, arrests, "disappearances," and, in some parts of the country, rapes, tortures, and murders. Nevertheless, we should point out, police behavior varies widely in the different cities, states, and political jurisdictions throughout India. See Focus on Practice 15-6.

Police officers have the option of taking juveniles before either the welfare boards or the juvenile courts, depending on the characteristics of the offenders, their situations, and their offenses. Most of the offenses for which police make arrests under the Indian Penal Code are property crimes and gambling, whereas offenses under Local and Special Laws consist primarily of alcohol prohibitions; the number of drug violations is very small. The distrust of police and formal law leads most communities to deal with the problems of the juveniles informally and in *Panchayats.*

FOCUS ON PRACTICE   **15–6**
CHILDREN IN CUSTODY IN INDIA

Seema has been tortured, ill-treated, and harassed. She is still only 12 years old. The adults responsible for her suffering are police officers, the very people who should protect her from harm. The daughter of a landless labourer, Seema was sent from Bihar to live with her grandparents in a slum in Delhi, India. She found work as a domestic servant, but the day after she got the job, her employer was murdered. Seema was arrested by police on 10 December 1997 and illegally detained for two days. She was never charged but was questioned repeatedly about the events surrounding the murder. She subsequently told members of the South Asia Coalition on Child Servitude that in custody she had been tied with electric cord and thrashed with a ruler. She was also hung upside-down and slapped on her ears. She was not provided with proper food or blankets to keep warm. She was released on the morning of 12 December, but continues to be called to the police station and questioned. On 24 January she filed a complaint with police which remains pending.

Children like Seema are arbitrarily detained, tortured, and ill-treated by police and other state authorities in lockups, prisons and army camps throughout South Asia. Far from giving them special protection, their status as children makes them especially vulnerable to abuse. The majority come from extremely poor families or have had to fend for themselves, outside family and social structures, from a very young age. Their poverty brings them into the path of the law, as they are forced into begging, prostitution, and exploitative forms of labour in order to survive. Often they are additionally vulnerable because of other aspects of their identity, such as their gender, ethnicity or caste background, for which they are discriminated against by state officials.

Source: http://web.amnesty.org/library/print/ENGASA040011998. Accessed July 24, 2003.

The Courts

Delinquent youths come before special juvenile courts whose membership is mandated by the state to be either metropolitan or judicial magistrates. Each court has a panel of two honorary social workers, one of whom, as in the case of the welfare boards, must be a woman.[89] Citizens appointed to the welfare boards or courts must have some understanding of the psychology and needs of youths. A wide range of sentences is available to judges. Youths may be sent home after consultation, released to parents, placed on probation or with responsible persons in the community, fined, or confined in community facilities, special homes, jails, or prisons.[90]

The Indian point of view is that both the courts and the police are to be avoided at all costs. Nevertheless, police do occasionally bring juveniles before the courts for violation of both the Indian Penal Code and the Local and Special Laws. Court hearings are closed to the public, although either the juvenile or the court may request anyone relevant to the case to appear.

Institutions

Although the Children's Act of 1960 and the Juvenile Justice Act of 1986 state that juveniles may not be held in the same facilities as adults, youths are confined with adults in both jails and prisons across India. The problems of confined youths are undoubtedly increased in that prisoners are classified by their social status. Wealthy prisoners and prominent citizens are classified as Class A prisoners. They are held in private rooms and government guest houses and may have their food supplemented by their families. Class B prisoners consist of college students and taxpayers and are held in less auspicious facilities with poorer support services. Class C prisoners often are held in overcrowded cells with dirt floors, no furnishings, and poor-quality food.[91] Juveniles from the lower castes and *jatis* are most frequently found in facilities for Class C prisoners.

Only a small minority of youths are ever confined, as most are either acquitted of the charges, released to their parents or placed under supervision in the community. Some children are placed in observation homes or "places of safety" until their cases are decided. Youths who are considered neglected or incorrigible may be placed in juvenile homes for a period of time up to age twenty for males and age eighteen for females.[92] Children who violate their probation often end up in these special homes.

Current Concerns

India's expanding population, lack of natural resources, and abject poverty characterize the struggle of its citizens for survival. Children growing up under these conditions, especially those in the remnants of the lower castes and *jatis*, find themselves hungry and disease-ridden. A nationwide shortage of jobs means that most children have no economically viable future. If they are poor, and most are, children must attempt to survive in any way possible. The options for most are child labor, wandering the streets, prostitution, begging, and crime. Estimates are that India has some five hundred thousand street children nationwide and another three hundred thousand who are bonded, that is, forced to work for others to help pay back their parents' debts. Trafficking in young females for purposes of prostitution and begging is common.[93] Dramatically, an estimated 34 percent of all primary school children drop out of school, many of whom enter the illegal labor markets. Given the economic importance of children to the ruling classes, little incentive exists for the central government to crack down on those who violate child labor laws and even less incentive for police and local authorities to try to dissuade youths or those who exploit them from undesirable activities.

The plight of females in India also must not be overlooked. Already noted is that females are sold into prostitution and frequently are the victims of infanticide. Females also are given as child brides to males in exchange for dowries that are paid to the male's family. When these dowries are considered inadequate, the brides, more than one-half of whom are under the age of sixteen, are often beaten and/or killed. The assumption in India is that any woman under the age of sixteen who dies is the victim of murder by either her husband or his family.

The Indian government is trying to improve its justice system. Nevertheless, the challenge for the government is to generate the financial resources necessary to expand and professionalize its police forces. Resources must also be found to train professionals in child care, rehabilitation, and the administration of justice. Facilities exclusively for juveniles must be built and staff sensitive to the needs of children hired. Finally, the ethnic and social class divisions found throughout India result in almost unlimited sources of conflict between the rulers and the ruled.

BRAZIL

Brazil has the largest population of any country in South America and is the fifth most populous nation in the world, with 174 million people.[94] Its legislative history in dealing with children has its roots in European law, particularly the Napoleonic and Rocco Codes, and has long called for differential treatment of juveniles and adults. The Penal Code of the Empire and the First Penal Code of the Republic, for example, differentiate between adults and juveniles by focusing on the ways minors' degree of "moral responsibility" and "discernment" exempt them from criminal culpability. The Penal Code of 1940 established that minors under the age of eighteen lack criminal responsibility entirely, and this assumption was continued through the enactment of a juvenile code in 1979 and the Statute of the Child and Adolescent (SEA) in 1990. The latter act specifically identifies a "child" as any person up to the age of twelve and an "adolescent" as any youth between the ages of twelve and seventeen.[95] The main thrust of Brazilian laws and codes is on the "protection of fundamental rights to physical, intellectual, emotional, social, and cultural development."[96] In 1988, the SEA called for the government to protect the rights of children. Reform groups and the government continue to call for human rights for children and for setting up a wide range of social service facilities throughout the country.[97] The first stop for a child in trouble is often a guardianship council.

Guardianship Council

Guardianship councils are composed of five members chosen by local citizens of local communities. The proceedings of these councils begin upon the referral of a youth by a judge to the council. The charge of these agencies is to guarantee that any youth who gets into difficulties receives any of a number of protective measures. The councils may, for example, recommend that children be placed under the care of their parents, basic education schools, government or community programs for youths or their families, hospitals, shelter foster families, or treatment.[98] Adolescents, in addition to being subject to protective measures, may be reprimanded, required to pay restitution or perform community service, or placed on probation. Youths caught committing serious crimes are subject to the deprivation of liberty if approved by the proper judicial authority.[99]

The Police

Police officers vary widely in how they handle juveniles. Reports of police brutality and vigilante murders continue to shock the world as three children are estimated murdered in Brazil each day. A disturbing number of these children are murdered on the streets and in custody by both on- and off-duty police officers.[100] Youths of African descent, mixed parentage, and Native Indian heritage are the primary targets, with males outnumbering females by a ratio of seven to one. Estimates are that many impoverished youths engage in begging, petty theft, shoplifting, loitering, and prostitution in an attempt to supplement family incomes.

In an effort to reduce police arbitrariness in dealing with juveniles, police must take any youth caught in the act of committing a crime directly to a guardianship council or a juvenile court judge as soon as possible. In rural areas, the youth usually is taken to a regular police station and often is confined with adult offenders. Once the police investigate the offense as well as the needs of the minor, the youth may either be released or, if the evidence warrants, sent to the prosecutor.

The Courts

Once a prosecutor decides how to dispose of a case, it is sent to either a juvenile judge, if one is available, or, more likely, to a judge of the adult court who handles the review. This judge then evaluates the characteristics of the juvenile, the juvenile's family situation, and the seriousness of the behavior. If the judge agrees with the prosecutor's procedures and decisions, the judge then

Brazil's policies on handling children, both formally and informally, are under fire from nations around the world. Here, confined children look out of an overcrowded, poorly equipped jail cell. (Photo by Inacio Teixeira, AP Wide World Photos.)

calls for the sentence to be carried out. If the judge does not agree, the case is sent back to the chief prosecutor's office for another hearing.

The courts work closely with the guardianship councils to maintain the juvenile's ties to the family and community and to provide juveniles with the proper educational experiences. Like the councils, judges have available to them such mechanisms as enrolling youths and parents in specialized schools and programs in order to assist them in solving their problems.[101]

Institutions

New laws provide for community centers for youths and include Integrated Screening Centers, which are open twenty-four hours a day and are available to all street youths who need help. Also available are training centers that operate as day-care centers and shelters that offer children a safe place to sleep. Actual penalties include reprimands, requiring the payment of restitution, performing community service, or, in more extreme instances, depriving youths of their liberty.[102] This latter sanction may involve either semiliberty, in which youths work or go to school during the day and return to a facility at night, or internment, which is confinement in a juvenile institution.

Maximum-security institutions are used only as a last resort for youths who are guilty of particularly serious offenses, who are repeat offenders, and who are capable of understanding and evaluating their own behavior. In fact, all types of youths, including the dependent and neglected, status offenders, and minor offenders, are often institutionalized. Once confined, juveniles are supposed to be evaluated every six months and are confined for no more than three years. In spite of today's welfare orientation, children are beaten, sexually abused, and packed in small cells without bathrooms or ventilation. In a 1999

FOCUS ON INSTITUTIONS   15-7
BRAZIL

An international expert on prison conditions, invited to accompany an Amnesty International delegation to Brazil in October 1999, wrote in his report of São Paulo's juvenile detention centers: " I should say as clearly as possible that I have never seen children kept in such appalling conditions . . . In my view the place should be closed down." A few days later, on 24 October, a riot broke out that shocked even those most hardened to the torture and neglect in São Paulo's juvenile detention system, the Foundation for the Well-Being of Minors, FEBEM. Eighteen hours later, four boys were dead, 58 people were injured, including 29 FEBEM staff, dozens of boys had escaped and the complex had been completely destroyed.

FEBEM has been the subject of scrutiny for decades. Thousands of adolescents have passed through FEBEM detention units since the Foundation came into being in 1976. Throughout this time Amnesty International has received denunciations of torture, ill-treatment, and cruel, inhuman and degrading conditions of detention affecting hundreds of adolescents. A number of boys have died in violent circumstances because the São Paulo government has failed to protect their safety.

Throughout the decade since the launch of Brazil's much-fêted Statute of the Child and Adolescent, Estatuto da Criana e do Adolescente, public prosecutors, bar associations, parliamentary commissions of inquiry, state human rights councils, guardianship councils, FEBEM staff unions and human rights organizations have all submitted to the São Paulo authorities detailed reports, denouncing the inhuman and dehumanizing conditions in FEBEM detention units. They have all made concrete and detailed recommendations aimed at putting an end to the decades-long pattern of violence, riots and escapes, and calling for the outdated repressive model of juvenile detention to be brought into line with Brazil's own Constitution and legislation regarding children and adolescents. Yet the São Paulo authorities have persistently avoided meeting their obligations to reform the juvenile detention system in line with the law, abandoning both FEBEM detainees and FEBEM staff to cope with a situation of violence and chaos.

Source: http://web.amnesty.org/ai.nsf/Index/AMR190142000?OpenDocument&of=COUNTRIES/E. Accessed June 17, 2002.

Critical Thinking Question:
To what extent should the United States develop a formal policy concerning situations such as this in other countries?

riot in a juvenile institution in São Paulo, residents killed four inmates, one of whom was beheaded. Forty other people were injured, including sixteen guards.[103] Life in institutions is often as brutal as life on the streets. For a report on Brazilian juvenile facilities, see Focus on Institutions 15-7.

Current Concerns

Brazil is a society of extremes. Industrially and agriculturally based wealth qualifies Brazil to be listed in some reports as an emerging nation. Yet Brazil has poverty and discrimination as deep as those in any country in South America. In addition, wild economic fluctuations over the past several decades have frequently destabilized Brazilian society to the point that few have confidence that their economic status will remain stable for long. The poor do not have these concerns, as their status at the bottom of the Brazilian socioeconomic structure remains unchanging.

Brazil's task in achieving justice for its juveniles is as daunting as that of India or China. While the government's statements and commitments to a better system of justice undoubtedly are genuine and the work of nongovernmental organizations is impressive, historical legacies and economic realities also are impinging and restrictive. Add a police force that only recently has had its repressive tactics challenged, and some of whose members believe literally in "cleaning the streets" by killing children, and Brazil's task becomes clear. More resources must be devoted to the training of all justice personnel. Old structures of justice must be reformed and efforts undertaken to provide an economic base sufficient to support all citizens.

✓**Progress Check 15.2**
Review this section at
www.prenhall.com/bartollas

SUMMARY

- Few if any countries around the world meet the standards set by the *Beijing Rules.*
- Even democratic, industrialized, bureaucratic societies such as the United States, Canada, England, and Australia fall short of the ideas accepted as necessary by many of the top justice and human rights advocates in the world.
- The proposed standards are based on the basic needs of all children for protracted and protected childhoods that are free of physical, emotional, and sexual abuse and neglect.
- The guidelines are based on the principle that juveniles up to the age of eighteen are still maturing physically, emotionally, and spiritually.
- They are grounded in the belief that children need tutoring, guidance, and the ability to grow into mature adults capable of making positive contributions to their societies.
- Damaged children become damaged adults who often perpetuate the cycles of violence, abuse, poverty, and neglect they experienced themselves.
- In recognition of this, the leaders of most countries do accept that very young children, that is, those under the age of seven, and those fourteen to eighteen, also need help.
- The three industrialized countries—Canada, England, and Australia—examined in this chapter have a more formalized approach to juvenile justice, much like that which is used in the United States.
- The four emerging countries—South Africa, China, India, and Brazil—have a more informal approach to juvenile justice. Communities and families are expected to provide more of the social control of children, and there is great reluctance to confine juveniles in institutions.

WEB SITES OF INTEREST

Amnesty International is a human rights organization with an excellent reputation for documenting injustices to individuals who are the victims of persecution in their own countries. Amnesty International's annual report for 2006 discusses human rights violations in 150 countries and territories. See

    http://www.amnesty.org

The *United Nations* also has many sites in the area of human rights, children's rights, and criminal and juvenile justice. To get started, see

    http://www.un.org

The *U.S. Department of Justice* has set up the National Institute of Justice, which in turn has a web page for the United Nations Online Crime and Justice Clearinghouse (UNOJUST) to assist member criminological institutes around the world in developing their capacity to exchange information electronically. For these different sites, see

http://www.justinfo.net

The *U.S. Department of State* issues reports on human rights practices in countries around the world. To access the regions site map for 2005, see

http://www.state.gov/g/drl/rls/hrrpt/2005/

CRITICAL THINKING QUESTIONS

1. What are the major differences and similarities between the U.S. approach to juvenile justice and those of the countries discussed in this chapter?
2. What is the influence of the different historical backgrounds of the countries discussed in this chapter on their delinquency rates and their juvenile justice systems?
3. How are the changing social and economic conditions of the countries discussed in this chapter likely to influence both their delinquency rates and the way they approach juvenile justice?
4. Should the United States try to develop some informal methods of social control of youths similar to those found in other countries?
5. Should states in the United States follow, or be required to follow, the *Beijing Rules*?
6. Do you believe that the techniques of juvenile justice used by other countries would work in the United States? Why or why not?

NOTES

1. John A. Winterdyk, ed., *Juvenile Justice Systems: International Perspectives* (Toronto: Canadian Scholar's Press, 1997), ix.
2. United Nations, "United Nations Standard Minimum Rules for the Administration of Juvenile Justice: The *Beijing Rules*" (New York: United Nations, 1986), 1–15. For a synopsis of the rules, see Geraldine Van Bueren and Anne-Marie Tootell, "United Nations Standard Minimum Rules for the Administration of Juvenile Justice: *Beijing Rules*," http://childhouse.uio.no/ childrens_rights/dci_html, 1–28.
3. United Nations, "United Nations Standard Minimum Rules: *Beijing Rules*," Rule 7.1, 6; see also Van Bueren and Tootell, "United Nations Standard Minimum Rules," 4.
4. Van Bueren and Tootell, "United Nations Standard Minimum Rules," 5.
5. United Nations, "United Nations Standard Minimum Rules: Beijing Rules," Part 1, Rule 2.1.
6. Maureen McGuire, "C.19: An Act to Amend the Young Offenders Act and the Criminal Code—Getting Tougher?" *Canadian Journal of Criminology* 39, no. 2 (April 1997), 186.
7. John A. Winterdyk, "Juvenile Justice and Young Offenders: An Overview of Canada," in *Juvenile Justice Systems,* edited by Winterdyk, 141. See also McGuire, "C.19: An Act to Amend the Young Offenders Act," 186.
8. McGuire, "C.19: An Act to Amend the Young Offenders Act," 186.
9. For a listing of some of the major juvenile justice legislation leading up to the YOA as well as the major tenets of the YOA, see Winterdyk, "Juvenile Justice and Young Offenders," 143–46.

10. McGuire, "C.19: An Act to Amend the Young Offenders Act," 188.

11. Raymond Corrado and Alan Markwart, "Canada," in *International Handbook on Juvenile Justice* (Westport, CT: Greenwood Press, 1996), 44.

12. Ibid., 41.

13. Ibid., 42.

14. Alan W. Leschied, Peter G. Jaffe, Dan Andrews, and Paul Gendreau, "Treatment Issues and Young Offenders: An Empirically Derived Vision of Juvenile Justice Policy," in *Juvenile Justice in Canada: A Theoretical and Analytical Assessment*, edited by Raymond R. Corrado et al. (Toronto: Butterworth, 1992).

15. McGuire, "C.19: An Act to Amend the Young Offenders Act," 191.

16. Corrado and Markwart, "Canada," 48.

17. Ibid.

18. Leon A. Radzinowicz, *A History of English Criminal Law and Its Administration from 1750–1833* (London: Stevens and Sons, 1948).

19. Chris Cunneen and Rob White, *Juvenile Justice: An Australian Perspective* (Melbourne: Oxford University Press, 1995), 18–20. For a detailed discussion of the history of English juvenile law as it relates to competing British conservative and labor ideologies, see Loraine Gelsthorpe and Mark Fenwick, "Comparative Juvenile Justice: England and Wales," in *Juvenile Justice Systems*, edited by Winterdyk, 79–80.

20. William Wakefield and David Hirschel, "England," in *International Handbook on Juvenile Justice*, 94.

21. Winterdyk, "Overview of the Juvenile Justice System," 79–80; and Cunneen and White, *Juvenile Justice*, 19.

22. Gelsthorpe and Fenwick, "Comparative Juvenile Justice," 79–80.

23. Wakefield and Hirschel, "England," 94.

24. Ibid., 95.

25. Michael Cavadino and James Dignan, *The Penal System* (London: Sage Publications, 1992).

26. Gelsthorpe and Fenwick, "Comparative Juvenile Justice," 96.

27. Wakefield and Hirschel, "England," 97.

28. David P. Farrington and Trevor Bennett, "Police Cautioning of Juveniles in London," *British Journal of Criminology* 21 (1981), 123–35.

29. Bryan Gibson, Paul Cavadino, Andrew Rutherford, and John Harding, *The Youth Court: One Year Onwards* (Winchester, England: Waterside Press, 1994).

30. Gelsthorpe and Fenwick, "Comparative Juvenile Justice," 96. For a comparison of crime rates in the United States and England, see Patrick A. Langan and David P. Farrington, "Crime and Justice in the United States and England and Wales: 1981–1996" (Washington, DC: Bureau of Justice Statistics, Executive Summary, 1998).

31. Wakefield and Hirschel, "England," 99–100.

32. B. F. Harrison and A. J. Maddox, *The Work of a Magistrate*, 3d ed. (London: Shaw and Sons, 1975).

33. Wakefield and Hirschel, "England," 101.

34. Ibid., 102–3.

35. Ibid., 104.

36. Gelsthorpe and Fenwick, "Comparative Juvenile Justice," 103–4.

37. Cunneen and White, *Juvenile Justice*, 10.

38. Ibid., 10, 13, 18–20.

39. Ibid., 147.

40. Ibid., 250–51. Cunneen and White note that these "conferences" are known by a variety of names, including Children's Aid Panels, Family Group Conferences, Community Aid Panels, Community Justice Panels, and Koori Justice Programs.

41. David B. Moore, "Transforming Juvenile Justice—Transforming Policing: The Introduction of Family Conferencing in Australia," in *Comparative Criminal Justice: Traditional and Nontraditional Systems of Law and Control,* edited by Charles B. Fields and Richter H. Moore, Jr. (Prospect Heights, IL: Waveland Press, 1996), 583–600.

42. Cunneen and White, *Juvenile Justice,* 250–51.

43. Ibid., 251–53.

44. Ibid., 203–6, 247–48.

45. Ibid., 203–6; John Seymour, "Australia," in *International Handbook on Juvenile Justice,* 3.

46. Cunneen and White, *Juvenile Justice,* 231–38.

47. See Amnesty International, "Australia: Juvenile Aboriginal Detention a Key Human Rights Concern," January 18, 1996, http://www.amnesty.org/news/1996/31200196.htm.

48. Fay Gale, Rebecca Bailey-Harris, and Joy Wondersitz, *Aboriginal Youth and the Criminal Justice System: The Injustice of Justice* (Cambridge: Cambridge University Press, 1990); see also Amnesty International, "Australia."

49. Herman Conradie, "The Republic of South Africa," in *International Handbook, on Juvenile Justice,* 287.

50. South African Law Commission, "Issue Paper 9: Juvenile Justice" (Pretoria, South Africa: South African Law Commission), October 20, 1999, http://www.law.wits.ac.za/sale/sale.html, 2.

51. Conradie, "Republic of South Africa," 286–300.

52. Wilfried Scharf and Rona Cochrane, "South Africa," *World Factbook of Criminal Justice Systems* (Washington, DC: U.S. Department of Justice, Office of Justice Programs, Bureau of Justice Statistics), http://www.ojp.usdoj.gov/bjs/abstract/wfcj.htm#new.

53. Mark Shaw, "South Africa: Crime and Policing in Post-Apartheid South Africa," in *War and Peace in Southern Africa: Crime, Drugs, Armies, Trade,* edited by Robert I. Rotberg and Greg Mills (Washington, DC: Brookings Institution Press, 1998), 31, 34–37.

54. Sheena Adams, "South Africa's One-Stop Child Justice Centers," http://www.unicef.org/southafrica/reallives_2143.html.

55. South African Law Commission, "Issue Paper 9, " 9.

56. Ibid., 50–51.

57. Ibid., 59–65.

58. Scharf and Cochrane, "South Africa," 15.

59. Conradie, "Republic of South Africa," 293–94, 297.

60. Scharf and Cochrane, "South Africa," 20–21.

61. Saffer, "South Africa's Youngest Prisoners," 31.

62. Conradie, "Republic of South Africa," 298–99.

63. Johann Le Roux, "Street Children in South Africa: Findings from Interviews on the Background of Street Children in Pretoria, South Africa," *Adolescence* 13, no. 122 (Summer 1996), 423–31.

64. John R. Weeks, *Population: An Introduction to Concepts and Issues,* 7th ed. (New York: Wadsworth, 1999), 14, 461.

65. Xin Ren, "People's Republic of China," in *International Handbook on Juvenile Justice*, 55–79.

66. Judge Emily Baker, "People's Republic of China Today: A View of Its Juvenile Justice System," *Juvenile and Family Court Journal* 37 (1986), 51; Xin Ren, "People's Republic of China," 57.

67. Xin Ren, "People's Republic of China," 57–59.

68. Dorothy Bracey, "'Like a Doctor to a Patient, Like a Parent to a Child'—Corrections in the People's Republic of China," *Prison Journal* 68, no. 1 (1988), 25.

69. *Gongdu* schools are middle schools that administer to children ages twelve to seventeen. For a discussion of these facilities, see Daniel J. Curran and Sandra Cook, "Growing Fears, Rising Crime: Juveniles and China's Justice System," *Crime and Delinquency* 39, no. 3 (July 1993), 296–315.

70. Baker, "People's Republic of China Today," 51–57.

71. Curran and Cook, "Growing Fears, Rising Crime," 302.

72. Baker, "People's Republic of China Today," 54. Curran and Cook, in "Growing Fears, Rising Crime," state that the juveniles face a five-stage hierarchy of control: education assisted by the community, education through work and study, reeducation through labor, reform through labor, and discipline in the reformatory.

73. Amnesty International, "China: Gross Human Rights Violations Continue," *Amnesty International Report* (February 1996), 3.

74. Baker, "People's Republic of China Today," 52.

75. Bracey, "Like a Doctor to a Patient, Like a Parent to a Child," 24–33.

76. Baker, "People's Republic of China Today," 55.

77. Ibid., 55.

78. Xiaogang Dent and Ann Cordilia, "To Get Rich Is Glorious: Rising Expectations, Declining Control, and Escalating Crime in Contemporary China," *International Journal of Offender Therapy and Comparative Criminology* 43, no. 2 (1999), 211–28. See also Curran and Cook, "Growing Fears, Rising Crime," 307–9.

79. Curran and Cook, "Growing Fears, Rising Crime," 304–5.

80. Ren, "People's Republic of China," 72–75.

81. Weeks, *Population*, 17–23.

82. Arvind Verma, "Cultural Roots of Police Corruption in India," *Policing: An International Journal of Police Strategies and Management* 22, no. 3 (1999), 264–79; see also Clayton Hartjen, "Legal Change and Juvenile Justice in India," *International Criminal Justice Review* 5 (1995), 6.

83. For a list of acts related to juveniles, see K. S. Shukla, "Role of the Police in Juvenile Justice," *Indian Journal of Criminology* (September 1981), 163.

84. Hartjen, "Legal Change and Juvenile Justice in India," 2–3.

85. Ibid.

86. Clayton A. Hartjen and G. Kethineni, "India," *International Handbook on Juvenile Justice*, 184–87.

87. Ibid.

88. Ibid., 185.

89. Hartjen, "Legal Change and Juvenile Justice in India," 4.

90. Ibid.

91. U.S. Department of State, "India Report on Human Rights Practices for 1997," Bureau of Democracy, Human Rights and Labor (January 30, 1998), 10.

92. Hartjen, "Legal Change and Juvenile Justice in India," 5.

93. U.S. Department of State, "India Report on Human Rights," 21, 25–26.

94. Weeks, *Population,* 17–23.

95. Annina Lahalle, "Modern Legislation for a Country of Contrasts: The Example of Brazil," in *Juvenile Delinquents and Young People in Danger in an Open Environment,* edited by Willie McCarney (Winchester, NM: Waterside Press, 1966), 177–83.

96. Lahalle, "Modern Legislation for a Country of Contrasts," p. 180.

97. Chuck Pfister, "Not for Kids," September 1995, http://www.brazil-brazil.com/cvrsep95.htm.

98. Lahalle, "Modern Legislation for a Country of Contrasts," 182.

99. Ibid., 182–88. This legislative act also calls for programs that offer assistance to parents.

100. Vincent A. Keeton and Michael P. McConnell, "Street Children in Brazil: The Policy Issue, Policy Background, and Current Policy and Programs," Chapter 11, PRP Papers, 1994–1995, http://lanic.utexas.edu/project/ppb/papers94–95/mcconnel.html.

101. Lahalle, "Modern Legislation for a Country of Contrasts," 182–83.

102. Keeton and McConnell, "Street Children in Brazil," 16.

103. Reuters, "Brazil Youth Riot Ends with Four Boys Dead," October 25, 1999, http://www.nytimes.com/reuters/international/international-brazil-html.

16

JUVENILE JUSTICE IN THE TWENTY-FIRST CENTURY

Kids are kids, not adults . . . . But it troubles me deeply that our focus is on juvenile justice and not juvenile education. It's about trials and not about schools or discipline. It's about punishment and not about mentoring. No, I can't understand it and I don't agree with it. We will never, in my view, solve our problems on the back end with punishment. We will solve our problems only if we are united with a higher purpose of doing better on the front end with day care, preschool, schools, churches, other institutions and yes, families. Kids are our future and we need to invest in them. Treating kids as adults solves very little; it's another quick-fix solution to a complex problem that took years to reach and will take years to resolve.

—Barry Glick and William Sturgeon[1]

OUTLINE

OBJECTIVES

1. To review the basic problems in American society that have an impact on juveniles
2. To review the basic problems in the administration of juvenile justice
3. To discuss the individual, systemic, and societal changes necessary for a promising future for juvenile justice

KEY TERMS

habilitation   honor   hope
healing

Barry Glick and William Sturgeon, in the chapter-opening quote, do not deny that juvenile crime is both a serious matter and a common phenomenon today.[2] Yet they contend that what is needed is more effective front-end programs, including day care, preschool, schools, and community programs. They believe that such an investment in youngsters will have far greater success than punishment programs on the back end.

The long-standing mission of juvenile justice is to correct youthful offenders so that they will neither return to the juvenile justice system nor continue on into the life of an adult criminal. Indeed, the opposite often appears to be true, for once trouble-making youths are processed through the correctional system, the chances of their returning are increased, not reduced. Juvenile corrections often breeds rather than reforms offenders.[3] A more recent mission is to provide justice to juveniles who are referred to the juvenile justice system.[4] As this book repeatedly documents, there is a long way to go to achieve the goals of either rehabilitation or justice.

Many intervention methods have been tried in order to accomplish the mission of rehabilitation. These include diversion, community-based corrections, radical nonintervention, the closing of training schools, mandatory sentencing, punishment, transactional analysis, guided group interaction, positive peer culture, behavior therapy, work release, home furloughs, and coeducational institutionalization. Although we know that some things work in some situations with some offenders, overall these strategies fall short of accomplishing the goal of preventing youngsters from returning to the system.

The juvenile justice system is under attack from all quarters. Few support keeping the system as it has been. Some urge the decriminalization of status offenders; others want to increase the number of youths transferred to the adult court. An increasingly vocal minority even propose merging the juvenile system into the adult justice system.

This chapter depicts the problems facing juveniles in their communities and the problems limiting the juvenile justice system; then it recommends a credo for society and for the juvenile justice system that is compatible with this new vision.

HOW DO THE PROBLEMS OF MODERN SOCIETY AFFECT YOUTHS AT RISK?

The problems of juveniles start well before they come to the attention of juvenile justice authorities. Accordingly, for real progress to be made in understanding the problems of high-risk youths, the larger social context of their lives must be examined.

THE FAMILY

The American family has changed rather dramatically in recent decades. Inflation has eroded the economic support of the traditional family. Even in intact families, both parents often must work to make ends meet. Single parents experience greater financial difficulties because they have only one source of income; some qualify only for unskilled and minimum-wage jobs. The result in too many families is that children find themselves on their own for significant portions of the day as parents attempt to survive financially.

To add to their problems, many children are members of dysfunctional families, in which neglect, emotional abuse, physical abuse, and sexual abuse are regular occurrences. Dysfunctional families also have more than their share of parents who are emotionally disturbed, alcoholics, drug users, or in prison. Children in some dysfunctional families may have no contact with one parent or may not even remember that parent. But even in what appear to be stable family units, parents may be struggling with problems stemming from long-repressed violence, neglect, or sexual or emotional abuse from their own childhood. The result is that many youths never receive the love, affection, and acceptance they need from parents.

THE SOCIOECONOMIC STRUCTURE

The American social class structure has come under increased scrutiny over the past decade. Such headlines as "The Rich Get Richer" and "Income Disparity Between the Rich and Poor Increases" frequently are found in the media. Increased references to a "shrinking middle class" and the "development of the underclass" are also found. These media trends reflect statistics indicating that a rather small percentage (20 percent) of the population controls more than 86 percent of the wealth in the nation and receives more than 45 percent of the income. The bottom 20 percent of the population controls less than 1 percent of the wealth and receives less than 5 percent of the income. The gap between the bottom 20 percent and the top 20 percent is increasing. In addition, the middle class has more people moving down than up in the social class structure.

The rapidly expanding underclass is one of the most serious social problems facing the United States. The underclass is made up of the poorest of the poor. Joblessness pervades the inner cities, as young males find employment increasingly difficult to find. The lack of suitable jobs tends to make the underclass welfare dependent, but its members do not receive enough welfare support to escape the ravages of poverty—high rents, dilapidated and inadequate housing, deteriorated neighborhoods, and ineffective schooling for their children.[5] Another feature of underclass life is the tendency of adolescent females to have children out of wedlock, which only extends the welfare and poverty cycle to another generation. Drugs, especially crack cocaine, are readily available as an escape from this dreary existence.

THE NEIGHBORHOOD

As children reach an age that allows them to spend time outside the home and away from direct supervision of parents or guardians, the neighborhood becomes an important focus of their expectations. For urban children, exploration of the neighborhood brings them in contact with a variety of social groups and institutions. Unfortunately, they find their inner-city neighborhoods too frequently to be battlegrounds where wars are waged among different ethnic groups. The battles are fought for reasons of misunderstanding, for imagined slights, and sometimes to protect the markets in which drugs are the sole means of making a living.

These neighborhoods reflect the downside of American society. Residents of such communities are poor, face prejudice, and feel powerless. On a daily basis, they must deal with an absence of jobs, vermin-filled housing, untreated diseases, scarcity of food, unwanted pregnancies, and a lack of community political and social organization. Weighed down with such problems, residents come to believe in fate rather than in their ability to bring positive change to their lives.

THE SCHOOL

Inner-city schools, especially, are under increased criticism. Although such schools have long been targeted as in need of reform, society has yet to take more than a piecemeal approach to the problems of uninterested and bored students, disillusioned and detached teachers, antiquated facilities, and inadequate curriculums. Gang battles of the streets are often carried into the halls of the schools, and innocent youths have been beaten and killed on school steps, hallways, classrooms, and playgrounds. Not surprisingly, these schools have become dens of fear and frustration for the remaining students and teachers. Drugs are frequently available, as police and security staff attempt to bring some semblance of order to the disorder. Too frequently, juveniles caught up in the environments of these schools make poor grades, become disruptive, skip school, are suspended, assault others, join gangs, traffic in drugs, and drop out. These problems help ensure that this nation has more uneducated citizens, higher dropout rates, and more people with minimal reading skills than do most of the industrialized countries in the world. African-American, Hispanic, and Native American students are particularly vulnerable to these problems.

THE GANG

Almost all adolescents are members of peer groups. This grouping together with peers is a normal rite of passage to adulthood. What is not normal from society's viewpoint is the weaponry and violence, drug trafficking, and other antisocial behaviors of urban and emerging gangs. Measures taken to deal with these gangs are often repressive and fail to recognize the major functions of the gangs for their members.

Many juveniles, especially those from the inner cities, see gangs as substitutes for their families. Gangs provide their members with roots, respect, and identity, which they can carry either to an early grave or into prison—the only futures on the horizons of many gang youths. For the first time in their lives, many feel a sense of respect and belonging they can get nowhere else. The gang gives them a sense of loyalty and an identity marked by the turf of their neighborhood. Finally, the gang offers the belief that only in this social group can they really belong to something and attain what is missing in their lives.

But gang participation is ultimately as self-defeating or destructive as, or perhaps even more than, the family and school have been. Gang involvement thrusts a youth into dangerous and deadly games. Gang members are more likely than nongang members to commit offenses and to become victims. Gang involvement also is one of the best ways for a juvenile to increase the likelihood of confinement in juvenile and adult facilities. Moreover, gangs poorly prepare a youth for marriage, employment, or learning to adapt to the adult world.[6]

Neighborhood centers provide one-on-one help to youths from impoverished areas. (Photo by Kathryn Miller.)

YOUTH ATTITUDES

Juveniles can be divided into high-risk, middle-risk, and low-risk groups. High-risk children, making up about one-fourth of the adolescent population, frequently are involved in problem-oriented behaviors. Middle-risk children, making up another one-fourth of the population, occasionally become involved in problem behaviors, especially minor forms of juvenile lawbreaking, drug and alcohol use, and sexual behaviors. Low-risk children, constituting the other 50 percent of the adolescent population, become involved in few problem behaviors.[7] The high-risk children are those with the most problematic social contexts shaping their lives. Middle-risk children have some problems in their social backgrounds but usually have positive forces balancing the negative ones. Low-risk children tend to have positive social and family backgrounds.

High-risk children frequently come out of their experiences with families, neighborhoods, and schools with the self-concepts of losers. Told all of their lives that they are dumb, worthless, and troublemakers and that they will never amount to anything, they tend to be self-absorbed, look down upon themselves, and resent anyone who confronts them. Once immersed in alcohol and drugs, they may assume that no legitimate avenues of success will ever open to them and that a life of trouble and an early death are their inevitable future. These youngsters blame society and others for their failures and have no confidence in themselves or in their ability to turn their lives around.

WHY IS IT HARD FOR A JUVENILE OFFENDER TO "GO STRAIGHT"?

The four key words in juveniles' ability to turn their lives around are **habilitation, healing, hope,** and **honor.** These four interrelated concepts go to the heart of why youths at risk feel alienated from modern society. Whether at home, on the streets, or in juvenile correctional institutions, all youths need to feel that they have the capacity to attain their goals.

HABILITATION

In a large gathering of juvenile justice practitioners, a seasoned probation officer raised the question, "How can we rehabilitate kids who have not first been habilitated?"[8] This person went on to say that a juvenile is not likely to be a good citizen if he or she has not learned how to get along with others and is unable to accept responsibility for his or her own behavior.

This reality goes to the heart of the problem facing many youths today. It reflects the fact that impoverished and dysfunctional families have difficulty raising children who will become contributing members of society. Nor are youths from these families likely to receive much positive reinforcement at school, in the workplace, or anywhere else. Accordingly, they do not believe that they have useful social roles to play, and, not surprisingly, they lack any real stake in the system or any basic respect for social norms, values, or institutions.

This discussion leads to several questions. Is it possible to make up for what was lacking at home? Is it possible to make up for deficient social skills, for the inability to function in school, and for the lack of job marketability? These questions continue to come up in working with hard-core delinquents, whether they are violent offenders, gang delinquents, drug-addicted or drug-trafficking offenders, or repetitive property offenders.

Clearly, the place to achieve habilitation is in the home before the child leaves the family. Society needs to support families in such a manner that the habilitation of all children is guaranteed from the very beginning of their lives. Other early possibilities for habilitation include day-care centers, preschools, and Head Start programs. Sensitive teachers and innovative approaches can help the school socialize children. For those children who fail to receive positive socializing influences at home or at school, the task of habilitation falls to neighbors, extended family, staff of community organizations, gang workers, juvenile justice personnel, and social service agencies.

HEALING

Healing is a crucial need in the lives of most youthful offenders because youths at risk frequently have a long litany of painful experiences. Pain, of course, is a normal part of life, but youths today appear to be experiencing pain in unparalleled numbers. Many are reared in one-parent families, in which they have experienced financial and perhaps emotional deprivation. Others have been neglected and/or abused. Incest is especially traumatic and may require a lifetime to overcome its destructiveness. As youths attempt to cope with emotional and/or material deprivations at home, they also face problems in school. Academic success can help ease this pain, but those who lack support from home all too often find school difficult or nonrewarding. Minority youths, particularly those faced with lack of support from home and with a history of failure in school, often are unable to find jobs. But even if youths can locate low-paying jobs in fast-food restaurants or convenience stores, they are aware that this type of employment has no future and may result in ridicule from members of their peer group.

Their painful experiences, not surprisingly, flood these youths with negative emotions. Many react with anger, resentment, rage, guilt, or depression. Some become self-destructive, engaging in prostitution or excessive drug or alcohol use. Their anger may explode toward others as they strike out in homicide, assaultive behavior, or gang violence.

These youths soon discover that painful consequences accompany their acting-out behaviors. Labeled at school, suspended, or perhaps even expelled, some are removed from their homes and placed in foster care or in residential facilities. Others are adjudicated to training schools or are waived to adult courts. Placement in long-term correctional facilities, especially, is extremely painful because of the freedom the youths lose.

The concept of healing is as old as human society. Yet today, the concept is usually limited to problems of physical healing designated to the care of a medical doctor. Emotional healing is left to the psychiatrists, psychologists, professional social workers, and caseworkers of the world. Clergy are sometimes seen as spiritual healers with family counseling offered with a Judeo-Christian emphasis.

Paradoxically, most treatment technologies in juvenile justice are based on the need for healing among correctional clients, yet few treatment modalities are able to reach the inner selves where healing can be effected. A further problem with treatment in juvenile justice is that it is imposed on juveniles. When receptivity to treatment becomes a necessary prerequisite of release from correctional service or confinement, treatment will always be viewed as involuntarily imposed on offenders.

Only within the past decade or so has much effort gone into understanding how individuals can open themselves to the healing process. What we have learned is that prevention is the best approach to avoid the pain that arrests self-development. Prevention, as previously suggested, is largely ignored in modern society. Hence, we are left with the necessity of having to heal what we have failed to prevent.

We have also learned that the desire, or impetus, for healing must begin with an individual. For youths to become useful members of society and to experience a turning point, they must overcome the negative emotions of fear, anger, resentment, and hate and must create or experience positive emotions that will help their minds and bodies stay healthy.

Finally, we are aware that this healing process is one in which an individual needs continual reinforcement from a supportive network of significant others. When a juvenile has been going down one street and tries to change and go the other way, which is exactly what needs to happen with many youthful offenders, the process requires a much more dependable support system than is typically found in juvenile justice.

HOPE

Hopelessness—the absence of hope—is being experienced by increasing numbers of individuals today. They feel that future possibility is defined by already known limits; in effect, the past exercises absolute tyranny over their future.[9]

The absence of hope is especially found among the underclass in this nation. The feeling of hopelessness is generated by a history of poverty without any apparent means to escape in the present or the future. This feeling contributes to high rates of child and spousal abuse and to frequent use of drugs and alcohol. The feeling of hopelessness among the underclass has also contributed to large numbers being sentenced to correctional care and imprisonment.

For juveniles, the feeling of hopelessness is also related to the high rates of teenage pregnancy and unwed motherhood as young girls often have babies in the hope that the babies will love them when no one else has. Hopelessness increases the appeal of drugs, especially crack cocaine. Hopelessness provides the stimulus for the development of drug-trafficking gangs, initially in our inner cities and now throughout the nation. It leads to involvement in crime, even though offenders know they face the possibility of incarceration in jail and prison. Finally, the feeling of hopelessness leads to a fatalistic approach to life. For example, gang youths often believe that life will be short, perhaps extending barely into their twenties.

"Where there is no hope," the Old Testament prophet tells us, "the people perish." The dimensions of *hopefulness* include an accurate portrayal of self, an ability to establish realistic goals for the future, the willingness to reach out to positive support systems, and the acknowledgment of one's sense of power. Hope is contained in the desire for some good to be accomplished with the belief that it is obtainable. Hope enables us to trust in the future. It is fostered by a belief in personal freedom based on the choices presented. The philosopher Marcel adds that hope is the radical refusal to calculate the limits of the possible.[10]

Hope gives adolescents something to anticipate—a reason to obey the law, to attend school, to avoid drug involvement, and to stay out of gangs. Those who have hope are more likely to be bonded to society.[11] They are more able to delay gratification. They believe that good things will happen in the future, including employment, education, marriage, and family.

Our challenge is to provide nourishing environments so that young people can be hopeful about their futures. Of course, achieving this with younger children is easier than with older adolescents. Prevention programs must be developed with young children before they become involved in antisocial groups and commit illegal activities. Adolescents pose a more challenging problem, because many may have already been socialized into a deviant lifestyle. For these youngsters to feel hopeful, they must come to believe that (1) they can attain their goals, (2) the future has possibilities for them, and (3) there are others who will support them in attaining their goals.

HONOR

Juveniles worry a great deal about their reputation with valued peer groups. Prosocial youngsters want to wear stylish clothing. They try to do what is socially acceptable, and they usually attempt to avoid anything that will bring embarrassment to themselves. Similarly, youngsters who support negative practices, such as satanic worship, pursue the same strategy for peer approval. Their clothing, tattoos, jewelry, and interactions with outsiders must be approved by other youngsters who believe in satanic worship and beliefs.

The need for peer approval, of course, will not change. But what is important are the values of the peer groups to which a youth turns for acceptance and guidance. The aspirations, values, and worldviews of one peer group might lead to confinement in a training school and to a continuation of crime as an adult, whereas another peer group might lend support to positive directions and socially approved goals for its members.

The peer groups to which juveniles turn depend largely on their definitions of self and where they feel they fit in the social fabric. Those who feel powerless, for example, will turn to groups that will provide what they feel they cannot provide for themselves. One problem with seeking answers "out there" is that many youths join gangs that inevitably lead to drug addiction, to violent gang activity, and to crime as the best or only options for achieving the good life.

An alternative direction for youths to take is to affirm their honor in socially acceptable ways. This affirmation refers to developing a sense of self-worth, of personal dignity, and of meaningful and important lives. Youths must respect themselves and believe they are entitled to achieve their goals.

In sum, habilitation, healing, hope, and honor are the processes that must take place for a juvenile to turn his or her life around from a negative to a positive direction. A youth who is receptive to change or is fed up with the ways of crime needs support from helpful and caring adults to stay on the path to good citizenry.

WHAT PROBLEMS ARE FOUND IN THE ADMINISTRATION OF JUVENILE JUSTICE?

The administrative problems facing the juvenile justice system likewise are formidable and extensive. Inadequate funding, fragmentation within the system, the lack of a unifying philosophy, a sharp upsurge in the public's fear of the violent juvenile, poorly developed prevention strategies, and the overuse of intervention are some of the many problems that demand solutions if the offending juvenile is to be successfully reintegrated into the daily life of the community.

The meagerness of the funding of juvenile justice sorely handicaps social policy advances. Juvenile justice presently is a relatively marginal area of governmental concern in most states. Regardless of how large certain budget line items for justice may seem, or how pressing litigation or code revision may be, the dollars involved are almost insignificant compared to the state resources allocated to public education, or to overcoming energy shortages and unemployment, or even to adult corrections. Consequently, it is not surprising to find that juvenile justice has no general backing in most states, that few interest groups regularly support juvenile justice measures, that coalitions of interest groups and political and governmental leaders seldom push for change, and that reports on important events relating to juvenile justice (other than incidents of crime) are usually relegated to the back pages of the newspapers.[12] It becomes much easier to explain why progress does not occur in this area than to trace the reasons for juvenile justice's varying directions and rate of change among the states.[13]

The fragmentation of the juvenile justice system also presents a barrier to those who would bring change to juvenile justice. Fragmentation clearly prevents juveniles from receiving just treatment under the law, because state and local units operate autonomously, with little coordination or cooperation at any level. Furthermore, the policy and program concerns of some states are quite different from those of other states: In fact, the policy, structure, or program solutions chosen by some states are the very ones rejected by other states as unworkable or undesirable.

The lack of a unifying philosophy is another barrier to change. Should our child-saving philosophy be based on the treatment, the justice, the balanced, or the punishment model? Should our strategy with juveniles in trouble be nonintervention, diversion, deinstitutionalization, or institutionalization? If a juvenile must be institutionalized, should our aim be treatment, punishment, or merely warehousing? The net effect of these philosophical differences works to form pressure groups and professional associations. These groups take specific, sometimes narrow, positions as each attempts to convince others that its position is the only one that deserves to be heard. Each stance is defended emotionally, and often more effort goes into argument than into a genuine concern with the needs of children.

Furthermore, a sharp upsurge in the public's fear of juvenile and adult crime has created a national mood of "let's get tough with juvenile criminals." The trilogy of gangs, drugs, and guns is doing much to contribute to this get tough approach. This attitude is producing a rise in the populations of juvenile correctional institutions and a loss of support for community-based corrections and diversionary programs. Determinate sentencing for juveniles has become the established policy in several states, and mandatory sentencing laws for youthful offenders have been adopted throughout the nation. More juvenile offenders are being transferred to the adult courts. In some states, the death penalty may be imposed on sixteen-year-old juveniles who commit what for adults would be a capital offense. Overall, as the crime control, or punishment, model gathered momentum during the 1970s and 1980s, retrenchment rather than innovation became the predominant characteristic of juvenile justice.

The juvenile justice system has too long been a disposal unit for the children of the poor. The lack of social justice for poor and minority groups is a grave indictment of our society. At the same time that the heavy-handed ministrations of the state have harshly processed the poor, the justice system has worked very hard at saving the "saved"—the middle-class youths who have committed minor offenses. These juveniles are usually the ones diverted from the system, placed on probation, and retained in community-based corrections.

When minor offenders and noncriminal youths, such as status offenders, go into the system, they typically stay a long time and have painful experiences; nothing testifies so well to the fact that the juvenile justice system does not work as the tossing of all youths into the same bag, the rapist with the runaway. The reality is that the system too often refuses to sort the youths who come into it.[14] The unfortunate consequence is that youths who either are noncriminal or have committed only minor offenses often end up being confined for months longer than those who have committed violent crimes. In the past, status offenders tended to become the institutional scapegoats and sometimes chose to take their own lives because they could not survive in the institutional context. Today, they are more likely to be sent to private placements where they end up spending two or three times as long as delinquent youths sent to state institutions.

In addition, juvenile institutionalization is for many youngsters a dehumanizing, brutal, and criminogenic experience. Exploitation has reached epidemic proportions in some training schools, where the weak give up everything, including their bodies, to the strong. Some youngsters come out of institutions psychologically devastated; others emerge much more committed to crime as a way of life and further alienated from conventional values and institutions than before their stay.

Prevention strategies are underdeveloped and inefficient.[15] We have not been able to prevent delinquency, and once youngsters become involved in lawbreaking behavior, we have not been able to exercise control. Problems in prevention strategies emerge on at least three fronts: First, although crime prevention must begin in the local community or on the grassroots level, little progress has been made in community organization since the Chicago Area

Projects; second, basic concepts in the prevention field are not precise, and few attempts have been made to design programs around theoretical constructs; and third, we have failed to appreciate fully the negative effects of removing juvenile offenders from such mainstream institutions as the home and school to rehabilitate them.

The overuse of intervention has too frequently characterized juvenile justice. Confined youths usually are required to participate in treatment programs because of our desire to help them. Faced with the options of locking up, giving up, or trying harder with certain youths, we have tried harder to treat them. Consequently, a treatment sprawl has resulted, in which these offenders are faced with what must seem like an endless variety of ways to "recycle" them. The treatment goes on and on, sometimes involving contradictory methods.

Closely related to overintervention is the failure of many community-based and diversionary programs to deliver. Too many programs set their goals too high and promise too much in order to obtain federal funding. In effect, each program promises to be the panacea for youth crime. Not only are these programs unable to achieve projected goals, but they also tend to evade accountability for the quality of their work with youths. For example, while these programs may do the necessary evaluation for funding renewal, the follow-up on program effectiveness is not done, with the result that poor programs are sometimes perpetuated rather than allowed to die.

Juvenile justice is in a quandary on what to do with the hard-core or difficult-to-handle juvenile. In the past, isolation, padded cells, Thorazine, handcuffs, and corporal punishment were usually reserved for these youths, who were shipped to maximum-security juvenile facilities. Hard-core offenders now face transfer to the adult court, mandatory sentencing, and if they have committed a heinous crime and are eighteen years of age, perhaps even the death penalty. But our strategies and programs are not rehabilitating these youngsters. The public says that hard-core youthful criminals must be locked up because the innocent deserve protection, but in places of juvenile confinement, these youths become inmate leaders and set the mood and the rules for a violent inmate subculture. In adult prisons and jails, juvenile thugs become the prey of adult predators.

In sum, a critical examination of juvenile justice easily leads the observer to cynicism and to the feeling that nothing can be done. The agencies that run our political system do not provide enough money for the juvenile justice system to be effective. Innovative methods are fought tooth and nail by those

Video monitoring cameras are found in an increasing number of schools and on community streets today. (Photo by Kathryn Miller.)

who benefit from keeping things the way they are. High-risk youths often have too much against them even if the system could be substantially improved. In addition, the skyrocketing growth of gangs across the nation, the lure of drugs and alcohol, the increased use of guns, and the rising number of hate crimes all contribute to rebellion against adult rules and law.

WHAT DOES JUVENILE JUSTICE LOOK LIKE FOR THE TWENTY-FIRST CENTURY?

This unsettling review of the present status of juvenile crime in the United States needs to be supplemented by the grim picture of what may take place with juvenile crime in the twenty-first century.

- The U.S. Census Bureau estimates that the population of juveniles under the age of eighteen will increase 14 percent between 2000 and 2025—about one-half of 1 percent per years. By 2050, it is estimated that the juvenile population will be 36 percent larger than it was in 2000.[16] Given this population growth of juveniles in the years to come, it is likely that juvenile justice will have greater demands placed on it.

- Many members of this increased population of juveniles will come from impoverished homes headed by single mothers. In 2002, African-American and Hispanic juveniles were more than three times as likely to live in poverty as non-Hispanic white juveniles. Since juvenile poverty appears to be associated with juvenile crime, it is likely that minority juveniles will continue to be the focus of social control in American society.[17]

- With this increased population of poor juveniles, the rate of juvenile violence, including homicide, may again grow, as it did in the late 1980s and early 1990s.

- The widespread feeling today that there are more troubled teenagers than in the past will be even more pronounced in the next twenty years. Adolescent psychiatry will be more frequently called on to treat these youths, but it will be the children of the haves who will benefit the most, as they will be placed in private hospitals and treatment centers.

- The *Roper v. Simmons* decision reveals that the debate about the death penalty for juveniles under the age of eighteen has been resolved at least for now, and it is unlikely that any changes will take place in the near future.[18]

- The trilogy of gangs, drugs, and guns will continue to be a social problem. Youth gangs are increasingly becoming a minority problem, and this trend is likely to increase in the decades to come.

- The drug choices of juveniles may well change in the future, but there is no evidence that drug use will be less of a problem than it presently is. There is currently a widespread movement among juveniles from the use of crack cocaine to the use of methamphetamine.

- Juveniles will continue to drink alcohol, and there is no reason to believe that the use of alcohol will be less of a problem than at present.

- The issue of gun control will remain a serious problem facing juvenile justice.

- The current tendency to create uniformity and reduce discretion in juvenile sentencing procedures is likely to continue.
- The deinstitutionalization movement is likely to continue and even expand, given the high costs of institutionalization.
- The use of restorative justice will continue to spread throughout the United States.
- The use of private programs will continue to be an important part of the landscape of juvenile corrections.
- State legislatures will become increasingly involved in passing laws related to the social control of juveniles.
- A structural change that will likely be implemented in those states that do not have it is the removal of serious crimes from the jurisdiction of the juvenile court. What will probably be imposed is some mechanism for the direct referral of juvenile crimes to the adult court.
- Disproportionate minority confinement, in spite of the efforts of the JJDPA, will remain a problem, and juvenile institutions will become even more emphatic dumping grounds for poor and minority children.
- The number of juveniles in adult prisons will probably not decrease. Wardens and their staffs will view the protection of these youngsters as one of their most difficult management problems.
- The dissatisfaction with the juvenile justice system will probably continue to increase. Those who want to eliminate the juvenile justice system and the juvenile court will be more vocal and will receive much greater support.
- Yet it remains unlikely that this nation will give up any time in the near future on the more than century-long experiment with a separate system for juveniles.

WHAT IS A VIABLE CREDO FOR JUVENILE JUSTICE IN THE NEXT ONE HUNDRED YEARS?

Changes to promote the vision of juvenile justice found in this text must consist of systemic changes in the juvenile justice system and structural changes in the wider society.

SYSTEMIC CHANGES IN JUVENILE JUSTICE

Let us turn to the grim reality of the juvenile justice process—a reality that includes drug trafficking, extortion, drive-by shootings, rape, and murder. The fact is that the history of juvenile justice has been filled with individuals who have made a difference in juvenile justice agencies. One of the authors worked with one such person for four years in a maximum-security training school. He had an absolutely astounding positive impact on these older, aggressive offenders.

The administrative system of this "jungle," as residents were fond of calling this institution, did not treat this person well. Nor have many other such individuals been treated well by the justice systems in which they worked. They are sometimes fired. They are often ignored. They are likely to experience burnout. They receive frequent harassment. And they may leave their jobs emotionally broken.

We need to be proud of the fact that some outstanding individuals make the difference they do against what appear to be overwhelming odds. We need to admire what they achieve but, at the same time, be aware that their contributions frequently are limited and often short-lived because they stand alone. Superior workers need support and encouragement from peers who believe in similar ideas.

The lesson to be learned is that those individuals who want to create a more humane, just, and effective criminal justice process must establish networks with others. As these individuals develop their networks and express the visions of systemic reform, they will eventually become a critical mass. Interestingly, once certain numbers of supporters are attained—the critical mass—a movement suddenly, dramatically increases its power and persuasiveness.

Specifically, the vision of juvenile justice described in this text points to the following systemic emphases to achieve a more hopeful juvenile crime prevention and control strategy.

- Grassroots participation is essential for any hopeful response to prevent and control youth crime; the community must participate in efforts of crime prevention and control.
- The concern for human dignity and wholeness requires that ethical considerations and personal integrity be viewed as essential components of working in the juvenile justice system.
- The spirit of cooperation and assistance of those who work in the juvenile justice system must replace competition, jealousy, and indifference.
- Conflict resolution approaches are much more efficient and effective means to resolve differences among young people. In order to mediate conflict and violence, these approaches can be more widely used at home, in the school and community, and in correctional settings.
- The more young people's basic needs are met, the less likely it is that they will turn to antisocial behaviors and drug use.
- Upholding the dignity of the human being requires that each person is treated fairly and that discriminatory treatment becomes a relic of the past.
- The more emphasis placed on prevention, the more likely it is that negative individual behavior patterns can be avoided before they become fixed and permanent features of the personality structure.
- The principle that good people make a difference is readily seen by those who are making a difference in improving systems and in motivating colleagues and offenders to be the best they can be. At a time in which so much powerlessness is evident among the public, youthful and adult offenders, and juvenile justice practitioners, there is increased need for those who have a positive vision for change and are able to lead others toward this vision.

STRUCTURAL CHANGES IN MODERN SOCIETY

Modern societies must take positive steps to reduce the problems of society and the juvenile justice system. Whereas the elimination of crime is clearly unrealistic, the possibility that some problems can be reduced, or at least stabilized, does remain. The following are some goals to attain, at least in part, the vision of a better society for youngsters as well as adults.

- Systemwide planning is required to guarantee a social structure that is sensitive to the needs of all people, regardless of their social class.

- The activities of social service agencies must be coordinated to provide integrated services to all families and youths in a caring manner.
- Disorganized and dangerous neighborhoods must be changed to make them safe and secure.
- All families must believe that they have ready access to agencies capable of providing them direction in solving their problems.
- All families must have access to jobs that provide them with the adequate necessities of life.
- Youths must grow up experiencing a positive social and economic milieu that gives them hope for the future.
- Schools must become responsive to the realities faced by youngsters and must attempt to prepare them realistically for life after graduation.

✓**Progress Check 16.1**
Review this section at
www.prenhall.com/bartollas

SUMMARY

- Our experience in working with juvenile offenders, in researching juvenile justice publications, and in writing about the rhetoric and reality of juvenile justice operations has convinced us that a new direction is needed.
- We hope that the student shares our enthusiasm and aspirations about the possibility of creating a better day for youngsters in our society.
- The challenge in juvenile justice is great at this time.

If we care for children, we will increase our efforts to diminish the negative effects of the hard-line and punitive approaches to corrections.

If we care for children, we will see to it that our ideas are presented forcefully and clearly to policymakers.

And if we care for children, we will not wait until the system finally works; instead, we will reach out and help those youths seeking to find themselves.

CRITICAL THINKING QUESTIONS

1. Is it possible to have hope in the midst of our hopelessness?
2. What is needed to improve juvenile justice in the United States?
3. What is the present status of juvenile corrections in social policy?
4. What is the most serious problem in developing a new vision for juvenile corrections?

NOTES

1. Barry Glick and William Sturgeon, *No Time to Play: Youthful Offenders in Adult Correctional Systems* (Lanham, MD: American Correctional Association, 1998), 10.
2. Refer to the self-report and cohort studies in Chapter 2.
3. See Lyle Shannon, *Assessing the Relationships of Adult Criminal Careers to Juvenile Careers* (Washington, DC: Government Printing Office, 1982); and Donna Martin Hamparian et al., *The Violent Few: A Study of Dangerous Juvenile Offenders* (Lexington, MA: Lexington Books, 1980).

4. See David Fogel, *We Are the Living Proof: The Justice Model for Corrections* (Cincinnati: Anderson, 1975); and David Fogel and Joe Hudson, eds., *Justice as Fairness: Perspectives on the Justice Model* (Cincinnati: Anderson, 1981).

5. Recent welfare legislation promises to make it even more difficult for the underclass.

6. James F. Short, Jr., "Exploring Integration of Theoretical Levels of Explanation: Notes on Gang Delinquency," in *Theoretical Integration,* edited by S. F. Messner, M. D. Krohn, and A. E. Liska (Albany: State University of New York Press, 1989), 3.

7. Joy G. Dryfoos, *Adolescents at Risk: Prevalence and Prevention* (New York: Oxford University Press, 1990).

8. Statement made in a conference one of the authors attended in 1978.

9. Sam Keen, *Apology for Wonder* (New York: Harper & Row, 1969), 174.

10. Cited in ibid.

11. Travis Hirschi, *Causes of Delinquency* (Berkeley: University of California Press, 1969).

12. Cited in Rosemary C. Sarri and Robert D. Vinter, "Justice for Whom? Varieties of Juvenile Correctional Approaches," in *The Juvenile Justice System,* edited by Malcolm W. Klein (Beverly Hills, CA: Sage Publications, 1976), 169.

13. Sources that explore the many directions of juvenile corrections include Barry Krisberg and Ira Schwartz, "Rethinking Juvenile Justice," *Crime and Delinquency* 21 (July 1983); Barry Krisberg, Ira Schwartz, Paul Litsky, and James Austin, "The Watershed of Juvenile Justice," *Crime and Delinquency* 23 (January 1986); and Dennis Maloney, "The Challenge for Juvenile Corrections: To Serve Both Youths and the Public," *Corrections Magazine* (August 1989).

14. Ira M. Schwartz, *(In)justice for Children: Rethinking the Best Interests of the Child* (Lexington, MA: Lexington Books, 1989), 167.

15. Richard J. Lundman, *Prevention and Control of Juvenile Delinquency* (New York: Oxford University Press, 1984); Richard J. Lundman, Paul T. McFarlane, and Frank R. Scarpitti, "Delinquency Prevention: A Description and Assessment of Projects Reported in the Professional Literature," *Crime and Delinquency* 22 (July 1976).

16. Howard N. Snyder and Melissa Sickmund, *Juvenile Offenders and Victims: 2006 National Report* (Washington, DC: National Center for Juvenile Justice, 2006), 2.

17. Ibid., 7.

18. *Roper v. Simmons,* No. 03-633.543 US.161 L Ed 2d 1,125 S Ct.

NAME INDEX

SUBJECT INDEX